The American Choice-of-Law Revolution

THE HAGUE ACADEMY OF INTERNATIONAL LAW MONOGRAPHS

Volume 4

The titles in this series are listed at the end of this volume.

THE HAGUE ACADEMY OF INTERNATIONAL LAW

The American Choice-of-Law Revolution:
Past, Present and Future

by

Symeon C. Symeonides

MARTINUS NIJHOFF PUBLISHERS

LEIDEN • BOSTON

A C.I.P. record for this book is available from the Library of Congress.

Printed on acid-free paper.

ISBN 90 04 15219 9

© 2006 by Koninklijke Brill NV, Leiden, The Netherlands.
Koninklijke Brill NV incorporates the imprints Brill, Hotei Publishers, IDC Publishers, Martinus Nijhoff Publishers and VSP.

http://www.brill.nl

Printed and bound in The Netherlands.

To Haroula

Foreword

On Labor Day 1980, I wrote the last words of my first book on American conflicts law. The book was appropriately titled "An Outsider's View" of the American Approach to Choice of Law[1]. And it was. It was a typical attempt by a foreign student to understand and make sense out of a system that was alien in both language and logic. The attempt was hopeless, but apparently the effort was valiant enough to earn a passing grade.

On Labor Day 2005, I write the last words of this book on the same subject, and for once I write in the first person. In the intervening years, I have not tried to become an "insider", but I have continued to explore, observe, question, and absorb. In particular, by choice or necessity, I have studied at least a myriad of judicial decisions. Like so many foreign observers, I gradually moved from extreme skepticism to unabashed admiration before I settled somewhere in the middle. This book is the result of what I have learned in these years.

The first version of this book comprised my 2002 lectures at the Hague Academy of International Law and appeared as part of the Academy's Collected Courses[2]. The Curatorium of the Academy has graciously authorized republication of the lectures as a free-standing volume. This provided the opportunity for both updating and substantial rewriting.

Among the book's readers, I am particularly partial toward those young, foreign or domestic students who are striving to make sense of either American conflicts law in particular or Private International Law in general. One way to assist them is to support as many of them as possible to study in that glorious temple of international

---

1. See S. Symeonides, *An Outsider's View of the American Approach to Choice of Law: Comparative Observations on Current American and Continental Conflicts Doctrine* (S.J.D. Dissertation, Harvard Law School, 1980).
2. See S. Symeonides, "The American Choice-of-Law Revolution in the Courts: Today and Tomorrow", 298 *Recueil des Cours* 1 (2003). For a review of this version of the book, see L. Weinberg, "Theory Wars in the Conflict of Laws", 103 *Mich. L. Rev.* 1631 (2005); 6. Shreve, "Symeonides, The American Choice-of-Law Revolution", 52 *Am. J. Comp. L.* 1003 (2004).

justice – the Hague Academy of International Law. To this end, the royalties from this book have been donated to the Academy for the establishment of scholarships.

Salem, Oregon, USA
S.C.S

Table of Contents

Tables

Charts and Maps

Maps

Biographical Note

Symeon C. Symeonides, born on 28 April 1949, in Lythrodontas, Cyprus.

Legal education: Aristotelian University of Thessaloniki, Greece: LL.B. *summa cum laude* (Private Law) (1972), LL.B. *summa cum laude* (Public Law & Pol. Sc.) (1973); Harvard Law School: LL.M. (1974), S.J.D. (1980).

Present and previous academic positions: Dean and Professor of Law, Willamette University College of Law, Salem, Oregon (1999-present); Judge Albert Tate Professor of Law (1989-1999), Vice Chancellor (1991-1997), Professor (1984-1989), Associate Professor (1981-1984); Assistant Professor (1978-1981), Louisiana State University Law Center; Assistant Professor, University of Thessaloniki (1976-1978). Visiting positions: Université Paris I, (2005, 2006); Université Paris V (2002, 2003); Louvain-la-Neuve (1997); Tulane (1985); Loyola (1982).

Work in law reform: Commissioner, Oregon Law Commission (since 1999); Chairman, Project for Choice-of-Law Codification, Oregon Law Commission (since 2001); Rapporteur and Chairman, Codification of Louisiana Conflicts Law, Louisiana State Law Institute (since 1984); Rapporteur and Chairman, Revision of the Law of Leases, Louisiana State Law Institute (since 1992); Rapporteur, Codification of Puerto Rican Private International Law, Puerto Rican Academy of Legislation and Jurisprudence (1987-1991); Consultant, Joint Permanent Commission for the Revision of the Puerto Rican Civil Code (2002).

Other activities, memberships, etc.: Vice-President (since 2002), Secretary (1994-2002) American Society of Comparative Law; Chairman, Association of American Law Schools Section on Conflicts of Laws (1999); Titular Member (since 2000), Associate Member (1994-2000), International Academy of Comparative Law; Member, American Law Institute (since 1988); Rapporteur General on Private International Law, 15th Quadrennial Int'l Congress of Comparative Law, Bristol, United Kingdom (1998); United States National Reporter on Private Int'l Law, 14th Quadrennial Int'l Congress of Comparative Law, Athens (1994); Member: Executive Editorial Board, *American Journal of Comparative Law*; Board of Editors *Yearbook of Private International Law* and *Electronic Journal of Comparative Law*; Honorary Consul, Republic of Cyprus (1985-1999).

Honours: Friedrich K. Juenger Prize in Private International Law (American Society of Comparative Law, 2002); Honoured in "Conflict of Laws, Comparative Law and Civil Law: A Tribute to Symeon C. Symeonides", 60 *Louisiana Law Re-*

view 1035-1399 (2000); *Resolution of Appreciation,* Association of American Law Schools Section on Conflict of Laws (1999); LL.B. 1972: recipient of the highest graduation grade (10 out of 10) in the history of the University of Thessaloniki Law School.

Principal Publications

(In reverse chronological order)

A. Books

Conflict of Laws (with E. Scoles, P. Hay and P. Borchers), Thomson-West Publ. Co., Hornbook Series (4th ed. 2004).

Conflict of Laws: American, Comparative, International (with W. C. Perdue and A. T. von Mehren), Thomson-West Publ. Co., American Casebook Series (2nd ed. 2003).

The American Choice-of-Law Revolution in the Courts: Today and Tomorrow, 298 Recueil des Cours 1 (Hague Academy of International Law, 2003).

Law and Justice in a Multistate World: Essays in Honor of Arthur T. von Mehren (with J. Nafziger, eds.) (2002).

American Law in a Time of Global Interdependence (with J. Reitz, eds., US National Reports to the 16th Int'l Congress of Comparative Law) (2002).

Droit international privé vers la fin du vingtième siècle: Progrès ou recul? – Private International Law at the End of the 20th Century: Progress or Regress? (Kluwer Publ. International, 1999).

Teacher's Manual for *Conflict of Laws: American, Comparative, International* (with W. Perdue), Thomson-West Publ. Co. (1998, 2003).

American Law at the End of the Twentieth Century (with G. Bermann. eds., US National Reports to the 15th Int'l Congress of Comparative Law) (1998).

Comparative Private International Law: Materials for the Comparative Study of American and European Approaches to Choice of Law in Torts and Contracts (Course-Book, 4th ed., 1996, P. M. Hebert Publ. Inst.).

American and Comparative Conflicts Law (Casebook, P. M. Hebert Publ. Inst., 1995).

Louisiana and Comparative Conflicts Law (Coursebook, 4th ed., 1993, P. M. Hebert Publ. Inst.).

An Introduction to the Louisiana Civil Law System (Coursebook, 6th ed., 1991, P. M. Hebert Publ. Inst).

A Projet for the Codification of Puerto Rican Private International Law (P.R. Acad. Jurispr. Legisl., 1991).

A Sourcebook for the Codification of Puerto Rican Private International Law (P.R. Acad. Jurispr. Legisl., 1991).

An Outsider's View of the American Approach to Choice of Law: Comparative Observations on Current American and Continental Conflicts Doctrine (S.J.D. Dissertation, Harvard Law School, 1980).

Comparative Law (with Dimitrios Evrigenis and Phocion Francescakis) (in Greek), Sakkoulas Publications (1978).

Introduction to Cypriot Law (in Greek), University of Thessaloniki Press (1977).

B.   Articles in Law Reviews or Chapters in Books

"Accommodative Unilateralism as a Starting Premise in Choice of Law", in *Balancing of Interests –Liber Amicorum Peter Hay* 417-434, Verlag Recht und Wirtschaft GmbH, 2005.

"The Quest for the Optimum in Resolving Product-Liability Conflicts", in *Essays in Honor of P. John Kozyris* (2005).

"A Choice-of-Law Rule for Conflicts Involving Stolen Cultural Property", 38 *Vanderbilt Journal of Transnational Law* 1177-98 (2005).

"Of Teleology, State Interests and Pluralism in Choice of Law: In Loving Memory of Friedrich K. Juenger", in Friedrich K. Juenger, *Choice of Law and Multistate Justice* xxxiii (Special ed. 2005).

"Choice of Law in the American Courts in 2003: Eighteenth Annual Survey", 53 *American Journal of Comparative Law* 919-994 (2005).

"Choice of Law for Products Liability: The 1990s and Beyond", 78 *Tulane Law Review* 1247-1349 (2004).

"Tort Conflicts and Rome II: A View from Across", in *Festschrift für Erik Jayme* 935-954 (2004).

"Choice of Law in the American Courts in 2003: Seventeenth Annual Survey", 52 *American Journal of Comparative Law* 1-76 (2004).

"Territoriality and Personality in Tort Conflicts", in *Intercontinental Cooperation Through Private International Law: Essays in Memory of Peter Nygh*, (T. Einhorn & K. Siehr, eds) 401-433 (2004).

"Resolving Punitive-Damages Conflicts", 5 *Yearbook of Private International Law* 1-34 (2003).

"Codifying Choice of Law for Contracts: The Oregon Experience", 67 *RabelsZ* 726-751 (2003).

"Choice of Law in the American Courts in 2002: Sixteenth Annual Survey", 51 *American Journal of Comparative Law* 1 (2003).

"The Mixed Legal System of the Republic of Cyprus", 78 *Tulane Law Review* 441 (2003).

"Choice of Law in the American Courts in 2001: Fifteenth Annual Survey", 50 *American Journal of Comparative Law* 1-95 (2002).

"Codifying Choice of Law for Contracts: The Puerto Rico Project", in *Law and Justice in a Multistate World: Essays in Honor of Arthur T. von Mehren* 419-437 (J. Nafziger and S. Symeonides, eds., 2002).

"Choice of Law in the American Courts in 2000: As the Century Turns", 49 *American Journal of Comparative Law* 1-47 (2001).

"Material Justice and Conflicts Justice in Choice of Law", in *International Conflict of Laws for the Third Millennium: Essays in Honor of Friedrich K. Juenger* 125-140 (P. Borchers and J. Zekoll, eds., 2001).

"American Conflicts Law at the Dawn of the 21st Century", 37 *Willamette Law Review* 1-87 (2000).

"On the Side of the Angels: Choice of Law and Stolen Cultural Property", in *Private Law in the International Arena – Liber Amicorum Kurt Siehr* 649-664 (J. Basedow, *et al.*, eds. 2000).

"The Need for a Third Conflicts Restatement (and a Proposal for Tort Conflicts)", 75 *Indiana Law Journal* 437-474 (2000).

"Choice of Law in the American Courts in 1999: One More Year", 48 *American Journal of Comparative Law* 143-180 (2000).

"Mandate, Agency, and Representation: A Kommentar" (with Wendell H. Holmes), 73 *Tulane Law Review* 1087-1159 (1999).

"Covenant Marriage and the Conflict of Laws" (with Katherine S. Spaht), 32 *Creighton Law Review* 1085-1120 (1999).

"Choice of Law in the American Courts in 1998: Twelfth Annual Survey", 47 *American Journal of Comparative Law,* 327-392 (1999).

"The Louisiana Judge: Judge, Statesman, Politician", in *Louisiana: Microcosm of a Mixed Jurisdiction* 89-104 (Vernon Palmer, ed., Carolina Academic Press, 1999).

"Historical Evolution and Diversity of Cypriot Law" (Chapter in a book on the law of Cyprus, Institut universitaire européen, Florence, 1999).

"Choice of Law in the American Courts in 1997", 46 *American Journal of Comparative Law* 233-285 (1998).

"The Judicial Acceptance of the Second Conflicts Restatement: A Mixed Blessing", 56 *Maryland Law Review* 1246-1283 (1997).

"Resolving Six Celebrated Conflicts Cases through Statutory Choice-of-Law Rules", 48 *Mercer Law Review* 837-869 (1997).

"Choice of Law in the American Courts in 1996: Tenth Annual Survey", 45 *American Journal of Comparative Law* 447-503 (1997).

"The Romanist Tradition in Louisiana: One Day in the Life of Louisiana Law", 56 *Louisiana Law Review* 249 (1995).

"Choice of Law in the American Courts in 1995: A Year in Review", 44 *American Journal of Comparative Law* 181-241 (1996).

"Choice of Law in the American Courts in 1994: A View 'From the Trenches'", 43 *American Journal of Comparative Law* 1-92 (1995).

"Les clauses d'exception en matière de conflits de lois – Etats-Unis", in *Les clauses d'exception en matière de conflits de lois et de conflits de juridictions – ou le principe de proximité* (D. Kokkini-Iatridou, ed.), 77-195 (Martinus Nijhoff Publishers, 1994). Also published as "Exception Clauses in American Conflicts Law", 42 *American Journal of Comparative Law* 813-865 (1994) (U.S. National Report to the XIVth Int'l Congress of Comp. L. (1994)).

"The ALI's Complex Litigation Project: Commencing the National Debate", 54 *Louisiana Law Review* 843-879 (1994).

"Choice of Law in the American Courts in 1993 (and in the Six Previous Years)", 42 *American Journal of Comparative Law* 559-653 (1994).

"Syngchroni kodikopoiitiki techniki sto Idiotiko Diethnes Dikaio" (Modern Codification Techniques in Private International Law), 14 *Revue hellénique de droit européen* 951-984 (1994).

"Louisiana Conflicts Law: Two 'Surprises'", 54 *Louisiana Law Review* 497-549 (1994).

"The New Law of Co-Ownership: A Kommentar" (with Nicole D. Martin) 68 *Tulane Law Review* 69-160 (1993)

"La nuova normativa della Louisiana sul diritto internazionale privato in tema di responsabilità extracontrattuale", 29 *Rivista di diritto internazionale privato e processuale* 43-68 (1993).

"Private International Law Codification in a Mixed Jurisdiction: The Louisiana Experience", 57 *Rabels Zeitschrift für ausländisches und internationales Privatrecht*, 460-516 (1993).

"Louisiana's New Law of Choice of Law for Tort Conflicts: An Exegesis", 66 *Tulane L. Rev.* 677-770 (1992).

"Les grands problèmes de droit international privé et la nouvelle codification de Louisiane", 81 *Revue critique de droit international privé* 223-281 (1992).

"Ruminations on Real Actions", 51 *Louisiana Law Review* 493-522 (1991).

"Problems and Dilemmas in Codifying Choice of Law for Torts: The Louisiana Experience in a Comparative Perspective", 38 *American Journal of Comparative Law* 431-73 (1990).

"Choice of Law in the American Courts in 1989: An Overview" (with J. P. Kozyris), 38 *American Journal of Comparative Law* 601-651 (1990).

"Revising Puerto Rico's Conflicts Law: A Preview", 28 *Columbia Journal of Transnational Law*, 601 (1990).

"Choice of Law in the American Courts in 1988", 37 *American Journal of Comparative Law* 1001-1039 (1989).

"The Swiss Conflicts Codification: An Introduction", 37 *American Journal of Comparative Law* 187 (1989).

"Swiss Federal Statute on Private International Law of December 18, 1987: An English Translation" (with J. Cornu and S. Hankins), 37 *American Journal of Comparative Law* 193-246 (1989).

"The General Principles of the [Greek] Civil Law", in K. Kerameus and J. P. Kozyris (eds), *Introduction to Greek Law*, 49-69 (Kluwer Publ. Co., 1988) (2nd ed., 1993).

"Exploring the 'Dismal Swamp': The Revision of Louisiana's Conflicts Law on Successions", 47 *Louisiana Law Review* 1029-1104 (1987).

"Louisiana Conflicts Jurisprudence, A Student Symposium: Introduction", 47 *Louisiana Law Review* 1105-1108 (1987).

"Louisiana's Draft on Successions and Marital Property", 35 *American Journal of Comparative Law* 259-293 (1987).

"Developments in the Law, 1985-1986: Property", 47 *Louisiana Law Review* 429-452 (1987).

"In Search of New Choice-of-Law Solutions to Some Marital Property Problems of Migrant Spouses: A Response to the Critics", 13 (3) *Community Property Journal* 11-31 (1986).

"Developments in the Law, 1984-85: Property", 46 *Louisiana Law Review* 655-693 (1986).

"Revolution and Counter-Revolution in American Conflicts Law: Is There a Middle Ground?", 46 *Ohio State Law Journal* 549-568 (1985).

"Developments in the Law, 1983-84: Property", 45 *Louisiana Law Review* 541-557 (1984).

"Developments in the Law, 1982-83: Property", 44 *Louisiana Law Review* 505-533 (1983).

"One Hundred Footnotes to the New Law of Possession and Acquisitive Prescription", 44 *Louisiana Law Review* 69-1108 (1983).

"Maritime Conflicts of Law from the Perspective of Modern Choice of Law Methodology", 7 *Maritime Lawyer* 223-264 (1982).

"Zypern" in *Internationales Ehe-und Kindschaftsrecht* (with Erik Jayme) (Bergmann and Ferid, eds.), Gmb H and Co. K.G. Frankfurt (1979).

C.   Shorter Pieces

"Party Choice of Law in Product-Liability Conflicts", 12 *Willamette J. of Int'l L. & Dispute Resolution* 263-286 (2004)

"Conflict of Laws", in *Oxford Companion to American Law* (Oxford University Press, 2001).

"On Deaning, Writing, and Roses", 33 *University of Toledo Law Review* 217 (2001).

"Conflict of Laws" in *International Encyclopedia of Social & Behavioral Sciences* (Kluwer, 2001).

"In Memoriam Friedrich K. Juenger", 35 *University of California – Davis Law Review* 249 (2002).

Chapter I   Introduction

A.   Book Coverage and Structure

1. This book discusses a phenomenon known as a "revolution" in private international law (PIL) or the law of conflict of laws in the United States. To be sure, the use of the term "revolution" in any field of law, especially one as esoteric as conflicts law is reputed to be[1], is hyperbolic and simplistic at the same time. Nevertheless, this term has prevailed in the literature as a shorthand description of the intellectual movement that challenged and eventually demolished the foundations of the established American system of conflicts law. Beginning in the 1960s, this movement had the appearances, and eventually acquired the dimensions and intensity, of a figurative rebellion against the established system, although it confined itself primarily to the area of choice of law in torts and contracts. This book chronicles this revolution, but also looks to the future and explores the question of what is, or should be, the next phase in the development of American conflicts law.

This is neither the first nor the last study of this phenomenon[2]. However, much of the literature has been at the level of academic theory and methodology. Without denying the role of academic theory in the development of American conflicts law, this book focuses on the role of the courts "where things matter more[3] in resolving actual conflicts and building or rebuilding American conflicts law, case by case. The book covers the choice-of-law decisions of American state

---

1.   It is hard to resist reciting Prosser's oft-quoted if trite description of conflicts law as a "dismal swamp, filled with quaking quagmires, and inhabited by learned but eccentric professors who theorize about mysterious matters in a strange and incomprehensible jargon." W. Prosser, "Interstate Publication", 51 *Mich. L. Rev.* 959, 971 (1953). Prosser's description was also hyperbolic but, as with the term "revolution", this has not prevented it from being so widely recited. In any event, without denying the role of scholars, which has been more constructive than Prosser implied, this course explores the role of the less eccentric, less theorizing courts in making American conflicts law.

2.   For a convenient collection of the voluminous literature, see E. Scoles, P. Hay, P. Borchers and S. Symeonides, *Conflict of Laws* 25-102 (4th ed. 2004).

3.   Cf. R. Weintraub, *Commentary on the Conflict of Laws* 347 (4th ed. 2001) ("More important than what the commentators are up to as they deforest the land with the mountains of conflicts articles, is the results that the courts are reaching").

and federal courts in the last four decades, with more emphasis on the last two decades. It examines the methodological and philosophical foundations of these decisions and attempts to extract from them precepts and principles that can be recast into new rules for future cases.

2. The book consists of ten chapters, including this introduction. Chapter II discusses the traditional American choice-of-law system and the academic dissent it generated – the "scholastic revolution". Chapter III chronicles the judicial manifestations of the same phenomenon – the "judicial revolution" – and the eventual abandonment of the traditional system. Chapter IV surveys and charts the methodological landscape as it exists in the various states and jurisdictions of the United States at the beginning of the twenty-first century.

Chapters V-VIII, which comprise the bulk of this book, concentrate on tort conflicts. The reason for this concentration is that tort conflicts make up the main arena of the conflicts revolution and have been the focus of, and the catalyst for, a fundamental reorientation of choice-of-law thinking in the United States. Thus, tort conflicts are an excellent vehicle for re-examining the methodological and philosophical foundations of American choice of law in general. Furthermore, because tort conflicts are not only the most challenging, but also the most numerous of conflicts cases, this book could not discuss other conflicts without exceeding the space limitations allotted to it.

Chapter V explores the distinction between tort rules that primarily regulate conduct (conduct-regulating rules) and rules that primarily allocate or distribute the losses caused by tortious conduct (loss-distributing rules). Chapter VI discusses loss-distribution conflicts, Chapter VII discusses conduct-regulating conflicts, and Chapter VIII discusses products-liability conflicts.

Finally, Chapters IX and X gauge the current position of American conflicts law with regard to six basic methodological and philosophical benchmarks, and then explore the question of what should be the next step in the evolution of American conflicts law. The thesis posited here is that the next step should include the development of new "smart" choice-of-law rules based on the lessons of the American conflicts experience. Chapter X concludes by describing the essential and desired features of these rules.

B.   The American Framework

3. The fact that the United States is a federal, multistate, plurilegal system entails certain challenges and limitations to this book. Strictly speaking, the term "American conflicts law" is a misnomer – there is no single American conflicts law[4]. Rather, there are as many conflicts laws in the United States as there are states or jurisdictions that constitute the United States. Today this includes 50 states and

---

4.   To be sure, the use of the term "American" when referring to only one of the countries of the American continent is also a misnomer. Nevertheless, it is used solely for the sake of brevity and in full awareness of its technical inaccuracy.

the District of Columbia[5], as well as the United States itself as a separate sovereign with its own system of laws.

The United States Constitution allocates law-making powers between the federal government and the constituent states by assigning to the federal government certain enumerated powers on matters of national concern[6] and reserving to the states the remaining powers, including the great bulk of private law[7]. Thus, by establishing and preserving a plurilegal federal union, the Constitution creates the conditions for the occurrence of conflicts of laws, of both the vertical and the horizontal type.

4. Vertical conflicts are those that occur between federal law and state law. Horizontal conflicts are those that occur between or among: (a) the laws of the states of the United States (interstate conflicts); or (b) between the laws of these states and the laws of foreign countries (international (state) conflicts); or (c) the laws of the United States and foreign countries (international (federal) conflicts). The following chart depicts these categories.

Chart 1. Interstate and international conflicts in the United States

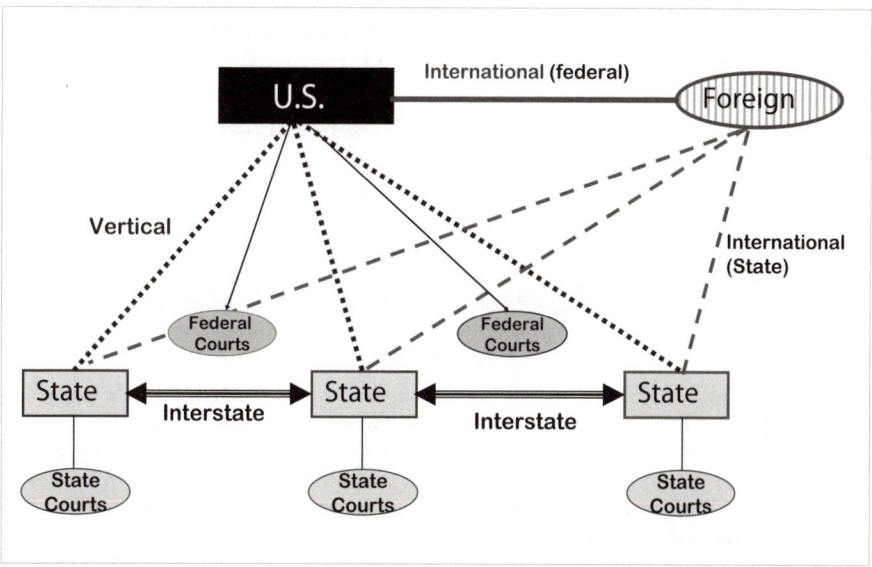

In theory, the resolution of all four categories of conflicts is a matter of federal law. In practice, this is true only with regard to vertical conflicts. Under the Con-

---

5.   The Commonwealth of Puerto Rico, which enjoys a special relation described as free association *(estado libre associado)* with the United States, is also included in this study. For a discussion of this status and Puerto Rico conflicts law, see S. Symeonides, "Revising Puerto Rico's Conflicts Law: A Preview", 28 *Colum J. Transnat'l L.* 601 (1990).

6.   See US Const. art. I § 8.

7.   See US Const. Amend. X.

stitution's supremacy clause[8], principles of federal law govern conflicts between federal and state law. Federal principles also govern conflicts between federal and foreign law, but these principles have grown out of, and continue to draw from, the states' experience with interstate conflicts.

The Constitution also addresses horizontal interstate conflicts by enunciating the obligation of each state to give "full faith and credit" to the laws and judgments of sister states, and by assigning to Congress the power to enact laws governing the manner in which each state will discharge this obligation[9]. For better or worse[10], however, Congress has exercised this power very sparingly[11]. Thus, by default, the power and the initiative of resolving interstate conflicts remain with the states, subject only to mild restraints imposed by the Constitution as interpreted by the United States Supreme Court.

The states possess the same power with regard to international conflicts between state law and foreign law, subject to some but not all of the same constitutional restraints as interstate conflicts[12], as well as an infrequently utilized admonition that, in addressing these conflicts, states should not interfere with the federal government's conduct of foreign affairs[13].

Thus, by default, the resolution of most interstate and international conflicts in the United States is a matter of state law rather than federal law.

5. Although each state legislature has the inherent power to enact choice-of-law legislation, very few states have exercised this power. Only one state has a comprehensive conflicts codification[14] and, although many other states have

---

8. See US Const. art. VI.
9. See US Const. art. IV § 1 (providing that "Full Faith and Credit shall be given in each State" to the "laws and judgments of every other State" and authorizing Congress to enact laws prescribing "the Effect" of such laws and judgments.)
10. Many commentators seem to applaud the inaction of the US Congress in the choice-of-law area. See M. McConnell, "A Choice-of-Law Approach to Products-Liability Reform", in *New Directions in Liability Law* (W. Olson ed. 1988) ("Congress ... generally and wisely refrains from engaging from experimental legislation, since federal mistakes are notoriously difficult to correct. It is hazardous to impose a single national 'solution' to a problem without a reasonable confidence that the solution can be tolerated for years to come").
11. See, e.g., 28 USCA § 1738A (Federal Parental Kidnaping Prevention Act); 28 USCA § 1738C ("Defense of Marriage Act").
12. The full faith and credit clause does not apply to international conflicts, and the privileges and immunities clause does not apply to non-US citizens.
13. See *American Ins. Ass'n v. Garamendi*, 539 U.S. 396 (2003); S. Symeonides, "Choice of Law in the American Courts in 2003: Seventeenth Annual Survey", 52 *Am. J. Comp. L.* 9, 12-15 (2005).
14. This state is Louisiana. See Book IV of the Louisiana Civil Code, enacted in 1991 (hereinafter referred to as the "Louisiana Codification"). For a discussion of this codification by its drafter, see, e.g., S. Symeonides, "Private International Law Codification in a Mixed Jurisdiction: The Louisiana Experience", 57 *RabelsZ* 460 (1993). See

piecemeal, narrowly drawn statutes[15], the great bulk of American conflicts law is found in the law reports, not the statute books. It has been created judicially through the pronouncements of the courts in adjudicating conflicts cases and through the operation of the doctrine of *stare decisis*.

Under the American system of dual sovereignty, conflicts cases can be adjudicated either by state courts or by federal courts[16]. The applicable choice-of-law principles depend not on whether the adjudicating court is state or federal, but rather on the category to which the particular conflict belongs. If, as described above, state choice-of-law principles govern a particular case, then those principles govern even if a federal court adjudicates the case[17]. Likewise, when a state court encounters one of the conflicts that are governed by federal choice-of-law principles, such as a conflict between federal maritime law and foreign law, the state court must follow the federal principles.

6. This book does not discuss vertical conflicts. Rather it focuses on horizontal interstate and international conflicts, the first of which are by far the most numerous. Since, as said above, state rather than federal law governs these conflicts, and since each state has its own body of law for these conflicts, it should follow that one should not be speaking of "American" conflicts law but rather of 50 or more state conflicts laws, and, in addition, a federal conflicts law. Technically, this is entirely accurate. Nevertheless, the practical question is whether and to what extent the various American conflicts laws share sufficient common denominators and similarities as to constitute – at least for certain purposes – a single law susceptible to meaningful treatment as such. As discussed shortly, an affirmative answer was more accurate during the first than during the second half of the twentieth century. One question this book explores is to what extent, as we proceed down the path of the twenty-first century, we approach again the part of the cycle that will bring about a new period of uniformity among the various American laws of choice of law.

---

also *infra* 102. For Puerto Rico and Oregon, see *infra* 103-104. Unless otherwise indicated, all cross-references are to paragraph numbers.

15.   See *infra* at 311-312, 376.

16.   According to a recent survey, conflicts cases do not exceed 2% of all cases. See S. Symeonides, "A Choice of Law in the American Courts in 2004: Eighteenth Annual Survey", 53 *Am. J. Comp. L.* 919, 921-923 (2005). For example, in 2004, Westlaw reported a total of 2,801 conflicts cases, and this represented 1.29% of all cases. Most of the conflicts cases are decided by federal courts. For example, in 2004, 72.3% (or 2,025) of the 2,801 conflicts cases were decided by federal courts and 27.7% (or 776) of the cases were decided by state courts. However these numbers are slightly misleading in that while Westlaw reports all the federal cases, it does not report most of the cases decided by state courts of first instance.

17.   See *Klaxon Co. v. Stentor Elec. Mfg. Co. Inc.*, 313 US 487 (1941) (holding that, when a federal court's jurisdiction is based on the parties' diversity of citizenship and the conflict in question is of the type that is governed by state choice-of-law principles, the court must follow the choice-of-law rules of the state in which the court sits).

C.   The Relative Insignificance of Interstate Boundaries

7. In an oft-quoted statement made more than four decades ago, the Supreme Court of Illinois observed that "[a]dvanced methods of distribution and other commercial activity ... [and] modern methods of doing business ... have largely effaced the economic significance of State lines"[18]. What was beginning to be true then is unquestionably true today, not only in the United States, but around the world as well. The new word "internet" is simply the latest manifestation of this reality.

However, state boundaries are even less important within the United States than are international boundaries in the rest of the world. While state lines divide the United States into more than fifty jurisdictions each with its own system of law, these lines generally have little effect on the economic, political, and cultural unity of the country[19]. It is not simply that people travel and goods circulate freely and constantly throughout the country, that many people live in one state and work in another[20], or that, as in the movies, a police car chase may begin in one state and end abruptly in another[21]. It is also that, in their everyday lives, people

---

18.   *Gray* v. *Am. Radiator & Standard Sanitary Corp.*, 176 NE 2d 761, 766 (Ill. 1961).

19.   But see L. Brilmayer, "Shaping and Sharing in Democratic Theory: Towards a Political Philosophy of Interstate Equality", 15 *Fla. St. U. L. Rev.* 389, 408 (1987) ("Maine has a different character than Texas, Nevada emphasizes different values than South Carolina, and ... Northern and Southern Californians joke about dividing the state in two precisely because it is thought that statehood appropriately reflects value choices, and two such different cultures are incongruously joined into a single state").

20.   See, e.g., *Allstate Ins. Co.* v. *Hague*, 449 US 302 (1981) (victim lived in Wisconsin and worked in Minnesota); *Bledsoe* v. *Crowley*, 849 F. 2d 639 (DC 1988) (plaintiff lived in the District of Columbia and worked in Maryland); *Foster* v. *Leggett*, 484 SW 2d 827 (Ky. 1972) (defendant lived in Ohio but worked in Kentucky); *Cipolla* v. *Shaposka*, 267 A. 2d 854 (Pa. 1970) (plaintiff lived in Pennsylvania but attended school in Delaware); *Kaiser-Georgetown Cmty. Health Plan, Inc.* v. *Stutsman*, 491 A. 2d 502 (DC 1985) (plaintiff lived in Virginia but worked in the District of Columbia); *Biscoe* v. *Arlington County*, 738 F. 2d 1352 (DC Cir. 1984) (plaintiff lived in Maryland but worked in the District of Columbia).

21.   See, e.g., *Jones* v. *Prince George's County*, 835 A.2d 632 (Md. 2003) (chase began in the District of Columbia, continued into Maryland, then back to D.C. and ended in Virginia with the death of a Maryland domiciliary); *Lommen* v. *The City of East Grand Forks*, 522 NW 2d 148 (Minn.App. 1994) (chase began in Minnesota and ended in North Dakota, injuring a North Dakota resident); *Biscoe* v. *Arlington County*, 738 F. 2d 1352 (DC Cir. 1984) (chase began in Virginia and ended in the District of Columbia, injuring a Maryland resident); *Skipper* v. *Prince George's County*, 637 F. Supp, 638 (DDC 1986) (chase began in Maryland and ended in the District of Columbia, injuring a DC resident); *Bays* v. *Jenks*, 573 F. Supp. 306 (WD Va. 1983) (chase began in West Virginia and ended in Virginia); *Tribe* v. *Borough of Sayre*, 562 F. Supp. 419 (WDNY 1983) (chase began in Pennsylvania and ended in New York, injuring a New York resident).

cross state lines with very little awareness of doing so[22]. Many large population centres spread across state boundaries. City names like Texarkana, or Kansas City (Missouri)/Kansas City (Kansas) amply illustrate this American phenomenon of "economically and socially integrated greater metropolitan area[s]"[23] that defy state boundaries[24].

While cross-border torts are quite common around the world, it is doubtful that courts in other countries encounter cases in which the tort occurs literally *at* the boundary line. Yet one finds such cases in the United States. One recent example is *Pittman* v. *Maldania, Inc.*[25], a case in which the defendant's business office was located squarely on the Delaware/Maryland border. The building was on the Delaware side of the border, but its door opened into Maryland. The plaintiff, a Pennsylvania resident, rented water skis inside the building in Delaware and then used them a few feet away in Maryland waters, where he was injured. Predictably, the laws of the two states differed, thus producing a conflict of laws[26].

The same border was also involved in two other cases arising out of traffic accidents. In *Sacra* v. *Sacra*[27], a collision of two cars occurred in Delaware, but the impact of the collision pushed one car across the border into Maryland, where it struck a Maryland utility pole and exploded. One of the parties argued that the injury occurred in Maryland, and thus Maryland law should govern. The court rejected the argument, reasoning that this was "a single, integrated accident, which occurred in Delaware and ... [t]he fact that the state line intervened between the impact and death was merely a fortuitous situation"[28].

Indeed, in retrospect, many state boundaries seem to have been drawn fortuitously. In *Judge Trucking Co. Inc.* v. *Cooper*[29], the state of the accident was in dispute because the very location of the border was in dispute. The two-car col-

---

22. For example, in many cases, a drive between two points in state A may go through state B. See, e.g., *Dist. of Columbia* v. *Coleman*, 667 A. 2d 811 (DC 1995) (defendant lived in Maryland, worked as policeman in the District of Columbia, and, while driving between two points in DC, drove through Maryland where he committed a tort).

23. *Gaither* v. *Myers*, 404 F. 2d 216, 223 (DC Cir.1968) ("It is a commonplace that residents of Maryland [and Virginia] are part of the Washington metropolitan trading area, and that District residents and businesses have an interest in the well-being of the[ ] citizens of [those] State[s].").

24. Other examples are New York (New York) and Newark (New Jersey), Philadelphia (Pennsylvania), Camden (New Jersey), and Wilmington (Delaware); Memphis (Tennessee), West Memphis (Arkansas); and Portland (Oregon) and Vancouver (Washington).

25. 2001 WL 1221704 (Del. Super. 2001). For another recent example, see *Greenwell* v. *Davis*, 180 SW3d 287 (Tex. App. 2005) (accident on road at Texas-Arkansas boundary in city of Texarkana).

26. *Pittman* is discussed *infra* at 176.

27. 426 A.2d 7 (Md.Ct. Spec.App. 1981).

28. *Id.* at 9.

29. 1994 WL 750369 (Del. Super. Ct. 1994).

lision occurred on the northern lane of US Route 54, which runs east-west along the Delaware/Maryland border (with Delaware to the North and Maryland to the south). The plaintiffs argued that the accident occurred in Delaware, because "people in the area consider the state line to run down the centerline of Route 54"[30]. After a long discussion of the history of the Delaware/Maryland boundary, which included detailed description of geodetic surveys and boundary agreements, the court concluded that the boundary was actually located at the northern shoulder of Route 54, and thus the accident had occurred in Maryland.

While cases like the above do not occur every day, they do say something about the nature and frequency of American interstate conflicts, which vastly outnumber the international conflicts American courts encounter. These cases also offer a hint as to why strict adherence to territorial notions makes less sense in the United States than in the rest of the world[31].

---

30.   *Id.* at *2.
31.   See discussion *infra* at 322-327.

Chapter II   The Scholastic Revolution

A.   Introduction

8. Although the focus of this book is on the judicial choice-of-law experience, one needs a basic familiarity with the academic writings that influence and reinforce the predilections and decisions of the courts to fully appreciate this experience. Indeed, American conflicts law, and choice of law in particular, is one of the few branches of American law that has been heavily influenced by scholastic writings. Whether this is due to the perceived esoteric nature of the subject matter[1], the dearth of English precedent or doctrine during the formative period of American conflicts law[2], or the relatively infrequent occurrence of conflicts cases in general – which retards the accumulation of judicial expertise on the subject – is beside the point. The fact remains that it is academic commentators like Story[3], and later Beale[4], who provided the theoretical underpinnings of the traditional choice-of-law system that lasted for more than a century. It is also academic commentators like Cook, Cavers, and Currie who have pinpointed and articulated that system's deficiencies and have instigated dissension from it. This chapter focuses on this dissension[5], which eventually acquired the dimensions of a revolution.

---

1.   See F. Juenger, *Selected Essays on the Conflict of Laws* ix (2001) ("Regarded as an arcane science far removed from real world concerns, and characterized by an esoteric vocabulary, [conflicts law] inevitably attracts speculative minds whose forte is not necessarily common sense.").

2.   See S. Symeonides, W. Perdue and A. von Mehren, *Conflict of Laws: American Comparative International* 12 (2nd ed. 2003).

3.   See J. Story, *Commentaries on the Conflict of Laws* (1834).

4.   See J. Beale, *A Treatise on the Conflict of Laws* (3 vols. 1935).

5.   This chapter is confined to the writings of the most influential members of the revolution's first generation, all but three of whom are now deceased. For a more complete discussion, see E. Scoles, P. Hay, P. Borchers and S. Symeonides, *Conflict of Laws* 22-68 (4th ed. 2004). The next generation, the present, is a diverse and prolific group that includes revolutionaries, counter-revolutionaries, and reformers, such as (alphabetically) P. Borchers, L. Brilmayer, P. Dane, R. Felix, P. Hay, A. Hill, F. Juenger, H. Kay, L. Kramer, P. Kozyris, D. Laycock, H. Maier, L. McDougal, J. Nafziger, C. Peterson, B. Posnak, M. Reimann, W. Reppy, W. Reynolds, W. Richman, R. Sedler, G. Shreve,

B.   The Traditional American Choice-of-Law System

9. Once upon a time, there existed in the United States a choice-of-law *system*. Its foundations were established by the careful and cosmopolitan scholarship of Joseph Story who was well-versed in, and made use of, the European conflicts literature[6]. On those foundations, Joseph Beale erected a new and somewhat artificial edifice – the first conflicts Restatement, which he drafted under the auspices of the American Law Institute[7]. Although academic commentators criticized the Restatement from its very inception, most American courts eventually adopted it, albeit with varying degrees of enthusiasm. As late as the middle of the twentieth century, the Restatement enjoyed an almost universal judicial following. This is as far as the United States came to having a *national system* of choice of law.

Although the Restatement was far from a flawless document, it provided a *system* – a complete, organized and disciplined network of bilateral, fixed, neutral[8] and detailed choice-of-law rules designed to provide solutions for all possible conflicts situations. Unfortunately, these rules were also rigid and mechanical. They completely sacrificed flexibility on the altar of certainty and, in the pursuit of an ill-conceived theoretical purity, they ignored the lessons of experience. They chose not among laws, but among states, based solely on a single, predesignated, territorial, or other factual contact. Subject only to limited post-choice exceptions, the chosen law applied almost automatically, regardless of its content, its underlying policy, or the substantive quality of the solution it would bring to the case at hand. Indeed, the Restatement's objective was to find the spatially appropriate law ("conflicts justice") rather than to ensure a substantively just result ("material justice")[9]. However, the Restatement's rules were also neutral in that they did not give preference to the forum *qua* forum. Indeed, they explicitly aspired to eliminate or curtail forum shopping and to foster international or interstate uniformity of result by ensuring that a case would be resolved in the same way regardless of where it was litigated.

In recent years, it has become habitual practice to describe the Restatement with derision. Indeed, it is hard to find any academic commentary published in the last three decades that contains a favourable reference to the Restatement. Yet, the Restatement was no worse than the intellectual movement that produced it – the school of conceptual jurisprudence – which in turn was no worse than any other intellectual movement of that period. The Restatement had many flaws, but

---

L. Silberman, G. Simpson, J. Singer, A. Twerski, L. Weinberg, and R. Whitten. Their writings are cited in the Bibliography.

6.   See S. Symeonides, W. Perdue and A. von Mehren, *Conflict of Laws: American, Comparative, International* 12-13 (2nd ed. 2003).

7.   See American Law Institute, *Restatement of the Law of Conflict of Laws* (1934).

8.   But see L. Weinberg, "Theory Wars in the Conflict of Laws", 103 *Mich. L. Rev.* 1631, 1645 (2005) (describing the traditional approach as "at least superficially 'neutral,' striking with even-handed ferocity now at plaintiffs, now at defendants".).

9.   See *infra* 349-357.

it was not the abomination that recent scholarship assumes it to be. Among these flaws was an excessive reliance on territoriality and vested rights as the guiding principles for delineating the spatial operation of conflicting laws[10], a Prussian-like fixation with over-regulating, the rigidity of its rules, the failure to consider the content and policies of the conflicting substantive laws[11], and an unyieldingly negative stance towards material-justice considerations.[12] Although this list of flaws is a long one, the Restatement also had virtues, such as its completeness, its lack of parochialism exhibited by its non-partiality towards the forum, its laudable aspiration to produce interstate uniformity and reduce forum shopping, and its persistence, albeit *in extremis,* to ensure legal certainty and predictability.

Whether the Restatement's flaws surpassed its virtues is a question of only historical importance today. The answer that came to prevail at the critical time in the United States was a decidedly affirmative one. This is why a "revolution" rather than a reform appeared to be the only promising option. The discussion now turns to this revolution.

C.   The First Critics: Cook and Cavers

10. One of the earliest and most outspoken critics of the established choice-of-law system was Professor Walter W. Cook[13]. Together with Judge Learned Hand, Cook is usually described as the author of the "local law" theory, which is no more memorable than the theory Cook intended to displace – the vested rights theory. The local law theory was Cook's attempt to explain the seemingly paradoxical application of foreign law by the forum, and to reconcile such application with the forum's sovereignty. Cook argued that, in adjudicating cases with foreign elements that would otherwise be "governed" by foreign law, the forum neither applies foreign law, nor enforces a foreign vested right. Rather, it fashions a local-law remedy that approximates the result provided by the pertinent foreign law[14]. While this theory is of dubious explanatory value, it did have the effect of placing the *lex fori* at the centre of choice-of-law thinking. Cook's subliminal message was that the function of conflicts law is not to preserve the international order, but rather to carry out local law and policy. This was a drastic departure from the universalistic conception of private international law that characterized earlier generations of American scholars, including Story and Beale.

---

10.   See *infra* 323.

11.   See *infra* 336-339.

12.   See *infra* 349-357.

13.   See W. Cook, "The Logical and Legal Bases of the Conflict of Laws", 33 *Yale LJ* 457 (1924); W. Cook, "An Unpublished Chapter of the Logical and Legal Bases of the Conflict of Laws", 37 *Ill. L. Rev.* 418 (1943). See also E. Lorenzen, "Territoriality, Public Policy, and the Conflict of Laws", 43 *Yale LJ* 736 (1924); H. Yntema, "The Hornbook Method and the Conflict of Laws", 37 *Yale LJ* 468 (1928).

14.   See W. Cook, *The Logical and Legal Bases of the Conflict of Laws* 20-21 (1942).

11. Cook's main contribution to American conflicts law lies not in enunciating a new theory, but in deconstructing the traditional theory, and thus freeing the "intellectual garden" of conflicts law of "rank weeds" so that useful vegetables could grow and flourish[15]. Cook argued that the Restatement's professed goals of certainty, predictability, and uniformity were illusory because of the multiple escape devices that judges could and did use; that the Restatement's seemingly simple, but excessively broad, principles were "inadequate," both in describing what the courts were doing and in directing what courts should do[16]; and that a simplistic, static system based on prefabricated rules could not provide workable solutions to complex problems. He advocated for "a set of guiding principles, which make provision for as much certainty as may reasonably be hoped for in a changing world, and at the same time provide for not only needed flexibility but also continuity of growth"[17]. This statement was the harbinger of the notion that later prevailed in American conflicts thought – that an "approach" is superior to a system of rules.

12. Although Cook fell short of articulating an affirmative approach of his own, his writings contained many of the seeds of modern theories. For example, on the basic question of how the forum court should select the foreign law on which to "model" its rule of decision in multistate cases, Cook simply said that "the problem involved is that of legal thinking in general", and that the forum should use "the same method actually used in deciding cases involving purely domestic torts, contracts, property, etc."[18]. This resort to the "domestic method" for handling conflicts cases anticipated Brainerd Currie's conception of the choice-of-law process as being based on the "ordinary process of construction and interpretation"[19]. Cook's reference to "socially useful" solutions to conflicts problems also anticipated the result-selectivity of many judicial decisions and academic commentators, and the notion that courts should not sacrifice material justice in the pursuit of "conflicts justice"[20]. Moreover, Cook's admonition that one should consider legislative purposes and policies "before a wise choice *between conflicting rules* can be made"[21] reveals that, like many modern American scholars, Cook thought of the choice-of-law problem as one of choosing between competing rules, not competing legal orders or "jurisdictions" in the abstract.

13. Professor David F. Cavers, who at the time shared many of Cook's legal-realist convictions, continued the attack on the traditional system. In a pioneering law review article, Cavers further exposed the mechanical nature of the traditional methodology, which he compared to a slot-machine programmed to select

---

15. *Id.* at p. x.
16. See W. Cook, *An Unpublished Chapter* at 422.
17. W. Cook, *Logical Bases* at 97.
18. *Id.* at 43.
19. See B. Currie, *Selected Essays on the Conflict of Laws* 183-184 (1963), discussed *infra* at 16, 338-339.
20. See *infra* 349-355.
21. W. Cook, *Logical Bases* at 46 (emphasis added).

the applicable law in a "blindfold" fashion, based solely on territorial contacts and without regard to the content of the implicated laws[22]. In his view, this exclusive reliance on territorial contacts and the insistence on using "jurisdiction-selecting" rules not only prevented a more individualized treatment of conflicts cases, but also prevented intelligent choices. After all, Cavers observed, "[t]he court is not idly choosing a law; it is deciding a controversy. How can it choose wisely without considering how that choice will affect that controversy?"[23]

Cavers argued for a drastic rearrangement of the priorities of the choice-of-law process. Rather than choosing between states or "jurisdictions" without regard to the way their laws would regulate the case at hand, Cavers advocated choosing between the conflicting legal rules based, in large part, on the result each rule would produce in the particular case. Rather than choosing on the basis of territorial contacts, Cavers would focus directly on the content of the competing rules and their underlying policies, the peculiarities of the particular case, and the need to ensure justice for the involved parties. Although falling short of articulating a comprehensive methodology to replace the first Restatement, Cavers's analysis provided useful markers on the path on which the quest for alternative methodologies should proceed. More than thirty years later, Cavers returned to the conflicts scene with a set of "principles of preference" for the solution of tort and contract conflicts. These principles are discussed later[24].

D.   An Open Revolution: Brainerd Currie

14. With their incisive and pioneering work, Cook and Cavers demonstrated the deficiencies of the traditional system, and helped to discredit the first Restatement in its infancy. Professor Brainerd Currie inflicted the decisive blow. Building on the works of Cook, Cavers, and others, Currie enunciated his approach in a series of law review articles published in the 1950s and early 1960s[25]. The basic components of Currie's approach are: (1) his rejection of choice-of-law rules in favour of the "domestic method" of statutory construction and interpretation; (2) the notion that states have a "governmental interest" in the outcome of conflicts cases; (3) his narrow conception of those interests; (4) the concepts of "true" and "false" conflicts and "unprovided-for" cases; and (5) a *de facto* and *de jure* forum favouritism. These components are described below and critiqued later[26].

---

22.   See D. Cavers, "A Critique of the Choice-of-Law Problem", 47 *Harv. L. Rev.* 173, 178 (1933).

23.   *Id.* at 189.

24.   See *infra* 124, 135, 141, 144-145, 156, 174, 343.

25.   These articles are collected in B. Currie, *Selected Essays on the Conflict of Laws* (1963).

26.   See *infra* 307-309, 331-335, 338-339, 360, 371-373.

1.   *Antirulism*

15. Currie issued a categorical indictment not only of the particular choice-of-law rules of the first Restatement, which "have not worked and cannot be made to work"[27], but also of all choice-of-law rules in general. Assuming that all such rules were not only bad but also harmful, he proclaimed that "[w]e would be better off without choice-of-law rules"[28].

Although this is the least noticed and least criticized of Currie's postulates, it is also directly responsible for why American conflicts law rejected the route of reform in favour of revolution. We will return to this postulate later[29].

2.   *The "domestic method"*

16. To fill the vacuum left by his rejection of choice-of-law rules, Currie resorted to the method of statutory construction and interpretation that courts employ in fully domestic cases. In Currie's words, "[j]ust as we determine by that process how a statute applies in time, and how it applies to marginal cases, so we may determine how it should be applied to cases involving foreign elements"[30].

Although this was not a new notion, it was pregnant with several interrelated consequences, including the following[31]:

(a) a rejection of the theretofore prevailing assumption that conflicts cases are so different from fully domestic cases as to require a distinctive mode of refereeing that draws from principles superior, or at least external, to the involved states. Indeed, Currie rejected the existence of an overarching legal order that delineates affirmatively and *a priori* the legislative jurisdiction of each state. He believed that in searching for choice-of-law solutions, the forum should look inward rather than upward;

(b) the rejection of pre-established choices in favour of an *ad hoc* judicial choice of the applicable law;

(c) the rejection of multilateralism in favour of unilateralism; and

(d) a rejection of the notion that the choice of the applicable law could be made on the basis of territorial contacts alone and without regard to the content of the substantive laws of the states that have those contacts.

In short, rather than selecting the applicable law through preordained choice-of-law rules that were oblivious to the content of the conflicting laws, Currie,

---

27.   B. Currie, *Selected Essays* 180.

28.   *Id.* at 183. See also *id.* at 180 ("The [traditional] rules ... have not worked and cannot be made to work ... But the root of the trouble goes deeper. In attempting to use rules we encounter difficulties that stem not from the fact that the particular rules are bad, ... but rather from the fact that we have such rules at all.").

29.   See *infra* 360, 364, 371-389.

30.   B. Currie, *Selected Essays* at 184.

31.   These consequences are discussed *infra* at 307, 336-340.

like Cavers, focused directly on the content of the substantive laws of the states implicated in the conflict. He argued that the "ordinary process of construction and interpretation" would reveal the policies underlying those laws and would, in turn, determine their intended sphere of operation in terms of space.

3.   The concept of governmental interests

17. According to Currie, whenever a case falls within a law's spatial reach as delineated by the interpretative process, the state from which that law emanates has a governmental interest in applying it so as to effectuate its underlying purposes[32]. Despite what the term might imply, a governmental interest is not the unilateral wish of the enacting state to apply its law in a given case. Rather, it is the result of a judge's evaluation of the reasonableness of this wish, in light of the factual elements that connect the enacting state with the case at hand. In Currie's words, an "interest ... is the product of *(a)* a governmental policy and *(b)* the concurrent existence of an appropriate relationship between the state having the policy and the transaction, the parties, or the litigation"[33]. In the words of one of Currie's followers, a state's interest consists of "mak[ing] effective, in all situations involving persons as to whom it has responsibility for legal ordering, that resolution of contending private interests the state has made for local purposes"[34]. Thus, Currie projected his legal-realist conception of law as "an instrument of social control"[35] at the interstate level by postulating that states do have an interest in the outcome of litigation between private parties.

4.   Currie's assumptions about state interests

18. The notion of a state interest in private-law disputes was not new in American law, domestic or interstate. For example, this notion had figured prominently in a cluster of US Supreme Court decisions in the 1930s interpreting the full faith

---

32.   In Currie's words,

>   "[T]he court should ... inquire whether the relationship of the forum state to the case at bar ... is such as to bring the case within the scope of the state's governmental concern, and to provide a legitimate basis for the assertion that the state has an interest in the application of its policy in this instance."

>   B. Currie, *Selected Essays* at 189.

33.   *Id.* at 621. But see L. McDougal, "Choice of Law: Prologue to a Viable Interest-Analysis Theory", 51 *Tul. L. Rev.* 207, 212 (1977) ("[A]n interest is not the 'product' of a policy; rather a policy reflects underlying interests.... . Interests give rise to the promulgation of policies and not vice versa.").

34.   W. Baxter, "Choice of Law and the Federal System", 16 *Stan. L. Rev.* 1, 17 (1963).

35.   B. Currie, *Selected Essays* at 64. For the influence of American Legal Realism and other philosophical trends on American choice-of-law thinking, see S. Symeonides, *An Outsider's View of the American Approach to Choice of Law: Comparative Observations on Current American and Continental Conflicts Doctrine* 202-234 (1980).

and credit clause of the Constitution[36]. What was new, and what evoked the criticism of many commentators[37], was Currie's partisan articulation of this concept. He thought and wrote in terms of a state's yearning to maximize its gains at the expense of other states' policies, rather than in terms of a state's need to avoid impairment of its own strongly held policies. As we shall see later[38], the main problem with Currie's interest-theory was not the core concept of state interests, but rather his narrow assumptions about the nature and scope of those interests.

In particular, Currie refused to consider a state's "multistate" interests, namely, interests which, though not reflected directly in a state's domestic law, stem from the state's membership in a broader community of states. For example, he specifically dismissed the view that a state should be guided in its choice-of-law decisions by the "needs of the interstate and international system"[39]. Currie thought that, because of its international origins, the traditional theory was overtaken by "the compulsion of internationalist and altruist ideals"[40]; it had "guiltily suppressed the natural instincts of community self-interest ... [and] enforce[d] a purposeless self-denial"[41]. To compensate for this, Currie's approach championed "the rational, moderate and controlled pursuit of self-interest"[42]. These adjectives offered some reassurance, as did his statements that "[t]he short-sighted, selfish state is nothing more than an experimental model"[43], and that "[n]o such state exists, at least in this country"[44]. Nevertheless, both the whole tenor and many of the specifics of his theory were far less moderate.

For example, Currie assumed that, in the vast majority of cases[45], a state has an interest in applying its law only when it benefits its domiciliaries, but not when it benefits similarly situated out-of-staters[46]. Thus, a state has an interest in applying

---

36. See *Bradford Elec. Light Co.* v. *Clapper*, 286 US 145 (1932); *Alaska Packers Ass'n* v. *Indus. Accident Comm'n*, 294 US 532 (1935); *Pacific Employers Ins.* Co. v. *Indus. Accident Comm'n*, 306 US 493 (1939). See also Watson v. *Employers Liab. Assur. Corp. Ltd.*, 348 US 66 (1954).

37. See *infra* 308-309; A. Ehrenzweig, *Private International Law* 63 (v. 11967); P. Hay, "Reflections on Conflict-of-Laws Methodology: A Dialogue", 32 *Hastings LJ* 1644, 1660 (1981); F. Juenger, "Choice of Law in Interstate Torts", 118 *U. Pa. L. Rev.* 200, 206 (1969); G. Kegel, "The Crisis of Conflict of Laws", 112 *Recueil des cours* 91, 180-182 (1964); M. Rheinstein, "How to Review a Festschrift", 11 *Am. J. Comp. L.* 632, 664 (1962).

38. See *infra* 308-309, 313-321.

39. B. Currie, *Selected Essays* at 614.

40. *Id.* at 525.

41. *Id.*

42. *Id.*

43. *Id.* at 616.

44. *Id.*

45. For an exception, see B. Currie, *Selected Essays* at 58-61, 69, where Currie distinguishes between "compensatory" rules and conduct-regulating rules and recognizes that the latter are territorially oriented.

46. See *id.* at 705.

its pro-plaintiff rules only for the benefit of local plaintiffs[47] and its pro-defendant rules only for the benefit of local defendants[48]. Because of this postulate (which is referred to hereafter as Currie's *"personal-law principle"*), some critics have charged that Currie's approach was constitutionally infirm[49]. Anticipating these criticisms, Currie argued, in essence, that his theory was not unconstitutional because the Constitution would not allow it to be[50]. Ironically, Currie was correct in the sense that: (1) the Supreme Court does not judge the constitutionality of theories in the abstract, but rather judges whether their application in the particular case produces an unconstitutional *result*[51], and (2) knowing this, reasonable courts will be careful not to apply Currie's theory in an unconstitutional manner, and thus the theory will not be found unconstitutional. This is what Currie must have had in mind when he stated that the Equal Protection and Privileges and Immunities clauses of the Constitution would help control undue protectionism[52], while the Due Process and Full Faith and Credit clauses would help control excessive forum favouritism[53]. However, it is a questionable policy to instigate protectionism and favouritism and then invoke constitutional compulsion to curtail it.

Finally, by Currie's own admission, his analysis is indifferent to the interests of individuals involved in the conflict. In his words, Currie found "no place in conflict-of-laws analysis for a calculus of private interests [because] [b]y the time the

---

47.　See *id.* at 691-721 (arguing that New York's unlimited compensatory-damages law "is not for the protection of all who buy tickets in New York, or board planes there. It is for the protection of New York people.").

48.　See *id.* at 724, and 85-86 (arguing that a state that has a guest-statute or a pro-defendant contract rule has an interest in applying them only if the defendants are domiciled in that state).

49.　See J. Ely, "Choice of Law and the State's Interest in Protecting its Own", 23 *Wm. & Mary L. Rev.* 173, 173-178 (1981) (charging that Currie's notion that states are interested in "generat[ing] victories for their own people in a way that they are not interested in generating victories for others", violates the Privileges and Immunities Clause of the Constitution); D. Laycock, "Equal Citizens of Equal and Territorial States: The Constitutional Foundations of Choice of Law", 92 *Colum. L. Rev.* 249 (1992).

50.　Currie acknowledged the potential for discrimination inherent in his analysis (see B. Currie, *Selected Essays* at 185-186), but expressed the confidence that the Equal Protection and Privileges and Immunities clauses of the Constitution would help control undue protectionism (*id.* at 123-126, 185, 191, 280, 285), while the Due Process and Full Faith and Credit clauses would help control excessive forum favouritism (*id.* at 271, 280-281, 191).

51.　See, e.g., *Allstate Ins. Co. v. Hague*, 449 US 302 (1981), in which a majority of the members of the Court expressed their disagreement with Minnesota's better-law approach but nevertheless found its application in the particular case to be constitutionally permissible.

52.　See *supra* footnote 50.

53.　See *id.*

interstate plane is reached the resolution of conflicting private interests has been achieved; it is subsumed in the statement of the laws of the respective states"[54].

5.   *False, true, and in-between conflicts*

19. In Currie's view, when a litigant argues that the court should apply foreign law to a multistate case, the court should first inquire into the policies embodied in the laws of the involved states, asking whether it is reasonable for each state to assert an interest in applying these laws to effectuate these policies. This inquiry may lead to three possibilities, which in turn correspond to the three well-known, if not well-accepted, categories of conflicts:
(a)   only one of the involved states is interested in applying its law (the *"false conflict"* pattern);
(b)   more than one state is interested (the *"true conflict"* pattern); or
(c)   none of the states are interested (the "no-interest" pattern or *"unprovided-for* case").

In his later work, Currie recognized a fourth category, what he called an *"apparent conflict"*, which is something between a false and a true conflict[55]. This category is terminologically useful, in that it names the grey area that lies between false and true conflicts. However, the practical utility of this category is questionable, if only because of the fluidity and manipulability of its outer limits[56]. In fact, the same fluidity characterizes all four of Currie's categories, because the primordial question of whether a state has an "interest" is one that different analysts often answer differently. Nevertheless, the above terms are useful in providing a common vocabulary and a framework for analysis and discussion.
20. In short, Currie argued that, subject only to constitutional restraints, the forum is entitled to, and should, apply its law to all of the above cases, except some false and apparent conflicts.
In false conflicts, Currie would apply the law of the only interested state, which in the majority of cases is likely to be the forum state. This part of Currie's analysis is neither controversial nor controvertible, at least for those who sub-

---

54.   B. Currie, *Selected Essays* at 610. But see Currie's letter to Cavers in D. Cavers, "A Correspondence with Brainerd Currie, 1957-58", 34 *Mercer L. Rev.* 471, 488 (1983) ("I shall not admit that I am unwilling to consider the claims of human beings to justice unless I can fit them into the conception of state interests.").
55.   In Currie's words, an apparent conflict is a case in which "each state would be constitutionally justified in asserting an interest, but on reflection the conflict is avoided by a moderate definition of the policy or interest of one state or the other", or "a case in which reasonable men may disagree on whether a conflicting interest should be asserted." B. Currie, "The Disinterested Third State", 28 *Law & Contemp. Prob.* 754, 763, 764 (1963).
56.   Currie conceded this fluidity when he stated that "indeed, the three classes of cases [i.e., false, apparent, true] are a continuum with no clear internal boundaries." B. Currie, *The Disinterested Third State* at 764.

scribe to the view that consideration of state interests is a proper starting point for resolving conflicts of laws[57]. In contrast to the traditional theory which, by failing to inquire into state interests, had the propensity to randomly sacrifice the interests of one state without promoting the interests of another state[58], Currie's solution to an admittedly false conflict can effectuate the policies of an interested state without sacrificing any policies of an uninterested state. In this sense, the concept of a false conflict was an important breakthrough in American choice-of-law thinking, and has become an integral part of all modern policy-based analyses[59].

21. However, Currie's solutions to the other categories of conflicts are questionable. Under Currie's analysis, true conflicts are to be resolved by the application of the law of the forum[60], because a court *may not* subordinate the forum's interests to those of another state[61]. Indeed, the very possibility of such a subordination impels Currie to insist that judges should not even attempt to weigh the interests of the two states. His explanation is that judges do not have the constitutional power, nor the necessary resources, to weigh conflicting governmental interests, and should not be put in the position of having to subordinate the forum's interests. Currie thought that such a weighing is a "political function of a very high order ... that should not be committed to courts in a democracy"[62].

---

57. See *infra* 308-309.

58. See B. Currie, *Selected Essays* at 191. See also *id.* at 589-590.

59. See S. Symeonides, "Revolution and Counter-Revolution in American Conflicts Law: Is There a Middle Ground?", 46 *Ohio St. LJ* 549, 564 (1985) ("That this [concept] is by now taken for granted, even by [Currie's] critics, and forms the common denominator of all current choice of law methodologies is no reason to deny him the credit rightfully due to him. Even if this were Currie's only contribution to conflicts theory, it would be sufficient to secure him a permanent position in the conflicts 'Hall of Fame.'").

60. A true conflict may arise before an interested or a disinterested forum. In the first situation, Currie advocated the application of the law of the forum for reasons stated in the text. In the second situation, Currie argued that the court should dismiss on *forum non conveniens* grounds and, if such dismissal is not possible, then apply forum law, at least when that law corresponds with the law of one of the interested states. See B. Currie, *The Disinterested Third State*, 765, 777 ff. Alternatively, Currie suggested, "the court might decide the case by a candid exercise of legislative discretion, resolving the conflict as it believes it would be resolved by a supreme legislative body having power to determine which interest should be required to yield". Currie's summary reproduced in S. Symeonides, W. Perdue and A. von Mehren, Conflict of Laws: *American Comparative International* 116 (2nd ed. 2003).

61. See B. Currie, "Comments on *Babcock* v. *Jackson* – A Recent Development in Conflict of Laws", 63 *Colum. L. Rev.* 1233, 1237-1238 (1963) ("In the absence of action by higher authority, each state must be conceded the *right* to apply its own laws for the reasonable effectuation of its own policies.") (Emphasis added).

62. B. Currie, *Selected Essays* at 182. See also *id.* (where Currie speaks of the "embarrassment of [a court] having to nullify the interests of its own sovereign"); *id.* at 278-279, 357; B. Currie, "The Disinterested Third State", 28 *Law & Contemp. Prob.* 754, 778 (1963).

In light of Currie's proud adherence to the common-law tradition[63], the above explanation is surprising in that it assumes a conception of the judicial process that does not reflect the realities of the American common-law tradition, in which judges almost routinely engage in evaluating and weighing conflicting social policies[64]. This explanation also contradicts the basic tenets of his theory, which in every other respect assumes an activist judge. For example, according to Currie's own analysis, in order to determine whether the conflict is a false or a true one, the judge must identify and articulate the interests of the involved states. The judicial application of this part of Currie's analysis suggests that this task is no less subjective or politically sensitive than the weighing of interests. The two tasks differ only in degree. If judges are qualified and empowered to identify governmental interests, they do not lose nor abdicate that power the moment they encounter a true conflict[65].

In one of his last writings, Currie advised that in some cases the judge should subject the laws of the involved states to a more moderate and restrained interpretation, which could lead to the conclusion that one of those states is not as interested as it might appear at first blush. If so, this would be an *apparent conflict* in which the judge should apply the law of the other state[66]. Although Currie asserted that this process of re-evaluating the two states' interests is qualitatively

---

63. See B. Currie, *Selected Essays* at 627 ("I am proud to associate myself with the common law tradition.").

64. As one observer put it, "[e]ver since conflicts law first developed, courts did precisely what Currie would forbid them to do; no judge has ever been impeached for inventing or applying a choice of law rule that sacrifices forum interests". F. Juenger, "Choice of Law in Interstate Torts", 118 *U. Pa. L. Rev.* 200, 206-207 (1969). See also A. Ehrenzweig, "A Counter-Revolution in Conflicts Law?", 80 *Harv. L. Rev.* 377, 389 (1966) ("[A]ll courts and writers who have professed acceptance of Currie's interest language have transformed it by indulging in that very weighing and balancing of interest from which Currie refrained."). Currie's response to such observations was sharp and short: "I do not care whether courts undertake to weigh and balance conflicting interests or not", he said, but when they do, "such action can find its justification in politics, not in jurisprudence". B. Currie, *Selected Essays* at 600-601. See *id.* at 183, 274 for a more moderate response.

65. As Cavers put it, in Currie's analysis, "[w]eighing of interests after interpretation is condemned: weighing of interests in interpretation, condoned, not to say, encouraged". D. Cavers, "Contemporary Conflicts in American Perspective", 131 *Recueil des cours* 75, 148 (1970).

66. See B. Currie, *The Disinterested Third State*, *supra* at 763, 764.

different from the weighing of the interests[67], this assertion seems to stretch the meaning of words[68].

22. Finally, under Currie's analysis, the law of the forum applies to his third category of conflicts – the "unprovided-for" or "no-interest" cases – even though in these cases the forum is, *ex hypothesi*, a disinterested state. Currie's explanation for applying the law of the forum is that "no good purpose will be served by putting the parties to the expense and the court to the trouble of ascertaining the foreign law"[69]. This is a practical explanation. Unfortunately, it overlooks the problem grammarians call *prothysteron*: one cannot know whether the case is a no-interest case without first knowing whether the foreign state is uninterested; and one cannot know whether that state is uninterested without first ascertaining the content of its law and identifying the policies underlying it.

6.   *Forum favouritism*

23. In sum, therefore, under Currie's analysis, almost all roads lead to the *lex fori*. Currie would apply foreign law in only two situations, both of which are fairly infrequent: *(a)* false conflicts in which the forum is not interested; and *(b)* apparent conflicts in which the judge chooses to subject the law of the forum, rather than that of the foreign state, to a restrained interpretation. In all other cases, Currie would apply the *lex fori*, to wit: *(1)* in a false conflict in which the forum is the interested state; *(2)* in a true conflict in which the forum is one of the interested states; *(3)* in the no-interest or unprovided-for case; and *(4)* even in a true conflict

---

67.   See B. Currie, *Selected Essays* at 759 ("[T]here is an important difference between a court's construing domestic law with moderation in order to avoid conflict with a foreign interest and its holding that the foreign interest is paramount. When a court avowedly uses the tools of construction and interpretation, it invites legislative correction of error. ... When it weighs state interests and finds a foreign interest weightier, it inhibits legislative intervention and confounds criticism.").

68.   Although Currie's statements regarding *which* state's interests should be subjected to a "restrained interpretation" are ambiguous, it seems that in most cases this aspect of his analysis presupposes the very kind of judicial discretion that he proscribes. This is clearer if the judge is to *choose between the two interests* in deciding which one to re-evaluate, or if the judge is to subject *both* interests to this re-evaluation. On the other hand, if the judge is to subject only the *forum's* interests to this "restrained interpretation", then this will entail a subordination of those interests, which (in Currie's conception of courts as instruments of state policy) is something judges may not do. Finally, if the judge is to subject only the *foreign* interest to this "restrained interpretation", then this would seem to defeat the purpose for which Currie proposed this re-evaluation (i.e., to rebut accusations that his theory was unduly parochial and forum-oriented). Even Justice Traynor (who, according to Currie, engaged in such a re-evaluation in some of his decisions) conceded that this process involved interest weighing. See R. Traynor, "Conflicts of Laws: Professor Currie's Restrained and Enlightened Forum", 49 *Calif. L. Rev.* 845, 855 (1961). See also *id.* at 853 (noting that "Currie's proscription of interest weighing seems to strike at the heart of the judicial process").

69.   B. Currie, *Selected Essays* at 156, 152-156.

before a disinterested forum, if the court cannot dismiss on grounds of *forum non conveniens*[70].

Although Currie defended his forum favouritism with arguments that ranged from the practical to the philosophical[71], his defense was not persuasive. In the words of one commentator, "Currie's analysis, which compels him to give to the forum's law such broad effects, would tend to fasten upon the international and the inter-state communities ... a legal order characterized by chaos and retaliation"[72].

7.   Currie's contribution

24. Currie's theory dominated choice-of-law thinking in the United States for almost three decades[73]. His "seductive style" of writing "hypnotized a whole generation of American lawyers"[74], perhaps in the same way that Beale's teachings had indoctrinated the previous generation[75]. While judicial support for Currie's approach has decreased dramatically in recent years[76], his analysis "still controls the academic conflicts agenda"[77], perhaps because this analysis remains the most popular pedagogical vehicle for teaching conflicts law in American law schools[78].

---

70. See *id.* at 182 (suggesting that a disinterested forum should apply its own law if it is similar to one of the competing laws or if the conflict between those laws is otherwise unavoidable).

71. See, e.g., *id.* 89, 93-94, 191, 197, 278-280, 323, 447, 489-490, 592, 627, 697.

72. A. von Mehren, "Book Review", 17 *J. Legal Ed.* 91, 97 n. 2 (1964). For similar criticisms, see P. Hay, "Flexibility versus Predictability and Uniformity in Choice of Law", 226 *Recueil des cours* 281 (1991); G. Kegel, "The Crisis in the Conflict of Laws", 112 *Recueil des cours* 95, 207 (1964).

73. The intense academic interest in Currie's theory is illustrated, *inter alia*, by the many Symposia devoted to interest analysis. See "Symposium on Interest Analysis in Conflict of Laws", 46 *Ohio St. LJ* 457 (1985) (contributions by Kozyris, Brilmayer, Sedler, Weintraub, Juenger, Evrigenis, Berman, Zaphiriou, Shreve, Luneburg, and Symeonides); "New Directions in Choice of Law: Alternatives to Interest Analysis", 24 *Cornell Int'l LJ* 195 (1991) (contributions by Simson, Singer, Brilmayer, and Kramer); "Choice of Law: How It Ought to Be", 48 *Mercer L. Rev.* 623 (Roundtable discussion by David Currie, Felix, Kay, Knowles, Posnak, Rees, and Sammons; Articles by Borchers, Cox, Juenger, Kay, O'Hara, Ribstein, Reynolds, Sedler, Shreve, Singer, Symeonides, and Weintraub).

74. H. Korn, "The Choice-of-Law Revolution: A Critique", 83 *Colum. L. Rev.* 772, 812 (1983).

75. In the words of Professor Juenger, one of Currie's harshest critics, "the single most influential American book on the conflict of laws published during the twentieth century was not Joseph Beale's three-volume treatise or Ernst Rabel's monumental four-volume comparative study, but Currie's collection of ... articles." F. Juenger, *Selected Essays on the Conflict of Laws*, vii-viii (2001).

76. See *infra* 65-66.

77. F. Juenger, "Conflict of Laws: A Critique of Interest Analysis", 32 *Am. J. Comp. L.* 1, 4 (1984).

78. See C. Peterson, "Restating Conflicts Again: A Cure for Schizophrenia?", 75 *Ind. LJ* 549, 559 (2000) (concluding that "the survival of interest analysis as a dominant

As Professor Weinberg aptly stated, "interest analysis is the very language of contemporary conflicts theory"[79].

In recent years, Currie's critics[80] clearly outnumber his old and new allies[81]. As explained later[82], there is much to criticize in Currie's theory. However, there is also much to praise. Some of Currie's critics seem to have focused more on debunking Currie's theory than on separating the tenable from the untenable elements of his analysis[83]. It would seem that, even if the latter elements outnumber

---

aspect of conflicts theory is the result of the fact that law professors use it to teach the subject of conflict of laws – even if they do not personally subscribe to its methodology").

79. L. Weinberg, "Theory Wars in the Conflict of Laws", 103 *Mich. L. Rev.* 1631, 1649 (2005).

80. In addition to works cited elsewhere in this chapter, the following are among Currie's early critics in the United States: A. Hill, "Governmental Interest and the Conflict of Laws – A Reply to Professor Currie", 27 *U. Chi. L. Rev.* 463 (1960); F. Juenger, "Choice of Law in Interstate Torts", 118 *U. Pa. L. Rev.* 202 (1969); M. Rosenberg, "Comments on *Reich* v. *Purcell*", 15 *UCLA L. Rev.* 641 (1968); A. Twerski, "*Neumeier* v. *Kuehner*: Where are the Emperor's Clothes?", 1 *Hofstra L. Rev.* 93 (1973); A. von Mehren, "Book Review", 17 *J. Legal Ed.* 91 (1964). For early European criticisms, see D. Evrigenis, "Tendances doctrinales actuelles en droit international privé", 118 *Recueil des cours* 313 (1966); G. Kegel, "The Crisis of Conflict of Laws", 112 *Recueil des cours* 91 (1964). For later American criticisms, see E. Bodenheimer, "The Need for a Reorientation in American Conflicts Law", 29 *Hastings LJ* 731 (1978); P. Borchers, "Conflicts Pragmatism", 56 *Alb. L. Rev.* 883 (1993); L. Brilmayer, "The Role of Substantive and Choice of Law Policies in the Formation of Choice of Law Rules", 252 *Recueil des cours* 9 (1995); J. Ely, "Choice of Law and the State's Interest in Protecting Its Own", 23 *Wm. & Mary L. Rev.* 173 (1983); P. Hay, "Reflections on Conflict-of-Laws Methodology: A Dialogue", 32 *Hastings LJ* 1644 (1981); H. Korn, "The Choice-of-Law Revolution: A Critique", 83 *Colum. L. Rev.* 772 (1983); P. Kozyris, "Reflections on *Allstate* – The Lessening of Due Process in Choice of Law", 14 *UC Davis L. Rev.* 889 (1981); J. Singer, "Real Conflicts", 69 *B.U. L. Rev.* 1 (1989); D. Trautman, "Reflections on Conflict-of-Law Methodology: A Dialogue", 32 *Hastings LJ* 1609 (1981).

81. See, in particular, H. Kay, "Currie's Interest Analysis in the 21st Century: Losing the Battle, but Winning the War", 37 *Willamette L. Rev.* 123 (2001); H. Kay, "A Defense of Currie's Governmental Interest Analysis", 215 *Recueil des cours* 9 (1989); B. Posnak, "Choice of Law: Interest Analysis and Its 'New Crits'", 36 *Am. J. Comp. L.* 681 (1988); R. Sedler, "Interest Analysis and Forum Preference in the Conflict of Laws: A Response to the 'New Critics'", 34 *Mercer L. Rev.* 593 (1984). See also H. Baade, "Counter-Revolution or Alliance for Progress? Reflections on Reading Cavers, *The Choice-of-Law-Process*", 46 *Tex. L. Rev.* 141 (1967); L. Kramer, "Interest Analysis and the Presumption of Forum Law", 56 *U. Chi. L. Rev.* 1301 (1989); L. Weinberg, "On Departing from Forum Law", 35 *Mercer L. Rev.* 595 (1984); R. Weintraub, "Interest Analysis in the Conflict of Laws as an Application of Sound Legal Reasoning", 35 *Mercer L. Rev.* 629 (1984).

82. See *infra* 307-309, 313-316, 318-321, 331-335, 338-339, 360, 371-373.

83. For an effort to separate the two, see S. Symeonides, "Revolution and Counter-Revolution in American Conflicts Law: Is There a Middle Ground?" 46 *Ohio St. LJ* 549 (1985).

the former, Currie's overall contribution to the advancement of American conflicts law is a decidedly positive one, if only because he stirred the stagnant waters of the "dismal swamp" of American conflicts law. But Currie did much more. His analysis was intentionally provocative and unintentionally extreme. However, in its basic core of making state interests the basis for resolving conflict of laws, it was new for American conflicts law and fundamentally correct.

Because Currie's framework of analysis, as well as his categorization of conflicts into false, true, and unprovided-for cases, remain the best analytical framework for discussing the cases, this book follows both.

E.   Comparative Impairment

25. Professor William F. Baxter took interest analysis to the next step, or perhaps in a different direction, with his "comparative impairment" theory[84]. Baxter agreed with Currie on two points: first, on the process of identifying and resolving false conflicts, and second, on the impropriety of weighing interests as a means of resolving true conflicts[85]. Baxter did not, however, accept Currie's view that the application of the *lex fori* is the only possible solution for true conflicts. Baxter argued that a "normative resolution of real conflicts cases is possible", and that an examination of the basic premises underlying the federal system would reveal "normative principles which could and should serve as a foundation for choice-of-law rules"[86]. To that end, Baxter proposed his "comparative impairment"[87] formula.

Baxter distinguished between two types of governmental interests or objectives – the "internal" and the "external." The internal objectives underlie each state's resolution of conflicting private interests in wholly domestic situations. The external objectives embody each state's goal "to make effective in all situations involving persons as to whom it has responsibility for legal ordering, the resolution of contending private interests the state has made for local purposes"[88]. In a true conflict, *ex hypothesi*, this external objective conflicts with the corresponding external objective of a foreign state. Rather than subordinating the external objective of the foreign state to that of the forum, as would Currie, Baxter would "subordinate ... the external objective of the state whose internal objective will be least impaired in general scope and impact by subordination in cases like

---

84.   See W. Baxter, "Choice of Law and the Federal System", 16 *Stan. L. Rev.* 1 (1963).

85.   See *id.* at 8, 5-6, 18-19. Echoing Currie, Baxter stated that weighing of interests involves super-value judgments that are incompatible with the judge's "non-political status." *Id.* at 5.

86.   *Id.* at 8-9.

87.   See also H. Horowitz, "Toward a Federal Common Law of Choice of Law", 14 *UCLA L. Rev.* 1191 (1967); H. Horowitz, "The Law of Choice of Law in California – A Restatement", 21 *UCLA L. Rev.* 719 (1974).

88.   W. Baxter, "Choice of Law and the Federal System", 16 *Stan. L. Rev.* 1, 18 (1963).

the one at hand"[89]. In simpler words, Baxter would apply the law of that state whose interests would be most impaired if its law were not applied.

26. In essence, rather than weighing the interests, comparative impairment weighs the *loss* that would result from subordinating the interests of one state to those of another state. However, inasmuch as the gravity of the loss depends on the strength and importance of each state's interest, one cannot avoid the conclusion that comparative impairment does weigh the interests. This is not a criticism of comparative impairment. Indeed, this author, having used comparative impairment *terminology* in drafting the Louisiana conflicts codification[90], does not consider himself a critic of Baxter's approach. Moreover, the undersigned subscribes to the view that weighing of state interests is an appropriate, if not inevitable, means of resolving conflicts in any approach that acknowledges the existence of state interests.

The question is not whether courts can or should weigh state interests, but rather how to weigh them, and how to resolve the resulting conflicts.

F.   Leflar and the "Better Law" Approach

27. Despite their criticism of the traditional theory in other respects, Cook, Currie, and to a lesser extent Cavers remained within the confines of the classical view of private international law in one core respect – they subscribed to the same basic premise that the goal of conflicts law is to achieve "the *spatially* best solution"[91] ("conflicts justice"), rather than "the *materially* best solution"[92] ("material justice")[93]. Professor Robert A. Leflar was among the first proponents of the material-justice view in the United States[94]. In two successive law review arti-

---

89.   *Id.*

90.   See *infra* 102.

91.   G. Kegel, "Paternal Home and Dream Home: Traditional Conflict of Laws and the American Reformers", 27 *Am. J. Comp. L.* 615, 616-17 (1979).

92.   *Id.*

93.   The tension between these two conceptions of private international law is discussed later. See *infra* 349-357. See also S. Symeonides, "Material Justice and Conflicts Justice in Choice of Law", in *International Conflict of Laws for the Third Millennium: Essays in Honor of Friedrich K. Juenger* 125 (P. Borchers and J. Zekoll eds. 2000).

94.   Another prominent proponent of this view was Professor Friedrich K. Juenger. See F. Juenger, *Choice of Law and Multistate Justice* 145-173, 191-208 (1993). In this fascinating book, Professor Juenger advocated a type of better-law approach, although he prefers to call it the "substantive-law" approach. By using the latter terminology Juenger intended to connect his approach with the most ancient approach to resolving conflicts problems – the approach of the Roman *Praetor peregrinus* who, in resolving disputes between Roman and non-Roman citizens, constructed *ad hoc* substantive rules derived from the laws of the involved countries. Juenger argued that in today's multistate cases, the court should construct from among the involved states a rule of law that best accords with modern substantive-law trends and standards. For example, for products liability conflicts, Juenger proposed that from among the

cles[95], Leflar proposed a non-hierarchical list of five choice-influencing considerations for guiding courts in resolving conflicts problems. The list consisted of: (1) predictability of results, (2) maintenance of interstate and international order, (3) simplification of the judicial task, (4) advancement of the forum's governmental interest, and (5) the application of the "better rule of law"[96].

Leflar argued that through reference to these considerations, "courts can replace with statements of real reasons the mechanical rules and circuitously devised approaches which have appeared in the language of conflicts opinions, too often as cover-ups for the real reason that underlay the decisions"[97].

28. As the above list indicates, there is much more to Leflar's approach than the "better-law" criterion. As Leflar said, "this fifth consideration ... is only one of five, more important in some types of cases than in others, almost controlling in some but irrelevant in others"[98]. This statement reiterates the non-hierarchical nature of Leflar's list, but also reveals the potentially controlling role of the better-law criterion. By not expressly assigning a residual role to this criterion, Leflar allowed it to become the decisive criterion in all the close cases. At least in the early years, this is precisely how courts employed this criterion, while paying lip service to the

---

laws of the places of conduct, injury, acquisition of the product, and domicile of the parties, the court should choose "[a]s to each issue ... that rule of decision which most closely accords with modern standards of products liability". *Id.* at 197. For a symposium on Juenger's writings, see F. Juenger, *Choice of Law and Multistate Justice* (Special ed. 2005).

95.   See R. Leflar, "Choice-Influencing Considerations in Conflicts Law", 41 *NYU L. Rev.* 367 (1966); R. Leflar, "Conflicts of Law: More on Choice Influencing Considerations", 54 *Cal. L. Rev.* 1584 (1966).

96.   As the word "better" indicates, Leflar envisioned *choosing*, between or among the laws of the involved states, the one law that is better. Thus, although unconventional in one sense, Leflar's approach is conventional in another sense – it is a "conflictual" or "selectivist" approach. See S. Symeonides, "American Choice of Law at the Dawn of the 20th Century", 37 *Willamette L. Rev.* 1, 4, 11-16 (2001). In contrast, Professor Luther McDougal took the material-justice view beyond the confines of the selectivist method by advocating a search for the "best" rule of law, which (unlike the "better law") assumes that "[c]ourts are not so limited in their choice [and that they] can, and should, in many cases construct and apply a law specifically created for the resolution of choice of law cases". L. McDougal, "Towards the Application of the Best Rule of Law in Choice of Law Cases", 35 *Mercer L. Rev.* 483, 483-484 (1984). McDougal described the best rule of law as the "one that best promotes net aggregate long-term common interests", *id.* at 484, and gave two examples of such rules: for non-economic loses, he proposed a rule that permits "complete recovery of all losses, pecuniary and nonpecuniary, and of all reasonable costs incurred in obtaining recovery, including reasonable attorneys' fees and litigation costs", *id.* at 533. For claims concerning punitive damages, he proposed a rule that imposes such damages "on individuals who engage in outrageous conduct and who are not adequately punished in the criminal process". *Id.*

97.   R. Leflar, "Conflicts of Law: More on Choice Influencing Considerations", 54 *Cal. L. Rev.* 1584, 1585 (1966).

98.   R. Leflar, L. McDougal and R. Felix, *American Conflicts Law* 300 (4th ed. 1986).

other four. If one adds the fact that, but for the better-law criterion, Leflar's list differs little from the lists proposed by others[99] or the list of §6 of the Second Restatement, then one can understand why Leflar's approach is deservedly known as "the better-law approach" and may be criticized or praised on that basis[100].

29. The undersigned is not alone in having more criticism than praise. The main criticisms are that a better-law approach entails either, or both, of the following risks: *(1)* becoming a euphemism for a *lex fori* approach; and *(2)* providing convenient cover for judicial subjectivism. Although Leflar admonished against subjective choices and argued that judges are capable of recognizing when foreign law is better than forum law[101], there is considerable evidence to support a conclusion that these risks are real. For example, as documented below[102], in the five states that adopted Leflar's approach for tort conflicts, one finds only five supreme court cases that have applied foreign law. Two of those cases were decided by the Supreme Court of Minnesota[103], and although in one of them the court admitted that the foreign law was better[104], this was a case in which one could not avoid that law under any theory, traditional or modern[105].

---

99. See, e.g., the list proposed in E. Cheatham and W. Reese, "Choice of the Applicable Law", 52 *Colum. L. Rev.* 959 (1952).

100. Most of the criticism comes from academic circles. See, e.g., E. Scoles, P. Hay, P. Borchers and S. Symeonides, *Conflict of Laws* 52-58 (4th ed. 2004); H. Baade, "Counter-Revolution or Alliance for Progress?", 46 *Tex. L. Rev.* 141, 155ff. (1947); D. Cavers, "The Value of Principled Preferences", 49 *Tex. L. Rev.* 211, 212-213, 214, 215 (1971); G. Kegel, "Paternal Home and Dream Home: Traditional Conflict of Laws and the American Reformers", 27 *Am. J. Comp. L.* 615 (1979); S. Symeonides, "Material Justice and Conflicts Justice in Choice of Law", in *International Conflict of Laws for the Third Millennium: Essays in Honor of Friedrich K. Juenger*, 125 (P. Borchers and J. Zekoll eds. 2000); A. von Mehren, "Recent Trends in Choice-of-Law Methodology", 60 *Cornell L. Rev.* 927, 952-953 (1975). For praise by academic writers, see a Symposium in 52 *Ark. L. Rev.* 1 (1999) (containing articles by Watkins, Cox, Felix, McDougal, Simson, Weintraub, and Whitten); F. Juenger, "Leflar's Contributions to American Conflicts Law", 31 *SC L. Rev.* 413 (1980). Judges generally are more receptive, perhaps understandably, and some are enthusiastic supporters. For warm praise by Justice Todd, the author of the majority opinion in *Milkovich* v. *Saari*, 203 NW 2d 408 (Minn. 1973) (discussed *infra* at 131), see J. Todd, "A Judge's View", 31 *SC L. Rev.* 435 (1980).

101. See R. Leflar, L. McDougal and R. Felix, *American Conflicts Law*, 298-299 (4th ed. 1986) ("Judges can appreciate ... the fact that their forum law in some areas is anachronistic ... or that the law of another state has these benighted characteristics.").

102. See *infra* 73-76.

103. See *Bigelow* v. *Halloran*, 313 NW 2d 10 (Minn. 1981); *Jepson* v. *Gen. Cas. Co. of Wisconsin*, 513 NW 2d 467 (Minn. 1994). For further discussion, see *infra* 73-76.

104. See *Bigelow* v. *Halloran*, 313 NW 2d 10 (Minn. 1981).

105. *Bigelow* involved an intentional tort committed in Iowa against a resident of that state by a Minnesota resident who later shot himself. The plaintiff worked in Minnesota and later moved her domicile to that state. Under the law of Iowa, but not Minnesota, the plaintiff's action survived the death of the tortfeasor. One year after *Bigelow*, the

In another case, *Allstate Ins. Co.* v. *Hague*[106], the court's application of forum law as the better law barely passed constitutional muster under a very loose standard[107]. In *Milkovich* v. *Saari*[108], the same court expressed its firm conviction of the "superiority"[109] of the forum's rule, and held it applicable primarily on that basis.

Similarly, the New Hampshire Supreme Court[110] as well as some lower Minnesota courts[111], have proclaimed that the forum's law remained "better" than that of the corresponding foreign law, even after the forum's legislature had repealed that law and replaced it with a law similar to the rejected foreign law.

G.   Functional Analyses

1.   Von Mehren and Trautman

30. In 1965, Professors Arthur T. von Mehren and Donald T. Trautman developed an approach to conflicts which they called "functional analysis"[112]. The fact that the authors formulated this approach in the context of a casebook, coupled with the approach's subtlety and sophistication, impedes any attempt at summarization. It is fair to say, however, that the first four steps of functional analysis are

---

same Minnesota court declared unconstitutional Minnesota's non-survival rule. See Thompson v. Estate of Petroff, 319 NW 2d 400 (Minn. 1982)

106. *Hague* v. *Allstate Ins. Co.*, 289 NW 2d 43, 48 (Minn. 1978), *aff'd*, 449 US 302 (1981).

107. See *Allstate Ins. Co.* v. *Hague*, 449 US 302 (1981).

108. 203 NW 2d 408 (Minn. 1973) (involving a suit between Ontario parties for injuries sustained in a single-car accident in Minnesota).

109. *Milkovich*, 203 NW 2d at 417 (1973): "In our search for the better rule, we are firmly convinced of the superiority of the common-law rule of liability to that of the Ontario guest statute ... . Accordingly, we hold that Minnesota law should be applied."

110. See *Keeton* v. *Hustler Magazine, Inc.*, 549 A. 2d 1187 (NH 1988) (holding that New Hampshire's six-year statute of limitation was better than the shorter statutes of other states, even after the New Hampshire legislature had voted to shorten that statute).

111. See *Wille* v. *Farm Bureau Mut. Ins. Co.*, 432 NW 2d 784 (Minn. App. 1988) and *Meir* v. *Auto Owners Ins. Co.*, 1989 Minn. App. Lexis 222 (1989) (holding that Minnesota's insurance stacking rule was "better" than Indiana's anti-stacking rule, even though by the time of the trial the Minnesota rule had been replaced by an anti-stacking rule that was identical to Indiana's). But see *Stenzel* v. *State Farm Mut. Auto Ins. Co.*, 379 NW 2d 674 (Minn. App. 1986) (concluding that, *because* of its repeal, the same Minnesota rule could no longer be considered the better rule of law). Both *Wille* and *Stenzel* were eventually disapproved by the Minnesota Supreme Court in *Jepson* v. *Gen. Cas. Co. of Wisconsin*, 513 NW 2d 467, 473 (Minn. 1994): "We disagree with the views expressed in *Stenzel* and *Wille*, as well as by the parties, as to which is the better rule of law. From our present day vantage point, neither the law Minnesota had then, nor the law we have now, is clearly better."

112. A. T. von Mehren and D. T. Trautman, *The Law of Multistate Problems*, 76, 102-105, 109-115, 178-210 (1965). See also A. von Mehren, "Recent Trends in Choice-of-Law Methodology", 60 *Cornell LQ* 927 (1975).

methodologically, though not philosophically, similar to interest analysis and its identification of false conflicts and apparent conflicts.

The major differences between the two methods appear in the handling of true conflicts. Unlike interest analysis, functional analysis openly advocates policy weighing, guided by specific criteria[113]. The first criterion is the relevant strength of the policies of the involved states. In measuring the strength of the respective policies, the court is to consider the conviction with which a state adheres to a policy, the appropriateness of that state's rule to the effectuation of its underlying policy, and the relative significance, to the states concerned, of the vindication of their policies. For example, all other factors being equal, the court should prefer an emerging rather than a regressing policy, or a policy underlying a specific rule rather than a policy underlying a general principle. The court also should engage in a comparative evaluation of the asserted policies, judging their strength and merits not only in comparison with the policies of other concerned states, but also in comparison with the policies of all states sharing the same legal and cultural tradition. For cases that the court cannot resolve by a rational choice among the various domestic or multistate policies, the court may select a commonly held multistate policy, or construct a new multistate rule[114], or, finally, apply the rule of the state that has the most effective control over the subject matter.

For those cases that remain unresolved after all these steps, functional analysis proposes certain other guidelines, such as applying the rule that best promotes multistate activity, or interferes least with the parties' intentions[115]. Only when all other routes have been explored and found ineffectual do von Mehren and Trautman admit that the forum may apply its own law, but on the condition that, all other factors being equal, the forum is also a concerned state. A neutral forum, in contrast, should not apply its own law, but it may apply the rule of a concerned state that approximates most closely the forum's rule. It is, however, desirable that such a forum exploit its impartial position and choose solutions that promote multistate activity and uniformity of decisions[116].

---

113. See A. von Mehren and D. Trautman, *supra*, at 376-406.

114. See A. von Mehren, "Special Substantive Rules for Multistate Problems: Their Role and Significance in Contemporary Choice of Law Methodology", 88 *Harv. L. Rev.* 347 (1974).

115. A. von Mehren and D. Trautman, *supra*, 406-408.

116. In 1974, Professor von Mehren suggested that certain true conflicts can be resolved expediently through a compromise of the conflicting state policies, rather than by fully vindicating the policies of the one state and completely subordinating those of the other state. This compromise would take the form of a special substantive rule, constructed *ad hoc*, for the case at hand and derived from the laws of both, or all involved states. For example, a court could resolve a true conflict between one state's strict-liability law and another state's non-liability law through a new substantive rule that would allow the recovery of only half of plaintiff's actual damages. See A. von Mehren, "Special Substantive Rules for Multistate Problems: Their Role and Significance in Contemporary Choice of Law Methodology", 88 *Harv. L. Rev.* 298, 367-369 (1974). The above suggestions resemble the substantive-law method of the Roman *praetor pereg-*

2.   Weintraub's consequences-based approach

31. In his early writings, Professor Russell J. Weintraub developed a "functional approach" that also advocated a weighing of interests but identified with more specificity the relevant criteria[117]. Weintraub also took the next step of distilling these criteria into two result-oriented rules – a plaintiff-favouring rule for non-false tort conflicts[118], and a "rule of validation" for contract cases[119]. In the 2001 edition of his *Commentary*, Weintraub conceded that his earlier proposed tort rule "was really an attempt at 'better law' analysis"[120], which was necessary at a time when tort laws were so drastically different from state to state, with some states holding on to anachronistic anti-recovery rules. With so many states having since moved and continuing to move in the opposite direction, says Weintraub, "[t]imes have changed"[121].

Weintraub now proposes a new "consequences-based approach"[122], which "chooses law with knowledge of the content of the laws of each of the [involved] states ... [and] seeks to minimize the consequences that any such state is likely to experience if its law is not applied"[123]. According to this approach, the court should (1) identify the policies underlying the conflicting laws of the involved states; (2) determine whether the non-application of a state's law would cause that state "to experience consequences that it is its policy to avoid"[124]; and (3) ensure that "ap-

---

rinus. Today, they may sound anomalous, perhaps because in the meantime, as Trautman suggests, "[w]e have become so accustomed by tradition and theory to ideas of conflict, choice and selection". D. Trautman, "The Relation between American Choice of Law and Federal Common Law", 41 *Law & Contemp. Prob.* 105, 118 (1977). Yet, it may be worth asking whether it is a good idea, in a discipline devoted to resolving conflicts, to reject *a priori* the notion of a compromise, of seeking a middle ground.

117. These writings, which began in the 1970s, are summarized in R. Weintraub, *Commentary on the Conflict of Laws* 284 *et seq.* (3rd ed. 1986). For torts cases, Weintraub's criteria included: *(a)* the advancement of clearly discernible trends in the law, such as the trend in tort law toward distribution of loss through liability insurance; *(b)* the prevention of unfair surprise to the defendant, a factor weakened by the presence of insurance; *(c)* the suppression of anachronistic or aberrational laws; and *(d)* consultation of the conflicts rules of the other interested states in order to determine whether such states have, through functional analysis, declared their policies with regard to similar cases.

118. See *id.* at 360 (proposing that "true conflicts" and "no interest" cases be resolved by applying the law that favors the plaintiff, unless that law is "anachronistic or aberrational" or the state with that law "does not have sufficient contact with the defendant or the defendant's actual or intended course of conduct to make application of its law reasonable").

119. See *id.* at 397-398.

120. R. Weintraub, *Commentary on the Conflict of Laws* 356 (4th ed. 2001).

121. *Id.*

122. See *id.* at 347ff.

123. *Id.* at 347.

124. *Id.* at 350.

plication of the law of a state that will experience consequences ... [is] fair to the parties in the light of their contacts with that state"[125].

Weintraub apparently believes that this approach is different from comparative impairment[126], but he states that "[t]he Louisiana Conflicts Code ... is an attempt to codify a consequences-based approach"[127]. He acknowledges that his approach may not provide an answer for cases that present either the true-conflict or the no-interest paradigms[128], and suggests that "courts need default rules"[129]. Among the default rules, or rather approaches, he proposes are comparative impairment and the better law criterion. However, he emphatically states that the better-law criterion should only be used in non-false conflicts and that "the better law should be selected by an objective determination that the disfavored law is anachronistic or aberrational"[130].

H.   The First Synthesis: The Second Conflicts Restatement

32. In 1953, the American Law Institute (ALI) began drafting the Restatement Second, partly in response to the challenge of the conflicts revolution. The task of Reporter was assigned to Professor Willis L. Reese, who was a member of the new school of conflicts thought, although not of its revolutionary branch. Reese agreed with many of the criticisms levelled against the first Restatement, but more importantly, he was receptive to the criticisms of his own drafts of the second Restatement. A cursory look at the successive versions of what eventually became §6 of the Restatement Second reveals this evolution in the Reporter's own thinking, as well as the gradual gains of the new school over the old. The final version of the Restatement Second, promulgated in 1969, did not join the revolution, but was a conscious compromise and synthesis between the old and new schools, as well as among the various branches of the new schools.

1.   Section 6

33. The cornerstone of the Restatement Second is section 6. It instructs the court to consider the following factors in searching for the applicable law: *(a)* the needs of the interstate and international systems; *(b)* the relevant policies of the forum; *(c)* the relevant policies of other interested states and their interests in applying

---

125. *Id.*
126. See *id.* at 355, where Weintraub states that "a rule of comparative impairment" can serve as a *default* rule for those non-false conflicts that his approach does not resolve.
127. *Id.*
128. Weintraub questions the "no interest" or "unprovided for" labels and suggests that many of these conflicts can be resolved by "re-examin[ing] the tentative conclusion that neither state has a policy that it will advance by applying its law" *Id.* at 407.
129. *Id.* at 355.
130. *Id.* at 417.

their law to the particular issue; *(d)* the protection of justified party expectations; *(e)* the basic policies underlying the particular field of law; *(f)* the objectives of certainty, predictability, and uniformity of result; and *(g)* the ease in determining and applying the governing law[131].

From a philosophical perspective, §6 is important in that it enunciates the Restatement's ideology, which distinguishes it from other modern theories such as that of Leflar or Currie. For example, the "better-law" criterion is noticeably absent from the factors listed in §6. Moreover, the list of §6 is broader and qualitatively different from the policies relied upon by Currie, whose analysis disregards, de-emphasizes, or expressly rejects most of the §6 factors, except the policies of the forum and other involved states. The contrast between interest analysis and the Restatement is clearest in their varying degrees of sensitivity towards "the needs of the interstate and international systems" and the need for "uniformity of result." To Currie's ethnocentric attitude toward both of these goals, the Restatement juxtaposes an universalistic conception of private inter-national law reflected in the statement that

> "the most important function of choice-of-law rules is to make the interstate and international systems work well[,] ... to further harmonious relations between states and to facilitate commercial intercourse between them"[132].

The contrast is hardly surprising, since, unlike interest analysis which Currie conceived from the perspective of the forum judge confined to the role of the "hand-maiden"[133] of the forum legislature, the Restatement was drafted from the perspective of a neutral forum[134] under the auspices of the American Law Institute, a body that strives for national uniformity.

From a methodological viewpoint, §6 is important in that it provides a guiding, as well as a validating, test for applying almost all other sections of the Restatement, most of which incorporate §6 by reference[135]. Because the §6 factors are not listed in a hierarchical order, and in fact they may point in different directions in a given case[136], they fall short of providing an actual choice of law for the court. Nevertheless, they can help steer courts away from a jurisdiction-selecting choice based solely on factual contacts. Although the specific sections of the Restatement call for the application of the law of the state with the "most significant

---

131. American Law Institute, *Restatement (Second) of Conflict of Laws* §6 (2).
132. Restatement (Second) §6, cmt. d.
133. See C. Peterson, "Weighing Contacts in Conflicts Cases: The Hand-Maiden Axiom", 9 *Duq. L. Rev.* 436 (1971).
134. W. Reese, "Discussion of Major Areas of Choice of Law", 111 *Recueil des cours* 315, 357 ff. (1964).
135. See, e.g., Restatement (Second) § 145, which provides that a tort issue is governed by the law of the state that, with respect to that issue, has the most significant relationship to the occurrence and the parties "under the principles stated in § 6".
136. Restatement (Second) §6, cmt. (c).

relationship" – a term that evokes jurisdiction-selecting notions, the choice of that state is to be made "under the principles stated in §6"[137], and by taking into account the contacts listed in the specific sections. This constantly repeated cross-reference to §6 also helps supplement the multilateral approach of the specific Restatement sections with elements from a unilateral approach[138].

2.   The "most significant relationship"

34. The "most-significant relationship" formula is the other cornerstone of the Second Restatement. While §6 articulates the principles and policies that should guide the choice-of-law process, the ubiquitous most-significant-relationship formula describes the objective of that process – to apply the law of the state that, with regard to the particular issue, has the most significant relationship with the parties and the dispute. This catch phrase resembles both Savigny's "seat" of a legal relationship, and more recent European catch phrases, such as the state with the "closest" or "strongest" connection. However, the similarities are only terminological. The Restatement is built around narrowly defined "issues" rather than entire legal relationships, and requires an individualized issue-by-issue analysis with the concomitant un-Savignian possibility of *dépeçage*. Furthermore, as said above, the Restatement's approach is a blend of multilateralism and unilateralism. Finally, although acoustically the Restatement's catch phrase may suggest otherwise, the state of the most significant relationship is not to be chosen by the quantity or even the closeness of its factual contacts, but rather "under the principles stated in §6", which include consideration of the policies and interests of the contact states. Herein lies an essential difference between the Restatement and one of its precursor movements, the "center of gravity" or "significant-contacts" approach.

3.   Rules

35. In relatively few cases, primarily in the areas of property and successions, the Restatement identifies *a priori* the state of the most significant relationship through black-letter rules[139]. In cases involving land, the applicable law is almost invariably the "law that would be applied by the courts of the situs"[140]. This is as close as the Restatement comes to prescribing black-letter choice-of-law rules. These rules are subject to the traditional escape mechanisms of the generic type,

---

137. Restatement (Second) §145, *supra* footnote 135.
138. See *infra* 310.
139. See §§260-265 (succession to movables); §§245-255 (*inter vivos* trans-actions involving movables). See also the unilateral choice-of-law rules contained in §§285 (divorce), 286 (nullity of marriage), and 289 (adoption).
140. See §§223, 225-232 (*inter vivos* transactions involving land); §§236, 239-242 (succession to land). This phrase is often accompanied by the prediction that these courts "usually" will apply their own law.

such as *ordre public* and *renvoi*. For example, the above-quoted phrase regarding land is an explicit authorization for *renvoi*, which contains the potential for applying, in appropriate cases, a law other than that of the situs state.

4.   Presumptive rules

36. In other cases, the Restatement identifies the state of the most significant relationship only tentatively through presumptive rules that instruct the judge to apply the law of a certain state, unless it appears that in the particular case another state has a more significant relationship. For example, all ten of the Restatement sections that designate the law applicable to different types of torts conclude with the following escape clause: "unless, with respect to the particular issue, some other state has a more significant relationship under the principles stated in §6 to the occurrence and the parties, in which event the local law of the other state will be applied"[141]. This clause is repeated throughout the entire Restatement[142].

5.   Pointers

37. In some instances, the presumptive rules are even more equivocal, and amount to no more than mere pointers in the direction of the presumptively applicable law. The pertinent sections provide that the state with the most significant relationship will "usually" be one particular state. For example, in tort conflicts, eleven of the nineteen sections devoted to specific tort issues conclude with the adage that "[t]he applicable law will usually be the local law of the state where the injury occurred"[143]; one section, §169, provides that for intra-family immunity the applicable law "will usually be the local law of the state of the parties' domicil"; and only the remaining seven sections are unaided by such a presumption[144].

In contract conflicts, §188 provides that, subject to some exceptions, "[i]f the place of negotiating the contract and the place of performance are in the same state, the local law of this state will usually be applied". Similarly, §198 provides that "[t]he capacity of a party to contract will usually be upheld if he has such capacity under the local law of the state of his domicil", while §199 provides that contractual "[f]ormalities which meet the requirements of the place where the

---

141. See, e.g., §152 which provides that, in an action for an invasion of privacy, the applicable law is the local law of the state where the invasion occurred, "unless, with respect to the particular issue, some other state has a more significant relationship."

142. See, e.g., §§146-151, 153-155, 175. In the area of contract conflicts, the "unless" clause appears in most of the sections devoted to particular contracts. See, e.g., §§189-193, 196.

143. See §156 (tortious character of conduct); §157 (standard of care); §158 (interest entitled to legal protection); §159 (duty owed to plaintiff); §160 (legal cause); §162 (specific conditions of liability); §164 (contributory fault); §165 (assumption of risk); §166 (imputed negligence); and §172 (joint torts).

144. See §§161, 163, 168, 170-171, and 173-174.

parties execute the contract will usually be acceptable". Similar language is found in other sections of the Restatement Second.

6.   Ad hoc *analysis*

38. Finally, in the remaining and most difficult cases, the Restatement does not even attempt to enunciate presumptive rules. It simply provides a non-exclusive, non-hierarchical list of the factual contacts or connecting factors that should be "taken into account" by the judge in choosing the applicable law. This choice is to be made "under the principles stated in §6" by "taking into account" the above factual contacts "according to their relative importance with respect to the particular issue"[145]. This language suggests that the policy part of this analysis should carry more weight than the evaluation of the factual contacts. Yet, courts tend to do the opposite by first focusing on the factual contacts listed in the pertinent section of the Restatement, and then, if ever, on the policies of §6. When the contacts of one state are clearly more numerous than are those of another state, some courts tend to assume that the first state is the one that has the more significant relationship without testing that assumption under the principles of §6[146]. In contrast, when the factual contacts are split evenly between the two states, courts look to the policies of §6, but many courts pay lip service to most of the policies listed therein, and confine themselves to examining "the relative policies of the forum" and of "other interested states"[147]. It seems that cases that follow the first type of practice differ little from cases that follow a "grouping of contacts" approach, while cases that follow the latter type of practice differ little from cases that follow interest analysis.

---

145. See, e.g., §§145, 188.
146. See S. Symeonides, "The Judicial Acceptance of the Second Conflicts Restatement: A Mixed Blessing", 56 *Md. L. Rev.* 1248, 1263 (1997).
147. Restatement (Second) §6. See S. Symeonides, *supra* footnote 146, at *id*.

Chapter III   The Judicial Revolution

A.   Introduction

39. The scholastic dissent against the established conflicts system described in the preceding chapter is interesting, but it would have been practically inconsequential had it not been followed by a similar dissent in the judicial ranks. Indeed, inspired in part by these academic commentators, many judges gradually questioned the premises of the established system and soon began to openly depart from it. This judicial movement away from the traditional ways of thinking can be seen more visibly in the initially gradual, and eventually not so gradual, erosion of two typical and important traditional choice-of-law rules – the *lex loci delicti* and the *lex loci contractus*[1]. This chapter chronicles this judicial movement.

B.   The Erosion of the *Lex Loci Delicti* Rule

40. Although revolutions seem to erupt overnight, discerning eyes can see the harbingers long before the actual eruption. The same was true of the conflicts revolution. Conflicts casebooks are replete with cases in which courts created exceptions to, or openly manipulated, the *lex loci delicti* rule. Many of these cases spoke in language that was indicative of later developments.

For example, *Levy* v. *Daniels' U-Drive Auto Renting Co.*[2], and *Haumschild* v. *Continental Cas. Co.*[3] are correctly cited as examples of manipulative characterization, but they were also harbingers of things to come in that each case spoke of the policies or purposes of the substantive rules involved in the conflict. Similarly,

---

1. At the same time, it should be pointed out that most other traditional choice-of-law rules have survived the conflicts revolution virtually unscathed.
2. 143 A. 163 (Conn. 1928) (applying Connecticut's pro-recovery law to a dispute between Connecticut parties and arising from a Massachusetts accident, after characterizing the plaintiff's action as one of contract rather than of tort).
3. 95 NW 2d 814 (Wis. 1959) (applying Wisconsin's pro-recovery law to a dispute between Wisconsin parties and arising from a California accident, after characterizing the plaintiff's action as one of family law rather than of tort).

Grant v. *McAuliffe*[4] and *Kilberg* v. *Northeast Airlines, Inc.*[5] are correctly cited as examples of a misuse of the substance versus procedure dichotomy, but they also exemplified the courts' increasing impatience with the fortuitous way in which the *lex loci delicti* rule operated. Finally, although seemingly unrelated, *Lauritzen* v. *Larsen*[6] was a cue from the Supreme Court of the United States that reliance on multiple factors was not only acceptable, but also preferable to reliance on a single connecting factor for selecting the law applicable to tort conflicts.

41. Be that as it may, for all practical purposes, the revolution began in 1963 with the seminal New York case of *Babcock* v. *Jackson*[7], which was the first case to openly abandon the traditional *lex loci delicti* rule. By 1977, half of the states had abandoned that rule, and by 2000 a total of 42 jurisdictions[8] had done so. The chronology of this movement is shown in Chart 1 and Table 1 below, and is documented in the accompanying text and footnotes. Chart 2, *infra*, shows the parallel erosion of the *lex loci contractus* rule, which is discussed later in this section.

---

4.   264 P. 2d 944 (Cal. 1953) (applying California's pro-recovery law to a dispute involving California parties and arising from an Arizona accident, after characterizing the issue as procedural and, alternatively, as one involving the administration of estates).

5.   172 NE 2d 526 (NY 1961) (applying New York's pro-recovery law to an action arising from a Massachusetts accident, after characterizing the issue as procedural, and alternatively reasoning that Massachusetts' law that limited recovery was contrary to New York's public policy).

6.   345 US 571 (1953) (enunciating a multifactor test for delineating the extraterritorial application of the Jones Act and selecting the law governing certain maritime torts).

7.   191 NE 2d 279 (NY 1963) (discussed *infra* at 89-92). *Babcock* is generally considered as marking the beginning of the revolution, even though two earlier contract cases had laid the foundation. See *W. H. Barber Co.* v. *Hughes*, 63 NE 2d 417 (Ind. 1945) (adopting a significant-contacts approach); *Auten* v. *Auten*, 124 NE 2d 99 (NY 1954) (adopting a center-of-gravity approach, but also examining the interests of the competing jurisdictions).

8.   This number includes the District of Columbia and the Commonwealth of Puerto Rico. The number was the same as of 2005.

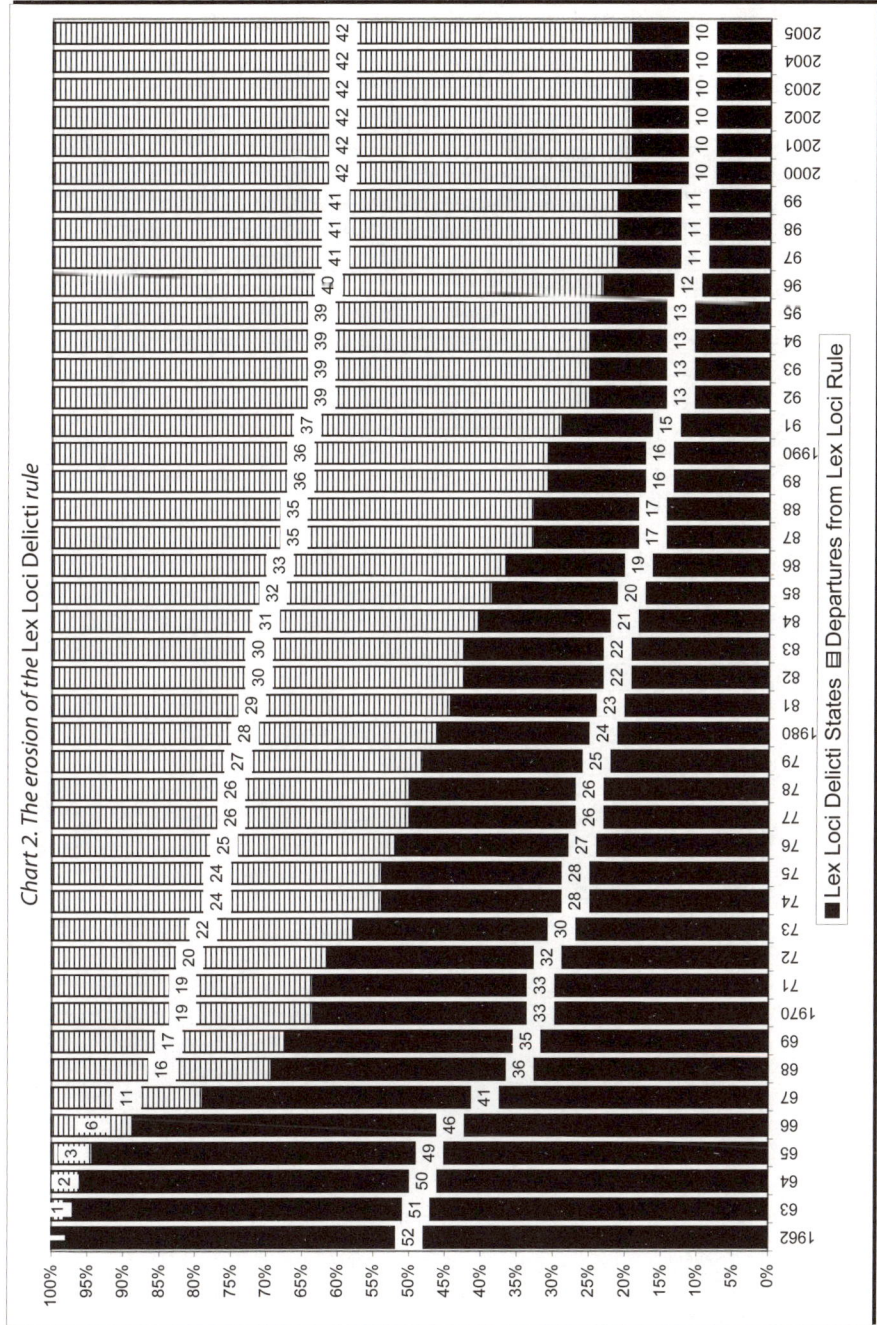

Chart 2. The erosion of the Lex Loci Delicti rule

■ Lex Loci Delicti States   ▥ Departures from Lex Loci Rule

Table 1. Chronological Table of Departures from the Lex Loci Delicti *Rule*

Lex loci states		Departures from lex loci rule					
1962	**52**						
1963	51	1	New York				
1964	50	1	Pennsylvania				
1965	49	1	Wisconsin				
1966	46	3	Minnesota	New Hampshire	Puerto Rico		
1967	41	5	California	Dist. of Columbia	Kentucky	New Jersey	Oregon
1968	36	5	Alaska	Arizona	Iowa	Mississippi	Rhode Islan
1969	35	1	Missouri				
1970	33	2	Illinois	Maine			
1971	33						
1972	32	1	North Dakota				
1973	30	2	Colorado	Louisiana			
1974	28	2	Oklahoma	Washington			
1975	28						
1976	27	1	Massachusetts				
1977	**26**	1	Arkansas				
1978	26						
1979	25	1	Texas				
1980	24	1	Florida				
1981	23	1	Hawaii				
1982	22	1	Michigan				
1983	22						
1984	21	1	Ohio				
1985	20	1	Idaho				
1986	19	1	Connecticut				
1987	17	2	Indiana	Nebraska			
1988	17						
1989	16	1	Utah				
1990	16						
1991	15	1	Delaware				
1992	13	2	South Dakota	Tennessee			
1993	13						
1994	13						
1995	13						
1996	12	1	Nevada				
1997	11	1	Vermont				
1998	11						
1999	11						
2000	10	1	Montana				
2001	10						
2002	10						
2003	10						
2004	10						
2005	**10**	**42**					

Alabama
Georgia
Kansas
Maryland
New Mexico
North Carolina
South Carolina
Virginia
West Virginia
Wyoming

42. As Table 1 indicates, most of the departures from the *lex loci delicti* rule (a total of 17) occurred in the 1960s, thus establishing that decade as the decade of the
conflicts revolution[9]. The period of 1966-1969, during which the American Law
Institute (ALI) published the Official Proposed Drafts of the Second Restatement,
was particularly active. This may explain why twelve jurisdictions abandoned the
lex loci rule during that period, and nine opted for the Restatement[10]. Apart from
these nine jurisdictions, the break-down for the decade of 1960-1969 was as follows: five jurisdictions opting for interest analysis[11], two jurisdictions for Leflar's
approach[12], and one for the significant-contacts approach[13].

During the 1970s, ten additional jurisdictions abandoned the *lex loci delicti*
rule. The equipoise point was 1977, at which time as many jurisdictions (26) adhered to the *lex loci* rule as had abandoned it. The break-down among the states
that abandoned the rule during this decade was: six states opting for the Second

---

9. In chronological order, the cases in which these jurisdictions abandoned the *lex loci*
    rule are: *Babcock v. Jackson*, 191 NE 2d 279 (NY 1963); *Griffith v. United Air Lines, Inc.*,
    203 A. 2d 796 (Pa. 1964); *Wilcox v. Wilcox*, 133 NW 2d 408 (Wis. 1965); *Balts v. Balts*,
    142 NW 2d 66 (Minn. 1966); *Kopp v. Rechtzigel*, 141 NW 2d 526 (Minn. 1966); *Clark
    v. Clark*, 222 A. 2d 205 (NH 1966); *Widow of Fornaris v. American Sur. Co.*, 93 PRR
    28 (1966); *Reich v. Purcell*, 432 P. 2d 727 (Cal. 1967); *Myers v. Gaither*, 232 A. 2d 577,
    583 (DC 1967); *Wessling v. Paris*, 417 SW 2d 259 (Ky. 1967); *Mellk v. Sarahson*, 229 A.
    2d 625 (NJ 1967); *Casey v. Manson Constr. & Eng'g Co.*, 428 P. 2d 898 (Or. 1967); *Arm-
    strong v. Armstrong*, 441 P. 2d 699 (Alaska 1968); *Schwartz v. Schwartz*, 447 P. 2d 254
    (Ariz. 1968); *Fuerste v. Bemis*, 156 NW 2d 831 (Iowa 1968); *Mitchell v. Craft*, 211 So. 2d
    509 (Miss. 1968); *Woodward v. Stewart*, 243 A. 2d 917 (RI 1968); *Kennedy v. Dixon*, 439
    SW 2d 173 (Mo. 1969).

10. These jurisdictions were Minnesota, the District of Columbia, Kentucky, Oregon,
    Alaska, Arizona, Iowa, Mississippi, and Missouri. The first four jurisdictions later
    switched to another approach.

11. These jurisdictions were New York, Pennsylvania, Wisconsin, California, and New
    Jersey. Pennsylvania later switched to a combined approach that includes interest
    analysis, the Second Restatement, and Professor Cavers's "principles of preference".
    See, e.g., *Cipolla v. Shaposka*, 267 A. 2d 854 (Pa. 1970) (Cavers); *Miller v. Gay*, 470
    A. 2d 1353 (Pa. 1984) (interest analysis and Second Restatement). Wisconsin later
    switched to Leflar's choice-influencing considerations. See, e.g., *Heath v. Zellmer*, 151
    NW 2d 664 (Wis. 1967); *Lichter v. Fritsch*, 252 NW 2d 360 (Wis. 1977).

12. These jurisdictions were New Hampshire and Rhode Island. See *Clark v. Clark*, 222
    A. 2d 205, 210 (NH 1966); *Woodward v. Stewart*, 243 A. 2d 917, 923 (RI 1968).

13. This jurisdiction was Puerto Rico. See *Widow of Fornaris v. American Sur. Co.*, 93 PRR
    28, 46 (1966).

Restatement[14], two states opting for a mixed approach[15], one state opting for Leflar's approach[16], and one state for a significant-contacts approach[17].

During the 1980s, nine jurisdictions abandoned the *lex loci* rule, of which six opted for the Second Restatement[18], one state opted for the significant-contacts approach[19], another for the *lex fori* approach[20], and another for a mixed approach[21].

During the 1990s, five more states followed suit in abandoning the *lex loci rule*, and all but one of them[22] opted for the Second Restatement[23].

---

14. These jurisdictions were Illinois, Maine, Colorado, Oklahoma, Washington, and Texas. See *Ingersoll* v. *Klein*, 262 NE 2d 593 (Ill. 1970); *Beaulieu* v. *Beaulieu*, 265 A. 2d 610 (Me. 1970); *First Nat'l Bank* v. *Rostek*, 514 P. 2d 314 (Colo. 1973); *Brickner* v. *Gooden*, 525 P. 2d 632 (Okla. 1974); *Johnson* v. *Spider Staging Corp.*, 555 P. 2d 997 (Wash. 1976); *Werner* v. *Werner*, 526 P. 2d 370 (Wash. 1974); *Gutierrez* v. *Collins*, 583 SW 2d 312 (Tex. 1979).

15. These states were Louisiana and Massachusetts. See *Jagers* v. *Royal Indem. Co.*, 276 So. 2d 309 (La. 1973); *Pevoski* v. *Pevoski*, 358 NE 2d 416 (Mass. 1976).

16. This state was Leflar's home state of Arkansas. See *Wallis* v. *Mrs. Smith's Pie Co.*, 550 SW 2d 453 (Ark. 1977). In the meantime, Minnesota also switched to Leflar's approach. See *Milkovich* v. *Saari*, 203 NW 2d 408 (Minn. 1973).

17. That state was North Dakota. See *Issendorf* v. *Olson*, 194 NW 2d 750 (ND 1972).

18. These states were Florida, Ohio, Idaho, Connecticut, Nebraska, and Utah. See Bishop v. Florida Specialty Paint Co., 389 So. 2d 999 (Fla. 1980); Morgan v. Biro Mfg. Co., 474 NE 2d 286 (Ohio 1984); Johnson v. Pischke, 700 P. 2d 19 (Idaho 1985); O'Connor v. O'Connor, 519 A. 2d 13 (Conn. 1986); Crossley v. Pacific Employers Ins. Co., 251 NW 2d 383 (Neb. 1977) (relying alternatively on the Second Restatement and the lex loci delicti with the same result); Harper v. Silva, 399 NW 2d 826 (Neb. 1987) (interpreting Crossley as having adopted the Second Restatement); Forsman v. Forsman, 779 P. 2d 218 (Utah 1989).

19. This state was Indiana. See *Hubbard Mfg. Co.* v. *Greeson*, 515 NE 2d 1071, 1073-74 (Ind. 1987) (holding that "when the place of the tort is an insignificant contact", the court will turn to the Second Restatement, but stopping short of embracing the policy-analysis component of the Second Restatement or of abandoning the *lex loci rule* in general).

20. That state was Michigan. See *Sexton* v. *Ryder Truck Rental, Inc.*, 320 NW 2d 843 (Mich. 1982).

21. That state was Hawaii. See *Peters* v. *Peters*, 634 P. 2d 586 (Haw. 1981) (applying a blend of interest analysis and Leflar's choice-influencing considerations).

22. That state is Nevada. See *Motenko* v. *MGM Dist., Inc.*, 921 P. 2d 933 (Nev. 1996) (adopting a *lex fori* approach in tort cases unless "another State has an overwhelming interest").

23. The four states that adopted the Second Restatement are Delaware, South Dakota, Tennessee, and Vermont. See *Travelers Indem. Co.* v. *Lake*, 594 A. 2d 38 (Del. 1991); *Chambers* v. *Dakotah Charter, Inc.*, 488 NW 2d 63 (S.D. 1992); *Hataway* v. *McKinley*, 830 SW 2d 53 (Tenn. 1992); *Amiot* v. *Ames*, 693 A. 2d 675 (Vt. 1997).

Finally, on the turn of the century, one more state (Montana) abandoned the *lex loci* rule in favour of the Second Restatement[24].

By the time of this writing (in 2005), a total of forty-two jurisdictions had abandoned the *lex loci delicti* rule, while ten jurisdictions appeared to adhere to it. This corresponds to a ratio of 81% to 19%. From a population perspective, the ratio is 84.5% to 15.5%[25]. (See Chart 3, below.) Map 1, below, shows the geographical distribution of these states, while Map 2 shows the same with regard to contract conflicts, which are discussed later.

C.   The Erosion of the *Lex Loci Contractus* Rule

43. In contract conflicts, the first abandonment of the *lex loci contractus* rule occurred as early as 1945, in the Indiana case of *W. H. Barber Co.* v. *Hughes*[26]. *Barber* employed "a method used by modern teachers of Conflict of Laws in rationalizing the results obtained by the courts in decided cases"[27], called the "center of gravity"[28] approach. Nine years later, the New York Court of Appeals employed the same approach in *Auten* v. *Auten*[29].

Although *Auten* is generally considered as marking the beginning of the revolution in contract conflicts, it did not garner a following until the 1960s. Even then, dissension against the *lex loci contractus* rule was slow. It took three decades for half of the states to abandon the *lex loci contractus* rule. By the time of this writing (in 2005), forty-one jurisdictions have done the same[30]. The chronological order in which they did so is shown in Chart 2 and Table 2, below, and is documented in the accompanying text and footnotes.

---

24. See *Phillips* v. *Gen. Motors Corp.*, 995 P. 2d 1002 (Mont. 2000).
25. Of the 281,421,906 inhabitants of the United States, 43,879,469, or 15.5%, are domiciled in states that adhere to the *lex loci delicti* rule. These figures are based on the US Census 2000.
26. 63 NE 2d 417 (Ind. 1945).
27. *Id.* at 423.
28. *Id.*
29. 124 NE 2d 99 (NY 1954).
30. 206. This number includes the District of Columbia and the Commonwealth of Puerto Rico.

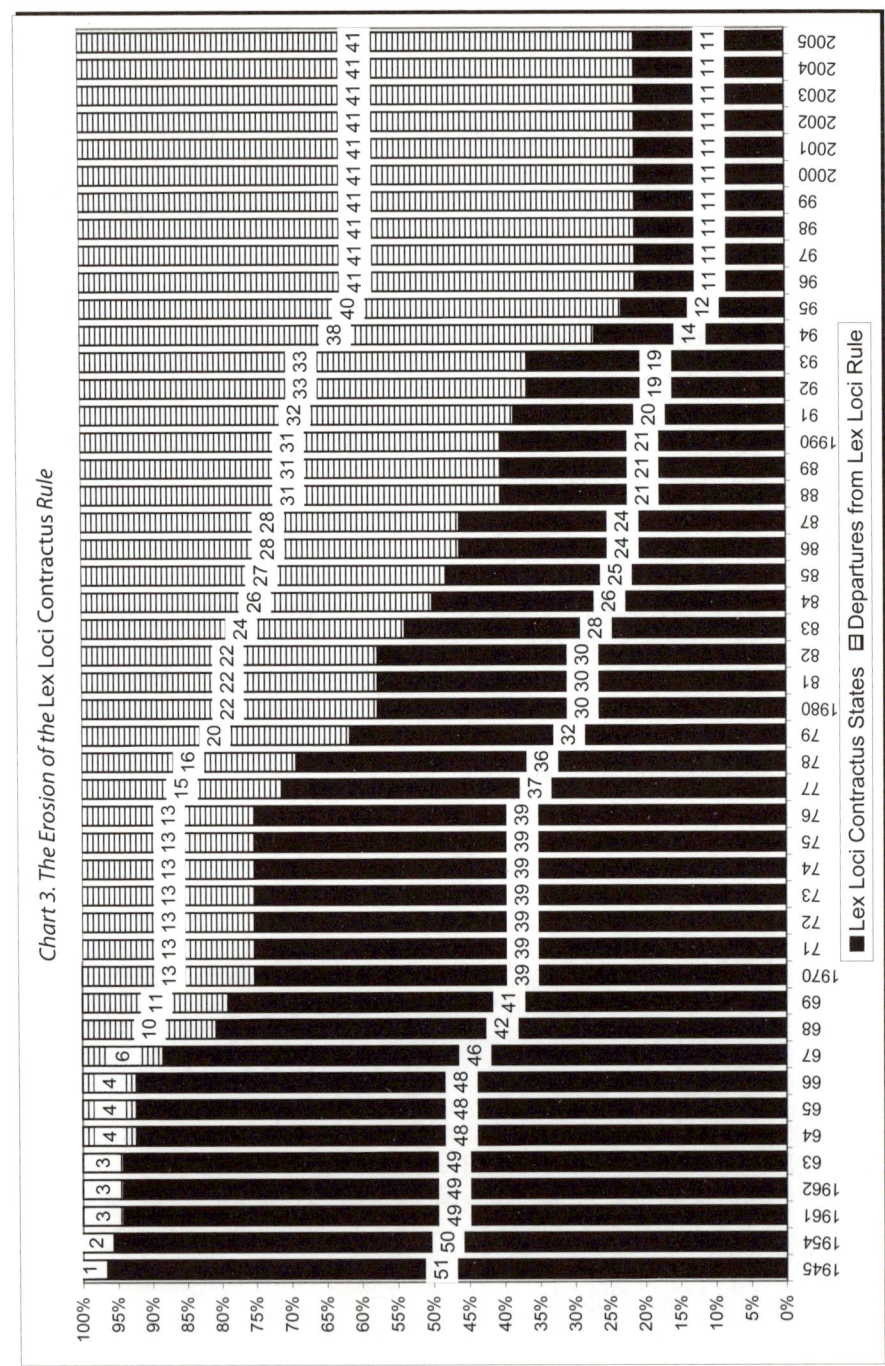

Chart 3. The Erosion of the Lex Loci Contractus Rule

Table 2. Chronological Table of Departures from the Lex Loci Contractus *Rule*

Lex loci states		Departures from the *lex loci contractus* rule				
1944	**52**					
1945	51	1	Indiana			
1954	50	1	New York			
1961	49	1	Puerto Rico			
1962	49					
1963	49					
1964	48	1	Oregon			
1965	48					
1966	48					
1967	46	2	California	Washington		
1968	42	4	Idaho	New Hampshire	Vermont	Wisconsin
1969	41	1	Dist. Columbia			
1970	39	2	Arizona	Delaware		
1971	39					
1972	39					
1973	39					
1974	39					
1975	39					
1976	39					
1977	37	2	Iowa	Kentucky		
1978	36	1	Missouri			
1979	32	4	Arkansas	Colorado	Illinois	Minnesota
1980	30	2	Mississippi	New Jersey		
1981	30					
1982	30					
1983	28	2	Maine	Pennsylvania		
1984	**26**	2	Ohio	Texas		
1985	25	1	Massachusetts			
1986	24	1	North Dakota			
1987	24					
1988	21	3	Hawaii	North Carolina	W. Virginia	
1989	21					
1990	21					
1991	20	1	Oklahoma?			
1992	19	1	Louisiana			
1993	19					
1994	14	5	Connecticut	Montana	Nebraska	Nevada	S. Dakota
1995	12	2	Alaska	Michigan		
1996	11	1	Utah			
1997	11					
1998	11					
1999	11					
2000	11					
2001	11					
2002	11					
2003	11					
2004	11					
2005	**11**	**41**				

Alabama
Florida
Georgia
Kansas
Maryland
New Mexico
Rhode Island
South Carolina
Tennessee
Virginia
Wyoming

44. As both Chart 2 and Table 2 indicate, the revolution spread at a much slower and more even pace in contracts than it had in torts. During the 1960s, only nine jurisdictions abandoned the *lex loci contractus* rule, with seven of them doing so in the 1967-1969 period, which coincided with the ferment surrounding the publication of the Second Restatement drafts. Four of those jurisdictions adopted the Restatement[31], two jurisdictions adopted a significant-contacts approach influenced by the Restatement[32], and three jurisdictions adopted interest analysis[33].

During the 1970s, nine additional states abandoned the *lex loci contractus* rule, and all but two of them[34] opted for the Second Restatement[35].

The decisive decade was the 1980s, during which eleven additional states abandoned the *lex loci contractus* rule, thus shifting the balance against it in 1985.

31.   These states are Idaho, New Hampshire, Vermont, and Washington. See *Rungee v. Allied Van Lines, Inc.*, 449 P. 2d 378 (Idaho 1968); *Consol. Mut. Ins. Co.* v. *Radio Foods Corp.*, 240 A. 2d 47 (NH 1968); *Pioneer Credit Corp.* v. *Carden*, 245 A. 2d 891 (Vt. 1968); *Baffin Land Corp.* v. *Monticello Motor Inn, Inc.*, 425 P. 2d 623 (Wash. 1967).

32.   These jurisdictions are Puerto Rico and Wisconsin. See *Maryland Cas. Co.* v. *San Juan Racing Ass'n*, 83 PRR 538 (1961); *Green Giant Co.* v. *Tribunal Superior*, 104 PR Dec. 489 (1975); *Urhammer v. Olson*, 159 NW 2d 688 (Wis. 1968). Wisconsin later switched to Leflar's approach. See *Haines v. Mid-Century Ins. Co.*, 177 NW 2d 328 (Wis. 1970); *Schlosser* v. *Allis-Chalmers Corp.*, 271 NW 2d 879 (Wis. 1978).

33.   These jurisdictions are Oregon, California, and the District of Columbia. See *Lilienthal* v. *Kaufman*, 395 P. 2d 543 (Or. 1964); *Travelers Ins. Co.* v. *Workmen's Comp. Appeals Bd.*, 434 P. 2d 992 (Cal. 1967); *McCrossin v. Hicks Chevrolet, Inc.*, 248 A. 2d 917 (DC 1969). All three of these jurisdictions later switched to a combined approach that includes interest analysis.

34.   The two states are Arkansas and Minnesota. See *Standard Leasing Corp.* v. *Schmidt Aviation, Inc.*, 576 SW 2d 181 (Ark. 1979) (significant-contacts approach); *Hague v. Allstate Ins. Co.*, 289 NW 2d 43 (Minn. 1979) (Leflar's choice-influencing considerations).

35.   See *Burr v. Renewal Guar. Corp.*, 468 P. 2d 576 (Ariz. 1970); *Oliver B. Cannon & Son, Inc.* v. *Dorr-Oliver, Inc.*, 394 A. 2d 1160 (Del. 1978); *Joseph L. Wilmotte & Co. v. Rosenman Bros.*, 258 NW 2d 317 (Iowa 1977); *Lewis v. American Family Ins. Group*, 555 SW 2d 579 (Ky. 1977); *Nat'l Starch & Chem. Corp. v. Newman*, 577 SW 2d 99 (Mo. App. 1978), cited with approval in *Fruin-Colnon Corp. v. Missouri Hwy. Transport. Comm'n*, 736 SW 2d 41 (Mo. 1987); *Wood Bros. Homes, Inc. v. Walker Adjustment Bureau*, 601 P. 2d 1369 (Colo. 1979); *Champagnie v. W. E. O'Neil Constr. Co.*, 395 NE 2d 990 (Ill. App. 1979).

These states split almost evenly between the Second Restatement[36] and a mixed approach which, in most instances, includes reliance on the Restatement[37].

The twentieth century ended with ten additional states abandoning the *lex loci* rule, with seven states opting for the Second Restatement[38] and three for other approaches.[39]

---

36. See *Spragins v. Louise Plantation, Inc.*, 391 So. 2d 97 (Miss. 1980); *Boardman v. United Servs. Auto. Ass'n*, 470 So. 2d 1024 (Miss. 1985); *Baybutt Constr. Corp.* v. *Commercial Union Ins. Co.*, 455 A. 2d 914 (Me. 1983); *Gries Sports Enters.* v. *Modell*, 473 NE 2d 807 (Ohio 1984); *Duncan* v. *Cessna Aircraft Co.*, 665 SW 2d 414 (Tex. 1984). See also the following West Virginia cases relying heavily on the Second Restatement in insurance contract conflicts: *Cannelton Indus., Inc. v. Aetna Cas. & Sur. Co. of America*, 460 SE 2d 1 (W. Va. 1994); *Adkins v. Sperry*, 437 SE 2d 284 (W. Va. 1993); *Clark v. Rockwell*, 435 SE 2d 664 (W. Va. 1993); *Nadler v. Liberty Mut. Fire Ins. Co.*, 424 SE 2d 256 (W. Va. 1992); *Lee v. Saliga*, 373 SE 2d 345 (W. Va. 1988); see also *New v. Tac & C Energy, Inc.*, 355 SE 2d 629 (W. Va. 1987) (applying Second Restatement §196 to an employment contract).

37. See *State Farm Mut. Auto. Ins. Co.* v. *Estate of Simmons*, 417 A. 2d 488 (NJ 1980); *Guy v. Liederbach*, 459 A. 2d 744 (Pa. 1983); *Bushkin Assocs., Inc.* v. *Raytheon Co.*, 473 NE 2d 662 (Mass. 1985); *Apollo Sprinkler Co.* v. *Fire Sprinkler Suppliers & Design, Inc.*, 382 NW 2d 386 (ND 1986); *Boudreau v. Baughman*, 368 SE 2d 849 (NC 1988) (interpreting the phrase "appropriate relation" in the forum's version of UCC Art. 1-105 as equivalent to the phrase "most significant relationship" as used in the Second Restatement); *Lewis v. Lewis*, 748 P. 2d 1362 (Haw. 1988) (interpreting *Peters v. Peters*, 634 P. 2d 586 (Haw. 1981), a tort conflict, as having adopted a significant-relationship test with primary emphasis on the state with the "strongest interest").

38. See *Williams v. State Farm Mut. Auto. Ins. Co.*, 641 A. 2d 783 (Conn. 1994); *Casarotto v. Lombardi*, 886 P. 2d 931 (Mont. 1994); *Powell v. American Charter Fed. S & L Ass'n*, 514 NW 2d 326 (Neb. 1994) (explicitly adopting the Second Restatement. An earlier case, *Shull v. Dain, Kalman & Quail, Inc.*, 267 NW 2d 517 (Neb. 1978), had also applied the Second Restatement. *Id.* at 520-521); *Stockmen's Livestock Exch.* v. *Thompson*, 520 NW 2d 255 (SD 1994); *Palmer G. Lewis Co.* v. *ARCO Chem. Co.*, 904 P. 2d 1221 (Alaska 1995) (interpreting *Ehredt v. DeHavilland Aircraft Co. of Canada, Ltd.*, 705 P. 2d 446 (Alaska 1985), a tort case, as having adopted the Second Restatement for contract conflicts as well); *Chrysler Corp.* v. *Skyline Indus. Servs., Inc.*, 528 NW 2d 698 (Mich. 1995); *American Nat'l Fire Ins. Co.* v. *Farmers Ins. Exch.*, 927 P. 2d 186 (Utah 1996).

39. The three states that adopted other approaches are: Louisiana (see La. Civ. Code. Arts. 3537-3540, enacted in 1992, described *infra* 102, providing rules based on the notion that the applicable law should be the law of the "state whose policies would be most seriously impaired if its law were not applied"); Nevada (see *Hermanson v. Hermanson*, 887 P. 2d 1241 (Nev. 1994), a status case re-interpreting earlier contract cases as having adopted a "substantial relationship test"); and Oklahoma. See *Bohannan* v. *Allstate Ins. Co.*, 820 P. 2d 787 (Okla. 1991) (stating that the court would be willing to apply the law of a state other than that of the *locus contractus* upon a showing that such state "has the most significant relationship with the subject matter and the parties"). Some commentators believe that Oklahoma should be listed as a *lex loci contractus* state, however, because an Oklahoma statute, although often disregarded, compels adherence to that rule. See Symeonides, "Choice of Law in the American Courts in 1994: A View 'From the Trenches'", 43 *Am. J. Comp. L.* 1 at 3 n. 6 (1995).

By the time of this writing (in 2005), a total of 41 jurisdictions had abandoned the *lex loci contractus* rule, while 11 continued to adhere to it. This corresponds to a ratio of 79% to 21%. From a population perspective, the ratio is 80% to 20%[40] (see Chart 3 below). The geographical distribution of these states is shown in Map 2, below.

Map 1. Methodological camps in tort and contract conflicts – tort conflicts

MAP 1. TORT CONFLICTS

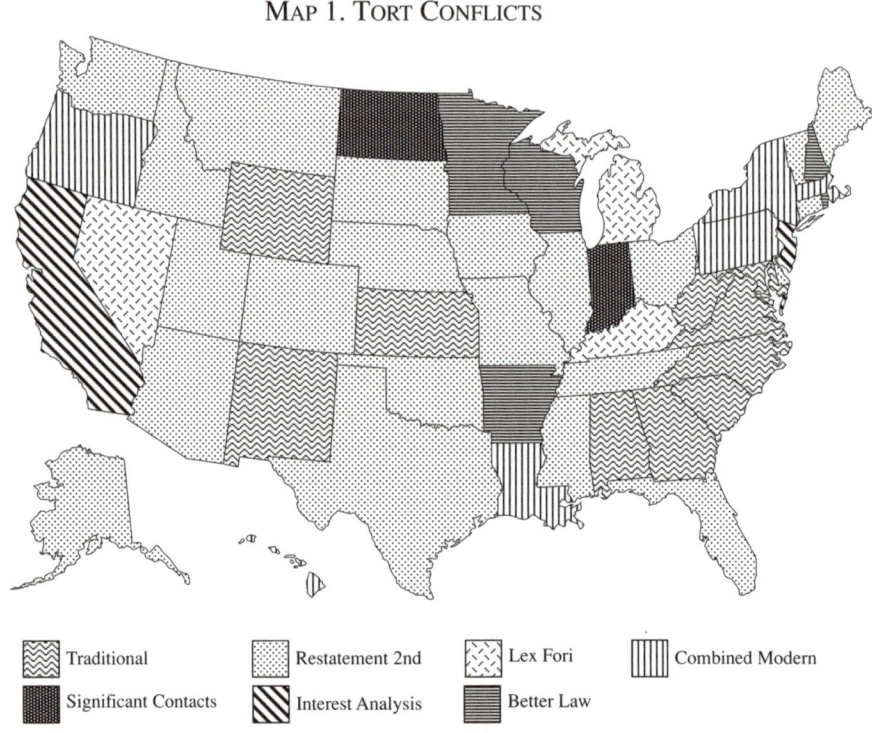

Traditional	Restatement 2nd	Lex Fori	Combined Modern
Significant Contacts	Interest Analysis	Better Law	

---

40.   Of the 281,421,906 inhabitants of the United States, 56,741,792, or 20%, are domiciled in states that adhere to the *lex loci contractus* rule. These figures are based on the US Census 2000.

Map 2. Methodological camps in tort and contract conflicts – contract conflicts

Map 2. Contract Conflicts

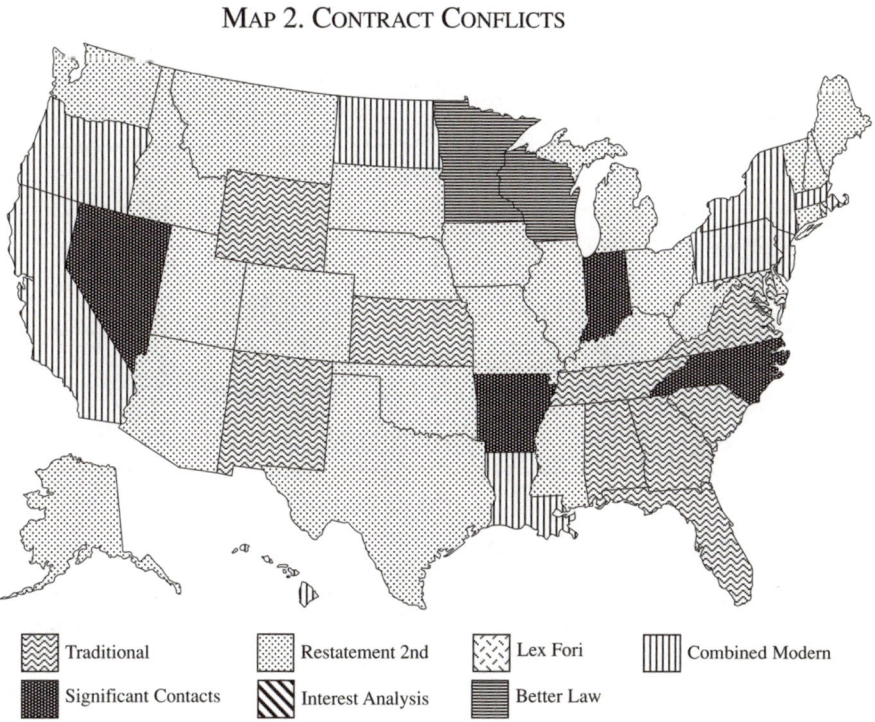

| Traditional | Restatement 2nd | Lex Fori | Combined Modern |
| Significant Contacts | Interest Analysis | Better Law | |

Chart 4. States and populations in traditional and modern methodological camps

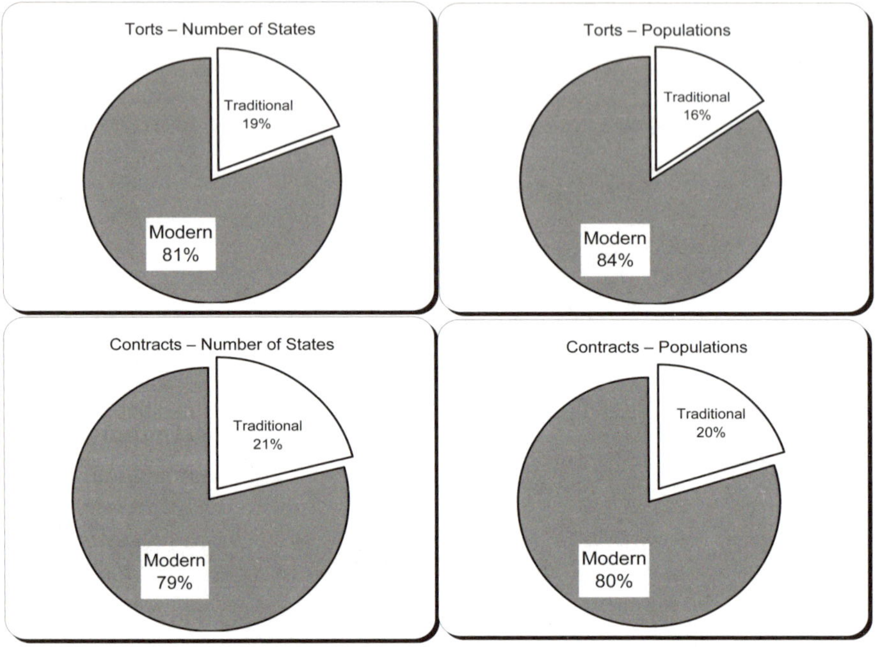

Torts – Number of States

Traditional
19%

Modern
81%

Torts – Populations

Traditional
16%

Modern
84%

Contracts – Number of States

Traditional
21%

Modern
79%

Contracts – Populations

Traditional
20%

Modern
80%

D.   The Remaining Traditional States

45. The above tables and charts indicate that ten states continue to follow the traditional theory in tort conflicts and eleven states do so in contract conflicts. For the reader's convenience these states are shown again in Table 3. This section discusses recent developments in these states.

Table 3. Traditional states

TORTS		CONTRACTS	
Alabama		Alabama	
		Florida	
Georgia		Georgia	
Kansas		Kansas	
Maryland		Maryland	
New Mexico		New Mexico	
North Carolina			
		Rhode Island	
South Carolina		South Carolina	
		Tennessee	
Virginia		Virginia	
West Virginia			
Wyoming		Wyoming	
Total	10	Total	11

As Table 3 indicates, the torts and contracts lists are not identical. Florida, Rhode Island, and Tennessee have abandoned the traditional theory in tort conflicts but not in contract conflicts, while North Carolina and West Virginia have done the reverse. In any event, it would be a mistake to assume that all the states listed in the above table are equally committed to the status quo, or that they will remain so for the same length of time.

1.   Tort conflicts

46. Of the ten states listed above as following the traditional theory in tort conflicts, only Alabama has recently and categorically reaffirmed its adherence to the *lex loci delicti* rule[41].

---

41.   See *Fitts v. Minnesota Mining & Mfg. Co.*, 581 So. 2d 819 (Ala. 1991); *Powell v. Sappington*, 495 So. 2d 569 (Ala. 1986); *Holman v. McMullan Trucking*, 684 So. 2d 1309 (Ala. 1996); *Griffin v. Summit Specialties, Inc.*, 622 So. 2d 1299 (Ala. 1993); *Etheredge v. Genie Indus., Inc.*, 632 So. 2d 1324 (Ala. 1994). See also *Ex parte* Exxon Corp., 1998 WL 397789 (Ala. 1998). Since completion of the manuscript, Georgia also reaffirmed its adherence to the *lex loci delicti* rule. See *Dowis v. Mud Slingers, Inc.*, 621 SE 2d 413 (Ga. 2005).

The highest courts of Kansas[42], Maryland[43], Virginia[44], and Wyoming[45] have

---

42. See *Ling* v. *Jan's Liquors*, 703 P. 2d 731 (Kan. 1985). Also, in 2003, the Kansas Supreme Court decided not to review a decision of the intermediate court that provided a good opportunity for reconsidering the *lex loci delicti* rule. See *Raskin* v. *Allison*, 57 P.3d 30 (Kan. App. 2002), *rev. denied* Feb 05, 2003 (applying Mexican compensatory-damages law to a *Babcock*-pattern case arising out of a boating accident in Mexico involving only Kansas domiciliaries vacationing in Mexico). However, in dealing with insurance conflicts, the Supreme Court of Kansas has employed policy-analysis, although disguised in traditional *ordre public* jargon. See *Hartford Accident & Indem. Co.* v. *American Red Ball Transit Co.*, 938 P. 2d 1281 (Kan. 1997); *Safeco Ins. Co.* v. *Allen*, 941 P. 2d 1365 (Kan. 1997); *St. Paul Surplus Lines* v. *Int'l Playtex, Inc.*, 777 P. 2d 1259 (Kan. 1989).

43. See *CHAMBCO* v. *Urban Masonry Co.*, 659 A. 2d 297 (Md. 1995) (applying the *lex loci delicti*, virtually without discussion). However, since the early 1980s, Maryland's highest court has employed straight policy analysis in tort actions arising in the context of workers' compensation. See *Hauch* v. *Connor*, 453 A. 2d 1207 (Md. 1983) (holding that the choice-of-law decision in these conflicts "turned on the determination of which jurisdiction had the greater interest". *Id.* at 1214); *Bishop* v. *Twiford*, 562 A. 2d 1238 (Md. 1989) (holding that such conflicts are to be governed by the law of the state that has "the greatest interest". *Id.* at 1241). In both *Hauch* and *Bishop*, the court applied Maryland law and allowed a Maryland employee to recover tort damages against his Maryland employer, even though the accident occurred in another state whose worker's compensation statute precluded such recovery. In *Powell* v. *Erb*, 709 A. 2d 1294 (Md. 1998), the court employed the same analysis and, once again, applied Maryland's pro-recovery law to an action arising out of an employment accident in Pennsylvania, despite a Maryland statute that seemed to require the application of Pennsylvania law.

44. The last time the Supreme Court of Virginia had an opportunity to consider the question of abandoning the *lex loci delicti* rule was in 1979. In *McMillan* v. *McMillan*, 253 SE 2d 662 (Va. 1979), the court considered but rejected plaintiff's appeal to adopt the Second Restatement because it is "susceptible to inconstancy" and tends to create "uncertainty and confusion." *Id.* at 664. Applying the interspousal immunity rule of the *locus delicti*, the court refused to allow an action between Virginia spouses, which was allowed under Virginia law. The next time the court encountered a tort conflict was in 1993, in *Jones* v. *R. S. Jones Assoc., Inc.*, 431 SE 2d 33 (Va. 1993) and *Buchanan* v. *Doe*, 431 SE 2d 289 (Va. 1993), decided on the same day. However, none of the parties urged the court to abandon the *lex loci delicti* rule, and the court saw no reason to reconsider the issue. In *Jones*, the court applied the *lex loci* which was more favorable to the forum plaintiff than the *lex fori*. In *Buchanan*, where the situation was the reverse, the court found a way to apply the *lex fori*, while professing adherence to the *lex loci* rule.

45. See *Jack* v. *Enterprise Rent-A-Car Co. of Los Angeles*, 899 P. 2d 891 (Wyo. 1995). This was an action by a Wyoming resident against a California car rental company for injuries sustained in a Wyoming traffic accident, caused by defendant's car which was rented in California to a driver of unspecified domicile. Under the law of California, but not Wyoming, the rental company would be liable. The court's choice-of-law discussion was confined to a few sentences, concluding that Wyoming law should govern because "[t]he accident occurred in Wyoming ... , the [victims] resided in

applied the *lex loci delicti* rule in recent years, but their commitment to it does not appear to be as firm as Alabama's. As explained below, the remaining five states are even more lukewarm in their commitment to the *lex loci* rule. They appear to retain the rule in name only, by disingenuously evading it through transparent escape devices, such as the *ordre public,* or even "comity."

47. *Boone* v. *Boone*[46], a case decided by the South Carolina Supreme Court, is a typical example. *Boone* was an interspousal-immunity conflict in which two spouses domiciled in South Carolina, a state that allows interspousal tort suits, were involved in an accident in Georgia, a state that does not allow such suits. The court acknowledged its past adherence to the *lex loci delicti* rule[47], which in this case would dictate the application of the Georgia immunity rule. However, the court noted with relief, "foreign law may not be given effect in this State if it is 'against good morals or natural justice'"[48]. The court opined that it would be "contrary to 'natural justice'"[49] to preclude one spouse from suing the other, as the Georgia rule did, and hence the court declined to apply it.

Although few people would quarrel with this result, the process by which the court arrived at it left much to be desired. For example, while the interspousal immunity rule may be outmoded and arguably ill-advised, it is far fetched to say that it is "against natural justice", or that it is so repugnant and "shocking" to the forum's sense of justice and fairness as to meet Cardozo's classic *ordre public* test[50]. Moreover, from a methodological perspective, one would expect that the court would at least pause to consider whether the *lex loci* rule was worth preserving before shortcutting to, and misapplying, an exception to the rule. It is one thing to adhere to a rule because it is rationally and functionally defensible, and another thing to adhere to a rule because it can be easily evaded. Had the court followed through with its own analysis of South Carolina policies in abandoning the immunity rule[51], the court could have easily concluded that those policies would be promoted by their application to this case (which involved South Carolina spouses) without offending Georgia's policies of protecting Georgia marriages or, more likely, Georgia

---

Wyoming, the negligent operation of the vehicle occurred in Wyoming, and the damages were sustained in Wyoming". *Id.* at 894-895.

46.   546 SE 2d 191 (S.C. 2001).

47.   In an earlier case, *Dawkins* v. *State*, 412 SE 2d 407 (SC 1991), the same court refused to a apply the *ordre public* exception in an action brought against the State of South Carolina by a Georgia citizen who was injured in Georgia by a convict who escaped from a nearby South Carolina prison. The court applied Georgia law, which favoured the State of South Carolina.

48.   *Boone*, 546 SE 2d at 193.

49.   *Id.* at 194.

50.   See *Loucks* v. *Standard Oil Co. of New York*, 120 NE 198, 202 (NY 1918) (asking whether the foreign law "shock[s] our sense of justice" or "menaces the public welfare" or "violate[s] some fundamental principle of justice, some prevalent conception of good morals, some deep-rooted tradition of the common weal").

51.   See *Boone*, 546 SE 2d at 194 ("It is the public policy of our State to provide married person with the same legal rights and remedies possessed by unmarried persons.").

insurers. In other words, this was a classic false conflict. The court could have easily resolved it by applying the law of the common domicile (as other courts did in the vast majority of similar cases since *Haumschild*[52]) and without resorting to gimmicks that may have been necessary in the *Haumschild* days, but not today.

48. Georgia's adherence to the traditional theory is subject to the usual escapes, but also to a peculiar rule that forbids Georgia courts from applying the common law (as opposed to the statutory law) of another state[53].

This essentially means that the *lex loci delicti* and *lex loci contractus* rules are inapplicable whenever the locus of the tort or contract is in another state that has not enacted a statute on the matter. Even when these rules are applicable, however, Georgia courts tend to find a way to avoid them. For example, in a manner typical of courts that purport to like the traditional theory but not its solutions, the Georgia Supreme Court recently avoided the *lex loci delicti* rule by stretching the meaning of the traditional *ordre public* exception. The court held that a Virginia rule that did not impose strict liability on manufacturers was so "radically dissimilar"[54] to Georgia's strict-liability rule as to justify its rejection on public policy grounds. Observers who find it incongruous for a court to be conservative on conflicts law and liberal on substantive law may be tempted to conclude that a more pragmatic explanation for the court's refusal to apply the Virginia rule was that this rule was unfavourable to a Georgia plaintiff who purchased the product in Georgia[55].

---

52. *Haumschild* v. *Continental Cas. Co.*, 95 NW 2d 814 (Wis. 1959) (characterizing interspousal-immunity as a family-law issue to be governed by the law of the spouses' domicile rather than the *lex loci*). Eight state supreme courts have used cases of this pattern as the opportunity to abandon the *lex loci delicti* rule. Six of those cases involved interspousal immunity. See *Armstrong* v. *Armstrong*, 441 P. 2d 699 (Ala. 1968) (Alaska spouses, accident in Yukon territory); *Schwartz* v. *Schwartz*, 447 P. 2d 254 (Ariz. 1968) (New York spouses, Arizona accident); *Pevoski* v. *Pevoski*, 358 NE 2d 416 (Mass. 1976) (Massachusetts spouses, New York accident); and *Forsman* v. *Forsman*, 779 P. 2d 218 (Utah 1989) (California spouses, Utah accident). Two cases involved intrafamily immunity. See *Balts* v. *Balts*, 142 NW 2d 66 (Minn. 1966) (Minnesota parent and child, Wisconsin accident); *Jagers* v. *Royal Indem. Co.*, 276 So. 2d 309 (La. 1973) (Louisiana parent and child, Mississippi accident).

53. See *Trustees of Jesse Parker Williams Hosp.* v. *Nisbet*, 7 SE 2d 737 (Ga.1940); *Menendez* v. *Perishable Distrib., Inc.*,329 SE 2d 149 (Ga.1985); *Avnet, Inc.* v. *Wyle Labs., Inc.*, 437 SE 2d 302 (Ga. 1993); *Shorewood Packaging Corp.* v *Commercial Union Ins. Co.*, 865 F.Supp. 1577 (N.D.Ga. 1994); *In re Tri-State Crematory Litig.*, 215 FRD 660 (ND Ga. 2003).

54. *Alexander* v. *Gen. Motors Corp.*, 478 SE 2d 123, 124 (Ga. 1996). *Alexander* was a products liability action arising out of a traffic accident in Virginia in which a Georgia motorist was injured while driving a car manufactured by the defendant and sold to plaintiff in Georgia. Finding the laws of the two states to be "radically dissimilar", 478 SE 2d at 124, the court held that "the rule of *lex loci delicti* should not be applied", *id.* at 123, because its application would be "antithetical" to "the public policy of [Georgia]." *Id.* at 124. For a more recent case directly reaffirming the *lex loci* rule, see footnote 41, *supra*.

55. For a critique of *Alexander*, see Symeonides, "Choice of Law in the American Courts in 1996: Tenth Annual Survey", 45 *Am. J. Comp. L.* 447, 453-455 (1997).

49. New Mexico's highest court has acknowledged its past adherence to the *lex loci delicti* rule, but chose not to apply it. In *Torres* v. *State*[56], the court said that "[t]his rule is not utilized if such application would violate New Mexico public policy"[57]. While this statement does not in itself entail a departure from the traditional theory, the court's use of the forum's public policy is essentially incompatible with that theory which teaches that *ordre public* is to function only defensively (i.e., as a means of preventing the application of an objectionable foreign law that is found applicable under the forum's choice-of-law rule). In *Torres*, the court did not even examine the content of the foreign *locus delicti* – which it defined as the place of the injury – and instead applied the law of the forum state, which was also the place of conduct, under a reasoning that approximates a modern policy analysis[58]. It should therefore come as no surprise that lower courts have interpreted the above quoted phrase as meaning that "policy considerations may override the place-of-the-wrong rule"[59].

50. The Supreme Court of North Carolina also threatened to "abjure the *lex loci commissi* rule" if "the governmental interests and public policy of [North Carolina] would [so] require"[60]. But since it found another way to avoid the *lex loci* rule[61], the court did not follow up on the threat. Amazingly, the court concluded that the *locus* state had "[n]o law one way or another"[62] on the particular issue, and thus there was nothing for the court to apply. Thus, the court applied the law of the forum. Since then, the court has encountered two more tort conflicts. It

---

56.   894 P. 2d 386 (NM 1995).

57.   *Id.* at 390.

58.   In contrast to *Alexander, supra* footnote 54, the use of the public policy exception and the resulting application of the *lex fori* in *Torres* was not as self-serving because the forum state, which was also the state of the wrongful conduct, had a law that was favourable to a foreign plaintiff and unfavourable to a forum defendant (the State itself). In this sense, *Torres* can be contrasted with *Dawkins, supra* footnote 47, which involved the converse pattern (*lex fori* unfavourable to local defendant (the State) and favourable to foreign plaintiff, and foreign *lex loci* favourable the forum State). The *Dawkins* court applied the *lex loci* showing no sympathy for the plaintiff's *ordre public* argument.

59.   *Estate of Gilmore*, 946 P. 2d 1130 at 1135 (NM App. 1997). Despite acknowledging that the Supreme Court "ha[d] not embraced the Restatement Second ... in either tort or contract", *id.* at 1136, this court relied heavily on the Second Restatement. It described New Mexico's approach as "reflecting a desire for the greater certainty presumably provided by more traditional approaches ... [but] tempered by recognition that important policy considerations cannot be ignored." *Id.* This meant that the court, should begin with a strong *lex loci* presumption but should "not close [its] eyes to compelling policy arguments for departure from the general rule in specific circumstances". *Id.*

60.   *Leonard* v. *Johns-Manville Sales Corp.*, 305 SE 2d 528 at 532 (NC 1983).

61.   The court concluded that the *locus* state had "[n]o law one way or another on this issue". *Id.* at 532. Consequently, said the court, "the rule of *lex loci commissi* does not apply. Instead we hold that North Carolina law applies." *Id.*

62.   *Id.* at 532.

applied the *lex loci* in the first one[63], but not in the second[64], preferring instead to resolve the conflict on the basis of "public policy considerations"[65] derived from the forum's workers' compensation statute[66].

51. Finally, the Supreme Court of West Virginia provided a blunt explanation for its continued, albeit not enthusiastic, adherence to the *lex loci* rule – the availability of escapes which the court could employ at will to reach the desired substantive result. In *Paul v. National Life*[67], the court rejected an appeal to adopt the Second Restatement, stating:

> "[I]f we are going to manipulate conflicts doctrine in order to achieve substantive results, we might as well manipulate something we understand. Having mastered marble, we decline an apprenticeship in bronze. We therefore reaffirm our adherence to the doctrine of *lex loci delicti* today."[68]

In this case, the vehicle for reaching the desired substantive result was the *ordre public* exception, which enabled the court to avoid the Indiana guest statute in a case arising from an Indiana traffic accident involving only West Virginia parties.

The court's subsequent decisions live up to the court's declared intention to manipulate the *lex loci* rule whenever possible, if not always. For example, in *McKinney v. Fairchild Int'l, Inc.*[69], the court toyed once again with the idea of adopting the Second Restatement, but in the end applied the *lex fori* rather than the *lex loci* under both a traditional and a modern rationale[70]. In *Mills v. Quality*

---

63.   See *Boudreau* v. *Baughman*, 368 SE 2d 849 (NC 1988).

64.   See *Braxton* v. *Anco Elec., Inc.*, 409 SE 2d 914 (NC 1991) (Applying North Carolina law and allowing a tort action by a North Carolina worker, who was injured in a Virginia work accident, against a North Carolina employer who would have been immune under Virginia's workers' compensation law.)

65.   *Id.* at 916.

66.   The court also noted that the same result would be reached through a *renvoi* from the *lex loci* to the *lex fori*. See *id.* at 916-917. In *Gbye v. Gbye*, 503 SE 2d 434 (NC App. 1998), North Carolina's intermediate court concluded that the Supreme Court's adherence to the *lex loci* rule was "steadfast" and "strong", *id.* at 435, 436, and "decline[d] any request to carve out a more 'modern approach' to the rule's application". *Id.* at 436. The court applied the *lex loci*'s parental immunity rule to an action between two North Carolina domiciliaries.

67.   352 SE 2d 550 (W Va. 1986).

68.   *Id.* at 556.

69.   487 SE 2d 913 (1997). See also Oakes v. Oxygen Therapy Services, 363 SE 2d 130 (W. Va. 1987) (quoting in full Second Restatement §§145, 146 and 6 and determining the applicable law on a grouping-of-contacts basis); Vest v. St. Albans Psychiatric Hosp., Inc., 387 SE 2d 282 (W. Va. 1989) (acknowledging the lex loci delicti rule but eventually avoiding it through the use of the substance/procedure distinction).

70.   For a discussion of why this case should not be interpreted as an abandonment of the *lex loci* rule, see Symeonides, "Choice of Law in the American Courts in 1997", 46 *Am.*

Supplier Trucking, Inc.[71], the court refused on public policy grounds to apply the contributory negligence rule of the *lex loci* and applied instead the comparative negligence rule of the *lex fori*. Finally, in *Russell* v. *Bush & Burchett, Inc.*[72], the court invoked a doctrine of deference – comity – not in order to defer to foreign law, but rather to reject it. *Russell* was a workers' compensation case arising out of an employment accident on the Kentucky end of a bridge connecting Kentucky and West Virginia. The injured employee was a Kentucky domiciliary, hired by defendant, a Kentucky employer, who in turn was hired through a public bidding by the West Virginia Division of Highways (DOH) to construct the bridge.

The question in *Russell* was whether the plaintiff employee was entitled to invoke the "deliberate intention" provision of the West Virginia workers' compensation statute, which deprives the employer of its statutory tort immunity[73]. The court held that "this question is not determined by the doctrine of *lex loci delicti*, but rather under the principles of comity"[74]. The court explained that, although comity is often used as a shorthand term to explain why a court would defer to the laws of another state, the term comity was used here "in its meaning as a choice-of-law analytic approach that may lead to either applying *or* declining to apply the law of another jurisdiction"[75]. The court further explained that comity rests on several principles, including the proverbial kitchen sink, and "most important[ly], the forum court['s] [right to] ask itself whether these [foreign-created] rights are compatible with its own public law and policy"[76]. The court seized on this last "principle" and, without saying anything about the foreign law or any foreign-created right, concluded that West Virginia law should govern because West Virginia had "an *affirmative* public policy ... that all persons working on the ... bridge project would have all the benefits of West Virginia's workers' compensation law, including its 'deliberate intention' provisions"[77].

Again, few people would quarrel with the result. The court could have based this result on a simple factual finding that the plaintiff was a "covered employee" un-

---

J. Comp. L. 233, 248 (1998).

71. 510 SE 2d 280 (W. Va. 1998).

72. 559 SE 2d 36 (W. Va. 2001).

73. This provision allowed a tort action against an employer who "acted with a consciously, subjectively and deliberately formed intention" to cause injury to the employee. W. Va. Code 23-4-2 *(c)*. The Kentucky workers' compensation statute apparently did not contain a similar provision. Following the *lex loci delicti* rule, the lower court held that the West Virginia statute was inapplicable, and granted a summary judgment for defendant.

74. *Russell*, 559 SE 2d at 40.

75. *Id.* at n. 4.

76. *Id.* at 40. Among the other principles were "legal harmony and uniformity among the co-equal states" and protection of the "rights and expectations of a party who has relied on foreign law". *Id.*

77. *Id.* at 40-41 (emphasis added).

der West Virginia's workers' compensation statute[78]. Under these circumstances, the plaintiff should be entitled to the protection of that statute[79], and regardless of comity, public policy, or contrary provision, if any, in the Kentucky workers' compensation statute. The court could have reached this result directly based on West Virginia's "affirmative public policy"[80], without apologies and without the confused discussion of comity and vested rights, neither of which had anything to do with the case.

2.   *Contract conflicts*

52. Of the eleven states that follow the traditional system in contract conflicts, Alabama[81], Florida[82], Georgia[83], and Virginia[84] seem more committed to the *lex loci contractus* than any of the remaining seven states.

---

78.   The court did make such a finding when it stated that "the DOH required in its bidding process – and [the employer] contractually promised to the DOH in that process – that all ... bridge project workers would be covered by the West Virginia Workers' Compensation Act." *Id.* at 40.

79.   "'[A]ll employees covered by the West Virginia Workers' Compensation Act ... are entitled to all benefits and privileges under the Act, including the right to file a direct deliberate intention cause of action ...'" *Id.* at 41 (quoting *Bell* v. *Vecellio & Grogan, Inc.*, 475 SE 2d 138, 144 (W. Va. 1996)).

80.   See text at footnote 77, *supra*.

81.   See *American Nonwovens, Inc.* v. *Non Wovens Eng'g, S.R.I*, 648 So. 2d 565 (Ala. 1994).

82.   See *Sturiano* v. *Brooks*, 523 So. 2d 1126 (Fla. 1988) (reaffirming the *lex loci contractus* rule and specifically refusing to extend to contract conflicts the "most significant relationship" formula earlier adopted for tort conflicts).

83.   See *Gen. Tel. Co.* v. *Trimm*, 311 SE 2d 460 (Ga. 1984) (rejecting as "confusing" and "uncertain" the center-of-gravity approach and deciding to adhere to the *lex loci contractus* rule "[u]ntil it becomes clear that a better rule exists". *Id.* at 462.); *Convergys Corp.* v. *Keener*, 582 SE 2d 84 (Ga. 2003) (reaffirming adherence to the traditional, if peculiar, Georgia approach and expressly rejecting the Restatement Second in a case in which the Restatement would have produced the same outcome. *Convergys* is discussed in S. Symeonides, "Choice of Law in the American Courts in 2003: Seventeenth Annual Survey", 52 *Am. J. Comp. L.* 9, 27-29 (2004). But see *Amica Mut. Ins. Co.* v. *Bourgault*, 429 SE 2d 908 (1993) (relying on Second Restatement §193 to interpret a Georgia insurance statute). Georgia's adherence to the *lex loci contractus* rule is subject to several exceptions. In addition to the exception described *supra* at 48, regarding non-statutory foreign law, Georgia courts do not apply the *lex loci contractus* rule when: *(a)* the contract is to be performed in a state other than the state in which it was made, see *Trimm*, 311 SE 2d at 461; or *(b)* when the contract contains a valid choice-of-law clause. See *Carr* v. *Kupfer*, 296 SE 2d 560 (Ga. 1982). However, contracts made in Georgia and not containing a choice-of-law clause to the contrary are presumed to have been tacitly submitted by the parties to the law of Georgia. See *Gen. Elec. Credit Corp.* v. *Home Indem. Co.*, 309 SE 2d 152 (Ga. App. 1983); *Boardman Petroleum, Inc.* v. *Federated Mut. Ins. Co.*, 926 F. Supp. 1566 (SD Ga. 1995).

84.   See *Buchanan* v. *Doe*, 431 SE 2d 289 (Va. 1993); *Erie Ins. Exch.* v. *Shapiro*, 450 SE 2d 144 (Va. 1994); *Lexie* v. *State Farm Mut. Auto. Ins. Co.*, 469 SE 2d 61 (Va. 1996).

53. At the other extreme is Rhode Island which remains in the traditional camp only because the supreme court of that state has not had the opportunity to reconsider the *lex loci contractus* rule since the 1968 abandonment of the *lex loci delicti*[85]. Four years later, when the court encountered a contract conflict, the court found that the contract had been made in Rhode Island, that this state had "the most significant interest in th[e] matter"[86], and that Rhode Island law should govern "under whatever theory we follow"[87]. The court also noted that, based on the record before it, the court "need not and do[es] not"[88] decide whether to adopt the modern approach it had earlier adopted for tort conflicts. Some courts have interpreted this statement as an abandonment[89], and others as a reaffirmation[90] of the *lex loci contractus* rule. Because the Supreme Court of Rhode Island has yet to encounter a clear contract conflict, the court has not had the opportunity to clarify this question. However, a 1992 case involving security interests – which could also be characterized as a contract case – leaves the impression that the days of the *lex loci contractus* are numbered if not over[91].

54. Tennessee's classification as a *lex loci contractus* state is almost as doubtful as Rhode Island's. In 1975, the Supreme Court of Tennessee expressly rejected an appeal to adopt "the dominant-contacts rule" for contract conflicts because of the rule's failure to produce uniformity[92]. However, in 1992, the same court adopted the Second Restatement's approach for tort conflicts[93] and appeared unconcerned about the possibility that this approach may not be as conducive to certainty. Although the court has yet to encounter a contract conflict since 1992, it would not be unreasonable to expect that, when it does, the court will abandon the *lex loci contractus* rule, perhaps in favour of the Second Restatement.

55. The highest courts of Kansas and Maryland have recently had an opportunity to abandon the *lex loci contractus* rule, but had little incentive to do so because both courts were able to evade the results of the rule. Both courts employed escape devices which, though couched in traditional jargon, suggest

85. See *Woodward* v. *Stewart*, 243 A. 2d 917, 923 (RI 1968). In fact, the court did not encounter a contract conflict between 1937 and 1972. See *Owens* v. *Hagenbeck-Wallace Shows Co.*, 192 A. 158 (RI 1937); *A.C. Beals Co.* v. *Rhode Island Hosp.*, 292 A. 2d 865 (RI 1972).

86. *A.C. Beals Co.* v. *Rhode Island Hosp.*, 292 A. 2d 865, 871 (RI 1972).

87. Id at 871.

88. *Id.*

89. See *Everett/Charles Contact Prod., Inc.* v. *Centec, S.A.R.I*, 692 F. Supp. 83, 89 (DRI 1988); *Albany Ins. Co.* v. *Wisnieski*, 579 F. Supp. 1004, 1003 (DRI 1984); *Roy* v. *Star Chopper Co.*, 442 F. Supp. 1010, 1015 (DRI 1977) aff'd 584 F. 2d 1124 (1st Cir 1978).

90. See *Soar* v. *Nat'l Football League Players' Ass'n*, 550 F. 2d 1287, 1290 (1st Cir. 1977).

91. See *Gordon* v. *Clifford Metal Sales Co., Inc.*, 602 A. 2d 535 (RI 1992). *Gordon* is alternatively based on the "reasonable relation" language of the UCC §1-105 and Restatement Second §6.

92. See *Great American Ins. Co.* v. *Hartford Accident & Indemn. Co.*, 517 SW 2d 579 at 580 (Tenn. 1975).

93. See *Hataway* v. *McKinley*, 830 SW 2d 53 (Tenn. 1992)

an increasing discomfort with traditional thinking[94]. The Kansas Supreme Court found it unnecessary to abandon the *lex loci* rule and "reserve[d] consideration of the Restatement's 'most significant relationship' test for a later day"[95], because the traditional public policy exception – which the court employed offensively rather than defensively – enabled the court to avoid applying the *lex loci* so as to protect "[t]he interests of Kansas"[96].

56. Maryland's highest court also used a similar notion of public policy and spoke of state "interests" and "significant relations" in avoiding the results of the *lex loci* rule, all the while professing adherence to it[97]. In its latest major decision

---

94.   A similar discomfort appears in New Mexico and South Carolina. With regard to New Mexico, see *Reagan v. McGee Drilling Corp.*, 933 P. 2d 867 (NM App. 1997), cert. denied (applying alternatively the public policy exception to the *lex loci* and the Second Restatement). But see *Shope v. State Farm Ins. Co.*, 955 P. 2d 515 (NM 1996) (applying the *lex loci contractus* without discussion). With regard to South Carolina, see *Sangamo Weston, Inc.* v. *Nat'l Sur. Corp.*, 414 SE 2d 127 (SC 1992) (acknowledging that, "historically", the *lex loci contractus* rule had been followed in South Carolina and noting that, with the record presently before it, the court was "unable to address the question of whether South Carolina would adopt the more modern view of the [Second] Restatement". *Id.* at 147-148); *Lister v. NationsBank of Delaware, N.A.*, 1997 WL 723056 (SC App. 1997) (applying alternatively the *lex loci* rule and the Second Restatement).

The Wyoming Supreme Court has vacillated between the *lex loci* and the Second Restatement. *Cherry Creek Dodge Inc.* v. *Carter*, 733 P. 2d 1024 (Wy. 1987) cited the Restatement favourably but relied mostly on the "reasonable relationship" language of the forum's version of the *UCC*. *Amoco Rocmount Co.* v. *The Anschutz Corp.*, 7 F. 3d 909 (10th Cir. 1993), interpreted *Cherry Creek* as having adopted the Restatement. *BHP Petroleum (Americas), Inc.* v. *Texaco Explor. & Prod., Inc.*, 1 P. 3d 1253 (Wy. 2000) renounced the view that *Cherry Creek* had adopted the Second Restatement.

95.   *St. Paul Surplus Lines v. Int'l Playtex, Inc.*, 777 P. 2d 1259 at 1267 (Kan. 1989).

96.   *Id.* ("The interest of Kansas exceeds [that of the other states].") See also *Hartford Accident & Indem. Co.* v. *American Red Ball Transit Co.*, 938 P. 2d 1281 (Kan. 1997) (accord); *Safeco Ins. Co.* v. *Allen*, 941 P. 2d 1365 (Kan. 1997) (reaffirming both the *lex loci contractus* rule and the public policy exception enunciated in *St. Paul* but finding the exception inapplicable because the *lex loci* was "consistent with the stated policy of [Kansas law]". *Id.* at 1372).

97.   In *Bethlehem Steel Co.* v. *G.C. Zarnas & Co., Inc.*, 498 A. 2d 605 (Md. 1984), the court, using an expansive notion of public policy, refused to apply Pennsylvania law to a contract made in Pennsylvania. Speaking of the two states' contacts and interests and invoking a *renvoi* rationale, the court concluded that "Pennsylvania ha[d] no strong interest in [applying its law] ... [because] had [this] suit ... been brought in Pennsylvania, the Pennsylvania court would likely have decided the issue according to Maryland law [because of Maryland's 'significant contacts' with the case]." *Id.* at 609. See also *Nat'l Glass v. J.C. Penney*, 650 A. 2d 246 (Md. 1994) (following Restatement Second §187 in analyzing a choice-of-law clause); *Kronovet v. Lipchin*, 415 A. 2d 1096 (Md. 1980) (accord).

on the subject, *American Motorists Ins. Co.* v. *ARTRA Group, Inc.*[98], the court managed to avoid the *lex loci* rule by concluding, albeit erroneously[99], that according to the conflicts law of Illinois, the *locus contractus* state, "Maryland ha[d] the most significant relationship"[100], and thus its law should govern under the *renvoi* doctrine. The court described its decision as "holding that Maryland's adherence to *lex loci contractus* must yield to a test such as Restatement (Second) Conflict of Laws §188 when the place of contracting would apply Maryland law pursuant to that test"[101], but insisted that this "is not a total jettisoning of *lex loci contractus*"[102]. The court recognized that, "[w]ith modern technology and modern business practices, the place of contracting becomes less certain and more arbitrary"[103], and that "[t]he *lex loci contractus* rule ... frequently elevates fortuitous and insignificant circumstances to crucial importance in establishing controlling law"[104]. Nevertheless, the court concluded as follows:

---

98. 659 A. 2d 1295 (Md. 1995) (action for declaratory judgment between an Illinois insurer and an Illinois insured on whether insurance policies issued in Illinois provided coverage for environmental contamination caused by the operation of the insured's paint-manufacturing factory located in Maryland).

99. Relying on the parties' representations, the court assumed that under the Second Restatement which is followed in Illinois, an Illinois court would have applied Maryland law because, although both the insurer and the insured were Illinois corporations and the insurance policies had been issued and delivered in Illinois, Maryland, as the state in which the insured risk was located, would have a more significant relationship to the dispute. Yet, slightly more than a month before *ARTRA* was decided, the Supreme Court of Illinois had held in *Lapham-Hickey Steel Corp.* v. *Protection Mut. Ins. Co.*, 655 NE 2d 842, 845 (Ill. 1995), that an environmental insurance policy which, like the policy involved in *ARTRA*, was issued in Illinois to an Illinois insured by an insurer doing business in Illinois, was governed by Illinois law, even with regard to risks situated in other states.

100. *ARTRA*, 659 A. 2d at 1304. The court said that "in spite of the doctrine of *lex loci contractus*", Maryland courts should apply Maryland law to contracts made elsewhere when: "(1) Maryland has the most significant relationship, or, at least, a substantial relationship with respect to the contract issue presented; and (2) The state where the contract was entered into ... would apply Maryland substantive law to the issue before the court." *Id.* This excerpt, as well as the rest of the opinion, suggests that the *renvoi* exception is to be employed only when the other state involved in the conflict employs a flexible approach, such as the Restatement Second, and not when that state follows a mechanical rule such as the *lex loci solutionis* rule. What remains unclear is whether the determination that "Maryland has the most significant ... or, at least, a substantial relationship" is to be made independently by Maryland courts, or whether it is to be made under the precedents of the other involved state(s).

101. *Id.*

102. *Id.*

103. *Id.* at 1305.

104. *Id.* The court also said that its recent decisions invoking the *ordre public* exception and those adopting §187 of the Restatement Second which "in effect, allow[s] the parties in their contract to select the jurisdiction with the most significant relationship",

"*Lex loci contractus* is still the law in the majority of jurisdictions, although there is a significant modern erosion of the rule. If that erosion continues, however, this Court may, in the proper case, have to reevaluate what the best choice-of-law rules ought to be to achieve simplicity, predictability, and uniformity."[105]

One would hope that when the court realizes the inaccuracy of the first sentence in the above excerpt[106], the court will follow up on the promise contained in the second sentence.

---

signified "some movement away from rigidly following the rule of *lex loci contractus*". *Id.* The court seemed to be satisfied that these two developments, coupled with the "limited *renvoi* exception" adopted in *ARTRA*, would suffice to preserve the *lex loci contractus* rule for the immediate future.

105.   *Id.*
106.   283. See *supra* 43-44.

Chapter IV   The Choice-of-law Revolution Today

A.   Introduction

57. As discussed in the preceding chapter, well before the end of the twentieth century, the great majority of American jurisdictions had abandoned the traditional theory in tort and contract conflicts. By the beginning of the twenty-first century, there is little doubt that the old order has collapsed. In this sense, the revolution that began in the 1960s has prevailed.

However, the revolution did not consist of a single unified movement, but rather encompassed several parallel movements united only in their opposition to the old order. It is therefore no surprise that the revolution has not produced a new choice-of-law system but rather several alternative approaches that continue to vie for judicial following.

This chapter discusses how these approaches fare in the over-forty American jurisdictions that, as of the date of this writing, have abandoned the traditional system. This chapter attempts to identify the particular approach or combination of approaches each jurisdiction follows and then discusses representative cases from each group.

B.   The Methodological Camps

58. The tables and charts reproduced in this section show the various methodological camps in tort and contract conflicts and the jurisdictions that seem to belong to each. Table 4 is an alphabetical list by jurisdiction. Chart 5 shows the various methodological camps in tort conflicts, and Chart 6 does likewise with regard to contract conflicts.

Table 4. Alphabetical list of states and choice-of-law methodologies

States	Traditional	Signif. contacts	Restate-ment 2d	Interest Analysis	Lex Fori	Better Law	Combined Modern
Alabama	T+C						
Alaska			T+C				
Arizona			T+C				
Arkansas		C				T	
California				T			C
Colorado			T+C				
Connecticut			T+ C?				
Delaware			T+C				
District of Columbia				T			C
Florida	C		T				
Georgia	T+C						
Hawaii							T+C
Idaho			T+C				
Illinois			T+C				
Indiana		T+C					
Iowa			T+C				
Kansas	T+C						
Kentucky			C		T		
Louisiana							T+C
Maine			T+C				
Maryland	T+C						
Massachusetts							T+C
Michigan			C		T		
Minnesota						T+C	
Mississippi			T+C				
Missouri			T+C				
Montana			T+C				
Nebraska			T+C				
Nevada		C			T		
New Hampshire			C			T	
New Jersey				T			C
New Mexico	T+C						
New York							T+C
No. Carolina	T	C					
North Dakota		T					C
Ohio			T+C				
Oklahoma			T+C?				
Oregon							T+C
Pennsylvania							T+C
Puerto Rico		T+C					
Rhode Island	C					T	
So. Carolina	T+C						
So. Dakota			T+C				
Tennessee	C		T				
Texas			T+C				
Utah			T+C				
Vermont			T+C				
Virginia	T+C						
Washington			T+C				
West Virginia	T		C				
Wisconsin						T+C	
Wyoming	T+C						
TOTAL 52	Torts 10 Contracts 11	Torts 3 Contracts 5	Torts 22 Contracts 24	Torts 3 Contracts 0	Torts 3 Contracts 0	Torts 5 Contracts2	Torts 6 Contracts10

T = Torts   C = Contracts

Chart 5. Methodological camps in tort conflicts

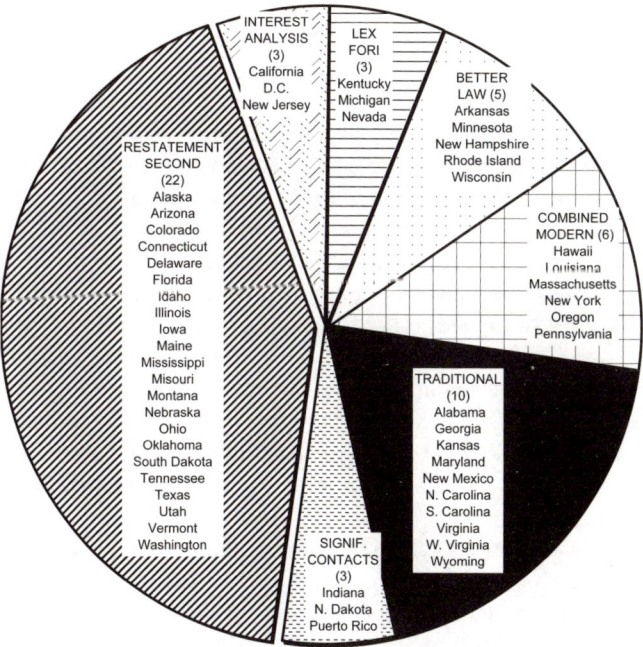

INTEREST ANALYSIS (3)
California
D.C.
New Jersey

LEX FORI (3)
Kentucky
Michigan
Nevada

BETTER LAW (5)
Arkansas
Minnesota
New Hampshire
Rhode Island
Wisconsin

RESTATEMENT SECOND (22)
Alaska
Arizona
Colorado
Connecticut
Delaware
Florida
Idaho
Illinois
Iowa
Maine
Mississippi
Misouri
Montana
Nebraska
Ohio
Oklahoma
South Dakota
Tennessee
Texas
Utah
Vermont
Washington

COMBINED MODERN (6)
Hawaii
Louisiana
Massachusetts
New York
Oregon
Pennsylvania

TRADITIONAL (10)
Alabama
Georgia
Kansas
Maryland
New Mexico
N. Carolina
S. Carolina
Virginia
W. Virginia
Wyoming

SIGNIF. CONTACTS (3)
Indiana
N. Dakota
Puerto Rico

Chart 6. Methodological camps in contract conflicts

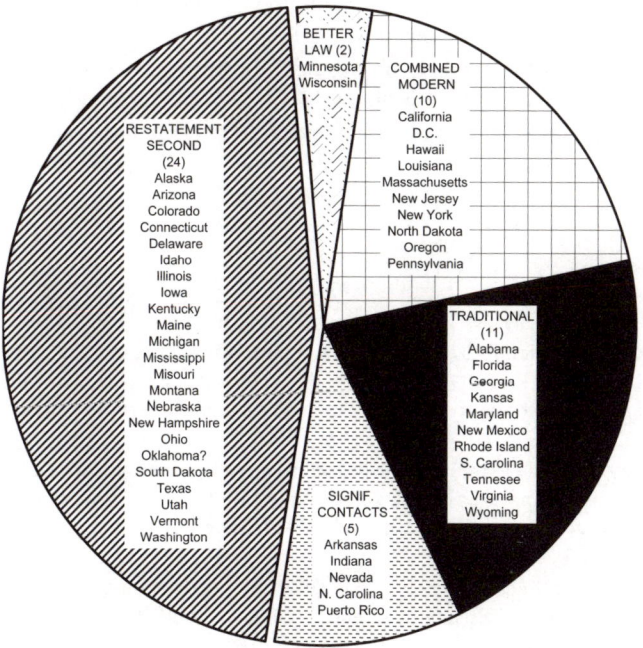

BETTER LAW (2)
Minnesota
Wisconsin

COMBINED MODERN (10)
California
D.C.
Hawaii
Louisiana
Massachusetts
New Jersey
New York
North Dakota
Oregon
Pennsylvania

RESTATEMENT SECOND (24)
Alaska
Arizona
Colorado
Connecticut
Delaware
Idaho
Illinois
Iowa
Kentucky
Maine
Michigan
Mississippi
Misouri
Montana
Nebraska
New Hampshire
Ohio
Oklahoma?
South Dakota
Texas
Utah
Vermont
Washington

TRADITIONAL (11)
Alabama
Florida
Georgia
Kansas
Maryland
New Mexico
Rhode Island
S. Carolina
Tennessee
Virginia
Wyoming

SIGNIF. CONTACTS (5)
Arkansas
Indiana
Nevada
N. Carolina
Puerto Rico

C.   Caveats and Qualifications

1.   *Lack of recent precedent*

59. These tables and charts should be used with caution. Classifying a state into a particular methodological camp is not an exact science. Difficulties arise from a variety of sources, ranging from the lack or dearth of authoritative precedent, to precedents that are either equivocal or exceedingly eclectic.

For example, for more than 60 years, the Supreme Court of Rhode Island has not had an occasion to reconsider its last precedent to apply the *lex loci contractus* rule[1]. Because this court was among the first to abandon the *lex loci delicti* rule[2], and has since remained in the forefront of the revolution in tort conflicts, one is tempted to infer that this court is likely to also abandon the *lex loci contractus* rule. Such an inference would be as plausible as the type of educated guesses federal courts make in diversity cases[3]. Even so, this guess would not be entirely safe, since some states have abandoned the traditional theory in torts, but not in contracts and vice versa[4], and in at least one of those states, Florida, this dichotomy is not accidental.[5]

Even if one concludes that Rhode Island no longer belongs in the traditional camp, there remains the more difficult question of placing this state into one or another of the modern methodological camps. Again, one could plausibly assume that the Rhode Island Supreme Court would adopt the same hybrid better-law approach for contract conflicts as it has for tort conflicts, but this assumption has its own hazards both because the better law approach seems to be losing it initial appeal and because there are states that follow a different modern choice-of-law methodology for torts and contracts. Because of these uncertainties, the tables reproduced here, perhaps erring on the side of caution, keep Rhode Island in the traditional camp for contract conflicts.

Another example is Tennessee's position in contract conflicts. The supreme court of that state has not encountered a contract conflict since its 1992 abandon-

---

1.   See *supra* 53.

2.   See *Woodward* v. *Stewart*, 243 A. 2d 917 (RI 1968).

3.   See, e.g., Judge Friendly's oft-quoted statement: "Our principal task ... is to determine what the New York courts would think the California courts would think on an issue about which neither court has thought." *Nolan* v. *Transocean Air Lines*, 276 F. 2d 280, 281 (2d Cir. 1960).

4.   West Virginia and Wyoming have abandoned the traditional theory in contracts but not in torts. See *supra* 45-46, 51. Also, in addition to Rhode Island, Florida and Tennessee have abandoned the traditional theory in torts but not in contracts. See 45, 52, 54.

5.   See *Sturiano* v. *Brooks*, 523 So. 2d 1126 (Fla. 1988) (reaffirming the *lex loci contractus* rule and specifically refusing to extend to contract conflicts the "most significant relationship" formula the court had earlier adopted for tort conflicts).

ment of the traditional theory in tort conflicts[6]. One could plausibly infer that, with the next available opportunity, that court will also abandon the traditional theory in contract conflicts and will likely opt for the Second Restatement. However, until then, it is better to err on the side of caution and to keep Tennessee in the traditional column for contract conflicts[7].

2.   Equivocal precedents

60. Another obstacle to accurate classifications results from the fact that in some cases the available supreme court precedents are equivocal, or even irreconcilable. For example, in contract conflicts, the precedents from North Carolina[8], Oklahoma[9], West Virginia[10], and Wyoming[11] are equivocal enough to be susceptible to different interpretations regarding the methodological orientation of those states. Similar doubts exist regarding Arkansas' classification as a significant-contacts state, because Arkansas precedents are virtually irreconcilable[12].

3.   Eclecticism

61. When methodological equivocation is intentional and appears in the same precedent, it can be described as eclecticism. This phenomenon, which appeared in the first years of the revolution, has become even more frequent in recent years. As said elsewhere,

---

6.   See *Hataway* v. *McKinley*, 830 SW 2d 53 (Tenn. 1992).

7.   On the other hand, the tables classify Illinois in the Second Restatement camp for contract conflicts, despite the lack of supreme court precedent to that effect. The reason for being less cautious here is that, for almost three decades, the Illinois Supreme Court has not only followed consistently and wholeheartedly the Second Restatement in tort conflicts, but also routinely left undisturbed lower court decisions that confidently applied the Restatement to contract conflicts. See, e.g., *Olsen* v. *Celano*, 600 NE 2d 1257 (Ill. App. 1992); *Soc'y of Mount Carmel* v. *Nat'l Ben Franklin Ins. Co.*, 643 NE 2d 1280 (Ill. App. 1994).

8.   See *supra* 44, footnote 37.

9.   See *supra* 44, footnote 39.

10.   See *supra* 44, footnote 36.

11.   See *supra* 55, footnote 94. See *BHP Petroleum (Americas), Inc.* v. *Texaco Explor. & Prod., Inc.*, 1 P. 3d 1253 (Wy. 2000) (holding that the court's earlier reliance on the Second Restatement was not intended as an adoption of the Second Restatement).

12.   For example, in *McMillen* v. *Winona Nat'l & Savings Bank*, 648 SW 2d 460 (Ark. 1983), and *Standard Leasing Corp.* v. *Schmidt Aviation, Inc.*, 576 SW 2d 181 (Ark. 1979), the Arkansas Supreme Court applied a significant-contacts approach. In *Stacy* v. *St. Charles Custom Kitchens, Inc.*, 683 SW 2d 225 (Ark. 1985), however, the same court appeared to revert to the *lex loci contractus* rule. In *Threlkeld* v. *Worsham*, 785 SW 2d 249 (Ark. App. 1990), a lower court applied the "better-law" approach to a sale contract. *Id.* at 252-253.

"... few cases rely exclusively on a single policy-based approach. Courts tend to be less interested in theoretical purity, and more interested in reaching what they perceive to be the proper result. The majority of cases that have abandoned the traditional approach tend to use modern approaches interchangeably, and often as *a posteriori* rationalizations for results reached on other grounds."[13]

Whatever its intrinsic virtues, eclecticism is another obstacle to an accurate methodological classification. The column called "combined modern" that appears in Table 4, above, reflects this eclecticism only to some extent in that it includes only those states that overtly, knowingly, and repeatedly combine more than one modern methodology. For, if one were to include instances of unknowing, latent, or occasional eclecticism, that column would absorb most other columns. Indeed, as said elsewhere, "[i]f one had to define *the* dominant choice-of-law methodology in the United States today, it would have to be called *eclecticism*"[14].

One example from Rhode Island illustrates this point. The Supreme Court of that state recently stated:

"In this jurisdiction ... we follow ... the interest-weighing approach. In so doing, we ... determine ... the rights and liabilities of the parties 'in accordance with the law of the state that bears the most significant relationship to the event and the parties'.... . That approach has sometimes been referred to as a rule of 'choice-influencing considerations'.

In applying the interest-weighing or choice-influencing considerations, we consider ... [Leflar's five choice-influencing considerations and the four factual contacts listed] in Restatement (Second) Conflict of Laws, §145 (2)."[15]

This excerpt suggests that this court follows a blend of at least three different approaches: *(a)* an "interest-weighing approach" (namely, governmental interest analysis, but combined with the very weighing of interests that Currie proscribed); *(b)* the Second Restatement; and *c)* Leflar's choice-influencing considerations. The court goes on to suggest that, in addition, Rhode Island follows a common-domicile rule for tort conflicts (perhaps inspired by New York's *Neumeier* rules), at least when the common domicile is in Rhode Island, and the parties have a pre-

---

13. S. Symeonides, W. Perdue and A. von Mehren, *Conflict of Laws: American, Comparative, International* 124 (2nd ed 2003).

14. P. Kozyris & S. Symeonides, "Choice of Law in the American Courts in 1989: An Overview", 38 *Am. J. Comp. L.* 601, 602 (1990).

15. *Cribb* v. *Augustin*, 696 A. 2d 285, 288 (RI 1997) (citations omitted). See also *Najarian* v. *Nat'l Amusements, Inc.*, 768 A. 2d 1253 (RI 2001) (blending choice-influencing considerations with Second Restatement); *Taylor* v. *Mass. Flora Realty Inc.*, 840 A 2d 1126 (RI 2004) (adding a presumptive *lex loci* rule, without mentioning the better-law approach).

existing relationship[16]. Ordinarily, such a virtually boundless eclecticism would justify placing Rhode Island in the "combined modern" column. However, because it is unclear whether this decision is an aberration, it is preferable to keep Rhode Island in the better-law group, where it has resided since 1968.

62. Another aspect of the eclecticism phenomenon is that certain courts' commitment to a particular methodology is less than full-hearted. This is particularly true in states that purport to follow the Second Restatement. For example, some cases seem to use the Restatement solely as an escape from a traditional choice-of-law rule that has survived the adoption of the Restatement[17], others as a camouflage for a grouping-of-contacts approach[18], and others as a vehicle for merely restraining, but not avoiding, interest analysis[19]. One can find examples of such disparate treatment of the Restatement even in the same jurisdiction[20]. Finally, some states prefer to use only the general, open-ended, and flexible sections of the Restatement (such as §§145, 187 and especially §6) and avoid using the specific sections that contain mildly confining presumptive rules[21].

---

16. See *Cribb*, 696 A. 2d at 288:

    "[I]n situations in which the [Restatement 146] factors *(a)* [place of injury] and *(b)* [place of conduct] are the only ones pointing to the law of another state and factors *c)* [parties' domicile] and *(d)* [seat of their relationship] point strongly to applying Rhode Island law, the latter two factors trump the earlier two, and Rhode Island law is applied."

    In its most recent decision, *Oyola v. Burgos*, 864 A 2d 624 (RI 2005), the Rhode Island Supreme Court followed this formula, without mentioning the better-law criterion or any of the other Leflar factors.

17. See, e.g., *Hubbard Mfg. Co.* v. *Greeson*, 515 NE 2d 1071, 1073 (Ind. 1987) (holding that, "when the place of the tort is an insignificant contact", the court will turn to the Second Restatement); *O'Connor* v. *O'Connor*, 519 A. 2d 13, 21 (Conn. 1986) (adopting the Second Restatement "for those cases in which application of the doctrine of lex loci [delicti] would produce an arbitrary, irrational result").

18. See, e.g., *Palmer G. Lewis Co.* v. *ARCO Chem. Co.*, 904 P. 2d 1221 (Alaska 1995); *Powell* v. *American Charter Fed. S & L Ass'n*, 514 NW 2d 326 (Neb. 1994); *Stockmen's Livestock Exch.* v. *Thompson*, 520 NW 2d 255 (SD 1994) *(per curiam)*; *Selle v. Pierce*, 494 NW 2d 634 (SD 1992); *Hataway v. McKinley*, 830 SW 2d 53 (Tenn. 1992); *American Nat'l Fire Ins. Co.* v. *Farmers Ins. Exch.*, 927 P. 2d 186 (Utah 1996); *Forsman v. Forsman*, 779 P. 2d 218 (Utah 1989).

19. See, e.g., *Williams v. State Farm Auto. Mut. Ins. Co.*, 641 A. 2d 783 (Conn. 1994); *O'Connor* v. *O'Connor*, 519 A. 2d 13 (Conn. 1986); *Esser v. McIntire*, 661 NE 2d 1138 (Ill. 1996); *Nelson v. Hix*, 522 NE 2d 1214 (Ill. 1988); *Veasley v. CRST Int'l, Inc.*, 553 NW 2d 896 (Iowa 1996); *Chrysler Corp.* v. *Skyline Indus. Servs., Inc.*, 528 NW 2d 698 (Mich. 1995); *Gilbert Spruance Co.* v. *Pennsylvania Mfgrs. Ass'n Ins. Co.*, 629 A. 2d 885 (NJ 1993).

20. Compare *Stockmen's Livestock Exchange* v. *Thompson*, 520 NW 2d 255 (SD 1994), and *Selle v. Pierce*, 494 NW 2d 634 (SD 1992), both of which relied more on state contacts than on state interests, with *Chambers v. Dakotah Charter, Inc.*, 488 NW 2d 63 (SD 1992), which relied more on state interests and less on state contacts.

21. See P. Borchers, "Courts and the Second Restatement: Some Observations and an Empirical Note", 56 *Md. L. Rev.* 1232 (1997).

4.   The relative inconsequence of methodology

63. Even if the above uncertainties did not exist, one might have good reason to object to classifying states on the basis of choice-of-law methodology, because such classifications tend to inflate the importance of methodology in explaining or predicting court decisions. Reality is much different. As stated elsewhere, "*of all the factors that may affect the outcome of a conflicts case, the factor that is the most inconsequential is the choice-of-law methodology followed by the court*"[22]. Indeed, methodology rarely drives judicial decisions. The converse is closer to the truth: "the result in the case often appears to have dictated the judge's choice of law approach at least as much as the approach itself generated the result"[23].

5.   The relative value of methodological classifications

64. The above discussion illustrates the difficulties and uncertainties one encounters in attempting to draw bright demarcation lines between the various methodological camps. In light of these uncertainties, one might wonder whether classifications such as the ones reflected in the above tables are more harmful than helpful.

This question admits different answers. This author's view is that these classifications are helpful, at least as tentative indications of where a particular jurisdiction stands. The study of any plurilegal system, especially one as vast as that of the United States, would be far more difficult if not impossible, without a modicum of categorization and sorting out, of seeking and cataloguing the common denominators among the various units. Taxonomy is not an end in itself, but it is a necessary first step in any study of multiple objects. It is also a medium for seeing the forest from the trees.

Following this cautionary preface, the rest of this chapter discusses representative cases from, and features of, the various modern methodological camps[24].

---

22.   S. Symeonides, "Choice of Law in the American Courts in 1994: A View 'from the Trenches'", 43 *Am. J. Comp. L.* 1, 2 (1995).

23.   S. Sterk, "The Marginal Relevance of Choice of Law Theory", 142 *U. Pa. L. Rev.* 949, 951 (1994); see also *Sutherland* v. *Kennington Truck Serv.*, Ltd., 562 NW 2d 466, 468 (Mich. 1997) ("[I]n practice, all the modern approaches to conflicts of law are relatively uniform in the results they produce"); S. Sterk, *supra*, at 962 ("[C]itation to academic theory has served more as window dressing than as a dispositive factor in deciding choice of law cases.").

24.   For the states following the traditional camp, see *supra* 45-56.

D. Currie-Based Approaches

65. In the above tables, the interest-analysis column is completely blank in contract conflicts[25], and lists only three jurisdictions in tort conflicts[26] – California[27],
the District of Columbia[28], and New Jersey[29]. In light of the pivotal role that interest analysis played in the conflicts revolution, this development is nothing short
of astonishing. Worse yet, a more literal classification might place even these
three jurisdictions elsewhere, insofar as they engage in the very weighing of state
interests that Currie proscribed. New Jersey and the District of Columbia weigh
interests openly and unapologetically[30], while California prefers to weigh not the
interests themselves but rather the impairment that would result from subordinating them[31]. Thus, a more technical classification might move these states to
different columns, leaving completely blank the interest-analysis column, four
decades after Currie's death.

However, this should not suggest that Currie's influence has disappeared.
First, an interest analysis traceable to Currie forms the core of most of the "combined modern" approaches followed in other states. Second, interest analysis is
often heavily employed in states that generally follow the Second Restatement,
especially in cases in which the factual contacts are evenly divided between the
involved jurisdictions[32]. Thus, in the same manner that the high numerical following of the Second Restatement tends to inflate its importance in deciding actual
cases[33], the low numerical following of Currie's original approach tends to under-
value the importance of this approach in influencing judicial decisions.

Be that as it may, the three jurisdictions named above remain closer to the
core of Currie's approach than all other states that follow a modern methodology.

---

25. Three jurisdictions had initially adopted interest analysis for contract conflicts: Or-
     egon (see *Lilienthal* v. *Kaufman*, 395 P. 2d 543 (Or. 1964)); California (see *Travelers
     Ins. Co.* v. *Workmen's Comp. Appeals Bd.*, 434 P. 2d 992 (Cal. 1967)); and the District of
     Columbia (see *McCrossin* v. *Hicks Chevrolet, Inc.*, 248 A. 2d 917 (DC 1969)). However,
     all three jurisdictions eventually switched to a mixed approach.

26. Initially, two more states had adopted interest analysis for tort conflicts – Pennsylva-
     nia and Wisconsin. Pennsylvania later switched to a "combined modern" approach,
     and Wisconsin to Leflar's approach. New York is not listed as an interest-analysis
     state because of its adherence to the *Neumeier* rules, which in some instances deviate
     significantly from interest analysis. See *infra* 93. Similarly, with regard to contracts,
     New York is not an interest-analysis state, at least not since 1993, when it switched to
     a mixed approach. See *infra* 100.

27. See *Reich* v. *Purcell*, 432 P. 2d 727 (Cal. 1967).

28. See, e.g., *Rong Yao Zhou* v. *Jennifer Mall Rest., Inc.*, 534 A. 2d 1268 (DC 1987).

29. See *Mellk* v. *Sarahson*, 229 A. 2d 625 (NJ 1967).

30. See *infra* 66.

31. See *infra* 67.

32. See S. Symeonides, "The Judicial Acceptance of the Second Conflicts Restatement: A
     Mixed Blessing", 56 *Md. L. Rev.* 1248, 1262-1263 (1997).

33. See *infra* 80.

Similarly, for entirely different reasons, three other states that follow the *lex fori* approach – Kentucky, Michigan, and Nevada – are also in the close periphery of Currie's camp. For, although they do not overtly speak in terms of interests and thus methodologically appear removed from Currie, these states are statistically if not ideologically in tune with Currie's approach – they tend to produce the very results he advocated in the majority of cases, the application of the *lex fori*. The figure reproduced below attempts to portray the surroundings of the Brainerd Currie camp.

Chart 7. Currie-based approaches

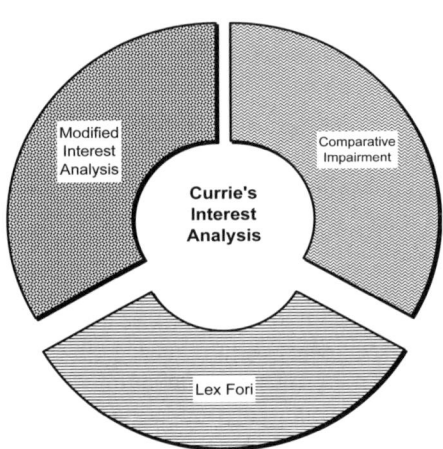

1. *Modified interest analysis*

66. New Jersey and the District of Columbia remain close to Currie's original analysis in that they resolve conflicts on the basis of state interests. However, neither jurisdiction appears constrained by Currie's proscription of interest-weighing, and both jurisdictions seem to have emancipated themselves from his parochial reading of such interests. Of course, one could argue that these two jurisdictions, as well as California, simply follow Currie's later call for "rational altruism" and for a "restrained and enlightened interpretation"[34] of the forum's interests, and thus they have not abandoned the Currie camp. However, they seem to be more outside than within the gates.

Eger v. E.I. Du Pont De Nemours Co.[35], a tort/workers' compensation case, is a good example of both interest-weighing and a non-parochial one. *Eger* was a true conflict between the laws of New Jersey, the forum state, and South Carolina. New Jersey law favoured the injured employee who was domiciled and hired in

---

34.   See D. Currie, "The Disinterested Third State", 28 *Law & Contemp. Prob.* 754, 763 (1963); *supra* 21.

35.   539 A. 2d 1213 (NJ 1988).

New Jersey, while South Carolina law favoured a defendant employer operating in South Carolina[36]. Without the slightest hesitation, the New Jersey court put the interests of the two states on the scale and concluded, over a strong dissent, that "New Jersey's interest in [protecting New Jersey employees and sub-contractors] was not strong enough to outweigh South Carolina's interest in [protecting its employers]"[37]. The court applied South Carolina law.

Gantes v. Kason Corporation[38], a products liability case, is another example of identifying state interests in a way that seems to liberate interest analysis from some of its congenital biases. Under Currie's assumptions, *Gantes* would be classified as a no-interest case, because New Jersey law favoured the Georgia plaintiff injured in Georgia, while Georgia law favoured the New Jersey defendant who manufactured the product in New Jersey[39]. After concluding that Georgia did not have an interest in protecting a New Jersey manufacturer, the New Jersey court took a broader view in identifying New Jersey's interests. The court concluded that, in addition to protecting plaintiffs (domestic *or foreign*), New Jersey law was intended to deter the manufacture of unsafe products in New Jersey[40]. Because the product had been "manufactured in, and placed into the stream of commerce from, [New Jersey]"[41], that state had a "cognizable and substantial interest in deterrence that would be furthered by the application of its ... law"[42]. Thus, by reading the forum's interests in a non-protectionist way, the court was able to conclude that this potentially no-interest case was a false conflict in which only New Jersey had an interest. The court applied New Jersey law, which benefited a foreign plaintiff at the expense of a forum defendant.

Kaiser-Georgetown Comm. Health Plan, Inc. v. Stutsman[43], a medical malpractice case, is another example of articulating the forum's interests in a non-protectionist way. Under Currie's assumptions, *Stutsman* would also qualify as a no-interest case. The law of the forum, the District of Columbia, favoured a Virginia plaintiff by providing unlimited tort damages, whereas the law of Virginia favoured a District defendant by limiting the amount of damages. The court found that "[t]he District ha[d] a significant interest ... in holding its [defendants] liable for the full extent of the negligence attributable to them"[44]. Thus, the court

---

36. The defendant was a general contractor who subcontracted with plaintiff's employer. The plaintiff was exposed to radioactivity while working for his employer in defendant's South Carolina plant. South Carolina, but not New Jersey, accorded defendant immunity from a tort action.

37. 539 A. 2d at 1218.

38. 679 A. 2d 106 (NJ 1996).

39. The plaintiff's action was timely under New Jersey's two-year statute of limitations, but was barred by Georgia's ten-year statute of repose for products-liability claims.

40. *Id.* at 111-112.

41. *Id.*

42. *Id.* at 113.

43. 491 A. 2d 502 (DC App. 1985).

44. *Id.* at 509-510.

applied the District's law, even though that law favoured a foreign plaintiff at the expense of a forum defendant[45].

2.   *Comparative impairment*

67. Interest-weighing, but with a different name, can also be seen in California. Two well-known California cases, *Bernhard* v. *Harrah's Club*[46], and *Offshore Rental Co.* v. *Continental Oil Co.*[47], illustrate this phenomenon.

Bernhard was a true conflict between the laws of California and Nevada. California law favoured the plaintiff who was domiciled and injured in California, while Nevada law favoured the defendant, a Nevada tavern owner who acted in Nevada. The defendant had served alcohol to an apparently intoxicated California patron, who then drove to California and caused the accident that resulted in plaintiff's injury. California, but not Nevada, imposed civil liability on the owner for injuries caused by the patron. The court followed Professor Baxter's comparative impairment approach, which the court described as "seek[ing] to determine which state's interest would be more impaired if its policy were subordinated to the policy of the other state"[48]. The court applied California's law, after finding that California's interest in imposing civil liability on tavern owners "would be very significantly impaired if its policy were not applied to defendant"[49], whereas "Nevada's interest in protecting its tavern keepers from civil liability ... will not be significantly impaired"[50] by imposing on them civil liability under California law[51].

---

45. Another basis for the court's decision was that the plaintiff, though domiciled in Virginia, was employed in the District, and, although the medical malpractice was committed in defendant's Virginia hospital, the relationship between plaintiff and defendant HMO arose out of plaintiff's employment in the District. The court found that "the District ha[d] an interest in protecting a member of its work force who contracts for health services with a District of Columbia corporation within this forum ..." 491 A. 2d at 510.

46. 546 P. 2d 719 (Cal. 1976), *cert. denied*, 429 US 859 (1976).

47. 583 P. 2d 721 (Cal. 1978).

48. *Bernhard*, 546 P. 2d at 723.

49. *Id.* at 725. The court reasoned that
     "California cannot reasonably effectuate its policy if it does not extend its regulation to include out-of-state tavern keepers such as defendant who regularly and purposely sell intoxicating beverages to California residents in places and under conditions in which it is reasonably certain these residents will return to California and act therein while still in an intoxicated state". *Id.*

50. *Id.*

51. This was so because "such liability involves an increased economic exposure, which, at least for businesses which actively solicit extensive California patronage, is a foreseeable and coverable business expense", *id.*, and because, "as in the instant case liability is imposed only on those tavern keepers who actively solicit California business". *id.*

The court reiterated Baxter's statements to the effect that the process of comparative impairment "is very different from a weighing process"[52]. However, the court apparently misunderstood the meaning of "weighing" by assuming it to be a process of "determining which conflicting law manifest[s] the 'better' or the 'worthier' social policy on the specific issue"[53]. Of course neither Currie nor Baxter ever advocated such a value-laden weighing. The court was closer to the mark when it described this process as one of "accommodation of conflicting state policies ... in multi-state contexts"[54].

Thus, when one looks beyond the confusion created by misused nomenclature, there remains little doubt that *Bernhard* is simply another example of interest-weighing by another name. As said elsewhere, "rather than weighing interests *as such*, comparative impairment weighs the *loss* that would result from subordinating the interest of one state to those of the other ... [and that] the gravity of the loss depend[s] on the strength and importance of the state interest at issue"[55].

Offshore Rental Co. v. *Continental Oil Co.*[56], another California case, could also be characterized as a true conflict between a California statute that favoured a California plaintiff, and a Louisiana rule that favoured a defendant operating in Louisiana[57]. The court applied the Louisiana rule, after concluding that Louisiana's interest in applying the rule was "stronger, [and] more current"[58] than California's corresponding interest, and that to apply California law "would strike at the essence of a compelling Louisiana law"[59]. In contrast, California was not really committed to its statute, which was "archaic and isolated in the context of the federal union"[60]. Hence California's interest in applying its "unusual and outmoded statute [was] comparatively less strong"[61].

Thus, *Offshore* appeared to repudiate not only Currie's proscription of interest-weighing, but also Baxter's more subtle formulation that the court should only weigh the *effects* of the application or non-application of a state's law. Indeed, in a very real sense, *Offshore* engaged in a comparative evaluation of the conflicting *laws themselves*, thus coming perilously close to a better-law approach.

---

52. *Id.* at 723.
53. *Id.*
54. *Id.*
55. S. Symeonides, W. Perdue, A. von Mehren, *Conflict of Laws; American Comparative International*, 220 (2nd ed. 2003).
56. 583 P. 2d 721 (Cal. 1978).
57. *Offshore* was an action by a California employer for the loss of the services of a key employee who was injured in Louisiana by defendant's employees. California, but not Louisiana, provided employers with an action for the loss of services of a key employee.
58. 583 P. 2d at 729.
59. *Id.* at 728.
60. *Id.*
61. *Id.*

3.   *The* lex fori *variant*

68. As explained earlier, Currie's interest analysis was heavily biased in favour of the *lex fori*, in both true conflicts and in unprovided-for cases[62]. The courts of Kentucky, Michigan, and Nevada seem to have turned this bias into a doctrine.

Foster v. *Leggett*[63] illustrates Kentucky's *lex fori* approach. Most casebooks classify *Foster* as an interest-analysis case, even though the majority opinion contains no reference to Currie's writings or, for that matter, any academic commentary. This classification is correct in the sense that the court reached the precise result Currie advocated. However, the court's heavy reliance on the forum's contacts and the absence of any discussion of policies suggest a contacts-based *lex fori* approach that is potentially more parochial than Currie's. According to this approach: *(a)* "[t]he basic law is the law of the forum which should not be displaced without valid reasons"[64]; and *(b)* such reasons are not present whenever the forum has "significant contacts – not necessarily the most significant contacts"[65].

Foster arose out of an accident in Ohio, which resulted in the death of a Kentucky domiciliary who was a guest-passenger in a car driven by the defendant, an Ohio domiciliary[66]. Ohio, but not Kentucky, had a guest-statute shielding the driver and his insurer from a suit brought on behalf of the guest-passenger. Thus, under the assumptions of interest analysis, this was a true conflict in which each state had an interest in applying its law to protect its own domiciliary. The court spoke of neither policies nor interests, nor did it cite any of Currie's writings. However, the court did echo Currie's views when it stated that the court's "primary responsibility is to follow its own substantive law"[67], and that "[t]he basic law is the law of the forum, which should not be displaced without valid reasons"[68]. Whether such a valid reason existed in this case is not free from doubt, but the court did not appear to entertain any. In a fashion that replicates Currie's solution to true conflicts, the court concluded that "if there are significant contacts – not necessarily the most significant contacts – with Kentucky, then Kentucky law should be applied"[69].The court acknowledged that its decisions could justify the inference that "we have accepted the rule of 'most significant contacts' ... to apply to Kentucky residents involved in another state and the rule of 'enough contacts'

---

62.   See *supra* 23.

63.   484 SW 2d 827 (Ky. 1972).

64.   *Id.* at 829.

65.   *Id.*

66.   The defendant worked in Kentucky, where he rented a room and had his social relationships, including a dating relationship with the deceased. Because of these Kentucky contacts, one could argue that *Foster* was sufficiently analogous to the common-domicile pattern as to justify the application of Kentucky law on this basis. However, as explained in the text, this was not the basis of the court's decision.

67.   484 SW 2d at 829.

68.   *Id.*

69.   *Id.*

for residents of other states involved in Kentucky"[70]. Nevertheless, said the court, "[s]uch is not the holding or policy of this court"[71].

While the court's interpretation of its holdings is entitled to respect, the court's failure to explain the absence of "valid reasons" for displacing forum law (other than reciting forum contacts) makes its analysis particularly vulnerable to the same criticism for parochialism as Currie's own theory.

69. *Sutherland* v. *Kennington Truck Service, Ltd.*[72] illustrates Michigan's *lex fori* approach[73]. *Sutherland* arose out of a traffic accident in Michigan involving an Ohio plaintiff and an Ontario defendant. The plaintiff's action was timely under Michigan's three-year statute of limitation, but was barred by the two-year statutes of Ohio and Ontario[74]. The court cited academic commentary according to which "each of the modern approaches tend to favour significantly the application of forum law ... between approximately fifty-five and seventy-seven percent of the time"[75], and that "courts employing the new theories have a very strong preference for forum law that frequently causes them to manipulate the theories so that they end up applying forum law"[76]. This preference, said the court, was "hardly surprising [because] the tendency toward forum law promotes judicial economy: judges and attorneys are experts in their state's law, but have to expend considerable time and resources to learn another state's law"[77].

Turning "preference" into virtue, the court elevated this "tendency" into a choice-of-law method. According to this method, a Michigan court should apply Michigan law, unless a "rational reason"[78] exists to do otherwise. In determining whether such a rational reason exists, the court is to undertake a two-step analysis. First, the court determines whether "any foreign state has an interest in having its law applied"[79]. If not, the analysis ends, and forum law applies. If a foreign state has an interest, then the court is to determine "if Michigan's interests

---

70. *Id.*

71. *Id.*

72. 562 NW 2d 466 (Mich. 1997).

73. For earlier application of this approach, see *Sexton* v. *Ryder Truck Rental, Inc.*, 320 NW 2d 843 (Mich. 1982) (abandoning the *lex loci delicti* rule in favor of the *lex fori* approach); *Olmstead* v. *Anderson*, 400 NW 2d 292 (Mich. 1987).

74. To its credit, the court refused to resolve the conflict through the traditional mechanical characterization of statutes of limitations as procedural, which, in the absence of a borrowing statute, would have led to the application of the *lex fori*. Rather, the court employed a full-fledged choice-of-law analysis, which led to the same result.

75. *Sutherland*, 562 NW 2d at 469 (citing P. Borchers, "The Choice-of-Law Revolution: An Empirical Study", 49 *Wash. & Lee L. Rev.* 357, at 374-375 (1992)).

76. *Id.* at 469-470. See also *id.* at 470, where the court opines that "only two distinct conflicts of law theories actually exist", the *lex loci delicti* and the *lex fori* approaches.

77. *Id.* at 470.

78. *Id.* at 471.

79. *Id.*

mandate that Michigan law be applied, despite the foreign interests"[80], in which case Michigan law again applies.

Applying this method, the court concluded that neither Ohio nor Ontario had an interest in applying their respective statutes of limitation. Thus, "the *lex fori* presumption [was] not overcome, and [the court] need not evaluate Michigan's interests"[81]. Ohio did not have an interest, said the court, because the application of Ohio law would "violat[e] the defendants' due process rights"[82]. The court did not explain how the application of a law that *favours* the defendant would somehow violate that defendant's due process rights[83]. The court also concluded that Ontario did not have an interest in applying its two-year statute (despite the fact that it favoured the Ontario defendant), because, "according to Canadian and Ontario law, Ontario has an interest in having Michigan's statute of limitations applied in this case"[84]. The basis for this conclusion was a decision of the Supreme Court of Canada that had adopted the *lex loci delicti* rule for both substantive tort matters and for statutes of limitation[85]. The *Sutherland* court did not explain how the *lex loci* rule, which the court had earlier discarded as being mechanical and oblivious to state interests, suddenly had become an accurate barometer of another state's "interest" in the modern sense of that word[86].

---

80.   *Id.* For the similarities with, and differences from, Albert Ehrenzweig's approach, see E. Scoles, P. Hay, P. Borchers and S. Symeonides, *Conflict of Laws*, 738 (4th ed. 2004).

81.   526 NW 2d at 473.

82.   *Id.* at 472 (citing *Allstate Ins.* Co. v. *Hague*, 449 US 302 (1981)). Noting that "the only contact that Ohio ha[d] with this litigation is that plaintiffs are Ohio residents", the court concluded that "the plaintiff's residence, with nothing more, is insufficient to support the choice of a state's law". *Id.*

83.   The court would have been closer to the mark if it were to base Ohio's lack of interests on other grounds. For example, Ohio's shorter statute of limitation could have been designed to either protect Ohio defendants or protect Ohio courts from the burden of hearing stale claims. Since neither an Ohio defendant nor an Ohio court were involved in this case, one could conclude that Ohio did not have an interest in applying its shorter statute of limitation at the expense of an Ohio *plaintiff*.

84.   562 NW 2d at 472. See also *id.* at 472-473: "[N]o Ontario court has expressed qualms about applying American law... . Ontario's courts have even applied American law when that law is detrimental to Canadian litigants."

85.   *Tolofson* v. *Jensen* and *Lucas* v. *Gagnon*, 3 SCR 1022, 120 DLR 4th 289 (1994).

86.   Nor did the court acknowledge that its reliance on a foreign choice-of-law rule essentially amounted to an adoption of the *renvoi* doctrine. Perhaps suspecting that *renvoi* does not mesh well with the *lex fori* approach, the court hastened to add: "[W]e in no way intend to breathe life into the doctrine of renvoi." *Sutherland*, 562 NW 2d at 473 n. 26. According to the court, *renvoi* occurs only when the forum "*applies* the entire law of th[e foreign] jurisdiction." *Id.* (emphasis added). That was not the case here, said the court, "because we decline to apply any of Ontario's law ... [and] look at Ontario's choice of law rules merely to determine Ontario's interests". *Id.* For further discussion of *Sutherland*, see S. Symeonides, "Choice of Law in the American Courts in 1997", 46 *Am. J. Comp. L.* 233, 240-244 (1998)

70. In *Motenko v. MGM Dist., Inc.*[87], the Supreme Court of Nevada used even starker terms in articulating that state's *lex fori* approach to tort conflicts. Under this approach, the *lex fori* governs, "unless another state has an *overwhelming* interest"[88]. However, the court defined this test in terms of contacts rather than interests, by stating that another state has an overwhelming interest if it has two or more of the following contacts:

> "*(a)* it is the place where the conduct giving rise to the injury occurred; *(b)* it is the place where the injury is suffered; *(c)* [it is the place where the parties have their common] domicile, residence, nationality, place of incorporation, or place of business ...; *(d)* it is the place where the relationship, if any, between the parties is centered"[89].

Applying this test, the court held that the *lex fori* governed because the other involved state, Massachusetts, had less than two of the above contacts. *Motenko* was an action for loss of parental consortium brought by a Massachusetts domiciliary whose mother had been injured in defendant's Nevada hotel. Massachusetts, but not Nevada, allowed the action. The result was entirely reasonable and would have been reached under any other choice-of-law approach, traditional or modern[90]: the victim's presence in Nevada was not fortuitous, the injury was caused by a defect in a Nevada *immovable*, the defendant was a Nevada corporation, and Nevada had a policy intended to protect that corporation. Thus, the court enunciated an approach that went far beyond the needs of the particular case[91]. This became evident in the next case to reach the same court, *Northwest Pipe v. Eight Judicial District Court*[92].

---

87.   921 P. 2d 933 (Nev. 1996).

88.   *Id.* at 935 (Nev. 1996) (emphasis added).

89.   *Id.* The quoted text is similar but also more flexible than § 145 of the Second Restatement. For example, the quoted text speaks of the "conduct giving rise to the injury" rather than of the "conduct causing the injury" as does the Restatement. More interestingly, *Motenko* speaks of "the place where the injury is suffered" rather than "the place where the injury occurred" as does the Restatement. Taking advantage of this phraseology, the court was able to conclude that the *Motenko* injury "has been suffered in [Massachusetts]," *Motenko*, 921 P.2d at 935, where the plaintiff lived, rather than in Nevada where the plaintiff's mother had been injured. Indeed, because of the nature of the injury involved in this case–loss of consortium– this conclusion was appropriate. More importantly, this may make it easier to rebut the lex-fori presumption in cases such as *Haumschild* v. *Continental Cas.* Co.,95 NW 2d 814 (Wis. 1959), in which both parties are domiciled in the same non-forum state and the conflict in question involves an issue like intrafamily immunity or other similar issues of loss distribution.

90.   See *infra* 139-141.

91.   For further discussion, see S. Symeonides, "Choice of Law in the American Courts in 1996: Tenth Annual Survey", 45 *Am. J. Comp. L.* 447, 448-451 (1997).

92.   42 P. 3d 244 (Nev. 2002).

Northwest Pipe arose out of a California traffic accident that caused the death of two Nevada domiciliaries and four California domiciliaries. Their survivors filed wrongful death actions in Nevada against the driver of the truck that caused the accident and his employer, both Oregon domiciliaries. The court rejected the defendants' argument that California law should govern, because they failed to rebut *Motenko's lex fori* presumption. This was so because, in the court's opinion, California had only one of the non-forum contacts – the place of conduct. The court opined that the injury occurred in Nevada because this "was a wrongful death action in which the injury is to the survivors ... [and] *almost* all the survivors are Nevada residents"[93] and, "although the deaths occurred in California, the injury to the survivors occurred in Nevada"[94].

Of course *not all* the survivors were Nevada residents. The survivors of the four California victims were California residents. For this reason, four of the court's seven members disagreed on this point, thus forming a majority for applying California law to the California plaintiffs' actions.

Two members of the court dissented from the application of Nevada law to the Nevada victims as well. One of them observed that, under the court's approach, "it is unlikely that anything but Nevada law will ever apply"[95]. He stated that Nevada had "no relationship, significant or otherwise, to the occurrence of the accident"[96], and that the application of Nevada law was "unreasonable" because "virtually every fact and circumstance giving rise to the causes of action, except the domicile of some of the plaintiffs, points to the application of California law"[97].

71. The three versions of the *lex fori* approach appear to differ in phraseology and nuance regarding the burden of rebutting the *lex fori* presumption. The Kentucky approach does not allow displacement of the presumption if the forum state has "significant contacts – *not necessarily the most significant* contacts"[98]. The Nevada approach speaks of "overwhelming interest", but actually contemplates contacts. The Michigan approach uses milder language ("rational reason"), but it is no less permissive[99]. All three approaches, however, remain statistically, if not ideologically, attuned with Currie's approach in that they tend to produce the very results he advocated in the majority of cases – the application of the *lex*

---

93. *Id.* at 245-246 (emphasis added).
94. *Id.* at 246. Technically, with regard to the two Nevada victims, this was a semi-plausible argument if the actions were indeed only "wrongful death" actions. However, if as usual, these actions were accompanied by "survival actions" which seek recovery for the decedents' losses, then the court would have to concede that their injuries had occurred in California, thus leading to the application of California law.
95. *Id.* at 248 (Agosti, J., dissenting).
96. *Id.*
97. *Id.*
98. *Foster* v. *Leggett*, 484 SW 2d at 829 (emphasis added).
99. See S. Symeonides, "Choice of Law in the American Courts in 1997", 46 *Am. J. Comp. L.* 233, at 243 (1998).

fori. In this sense they entail the risk of encouraging or legitimizing, especially in the lower courts, the very parochialism that private international law has always fought to minimize.

E.   The Better-Law Approach

72. The first state to adopt Professor Leflar's choice-influencing considerations, including the better-law criterion, was New Hampshire in 1966[100]. Since then, it has been adopted by Wisconsin[101], Minnesota[102], Rhode Island[103], and Arkansas[104] in tort conflicts. However, by the turn of the century, all of the latter states had begun combining this with other approaches. In contract conflicts, only Minnesota and Wisconsin follow Leflar's approach[105].

---

100. See *Clark* v. *Clark*, 222 A. 2d 205 (NH 1966). For later cases, see *Taylor* v. *Bullock*, 279 A. 2d 585 (NH 1971); *Gagne* v. *Berry*, 290 A. 2d 624 (NH 1972); *Maguire* v. *Exeter & Hampton Elec. Co.*, 325 A. 2d 778 (NH 1974); *Gordon* v. *Gordon*, 387 A. 2d 339 (NH 1978); *LaBounty* v. *American Ins. Co.*, 451 A. 2d 161 (NH 1982); *Ferren* v. *Gen. Motors Corp. Delco Battery Div.*, 628 A. 2d 265 (NH 1993); *Benoit* v. *Test Sys., Inc.* 694 A. 2d 992 (NH 1997). *LaBounty* and *Ferren* are the only cases that applied foreign law.

101. See *Heath* v. *Zellmer*, 151 NW 2d 664 (Wis. 1967). For later cases, see *Zelinger* v. *State Sand & Gravel Co.*, 156 NW 2d 466 (Wis. 1968); *Conklin* v. *Horner*, 157 NW 2d 579 (Wis. 1968); *Hunker* v. *Royal Indem. Co.*, 204 NW 2d 897 (Wis. 1973); *Lichter* v. *Fritsch*, 252 NW 2d 360 (Wis. 1977); *State Farm Mut. Auto. Ins. Co.* v. *Gillette*, 641 NW 2d 662 (Wis. 2002).

102. See *Milkovich* v. *Saari*, 203 NW 2d 408 (Minn. 1973). For later cases, see *Schwartz* v. *Consol. Freightways Corp. of Delaware*, 221 NW 2d 665 (Minn. 1974); *Blamey* v. *Brown*, 270 NW 2d 884 (Minn. 1978), cert. denied, 444 US 1070 (1980); *Hague* v. *Allstate Ins. Co.*, 289 NW 2d 43 (Minn.1978), aff'd 449 U.S. 302 (1981); *Bigelow* v. *Halloran*, 313 NW 2d 10 (Minn. 1981); *Nodak Mut. Ins. Co.* v. *American Fam. Mut. Ins. Co.*, 604 NW 2d 91 (Minn. 2000).

103. See *Woodward* v. *Stewart*, 243 A. 2d 917 (RI 1968). For later cases, see *Brown* v. *Church of the Holy Name of Jesus*, 252 A. 2d 176 (RI 1969); *Busby* v. *Perini Corp.*, 290 A. 2d 210 (RI 1972); *Pardey* v. *Boulevard Billiard Club*, 518 A. 2d 1349 (RI 1986); *Victoria* v. *Smythe*, 703 A. 2d 619 (RI 1997); *Cribb* v. *Augustin*, 696 A. 2d 285 (RI 1997); *Taylor* v. *Mass. Flora Realty Inc.*, 840 A 2d 1126 (RI 2004); *Oyola* v. *Burgos*, 864 A 2d 624 (RI 2005).

104. See *Wallis* v. *Mrs. Smith's Pie Co.*, 550 SW 2d 453 (Ark. 1977); *Schlemmer* v. *Fireman's Fund Ins. Co.*, 730 SW 2d 217 (Ark. 1987); *Gomez* v. *ITT Educ. Servs. Inc.*, 71 SW 3d 542 (Ark. 2002); *Schubert* v. *Target Stores, Inc.*, 2005 WL 174757 (Ark. 2005).

105. See *Hime* v. *State Farm Fire & Cas. Co.*, 284 NW 2d 829 (Minn. 1979); *Hague* v. *Allstate Insurance Co.*, 289 NW 2d 43 (Minn. 1978), affirmed 449 US 302 (1981); *Jepson* v. *Gen. Cas. Co. of Wisconsin*, 513 NW 2d 467 (Minn. 1994); *Nodak Mutual Ins. Co.* v. *American Family Mutual Ins. Co.*, 604 NW 2d 91 (Minn. 2000); *Haines* v. *Mid-Century Ins. Co.*, 177 NW 2d 328 (Wis. 1970); *Schlosser* v. *Allis-Chalmers Corp.*, 271 NW 2d 879 (Wis. 1978).

1.   Early cases: The biases

73. The early cases that followed Leflar's approach provided ample vindication for most of the philosophical and methodological criticisms levelled against this approach. Indeed, it is not surprising that an approach that authorizes an *ad hoc*, unguided, and *ex post* choice of the "better" law produces choices that reflect the subjective predilections of the judges who make the choices. To the extent that judges tend to prefer domestic over foreign law, plaintiffs over defendants (foreign or domestic), or domestic over foreign litigants (plaintiffs or defendants), these preferences are bound to be reflected in the judges' decisions. The early cases from the five states that follow Leflar's approach exhibit all three of these tendencies to a higher than usual degree. Although these tendencies are not parallel, they all stem from the same source – the judicial subjectivism that the better-law approach legitimizes.

(a)   Pro-forum law bias

74. A preference for forum law is a by-product of the human tendency to gravitate to the familiar. With human nature being what it is, one should not be surprised if judges tend to consider their own law, with which they are most familiar, as the better law. More often that not, this is precisely what judges applying the better-law approach have concluded. In this sense the Wisconsin Supreme Court was refreshingly forthright in essentially equating it own adherence to Leflar's approach with a strong presumption in favour of the *lex fori*[106].

Indeed, in the five states that follow Leflar's approach for tort conflicts, one finds only four supreme court cases in which the court admitted that the foreign law was better than the forum's. In three of those cases, the court applied the foreign law, but – perhaps not coincidentally – in two of these cases that law favoured a forum plaintiff[107]. In the third case, a legislative change before the trial had eliminated the difference between the forum and foreign law[108]. In the fourth case, the court did not apply the "better" foreign law, perhaps because that law disfavoured a forum defendant[109]. Finally, in the only other tort conflict in which

---

106. See *State Farm Mut. Auto. Ins. Co. v. Gillette*, 641 NW 2d 662, 676 (Wis. 2002) (prefacing its application of the five Leflar factors with a statement that the primary choice-of-law rule in Wisconsin is that "the law of the forum should presumptively apply unless it becomes clear that nonforum contacts are of greater significance."). See also S. Symeonides "Choice of Law in the American Courts in 2002: Sixteenth Annual Survey", 51 *Am. J. Comp. L.*, 1, 71 (2003) (discussing *Gillette* and concluding that, although the *lex fori* "rarely appeared on the surface of the opinions, ... it could describe the actual results of cases better than most of the rationalizations the courts had offered.")

107. See *Lichter v. Fritsch*, 252 NW 2d 360 (Wis. 1977); *Bigelow v. Halloran*, 313 NW 2d 10 (Minn. 1981).

108. See *Schlemmer v. Fireman's Fund Ins. Co.*, 730 SW 2d 217 (Ark. 1987).

109. See *Maguire v. Exeter & Hampton Elec. Co.*, 325 A. 2d 778 (NH 1974).

the court applied foreign law, that law produced the same result as a forum statute that was inapplicable on technical grounds[110].

The bias in favour of forum law is more visible in lower court cases, many of which never reach the state supreme court. For example, some lower Minnesota courts have applied a Minnesota rule after proclaiming it "better" than the conflicting foreign rule, even after the Minnesota legislature repealed the Minnesota rule and replaced it with a rule identical to the rejected foreign rule[111].

(b) Pro-plaintiff, pro-recovery bias

75. A preference for forum law often, but not always, translates into a preference for plaintiffs. This is because of the wide latitude plaintiffs usually enjoy in choosing a forum and the strong likelihood that they will choose a forum whose conflicts law and substantive law favour recovery. For example, in four of the five post-*lex loci* tort conflicts that reached the Rhode Island Supreme Court in which the plaintiff's recovery depended on the applicable law, the court applied the pro-recovery law of the forum for the benefit of a foreign plaintiff.[112] Similarly, of the

---

110. See *Victoria* v. *Smythe*, 303 A. 2d 619 (RI 1997). In addition to the four tort cases mentioned above, four workers' compensation cases applied non-forum law, thus bringing the total to eight cases applying non-forum law. See *Hunker* v. *Royal Indem. Co.*, 204 NW 2d 897 (Wis. 1973); *Busby* v. *Perini Corp.*, 290 A. 2d 210 (RI 1972); *LaBounty* v. *American Ins. Co.*, 451 A. 2d 161 (NH 1982); *Ferren* v. *Gen. Motors Corp. Delco Battery Div.*, 628 A. 2d 265 (NH 1993). In all four of the latter cases, the employment relationship had its center in the non-forum state, which also had most of the other relevant contacts.

111. See *Wille* v. *Farm Bureau Mut. Ins. Co.* 432 NW 2d 784 (Minn. Ct. App. 1988) (holding that Minnesota's stacking rule was "better" than Indiana's anti-stacking rule, even though in the interim the Minnesota legislature had repealed the Minnesota rule and replaced it with an anti-stacking rule identical to Indiana's). See also *Meir* v. *Auto Owners Ins. Co.*, 1989 Minn. App. Lexis 222 (1989) *(accord)*. But see *Stenzel* v. *State Farm Mut. Auto Ins. Co.* 379 NW 2d 674 (Minn. Ct. App. 1986) (concluding that, *because* of its recent repeal, the same Minnesota rule could no longer be considered the better rule of law). In *Jepson* v. *Gen. Cas. Co. of Wisconsin*, 513 NW 2d 467 (Minn. 1994), the Minnesota Supreme Court disapproved both *Wille* and *Stenzel*: "We disagree with the views expressed in *Stenzel* and *Wille* ... as to which is the better rule of law. From our present day vantage point, neither the law Minnesota had then, nor the law we have now, is clearly better". *Id.* at 473.

112. See *Woodward* v. *Stewart*, 243 A. 2d 917 (RI 1968); *Brown* v. *Church of the Holy Name of Jesus*, 252 A. 2d 176 (RI 1969); *Pardey* v. *Boulevard Billiard Club*, 518 A. 2d 1349 (RI 1986); *Cribb* v. *Augustin*, 696 A. 2d 285 (RI 1997). See also *LaPlante* v. *American Honda Motor Co., Inc.*, 27 F. 3d 731 (1st Cir. 1994) (decided under Rhode Island conflicts law; applying the forum's pro-recovery law to a products liability action in which the forum's only contact was the plaintiff's domicile). In *Victoria* v. *Smythe*, 703 A. 2d 619 (RI 1997), the court applied non-forum law, but that law favoured the forum plaintiff as much as the forum's law, while in *Taylor* v. *Mass. Flora Realty Inc.*, 840 A 2d 1126 (RI 2004), the parties agreed on the application of Massachusetts law. *Oyola* v. *Burgos*, 864 A 2d 624 (RI 2005) is the only case to apply a non-recovery law.

six tort conflicts cases decided by the New Hampshire Supreme Court, two cases applied forum law for the benefit of a forum plaintiff[113], three cases applied forum law for the benefit of a foreign plaintiff[114], and the sixth case applied forum law for the benefit of a forum defendant[115].

(c) Pro-forum-litigant bias

76. The last one of the above cases indicates that sometimes the preference for a forum litigant (plaintiff or defendant) prevails over other preferences, including the preference for forum *law*. For example, in two of the three cases in which the Minnesota Supreme Court applied foreign law (in both tort and contract conflicts), that law benefited a forum plaintiff[116]. If this is not coincidental, it suggests that, when forced to choose between applying forum law and protecting forum litigants, courts tend to choose the latter. Again, lower court cases present clearer evidence of this trend.

One example is *Boatwright* v. *Budak*[117], in which a Minnesota court applied Iowa law, because "Iowa law best serve[d] *Minnesota's* interests in compensating tort victims"[118] domiciled in Minnesota. All of this despite the fact that Minnesota law favoured the defendant by limiting the amount of damages. *Boatwright* arose out of a single-car accident in Iowa that caused injury to the car's passenger, a Minnesota domiciliary. The defendant was a national car-rental company that rented the car in Minnesota to the driver, another Minnesota domiciliary. Min-

---

113. See *Clark* v. *Clark*, 222 A. 2d 205 (NH 1966); *Benoit* v. *Test Sys.*, Inc. 694 A. 2d 992 (NH 1997).

114. See *Taylor* v. *Bullock*, 279 A. 2d 585 (NH 1971); *Gagne* v. *Berry*, 290 A. 2d 624 (NH 1972); *Gordon* v. *Gordon*, 387 A. 2d 339 (NH 1978).

115. See *Maguire* v. *Exeter & Hampton Elec. Co.*, 325 A. 2d 778 (NH 1974).

116. The two cases are *Bigelow* v. *Halloran*, 313 NW 2d 10 (Minn. 1981) and *Nodak Mutual Ins. Co.* v. *American Family Mut. Ins. Co.*, 604 NW 2d 91 (Minn. 2000). *Bigelow* applied Iowa law, which provided that an action for an intentional tort survived the tortfeasor's death, rather than Minnesota law which did not allow survival. The plaintiff had become a Minnesota domiciliary before the trial. *Nodak* applied North Dakota law to a subrogation dispute between a North Dakota insurer and a Minnesota insurer. North Dakota law favoured the Minnesota insurer, while Minnesota law favoured the North Dakota insurer. The third case, *Jepson* v. *Gen. Cas. Co. of Wisconsin*, 513 NW 2d 467 (Minn. 1994), applied North Dakota law which disfavoured a Minnesota plaintiff. However, except for plaintiff's domicile, all other pertinent factors and contacts pointed to North Dakota. The court found the better-law factor inapposite because the two states' laws were "neither better nor worse in an objective way, just different". 513 NW 2d at 473.

117. 625 NW 2d 483 (Minn. App. 2001). For another possible example, see *Lichter* v. *Fritsch*, 252 NW 2d 360 (Wis. 1977) (applying foreign law and providing recovery to a forum plaintiff who would not recover under forum law).

118. *Boatwright*, 625 NW 2d at 489. See also *id.* ("Application of Iowa law to this case will most advance Minnesota's significant interest in giving injured persons more certainty of recovery and imposing responsibility for the operation of vehicles on the owners of those vehicles").

nesota, but not Iowa, limited the rental company's liability to $100,000. The court noted that the Minnesota Supreme Court had "'refused to apply [Minnesota] law when the law of another state would better serve to compensate a tort victim'"[119], and concluded that "the better-rule-of-law analysis results in the application of Iowa law to this case"[120].

Lommen v. *The City of East Grand Forks*[121] indicates that sometimes the preference for forum litigants may outweigh the preference for recovery. *Lommen* arose out of a North Dakota accident caused by a Minnesota police officer who pursued a stolen pickup truck at high speeds from Minnesota into North Dakota. The car chase ended in a collision with another car in which plaintiff, an unsuspecting resident of North Dakota, was a passenger. She brought a personal injury action in Minnesota against the officer's employer, a Minnesota city. Minnesota, but not North Dakota, provided immunity for the city. The court concluded that "overall the relevant considerations favor application of Minnesota law ... [because] Minnesota's ability to define the immunity of its officials should not vary according to the fortuitous facts of either the location of the accident or the citizenship of the injured party."[122]

In case anybody had doubts, the court stated that it did "not prefer Minnesota law ... simply because Minnesota is the forum"[123].

2.   *Recent cases: Eclecticism and watering-down*

77. The above-described biases are less pronounced in the cases decided around and since the end of the twentieth century. This change is probably related to the fact that most of the states that initially adopted Leflar's approach began to combine it with other approaches and to de-emphasize the better-law factor.

(a)   Eclecticism

78. The trend towards an eclectic approach is more prominent in Rhode Island and Minnesota. As seen earlier, by its own admission, the Rhode Island Supreme Court tends to combine at least three distinct choice-of-law methodologies[124].

Even more eclectic, if not confusing, is the latest articulation of the Minnesota Supreme Court's approach. In *Nodak Mutual Insurance Co.* v. *American*

---

119.   *Id.* at 489 (quoting *Jepson* v. *Gen. Cas. Co.*, 513 NW 2d 467, 472 (Minn. 1994)).

120.   *Id.* at 490.

121.   522 NW 2d 148 (Minn. Ct. App. 1994).

122.   *Id.* at 152.

123.   *Id.* at 151.

124.   See *supra* 61, discussing *Cribb* v. *Augustin*, 696 A. 2d 285, 288 (RI 1997). Similarly, some Arkansas decisions combine this approach with the Second Restatement (see *Wallis* v. *Mrs. Smith's Pie Co.*, 550 SW 2d 453 (Ark. 1977); *Williams* v. *Carr*, 565 SW 2d 400 (Ark. 1978); *Schlemmer* v. *Fireman's Fund Ins. Co.*, 730 SW 2d 217 (Ark. 1987)), or with a presumptive *lex loci* rule (see *Gomez* v. *ITT Educ. Servs. Inc.*, 71 SW 3d 542 (Ark. 2002); *Schubert* v. *Target Stores, Inc.*, 2005 WL 174757 (Ark. 2005)).

Family Mutual Insurance Co.[125], this court twice described its approach as "the significant contacts test"[126] and noted that "this court has not placed any emphasis on [the better-law] factor in nearly 20 years"[127]. The court dutifully listed the five Leflar choice-influencing factors – including the better-law factor – but, after quickly finding the first three factors to be inconclusive, the court spent the balance of the opinion discussing the fourth factor – "advancement of the forum's governmental interest"[128]. Yet, at the end of this discussion, the court concluded that it was not the forum's, but the other state's interests that needed advancement[129]. Even more curiously, the court phrased its holding as follows: "[W]hen all other relevant choice-of-law factors favour neither state's law, the state where the accident occurred has the strongest governmental interest ... [and its law] should be applied."[130]

Thus, by its own statements, the Minnesota Supreme Court follows a "significant *contacts*"[131] approach, which, however, relies not on contacts, but on five choice-influencing *factors*, which are not really five, but rather one. This is because the first three factors (being no more than hortatory statements) are inconclusive in the vast majority of cases, while the fifth factor (the better-law) has not been employed "in nearly twenty years"[132]. Thus, Minnesota's approach boils down to the remaining factor – the "[a]dvancement of *the forum's* governmental interest"[133]. However, this does not mean that Minnesota is parochially bent on advancing the forum's governmental interests; on appropriate occasions, Minnesota may choose to advance the interests of a *non-forum* state[134]; In fact, Minnesota may have advanced beyond thinking in terms of forum versus non-forum

---

125. 604 NW 2d 91 (Minn. 2000).

126. *Id.* at 94, 96.

127. *Id.* at 96. The statement quoted in the text prompted a lower court to conclude that the better-law criterion "has been abandoned in recent years." *Montpetit* v. *Allina Health System, Inc.*, 2000 WL 1486581 at *3 (Minn.App. 2000). But see *Boatwright* v. *Budak*, 625 NW 2d 483 (Minn.App. 2001) (employing the better-law criterion and holding that non-forum law was better than forum law in that it provided recovery for a forum domiciliary against a national car rental company.)

128. *Nodak*, 604 NW 2d at 96.

129. The other state's law was more favourable to the Minnesota party than was Minnesota law.

130. When the losing litigant characterized this statement as "a return to the doctrine of *lex loci*", *id.*, the court responded that "this court ... ha[s] rejected *lex loci* in favour of the significant contacts approach". *Id.*

131. *Supra* footnote 126 (emphasis added).

132. *Supra* footnote 127.

133. *Supra* footnote 128 (emphasis added).

134. At least when the law of that state would benefit a forum litigant. See *supra* footnote 129.

interests in that it presumes *a priori* that the accident state, be it the forum or not, "has the strongest governmental interest"[135].

(b) De-emphasis of better-law factor

79. As *Nodak* indicates, the better-law criterion seems to play a far less significant role in recent decisions than it did three decades ago. Indeed, in recent years, some courts have expressed misgivings on their ability to determine which law is better[136], or have tried to dispel the notion that better law and forum law are synonymous terms[137], while other courts have employed the better-law criterion only as a tie-breaker[138], or ignored it altogether[139].

If this trend persists, then perhaps the better-law approach should resume its original name of [many] "choice-influencing considerations".

---

135. Supra footnote 130.Yet this is not a return to the *lex loci delicti* rule because that rule has been "rejected ... in favor of the significant contacts approach", *supra* footnote 130.

136. See, e.g., *Jepson v. Gen. Cas. Co. of Wisconsin*, 513 NW 2d 467 at 473 (Minn. 1994) ("Sometimes different laws are neither better nor worse in an objective way, just different. Because we do not find either stacking or anti-stacking to be a better rule in the sense Leflar intended, this consideration does not influence our choice of law"); *Lommen v. The City of East Grand Forks*, 522 NW 2d 148 at 152 (Minn. Ct. App. 1994) ("[N]either Minnesota's nor North Dakota's law is 'better' than the other ... neither ... is demonstrably antiquated or plainly unfair ... [They] simply differ"); *Kenna v. So-Fro Fabrics, Inc.*, 18 F. 3d 623 at 627 (8th Cir. 1994) ("[W]e are not in a position to decide that either [state's law] is the better rule of law"); *Lessard v. Clarke*, 736 A. 2d 1226 at 1229 (NH 1999) (expressing scepticism on whether "New Hampshire damages law is 'wiser, sounder, and better calculated to serve the total ends of justice', ... than the competing law of Ontario"); *Hughes v. Wal-Mart Stores, Inc.*, 250 F. 3d 618 at 621 (8th Cir. 2001) ("Courts often refrain from resolving a conflict of law question based on the better rule of law factor ... [because] laws do not necessarily lend themselves to being labeled either 'better' or 'worse'").

137. *Jepson*, 513 NW 2d at 473 ("If [it] were true [that] forum law would always be the better law ... [then] this step in our choice of law analysis would be meaningless."). See also *Boatwright v. Budak*, 625 NW 2d 483 (Minn. App. 2001) (holding that non-forum law was better than forum law).

138. See *Nesladek v. Ford Motor Co.*, 876 F. Supp. 1061 at 1070 (D. Minn. 1994) (stating that the better-law factor need not be considered when Minnesota's other choice-influencing factors "clearly dictate the application of one state's law); *Hughes v. Wal-Mart Stores, Inc.*, 250 F. 3d 618 at 621 (8th Cir. 2001) (stating that the court "has been especially hesitant to pronounce the better law when other Leflar factors point decidedly towards the application of one state's law"); *Ferren v. Gen. Motors Corp. Delco Battery Div.*, 628 A. 2d 265, 269 (NH 1993); *Nodak Mutual Ins. Co. v. American Family Mutual Ins. Co.*, 604 NW 2d 91 (Minn. 2000); *Lessard v. Clark*, 736 A. 2d 1226 (NH 1999).

139. See *Najarian v. Nat'l Amusements, Inc.*, 768 A. 2d 1253 (RI 2001).

F.   The Restatement Second

1.   *Judicial following*

80. Table 4, above, makes it clear that the Second Restatement is by far the most popular among the modern methodologies. It is followed in 22 states in tort conflicts and 24 states in contract conflicts. For the reader's convenience, another table showing only the Restatement states is reproduced below.

Table 5. States following the Second Restatement

TORTS	CONTRACTS
Alaska	Alaska
Arizona	Arizona
Colorado	Colorado
Connecticut	Connecticut
Delaware	Delaware
Florida	
Idaho	Idaho
Illinois	Illinois
Iowa	Iowa
	Kentucky
Maine	Maine
	Michigan
Mississippi	Mississippi
Missouri	Missouri
Montana	Montana
Nebraska	Nebraska
	New Hampshire
Ohio	Ohio
Oklahoma	Oklahoma?
South Dakota	South Dakota
Tennessee	
Texas	Texas
Utah	Utah
Vermont	Vermont
Washington	Washington
	West Virginia
Total 22	24

For all 22 states listed above as following the Restatement for tort conflicts, there is express supreme court precedent to that effect[140]. The same is true with regard

---

140. See *Ehredt* v. *DeHavilland Aircraft Co. of Canada, Ltd.*, 705 P. 2d 446 (Alaska 1985) (relying exclusively on the Second Restatement); *Armstrong* v. *Armstrong*, 441 P. 2d 699 (Alaska 1968) (relying partly on the Second Restatement); *Schwartz* v. *Schwartz*, 447 P. 2d 254 (Ariz. 1968); *First Nat'l Bank* v. *Rostek*, 514 P. 2d 314 (Colo. 1973); *O'Connor* v. *O'Connor*, 519 A. 2d 13 (Conn. 1986); *Travelers Indem. Co.* v. *Lake*, 594 A. 2d 38, (Del. 1991); *Bishop* v. *Florida Specialty Paint Co.*, 389 So. 2d 999 (Fla. 1980); *Johnson* v. *Pischke*, 700 P. 2d 19 (Idaho 1985); *Ingersoll* v. *Klein*, 262 NE 2d 593 (Ill. 1970); *Fuerste* v. *Bemis*, 156 NW 2d 831 (Iowa 1968); *Beaulieu* v. *Beaulieu*, 265 A. 2d 610 (Me. 1970);

to 23[141] of the 24 states listed as following the Restatement for contract conflicts[142]. The remaining state is Illinois which, for reasons explained earlier, is classified as a Restatement state despite the lack of express supreme court precedent to that effect[143].

As Table 5 indicates, while most jurisdictions have adopted the Second Restatement for both tort and contract conflicts, a few jurisdictions have done so

---

Collins v. *Trius, Inc.*, 663 A. 2d 570 (Me. 1995); *Mitchell* v. *Craft*, 211 So. 2d 509 (Miss. 1968); *Kennedy* v. *Dixon*, 439 SW 2d 173 (Mo. 1969); *Phillips* v. *Gen. Motors Corp.*, 995 P. 2d 1002 (Mont. 2000); *Crossley* v. *Pacific Employers Ins. Co.*, 251 NW 2d 383 (Neb. 1977) (relying alternatively on the Second Restatement and the *lex loci delicti* with the same result); *Harper* v. *Silva*, 399 NW 2d 826 (Neb. 1987) (interpreting *Crossley* as having adopted the Second Restatement); *Morgan* v. *Biro Mfg. Co.*, 474 NE 2d 286 (Ohio 1984); *Brickner* v. *Gooden*, 525 P. 2d 632 (Okla. 1974); *Chambers* v. *Dakotah Charter, Inc.*, 488 NW 2d 63 (SD 1992); *Hataway* v. *McKinley*, 830 SW 2d 53 (Tenn. 1992); *Gutierrez* v. *Collins*, 583 SW 2d 312 (Tex. 1979); *Forsman* v. *Forsman*, 779 P. 2d 218 (Utah 1989); *Amiot* v. *Ames*, 693 A. 2d 675 (Vt. 1997); *Johnson* v. *Spider Staging Corp.*, 555 P. 2d 997 (Wash. 1976); *Werner* v. *Werner*, 526 P. 2d 370 (Wash. 1974).

141.   See *Palmer G. Lewis Co.* v. *ARCO Chem. Co.*, 904 P. 2d 1221 (Alaska 1995) (interpreting *Ehredt* v. *DeHavilland Aircraft Co. of Canada, Ltd.*, 705 P. 2d 446 (Alaska 1985), a case involving a tort conflict, as having adopted the Second Restatement for contract conflicts as well); *Burr* v. *Renewal Guar. Corp.*, 468 P. 2d 576 (Ariz. 1970); *Wood Bros. Homes, Inc.* v. *Walker Adjustment Bureau*, 601 P. 2d 1369 (Colo. 1979); *Williams* v. *State Farm Mut. Auto. Ins. Co.*, 641 A. 2d 783 (Conn. 1994); *Oliver B. Cannon & Son, Inc.* v. *Dorr-Oliver, Inc.*, 394 A. 2d 1160 (Del. 1978) (relying in part on §188 of the Second Restatement); *Rungee* v. *Allied Van Lines, Inc.*, 449 P. 2d 378 (Idaho 1968); *Joseph L. Wilmotte & Co.* v. *Rosenman Bros.*, 258 NW 2d 317 (Iowa 1977); *Lewis* v. *American Family Ins. Group*, 555 SW 2d 579 (Ky. 1977); *Baybutt Constr. Corp.* v. *Commercial Union Ins. Co.*, 455 A. 2d 914 (Me. 1983); *Chrysler Corp.* v. *Skyline Indus. Servs., Inc.*, 528 NW 2d 698 (Mich. 1995); *Boardman* v. *United Servs. Auto. Ass'n*, 470 So. 2d 1024 (Miss. 1985); *Spragins* v. *Louise Plantation, Inc.*, 391 So. 2d 97 (Miss. 1980); *Fruin-Colnon Corp.* v. *Missouri Hwy. Transp. Comm'n*, 736 SW 2d 41 (Mo. 1987); *Casarotto* v. *Lombardi*, 886 P. 2d 931 (Mont. 1994), judgment rev'd on other grounds, 116 S. Ct. 1652 (1996); *Powell* v. *American Charter Fed. S & L Ass'n*, 514 NW 2d 326 (Neb. 1994) (explicitly adopting the Second Restatement); *Consol. Mut. Ins. Co.* v. *Radio Foods Corp.*, 240 A. 2d 47 (NH 1968); *Gries Sports Enters.* v. *Modell*, 473 NE 2d 807, 810 (Ohio 1984); *Stockmen's Livestock Exch.* v. *Thompson*, 520 NW 2d 255 (SD 1994); *Duncan* v. *Cessna Aircraft Co.*, 665 SW 2d 414 (Tex. 1984), judgment rev'd on other grounds sub nom. *Smithson* v. *Cessna Aircraft Co.*, 665 SW 2d 439, 445 (Tex. 1984); *American Nat'l Fire Ins. Co.* v. *Farmers Ins. Exch.*, 927 P. 2d 186 (Utah 1996); *Baffin Land Corp.* v. *Monticello Motor Inn, Inc.*, 425 P. 2d 623, 627-28 (Wash. 1967); *Pioneer Credit Corp.* v. *Carden*, 245 A. 2d 891 (Vt. 1968) (relying in part on §188 of the Second Restatement but not actually applying it). Later cases have assumed adoption of the Second Restatement. See, e.g., *Amiot* v. *Ames*, 693 A. 2d 675, 677 (Vt. 1997).

142.   However, in two of these states, Oklahoma and West Virginia, the available supreme court precedents are equivocal and thus the classification of these states in the Second Restatement column may be doubtful. See *supra* 60.

143.   See *supra* 59 footnote 7.

for only one or the other of these categories of conflicts. Florida and Tennessee follow the Restatement only in tort conflicts, whereas Kentucky, Michigan, New Hampshire, and West Virginia follow the Restatement only in contract conflicts. The reason for such divided loyalties is a deliberate choice in some instances[144] and lack of a good opportunity in other instances[145].

In addition to the above states, many federal courts follow the Second Restatement in federal question cases[146]. Furthermore, on the issue of choice-of-law clauses, many states follow §187 of the Restatement, even if on other issues they follow other approaches, including the traditional approach[147].

---

144. This is the case with Florida, Kentucky, Michigan, and New Hampshire. After adopting the Second Restatement for tort conflicts, Florida's highest court specifically refused to do the same for contract conflicts. See *Sturiano* v. *Brooks*, 523 So. 2d 1126, 1129 (Fla. 1988). Kentucky at first adopted the Second Restatement in tort conflict, see *Wessling* v. *Paris*, 417 SW 2d 259 (Ky. 1967), and later switched to the *lex fori* approach, see *Arnett* v. *Thompson*, 433 SW 2d 109 (Ky. 1968). When Kentucky's highest court encountered a contract conflict in 1977, the court held that its earlier adoption of the Restatement was appropriate for contract conflicts. See *Lewis* v. *American Family Ins. Group*, 555 SW 2d 579, 581-582 (Ky. 1977). Michigan followed the reverse sequence. In 1982, the Michigan Supreme Court abandoned the traditional theory for tort conflicts in favor of the *lex fori* approach, see *Sexton* v. *Ryder Truck Rental, Inc.*, 320 NW 2d 843, 857 (Mich. 1982), and in 1995, when it encountered a contract conflict, the court adopted the Restatement. See *Chrysler Corp.* v. *Skyline Indus. Servs., Inc.*, 528 NW 2d 698, 703 (Mich. 1995). New Hampshire adopted the better-law approach for tort conflicts in 1966, see *Clark* v. *Clark*, 222 A. 2d 205 (NH 1966), and the Restatement for contract conflicts in 1968. See *Consol. Mut. Ins. Co.* v. *Radio Foods Corp.*, 240 A. 2d 47 (NH 1968).

145. For example, the highest court of Tennessee simply did not encounter a tort conflict in recent years. See *supra* 59. The highest court of West Virginia and Wyoming did encounter such conflicts (see *supra* 60), but arguably not of the kind that would necessitate an abandonment of the *lex loci* rule.

146. See, e.g., *Schoenberg* v. *Exportadora de Sal*, 930 F. 2d 777 (9th Cir. 1991) ("Federal common law follows the approach of the Restatement (Second) of Conflict of Laws..."); *Alvarez-Machain* v. *United States*, 266 F. 3d 1045 (9th Cir. 2001) (Federal Tort Claims Act); *Wagner* v. *Islamic Republic of Iran*, 172 F.Supp.2d 128 (DDC 2001) (Antiterrorist and Effective Death Penalty Act); *Harris* v. *Polskie Linie Lotnicze*, 820 F. 2d 1000 (9th Cir. 1987) (Foreign Sovereign Immunities Act); *American Home Assurance Co.* v. *L & L Marine Serv., Inc.*, 153 F. 3d 616 (8th Cir. 1998) (admiralty jurisdiction); *Bickel* v. *Korean Air Lines Co.*, 83 F. 3d 127 (6th Cir. 1996) (arising under the Warsaw Convention), superseded on other grounds, 96 F. 3d 151 (6th Cir. 1996); *In re Lindsay*, 59 F. 3d 942 (9th Cir. 1995) (bankruptcy proceeding), cert. denied, 116 S. Ct. 778 (1996); *Edelmann* v. *Chase Manhattan Bank, N.A.*, 861 F. 2d 1291 (1st Cir. 1988) (Edge Act); *Corp. Venezolana de Fomento* v. *Vintero Sales Corp.*, 629 F. 2d 786 (2d Cir. 1980) (Edge Act); *Aaron Ferer & Sons* v. *Chase Manhattan Bank, N.A.*, 731 F. 2d 112 (2d Cir. 1984).

147. See, e.g., *Cherry, Bekaert & Holland* v. *Brown*, 582 So. 2d 502 (Ala. 1991) (relying on Second Restatement §187, even though Alabama follows the traditional rules in both contract and tort conflicts); *Nat'l Glass, Inc.* v. *J.C. Penney Prop., Inc.*, 650 A. 2d 246 (Md. 1994) (relying on §187, even though Maryland follows the traditional

Thus, three decades after its promulgation, the Second Restatement appears close to dominating the American methodological landscape. As explained elsewhere[148], however, this high numerical following does not necessarily entail a deep-seated commitment to, or intense loyalty toward, the Restatement. In many cases it simply means that the Restatement offers the most convenient, and also authoritative-sounding, rationalization for results that the court would have reached under any other modern methodology[149]. In any event, it is worth asking (1) why has the Restatement enjoyed such a high numerical success, and (2) whether this success has had a positive impact on American conflicts law. The next section addresses these questions.

2.   *Reasons for the Restatement's high judicial following*

81. The reasons for which the Restatement appears to have won the hearts and minds of so many American judges are many and varied, and some of them are not necessarily complimentary. They include the following.

(a)   The Restatement provides judges with virtually unlimited discretion

As explained earlier, of the Restatement's 423 sections, only a handful contain anything resembling a black-letter, unqualified rule[150]. The remaining sections allow the judge wide latitude in choosing the applicable law, ranging from mildly limited to virtually unlimited discretion. These sections can be divided into three groups:
(1)   those that provide presumptive and easily displaceable rules instructing the judge to apply the law of one state *"unless* ... some other state has a more significant relationship under the principles stated in section 6"[151];
(2)   those that do not even presumptively designate the applicable law, but simply provide gentle pointers mildly suggesting that the state of the applicable law will *"usually"* be one particular state[152]; and

---

rules in both contract and tort conflicts); *Kronovet* v. *Lipchin*, 415 A. 2d 1096 (Md. 1980) (same); *SBKC Serv. Corp.* v. *111 Prospect Partners, L.P.*, 1998 WL 436579 (10th Cir. 1998) (same with regard to Kansas); *Nedlloyd Lines B.V.* v. *Superior Court*, 834 P. 2d 1148 (Cal. 1992) (relying on §187, even though in other conflicts California follows a combination of interest analysis with comparative impairment); *Prows* v. *Pinpoint Retail Sys., Inc.*, 868 P. 2d 809 (Utah 1993) (relying on §187 before Utah adopted the Restatement for other contractual issues).

148. See S. Symeonides, "The Judicial Acceptance of the Second Conflicts Restatement: A Mixed Blessing", 56 *Md. L. Rev.* 1248, 1261-1263 (1997) (describing the various "gradations of commitment" to the Restatement and suggesting several other qualifications for such classifications).

149. See *id.* at 1261-1273.

150. See *supra* 35-38. All of these sections are confined to property and successions issues, which are outside the scope of this course. See *id.*

151. See *supra* 36 (italics added).

152. See *supra* 37 (italics added).

(3)   those residual sections, such as §145 for torts and §188 for contracts, in which the drafters make no suggestion whatsoever as to the applicable law, but leave the choice to the judge to be made on an *ad hoc* basis, guided only by a deliberately malleable list of contacts and §6 policies[153].

On the surface, it would seem that the sections of the third group allow judges more discretion than the sections of the second group, which in turn allow more discretion than the sections of the first group. In reality, however, all of these sections provide as much discretion as a judge is willing to exercise. Thus, if the particular case falls within the scope of a presumptive rule of the first group, the judge may avoid the rule by invoking the "unless" clause that qualifies the rule. If the particular issue fits within the scope of one of the sections of the second group which provide a "pointer," the judge may disregard the pointer by underscoring the word "usually" which qualifies the pointer. As for the many cases that do not fall within the scope of either a presumptive rule or a pointer, the judge need not evade anything because the Restatement does not purport to point to a particular choice of law. For example, in a case that falls within a general, *ad hoc* section, such as §145, the judge will determine on her own the state of the most significant relationship "under the principles stated in §6", by "taking into account" the contacts listed illustratively in §145. If the drafters intended "the principles stated in §6" to limit the judge's discretion, that intent was lost on the vast majority of judges that have applied §6.

Even more indicative of the judiciary's inclination to retain as much discretion as possible is the tendency of some courts to expressly bypass the specific Restatement sections that contain the mild restraints described above, and to resort directly to the general, laissez faire §6[154]. By going straight to §6, a court does not even have to explain its implicit decision to displace a presumptive rule or ignore a pointer. In this sense, the court's analysis differs little from a significant-contacts approach or, for that matter, Leflar's choice-influencing considerations. For, although the latter two approaches differ on the specifics from §6 of the Restatement[155], they nevertheless provide the judge with the same virtually unlimited discretion as §6 does.

---

153.   See *supra* 38.
154.   See *Dawson-Austin* v. *Austin*, 920 SW 2d 776 (Tex. App.-Dallas, 1996); *Duncan* v. *Cessna Aircraft Co.*, 665 SW 2d 414 (Tex. 1984), discussed in S. Symeonides, "Choice of Law in the American Courts in 1996: Tenth Annual Survey", 45 *Am. J. Comp. L.* 447, 495-500 (1997). See also P. Borchers, "Courts and the Second Conflicts Restatement: Some Observations and an Empirical Note", 56 *Md. L. Rev.* 1248, 1271 (1997).
155.   The significant contacts approach differs from §6 of the Restatement, in that it calls for a consideration of the factual contacts alone, rather than of a set of policies in light of the factual contacts as does §6. Leflar's list of choice-influencing considerations resembles the list of policies contained in §6 (2), but also differs in some respects, the most important of which is that it calls for the application of the "better rule of law".

The truth is that, as much as the Restatement can be rightfully accused of giving judges too much discretion, all other "modern" approaches, except one[156], allow even greater leeway. In this sense, a cynic may describe the whole conflicts revolution as a judicial movement to attain and retain more power in choice-of-law decisions. In the final analysis, the reason for the Restatement's higher appeal to judges is that, while it provides as much discretion as the other modern approaches, it also retains the facade of an orderly system.

(b) The Restatement, as applied by some judges, does not require hard thinking

82. Despite the drafters' contrary intentions and their instructions contained in the very valuable "comments", many judges apply the Restatement in a way that does not require hard thinking. As explained above, in the great majority of cases, the Restatement instructs the judge to determine the state of the most significant relationship "under the principles stated in §6," by "taking into account" the contacts listed in the pertinent Restatement section for the type of conflict in question. This process is supposed to be a sophisticated dialectical evaluation of the policies listed in §6 in light of the pertinent factual contacts, not a quantitative counting (nor a so-called qualitative assessment) of the factual contacts. Yet, many cases do only the latter. After an impressionistic counting of contacts, they conclude that the state with the most contacts has the most significant relationship. Even the cases that go through the trouble of examining the policies of §6, do so more in order to confirm, rather than to test, the conclusion they reach through contact counting.

Professor Willis Reese, the Restatement's chief drafter, observed once that "courts which purport to take a 'governmental interest' approach frequently engage in a judicial masquerade. In actual practice, they decide first upon the particular rule they wish to apply and then attribute policies to that rule that call for its application"[157]. Ironically, through no fault of his, the same is equally true of courts that follow his Restatement.

(c) The Restatement is not ideologically "loaded"

83. It is common knowledge that many of the other "modern" approaches either contain built-in biases or provide judges with the opportunity to rationalize certain biases. For example, Currie's interest analysis seems to harbour a certain pro-plaintiff, pro-recovery bias. Leflar's approach openly advocates the application of the "better law" in certain circumstances, and Weintraub's rule for tort conflicts calls for the application of the law that favours the plaintiff in certain cases.

---

156. The only exception is New York's *Neumeier* rules for tort conflicts. See *infra* 93. See also Louisiana's statutory choice-of-law rules in La. Civ. Code 3537-3541 and 3542-3548, for contract and tort conflicts, respectively.

157. W. Reese, "The Second Restatement of Conflict of Laws Revisited", 34 *Mercer L. Rev.* 501, 511 (1983).

In contrast, the Restatement is not laden with such biases. The list of policies contained in §6 is not only innocuous, but also balanced and ideologically unbiased. It begins with "the needs of the interstate and international systems" and includes "the protection of justified expectations", and "certainty, predictability and uniformity of result"[158]. These are policies with which no one would seriously disagree. They are also policies that appeal to judges who do not want to be perceived as pro-plaintiff or result-oriented.

Here again, however, one must distinguish between the drafters' pronouncements and the degree to which judges actually follow these pronouncements. For example, despite the Restatement's reminder that the decision-maker should keep in mind the "needs of the interstate and international systems"[159], cases following the Restatement do not seem to be any more "internationalist" than cases following other approaches.

Thus, another reason for the Restatement's appeal to judges may be that it provides an approach that is ideologically neutral, yet has ample room for accommodating just about any judicial ideology.

(d) The Restatement is a complete "system"

84. One common denominator of most other modern American choice-of-law methodologies is the rejection of choice-of-law rules in favour of *ad hoc* "approaches" or guidelines that ostensibly can resolve conflicts in all areas of the law. These approaches are very flexible, but provide little real guidance. While flexibility makes these approaches attractive to those judges who have both the time and the expertise in conflicts law, the lack of guidance makes them unattractive to most other judges.

In contrast, the Restatement successfully combines flexibility with real guidance. Although the Restatement does not provide fixed rules, it also rejects the notion that a mere list of principles such as the §6 list is sufficient to yield solutions to conflicts in all areas of the law. Instead, the Restatement provides flexible rules not only for various types of tort and contract conflicts, but also for conflicts in the area of property, marital property, succession, trusts, status, agency and partnership, business corporations, etc. Although most of these rules are open-ended or displaceable, they provide a starting point in the court's search for a solution; and they are accompanied by thoughtful comments and illustrations, both of which can further aid the court's analysis.

Thus, the fact that the Restatement offers a complete system of rules for almost every conceivable case or issue can only increase its usefulness to judges[160].

---

158. Restatement Second, §6.

159. *Id.*

160. For example, *NUCOR Corporation* v. *Aceros Y Maquilas de Occidente*, 28 F. 3d 572 (7th Cir. 1994) (decided under Indiana conflicts law), applied the Second Restatement to an issue of agency law (although the Indiana Supreme Court had not applied the Restatement to agency issues and had not expressly adopted it with regard to generic contract issues) because the Restatement "offers a provision that can be adapted to

At the same time, the fact that these rules are almost never confining explains the judges' willingness to follow them.

(e) The Restatement carries the prestige of the American Law Institute

85. Unlike approaches proposed by individual scholars whose persuasive power depends entirely on the inherent soundness of the proposed approach, the Restatement carries the imprimatur of the American Law Institute, a prestigious collective body with a record of success in reforming other sectors of American law. The process of approving an ALI project contains several layers of collective scrutiny that not only contribute to the overall quality of the final product, but also militate against adoption of extreme or one-sided views. Occasionally, as was the case with the second conflicts Restatement, the end result may be the product of too many compromises among opposing philosophies and too much of an effort to please everybody. Nevertheless, from the judges' perspective, this alone is very rarely a handicap. A judge who chooses to adopt a Restatement position has much less explaining to do than a judge who chooses to adopt the views of any individual academic author, even one considered an intellectual giant.

(f) The Restatement has "momentum"

86. As Chapter III documents[161], before the Second Restatement's promulgation in 1969, the states that had adopted the draft Restatement were slightly outnumbered by the states that had adopted other modern approaches[162]. Since then, the trend has been steadily and clearly in favour of the Restatement. Since 1969, twice as many states have adopted the Restatement in contract conflicts as have adopted other approaches (20 to 10),[163] while in the 1990s, the ratio was 8:2 in favour of the Restatement[164]. (See Charts 8 and 9, below.)

---

areas for which particularized rules have not yet been developed". *Id.* at 583. See also *Fasa Corp.* v. *Playmates Toys, Inc.*, 869 F. Supp. 1334 (ND Ill. 1994) (predicting that the Illinois Supreme Court would adopt the Restatement with regard to agency issues, and applying same.); *Stockmen's Livestock Exchange* v. *Thompson*, 520 NW 2d 255 (SD 1994), (applying the Restatement to an agency issue although the court had not applied the Restatement in contracts in general).

161. See *supra* 42.

162. In tort conflicts, eight jurisdictions had adopted the draft Restatement by 1969, and nine had adopted other approaches. See *supra* 41-42. In contract conflicts, only four jurisdictions had adopted the draft Restatement by 1969, and seven jurisdictions adopted other approaches. See *supra* 43-44.

163. See *supra* 44. In tort conflicts, 12 states have adopted the Restatement since 1969, and 11 states have adopted other approaches. See *supra* 42.

164. Eight states adopted the Restatement and two states adopted other approaches. See *supra* 43-44. In tort conflicts, five states adopted the Restatement and only one state adopted another approach. See *supra* 41-42.

Chart 8. The Restatement Second's momentum in tort conflicts

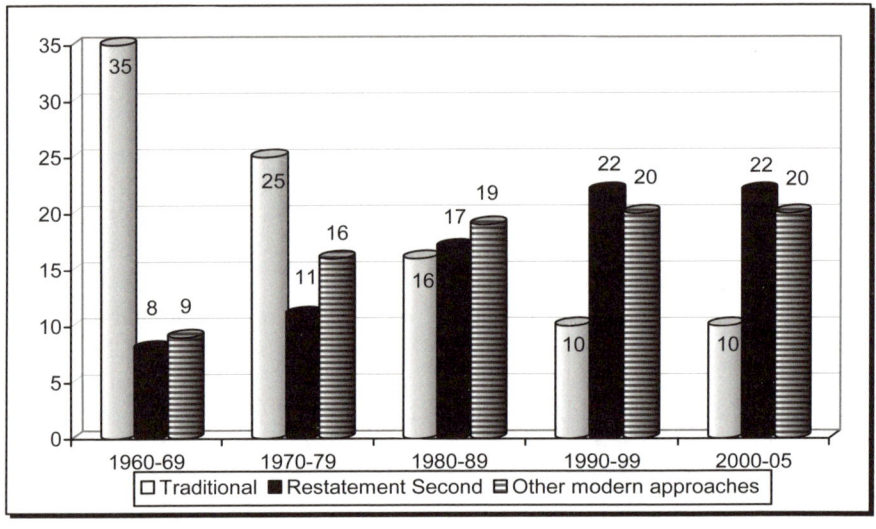

Chart 9. The Restatement Second's momentum in contract conflicts

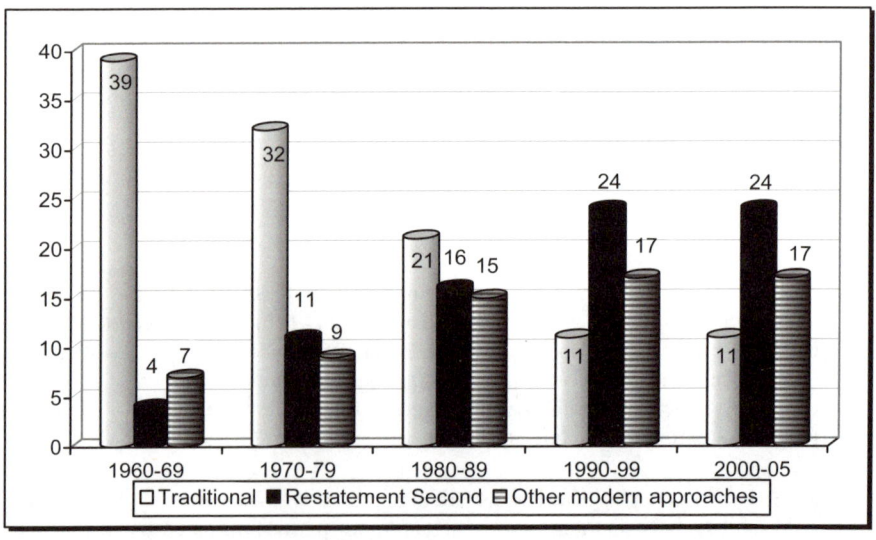

Thus, as time went by, the appeal of other approaches, such as interest analysis or the better-law approach, subsided while the Restatement's appeal increased. It seems that, at this point, the Restatement has enough "momentum" as to justify a prediction that, if any of the jurisdictions that continue to adhere to the traditional theory choose to abandon that theory, they will likely adopt the Restatement.

3.   The Restatement's contribution

87. The Restatement's dominance of the American conflicts scene is a mixed blessing for American conflicts law. The Restatement's contribution has been positive to the extent that it facilitated the abandonment of the traditional rules of *lex loci delicti* and *lex loci contractus* and of all the accompanying artificial and mechanical logic. It is true that persistent academic attacks had undermined the traditional theory even before 1953, the year the Restatement's drafting began, and certainly before 1969, the year the Restatement was officially promulgated. However, before 1953, these academics attacks had made only marginal inroads in judicial opinions. From 1953 and thereafter, these inroads began to increase and by 1966 five states had abandoned the traditional theory in tort conflicts, led by the New York Court of Appeals in *Babcock* v. *Jackson*[165]. Although none of these states adopted the Restatement, its influence helped move the courts in that direction, as the *Babcock* court acknowledged[166]. More importantly, between 1967 and 1969, the years during which the ALI publicized the Proposed Official Drafts of the Second Restatement, eleven more states abandoned the traditional theory and eight of them adopted these drafts[167].

Thus, although it did not cause the conflicts revolution, the Second Restatement was a major contributing factor in the courts' cascading decisions in the 1960s and 1970s to abandon the traditional theory. Without the Restatement, the ranks of the revolutionaries during the 1960s would have been much more sparse. They would have included New York, California and a few other "progressive" states, but probably not states as diverse as Alaska, Arizona, Idaho, Iowa or Mississippi. More than likely, the latter states would have retained the traditional theory and simply increased the use of escape devices. Largely because of the Restatement's influence, these and many other states have abandoned the traditional theory, a development that was both necessary and positive in American conflicts law.

Naturally, whether the decision of these states to adopt the Restatement, as opposed to other modern approaches, is a positive development depends on one's opinion of the Restatement[168]. Nevertheless, one clearly positive contribution of

---

165. 191 NE 2d 279 (NY 1963). The other four jurisdictions were Pennsylvania, Wisconsin, New Hampshire and Puerto Rico. See Table 1, *supra* 41.

166. See *Babcock*, 12 NY 2d at 479, relying in part on a 1960 Tentative Draft of the Second Restatement.

167. These jurisdictions were: Kentucky, Oregon and the District of Columbia in 1967, Alaska, Arizona, Idaho and Mississippi in 1968, and Missouri in 1969. See Table 1, *supra* 41. The first three jurisdictions later abandoned the Restatement in favour of other approaches.

168. All viewpoints are represented in a scholarly symposium devoted to the Restatement. See "The Silver Anniversary of the Second Conflicts Restatement", 56 *Md. L. Rev.* 1193-1410 (1997) (containing articles by Borchers, Reynolds, Richman, Symeonides, Weintraub and Weinberg)

the Restatement is that it has helped avoid polarization among American courts, and has laid the foundations for a new synthesis from among competing choice-of-law theories. Contrary to the first Restatement's rigidity and dogmatism, which caused the revolution, the Second Restatement's lack of dogmatism and flexible and compromissory content have helped spawn a benign, albeit uncertain, evolution. Had the Second Restatement aspired for ideological purity rather than philosophical pluralism, it would have pleased some of its academic critics but it would have been far less attractive to judges. Its followers would have been more devoted but fewer in number, and the polarization among American courts would have been inevitable.

To date, this polarization has been avoided. As the majority of American courts abandoned the old dogma, they moved not in a single direction, but in parallel and arguably fungible directions, one of which is that of the Second Restatement. As much as academics tend to accentuate the differences between these directions, the courts tend to do the opposite. For example, the fact that judges tend to move so easily from the Restatement to other policy-based analyses suggests that, correctly or not, judges believe that these analyses do not differ in essential respects. Although academic critics tend to vilify this eclecticism[169], it is a fact of life. One can continue to decry this phenomenon, or one can exploit its positive aspects.

For what is worth, this author continues to subscribe to the hope that this eclecticism can become the basis for a productive synthesis of the American conflicts experience of the twentieth century. This author also subscribes to the view that the Second Restatement, being conceived and designed as a transitional document, has successfully discharged the task of steering American conflicts law from revolution to evolution. The time has come for this Restatement to be replaced with a third Restatement[170]. These points are discussed later[171].

G.   Significant-Contacts Approaches

88. The approach known as "significant-contacts", "grouping of contacts", or "center of gravity" is followed by three jurisdictions in tort conflicts and by five in

---

169. See, e.g., W. Reppy, "Eclecticism in Choice of Law: Hybrid Method or Mishmash?", 34 *Mercer L. Rev.* 645 (1983).

170. See S. Symeonides, "The Need for a Third Conflicts Restatement (and a Proposal for Tort Conflicts)", 75 *Ind. LJ* 437 (2000). For different viewpoints, see "Symposium: Preparing for the Next Century – A New Restatement of Conflicts", 75 *Ind. LJ* 399-686 (2000) (containing articles by Shreve, Juenger, Richman, Reynolds, Symeonides and Weinberg, and comments by Borchers, Dane, Gottesman, Hill, Maier, Peterson, Posnak, Reimann, Reppy, Sedler, Silberman, Lowenfeld, Simson, Singer, Twerski and Weintraub).

171. See *infra* 371-389.

contract conflicts[172]. The above quoted terms are interchangeable and descriptive of this approach's reliance on physical contacts, rather than on state policies or interests. The state that has the "most significant contacts" with the case and the parties is the center of gravity of the dispute, and thus its law governs, essentially regardless of its content or underlying policy.

When this approach first appeared on the American conflicts scene [173], it was a significant and hopeful step in the right direction. By abandoning the traditional system's reliance on a single connecting factor and relying instead on multiple contacts, this approach opened the door to new and promising ways of thinking. This was meant to be a transitional point between the traditional system and modern approaches. Some states, however, have chosen not to make this transition, such as by switching to the Second Restatement which, although itself a transitional document, was the next logical step.

One of the differences between the two approaches is that, although they both tend to consider the same contacts, the Restatement also requires a *policy analysis* by providing that the contacts must be evaluated "in light of the policies of §6," which include the policies of the contact states as well as multistate policies. In contrast, the significant-contacts approach does not require, and according to some courts does not even contemplate, examination of these policies but confines itself to a comparison of contacts alone. Worse yet, it is rarely clear whether the court is looking for the *most* contacts or rather the most *significant* contacts. The comparison is supposed to be qualitative rather than quantitative, but even assuming that this is a meaningful exercise, few courts discharge it convincingly.

---

172. For torts, the three jurisdictions are: Indiana (see *Hubbard Mfg. Co., Inc.* v. *Greeson*, 515 NE 2d 1071 (Ind. 1987)); North Dakota (see *Issendorf* v. *Olson*, 194 NW 2d 750 (ND 1972)); and Puerto Rico (see *Widow of Fornaris* v. *American Sur. Co.*, 93 PRR 28 (1966)). For contracts, the five jurisdictions are: Arkansas (see *Standard Leasing Corp.* v. *Schmidt Aviation, Inc.*, 576 SW 2d 181 (Ark. 1979); *McMillen* v. *Winona Nat'l & Savings Bank*, 648 SW 2d 460 (Ark. 1983); for caveats, see *supra* 60)); Indiana (see *W. H. Barber Co.* v. *Hughes*, 63 NE 2d 417 (Ind. 1945); *Dohm & Nelke* v. *Wilson Foods Corp.*, 531 NE 2d 512 (Ind.App. 1988); *Barrow* v. *ATCO Mfg. Co.*, 524 NE 2d 1313 (Ind. App. 1988)); Nevada (see *Hermanson* v. *Hermanson*, 887 P. 2d 1241 (Nev. 1994)); Puerto Rico (see *Maryland Cas. Co.* v. *San Juan Racing Ass'n*, 83 PRR 538 (1961); *Green Giant Co.* v. *Tribunal Superior*, 104 PR Dec. 489 (1975)); and arguably North Carolina (see *Boudreau* v. *Baughman*, 368 SE 2d 849 (NC 1988) (interpreting the phrase "appropriate relation" in the forum's version of UCC Art. 1-105 as being equivalent to the phrase "most significant relationship". *Id.* at 855)). Also, after many years of employing a policy-based approach, New York has partly reverted to the center of gravity approach in contract conflicts. See *infra* 100.

173. The first case to employ this approach was *W. H. Barber Co.* v. *Hughes*, 63 NE 2d 417, 423 (Ind. 1945), but *Auten* v. *Auten*, 124 NE 2d 99 (NY 1954) is the case that brought it to prominence. One year earlier, the US Supreme Court decided *Lauritzen* v. *Larsen*, 345 US 571 (1953), a maritime case, that also employed a multi-factor choice-of-law test.

The Supreme Court of Indiana, the first state to adopt the significant-contacts approach, recently reiterated its adherence to it as well as its differences from the Second Restatement. In *Simon* v. *United States*,[174] the court recited academic commentary criticizing the Restatement as a "hodgepodge of all theories" and a "kitchen-sink concoction"[175] and, as if this were an example of superiority, self-assuredly proclaimed that, unlike the Restatement, the Indiana approach does *not* contemplate an examination of the policies underlying the conflicting laws. Identifying and weighing policies is a "difficult and ultimately speculative" task, said the court, whereas it is much easier – and presumably less speculative – to "simply look at the contacts that exist between the action and the relevant states and determine which state has the most significant relationship with the action"[176]. Yet, the better question is whether weighing the contacts of a state without examining its policies is at all a *meaningful* task. Without such an examination, one cannot know whether that state is "most intimately concerned"[177], or indeed concerned at all, even if it otherwise has the most significant contacts (whatever that means).

The Indiana court also denounced *dépeçage*, albeit after erroneously defining it as "the process of *analyzing* different issues within the same case separately under the laws of different states"[178]. The court reasoned that dépeçage is undesirable because it "amalgamates the laws of different states, producing a hybrid that may not exist in any state"[179], which in turn may "produce unfair results because the hybrid law may be more favorable to one party than another", or it may "hinder the policy of one or more states without furthering the considered policy dépeçage any state."[180]

While these may be problems, they only appear in *some* cases, and even then they are easily avoidable. By completely rejecting the possibility of dépeçage, a court unnecessarily deprives itself of useful flexibility. This is particularly true of this court, which apparently rejected not only dépeçage itself but also the process

---

174. 805 NE 2d 798 (Ind. 2004). *Simon* is discussed extensively in S. Symeonides, "Choice of Law in the American Courts in 2004: Eighteenth Annual Survey", 53 *Am. J. Comp. L.* 919, 943-948 (2005).

175. *Simon*, 805 N.E.2d at 804.

176. *Id*. at 803.

177. *Auten* v. *Auten*, 124 NE 2d 99 at 101 (NY 1954). For a discussion of this point, see S. Symeonides, W. Perdue and A. von Mehren, *Conflict of Laws* 123-124 (2nd ed. 2003).

178. *Simon*, 805 NE 2d 7 at 801 (emphasis added). Dépeçage is the *application* (not the analysis) of the laws of different states to different issues in the same cause of action (not case). See S. Symeonides, W. Perdue and A. von Mehren, *Conflict of Laws* 259 (2nd ed. 2003).True enough, dépeçage is possible only when the court undertakes a separate analysis of each issue ("issue-by-issue analysis"), but this does not mean that this analysis always leads to dépeçage.

179. *Id*. at 802

180. *Id*. at 803

that leads there, namely *issue-by-issue analysis*.[181] Indeed, the court seemed to assume: (1) that, in each cause of action in each case, there will be more than one issues on which there is a conflict of laws; (2) that a separate analysis of each of those issues will always lead to the application of the laws of different states; and (3) that such application will be inappropriate or problematic in *all* cases.

For reasons explained in detail elsewhere[182], all three assumptions are at least partly wrong. First, as *Simon* itself illustrates, in many cases the conflict is confined to a single issue and in such a case it is hardly sensible to engage in a global search for the law that would govern "the tort" as a whole. Second, even a cursory review of the cases confirms that, although an issue-by-issue analysis entails the potentiality of dépeçage, it does not always lead there. And, third, there is no reason to assume that dépeçage is always inappropriate. Sometimes it is, and sometimes it is not. The obvious and difficult question is how to distinguish the one from the other. One answer is that, generally speaking, dépeçage is inappropriate "when the rule of one state that is chosen is so closely interrelated to a rule of the same state that is not chosen that applying the one rule without the other would drastically upset the equilibrium established by the two rules and would distort and defeat the policies of that state."[183] The *Simon* court is perfectly capable of providing much better answers. Rather than attempting to do so, the court chose to reject dépeçage in all cases, thus depriving itself, and lower courts, of the opportunity for a more nuanced and individualized analysis of choice-of-law cases.

H.   The New York Experience

1.   *Tort Conflicts*

(a)   *Babcock v. Jackson*

89. The state of New York is justifiably considered the birthplace of the American conflicts revolution. The preparatory steps became evident in the 1954 case *Auten v. Auten*[184], a contract case in which New York's highest court, the Court of Appeals, abandoned the *lex loci contractus* rule in favour of the "center of gravity" approach. The next and most important step came in the landmark 1963 case *Babcock v. Jackson*[185], a tort case in which the court abandoned the *lex loci delicti* rule in favour of a policy-based choice-of-law analysis.

---

181. See id. at 801 ("Although Indiana allows different claims to be analyzed separately, it does not allow issues within those counts to be analyzed separately.")

182. See S. Symeonides, "Choice of Law in the American Courts in 2004: Eighteenth Annual Survey", 53 *Am. J. Comp. L* 919, 943-948 (2005).

183. S. Symeonides, W. Perdue & A. von Mehren, *Conflict of Laws* 260 (2nd ed. 2003).

184. 124 NE 2d 99 (NY 1954).

185. 191 NE 2d 279 (NY 1963). *Babcock* is the single most important case in modern American conflicts law. One of many indications of its importance is the fact that it has been the subject of two symposia devoted exclusively to it. See "Comments on *Babcock* v. *Jackson*; A Recent Development in Conflicts of Laws", 63 *Colum. L. Rev.*

Babcock arose out of a single-car accident in Ontario, which resulted in injury to a New York domiciliary who was a guest-passenger in a car driven by a New York host-driver, and insured and garaged in New York. New York law allowed the passenger to bring a tort action against the host-driver, whereas Ontario's "guest statute" immunized the driver and his insurer from suits brought by a gratuitous guest-passenger.

The *Babcock* court resolved the resulting conflict by enunciating a new approach for tort conflicts that drew from the "center of gravity" approach, but also went far beyond. The court described the new approach as one based on a "[c]omparison of the relative 'contacts' and 'interests'"[186] of the involved states. The court asked the rhetorical question of whether "the place of the tort [should] *invariably* govern the availability of relief for the tort or [whether] the applicable choice of law rule [should] also reflect a consideration of other factors which are relevant to the *purposes served* by the enforcement or denial of the remedy."[187]

The court ultimately answered the question by deciding to apply the law of the state which, "because of its *relationship* or contact with the occurrence of the parties, has the *greatest concern* with the *specific issue* raised in the litigation"[188]. The italicized phrases illuminate the four important elements of the court's approach, which are discussed below.

(1) Issue-by-issue analysis

90. First, the word "invariably" suggests that the court sought not a wholesale abandonment of the *lex loci* rule, but rather a narrowing of its scope depending on the *particular issue* with regard to which the laws of the involved states conflicted. Here the conflict was confined to a single issue – the driver's immunity from suit because of the Ontario guest-statute, and the absence of such statute in New York. The court was no longer thinking in broad global terms, such as whether the problem at hand should be characterized as one of tort or contract, or which law should apply to the tort as a whole. Rather, the court isolated the particular issue with regard to which a conflict existed in the actual case and focussed its analysis on that issue.

This issue-by-issue analysis, which has become an integral feature of all modern policy-based analyses, was a return to the familiar schemes of common-law decision making – temporarily submerged by Bealian systematics – which is characterized by small, cautious steps of inductive reasoning. At least in the ab-

---

1212 (1963) (contributions by D. Cavers, E. Cheatham, B. Currie, A. Ehrenzweig, R. Leflar and W. Reese); "Symposium on Conflict of Laws: Celebrating the 30th Anniversary of *Babcock* v. *Jackson*", 56 *Alb. L. Rev.* 693 (1993) (contributions by D. Siegel, R. Weintraub, F. Juenger, H. Maier, M. Solimine, L. McDougal, L. Weinberg, R. Sedler, P. Borchers, G. Simson and H. Korn).

186. *Babcock*, 191 NE 2d at 284.

187. *Id.* at 280-281 (first emphasis in original, second emphasis added).

188. *Id.* at 283 (emphasis added).

stract, such an analysis is more conducive to a nuanced, individualized, and thus more rational, resolution of conflicts problems.

(2) Dépeçage

One of the reasons for which *Babcock* was an easy case was because it involved a conflict with regard to one issue only. When a case, or more precisely a cause of action, involves conflicts with regard to more than one issue, then the court is to analyse each conflict separately. Depending on the circumstances, this analysis may lead to the conclusion that: (a) one and the same state is interested in applying its law to all issues; or (b) one involved state is interested in one issue, while another state is interested in another issue. In the latter situation, if the court applies the laws of the each state to the issue in which each state is respectively interested, the resulting phenomenon is called *dépeçage*.

Today, *dépeçage* is widely practised by American courts. It is neither a choice-of-law "doctrine" nor a goal of the choice-of-law process. Rather, it is the result, often unintended, of the abandonment of the traditional theory's broad categories and the adoption of issue-by-issue analysis. It is also a natural consequence, and an appropriate recognition, of the fact that the states involved in the case may be interested in different aspects of it or interested in varying degrees. As such, *dépeçage* is, *per se*, neither good nor bad. However, as noted earlier, in some cases the application of the law of two different states to different issues in the same case may unintentionally defeat the policies of both states. In such cases, *dépeçage* is inappropriate and must be avoided[189].

(3) The distinction between loss-distribution and conduct-regulation issues

91. Because *Babcock* was a single-issue conflict, the court did not need to engage in *dépeçage* in the sense of actually applying the laws of two different states. However, the *Babcock* court clearly signalled its willingness to engage in *dépeçage* by stating in dictum that it would have reached a different conclusion with regard to Ontario's interest "had the issue related to the manner in which the defendant had been driving his car at the time of the accident ... [or to] the defendant's exercise of due care"[190].

At the same time, through this dictum, the court enunciated a distinction between, on the one hand, issues of regulation of conduct, such as "whether the defendant offended against a rule of the road prescribed by Ontario for motorists generally or whether he violated some standard of conduct imposed by that jurisdiction"[191], and, on the other hand, issues like those actually involved in *Babcock*, namely, "whether the plaintiff, because she was a guest in the defendant's automo-

---

189. For the criteria for distinguishing permissible from inappropriate *dépeçage*, see S. Symeonides, W. Perdue and A. von Mehren, *Conflict of Laws: American, Comparative, International*, 260-261(2nd ed. 2003).

190. *Babcock*, 191 NE 2d at 284.

191. *Id*

bile, is barred from recovering damages for a wrong concededly committed"[192]. The latter issues are hereinafter referred to as "issues of loss distribution". They include guest-statutes such as Ontario's in *Babcock*, as well as New York's opposite common-law rule which provided recovery to the victim despite her status as a gratuitous guest, rules eliminating or limiting the defendant's liability, such as rules of intrafamily or charitable immunity, or rules imposing a ceiling on the amount of recovery. With regard to conduct-regulation issues, the court stated that the state in which the conduct occurred "will usually have a predominant, if not exclusive, concern"[193] and that "it would be almost unthinkable to seek the applicable rule in the law of some other place"[194]. Thus, according to *Babcock*, rules that regulate conduct operate territorially. In contrast, rules that regulate loss distribution, *do not necessarily operate territorially*. According to Currie, these rules "follow the person"[195].

As we shall see later[196], the distinction between conduct-regulating rules and loss-distributing rules is conceptually easy, but often is difficult to apply in practice. Not only do reasonable people disagree about whether a particular rule falls within the one category or the other, but they often agree that a given rule of law may both regulate conduct *and* effect or affect loss distribution. *Babcock* assumed that a guest statute does not affect a driver's conduct in that a driver does not drive differently depending on whether the state in which she drives has a guest statute. If this assumption is correct, then this is another reason for which *Babcock* is an easy case.

(4) Policy analysis

92. According to *Babcock*, the search for the applicable law should take account of more factors and contacts than the place of the tort and should include the overall relationship of each involved state with the occurrence and the parties. More importantly, the search should seek to identify the state that, because of this relationship and the "purposes" sought to be served by its laws, has the "greatest concern" with regard to the specific issue in dispute. Thus, *Babcock* introduced a policy-based analysis that went beyond the center-of-gravity approach the court had enunciated in *Auten*.

The *Babcock* court identified the policies underlying the respective rules of Ontario and New York, and then examined whether the application of each rule would further its underlying purpose or policy. Assuming that the purpose of the Ontario guest statute was to protect insurers – and only Ontario insurers[197]480

---

192. *Id.*
193. *Id.*
194. *Id.*
195. See *supra* 18.
196. See *infra* 113-121.
197. Implicitly adopting Currie's personal law principle (see *supra* 18), the court assumed that the statute was intended to protect "only Ontario defendants and their insurance carriers". *Babcock* 191 NE 2d at 289.

– from collusion between drivers and their gratuitous guests[198], the court concluded that the application of the statute would not further its purpose in this case, which did not involve an Ontario insurer. Thus, Ontario was "not interested" in applying that statute.

Conversely, assuming that the policy underlying New York's refusal to enact a guest-statute was to compensate traffic-accidents victims regardless of their status as gratuitous guests, the court concluded that the application of New York law to this case, which involved a New York victim injured by a New York driver, would further this policy by allowing a New York victim to recover damages. Hence, New York was interested in applying its law, and since Ontario was not, this was a false conflict which the court resolved by applying the law of the only interested state — New York.

(b)   The *Neumeier* rules

93. The *Babcock* approach evolved further in subsequent guest statute cases[199] and other tort conflicts[200]. This evolution, however, was far from consistent and often left the lower courts in a state of confusion. To remedy this problem, the New York Court of Appeals took the next step, in the 1973 case *Neumeier* v. *Kuehner*[201], of pronouncing in a quasi-legislative fashion[202] a new set of choice-of-law rules for guest-statute conflicts. These rules provide as follows:

> "[Rule 1]. When the guest-passenger and the host-driver are domiciled in the same state, and the car is registered there, the law of that state should control and determine the standard of care which the host owes to his guest.

---

198. Of course, one could argue that the, or a, purpose of the Ontario statute was to protect the driver from the burden and aggravation of litigation initiated by his gratuitous guest and/or to punish the guest's potential ungratefulness. The history of the enactment of that statute seems to suggest such a possibility. The bill that led to the statute's enactment was sponsored by a driver who had been sued by two hitchhikers to whom he had offered a ride on a snowy winter night and who had been injured in an accident during that ride. See W. Reese, "Choice of Law", 71 *Colum. L. Rev.* 548, 558 (1971); D. Trautman, "Two Views on *Kell* v. *Henderson*: A Comment", 67 *Colum. L. Rev.* 465, 469 (1967).

199. See *Dym* v. *Gordon*, 209 NE 2d 792 (NY 1965); *Macey* v. *Rozbicki*, 221 NE 2d 380 (NY 1966); *Tooker* v. *Lopez*, 249 NE 2d 394 (NY 1969).

200. See *Long* v. *Pan American World Airways, Inc.*, 213 NE 2d 796 (NY 1965); *Miller* v. *Miller*, 237 NE 2d 877 (NY 1968). See also the decedents' estates cases *In re Crichton's Estate*, 228 NE 2d 799 (NY 1967) and *In re Estate of Clark*, 236 NE 2d 152 (NY 1968).

201. 286 NE 2d 454 (NY 1972), appeal after remand 43 AD 2d 109, 349 NYS 2d 866 (1973).

202. Indeed, only some parts of the *Neumeier* rules could be grounded on previous New York precedents. For example, part of Rule 1 can be grounded on *Babcock, Macey* and *Tooker, supra* footnote 199, but the other part (common domicile in a guest-statute state and accident in a recovery state), as well as Rule 2, are not derived from any pre-*Neumeier* precedent.

[Rule 2a]. When the driver's conduct occurred in the state of his domicile and that state does not cast him in liability for that conduct, he should not be held liable by reason of the fact that liability would be imposed upon him under the tort law of the state of the victim's domicile. [Rule 2b]. Conversely, when the guest was injured in the state of his own domicile and its law permits recovery, the driver who has come into that state should not – in the absence of special circumstances – be permitted to interpose the law of his state as a defence.

[Rule 3]. In other situations, when the passenger and the driver are domiciled in different states, the rule is necessarily less categorical. Normally, the applicable rule of decision will be that of the state where the accident occurred but not if it can be shown that displacing the normally applicable rule will advance the relevant substantive law purposes without impairing the smooth workings of the multi-state system or producing great uncertainty for litigants."[203]

Neumeier, like *Babcock*, arose out of a single-car accident in Ontario involving a New York host-driver and a car insured and garaged in New York. The difference was that in *Neumeier* the guest-passenger was an Ontario domiciliary. Because of this difference, Rule 1 was inapplicable and the case fell within the scope of Rule 3, which calls for the application of Ontario law, subject to the escape provided in the rule. The court refused to apply the escape because displacing the *lex loci* would not advance New York's "substantive law purposes", and would impair the smooth functioning of the multi-state system by sanctioning forum shopping.

(c)   Extending the *Neumeier* rules to other loss-distribution conflicts: *Schultz* and *Cooney*

94. For some time after *Neumeier*, it was unclear whether the rules enunciated in that case could, or should, be extended to include tort situations beyond guest-statute cases or at least whether they could serve as useful analogies. The New York Court of Appeals resolved this uncertainty in the 1985 case *Schultz v. Boy Scouts of America, Inc.*[204] *Schultz* involved a fact pattern that was the reverse of *Babcock*: the plaintiffs and one of the defendants, the Boy Scouts, were domiciled in New Jersey[205], the law of which accorded the Boy Scouts charitable immunity, whereas the injury was deemed to have occurred in New York[206], which did not accord such immunity. The court characterized the immunity rules as loss-dis-

---

203. *Neumeier*, 286 NE 2d at 457-458.

204. 480 NE 2d 679 (NY 1985).

205. By the time of the trial, Boy Scouts had moved its domicile to Texas, the law of which denied charitable immunity. The court ignored the post-event change of domicile and treated Boy Scouts as a New Jersey domiciliary, noting that the change of domicile "provides New York with no greater interest in this action than it would have without the change". *Schultz*, 480 NE 2d at 682. Thus the court treated the problem as involving a choice between the laws of New York and New Jersey.

206. Two counts alleged injuries sustained in New Jersey and were dismissed under New Jersey's charitable immunity law. The remaining two counts alleged injuries suffered

tributing rather than as conduct-regulating, and concluded that the law of the parties' common domicile should govern this conflict[207]. Thus *Schultz* confirmed the applicability of the first *Neumeier* rule to cases of the reverse-*Babcock* pattern which, as we shall see later, are more difficult than the *Babcock*-pattern cases[208].

The second defendant, the Franciscan Brothers, had its domicile in Ohio[209]. Since the parties had their domiciles in different states, *Neumeier* Rule 1 was inapplicable. Rule 2 was also inapplicable because neither party was domiciled in a state whose law favoured that party. Thus, this case fell within the residual provisions of Rule 3, which calls for the application of the law of the state "where the accident occurred"[210], subject to an escape contained in that rule. The court chose to apply the escape, displacing the *lex loci* in favour of New Jersey law. The court reasoned that application of the law of New Jersey "would further that State's interest in enforcing the decision of its domiciliaries to accept the burdens as well as the benefits of that State's loss-distributing tort rules and its interest in promoting the continuation and expansion of defendant's charitable activities in that State."[211]

95. Although the substantive fairness of the *Schultz* result is open to intense debate[212], from a methodological perspective, *Schultz* is important for several reasons. First, it confirmed the New York court's commitment to adhering to the *Neumeier* rules even in difficult cases. Second, it reaffirmed and solidified the *Babcock* distinction between conduct-regulating rules and loss-distributing rules. The importance of this distinction, both for New York and American conflicts law is discussed later[213]. Third, it expanded the scope of the *Neumeier* rules to encompass conflicts between loss-distribution rules other than the now obsolete guest statutes.

---

in both New York and New Jersey. The court treated these injuries as having occurred in New York. See *infra* footnote 216.

207. Application of the law of the parties' common domicile "reduces forum-shopping opportunities ..., rebuts charges that the forum-locus is biased in favor of its own law ..., [furthers] mutuality and reciprocity [through] consistent application of the common-domicile law [and] produces a rule that is easy to apply and brings a modicum of predictability and certainty to an area of the law needing both". 480 NE 2d 687.

208. See *infra* 130-134.

209. Ohio law denied charitable immunity in actions based on negligent hiring.

210. *Neumeier* Rule 3, *supra* 93.

211. *Schultz*, 480 NE 2d at 687.

212. See. e.g., P. Borchers, "Conflicts Pragmatism", 56 *Alb. L. Rev.* 883, 909-911 (1993); G. Simson, "The *Neumeier-Schultz* Rules: How Logical a 'Next State in the Evolution of the Law' after *Babcock*?", 56 *Alb. L. Rev.* 913 (1993); S. Symeonides, "Resolving Six Celebrated Conflicts Cases through Statutory Choice-of-Law Rules", 48 *Mercer L. Rev.* 837, 847-858 (1997) (discussing how *Schultz* could be decided under the Louisiana codification).

213. See *infra* 113-123.

The latter development, however, created some new technical problems arising from the fact that the *Neumeier* rules do not differentiate between the place
of injurious conduct and the place of the resulting injury. Indeed, such differentiation was unnecessary because the *Neumeier* rules were devised for guest-statute conflicts in which the driver's conduct and the guest's injury coincide in the
same state. Thus, when the first sentence of *Neumeier* Rule 2 (hereafter "Rule 2a")
speaks of the "driver's conduct", it presupposes that any injury resulting from that
conduct will also occur in the same state. Likewise, when the second sentence of
the same rule (hereinafter "Rule 2b") speaks of a "guest [being] injured in the state
of his own domicile", it assumes that the injury is the result of the host-driver's
conduct and that this conduct also must have occurred in the same state[214]. These
assumptions are both natural and logical. Traffic accident cases in which a driver's
conduct in one state causes injury in another state are rare, even when the collision occurs *at* a state border[215].

However, in many other torts, the conduct may occur in one state and the
injury in another. By extending the scope of the *Neumeier* rules beyond guest-
statute conflicts, the *Schultz* court made the rules applicable to these cross-border torts. Besides other complications, these cases also raise the old question of
"localizing" the tort. Where one places the locus of the tort determines which of
the *Neumeier* rules is applicable and ultimately determines the outcome of the
case. Unfortunately, the *Schultz* court did not elaborate on this question, apparently because the answer would not have affected the outcome in that case[216].

---

214. Judge Weinstein's restatement of *Neumeier* Rule 2 in a non-guest-statute conflict uses
the broader terms defendant (rather than host-driver) and plaintiff (rather than guest-
passenger) but also makes clear that in non-guest statute conflicts only the conduct
need be at the defendant's domicile and only the injury need be at the victim's domicile. See *Hamilton* v. *Accu-Tek*, 1999 WL 167672 (EDNY 1999) at *4:

> "When the conduct occurs in the state of defendant's domicile, and he would not be
> liable under that state's laws, he should not be held liable under the tort law of the
> plaintiff's domicile. Conversely, when a plaintiff is injured in his own domicile, and the
> law of that state would permit him to recover, the defendant should not be allowed to
> interpose his own state's law as a defense."

215. In *Judge Trucking Co. Inc.* v. *Cooper*, 1994 WL 164519 (Del. Super. Ct. 1994), the traffic
accident occurred at the Delaware-Maryland border. After the impact, the involved
vehicles ended up in Maryland, but there was a factual question as to whether the
impact itself had occurred in Delaware. The court opined that, "if the impact occurred in Delaware, then Delaware is the place where the negligent conduct *and the
injury* took place". *Id.* at *3. (emphasis added). In *Amiot* v. *Ames*, 693 A. 2d 675 (Vt.
1997), it was argued that a traffic accident in Quebec was caused by the negligence of
a Vermont driver in Vermont where he failed to deliver himself the insulin necessary
to control his diabetes and that, because of that failure, he lost control of his car in
Vermont and struck plaintiff's car which was parked at the Canadian customs check
point.

216. *Schultz* involved tortious acts that occurred in two states, New York and New Jersey,
and produced injuries in both of those states, but primarily in New Jersey. Rather than
discussing the problem that such a split between conduct and injury might present

96. Eight years after *Schultz*, the localization problem reappeared in *Cooney v. Osgood Machinery, Inc.*[217] *Cooney* arose out of an employment accident in Missouri in which Cooney, a Missouri domiciliary, was injured by a machine owned by Mueller, his Missouri employer. Mueller bought the machine from a New York company which, ten years earlier, had bought the machine from its manufacturer Hill Acme through defendant Osgood Machinery, Inc., a New York sales agent. Cooney received workers' compensation through his employers under Missouri law, and then brought a product liability action in New York against Osgood. Osgood third-partied Mueller and Hill Acme, seeking contribution. Only this third-party action was at stake in *Cooney*. Mueller would be liable for contribution under New York law, but not under Missouri law, which provided that employers who provide workers' compensation benefits for the employee were immune from tort actions brought by the employee or by a third party.

The *Cooney* court reiterated the *Babcock-Schultz* distinction between conduct-regulating and loss-allocating rules, classified contribution rules into the latter category, and reaffirmed the applicability of the *Neumeier* rules to loss-allocating conflicts other than guest-statute conflicts. After noting that the first *Neumeier* rule was inapplicable because the disputants were domiciled in different states, the court stated that the case "presented a true conflict *in the mold of* Neumeier's second rule, where the local law of each litigant's domicile favors that party. Under that rule, the place of injury governs, which in this case means that contribution is barred."[218]

This statement would have been accurate if the dispute in *Cooney* concerned Mr. Cooney's initial product-liability action against Osgood, *and if* Missouri's product-liability law was more favourable to Cooney than to Osgood. In such a case, one could analogize Mr. Cooney to the guest-passenger under *Neumeier* Rule 2b who is injured in his home state whose law protects him, and then analogize Osgood to the host-driver who acts in his home state whose law favours him.

---

to the application of the *Neumeier* rules, the *Schultz* court designated one of the two states, New York, as the "locus of the tort", thus providing plaintiffs with a fighting chance to argue for the application of New York law. This designation, however, did not affect which of the *Neumeier* rules was applicable nor the outcome of the case. With regard to defendant Boy Scouts, a determination that the tort had occurred in New Jersey, rather than New York, would have made the case a false conflict which would be governed by New Jersey law because both parties were domiciled there. With regard to defendant Franciscan Brothers, a determination that the tort had occurred in New Jersey again would have led to the application of New Jersey law under the third *Neumeier* rule, rather than under the escape from that rule, as had occurred in the actual case.

217. 612 NE 2d 277 (NY 1993).
218. *Id.* at 283 (emphasis added). The words "in the mold of" may signify the court's understanding that the case did not fall precisely within the scope of Rule 2, first because the conduct and the injury occurred in different states and, second, because the dispute was one between joint-tortfeasors rather than between a victim and a tortfeasor. See *infra* 99.

The resulting conflict then would be a true conflict between the laws of Missouri and New York (each of which favoured the local party) as well as an internal conflict between Rules 2b and 2a, each of which would favour a different party[219]. However, the only action that was before the court in *Cooney* was Osgood's third-party action for contribution against Mueller. This makes the case much more difficult in that it raises the following questions:

(a) Which party should be analogized to the injured guest-passenger under Rule 2b? Should it still be Cooney (who actually was not a party to the third-party action), Osgood (who was the complaining plaintiff in the third-party action), or Mueller (who had paid worker's compensation for injury sustained in his home state whose law protects him)?[220]

(b) Which party should be analogized to the defendant host-driver under Rule 2a? Should it be Osgood who was the defendant in the products liability action but a plaintiff in the third-party action, and who acted in its home state whose law protected it; or should it be Mueller who was the actual defendant in the third-party action and who acted in his home state whose law favoured him?;

(c) Which injury is pertinent for purposes of the third-party action? Is it still Cooney's personal injury (which occurred in Missouri), Mueller's financial injury (which also occurred in Missouri), or Osgood's financial injury (having to pay compensation to Cooney) which occurred in New York?;

(d) Which conduct is pertinent for the purposes of the third-party action? Was it Osgood's conduct in doing or not doing something with regard to the sale of the machine in New York, or was it Mueller's conduct in modifying the machine in Missouri?; and

(e) In cases in which the conduct and injury occur in different states, is the place of conduct relevant for applying Neumeier Rule 2 or, for that matter, Rule 3?

The above are difficult questions that are susceptible to different answers. If nothing else, these questions suggest that, without further elaboration, the *Neumeier* rules may be ill-suited for cross-border torts in which the injurious conduct and the resulting injury occur in different states, or for cases in which the dispute is

---

219. See discussion *infra* 99. Judging from the court's ultimate decision to apply Missouri law to the third-party action between Osgood and Mueller, one could surmise that the court might also have applied Missouri law to Cooney's underlying products liability action against Osgood. If so, this would mean either that (a) the court considered the place of conduct to be irrelevant for Rule 2 purposes, or (b) the court believed that Rule 2b trumps Rule 2a.

220. In *Mihalic* v. *K-Mart of Amsterdam N.Y.*, 363 F.Supp.2d 394 (NDNY 2005), a case somewhat analogous to *Cooney*, the court treated the third-party plaintiff as the guest-passenger, and the third-party defendant as the host-driver.

not between the injured victim and the tortfeasor, but rather between joint tort-feasors[221].

97. The *Cooney* court seems to have recognized this deficiency, because it proceeded to resolve the conflict under a full-fledged policy analysis, if not interest analysis[222]. After concluding that the interests of the two states were "irreconcilable"[223], the court decided that on balance Missouri law should govern. The court explained that

> "this holding is consistent with the result reached historically, and reflects application of a neutral factor that favors neither the forum's law nor its domiciliaries ... . [The] locus *[delicti]* tips the balance ... [because] ordinarily it is the place with which both parties have voluntarily associated themselves."[224]

The problem was that, by the court's own admission: Osgood "did nothing to affiliate itself with Missouri"[225]; its sale activities were limited to New York and parts of Pennsylvania; the machine wound up in Missouri through no effort, or even knowledge, of Osgood; and consequently, Osgood "may not have reasonably an-

---

221. The Louisiana codification avoids both of these pitfalls. Article 3544 which, like the *Neumeier* rules, applies to conflicts between loss-distribution rules, differentiates between cases in which the conduct and the injury occurred in different states. Furthermore, the article is confined to disputes "between a person injured by an offense or quasi-offense and the person who caused the injury". Disputes between joint tortfeasors, or between a tortfeasor and a person vicariously liable for his acts, are relegated to the flexible choice-of-law approach of Article 3542, the residual article. For an explanation of the rationale of these two features by the article's drafter, see S. Symeonides, "Louisiana's New Law of Choice of Law for Tort Conflicts: An Exegesis", 66 *Tul. L. Rev.* 677, 715-731 (1992).

222. The court described its analysis as "evaluat[ing] the relative interests of jurisdictions with conflicting laws and, if neither can be accommodated *without substantially impairing* the other, finding some other sound basis for resolving the impasse." *Cooney*, 612 NE 2d at 282 (emphasis added). The italicized phrase reminds the reader of a comparative impairment analysis. Certainly, it has nothing of the selfishness of Currie's original analysis.

223. *Id.* at 283. See also *id.* ("To the extent we allow contribution against Mueller, the policy underlying the Missouri workers' compensation scheme will be offended. Conversely, to the extent Osgood is required to pay more than its equitable share of a judgment, the policy underlying New York's contribution law is affronted. It is evident that one State's interest cannot be accommodated without sacrificing the other's, and thus an appropriate method for choosing between the two must be found.").

224. *Id.* at 283. See also *id.* at 281-283 (referring to the *locus delicti*, the "traditional choice of law crucible", as an "appropriate ... 'tie breaker' because that is the only State with which both parties have purposefully associated themselves in a significant way ... [and because it] is a neutral factor, rebutting an inference that the forum state is merely protecting its own domiciliary or favoring its own law").

225. *Id.* at 283.

ticipated becoming embroiled in litigation with a Missouri employer"²²⁶. Once again, this recognition is a reminder that this case did not quite fit "in the mold" of *Neumeier* Rule 2, which was designed only for cases in which both parties associate themselves with the same state.

Nevertheless, the court offered another, ostensibly independent, reason for applying Missouri law – "the protection of reasonable expectations"²²⁷. The court reasoned that, although Osgood may not have reasonably anticipated the application of Missouri law, Osgood also had no reasonable expectation that contribution would be available to it because, at the time of the sale, New York law did not provide for such contribution. By contrast, said the court, "[i]n view of the unambiguous [Missouri] statutory language barring third-party liability ... Mueller could hardly have expected to be haled before a New York court to respond in damages for an accident to a Missouri employee at the Missouri plant"²²⁸. Thus, the court concluded that Missouri law should apply because, "although the interests of the respective jurisdictions are irreconcilable, the accident occurred in Missouri, and unavailability of contribution would more closely comport with the reasonable expectations of both parties in conducting their business affairs"²²⁹.

98. The *Cooney* court also thought it necessary to address Osgood's contention that the application of Missouri law offended New York's public policy. The court reiterated Cardozo's classic test for the *ordre public* exception²³⁰, and eventually concluded that the application of Missouri's contribution law was not repugnant to New York's public policy.

---

226. *Id.*

227. *Id.* (citing Restatement Second, §6 (2) *(d)*).

228. *Id.* at 284. In an important footnote, the court gave an additional reason as to why New York law should yield in this case – New York's law permitting contribution against an employer was "clearly a minority view" and thus it would be "undesirable" to impose that law "on the carefully structured workers' compensation schemes of other states – especially when the accident occurred there". *Id.* at n. 2. (Indeed, three years after *Cooney*, New York amended its law to make indemnification and contribution unavailable against the employer, except in cases of "grave injury" to the employee. See Omnibus Workers' Compensation Reform Act, L. 1996, ch. 635, 90). This footnote reminds one of the reasoning of the California Supreme Court in *Offshore Rental Co.* v. *Continental Oil Co.*, 583 P. 2d 721 (Cal. 1978), discussed *supra* 67. Professor Juenger thought that the footnote "holds forth the promise of a distinct improvement of New York conflicts law ... [in that] it relies on a teleological consideration ..., namely an assessment of the competing substantive rules' intrinsic quality". F. Juenger, "*Babcock* v. *Jackson* Revisited: Judge Fuld's Contribution to American Conflicts Law", 56 *Albany L. Rev.* 727, 741 n. 121 (1993). His conclusion seems to be that such a "value judgment about competing ... rules" (*id.* 751 n. 182) offers support for a choice-of-law rule Juenger proposed calling for the application of the law that "most closely accords with modern tort law standards". *Id.* at 751.

229. *Cooney*, 612 NE 2d at 284. By the same token, given the state of the law in 1958 when the machine was sold, Osgood could argue that mere sales agents could not have expected to be subject to strict liability for their involvement in the sale.

230. *Loucks* v. *Standard Oil Co.*, 224 NY 99, 111 (1918).

The reaffirmation of Cardozo's test is a positive development, especially in light of the abuse that test had suffered in the hands of the same court in *Kilberg*[231]. The *ordre public* exception remains necessary in cases subject to the first *Neumeier* rule, or any other rule that does not contain an escape clause. However, the fact that both the second and third *Neumeier* rules contain built-in escapes[232] that are capable of directly repelling an obnoxious foreign law should obviate the need for an additional *ordre public* inquiry for those cases that are disposed of under those rules[233].

99. What the *Neumeier* rules cannot resolve is the internal conflict between the rules themselves in cross-border torts in which the conduct and the injury occur in different states. One post-*Cooney* example suffices to illustrate the conflict between Rules 2a and 2b. *Bankers Trust Co. v. Lee Keeling & Associates, Inc.*[234], involved conduct in Oklahoma by an Oklahoma defendant, which caused injury in New York to a New York plaintiff[235]. Oklahoma law favoured the Oklahoma de-

---

231. See *Kilberg v. Northeast Airlines, Inc.*, 172 NE 2d 526 (NY 1961). *Cooney* does not even mention *Kilberg*.

232. Rule 2b contains a proviso allowing the showing or absence of "special circumstances", while Rule 3 is merely a presumptive rule. See *supra* 93.

233. *A fortiori*, this is true for cases handled under *ad hoc* free-wheeling analyses, such as interest analysis. As Brainerd Currie put it, interest analysis "summon[s] public policy from the reserves and place[s] it in the front lines where it belongs". B. Currie, *Selected Essays on the Conflict of Laws*, 88 (1963).

234. 20 F. 3d 1092 (10th Cir. 1994) (decided under New York conflicts law). Another case is *Venturini v. Worldwide Marble & Granite Co.*, 1995 WL 606281 (SDNY 1995), which is somewhat similar to *Cooney*. In *Venturini*, a New York company and a Michigan company filed third-party actions against a New Jersey employer, seeking contribution and indemnification in connection with an injury sustained in Michigan by a truck driver employed by the New Jersey company. Under New Jersey and Michigan law, an employer who provided worker's compensation benefits was immune from a claim for contribution by his joint tortfeasors. Under New York law, contribution was available. The court concluded that, under "the second *and* third Neumeier rules", 1995 WL 606281, at *3 (emphasis added), Michigan law governed both actions and barred both the contribution and indemnification claims. The court reasoned that, for purposes of applying the *Neumeier* rules, the "place of wrong" is "'where the last event necessary to make the actor liable occurred'". *Id.* The last event occurred in Michigan, where the truck driver was injured while unloading marble slabs that had been negligently loaded in New York.

235. The plaintiff, a New York banking corporation, agreed in New York to loan $105 million to a Texas oil producer. The loan was secured by the borrower's oil and gas reserves. In agreeing to provide the loan, plaintiff had relied on certain oil and gas reserve reports prepared in Oklahoma by defendant, an Oklahoma petroleum consultant. After the borrower defaulted on the loan, the plaintiff discovered that the defendant's reports had vastly overstated the value of the borrower's oil and gas reserves. The plaintiff sued the defendant in federal court in New York for negligence and negligent misrepresentation. The case was transferred to an Oklahoma federal court and, under *Van Dusen*, was decided under New York's choice-of-law rules.

fendant, thus making applicable Neumeier Rule 2a, while New York law favoured the plaintiff, thus making applicable Rule 2b[236].

The court assumed that the only way to resolve the conflict between the two rules was by "determin[ing] the place *of the injury*"[237], and that, under *Schultz*, that place is "where the last event necessary to make the actor liable occurred"[238]. Following this last-event rule, the court found that the injury had occurred in New York because the plaintiff's reliance on defendant's misrepresentation had taken place in New York and the resulting loss was suffered there. The court held that New York law governed under Rule 2b[239].

While the result is appropriate, the court's technical reading of *Schultz* is troublesome. Indeed, although several statements in *Schultz* may support the assumption that the "locus of the tort" is synonymous with the place of the injury, it is doubtful that these statements should be taken literally. Furthermore, although the *Schultz* court did restate the last-event concept, the court also prefaced it with the qualifier "*[u]nder traditional rules*"[240]. There is no reason to assume that the *Schultz* court intended to resuscitate those rules, especially since the court did not in fact *follow* the last-event rule[241]. In any event, this is one of the many technical problems resulting from the extension of the *Neumeier* rules to cross-border torts.

2.   *Contract conflicts*

100. As said above, in the 1954 case *Auten* v. *Auten*[242], the New York Court of Appeals abandoned the traditional *lex loci contractus* rule and adopted the "center of gravity" approach for resolving contract conflicts. Since then, the court has moved on to a full-fledged policy analysis, if not interest analysis, that relies more on policies and less on contacts.

However, in the 1993 case *In re Allstate Ins. Co.* v. *Stolarz*[243], a case involving the interpretation of an insurance contract, the court made a partial return to

---

236. The court recognized the tension between the *Neumeier* rules, although it assumed that the tension was between Rules 2 and 3, rather than between Rules 2a and 2b. See *Bankers Trust*, 20 F. 3d at 1097.
237. *Id.* (emphasis added).
238. *Id.* (quoting *Schultz*).
239. *Id.* at 1098. The court also noted the absence of any "special circumstances", which under Rule 2b may displace the law of the plaintiff's domicile and *locus delicti. Id.*
240. *Schultz*, 480 NE 2d at 683 (emphasis added) ("Under traditional rules, ... when the defendant's negligent conduct occurs in one jurisdiction and the plaintiff's injuries are suffered in another, the place of the wrong is considered to be the place where the last event necessary to make the actor liable occurred.")
241. *Schultz* treated New York as the "locus of the tort", even though New York was *not* the place of the "last event".
242. 124 NE 2d 99 (NY 1954).
243. 613 NE 2d 936 (NY 1993).

the center-of-gravity approach. After stating that interest analysis is the court's "preferred analytical tool in tort cases"[244] because "in a typical tort case ... strong governmental interests may underlie the choice of law issue"[245], the court stated the following:

> "By contrast, contract cases often involve only the *private* economic interests of the parties, and analysis of the public policy underlying the conflicting contract laws may be inappropriate to resolution of the dispute. It may even be difficult to identify the competing 'policies' at stake, because the laws may differ only slightly ... . The 'center of gravity' or 'grouping of contacts' choice of law theory applied in contract cases ... enables the court to identify which law to apply without entering into the difficult, and sometimes inappropriate, policy thicket."[246]

This statement, coupled with some other statements in *Stolarz*, suggests a dichotomy in the court's approach to contract conflicts: *(a)* interest analysis remains the "preferred approach" when "the policies underlying conflicting laws ... are readily identifiable and reflect strong governmental interests"; and *(b)* center of gravity is the preferred approach when the policies are not readily identifiable, when the policies do not reflect strong governmental interests, or when they "involve only the private economic interest of the parties".

I.   Other "Combined Modern" Approaches

101. The following states follow a combination of approaches other than the traditional one: New Jersey[247] and the District of Columbia[248] combine interest analysis with the Second Restatement in contract conflicts; Massachusetts does likewise in both tort and contract conflicts[249]; Oregon follows the same combination in

---

244. *Id.* at 938.
245. *Id.* at 939.
246. *Id.*
247. See *Gilbert Spruance Co. v. Pennsylvania Mfgrs. Ass'n Ins. Co.*, 629 A. 2d 885 (NJ 1993) *Pfizer, Inc. v. Employers Ins. of Wausau*, 712 A.2d 634 (NJ 1998); *Unisys Corp. v. Ins. Co. of North America*, 712 A.2d 649 (NJ 1998); *HM Holdings, Inc. v. Aetna Cas. & Sur. Co.*, 712 A.2d 645 (NJ 1998) .
248. See *Dist. of Columbia Ins. Guar. Ass'n v. Algernon Blair, Inc.* 565 A. 2d 564 (DC App. 1989) (applying interest analysis but also relying on the Restatement Second); *Owen v. Owen*, 427 A. 2d 933, 937 (DC 1981) (mixed approach, described as a search for the "more substantial interest", but reduced to contact counting).
249. See *Bushkin Assoc., Inc. v. Raytheon Co.*, 473 NE 2d 662 (Mass. 1985) (a contract case stating that the court would "not tie itself to any particular modern approach but would instead "feel free to draw from any of the various lists", as it had previously done in tort conflicts. The court drew from the Second Restatement and Leflar's lists, but applied them in a way that resembled interest analysis.).

tort conflicts, but "coupled with an almost irresistible forum presumption"[250]; Hawaii follows a combination of interest analysis, the Second Restatement, and Leflar's choice-influencing considerations for both tort and contract conflicts[251]; North Dakota follows the same combination in contract conflicts, but perhaps in different dosages[252]; and Pennsylvania combines interest analysis and the Second Restatement in contract conflicts but also draws from Cavers's principles of preference in tort conflicts[253].

J.   The Louisiana Codification

102. In 1991, Louisiana became the first state of the United States to enact a comprehensive choice-of-law codification[254]. The civil law heritage of that state explains why codification was a viable option there, but it does not mean that the resulting product was either easy or peculiarly civilian. The codification uses civilian drafting technique and draws elements from many European approaches but, more than anything, it draws from the general American conflicts experience[255].

The codification, which now forms Book IV of the Louisiana Civil Code, employs comparative-impairment *terminology*. Article 3515, which is the general and

---

250. S. Symeonides, "Choice of Law in the American Courts in 1994: A View 'From the Trenches'", 43 *Am. J. Comp. L.* 1 at 3 n. 6 (1995).

251. See *Lewis* v. *Lewis*, 748 P. 2d 1362 (Haw. 1988) (contract conflict interpreting *Peters* v. *Peters*, 634 P. 2d 586 (Haw. 1981), a tort conflict, as having adopted a "significant relationship" test with primary emphasis on the state with the "strongest interest").

252. See *American Family Mut. Ins. Co.* v. *Farmer's Ins. Exch.*, 504 NW 2d 307 (ND 1993); *Starry* v. *Central Dakota Printing, Inc.*, 530 NW 2d 323 (ND 1995).

253. See, e.g., *Cipolla* v. *Shaposka*, 267 A. 2d 854 (1970) (discussed *infra* 139).

254. For discussion of this codification by its drafter, see, *inter alia*, S. Symeonides, "Private International Law Codification in a Mixed Jurisdiction: The Louisiana Experience", 57 *RabelsZ* 460 (1993); S. Symeonides, "Les grands problèmes de droit international privé et la nouvelle codification de Louisiane", 81 *Revue critique* 223 (1992); S. Symeonides, "Louisiana's New Law of Choice of Law for Tort Conflicts: An Exegesis", 66 *Tul. L. Rev.* 677 (1992). For judicial applications of the codification, see P. Borchers, "Louisiana's Conflicts Codification: Some Empirical Observations Regarding Decisional Predictability", 60 *La. L. Rev.* 1061 (2000); R. Sedler, "The Louisiana Codification and Tort Rules of Choice of Law", 60 *La. L. Rev.* 1331 (2000); S. Symeonides, "Louisiana Conflicts Law: 'Two Surprises'", 53 *La. L. Rev.* 497 (1994); R. Weintraub, "Courts Flailing in the Waters of the Louisiana Conflicts Code: Not Waving but Drowning", 60 *La. L. Rev.* 1365 (2000).

255. See S. Symeonides, "Problems and Dilemmas in Codifying Choice of Law for Torts: The Louisiana Experience in a Comparative Perspective", 38 *Am. J. Comp. L.* 431, 443 (1990); S. Symeonides, "Private International Law Codification in a Mixed Jurisdiction: The Louisiana Experience", 57 *RabelsZ* 460, at 463 (1993) ("The raw material is mostly American, while the architecture and building technique bear unmistakable civilian imprints"); E. Scoles, P. Hay, P. Borchers and S. Symeonides, *Conflict of Laws*, 105 (4th ed., 2004) ("The Louisiana codification combines elements from many modern American and European approaches into a distinct identity.").

the residual article of the entire codification, calls for the application of the law of the state "whose policies would be most seriously impaired if its law were not applied to that issue"[256]. In his capacity as the codification's drafter, this author has explained the intended meaning of this terminology both in the legislatively approved "Revision Comments" and in subsequent publications. He has stated that the negative phrasing of the above article was "intended to disassociate its approach from Currie's governmental interest analysis, and other modern American approaches that seem to perceive the choice-of-law problem as a problem of interstate competition rather than as a problem of interstate co-operation in conflict avoidance"[257]. Although this negative phraseology, as well as the use of the key-word "impaired"[258], is bound to evoke comparison with California's comparative impairment approach, it is important to understand that the similarity is only phraseological[259]. One who looks at the specifics will find much fewer similarities[260].

This author has also stated that the Louisiana codification

"... is based on the premise that the choice-of-law process should strive for ways to minimize the impairment of the interests of the involved states, rather than to maximize the interests of one state at the expense of the interests of the other states. This is accomplished by identifying the state which, in light of its relationship to the parties and the dispute and its policies rendered pertinent by that relationship, would bear the most serious legal, social, economic, and other *consequences* if its law were not applied to that issue."[261]

---

256. La. Civ. Code, Art. 3515. The phrase quoted in the text is prefaced by a qualifier giving precedence to more specific articles contained in the same codification and to other special conflicts statutes of the forum state.

257. La. Civ. Code Art. 3515 cmt. (b); S. Symeonides, "Louisiana's New Law of Choice of Law for Tort Conflicts: An Exegesis", 66 *Tul. L. Rev.* 677, 690 (1992).

258. For the circumstances surrounding the somewhat accidental decision to use this word, see S. Symeonides, *Exegesis* at 691 n. 80.

259. See *id.* at 691-692: ("The assumption that such a [terminological] resemblance entails an ideological or philosophical affinity [between the two approaches] should not be taken for granted, but should be tested through a careful examination of the specifics ... . [S]uch an examination will reveal ... [that] the two approaches have much less in common than their acoustic resemblance might suggest. For example, the specific rules [of the Louisiana codification] deliberately steer away from the quantitative measurement of the impairment of state interests that is implicit, and sometimes even explicit, in Baxter's theory. Moreover, in designating the applicable law, these rules point to the law of a state other than the one to which Baxter would point.").

260. For specific differences, see S. Symeonides, *Exegesis*, 691-692, 707-708. See also *id.* at 691 n. 79 (suggesting that "curious students may find it more fruitful to compare the *substance* of Book IV" with the works of Evrigenis, Cavers, von Mehren and Trautman, who have been the drafter's teachers).

261. La. Civ. Code Art. 3515 cmt. (b) (emphasis added); S. Symeonides, *Exegesis*, 690.

Professor Weintraub has correctly concluded that this is a "consequences-based approach"[262].

Article 3515 provides that the state of the least impairment is to be determined

> "... by evaluating the strength and pertinence of the relevant policies of all involved states in the light of: (1) the relationship of each state to the parties and the dispute; and (2) the policies and needs of the interstate and international systems, including the policies of upholding the justified expectations of parties and of minimizing the adverse consequences that might follow from subjecting a party to the law of more than one state"[263].

With regard to tort conflicts, Article 3542, the general and residual article for such conflicts, provides that, except as otherwise provided by the more specific articles[264], these conflicts are governed by the law of the state whose policies would be most seriously impaired if its law is not applied to the particular issue. In turn this state is determined by evaluating the strength and pertinence of the relevant policies of the involved states in the light of:

> "(1) the pertinent contacts of each state to the parties and the events giving rise to the dispute, including the place of conduct and injury, the domicile, habitual residence, or place of business of the parties, and the state in which the relationship, if any, between the parties was centered; and (2) the policies referred to in Article 3515, as well as the policies of deterring wrongful conduct and of repairing the consequences of injurious acts"[265].

---

262. See R. Weintraub, *Commentary on the Conflict of Laws*, 355 (4th ed.,2001).
263. La. Civ. Code Art. 3515. Similar phraseology is contained in articles 3519, 3537 and 3542, which are the residual articles for status, contracts, and torts, respectively.
264. These articles cover certain fact-law patterns in cases involving: "issues of conduct and safety" (Art. 3543); "issues of loss distribution and financial protection" (Art. 3544); certain products liability cases with enumerated Louisiana connections regardless of the type of issue involved (Art. 3545); and punitive damages in cases other than the above products cases (Art. 3546). Article 3547 provides an "escape" from Articles 3543-3546; and Article 3548 contains a special rule with regard to the domicile of some corporate tortfeasors.
265. La. Civ. Code Art. 3542. For discussion by the article's drafter, see S. Symeonides, *Exegesis*, 692-699; S. Symeonides, "La Nuova Normativa della Louisiana sul DIP in Tema di Responsabilità Extracontrattuale", 29 *Riv. dir. int'le priv. e proc.* 43 (1993). For discussion by other authors, see Jean-Claude Cornu, *Choice of Law in Tort: A Comparative Study of the Louisiana Draft on Delictual and Quasi-Delictual Obligations and the Swiss Statute on Private International Law* (1989); E. Jayme, "Neue Kodifikation des Internationalen Privatrechts in Louisiana", 13 *Praxis des Internationalen Privat- und Verfarensrechts (IPRax)* 56 (1993-1); P. Kozyris, "Values and Methods in Choice of Law for Products Liability: A Comparative Comment on Statutory Solutions", 38 *Am. J. Comp. L.* 475 (1990); R. Weintraub, "The Contributions of Symeonides and Kozyris

The specific articles of the codification are discussed in some detail later[266].

K.   The Puerto Rico and Oregon Codifications

103. Another attempt at a comprehensive choice-of-law codification has been undertaken in the Commonwealth of Puerto Rico under the auspices of the Puerto Rican Academy of Jurisprudence and Legislation. In 1991, the undersigned completed a Draft Code of Private International Law[267], which was to be submitted to the Puerto Rican Legislature that year. However, for extraneous reasons unrelated to the merits of the project, this introduction to the Legislature was delayed for more than a decade. More than a decade later, this Draft Code became part of a broader project for the Revision of the Puerto Rican Civil Code. At the time of this writing, the Draft Code is pending before the Puerto Rico Legislature. This Code is more comprehensive and more civilian than the Louisiana code, but it too draws from the general American conflicts experience[268].

104. In the meantime, in 2001, Oregon became the second state to begin a comprehensive codification effort, under the auspices of the Oregon Law Commission[269]. The first installment of this effort was the 2001 enactment of a new choice-of-law statute for contract conflicts[270].

The statute's first operative provision contains an unilateral rule providing that forum law governs four types of contracts that have certain enumerated

---

in Making Choice of Law Predictable and Just: An Appreciation and Critique", 38 *Am. J. Comp. L.* 511 (1990). For discussion of cases decided under the new codification, see S. Symeonides, "Louisiana Conflicts Law: Two 'Surprises'", 54 *La. L. Rev.* 497 (1994). For discussion of how the codification would resolve some well-known non-Louisiana cases, see S. Symeonides, "Resolving Six Celebrated Conflicts Cases through Statutory Choice-of-Law Rules", 48 *Mercer L. Rev.* 837 (1997).

266. See *infra* 134, 136, 141, 145, 150, 156, 180, 199-200, 316, 345.

267. See Academia Puertorriqueña de Jurisprudencia y Legislacion, *Proyecto para la Codificación del Derecho internacional privado de Puerto Rico* (Symeon C. Symeonides and Arthur von Mehren, *Rapporteurs*, 1991).

268. For general discussion of the Code, see S. Symeonides, "Revising Puerto Rico's Conflicts Law: A Preview", 28 *Columbia J. Trans'l L.* 601 (1990). For a discussion of the Code's contracts provisions, see S. Symeonides, "Codifying Puerto Rico's Choice-of-Law for Contracts", in *Law and Justice in a Multistate World: Essays in Honor of Arthur T. von Mehren*, 419 (J. Nafziger and S. Symeonides, eds., 2002).

269. Established by statute, the Commission is Oregon's official law reform agency. Since 1999, the Commission has been housed at Willamette University College of Law and is directed by Associate Dean David R. Kenagy. The Commission has already produced a sizable body of work on subjects other than conflicts law. The Reporter for the conflicts project is Professor James A. R. Nafziger of Willamette University. The undersigned serves as chair of the project.

270. See Or. Rev. Stat. 81.100-135 (2001). For a discussion of this statute, see J. Nafziger, "Oregon's Conflicts Law Applicable to Contracts", 38 *Willamette L. Rev.* 397 (2002). S. Symeonides, "Codifying Choice of Law for Contracts: The Oregon Experience", *RabelsZ* (2003).

forum contacts, notwithstanding a choice-of-law clause to the contrary, or any other factors[271]. These are contracts in which the forum state's contacts and interests predominate, and in which the law of the forum would govern under almost any choice-of-law theory. In the interest of judicial economy, the statute singles out these contracts and essentially exempts them from the judicial choice-of-law process.

The next three provisions deal with form, capacity, and consent, respectively[272]. In general, these provisions facilitate upholding the contract through alternative references to certain validating laws, but also provide exceptions in favour of incapable parties[273], consumers, and employees. Importantly, in order to avoid the bootstrapping phenomenon, the statute removes issues of capacity and consent from the scope of party autonomy.

The next provision enunciates the principle of party autonomy, delineates its scope, and defines its modalities. Section 81.125 defines the limitations to party autonomy. It provides that the chosen law will not be applied to the extent its application would: *(a)* require a party to perform an act prohibited by the law of the state where the act is to be performed; *(b)* prohibit a party from performing an act required by the law of the state where it is to be performed; or *c)* contravene an established fundamental policy[274] embodied in the law that would otherwise govern the issue in dispute.

Section 81.130, the statute's general and residual rule, enunciates the general approach for issues other than those covered by the specific sections and in contracts that do not contain an effective choice-of-law clause. The aim of this approach is to find the law that, in light of the multistate elements of the contract, is "the most appropriate" for the resolution of the particular issue in dispute. This law is determined by:

> "(1)   Identifying the states that have a relevant connection with the transaction or the parties, ...;
>
> (2)   Identifying the policies underlying any apparently conflicting laws of these states that are relevant to the issue; and

---

271. See ORS 81.105 (providing for certain contracts involving a state entity, as well as construction, employment, and consumer contracts that have certain enumerated close connections with Oregon).

272. See ORS 81.110-115. Like much else in the Oregon statute, these sections are modeled after the Puerto Rico Draft Code. See *supra* 103, footnotes 267-268.

273. Even so, *Lilienthal* v. *Kaufman*, 395 P. 2d 543 (Or. 1964), the infamous Oregon spendthrift case, is overruled by ORS 81.110-115 (2), which provides in part that "[a] party that lacks capacity to enter into a contract under the law of the state in which the party resides may assert that incapacity against a party that knew or should have known of the incapacity at the time the parties entered into the contract".

274. The policy must be "established", as opposed to being invented *ad hoc*, and must be "fundamental". A policy is regarded as fundamental if it "reflects objectives or gives effect to essential public or societal institutions beyond the allocation of rights and obligations of parties to a contract at issue". ORS 81.125(2).

(3)   Evaluating the relative strength and pertinence of these policies in: *(a)* Meeting the needs and giving effect to the policies of the interstate and international systems; and *(a)* Facilitating the planning of transactions, protecting a party from undue imposition by another party, giving effect to justified expectations of the parties concerning which state's law applies to the issue, and minimizing adverse effects on strong legal policies of other states."[275]

Finally, recognizing that the choice-of-law process contemplated by the above provision can be both labourious and to some extent uncertain, the statute's next provision introduces presumptive rules for certain types of contracts[276]. The court is to apply the law designated by these rules, unless the opposing party demonstrates that the application of that law would be "clearly inappropriate under the principles of ORS 81.130"[277].

---

275. ORS 81.130.
276. See ORS 81.135 (providing for contracts involving the occupancy, land use, or recording of interests in real property (situs law); contracts for personal services (state where the services are to be primarily rendered); franchise contracts (state where the franchise is to operate); licensing contracts (state where the licensor has its place of business); agency contracts (state where the agent's duties are to be primarily performed)).
277. *Id.*

Chapter V   The Distinction between Conduct-regulation and Loss-distribution in Tort Conflicts

A.   Introduction

105. The previous chapters have chronicled the movement of American conflicts law from the rigid territorial system of the First Restatement, to the choice-of-law revolution, and to the new approaches that followed it. Because much of this movement has occurred in the arena of tort conflicts, the next three chapters concentrate on these conflicts. These chapters discuss cases decided by American courts since the abandonment of the *lex loci delicti* rule, focusing more on cases decided in the last two decades, and seek to identify common trends as well as potential lessons that emerge from this period.

One of the major developments of this period has been the emergence of a distinction between tort rules that are designed primarily to regulate conduct and tort rules that are designed primarily to allocate between parties the losses caused by admittedly tortious conduct. This chapter explores this distinction. Chapter VI focuses on loss-distribution conflicts, which are more numerous; Chapter VI discusses conduct-regulation conflicts; and Chapter VII discusses products liability conflicts, which deserve separate consideration because of their complexity and other factors.

B.   The Origins and Meaning of the Distinction

1.   Antecedents

106. At least since the time of the Italian statutists, private international law has struggled with the basic question of delineating the spatial operation of laws. The question can be phrased in different ways, but one of them is whether laws attach to a territory as such or to the citizens or domiciliaries of that territory (territoriality versus personality). The statutists thought they solved the problem – some laws operate territorially *(statuta realia)* and some laws follow the person *(statuta personalia)*. However the statutists' answer to the all-important question of which is which left much to be desired[1].

---

1.   See *infra* 303; E. Scoles, P. Hay, P. Borchers and S. Symeonides, *Conflict of Laws*, 10-14 (4th ed., 2004)); S. Symeonides, W. Perdue and A. von Mehren, *Conflict of Laws:*

Since then, various national PIL systems have answered the same basic question in various ways which are discussed later[2]. In the United States, Joseph Beale took the odd position that most law operates territorially, and essentially *all* torts law operates territorially[3], a position that he "codified" in his first Restatement as the *lex loci delicti* rule. The American conflicts revolution was a rebellion against many aspects of Beale's system, but in terms of actual results, the revolution was also, if not primarily, a rebellion against the *lex loci delicti* rule and its underlying holistic assumption that all of torts law operates territorially. Without denying that many tort rules operate territorially, many courts came to the realization that some tort rules, or some rules implicated in tort cases, do not, or should not, operate territorially.

As early as 1953, Justice Traynor of the California Supreme Court said as much, although not openly. In *Grant* v. *McAuliffe*[4], the court faced the question of whether a California victim's right to sue the estate of the deceased tortfeasor should be governed by the law of their common domicile, which permitted such suits, or instead by the law of the state of the tort, which prohibited the suit. Realizing that, if framed as a question of tort law, this question would be governed by the *lex loci delicti*, the court chose to characterize it as either a question of procedure or as a question of decedents' estates. Either characterization made applicable the law of California, which was both the forum and the decedent's domicile.

Two years later, the court faced a similar dilemma in *Emery* v. *Emery*[5] – whether a person should be allowed to sue a member of her family in tort. The law of the place of the tort prohibited such lawsuits (intrafamily immunity), whereas the law of the parties' common domicile permitted them. Again, realizing that, if framed as a question of tort law this question would have to be governed by the *lex loci*, the court, speaking again through Traynor, characterized this as a question of family law and applied to it the law of the parties' common domicile.

Four years after *Emery*, the same question appeared in *Haumschild* v. *Continental Cas. Co.*[6], and the Wisconsin court answered it the same way.

107. In essence, all three of the above cases created exceptions from the *lex loci* rule and its underlying principle of territoriality. They applied the law of a state that had the personal connections with the parties rather than the state that had the territorial connection with the tort. However, because the time was not

---

American Comparative International, 7-10 (2nd ed. 2003).

2. See *infra* 322-327.
3. See *infra* 323.
4. 264 P. 2d 944 (Cal. 1953).
5. 289 P. 2d 218 (Cal. 1955).
6. 95 NW 2d 814 (Wis. 1959) (applying Wisconsin's pro-recovery law to a dispute between Wisconsin parties and arising from a California accident, after characterizing the plaintiff's action as one of family law rather than of tort).

yet ripe for an open departure from the *lex loci* rule[7], these exceptions had to be camouflaged with characterization gimmicks. Thus the courts did not have the opportunity to articulate the criteria for determining when to follow the principle of territoriality and when not to. This step came in *Babcock* v. *Jackson*[8], the first case to openly depart from the *lex loci* rule.

2.   Babcock *and* Schultz

108. As previously noted, *Babcock* framed the question properly, if narrowly:

> "Shall the law of the place of the tort *invariably* govern the availability of relief for the tort, or shall the applicable choice of law rule also reflect a consideration of other factors which are relevant to the *purposes served* by the enforcement or denial of the remedy?"[9]

The answer the court gave is both well-known and important to American conflicts law[10]. But even more important was the explanation the court provided. Although the court refused to apply Ontario law on the issue of host-driver immunity, the court noted that it would have reached a different conclusion "had the issue related to the manner in which the defendant had been driving his car at the time of the accident ... [or to] the defendant's exercise of due care"[11]. In such a case, said the court, the state in which the conduct occurred "will usually have a predominant, if not exclusive, concern"[12], and that "it would be almost unthinkable to seek the applicable rule in the law of some other place"[13]. In contrast, the issue actually involved in *Babcock* was

> "not whether the defendant offended against a rule of the road prescribed by Ontario for motorists generally or whether he violated some standard of conduct imposed by that jurisdiction, but rather whether the plaintiff, because she was a guest in the defendant's automobile, is barred from recovering damages for a wrong concededly committed "[14].

---

7.   Justice Traynor explained later that, despite his efforts, he was unable to garner a majority vote for abandoning the *lex loci* rule at that time. See R. Traynor, "Is this Conflict Really Necessary?", 37 *Tex. L. Rev.* 658, 670 (1959).

8.   191 NE 2d 279 (NY 1963), discussed *supra* 89-92.

9.   *Id.* at 280-81 (first italics in original, second emphasis added).

10.   See *supra* 89.

11.   *Babcock*, 191 NE 2d at 284.

12.   *Id.*

13.   *Id.*

14.   *Id.* at 285.

On this issue, said the court, the state in which both parties were domiciled and their relationship was centred had "the dominant contacts and the superior claim for application of its law"[15].

Thus, this was no longer to be an all-or-nothing proposition – the *lex loci* for all issues, or not at all. Rather, the choice of the governing law was to depend on the particular issue. If the conflict involved an issue that implicated the conduct-regulation concerns of the state of conduct, territoriality was to remain the governing principle. If the issue was one that implicated reparation concerns for admittedly tortious conduct, the court was to look at other factors, including especially the personal connections of both the payor and the payee of the reparation. Thus was born the distinction between conduct-regulation issues or rules, on the one hand, and loss-distribution or loss-allocation issues or rules, on the other[16].

109. The New York court reiterated the above distinction in *Schultz* v. *Boy Scouts of America, Inc.*[17] The court explained that, in conflicts between conduct-regulating rules, the state where the tort occurs "'will usually have a predominant, if not exclusive, concern'"[18] because of that state's "interests in protecting the reasonable expectations of the parties who relied on it to govern their primary conduct and in the admonitory effect that applying its law will have on similar conduct in the future"[19]. Conversely, in conflicts between

> "rules [that] relate to allocating losses that result from admittedly tortious conduct, ... such as [rules] limiting damages in wrongful death actions, vicarious liability rules, or immunities from suit, considerations of the State's admonitory interest and party reliance are less important."[20]

In such conflicts, said the court,

---

15.   *Id.*

16.   Currie came to a similar distinction when he differentiated between compensatory and conduct-regulating laws. See B. Currie, *Selected Essays on the Conflict of Laws* 58-61, 69 (1963). The Second Restatement also alludes to this distinction when it states that the place of conduct has "peculiar significance" when the tort rule at issue is intended to deter misconduct. Restatement (Second) 145 cmt. e. For Ehrenzweig's theory of "local data", see A. Ehrenzweig, "Local and Moral Data in the Conflict of Laws", 16 *Buffalo L. Rev.* 55 (1966). For the same theory in Europe, see E. Jayme, "Versorgungsausgleich mit Auslandsberührung und Theorie des internationalen privatrechts – Begriffe und Instrumente", in Zacher (ed), *Der Versorgungsausgleich im internationalen Vergleich und in der zwissenstaatlichen Praxis*, 423 (1985).

17.   480 NE 2d 679 (NY 1985), discussed *supra* 94-95. See also *Miller* v. *Miller*, 237 NE 2d 877 (NY 1968) (noting that a rule limiting the amount of compensatory damages was not a conduct-regulating rule).

18.   *Schultz*, 480 NE 2d at 684 (quoting *Babcock*).

19.   *Id.* at 684-685.

20.   *Id.* at 685.

"[a]nalysis ... favors the jurisdiction of common domicile because of its interests in enforcing the decision of both parties to accept both the benefits and the burdens of identifying with that jurisdiction and to submit themselves to its authority."[21]

After concluding that both New Jersey's charitable-immunity rule and New York's no-immunity rule were loss-distribution rules, the *Schultz* court applied the law of the parties' common domicile, rather than the law of the place of the tortious conduct.

With *Babcock* and then *Schultz*, the distinction between conduct-regulation rules and loss-distribution rules had taken roots in New York conflicts law. Since then, courts in many other states have also adopted this distinction, explicitly or implicitly. As one recent study concluded, "[w]hile not every state has decided the issue, there are no states that have rejected [it]"[22]

3.   *Codifications*

110. The 1991 Louisiana codification also adopted a similar distinction, although it used terminology that was intended to narrow down the category of conduct-regulating rules. The pertinent provision of the codification, Article 3543, refers to rules or issues pertaining to "standards of conduct *and* safety"[23], terms which

---

21.   *Id.*

22.   Cross, "The Conduct-Regulating Exception in Modern United States Choice-of-Law", 36 *Creighton L. Rev.* 425, 441 (2003). For cases to this effect, see, e.g., *Collins* v. *Trius, Inc.*, 663 A. 2d 570 (Me. 1995); *O'Connor* v. *O'Connor*, 519 A. 2d 13 (Conn. 1986); *Miller* v. *White*, 702 A. 2d 392 (Vt. 1997); *Myers* v. *Langlois*, 721 A. 2d 129 (Vt. 1998); *Schwartz* v. *Schwartz*, 447 P. 2d 254 (Ariz. 1968); *Woodward* v. *Stewart*, 243 A. 2d 917 (RI 1968); *Mellk* v. *Sarahson*, 229 A. 2d 625 (NJ 1967); *Fu* v. *Fu*, 733 A. 2d 1133 (NJ 1999); *Veasley* v. *CRST Intern., Inc.*, 553 NW 2d 896 (Iowa 1996); *District of Columbia* v. *Coleman*, 667 A. 2d 811 (DC 1995); *Rong Yao Zhou* v. *Jennifer Mall Rest.*, 534 A. 2d 1268 (DC 1987); *Phillips* v. *Gen'l Motors Corp.*, 995 P. 2d 1002 (Mont. 2000); *Bauer* v. *Club Med Sales, Inc.*, 1996 WL 310076 (ND Cal. 1996); *Ellis* v. *Barto*, 918 P. 2d 540 (Wash. App. 1996), review den. 930 P. 2d 1229 (Wash. 1997); *Troxel* v. *A.I. duPont Institute*, 636 A. 2d 1179 (Pa. Super. 1994); *Spinozzi* v. *ITT Sheraton Corp.*, 174 F. 3d 842 (7th Cir. 1999); *Kuehn* v. *Childrens Hosp.*, Los Angeles, 119 F. 3d 1296 (7th Cir. 1997); *Moye* v. *Palma*, 622 A. 2d 935 (N.J. Super.1993); *Dorr* v. *Briggs*, 709 F. Supp. 1005 (D. Colo. 1989); *FCE Transp. Inc.* v. *Ajayem Lumber Midwest Corp.*, 1988 WL 48018 (Ohio App. 10 Dist. 1988); *Matson by Kehoe* v. *Anctil*, 979 F. Supp. 1031 (D. Vt. 1997); *Matson* v. *Anctil*, 7 F. Supp. 2d 423 (D. Vt. 1998); *Svege* v. *Mercedes Benz Credit Corp.*, 182 F. Supp. 2d 226 (D. Conn. 2002); *Burney* v. *PV Holding Corp.*, 553 NW 2d 657 (Mich. App. 1996); *Pittman* v. *Maldania, Inc.*, 2001 WL 1221704 (Del. Super. 2001). All of these cases are discussed in Chapters VI and VII, *infra*.

23.   La. Civ. Code Art. 3543 (emphasis added). Article 46 of the Puerto Rico Draft Code also uses the same terminology. Professor Weinberg surmises that this distinction must have been influenced by the "embarrassingly wrong" New York case *Schultz* v. *Boy Scouts of Am.* See L. Weinberg, "Theory Wars in the Conflict of Laws", 103 *Mich. L. Rev.* 1631, 1655 (2005). This is a reasonable inference. However, the first draft

suggest that the inspiration for this dichotomy came from Europe[24], rather than from New York.

Although the quoted terms are not self-definable (and this author has avoided the risk of defining them), they may provide an answer to the view that assumes, to some extent justifiably, that *all* rules of tort law are, at some level, conduct-regulating[25]. For even if all tort rules are conduct-regulating, *not* all of them prescribe "standards of conduct *and* safety". In any event, at least for the sake of brevity, the two sets of terms can be used interchangeably, and this author admits to having so used them. For this reason, and for the sake of brevity this book uses the term conduct-regulation, even when referring to the Louisiana codification.

The codification provides different choice-of-law rules for conduct-regulation conflicts than for loss-distribution conflicts. For the former category, Article 3543 discounts the parties' domicile and focuses on the places of conduct and injury[26]. For loss-distribution conflicts, the codification focuses on the parties' domicile, although it assigns a supporting role to the places of conduct and injury[27].

111. In the meantime, a parallel, but not identical, distinction had also emerged in Europe. For example, the Swiss codification provides that, regardless of which law governs a tort case, "[r]ules of safety and conduct in force at the place of the act are [to be] taken into consideration"[28]. The Belgian, Dutch, Portuguese, Hungarian, and Tunisian codifications contain similar provisions[29] as do the Hague

---

of the Louisiana codification that used this distinction was written before *Schultz* was published. Whether or not the codification's drafter approves of the particular result in *Schultz* is totally unimportant. What is important is that the codification has equipped the judge with the tools to avoid that result if the judge is so inclined. For a discussion of how a court applying the Louisiana codification can avoid the *Schultz* result, if the court is so inclined, see S. Symeonides, "Resolving Six Celebrated Conflicts Cases Through Statutory Choice-of-Law Rules", 47 *Mercer L. Rev.* 837, 848-854 (1997).

24. See the European codifications cited *infra* 111.

25. See *infra* 113-115.

26. Article 3543 provides that the law of the conduct state governs, unless the injury occurred in another state that imposes a higher standard of conduct. In the latter case, the law of the state of injury governs, provided that the occurrence of the injury in that state was objectively foreseeable. For a similar provision, see Article 46 of the Puerto Rico Draft Code.

27. See La. Civ. Code Art. 3544 (discussed *infra* 134, 136, 141, 145, 150, 156). This article provides, *inter alia*, that if the parties are domiciled in the same state, the law of that state governs, subject to escapes provided in other articles. For a similar provision, see Article 47 of the Puerto Rico Draft Code.

28. Swiss Federal Statute on PIL of 1987, Art. 142 (2).

29. See Belgian Code of PIL of 2004, Art. 102 (in determining liability "consideration must be given to the safety and conduct rules that are in force at the place and time of the tort"); Dutch Act Regarding the Conflict of Laws on Torts of 11 April 2001, Staatsblad 2001, 190, Art. 8 (the Act's other choice-of-law articles "shall not prevent the taking into account of traffic and other safety regulations, and other comparable regulations for the protection of persons or property in force at the place of the tort.");

conventions on traffic accidents and products liability[30], and some more recent proposals for a Regulation on tort conflicts currently under consideration in the European Union[31].

112. Implicit in all of the above developments are certain assumptions about state interests and the spatial operation of laws. One such assumption is that a state's policy of deterring substandard conduct is implicated whenever such conduct occurs in, or causes injury within, that state's territory, regardless of whether the involved parties are domiciled there. Another assumption is that, while a state's loss-distribution policy may or may not extend to non-domiciliaries acting within its territory, the policy does extend to state domiciliaries even when they act outside the state. In simpler words, conduct-regulating rules are territorially oriented, whereas loss-distribution rules are *usually* not territorially oriented.

C.   The Validity of the Distinction

113. While the above assumptions may or may not be questionable, what is questionable is the precision with which one can expect to classify conflicting tort rules into one or the other of the two categories. Indeed, as this author has previously acknowledged[32], the line between conduct-regulating and loss-distributing

---

Portuguese Civ. Code, Art. 45 (3) (application of law of parties' common nationality or residence shall be "without prejudice to provisions of local laws that must be applied to all persons without differentiation"); Hungarian PIL Decree of 1979, § 33.1 (regardless of the law applicable to the tort, "[t]he law of the place of the tortious conduct shall determine whether the tortious conduct was realized by the violation of traffic or other security regulations"); Tunisian Code of Private International Law of 1998, Art. 75 (regardless of the otherwise applicable law, "the rules of conduct and security in force at the place of the injurious event are taken into consideration.").

30.   See Hague Convention on the Law Applicable to Traffic Accidents of 1971, Art. 9 ("Whatever may be the applicable law, in determining liability account shall be taken of rules relating to the control and safety of traffic which were in force at the place and time of the accident"); Hague Convention on the Law Applicable to Products Liability of 1973, Art. 9 ("The application of Articles 4, 5 and 6 shall not preclude consideration being given to the rules of conduct and safety prevailing in the State where the product was introduced into the market.").

31.   See Proposal for a Regulation of the European Parliament and the Council on the Law Applicable to Non-contractual Obligations ("Rome II"), Art. 13, Brussels, 22.7.2003 COM (2003) 427 final, 2003/0168 (COD) ("Whatever may be the applicable law, in determining liability account shall be taken of the rules of safety and conduct which were in force at the place and time of the event giving rise to the damage."); European Group for Private International Law (GEDIP), Proposal for a European Convention on the Law Applicable to Non-Contractual Obligations of 27 September 1997, Art. 7.

32.   S. Symeonides, "Louisiana's New Law of Choice of Law for Tort Conflicts: An Exegesis", 66 *Tul. L. Rev.* 677, 704-705 (1992) (acknowledging difficulties of this distinction under the Louisiana codification); S. Symeonides, "Choice of Law in the American

rules is not always as bright as one would like[33]. While some tort rules are clearly conduct-regulating[34] and some are clearly loss-distributing[35], there are many tort rules that do not easily fit in either category, and some rules that appear to fit in *both* categories[36]. In fact, at least one erudite conflicts scholar who is also versed in law and economics, Professor Wendy Perdue, has contended that "*most* tort rules"[37] belong to both categories, and that "'the compensation and deterrence goals ascribed to the tort system cannot be separated'"[38].

114. Professor Perdue's contention deserves serious consideration, if only because it questions not only the manageability but also the validity of the above distinction. In a nutshell, the contention is that "*all* tort rules are loss-allocating ... and most [of them] affect conduct"[39]. The first prong of the contention is that "[a]ll tort rules determine who will bear the loss and thus are all are loss-allocating"[40].

On a general and abstract level, this statement is true; but it can also be made about any rule of law. For example, a rule invalidating a contract because of one party's incapacity has the effect of benefiting that party, and imposing a loss on the other contracting party; a rule authorizing the expropriation of private property for the construction of a public school has the effect of forcing upon the private owner a loss of property (rarely offset by the amount of compensation) for the benefit of the public; a regulation allowing factories to emit certain polluting substances may have the effect of producing a gradual loss on the public's health and a quick gain for factory owners; and a rule providing that the banks of navigable rivers are subject to a servitude or easement of public use also has the effect of imposing a loss on the riparian owner for the benefit of the navigating public.

Courts in 1994: A View 'From the Trenches'", 43 *Am. J. Comp. L.* 1, 17-18 (1995) (describing the difficulties encountered by New York courts).

33. See also P. Borchers, "The Return of Territorialism to New York's Conflicts Law: *Padula* v. *Lilarn Properties Corp.*", 58 *Alb. L. Rev.* 775 (1995); W. Reppy, "Codifying Interest Analysis in the Torts Chapter of a New Conflicts Restatement", 75 *Ind. LJ* 591, 594-97 (2000); W. Perdue, "A Reexamination of the Distinction between 'Loss Allocating' and 'Conduct-Regulating' Rules", 60 *La. L. Rev.* 1251 (2000); L. Weinberg, "Theory Wars in the Conflict of Laws", 103 *Mich. L. Rev.* 1631, 1655 (2005).

34. See *infra* 120.

35. See *infra* 121.

36. See S. Symeonides, *Exegesis, supra* footnote 32 at 704 ("a given rule of law may at the same time regulate safety and (or through) loss distribution").

37. W. Perdue, "A Reexamination of the Distinction between 'Loss Allocating' and 'Conduct-Regulating' Rules", 60 *La. L. Rev.* 1251, 1252 (2000) (emphasis added).

38. *Id.* (quoting M. Trebilock, "Incentive Issues in the Design of 'No-Fault' Compensation Systems", 39 *U. Tor. LJ* 19, 20 (1989)). Having had the privilege of working with Professor Perdue on a joint conflicts book, this author has benefited from her intellectual prowess. This mild disagreement among friends is simply an example of the admitted difficulty of this issue.

39. W. Perdue, *supra* at *id.* (emphasis in original).

40. *Id.*

Like so many other rules, each of the above rules has a detrimental effect on one class of people. However, this effect is not the rule's intended *purpose*. The purpose is, respectively, to protect the incapable party, promote public education, promote industrial development and job creation, and facilitate navigation. In the pursuit of these laudable objectives, these rules *produce* certain losses, but this is only a side effect. In contrast, the tort rules that qualify as loss-allocating do not produce the losses, but rather purport to repair or re-allocate losses which are bound to occur and which are caused by conduct found to be tortious.

115. Perdue's second contention is that, since all rules are loss-allocating, most of them are also conduct-regulating, because "[l]oss allocation creates incentives for those who must bear the loss to behave differently than they would if they did not have to bear the loss"[41].

This observation is true in many instances, but by no means all. For example, as Perdue acknowledges[42], a guest statute is clearly loss-allocating but it has practically zero effect on the driver's conduct. A driver will not drive less carefully in a guest-statute state just because of the assurance that, if she is involved in an accident and she survives it, she will be immune from a suit by her guest-passengers.

Perdue argues, however, that other immunity rules such as the charitable immunity rule involved in *Schultz*, are both loss-allocating and conduct-regulating, because *(a)* they "eliminate[] incentives for the tortfeasor to take care"[43]; and *(b)* they "provide[] incentives for charities to increase the quantity of service provided"[44].

The first observation may reflect the actual conduct of some charity employees such as the despicable child molester involved in *Schultz*, but it is hard to accept that it reflects the mind set of charity leaders. In any event, the *purpose* of a charitable immunity rule is clearly *not* to encourage or even condone substandard conduct. The same is true with regard to other immunity rules such as the interspousal or intrafamily immunity rules involved in *Haumschild* and *Emery*. These rules are neither intended to, nor have the effect of eliminating, the incentive to act carefully.

The second observation regarding incentives for charities to increase the quantity of their services is both accurate and within the intent of the charitable immunity rule, but it is totally inapplicable to other immunities, such as intrafamily immunities. Indeed, like guest statutes, intrafamily immunity rules are not intended to and do not affect conduct. The purpose of these immunities may be to preserve family harmony, to protect insurers, or to protect the community property and its creditors in some of the interspousal immunity cases, but it is not directed towards the conduct of family members. Even with regard to charitable immunities, the key word is "quantity". The charitable immunity rule affects the quantity of the services, but it is not intended to affect their quality.

---

41.   *Id.* See also *id.* ("all tort rules allocate loss and thereby affect conduct").
42.   See *id.* at 1256.
43.   *Id.* at 1254.
44.   *Id.*

116. One is on more solid ground in arguing that a *non*-immunity rule, such as New York's rule in *Schultz*, is both loss-distributive and conduct-regulating. It is loss-distributive to the extent it imposes financial responsibility on the actor and provides compensation for the victim, but it can also be conduct-regulating to the extent it affects the actor's conduct by providing an additional incentive to act more carefully. In his dissenting opinion in *Schultz*, Justice Jasen made a similar argument. Jasen agreed that the majority's characterization of New Jersey's immunity rule as loss-distributing was correct because, in his words, the rule reflected "a legislative paternalism towards resident charities"[45]. Jasen argued, however, that the majority's characterization of New York's non-immunity rule as loss-distributing was "obviously" erroneous, and that a state's policy of "deterring serious tortious misconduct" can be expressed either "in the form of imposing liability or denying immunity"[46]. The *Schultz* majority dismissed Jasen's argument rather summarily[47]. A subsequent case discussed later[48] sheds some light on why the court dismissed the argument. For even conceding that New York's rule was in part conduct-regulating, its primary purpose, the court must have thought, was loss-distributive.

117. Perdue also argues that rules limiting the amount of compensatory damages "have a significant impact on conduct ... [because] [t]he level of damages that an actor expects to pay directly affects the level of care the actor will take"[49]. A potential tortfeasor "will take precautions so long as it is cheaper to take precautions than to pay the expected damage award. If the damages are low, then the amount spent to avoid damages will also be low. Thus although damages limits have an allocative effect, they also affect conduct."[50]

Again there is much truth to this argument, especially in the American legal system which – perhaps more than any other system – employs civil sanctions and financial incentives to achieve objectives that other systems pursue through public-law means[51]. However, this argument can be carried a bit too far.

---

45.   *Schultz*, 491 NYS 2d 90 at 102 (Jasen, J., dissenting).

46.   *Id.*

47.   See *Schultz*, 491 NYS 2d 90 at 96 n.2 ("New York's rule holding charities liable for their tortious acts ... is also a loss-allocating rule, just as New Jersey's charitable immunity statute is"). More than a decade later, a New Jersey court ignored *Schultz* and held that New York's non-immunity rule served a two-fold purpose of "both assur[ing] payment of any obligation to the person injured and giv[ing] warning that justice and the law demand the exercise of care". *Butkera* v. *Hudson River Sloop "Clearwater," Inc.*, 693 A. 2d 520, 523 (NJ Super. 1997). With such a dual characterization, the New Jersey court convinced itself that it could justify applying the New York rule against a New York charity whose conduct in New Jersey had injured a New Jersey resident there.

48.   See *Padula* v. *Lilarn Props. Corp.*, 644 NE 2d 1001 (NY 1994), discussed *infra* 118.

49.   W. Perdue, "A Reexamination of the Distinction between 'Loss Allocating' and 'Conduct-Regulating' Rules", 60 *La. L. Rev.* 1251, 1253 (2000).

50.   *Id.* at 1253-1254.

51.   See S. Symeonides, "Resolving Punitive-Damages Conflicts", 5 *Ybk Priv. Int'l L.* 1, 5-9 (2004).

For example, in *Hurtado* v. *Superior Court*[52], the California Supreme Court concluded that a California rule that did *not* limit the amount of wrongful-death damages was designed in large part to deter people from wrongfully killing other people. This was long before the infamous O. J. Simpson case[53], but even then it was a huge stretch[54]. Indeed, regardless of time or place, it is difficult to accept the proposition that large damage awards have the effect of deterring wrongful deaths, especially in traffic-accident cases like *Hurtado* in which the tortfeasor's own safety is also at risk[55]. More importantly, leaving aside the actual impact on people's behaviour, it is just as difficult to accept that the *purpose* of a rule that allows unlimited damages is to deter wrongful conduct as it is to accept that the *purpose* of a rule that limits the amount of damages is to encourage or even condone wrongful conduct.

The more probable purpose of a rule that limits the amount of compensatory damages is to reduce the financial burden on the class of people engaging in the particular conduct, be they drivers, surgeons, or manufacturers. The purpose is not to encourage substandard conduct, which may even harm the lawmakers themselves. Rather the purpose is to affix in advance the financial consequences of conduct that experience tells us will occur and will cause harm. The lawmaker simply recognizes that the conduct will, and should, occur (people will drive, surgeons will operate, manufacturers will produce), that some of this conduct will cause injury, and a decision must be made on which class of people will bear the loss, and how much of it. These loss-allocative decisions are value judgments lawmakers make every day.

---

52. 522 P. 2d 666 (Cal. 1974), discussed *infra* 149.

53. In 1994, O. J. Simpson was charged with killing his wife and another person. Although he was not found guilty in the criminal trial, he was cast in judgment in the ensuing civil trial and ordered to pay a large amount in civil damages for the wrongful death of the two victims.

54. For a critique of *Hurtado* on this point, "offer[ing] a long list of reasons why this conclusion is untenable", see W. Reppy, "Eclecticism in Choice of Law: Hybrid Method or Mishmash?", 34 *Mercer L. Rev.* 645, 669 (1983).

55. It is conceivable that, over a long period of time, a rule that limits damages may affect the actor's conduct (by increasing the level of his activity), but only in cases of *non-*intentional torts in which the tortfeasor's activity does *not* endanger the actor's own safety. Even in these cases however, this does not seem to be the reason for which a state decides not to limit the amount of damages. After all, unlimited damages are the norm. The lawmaker allows them because ordinarily the victim is entitled to recover her entire loss. On the other hand, limited damages are the exception. The lawmaker limits their amount, not because the victim is undeserving, but rather because, on balance, the lawmaker decides to reduce the financial burden on a particular class of tortfeasors. In both cases, the lawmaker's motives are loss-distributive rather than conduct-regulating.

D.   The Manageability of the Distinction

118. This is not to deny that in many instances loss-allocative and conduct-reg-
ulative motives or even purposes can co-exist in the same rule. The law is too
complex a phenomenon to be viewed through such mono-dimensional lenses. As
previously conceded, some tort rules do fit into both categories. One example is
a dram shop act[56]. In enacting a dram shop act, a state may be motivated by both
conduct-regulating *and* loss-allocating objectives, namely: (1) providing additional incentives for tavern owners to act more carefully and refrain from serving
apparently intoxicated patrons; and (2) facilitating financial recovery for victims
by making available to them an additional defendant, the tavern owner, and placing on the latter the economic loss of accidents caused by his drunk patrons. In
contrast, in refusing to enact a dram shop act – or in enacting an anti-dram shop
act – a state may be motivated by loss-allocating rather than conduct-regulating
considerations, namely, to shield tavern owners or social hosts from financial responsibility, rather than to encourage them to act carelessly.

Other examples of dual-character rules include strict-liability rules[57], contributory-negligence rules[58], and "car-owner statutes," namely statutes that impose vicarious liability on car owners for injuries caused by a driver using the car
with the owner's consent[59]. Another well-known example is provided by a series
of New York cases involving §240 of New York's Labor Law, which imposes on
the owner of an immovable absolute liability for injury caused by a defective scaffold to a construction worker working on the premises. Six lower-court cases had
characterized this provision in three different ways[60], before the New York Court

---

56.   Cases involving dram shop acts are discussed in Chapter VII, *infra*, which deals with
       conduct-regulating conflicts, because most cases characterize dram shop acts as con-
       duct-regulating.
57.   See W. Perdue, "A Reexamination of the Distinction between 'Loss Allocating' and
       'Conduct-Regulating' Rules", 60 *La. L. Rev.* 1251, 1253 (2000).
58.   Professor Perdue, *id.* at 1257 n. 41, erroneously attributes to this author the view
       that contributory negligence rules are conduct-regulating. Apparently, Perdue has
       been misled by this author's approving discussion of the *Spinozzi* case (see *infra*, 120,
       169) which involved issues of building safety standards and contributory negligence.
       However, that discussion was approving only with regard to the safety-standards part
       of the case. For this author's position (actually non-position) on this matter, see S.
       Symeonides, W. Perdue and A. von Mehren, *Conflict of Laws: American, Compara-
       tive, International*, 162-164 (1998) (presenting both sides of the issue).
59.   Conflicts involving these statutes are discussed in Chapter VII, *infra*, which deals
       with conduct-regulating conflicts, because the majority of cases have characterized
       these statutes as conduct-regulating.
60.   The following cases classified §240 as conduct-regulating: *Zangiacomi v. Saunders*,
       714 F. Supp. 658 (SDNY 1989) (Connecticut accident, New York plaintiff, New York
       defendant – §240 not applied); *Salsman v. Barden & Robeson Corp.*, 564 NYS 2d 546
       (NYAD 3rd Dept. 1990) (Massachusetts accident, Pennsylvania plaintiff, New York
       defendant – §240 not applied). *Thompson v. IBM Corp.*, 862 F. Supp. 79 (SDNY 1994),

of Appeals had the opportunity to consider the matter in *Padula* v. *Lilarn Props. Corp.*[61]

After defining as conduct-regulating those rules that "have the prophylactic effect of governing conduct to prevent injuries from occurring"[62] and as loss-distributive those rules that "prohibit, assign, or limit liability after the tort occurs, such as charitable immunity statutes"[63], the *Padula* court acknowledged that §240 "embod[ied] both conduct-regulating and loss-allocating functions"[64]. However, the court concluded that the *primary* function of §240 was to regulate conduct[65]. Thus, the court provided a simple answer to a complex question: whenever a particular rule embodies both conduct-regulating and loss-distributing functions, one should focus on the rule's primary function and proceed accordingly.

E.   Looking at Primary Purpose and Function

119. While the answer of the *Padula* court is not profound, it is sensible and practical. It enunciates a criterion for distinguishing between the two categories and invites the parties and their experts to present their best arguments. The criterion may appear vague[66], but it is no more vague than the criteria courts employ in so

---

characterized §240 as primarily a loss-distributing rule and applied it to a New York accident involving Massachusetts parties, *inter alia* "to avoid giving a competitive advantage to out-of-state contractors utilizing out of state workers". *Id.* The following cases characterized §240 as both conduct-regulating and loss-distributing: *Calla* v. *Shulsky*, 543 NYS 2d 666 (NYAD 1st Dept. 1989) (Connecticut accident, New York plaintiff, New York defendant: "[T]he act of shifting financial responsibility often serves to regulate conduct by providing an inducement to exercise oversight in order to avoid the economic disincentive of vicarious liability" – §240 applied); *Huston* v. *Hayden Bldg. Maint. Corp.*, 617 NYS 2d 335 (NYAD 2d Dept.1994) (New Jersey accident, New York plaintiff, New York defendants: "[E]ven though [§240] serves a dual function at various times, our analysis should focus on which of those functions is applicable to the specific cause of action here" – §240 not applied.); *Aviles* v. *The Port Auth. of New York and New Jersey*, 615 NYS 2d 668 (NYAD 1994) (New Jersey accident, New York plaintiff, defendant domiciled in New York and New Jersey – §240 not applied).

61.   644 NE 2d 1001 (NY 1994). In this case, a New York worker invoked §240 in an action filed against a New York defendant for injuries the plaintiff sustained in Massachusetts, when he fell from a scaffold while working on defendant's building.

62.   *Id.* at 1002.

63.   *Id.*

64.   *Id.* at 1003. The conduct-regulating function was "requiring worksites be made safe", *id.*, while the loss-distributing function was the imposition of vicarious liability on the owner of the property for failure to provide a safe worksite. *Id.*

65.   See *id.* (characterizing §240 and its companion §241 as "primarily conduct-regulating rules, requiring that adequate safety measures be instituted at the work site" and holding them inapplicable to the Massachusetts accident).

66.   See, e.g., W. Perdue, "A Reexamination of the Distinction between 'Loss Allocating' and 'Conduct-Regulating' Rules", 60 *La. L. Rev.* 1251, 1255 (2000) (questioning wheth-

many other situations in resolving conflicts in interstate or domestic law. In fact one might question whether any further specificity would be possible or helpful. Despite contrary opinion, the process of determining the purpose, function, or "policy" underlying a rule of law is neither futile nor unworthy of the effort[67]. Moreover, this process of teleological interpretation is a road we chose to travel the moment we concluded that conflicts of laws can be resolved more rationally by looking at the policies and functions of the conflicting laws, rather than at metaphysical notions of legislative jurisdiction. This process is admittedly difficult at times, but attorneys and their tort experts can certainly handle this difficulty, and many of them would prefer it over mechanical rules that lead inexorably to a pre-ordained result.

This author lacks the necessary expertise in tort law to illuminate this debate. Nevertheless, looking at the cases discussed in the next three chapters, the following appear to be relatively clear examples of rules that belong primarily in the one category or the other.

120. As *Babcock* stated, "rules of the road" are a classic example of conduct-regulating rules, or "rules of conduct and safety". They are designed to ensure the safety of the public by defining permissible and impermissible conduct *and* by imposing sanctions on violators. This category is not as small as most commentators assume. It includes not only speed limits and traffic-light rules, but also rules that prescribe the civil sanctions for violating traffic rules, including presumptions and inferences attached to the violation. For example, a rule providing that drivers involved in collisions while driving intoxicated or while driving in excess of the speed limit are presumed negligent is primarily a conduct-regulating rule as is a rule providing that, in a rear-end vehicular collision, the driver of the rear car is presumed to be at fault.

Other examples are rules that prescribe safety standards for work sites, buildings, and other premises. These rules are primarily conduct-regulating, although they may well have an impact on loss-allocation. As Judge Posner noted in a case involving safety standards in a foreign hotel, it would be both non-sensical and dangerous to impose on the hotel operator a duty to follow the safety standards in force in the home-states of the hotel guests. This would subject the operator "to a hundred different bodies of tort law"[68], each imposing potentially inconsistent duties of care. "A resort might have a system of firewalls that under the law of some states or nations might be considered essential to safety and in others might be considered a safety hazard."[69]

---

er there is "any coherent methodology to determine which of multiple purposes is the more important or significant"). See also *id.* at 1256 (correctly warning that "one cannot assume that because one state's purpose in adopting a rule is loss allocation, another state's purpose for adopting a different rule is also loss allocation").

67. See *infra* 338-339 (discussing the criticisms leveled against the teleological approach to statutory interpretation).
68. *Spinozzi* v. *ITT Sheraton Corp.*, 174 F. 3d 842, 845 (7th Cir. 1999).
69. *Id.*

Finally, other examples of conduct-regulating rules are those that impose punitive damages. As the word "punitive" suggests, the purpose of these rules is to punish the individual tortfeasor, as well as to deter other potential tortfeasors, rather than to compensate the victim who is, *ex hypothesi*, made whole through compensatory damages. Do punitive damages have an impact on loss-allocation? Absolutely! Large punitive damages awards can drive a whole industry to the ground and may effect a massive transfer of wealth from the insurance industry to the plaintiffs' bar. Again, however, this transfer of wealth is simply an effect of the punitive damage rule, not its purpose, which is to deter egregious conduct[70].

121. On the loss-distributive side, the following appear to be examples of rules that are primarily loss-distributive, even if they have a bearing on conduct: guest statutes; rules providing intrafamily or charitable immunity; rules imposing ceilings on the amount of damages or excluding certain types of damages, such as for pain and suffering; rules defining the beneficiaries of wrongful death actions, survival actions, and loss of consortium actions; the old rules providing that a tort action does not survive the tortfeasor's death; rules dealing with contribution or indemnification among joint tortfeasors[71]; rules providing for no-fault automobile insurance[72], statutes of repose, which protect manufactures from suits filed after a designated number of years from the product's first use, corporate-successor liability or non-liability rules, and direct action statutes, namely statutes that allow the victim to directly sue the tortfeasor's insurer.

F.   The Usefulness of the Distinction

122. Even if some of the above examples were questionable, the remaining ones comprise a long enough list to support the usefulness of the basic distinction between conduct-regulating and loss-distributing rules. The fact that with regard to some other rules opinions may differ and the classification can go in either direction simply illustrates the difficulties of this distinction, but does not negate its usefulness. These difficulties are inherent in any teleological approach and are a fair price to pay in return for the rational resolution of conflicts that such an ap-

---

70.   On the other hand, one could argue that a state's decision not to impose punitive damages is motivated by loss-allocation factors, e.g., protecting an industry from potentially debilitating financial burdens. See W. Reppy, "Codifying Interest Analysis in the Torts Chapter of a New Conflicts Restatement", 75 *Ind. LJ* 591, 597 (2000). The author correctly concludes, however, that when two parties from such a jurisdiction are involved in a tort in a state that imposes punitive damages, the punitive-damages rule of the latter state should govern because "the conduct-regulating rule here trumps the contrary loss-distributive rule". *Id.*

71.   See P. Borchers, "The Return of Territorialism to New York's Conflicts Law: *Padula v. Lilarn Properties Corp.*", 58 *Alb. L. Rev.* 775, 785 (1995) ("[p]arties, obviously, can do little to choose their co-tortfeasors, and thus rules like this have, at most, minimal effect on conduct").

72.   See W. Perdue, "A Reexamination of the Distinction between 'Loss Allocating' and 'Conduct-Regulating' Rules", 60 *La. L. Rev.* 1251, 1255 (2000).

proach promises. Moreover, these difficulties should not be overestimated. They are no more insurmountable than, for example, the difficulties of distinguishing between substance and procedure[73] or, in some close cases, distinguishing between tort and contract actions[74].

While this comparison may evoke the difficulties encountered in the characterization process under the traditional theory, the similarity is only superficial. The traditional theory sought to ascribe labels to rules without regard to their underlying purposes. In contrast, the process of distinguishing between conduct-regulating and loss-distributing rules seeks to ascertain the rule's purpose, and does so in a much more nuanced and focused manner. It asks the right questions and, more importantly, it is expected to provide reasons for the answers to which it arrives. In any event, as Judge Weinstein observed, this distinction, far from being a rigid one, is no more than "a proxy for the ultimate question of which state has the greater interest in having its law applied to the litigation at hand"[75].

Indeed, at least in a judicial choice of law[76], the above distinction does no more than focus the parties' and the court's attention on the right questions and to draw the lines along which the battle will be fought. It stands for the simple proposition that in conflicts between conduct-regulation rules, one should focus on the place or places of conduct and injury, whereas in conflicts between loss-distribution rules, one should also focus on the parties' connections, if any, with other states. Surely, in hard cases or cases in which the distinction is unworkable, the lines may be adjusted or even stepped-over, but this does not mean that it is better to debate without lines[77].

---

73. See P. Borchers, "The Return of Territorialism to New York's Conflicts Law: *Padula v. Lilarn Properties Corp.*", 58 *Alb. L. Rev.* 775, 784 (1995) ("Many important and fundamental legal distinctions involve large areas of overlap. The distinction between substance and procedure is a good example.").

74. To paraphrase Professor Baxter, the process of distinguishing between the two categories "will sometimes be difficult, and reasonable disagreement may exist regarding the objectives of various internal rules. The process, however, is a familiar one rather than a unique concomitant of the choice analysis proposed." Baxter, "Choice of Law in the Federal System", 16 *Stan. L. Rev.* 1, 12 n. 28 (1963).

75. *Hamilton* v. *Accu-Tek*, 47 F. Supp. 330, 337 (EDNY 1999).

76. Even when the distinction is codified, as in the case of the Louisiana codification, the distinction is not so rigid as to leave no flexibility. To begin with, in many instances the codification's two articles (3543 and 3544) that provide for conduct-regulation and loss-distribution conflicts, respectively, lead to the same result, albeit for different reasons. See S. Symeonides, "Louisiana's New Law of Choice of Law for Tort Conflicts: An Exegesis", 66 *Tul. L. Rev.* 677, 731-732. For those instances in which the two articles lead to a different result (such as a *Babcock*-type case in which an accident in one state involves a tortfeasor and a victim domiciled in another state), the court has flexibility from deviating from the legislatively prescribed result by utilizing the escapes the codification provides. See *id.* 733-734, 704-705 n. 147.

77. Precisely because this distinction is only "a proxy for the ultimate question", many commentators justifiably prefer to move these lines in a direction that conforms to

123. Thus, one can conclude that, despite the difficulties in its application, the distinction between conduct-regulating and loss-distributing rules provides a useful framework for resolving many tort conflicts. In an earlier publication, this author contended that, despite the difficulties in its application, this distinction "may be one of the major breakthroughs in American conflicts thought and perhaps one of its major contributions to international conflicts thought"[78]. More than a decade later, this author cannot think of a better starting point or framework for determining when to apply the *lex loci* and when not to, for delineating, in other words, the respective scopes of territoriality and personality of the laws[79].

To a large extent, the story of private international law can be described as a contest between these two grand principles, with the pendulum swinging from one principle to the other in different periods in history. In the United States, Joseph Beale had pulled the pendulum all the way toward territoriality, and then Brainerd Currie pulled it almost all the way back toward personality. It is time to acknowledge that neither Beale nor Currie was entirely wrong or entirely right. It is also time to begin defining the parameters for seeking a new equilibrium between these two principles.

In this process, it helps to remember that these two principles parallel the two fundamental objectives of the substantive law of torts – deterrence and compensation – and that contemporary states, although still "territorially organized"[80], are also "welfare states". They seek to both "safeguard the health and safety of people and property within their bounds"[81], and to "prescribe modes of financial

---

their conflicts philosophy. For example, Professor Reppy, who generally subscribes to this distinction, suggests that "if a court is unable to determine whether a tort rule is primarily conduct-regulating or primarily loss-distributive, the latter [should be] the default classification". W. Reppy, "Codifying Interest Analysis in the Torts Chapter of a New Conflicts Restatement", 75 *Ind. LJ* 591, 597 (2000). Professor Weintraub, who is skeptical of the whole distinction, proposes that the category of conduct-regulating rules "should be limited to rules intended to regulate conduct in the most immediate manner ... [such as] speed limits or right of way". R. Weintraub, *Commentary on the Conflict of Laws*, 435 (4th ed. 2001). Professor Perdue, who argues that most tort rules are conduct-regulating, acknowledges that acceptance of her argument would lead to "a largely territorial choice of law rule for torts", a development which she welcomes because it is "consistent with the standard economic view of torts as primarily conduct-regulating". W. Perdue, "A Reexamination of the Distinction between 'Loss Allocating' and 'Conduct-Regulating' Rules", 60 *La. L. Rev.* 1251, 1258 (2000).

78. S. Symeonides, "Problems and Dilemmas in Codifying Choice of Law for Torts: The Louisiana Experience in a Comparative Perspective", 38 *Am. J. Comp. L.* 431, 441 (1990).

79. See *infra* 322-327; S. Symeonides, "Territoriality and Personality in Tort Conflicts", in *Inter-continental Cooperation Through Private International Law: Essays in Memory of Peter Nygh*, (T. Einhorn & K. Siehr, eds.) 401(2004).

80. D. Cavers, *The Choice-of-Law Process*, 139 (1965).

81. *Id.*

protection for those endangered"[82]. When the objectives of one state conflict with those of another, territoriality is the starting point in conduct-regulation conflicts, and personality is the starting point in loss-allocation conflicts. To quote Judge Weinstein, once again, "the conduct regulation-loss allocation dichotomy is a proxy for the balancing of competing state interests"[83]. Many of the cases discussed in the next two chapters seem to proceed on this basis.

---

82.   *Id.*
83.   *Hamilton* v. *Accu-Tek*, 47 F. Supp. 2d at 341.

Chapter VI Loss-distribution Tort Conflicts

A. Introduction

124. Logically one should discuss conflicts between loss-distributing rules after examining conflicts between conduct-regulating rules, for the same reasons that one should discuss reparation only after establishing culpability or at least liability. The fact is, however, that almost all the major cases that constitute the American conflicts revolution involved loss-distribution conflicts, precisely because it is with regard to these conflicts that the territorially based traditional system proved most deficient. Moreover, even today, loss-distribution conflicts are more common than conduct-regulation conflicts, apparently because the laws of the various states are more likely to differ on loss-distribution than on conduct-regulation issues.

For these reasons, this book discusses first loss-distribution conflicts (Chapter VI) and then conduct-regulation conflicts (Chapter VII).

This chapter focuses on the major loss-distribution conflicts cases decided since the abandonment of the *lex loci delicti* rule. First, it classifies the cases into eight typical, primary, fact-law patterns based on the most common combinations of the pertinent factual contacts (territorial and personal) and substantive laws of the contact-states. After discussing the cases in each pattern, the chapter compares their results with the solutions provided by three American rule-models[1]: a judicial model, the *Neumeier* rules[2]; a statutory model, the Louisiana codification[3]; and an academic model, Professor Cavers's "principles of preference"[4]. Finally this chapter attempts to summarize and recast the results of the cases into a form suitable for both descriptive and normative choice-of-law rules.

---

1.   Occasionally, comparisons are also made with foreign PIL codifications.
2.   See *supra* 93.
3.   See *supra* 102.
4.   See *supra* 13; D. Cavers, *The Choice of Law Process* 139-180 (1965).

B.   Defining the Typical Patterns

1.   The pertinent connecting factors or contacts

125. Unlike conduct-regulating rules which operate territorially, loss-distribut-ing rules operate in a more complex mode that focuses more on the individuals involved in the conflict rather than on the physical location of the events that caused the conflict. Because of its fixation with territoriality and its one-size-fits-all mentality, the traditional system was unable to recognize or accommodate this basic reality and thus precipitated the revolution in tort conflicts. It is therefore no surprise that one of the common points of reference among all branches of the revolution has been the acceptance of the parties' domicile[5] as the focal point around which to resolve conflicts between loss-distribution rules. In the span of a few years, the parties' domicile, which was an irrelevant factor under the *lex loci delicti* rule, became a primary factor in loss-distribution conflicts.

However, the new importance of domicile does not mean that the traditional contact of *locus delicti* has become irrelevant. Rather it means that domicile now shares the stage with the *locus delicti*, which remains an important, albeit not an exclusive factor, and that territoriality is no longer the exclusive governing prin-ciple in the resolution of tort conflicts.

Since many torts are committed across state boundaries, the *locus delicti* may be in more than one state. Rather than artificially place the *locus delicti* at the place of the "last event", proper analysis should consider both the place of the last event, the injury, *and* the place in which the injurious conduct occurred[6].

In summary, the pertinent contacts for resolving loss-distribution conflicts are: (1) the parties' domiciles; (2) the place of the injurious conduct; and (3) the place of the resulting injury[7]. Thus, if one were to classify loss-distribution con-

---

5.   As used hereafter, the term domicile includes other equivalent concepts, such as ha-bitual residence, "home state", or, in the case of juridical persons like corporations, the principal place of business. See, e.g., *Dorsey* v. *Yantambwe*, 715 NYS 2d 566 (NYAD 4th Dept. 2000) (holding that the domicile of a corporate defendant is in the state of its principal place of business and applying the law of that state, which was also the plaintiff's domicile, to a dispute arising from an accident in another state.); *Elson* v. *Defren*, 726 NYS 2d 407 (NYAD 2001) (holding that a nationwide rental company that had its principal place of business in New York should be treated as a New York domiciliary for purposes of applying the *Neumeier* rules); *Sheldon* v. *PHH Corp.*, 135 F. 3d 848 (2d Cir. 1998) (accord).

6.   Of course, in some cases the conduct may have occurred in more than one state, as in products liability cases in which the product was designed in one state, tested in an-other, and manufactured in another state. See *infra* 205. Similarly, in some cases the injury may be in more than one state, as in multistate defamation cases. Nevertheless, in order to keep things relatively simple, the following discussion focuses on typical cases which do not present these factual complexities.

7.   Naturally, the list of contacts could be longer so as to include, for example, the place of the parties' pre-existing relationship, if any. However, for the purposes of this dis-

flicts on the basis of factual contacts only, one would arrange them into: (1) common-domicile cases arising from torts in another case; (2) split-domicile cases involving intrastate torts; and (3) split-domicile cases involving cross-border torts.

2.   The content of the involved laws

126. Another important lesson of the modern American conflicts experience is that one cannot resolve conflicts intelligently and rationally without considering the substantive content of the laws of each involved state, and without making that content an integral part of the whole choice of-law process. This fundamental premise should be kept in mind, not only by the judge in resolving conflicts, but also by the commentator in discussing and analyzing them.

Loss-distribution laws may be grouped into two major categories, depending on whether their application benefits the injured party (hereafter "victim" or "plaintiff"), or the party whose conduct is claimed to have caused the injury (hereafter "tortfeasor" or "defendant"). Based on these categories, loss-distribution conflicts can be grouped into: (1) cases in which each involved state has a law that favors its own domiciliary; and (2) cases in which each state has a law that favours the domiciliary of the other state.

3.   The typical fact-law patterns in conflicts involving two states

127. Putting factual contacts and pertinent substantive laws in the mix produces multiple fact-law patterns, depending on how many states are involved in the conflict. In the most common cases which involve only two states, the combination of contacts and laws produces eight typical patterns, which are described below. These patterns are also depicted in Table 6, *infra*, and are numbered in the order in which they will be discussed.

a.   *Common-domicile cases.* These are cases in which the parties are domiciled in the same state and are involved as tortfeasor and victim in a tort committed entirely in another state. Depending on the content of each state's law, these cases can be subdivided into cases in which the law of the common domicile:
   (1)   favours the plaintiff (while the law of the state of the tort favours the defendant) *(Pattern 1)*; or
   (2)   favours the defendant (while the law of the state of the tort favours the plaintiff) *(Pattern 2)*[8];
b.   *Split-domicile intra-state tort cases.* These are cases in which the tortfeasor and the victim are domiciled in different states but in which *both* the conduct

---

cussion, which is to categorize cases into primary patterns rather than to resolve them in a judicial fashion, the list is confined to the primary contacts.

8.   A variation of these patterns occurs when the parties are domiciled in different states which, however, have loss-distribution laws that produce the same outcome. See *infra* 135-136.

and the injury occur in the home state of one of the parties. Depending on which of the two parties is domiciled in that state and which party its law favors, these cases can be divided into four patterns, as follows:

(1)   cases in which the conduct and the injury occur in the defendant's home state, and in which that state's law:

  (a) favours the defendant (while the law of the plaintiff's home state favours the plaintiff) *(Pattern 3)*; or

  (b) favours the plaintiff (while the law of the defendant's home state favours the defendant) *(Pattern 6)*; and

(2)   cases in which the conduct and the injury occur in the plaintiff's home state, and in which that state's law:

  (a) favours the plaintiff (while the law of the defendant's home state favours the defendant) *(Pattern 4)*; or

  (b) favours the defendant (while the law of the defendant's home state favours the plaintiff) *(Pattern 5)*;

c.   *Split-domicile cross-border tort cases.* These are cases in which the parties are domiciled in different states and in which the conduct and the injury also occur in different states. The most common cases of this broad category are those in which the conduct occurs in the tortfeasor's home state and the injury occurs in the plaintiff's home state. Depending on the content of the two states' laws, these cases can be subdivided into cases in which:

(1)   the law of each home-state favours the domiciliary of that state *(Pattern 7)*; or

(2)   the law of each home-state favours the domiciliary of the other state *(Pattern 8)*

Obviously, there are several additional variations, especially when one adds a third state to the mix. Nevertheless, the aforementioned eight patterns are the most common, and the following discussion is confined to them. Table 6, below, depicts these patterns for the reader's convenience. In this table, the letters A and B, in uppercase or lowercase, represent the two states involved in the conflict. The use of a boldface uppercase letter indicates that the state represented by that letter has a "higher standard of financial protection"[9] for the victim, i.e., it favours recovery, while the use of a lowercase letter indicates that the particular state has a "lower standard of financial protection", i.e., it does not allow or limits recovery.

9.   The quoted terms are borrowed from D. Cavers, *The Choice of Law Process*, 139, *et passim* (1965).

Table 6. Patterns in loss-distribution conflicts involving two states

Pattern #	Plaintiff's Domicile	State of injury	State of Conduct	Defendant's Domicile	Currie's Classification
Common-Domicile Cases – Intrastate Torts					
1	**A**	b	b	**A**	False
2	a	**B**	**B**	a	False
Split-Domicile Cases – Intrastate Torts					
3	**A**	b	b	b	True
4	**A**	A	A	b	True
5	a	a	a	**B**	Unprovided
6	a	**B**	**B**	**B**	Unprovided
Split-Domicile Cases – Cross-Border Torts					
7	**A**	A	b	b	True
8	a	a	**B**	**B**	Unprovided

C.   Common-Domicile Cases Arising from Torts in Another State

128. Of the 42 states that have abandoned the *lex loci delicti* rule, the vast majority (32 cases or 76%) did so in cases involving intra-state torts of the common-domicile pattern, namely cases in which parties domiciled in the same state were involved in a tort that was committed entirely in *another* state. Thus, it is appropriate to begin this discussion with these cases. Suffice it to say at the outset that all but one[10] (or 98%) of the 32 cases applied the law of the common domicile.

As explained above, common-domicile cases can be divided into two permutations, depending on the content of the law of the common domicile:

1.   Pattern 1 (the *Babcock* pattern), in which the law of the state of the common domicile favours recovery more than the law of the state of conduct and injury; and

2.   Pattern 2 (the converse-*Babcock* pattern), in which the law of the common domicile is less favourable to recovery than the law of the state of conduct and injury.

---

10.   The only case that applied the law of the place of the injury while abandoning general adherence to the *lex loci delicti* rule was *Peters* v. *Peters*, 634 P. 2d 586 (Haw. 1981). This case arose out of a Hawaii traffic accident in which a New York domiciliary was injured while riding in a rented car driven by her husband. Her suit against him and ultimately his insurer was barred by Hawaii's interspousal immunity law, but not by New York's law. The court applied Hawaii law because the insurance policy that had been issued on the rental car in Hawaii had been written in contemplation of Hawaii immunity law.

1.   *Pattern 1: The* Babcock *pattern*

129. The *Babcock* pattern appeared in 26 of the 32 common-domicile cases in which a court of last resort abandoned the *lex loci* rule. The same pattern appeared in at least nine more state supreme court cases decided after the particular court had abandoned that rule, thus raising the total number of *Babcock*-pattern cases to 35. Table 7 depicts these cases and uses shading to denote the state whose law the court applied.

Table 7. Babcock-pattern cases (Pattern 1)

#	Case name	Forum state	Contact States and their Laws			
			Plaintiff's Domicile **Pro-P**	State of injury Pro-D	State of Conduct Pro-D	Defendant's Domicile **Pro-P**
Guest-Statute Cases						
1	Babcock	**NY**	**NY**	ON	ON	**NY**
2	Wilcox	**WS**	**WS**	NE	NE	**WS**
3	Clark	**NH**	**NH**	VT	VT	**NH**
4	Mellk	**NJ**	**NJ**	OH	OH	**NJ**
5	Wessling	**KY**	**KY**	IN	IN	**KY**
6	Woodward	**RI**	**RI**	MA	MA	**RI**
7	Kennedy	**MO**	**MO**	IN	IN	**MO**
8	Beaulieu	**ME**	**ME**	MA	MA	**ME**
9	Rostek	**CO**	**CO**	SD	SD	**CO**
10	Bishop	**FL**	**FL**	NC	NC	**FL**
11	Dym	NY	NY	CO	CO	NY
12	Tooker	**NY**	**NY**	MI	MI	**NY**
13	Macey	**NY**	**NY**	ON	ON	**NY**
Inter-spousal-Immunity Cases						
14	Armstrong	**AK**	**AK**	YU	YU	**AK**
15	Schwartz	**AZ**	**NY**	AZ	AZ	**NY**
16	Pevoski	**MA**	**MA**	NY	NY	**MA**
17	Forsman	UT	**CA**	UT	UT	**CA**
18	Peters	HI	NY	HI	HI	NY
19	Nelson	ILL	**ON**	ILL	ILL	**ON**
Intra-family Immunity Cases						
20	Balts	**MN**	**MN**	WS	WS	**MN**
21	Jagers	**LA**	**LA**	MS	MS	**LA**
Compensatory Damages						
22	Fornaris	**PR**	**PR**	St.T	St.T	**PR**
23	Brickner	**OK**	**OK**	Mex	Mex	**OK**
24	Gutierrez	**TX**	**TX**	Mex	Mex	**TX**
25	Miller v. M	**NY**	**NY**	ME	ME	**NY**
26	Miller v. W	**VT**	**VT**	Qu	Qu	**VT**
27	Wendelken	**AZ**	**AZ**	Mex	Mex	**AZ**
Other Issues						
28	Fabricious	**IA**	**IA**	MN	MN	**IA**
29	Mitchell	**MS**	**MS**	LA	LA	**MS**
30	Sexton	**MI**	**MI**	VA	VA	**MI**
31	O'Connor	**CN**	**CN**	Qu	Qu	**CN**
32	Travelers	**DE**	**DE**	Qu	Qu	**DE**
33	Myers	**DC**	**DC**	VA	VA	**DC**
34	Esser	**ILL**	**ILL**	Mex	Mex	**ILL**
35	Cribb	**RI**	**RI**	NH	NH	**RI**

As the above table indicates, 33 of the 35 cases (or 94%) applied the law of the parties common domicile in conflicts involving guest statutes[11], inter-spousal[12] or intrafamily[13] immunity, compensatory damages[14], and other similar conflicts[15] between the loss-distribution rules of the common domicile and the state of the

11. These cases are: *Babcock* v. *Jackson*, 191 NE 2d 279 (NY 1963 (New York parties, Ontario accident and guest statute); *Wilcox* v. *Wilcox*, 133 NW 2d 408 (Wis. 1965) (Wisconsin parties, Nebraska accident and guest statute); *Clark* v. *Clark*, 222 A. 2d 205 (NH 1966) (New Hampshire parties, Vermont accident and guest statute); *Mellk* v. *Sarahson*, 229 A. 2d 625 (NJ 1967) (New Jersey parties, Ohio accident and guest statute); *Wessling* v. *Paris*, 417 SW 2d 259 (Ky. 1967) (Kentucky parties, Indiana accident and guest statute); *Woodward* v. *Stewart*, 243 A. 2d 917 (RI 1968) (Rhode Island parties, Massachusetts accident and guest statute); *Kennedy* v. *Dixon*, 439 SW 2d 173 (Mo. 1969) (Missouri parties, Indiana accident and guest statute); *Beaulieu* v. *Beaulieu*, 265 A. 2d 610 (Me. 1970) (Maine parties, Massachusetts accident and guest statute); *First Nat'l Bank* v. *Rostek*, 514 P. 2d 314 (Colo. 1973) (Colorado parties, South Dakota accident and guest statute); and *Bishop* v. *Florida Specialty Paint Co.*, 389 So. 2d 999 (Fla. 1980) (Florida parties, North Carolina accident and guest statute). For post-*lex loci* cases, see *Tooker* v. *Lopez*, 301 NYS 2d 519 (NY 1969) (New York parties, Michigan accident and guest statute); *Macey* v. *Rozbicki*, 221 NE 2d 380 (NY 1966) (New York parties, Ontario accident and guest statute).

12. These cases are: *Armstrong* v. *Armstrong*, 441 P. 2d 699 (Alaska 1968) (Alaska spouses, accident in Yukon territory); *Schwartz* v. *Schwartz*, 447 P. 2d 254 (Ariz. 1968) (New York spouses, Arizona accident); *Pevoski* v. *Pevoski*, 358 NE 2d 416 (Mass. 1976) (Massachusetts spouses, New York accident); *Forsman* v. *Forsman*, 779 P. 2d 218 (Utah 1989) (California spouses, Utah accident). See also *Nelson* v. *Hix*, 522 NE 2d 1214 (Ill. 1988), cert. denied, 488 US 925 (1988) (Ontario parties, Illinois accident).

13. These cases are: *Balts* v. *Balts*, 142 NW 2d 66 (Minn. 1966) (Minnesota parent and child, Wisconsin accident); and *Jagers* v. *Royal Indem. Co.*, 276 So. 2d 309 (La. 1973) (Louisiana parent and child, Mississippi accident).

14. These cases are: *Widow of Fornaris* v. *American Sur. Co.*, 93 PRR 28 (PR 1966) (Puerto Rico parties, accident in St. Thomas); *Brickner* v. *Gooden*, 525 P. 2d 632 (Okla. 1974) (Oklahoma parties, accident in Mexico); *Gutierrez* v. *Collins*, 583 SW 2d 312 (Tex. 1979) (Texas parties, Mexico accident); *Fox* v. *Morrison Motor Freight, Inc.*, 267 NE 2d 405 (Ohio 1971) (Ohio parties, Illinois accident). For post-*lex loci* cases, see *Miller* v. *Miller*, 290 NYS 2d 734 (NY 1968) (New York parties, Maine accident); *Miller* v. *White*, 702 A. 2d 392 (Vt. 1997) (Vermont parties, Quebec accident); *Wendelken* v. *Superior Court*, 671 P. 2d 896 (Ariz. 1983) (Arizona parties, Mexico accident).

15. These cases are: *Fabricious* v. *Horgen*, 132 NW 2d 410 (Iowa 1965) (eligibility for wrongful death action, Iowa parties, Minnesota accident); *Mitchell* v. *Craft*, 211 So. 2d 509 (Miss. 1968) (comparative negligence, Mississippi parties, Louisiana accident); *Sexton* v. *Ryder Truck Rental, Inc.*, 320 NW 2d 843 (Mich. 1982) (vehicle owner's liability law, Michigan parties, Virginia accident); *O'Connor* v. *O'Connor*, 519 A. 2d 13 (Conn. 1986) (tort action vs. administrative remedy, Connecticut parties, Quebec accident); *Travelers Indem. Co.* v. *Lake*, 594 A. 2d 38 (Del. 1991) (tort action vs. administrative remedy, Delaware parties, Quebec accident). For post-*lex loci* cases, see *Esser* v. *McIntire*, 661 NE 2d 1138 (Ill. 1996) (applying Illinois's pro-recovery law to action between Illinois parties arising out of injury sustained during the parties' common vacation in Mexico); *Cribb* v. *Augustin*, 696 A. 2d 285 (RI 1997) (applying Rhode

tort[16]. The two cases that did not apply the law of the common domicile were factually distinguishable, and one of them was subsequently over-ruled[17]. In addition, many cases decided during the lex loci era also applied the law of the common domicile, thus foreshadowing the eventual abandonment of the lex loci rule[18].

In the most recent of the 35 cases, *Miller* v. *White*[19], the court stated that "every American court"[20] that has considered cases of the *Babcock* pattern under a significant-contacts test has applied the law of the parties' common domicile. The court reasoned that the application of this law "correspond[s] with international norms and promote[s] consistent treatment of accident victims across borders"[21].

The *Miller* court applied Vermont law to an action between Vermont parties arising out of a single-car accident in Quebec. Vermont's law allowed a tort action, but Quebec's no-fault law confined the plaintiff to an administrative remedy and a much lower recovery. After reiterating the distinction between conduct-regulation and loss-distribution issues, the court characterized the issue in question as one that "raises competing policies that allocate postevent losses"[22] and concluded that, with regard to such an issue, "the domicile of the parties is the most significant contact bearing on the determination of the relevant law"[23].

Island's pro-plaintiff statute of limitation in dispute between Rhode Island domiciliaries arising from incident in New Hampshire).

16. The common domicile was in the forum state in all but three of these cases (*Schwartz* v. *Schwartz*, 447 P. 2d 254 (Ariz. 1968); *Forsman* v. *Forsman*, 779 P. 2d 218 (Utah 1989); *Nelson* v. *Hix*, 522 NE 2d 1214 (Ill. 1988)).

17. *Peters* v. *Peters*, 634 P. 2d 586 (Haw. 1981), was factually exceptional. See *supra* 128 footnote 10. Arguably, the same was true of the other case, *Dym* v. *Gordon*, 209 NE 2d 792 (NY 1965), in which the parties had a less-than-transient relationship with the accident state and which also involved third parties. In any event, *Dym* must be deemed overruled by *Tooker* v. *Lopez*, 301 NYS 2d 519 (NY 1969) or at least superseded by *Neumeier* Rule 1 (*supra* 93).

18. *Emery* v. *Emery*, 289 P. 2d 218 (Cal. 1955), and *Haumschild* v. *Continental Cas. Co.*, 95 NW 2d 814 (Wis. 1959), are among the oldest and best-known examples of such cases. Similar cases appear in the few states that continue to adhere to the *lex loci* rule. For example, in *Owen* v. *Owen*, 444 NW 2d 710 (SD 1989), the court refused on public policy grounds to apply the guest statute of the accident state, Indiana, and applied instead the law of the parties' common domicile, South Dakota. Three years later, this court abandoned the *lex loci* rule. See *Chambers* v. *Dakotah Charter, Inc.*, 488 NW 2d 63 (SD 1992) (applying South Dakota law to case arising out of Missouri accident involving South Dakota parties). Likewise, in *Boone* v. *Boone*, 546 SE 2d 191 (SC 2001), discussed *supra* 47, the court refused on public policy grounds to apply the interspousal immunity rule of the state of the accident, Georgia, and applied instead the non-immunity rule of the spouses' domicile, South Carolina.

19. 702 A. 2d 392 (Vt. 1997).

20. *Id.* at 397 n. 4.

21. *Id.* at 397.

22. *Id.* at 394.

23. *Id.* at 394-395.

The court found that Quebec's no-fault law was designed to "expedite compensation to victims of automobile accidents, reduce the amount of tort litigation in Quebec courts, and guarantee relatively low automobile-insurance rates"[24]. The court reasoned that Quebec had "'little interest in ... the rights of action of an United States citizen against another United States citizen in an United States court'"[25]. In contrast, said the court, Vermont, as the domicile of both parties and the place of their relationship, as well as the place where the "social and economic repercussions of personal injury will occur"[26], had a "strong interest in applying its law"[27].

The above cases indicate that, in common-domicile cases of the *Babcock* pattern, American courts that have abandoned the *lex loci* rule are virtually unanimous in applying the law of the parties' common domicile. According to one commentator, this is the revolution's "only unqualified success"[28] and perhaps its "most enduring contribution"[29].

2.   *Pattern 2: The converse-Babcock pattern*

130. In cases of the converse-*Babcock* pattern, there is also strong, though less than unanimous, support for applying the law of the common-domicile. This pattern appeared in six cases in which a court of last resort abandoned the *lex loci* rule, and in nine other state supreme court cases decided after the particular court had abandoned that rule. Table 8 depicts these 15 cases and uses shading to indicate the state whose law the court applied.

---

24. *Id.*
25. *Id.* at 395. The court noted: "Pursuit of this claim will not raise insurance rates in Quebec nor hinder the administration of its courts. Quebec does not seek to deter negligent conduct by a fault-based determination of liability." *Id.* at 395-396.
26. *Id.* at 396.
27. *Id.*
28. H. Korn, "The Choice-of-Law Revolution: A Critique", 83 *Colum. L. Rev.* 772, 788-789 (1983).
29. *Id.*

Table 8. Converse-Babcock pattern cases (Pattern 2)

#	Case name	Forum state	Contact states and their laws			
			Plaintiff's Domicile Pro-D	State of injury **Pro-P**	State of Conduct **Pro-P**	Defendant's Domicile Pro-D
1	Ingersoll	ILL	ILL	WS	WS	ILL
2	Issendorf	ND	ND	MN	MN	ND
3	Johnson	ID	SAS	ID	ID	SAS
4	Hubbard	IN	IN	ILL	IN	IN
5	Chambers	SD	SD	MO	MO	SD
6	Hataway	TN	TN	AR	AR	TN
7	Fuerste	IA	IA	WS	WS	IA
8	Schultz	NY	NJ	NY	NY	NJ
9	Collins	ME	CAN	ME	ME	CAN
10	Myers	VT	Quebec	VT	VT	Quebec
11	Lessard	NH	ON	NH	NH	ON
12	Conklin	WS	ILL	WS	WS	ILL
13	Milkovich	MN	ON	MN	MN	ON
14	Arnett	KY	OH	KY	KY	OH
15	Martineau	VT	Quebec	VT	VT	Quebec

As the table indicates, eleven of the 15 cases (or 73%) applied the pro-defendant law of the common domicile, rather than the pro-recovery law of the accident state[30], while four cases reached the opposite result[31].

131. Of the four cases that did *not* apply the law of the common domicile, the only one that is relatively recent, *Martineau* v. *Guertin*[32], is also factually atypical. Although the parties were domiciled in the same state, they resided together in another state, and the accident occurred in a third state, the law of which was identical to the residence state. This factor tipped the scales in favour of the accident state[33].

---

30. For cases abandoning the *lex loci* rule, see *Ingersoll* v. *Klein*, 262 NE 2d 593 (Ill. 1970) (Iowa accident, Illinois parties and less favourable law on damages); *Issendorf* v. *Olson*, 194 NW 2d 750 (ND 1972) (Minnesota accident, North Dakota parties and contributory negligence rule); *Johnson* v. *Pischke*, 700 P. 2d 19 (Idaho 1985) (Idaho accident, Saskatchewan parties and worker's compensation immunity); *Hubbard Mfg. Co.* v. *Greeson*, 515 NE 2d 1071 (Ind. 1987) (Illinois injury, Indiana parties and pro-manufacturer products liability law); *Chambers* v. *Dakotah Charter, Inc.*, 488 NW 2d 63 (SD 1992) (Missouri accident, South Dakota parties and contributory negligence rule); *Hataway* v. *McKinley*, 830 SW 2d 53 (Tenn. 1992) (Arkansas accident, Tennessee parties and contributory negligence rule). In all but one of these cases (*Johnson* v. *Pischke, supra*), the common domicile was in the forum state.

For cases decided after the abandonment of the *lex loci* rule, see *Fuerste* v. *Bemis*, 156 NW 2d 831 (Iowa 1968) (Wisconsin accident, Iowa parties and guest statute); *Schultz* v. *Boy Scouts of America, Inc.*, 480 NE 2d 679 (NY 1985) (discussed *supra* 94-95; applying the charitable immunity rule of New Jersey, the state where the plaintiffs and one of the defendants were domiciled rather than the law of New York where the wrongful conduct occurred and which did not provide for charitable immunity); *Collins* v. *Trius, Inc.*, 663 A. 2d 570 (Me. 1995) (discussed *infra* 132) applying Canadian law, which did not allow recovery for pain and suffering, to a case arising out of a Maine accident involving Canadian parties); *Myers* v. *Langlois*, 721 A. 2d 129 (Vt. 1998) (applying Quebec law and denying a tort action in a dispute between Quebec parties arising out of a Vermont accident); *Lessard* v. *Clark*, 736 A. 2d 1226 (NH 1999) (applying the law of Ontario, the parties' common domicile, which provided for lower-recovery, rather than the law of New Hampshire, the accident state). In four of these cases (except for *Fuerste*), the common domicile was in the non-forum state.

31. See *Conklin* v. *Horner*, 157 NW 2d 579 (Wis. 1968) (applying Wisconsin law allowing an action by Illinois guest-passenger against an Illinois host-driver and arising out of a Wisconsin accident. Illinois' guest statute barred the action); *Milkovich* v. *Saari*, 203 NW 2d 408 (Min. 1973) (applying Minnesota law allowing an action by Ontario guest-passenger against Ontario host-driver and arising out of a Minnesota accident. Ontario's guest statute barred the action); *Arnett* v. *Thompson*, 433 SW 2d 109 (Ky. 1968) (applying Kentucky law and allowing an action between Ohio spouses that was not allowed by Ohio's interspousal immunity rule and guest statute); *Martineau* v. *Guertin*, 751 A. 2d 776 (Vt. 2000) (discussed *infra* 131).

32. 751 A. 2d 776 (Vt. 2000).

33. The accident state was Vermont, which was also the forum state, whose law allowed a tort action. The parties were domiciled in Quebec, whose no-fault law confined the plaintiff to an administrative remedy and a low recovery. However, both parties had

The remaining three cases are rather old and discredited. They too applied the (pro-plaintiff) law of the accident state, but in all of them the accident state was also the forum state. This fact can explain the outcome much better than any other factor, especially since two of these cases, *Conklin* v. *Horner*[34] and *Milkovich* v. *Saari*[35], were decided under the usually pro-plaintiff and pro-forum better-law approach that now appears to be losing both steam and luster[36], while the third case, *Arnett* v. *Thompson*[37] was decided under Kentucky's unapologetically parochial *lex fori* approach. Indeed, the *Arnett* court was quite blunt in stating that "the conflicts question should not be determined on the basis of a weighing of interests, but simply on the basis of whether Kentucky has enough contacts to justify applying Kentucky law. Under that view if the accident occurs in Kentucky (as in the instant case) there is enough contact from that fact alone to justify applying

---

been living and working together in Connecticut for a long time, their relationship was centered there, and the accident occurred while they were returning from Quebec to Connecticut through Vermont. The car involved in the accident was registered in Connecticut and insured by a Connecticut insurer. Because Connecticut's law was identical to Vermont's, the court reasoned that "the Connecticut contacts must be grouped with the Vermont contacts in determining whether the Quebec contacts are significant enough", *id.* at 779, and that, with such a grouping, "the significance of the parties' common legal domicile is considerably reduced". *Id.* Thus, the court concluded, any interest Quebec might have was "not significant enough to overcome the [Restatement Second §175] presumption that the law of Vermont – the place where the injury and wrongful conduct occurred – should govern the dispute." *Id.* at 781. For another case in which the common domicile was outweighed by other more significant factors, see *Grover* v. *Isom*, 53 P.3d 821 (Idaho 2002) (although the parties were domiciled in Idaho, the defendant was practicing medicine in Oregon and the action arose out of a medical procedure he performed in his Oregon clinic).

In *Coutellier* v. *Ouellette*, 798 So. 2d 42 (Fla. App. 2001), the parties were domiciled in Quebec and had an accident in Florida where they resided separately for several months every year. Florida law allowed a tort action and unlimited damages, while Quebec's no-fault system confined the plaintiff to an administrative remedy and a much lower recovery. The court held that Florida law governed, after stating that this case could be classified as a false conflict in that it involved two persons who for several months each year resided in Florida and who were involved in an accident in the very community in which they resided. The court also noted that Florida had a substantial interest in compensating persons injured within its borders, that the plaintiff received extensive treatment in two Florida hospitals, and that those hospitals were protected by a special law with a lien on settlement proceeds.

34.   157 NW 2d 579 (Wis. 1968) (described *supra* footnote 31).

35.   203 NW 2d 408 (Minn. 1973) (described *supra* footnote 31).

36.   See *supra* 74-79. The two cases also invoked the interests of the forum-accident state in providing recovery for accident victims injured within the state, ensuring recovery of medical costs incurred by local hospitals, and deterring violation of local traffic laws.

37.   433 SW 2d 109 (Ky. 1968) (described *supra* footnote 31).

Kentucky law"[38]. This reasoning has little persuasive value, especially when juxtaposed to other Kentucky cases such as *Wessling* v. *Paris*[39] and *Foster* v. *Leggett*[40] in which the same court applied Kentucky's pro-plaintiff law even though the accidents did not occur there[41].

Despite their limited contemporary persuasive value, cases like *Conklin*, *Milkovich*, and *Arnett* deserve attention to the extent they articulated the interest of the accident state, *when it has a pro-recovery law*, to ensure recovery of medical costs resulting from the tort and, to a lesser extent, to deter wrongful conduct within that state. Although the New York Court of Appeals dismissed this interest in *Schultz*[42], other courts may be more hesitant to reject it, especially when the accident state is also the forum state[43]. This interest does not necessarily trump, but it rivals to some extent the interest of the parties' common-domicile in denying or reducing recovery. Thus, the very presence of an interest, even a weak one, on the part of the accident state prevents the easy classification of reverse-*Babcock* cases into the classic false conflict paradigm and suggests the need for an appropriate escape clause.

132. Be that as it may, the majority of cases involving the converse-*Babcock* pattern, including the most recent ones, have applied the law of the common domicile with little hesitation. For example, in *Collins* v. *Trius, Inc.*[44], the supreme court of Maine refused to apply Maine's pro-recovery law to the actions of Canadian passengers of a Canadian bus that was involved in an accident in Maine. The court noted that, "[a]lthough Maine ha[d] a significant interest in regulating conduct on its highways"[45], the issue at stake, recovery for non-economic loss, was "primarily loss-allocating rather than conduct-regulating"[46]. The court continued as follows:

---

38. *Id.* at 113. See also *id.* (reiterating that "the basis of the application [of Kentucky law] is not a weighing of contacts but simply the existence of enough contacts with Kentucky to warrant applying our law.").

39. 417 SW 2d 259 (Ky. 1967).

40. 484 SW 2d 827 (Ky.1972) (discussed *supra* 68 and *infra* 139).

41. *Wessling* applied Kentucky's pro-plaintiff law to an Ohio accident involving Kentucky parties. *Foster* did the same in a case involving an Ohio accident and defendant and a Kentucky plaintiff.

42. See *supra* 94.

43. See L. Weinberg, "Theory Wars in the Conflict of Laws", 103 *Mich. L. Rev.* 1631, 1665 (2005) (arguing that, in such a case, "the forum, as place of injury, has legitimate governmental interests in applying its own remedial law to benefit the nonresident plaintiff, notwithstanding the laws of the joint domicile, ... [and that] the interested forum not only can, but should, furnish the remedy to the nonresident plaintiff, if only to avoid a discriminatory departure from its own law").

44. 663 A. 2d 570 (Me. 1995).

45. *Id.* at 573.

46. *Id.*

"[O]ne incontestably valuable contribution of the choice-of-law revolution in the tort conflict field is the line of decisions applying common-domicile law ... The superiority of the common domicile as the source of law governing loss-distribution issues is evident. At its core is the notion of a social contract, whereby a resident assents to casting her lot with others in accepting burdens as well as benefits of identification with a particular community, and ceding to its lawmaking agencies the authority to make judgments striking the balance between her private substantive interests and competing ones of other members of the community."[47]

3.   A common-domicile rule

133. The above review indicates that, when both the tortfeasor and the injured party are domiciled in the same state, judicial opinions converge on the proposition that the state of the common domicile has a better claim to apply its law to loss-distribution issues than the state of conduct and/or injury. As the *Schultz* court stated, in these cases, "the locus jurisdiction has at best a minimal interest in determining the right of recovery or the extent of the remedy"[48], and proper analysis favours the jurisdiction of common domicile "because of its interest in enforcing the decisions of both parties to accept both the benefits and the burdens of identifying with that [state] and to submit themselves to its authority"[49].

Based on sheer numbers, one can safely conclude that, *regardless* of which modern choice-of-law methodology or philosophy they follow, American courts that have abandoned the *lex loci* rule have adopted the above thesis in cases of both the *Babcock* and the converse-*Babcock* patterns. All together, a total of 50 common-domicile cases have reached 34 state supreme courts with, and since, the abandonment of the *lex loci delicti* rule. Forty-four of these cases (or 88%) applied the law of the common domicile and six cases (12%) did not. (See chart 10 below.) Of the latter cases, two were factually exceptional[50], one was overruled[51], and the remaining three are probably discredited[52].

---

47. *Id.* The court concluded that, in light of the parties' common domicile in Canada and its other contact with the case, "Canada has the most significant interest with respect to the issue of damages for non-pecuniary harm in this case." *Id.*

48. *Schultz*, 491 NYS 2d at 96.

49. *Id.*

50. See *Peters* v. *Peters, supra* 128 footnote 10, and *Martineau, supra* 131.

51. See *Dym* v. *Gordon, supra* 129 footnote 17.

52. See *Conklin, Milkovich,* and *Arnett, supra* 131.

Chart 10. Cases applying common-domicile law

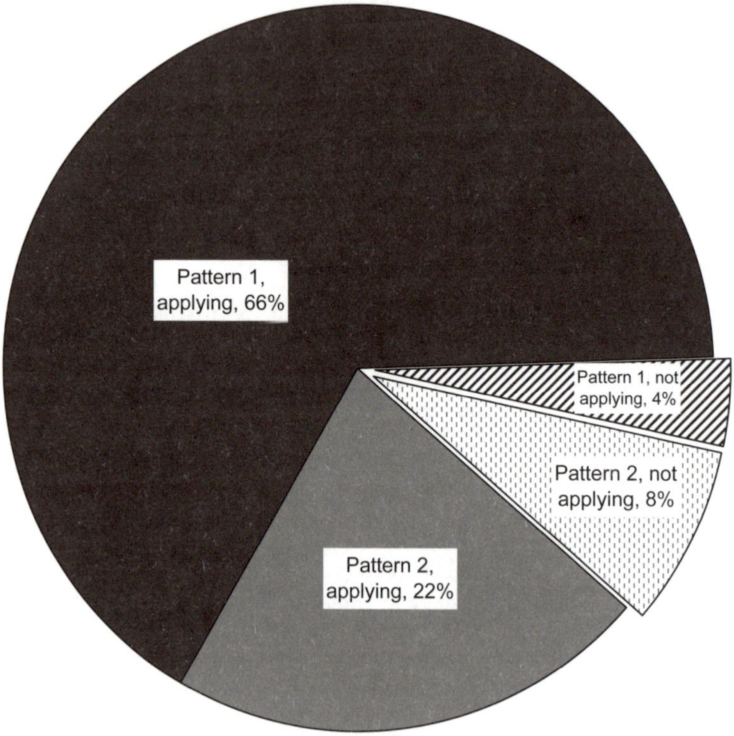

These numbers are convincing, especially because they originate in courts of all modern methodological and philosophical persuasions. Indeed, based on these numbers one may accurately speak of the emergence of a *de facto* common-domicile *rule*. This rule can be phrased in terms that are both content-neutral and forum-neutral, as follows:

> RULE I. *When the injured party (victim) and the party whose conduct caused the injury (tortfeasor) are domiciled in the same state, the law of that state governs* [whether it favours the victim (Pattern 1) or the tortfeasor (Pattern 2)].

134. In this sense, both *Neumeier* Rule 1[53] and the corresponding rule of the Louisiana codification[54] accurately reflect the contemporary American case law when

---

53.   See *supra* 93.

54.   The Louisiana rule is contained in Article 3544(1), which provides that the law of the common-domicile applies to "[i]ssues pertaining to loss distribution and financial protection ... as between a person injured by an offense or quasi-offense and the person who caused the injury". However, unlike the *Neumeier* rule, the Louisiana

they call for the application of the law of the common domicile in both the *Babcock* sub-pattern and its converse.

A "common-country" rule, for both of these, has also emerged in the rest of the world. As documented elsewhere[55], recent private international law codifications and international conventions have also adopted the notion of applying the law of the country with which both parties are affiliated, either through domicile or nationality. This notion is implemented either through a common-domicile rule (as in the Belgian, Swiss, Quebec, and Puerto Rico codifications, and the Hague Convention on Products Liability)[56], or through an exception from the *lex loci* rule. The exception is phrased either in common-domicile or common-habitual residence language (as in the proposed Rome II Regulation, and the Dutch, German, Hungarian, and Tunisian codifications)[57], or in common-nationality language (as in the Portuguese, Polish, Italian and Russian codifications)[58]. Other codifications contain exceptions which, though not explicitly phrased in common-domicile language, are very likely to be employed in common-domicile situations[59].

---

rule is subject to escapes contained in Articles 3547 ("exceptional cases") and 3548 ("corporate tortfeasors"). These articles authorize a judicial deviation from the common-domicile rule in appropriate cases. For the operation of these escapes in a case like *Schultz*, see S. Symeonides, "Resolving Six Celebrated Conflicts Cases through Statutory Choice-of-Law Rules", 48 *Mercer L. Rev.* 837, 853-854 (1997).

55. See E. Scoles, P. Hay, P. Borchers and S. Symeonides, *Conflict of Laws* 804-806 (4th ed. 2004).

56. See Belgian Code of PIL of 2004, Art. 99(1)(1); Swiss PIL Act, Art. 133; Quebec Civ. Code, Art. 3126; Puerto Rican Draft Code of PIL, Art. 47(a); Hague Convention on the Law Applicable to Products Liability of 1972, Art. 5.

57. See, Commission of the European Communities, Proposal for a Regulation of the European Parliament and the Council on the Law Applicable to Non-Contractual Obligations, Art. 3(2), COM(2003) 427 final, 2003/0168(COD), Brussels, 22.7.203; (Netherlands) Act Regarding Conflict of Laws on Torts, Art. 3(3), Staatsblad 2001, 190; EGBGB Art. 40 (2); Hungarian PIL Act of 1979, § 32(3); Tunisian Code of Private International Law (Law N. 98-97 of 27 November 1998), Art. 70(3).

58. See Portuguese Civ. Code, Art. 45; Polish PIL Act of 1966, Art. 31 (2); Italian PIL Act of 1995, Art. 62; Civil Code of the Russian Federation, Art. 1219(2) (2001). See also Chinese Society of Private International Law, "Model Law of Private International Law of the People's Republic of China (6th Draft, 2000)", Art. 114, 3 *Ybk. Priv. Int'l L.* 349 (2001).

59. This is the case, for example, in the Austrian codification, the English PIL statute of 1995, the Hague Traffic Accidents Convention, and some other international conventions. These exceptions are not expressly confined to issues of loss distribution. However, they are more likely to be so confined in actual application because these codifications contain varying admonitions to the effect that, in applying another law, the court should "not prejudice" or should "take into consideration" the laws of conduct and safety prevailing at the place of conduct. For citations and discussion, see E. Scoles, P. Hay, P. Borchers and S. Symeonides, *Conflict of Laws*, 805-806 (4 th ed. 2004).

All of the above rules are phrased in bilateral terms that are not only fo-rum-neutral, but also party-neutral and content-neutral as well[60]. They authorize the application of the law of the common domicile, whether that law favours the plaintiff (as in the *Babcock* pattern) or the defendant (as in the converse-*Babcock* pattern).

In the United States, a common-domicile rule enjoys universal approval in cases of the first pattern which, after all, present the classic false-conflict para-digm. However, as noted earlier, the rule encounters objections in cases of the second pattern where the accident state has a certain interest in applying its pro-recovery law so as to provide recovery to those injured within its borders and to ensure recovery of medical costs.[61] On balance, however, this interest is not strong enough to outweigh either the interests of the common domicile or the other benefits of the common-domicile rule. The *Schultz* court was correct to speak of the "concepts of mutuality and reciprocity"[62], and so was the *Collins* court in speaking of "a social contract notion"[63] whereby domiciliaries of the same state agree to "accept[] burdens as well as benefits of identification with a particu-lar community"[64].

For these reasons, a common-domicile rule that cuts both ways, is superior to a unilateral rule. Nevertheless, when such a rule is cast in statutory language, one must exercise caution not to completely deprive courts of the necessary flex-ibility to deviate from the rule in exceptional cases. This is why, unlike the judi-

---

60. Professor Sedler believes that the common-domicile rule emerging from the cases is tied to the parties' affiliation with the forum state. According to Sedler, when the parties' common domicile is in the forum state, the courts apply that state's law re-gardless of whether it favors recovery. However, when the common domicile is in the non-forum state, the courts apply that state's law when it favors recovery, but are divided when it does not favor recovery. See R. Sedler, "Choice of Law in Conflicts Torts Cases: A Third Restatement or Rules of Choice of Law?", 75 *Ind. LJ* 615, 619-622 (2000). Professor Posnak endorses a common-domicile rule that is forum-and content-neutral but which would be only a presumptive rule. See B. Posnak, "The Restatement (Second): Some Not So Fine Tuning for a Restatement (Third): A Very Well-Curried Leflar over Reese with Korn on the Side (or is it Cob?)", 75 *Ind. LJ* 561, 565 (2000).

61. See *supra* 131. Professor Weinberg states that the prevailing faith in the common do-micile "seems to be a species of mass mistake, something like the ineradicable com-mon belief that the Declaration of Independence is either in the Constitution, or is the Constitution". L. Weinberg, "Theory Wars in the Conflict of Laws", 103 *Mich. L. Rev.* 1631, 1665 (2005). Weinberg agrees that the law of the common domicile should govern in cases of the *Babcock* pattern. However, in cases of the converse-*Babcock* pattern, Weinberg would apply the law of the common domicile only if that domicile is in the *forum* state. See *id.* At 1665-66.

62. *Schultz*, 491 NYS 2d 90 at 98.

63. *Collins v. Trius, Inc.*, 663 A. 2d 570, 573 (Me. 1995). *Collins* is discussed *supra* 132.

64. *Id.*

cially enunciated *Neumeier* Rule 1, the Louisiana rule, which is statutory, is accompanied by appropriate escapes[65].

At the same time, a common-domicile rule can go too far if it is phrased so broadly as to extend beyond loss-distribution issues. This appears to be the case with some civilian formulations such as those in the Italian, Quebec, and Polish codifications[66], which provide for the application of the law of the parties' common domicile or nationality without any differentiation on whether the issue involved is a loss-distribution or conduct-regulation issue, and without allowing any escape.

4.   Cases analogous to common-domicile cases

135. A variation of Patterns 1 and 2 appear when the tortfeasor and the victim are domiciled in different states which, however, adhere to loss-distribution rules that produce the same result[67]. For example, in a case like *Babcock*, if the defendant had been domiciled in New Jersey (rather than in New York) and if New Jersey (like New York) did not have a guest statute (Pattern 1a), there would be little argument that the resulting conflict would be as false as *Babcock* itself, and that it should be resolved by allowing the action to proceed. Similarly, in a converse-*Babcock* case, if the two parties had been domiciled in Ontario and Quebec, respec-

---

65.   See *supra* footnote 54.

66.   See Italian PIL Act, Art. 62 (2); Quebec Civ. Code, Art. 3126(2); Polish PIL Act, Art. 31 (2).

67.   A somewhat similar pattern appears when the parties, though not domiciled in the same state, are nevertheless parties to a pre-existing relationship that is centred in a state other than the state of injury. European codifications such as the Swiss, German, and Dutch codifications, as well as the Proposed Rome II Regulation have adopted the notion that the law that governs the parties' pre-existing relationship displaces the law that would otherwise govern the tort. For citations, see E. Scoles, P. Hay, P. Borchers and S. Symeonides, *Conflict of Laws*, 808-809 (4th ed. 2004). See also Belgian Code of PIL of 2004, Art. 100.

In the United States, neither the literature nor the case law have sufficiently explored this notion. However, the place in which the parties' relationship, if any, is centered is one of the contacts that courts consider under the Restatement (Second), or other modern approaches, in selecting the applicable law. Professor Cavers's Principles 4 and 5 provide that in such cases the law of the state where the relationship is centred applies, whether that state has a higher (Principle 4) or lower (Principle 5) standard of financial protection for the victim than the state of injury, and without mention of whether the former state is also the parties' domicile. See D. Cavers, *The Choice-of-Law Process*, 166, 177 (1965). However, the fact that his discussion of Principles 4 and 5 is confined to cases in which the relationship in centred in the state of the parties' common domicile, as well as some of his other statements, see *id.* at 151, suggests that Cavers intended these Principles to function as a common-domicile rule rather than to displace such a rule.

tively, and both of these provinces had a guest statute (Pattern 2a), the resulting conflict would not differ in any material way from that present in *Milkovich*[68].

In *Bauer* v. *Club Med Sales, Inc.*[69], which was decided under California's comparative impairment, the court used the common-domicile analogy, although the parties were domiciled in different states. *Bauer* arose out of an accident in an American-owned hotel in Mexico that caused the death of a California vacationer. The court applied Mexican law to the conduct-regulating issue of premises liability[70]. However, with regard to the amount of damages for the victim's wrongful death, the court took note of the parties' common affiliation with the United States, including defendant's status as an American corporation, and held that California's pro-recovery law should govern. The court also reasoned that Mexico did not have an interest in applying its limited-damages rule because that rule was designed "to protect its resident defendants from excessive financial burdens" and since the defendant was "not a Mexico corporation, Mexico ha[d] no interest in having its damages rules apply."[71]

In contrast, in *Sutherland* v. *Kennington Truck Service, Ltd.*[72], a case decided under Michigan's *lex fori* approach, the court applied the law of the forum and accident state and allowed the foreign plaintiff's action, although both the plaintiff and the defendant were domiciled in states that had an identical statute of limitation barring the action. However, *Sutherland* is atypical for three reasons. First, it involved a statute-of-limitations conflict, to which most courts apply the law of the forum even when, as in *Sutherland*, they do not follow the traditional procedural characterization of limitations. Second, *Sutherland* was decided under the *lex fori* approach, which, more often than not, leads to forum law[73]. Third, *Sutherland* involved the converse-*Babcock* pattern because the accident state, in addition to being the forum, had a law that *allowed* recovery. As noted earlier, cases of this pattern are not as clear false conflicts as those of the *Babcock* pattern.

136. Be that as it may, the better view is that the cases of both Pattern 1a and Pattern 2a are functionally analogous to common-domicile cases and should be treated accordingly. New York courts have done so, even though the *Neumeier*

---

68. See *supra* 131.

69. 1996 WL 310076 (ND Cal. 1996).

70. See *infra* 169 footnote 27.

71. *Bauer*, 1996 WL 310076 at *6. The court rejected defendant's argument that the application of California law would impair Mexico's interest in fostering tourism in Mexico: "While Mexico's tourism interest may be served by [defendant]'s presence there, [defendant], as a United States corporation, benefits from that presence. Neither Mexico's nor California's interest is served by limitations on damages for California citizens when a United States corporation is found negligent".

72. 562 NW 2d 466 (Mich. 1997).

73. In *Olmstead* v. *Anderson*, 400 NW 2d 292 (Mich. 1987), the *lex fori* approach led to the application of Michigan law, even though Michigan was not the accident state. The accident occurred in Wisconsin and involved a Michigan tortfeasor and a Minnesota victim. Unlike Wisconsin, which limited recovery, Michigan and Minnesota law allowed unlimited recovery.

rules do not directly authorize this result. *Neumeier* Rule 1 is technically inapplicable because it requires that the parties be domiciled in "the *same* state"[74] for that state's law to apply. Thus, these cases fall within the scope of *Neumeier* Rule 3, which calls for the application of the law of the accident state, subject to the escape.

Among the New York cases involving this pattern, one case ignored the *Neumeier* rules altogether and allowed recovery by "[a]pplying the so-called 'interest analysis' of *Babcock* and *Schultz*"[75]. A second case recognized that *Neumeier* Rule 1 was "facially inapplicable", but concluded that the rationale underlying that rule justified the same result – since the parties were domiciled in "states that share a common perspective on this issue of law, neither can complain that this Court subjects them to the standard of care commensurate with the law of their respective domicile"[76]. The court concluded that the application of the law of either party's domicile "fully comports with the policies served by the first *Neumeier* rule"[77]. A third case followed the same reasoning and reached the same result through Rule 3[78]. Finally, a fourth case stated directly that "there should be no dif-

---

74. See *supra* 93.

75. *Reach* v. *Pearson*, 860 F. Supp. 141, 143 (SDNY 1994). In *Reach*, the plaintiffs and defendants were domiciled in New Jersey and New York, respectively, and were involved in a traffic accident in Quebec. Quebec's no-fault law limited the amount of damages, while both New Jersey and New York provided for unlimited recovery. The court did not cite *Neumeier*, but quoted *Schultz's* statement that "[t]he domicile of the parties ... becomes the more significant contact when the conflicting laws involve allocation of losses". *Id.* The court concluded that "New York's interests outweigh those of Quebec", *id.*, because "the conflict relates to the allocation of losses rather than the governing standard of conduct ..., [t]he significant contact ... is the parties' domiciles ..., [and] Quebec, the locus jurisdiction, has the less significant interest in disputes between nonresidents". *Id.*

76. *Diehl* v. *Ogorewac*, 836 F. Supp. 88, 92 (EDNY 1993). In this case, a New York plaintiff was injured in a North Carolina accident while riding as a passenger in a car driven by a New Jersey defendant. Although all three states required passengers to wear seat belts, only North Carolina prohibited the admission into evidence of a passenger's failure to wear a seat belt. The court implicitly characterized the North Carolina rule as substantive and then explicitly as loss-allocating because that rule "does not regulate conduct since it does not purport to limit the scope of permissible conduct in North Carolina". *Id.*

77. *Id.* at 92. The court also explained why the same result would follow under the escape provided in *Neumeier* Rule 3. See *id.* at 93-94. In *Sheldon* v. *PHH Corp.*, 135 F. 3d 848 (2d Cir. 1998), which arose out of a Michigan accident, the defendant corporation had its principal place of business in New York, which was also the plaintiff's domicile, thus leading to New York law under *Neumeier* Rule 1. The court held that, even if Rule 1 did not apply, New York law should still govern under the escape of Rule 3. Michigan, but not New York, law provided a loss of consortium action.

78. See *O'Connor* v. *U.S. Fencing Ass'n*, 260 F.Supp.2d 545, 559 (EDNY 2003) ("[T]he expectations of the parties could not be more clear. Both [parties] have 'chosen to identify themselves in the most concrete form possible, domicile, with jurisdiction[s]

ference in result where the plaintiff and defendant have the same domicile (where the first *Neumeier* rule governs and the law of the common domicile applies), and the plaintiff and defendant have a split domicile but with the same domiciliary law (where the third *Neumeier* rule governs)"[79].

Indeed, there should be no difference, and this result would have been reached more directly if *Neumeier* Rule 1 were phrased like the corresponding Louisiana rule, which provides that "[p]ersons domiciled in states whose law on the particular issue is substantially identical shall be treated as if domiciled in the same state"[80]. This legal fiction, which is particularly useful in cases with multiple victims or defendants, enables a court to resolve these false conflicts by applying the law of the domicile of either party, unless the general escape clause of the codification dictates a different result. The American Law Institute has recommended a similar rule for mass tort cases[81].

D.   Split-Domicile Cases – Intrastate Torts

137. This section discusses split-domicile cases involving intrastate torts, namely cases in which the tortfeasor and the victim are not domiciled in the same state, but are involved in a tort that occurs entirely in the home state of either the tortfeasor or the victim[82]. Obviously, some of these cases present the false conflict paradigm, such as when the laws of the two states produce the same outcome. Such cases need not occupy us here.

Instead, the following discussion focuses on cases in which the two states have different loss-distribution laws that produce a different outcome. If the law of each state favours the domiciliary of that state, the case presents a *direct* con-

---

that have weighed the [pertinent] interests' ... and resolved the conflict in favor of recovery." (quoting *Schultz*, 480 N.E.2d at 686). This case arose out of a fencing competition in California that resulted in injury to a New York amateur athlete who sued the competition's organizer, a Colorado-based corporation. New York and Colorado law, but not California law, allowed recovery. The court held for the plaintiff.

79.   *Gould Elect. Inc.* v. *United States*, 220 F. 3d 169, 187 (3d Cir. 2000) (decided under New York conflicts law).

80.   La. Civ. Code Art. 3544 (1). In addition, in certain cases involving corporate tortfeasors, the Louisiana common-domicile rule is subject to further expansion, or contraction, through Article 3548 which provides that a juridical person that is domiciled outside the forum state but transacts business in that state and incurs a tort obligation arising from such activity may be treated as a domiciliary of that state, if such treatment is appropriate under the principles of Article 3542. For pertinent discussion, see S. Symeonides, "Louisiana's New Law of Choice of Law for Tort Conflicts: An Exegesis", 66 *Tul. L. Rev.* 677, 759-763 (1992).

81.   See American Law Institute, *Complex Litigation: Statutory Recommendations and Analysis*, § 6.01 *(c)* (2) and (3) (1994) ("Plaintiffs shall be considered as sharing a common habitual residence or primary place of business if they are located in states whose laws are not in material conflict.").

82.   For split-domicile cross-border conflicts, see *infra* 151-159.

flict or what interests analysts call a *true* conflict. If the law of each state favours the domiciliary of the other state, the case presents an *inverse* conflict or what interest analysts call the *unprovided-for*, or *no-interest* paradigm. For the sake of convenience, the following discussion adopts the terminology of interest analysis, and begins with cases that fall within the true-conflict paradigm.

1.   True conflicts

138. This subsection discusses split-domicile cases of intrastate torts in which each domiciliary state has a loss-distribution rule that favours its own domiciliary, thus creating a direct or true conflict. Depending on which domiciliary state has the additional contacts of conduct and injury, these cases can be further subdivided into the following two primary patterns: *(a) Pattern 3*: Split-domicile cases in which both the conduct and the injury occur in the tortfeasor's home state, which has a law that favours the tortfeasor; and *(b) Pattern 4*: Split-domicile cases in which both the conduct and the injury occur in the victim's home state, which has a law that favours the victim.

(a)   Pattern 3: Split-domicile cases in which the conduct, the injury, and the tortfeasor's domicile are in a state whose law favours the tortfeasor

(1)   The cases

139. *Foster* v. *Leggett*[83] and *Cipolla* v. *Shaposka*[84] are both well-known, old illustrations of split-domicile cases falling within Pattern 3. In both cases, the conduct and injury (traffic accident) occurred in the defendant's home state, which had a guest statute favouring the defendant and his insurer. *Foster* applied the pro-plaintiff law of the victim's domicile (which was also the forum state), whereas *Cipolla* applied the pro-defendant law of the defendant's domicile, which was the accident and non-forum state.

In *Foster*, the Kentucky court acknowledged that its decision was based exclusively on the presence of contacts with the forum state *qua* forum, rather than on any other considerations. The court stated bluntly that its "primary responsibility is to follow its own substantive law"[85], that "[t]he basic law is the law of the forum, which should not be displaced without valid reasons"[86], and that "if there are significant contacts – *not necessarily the most significant contacts* – with [the

---

83.   484 SW 2d 827 (Ky. 1972) (discussed *supra* 68; refusing to apply Ohio's guest state and allowing under Kentucky law an action arising from an Ohio accident involving an Ohio host-driver and a Kentucky guest-passenger).

84.   267 A. 2d 854 (Pa. 1970) (applying Delaware's guest-statute and thus denying recovery to a Pennsylvania plaintiff injured in Delaware while riding as a guest-passenger in a car owned and driven by a Delaware host-driver).

85.   *Foster*, 484 SW 2d at 829.

86.   *Id.*

forum], then [forum] law should be applied"[87]. For reasons explained earlier[88], such a self-centered approach has little to contribute to the rational resolution of interstate or international conflicts and should be ignored for this reason.

In *Cipolla*, a Pennsylvania court took a non-parochial approach that resulted in the application of the Delaware guest statute, which favoured a Delaware host-driver at the expense of a Pennsylvania guest-passenger. The court found that Delaware's contacts were "qualitatively greater than Pennsylvania's"[89], and that Delaware's policies – protecting host-drivers and ensuring stability of insurance rates – were more pertinent because this case involved a Delaware host-driver and a car insured in that state. Hence, Delaware had "the greater interest in having its law applied"[90].

More meaningful than this debatable comparison of contacts was the court's reasoning regarding the parties' expectations or at least reliance, which was influenced by Professor Cavers. "It seems only fair", said the court, "to permit a defendant to rely on his home state's law when he is acting within that state ... . Inhabitants of a state should not be put in jeopardy of liability exceeding that created by their state's law just because a visitor from a state offering higher protection decides to visit there."[91] Conversely, "'[b]y entering the state ... the visitor has exposed himself to the risk of the territory and should not subject persons living there to a financial hazard that their law had not created'"[92]. As the old saying goes, "when in Rome do as Romans do,"[93] not because of Roman imperialism but rather because it is more in line with both party expectations and state policies.

---

87.   *Id.* (emphasis added).
88.   See *supra* 68.
89.   267 A. 2d at 856.
90.   *Id.*
91.   *Id.*
92.   *Id.*, quoting D. Cavers, *The Choice-of-Law Process*, 146-147 (1965).
93.   *Bledsoe* v. *Crowley*, 849 F. 2d 639, 647 (DC Cir. 1988) (Williams, J., concurring) (discussed *infra* 140).

140. Without explicitly subscribing to this precise maxim but following a similar rationale, the vast majority of cases falling within Pattern 3 cases have reached the same result as Cipolla. They resisted the temptation of applying the pro-plaintiff law of the plaintiff's home state, which in many of these cases was also the forum state, and instead applied the pro-defendant law of the defendant's home state, which was also the locus delicti. Some of these cases have been decided under the same "mixed" approach as Cipolla[94]. However, more numerous are the cases decided under other approaches, such as the Second Restatement,[95]

---

94.   See, e.g., *Shuder* v. *McDonald's Corp.*, 859 F. 2d 266 (3 rd Cir. 1988) (applying Virginia contributory-negligence law, rather than Pennsylvania comparative-negligence law, to an action filed against McDonald's by a Pennsylvania plaintiff who slipped and fell in the parking lot of one of defendant's Virginia restaurants); *Blakesley* v. *Wolford*, 789 F. 2d 236 (3d Cir. 1986) (applying Texas pro-defendant medical consent and damages-limitation law to medical malpractice action filed by Pennsylvania domiciliary against Texas oral surgeon for surgery performed in Texas); *Evans* v. *Valley Forge Convention Center*, 1996 WL 468688 (ED Pa. 1996) (applying Pennsylvania's pro-defendant parental supervision law to action filed by New Jersey parents against Pennsylvania defendants arising out of Pennsylvania accident).

95.   In addition to *Casey*, *Malena*, and *Grover*, which are discussed *infra*, see, e.g., *McBride* v. *Whiting-Turner Contracting Co.*, 1993 WL 489487 (Del. Super. 1993) aff'd. 645 A. 2d 568 (Del. 1994) (applying Maryland's law immunizing a Maryland employer from a tort suit brought by a Delaware worker injured in Maryland, while working for defendant's subcontractor.); *Byrn* v. *American Universal Ins. Co.*, 548 SW 2d 186 (mo. App. 1977) (applying Iowa guest-statute, rather than Missouri's pro-recovery law, and denying a remedy to the survivors of a Missouri domiciliary who was killed in an Iowa accident while riding as passenger in a car driven by an Iowa defendant and insured there); *Ricci* v. *Alternative Energy Inc.*, 211 F. 3d 157 (1st Cir. 2000) (decided under Maine's conflicts law; applying Maine's pro-defendant law to a work-related accident in Maine that caused the death of Rhode Island worker); *Bowman* v. *Koch Transfer Co.*, 862 F. 2d 1257 (6th Cir. 1988) (decided under Ohio conflict law; applying Illinois' limited-damages law to an action arising from an Illinois traffic accident involving an Illinois defendant and an Ohio victim); *Marion Power Co.* v. *Hargis*, 698 So. 2d 1246 (Fla. App. 1997) (applying Florida's pro-defendant law to action of Illinois employee of Indiana subcontractor against Florida contractor arising out of Florida injury).

interest analysis[96], New York's Neumeier Rule 2a[97], and even the lex-fori[98] and the better-law[99] approaches.

96. In addition to *Eger, Bledsoe,* and *Lebegern,* which are discussed *infra,* see *Herbert* v. *District of Columbia,* 808 A.2d 776 (D.C. 2002) (applying D.C's pro-defendant damages law to an action filed against a D.C. policeman and his employer for the wrongful death of Maryland domiciliary who was accidentally shot in D.C.); *Amoroso* v. *Burdette Tomlin Mem'l Hosp.,* 901 F. Supp. 900 (DNJ 1995) (applying New Jersey's pro-defendant law to survival action filed against New Jersey hospital and building-owner by Pennsylvania domiciliary whose son died during a New Jersey surgery following an injury in the owner's premises).

97. In addition to *Cooney* v. *Osgood Mach., Inc.,* 612 NE 2d 277 (NY 1993), discussed *supra* 96-99, see *Kranzler* v. *Austin,* 732 NYS 2d 328 (N.Y. Sup. Ct. 2001) (applying New York's pro-defendant law to a case arising out of a New York traffic accident involving a New York defendant and a New Jersey plaintiff); *Feldman* v. *Acapulco Princess Hotel,* 520 NYS 2d 477 (N.Y. Sup.Ct. 1987) (applying Mexico's limited-damages law to New York plaintiff's action arising from a swimming pool accident in Mexican defendant's hotel in Mexico); *Barkanic* v. *General Adm'n of Civil Aviation of the People's Republic of China,* 923 F. 2d. 957 (2d Cir. 1990) (applying China's limited-damages rule to American plaintiffs' action arising from the crash in China of an airplane operated by Chinese defendant); *Mascarella* v. *Brown,* 813 F. Supp. 1015, (SDNY 1993) (applying New York law to a wrongful death action resulting from medical malpractice committed in New York by a New York defendant against a North Carolina domiciliary. North Carolina law was more favourable to the victim than New York law); *Pascente* v. *Pascente,* 1993 WL 43502 (SDNY 1993) (applying Connecticut's pro-defendant contributory negligence law to action arising out of Connecticut accident involving Connecticut defendant and New York victim; characterizing contributory negligence rules as loss-allocating); *Ditonto* v. *Rent-A-Fence,* 2004 WL 1242742 (NDNY 2004) (adopting the same characterization and applying North Carolina's pro-defendant contributory negligence law to action arising out of North Carolina accident involving North Carolina defendant and New York victim); *Reale* v. *Herco, Inc.* 589 NYS 2d 502 (App. Div. 1992) (applying Pennsylvania's pro-defendant contribution law to action by a New York minor injured in a Pennsylvania amusement park owned by Pennsylvania defendant); *Miller* v. *Bombardier, Inc.,* 872 F. Supp. 114 (SDNY 1995) (applying Quebec's pro-defendant law, rather than Connecticut's pro-plaintiff law, to personal-injury and loss-of-consortium actions filed by Connecticut spouses after husband was injured during a snowmobiling trip in Quebec that was organized by a Quebec defendant); *Boxer* v. *Gottlieb,* 652 F.Supp. 1056 (SDNY 1987) (applying pro-defendant vicarious liability law of France in New Yorker's action against French car-owner arising from car accident in France). See also *Bankers Trust Co.* v. *Lee Keeling & Assoc., Inc.* 20 F. 3d 1092 (10th Cir. 1994) (discussed *supra* 99); *Venturini* v. *Worldwide Marble & Granite Co.,* 1995 WL 606281 (SDNY 1995) (discussed *supra* 99, footnote 234).

98. See *Motenko* v. *MGM Dist., Inc.,* 921 P. 2d 933 (Nev. 1996), (discussed *supra* 70; applying Nevada law to an action for loss of parental consortium brought by a Massachusetts domiciliary whose mother was injured in defendant's Nevada hotel. Massachusetts, but not Nevada, allowed the action.)

99. See, e.g., *Benoit* v. *Test Sys., Inc.,* 694 A. 2d 992 (NH 1997) (applying New Hampshire's pro-defendant law, rather than Massachusetts' pro-plaintiff law, to action arising out

The old case *Casey v. Manson Construction & Engineering Co.*[100] is representative of cases decided under the Restatement Second. In *Casey*, a Washington defendant acting in Washington caused injury to an Oregon domiciliary. The victim's wife sued the defendant in Oregon for loss of consortium, a remedy that was available under Oregon, but not Washington, law. The Oregon court applied Washington law, reasoning that Washington defendants "should not be required to accommodate themselves to the law of the state of any traveler whom they might injure in Washington; [and] and that Washington's interest in the matter, which was protective of Washington defendants, was paramount to Oregon's interest in having its resident recover for her loss"[101]. More recent cases decided under the Restatement Second have adopted a similar rationale.[102]

Eger v. E.I. Du Pont De Nemours Co.[103] is representative of cases decided under interest analysis. In *Eger*, a New Jersey court applied South Carolina's pro-de-

---

of New Hampshire employment accident and filed by a Massachusetts employee against a New Hampshire employer who had borrowed plaintiff from his Massachusetts employer); *Reed v. Univ. of North Dakota*, 543 NW 2d 106 (Minn. App. 1996) (applying North Dakota pro-defendant immunity law, rather than Minnesota non-immunity law, and dismissing action against North Dakota state entity filed by Minnesota plaintiff for injury in North Dakota – Distinguishing *Nevada v. Hall, infra* 142, on the ground that, unlike *Hall*, this case arose out of actions that occurred in defendant's home state. See 543 NW 2d at 110.).

100. 428 P. 2d 898 (Or. 1967).

101. *Erwin v. Thomas*, 506 P. 2d 494, 497-498 (Or. 1973) See also *Casey*, 428 P. 2d 898, 908 (Hollman, J. concurring) ("Washington citizens carrying on activities in Washington [should not] have to lift their financial protection to an unaccustomed level and one which would be dependent on the locality from which the injured party might come.").

102. For example, in *Malena v. Marriott Int'l, Inc.*, 651 NW 2d 850 (Neb. 2002), a Nebraska court applied California's pro-defendant rather than Nebraska's pro-plaintiff damages law to the action of a Nebraska domiciliary who was injured in a California hotel owned by a defendant doing substantial business in California. The court reasoned that California law reflected a "concern that unrestricted claims would adversely affect the availability and affordability of liability insurance", that since "the conduct and injury have occurred in California", that state's interests "should be considered the dominant interests", and that "the visitor should ordinarily anticipate that the foreign state's law will govern any tort which results from conduct and injury occurring there". *Id.* at 857. In *Grover v. Isom*, 53 P.3d 821 (Idaho 2002), an Idaho court applied Oregon's pro-defendant law rather than Idaho's pro-plaintiff law to a medical malpractice action filed by an Idaho plaintiff and arising from a medical procedure performed in the Oregon clinic of a doctor domiciled in Idaho. The court found that Oregon had the most significant relationship because, although the doctor was domiciled in Idaho, he was licensed and practiced in Oregon and "had every expectation that Oregon law would govern [his] business in Oregon" while Oregon had "an interest in making certain that oral surgeons practicing in Oregon are subject to Oregon laws". *Id.* at 824 Moreover, the plaintiff's presence in Oregon was "not fortuitous" in that she "purposefully went to Oregon for the operation". *Id.*

103. 539 A. 2d 1213 (NJ 1988).

fendant law, rather than New Jersey's pro-plaintiff law, to a New Jersey employee's action against a South Carolina employer arising out of an employment accident in South Carolina. South Carolina law immunized the South Carolina employer from a tort action, whereas New Jersey law provided a tort action for the employee and allowed his own employer, a New Jersey subcontractor, to recoup from the South Carolina contractor the compensation benefits paid to the employee. Nevertheless, the court concluded that New Jersey's interests in protecting its domiciliaries was "not strong enough to outweigh South Carolina's interest"[104] in immunizing employers operating in South Carolina from tort liability as a quid pro quo for requiring them to furnish workers' compensation coverage for their subcontractors' employees.

In *Tucci* v. *Club Méditerranée, S.A.*[105], the court, using California's comparative impairment, applied the pro-defendant law of the Dominican Republic to an action of a California domiciliary who was injured while working in the defendant's club in the Dominican Republic[106]. The court noted that California had an interest in adequately providing for employees hired in California, and in assuring that employers who solicited California employees were adequately insured through credit-worthy carriers regulated by California. However, the court found that the Dominican Republic also had an interest in making sure that employers in that country "face limited and predictable financial liability ... and in ... predictably defining the duties and liabilities of employers doing business within its border, all with the goal of encouraging business investment and development there"[107]. The court concluded that the law of the Dominican Republic should govern because that country's interests would be more impaired if its law was not applied.

Finally, in *Bledsoe* v. *Crowley*[108], a medical malpractice case decided under interest analysis, a District of Columbia court refused to apply the District's pro-plaintiff law to the action of a District domiciliary. Instead, the court applied the pro-defendant law of Maryland, where the medical services had been rendered, because that state was the "jurisdiction with the stronger interests"[109]. A concurring judge would accord this result the status of an all-encompassing rule for medical malpractice conflicts. After pointing out that "patients are inherently on notice that journeying to new jurisdictions may expose them to [unfavourable] rules"[110], the judge concluded that "[t]he maxim 'When in Rome do as Romans

---

104. *Id.* at 1218.
105. 107 Cal. Rptr. 2d 401 (Cal. App. 2001).
106. Under Dominican Republic law, the plaintiff would be confined to workers' compensation and Social Security benefits. Under California law, the plaintiff would be entitled to a tort action, because the employer had not procured workers' compensation insurance through a California carrier, as required by a California statute.
107. *Tucci*, 107 Cal. Rptr. 2d at 408-09.
108. 849 F. 2d 639 (DC Cir. 1988).
109. *Id.* at 641. Maryland, but not District of Columbia, required compulsory arbitration before a medical malpractice claim could be pursued judicially.
110. *Id.* at 647 (Williams, J., concurring).

do' bespeaks the common sense view that it is the traveler who must adjust"[111]. As seen above, many other courts have adopted the same rationale[112].

(2) Summary and rule

141. For the reader's convenience, the table reproduced below depicts the cases involving Pattern 3[113], with shading indicating the state whose law the court applied.

---

111. *Id.*

112. For example, in *Lebegern* v. *Forman*, 339 F.Supp.2d 613 (DNJ 2004), an action for the wrongful death of a Pennsylvania motorist who was killed in a New Jersey collision with a car driven by a New Jersey defendant, the court acknowledged the "natural inclination to sympathize with the loss sustained by the [plaintiffs]", *id.* at 622, but applied the pro-defendant law of New Jersey because the conduct and the injury occurred there and the defendants, being New Jersey domiciliaries, were "entitled to expect the financial protections afforded by New Jersey law". *Id.* Conversely, said the court, quoting Professor Cavers, "'[b]y entering the state .. the visitor has exposed himself to the risks of the territory and should not expect to subject persons living there to a financial hazard that their law had not created'". *Id.* New Jersey law favored the defendant driver by limiting the plaintiff's recovery to the decedent's pain and suffering. Pennsylvania law favored the plaintiff by allowing recovery for pain and suffering and for the decedent's expected earning capacity.

113. Unlike the common-domicile cases involving Patterns 1 and 2, *supra*, all of which were decided by state supreme courts, the cases involving Patterns 3-8 include many lower-court cases. Although technically the latter cases have no precedential value, they nevertheless are indicative of the current practices and trends in the American courts.

Table 9. Pattern 3 cases

#	Case name	Forum state	Contact states and their laws			
			Plaintiff's domicile **Pro-P**	State of injury Pro-D	State of conduct Pro-D	Defendant's domicile Pro-D
1	Foster	KY	KY	OH	OH	OH
2	Cipolla	PA	PA	DE	DE	DE
3	Casey	OR	OR	WA	WA	WA
4	Eger	NJ	NJ	SC	SC	SC
5	Tucci	CA	CA	DomRep	DomRep	DomRep
6	Bledsoe	DC	DC	MD	MD	MD
7	Malena	NEB	NEB	CA	CA	CA
8	Grover	ID	ID	OR	OR	OR
9	Shuder	PA	PA	VA	VA	VA
10	Blakesley	PA	PA	TX	TX	TX
11	Feldman	NY	NY	Mex	Mex	Mex
12	Barkanic	NY	US	China	China	China
13	Pascente	NY	NY	CN	CN	CN
14	Ditonto	NY	NY	NC	NC	NC
15	Miller	NY	CN	Quebec	Quebec	Quebec
16	Boxer	NY	NY	France	France	France
17	Reale	NY	NY	PA	PA	PA
18	Reed	MN	MN	ND	ND	ND
19	McBride	DE	DE	MD	MD	MD
20	Byrn	MO	MO	Iowa	Iowa	Iowa
21	Bowman	OH	OH	ILL	ILL	ILL
22	Hebert	DC	MD	DC	DC	DC
23	Lebegern	NJ	PA	NJ	NJ	NJ
24	Benoit	NH	MA	NH	NH	NH
25	Evans	PA	NJ	PA	PA	PA
26	Amoroso	NJ	PA	NJ	NJ	NJ
27	Kranzler	NY	NJ	NY	NY	NY
28	Mascarell	NY	PA	NY	NY	NY
29	Motenko	NV	MA	NV	NV	NV
30	Ricci	ME	RI	ME	ME	ME
31	Marion	FL	ILL	FL	FL	FL

The above table and preceding discussion support the following observations:

1. All 31 cases present the true conflict paradigm in that they all involved situations in which the two states had conflicting loss-distribution laws that protected their respective domiciliaries;

2. Although all 31 cases presented the true conflict paradigm, only 11 of them applied forum law. Moreover, except for *Foster*, which was decided under the *lex fori* approach a long time ago, the remaining 10 cases, all of which

are more recent, applied forum law, not because they subscribed to Currie's prescription that all true conflicts should be decided under the *lex fori*, but rather because of the forum state's other contacts and interests;

3.   The cases also do not follow Currie's proscription of weighing state interests in true conflicts;

4.   Courts are not as parochial as Currie's personal-law principle assumes or instructs them to be.[114] In fact, two thirds of the cases (19 out of 28) applied the pro-defendant law of the non-forum state for the benefit of a non-forum defendant and at the expense of a forum plaintiff[115]; and

5.   Thirty of the 31 cases (again *Foster* being the exception) applied the law of the defendant's home state, which was also the place of the conduct and injury.

If one were to restate these results in the form of a rule, this rule would provide as follows:

> RULE II. *When the conduct and the injury occur in the tortfeasor's home state and that state's law favours the tortfeasor, that law governs* (even if the law of the victim's home state favours the victim).

Neumeier Rule 2a[116] produces the same result as the rule stated above, as does the Louisiana codification[117]. However, unlike the *Neumeier* rule which is "phrased in non-discretionary terms"[118], the Louisiana rule is subject to escapes[119], and also makes explicit what is implicit in the *Neumeier* rule by requiring that *both* the

---

114.   See *supra* 18, 23.

115.   See cases Nos. 2-14, 16-21, in Table 9, *supra*. In all 11 cases that applied forum law, that law favoured a forum litigant but, as explained above, only one case, *Foster*, can be characterized as protectionist.

116.   Rule 2a provides that

> "[w]hen the driver's conduct occurred in the state of his domicile and that state does not cast him in liability for that conduct, he should not be held liable by reason of the fact that liability would be imposed upon him under the tort law of the state of the victim's domicile".

117.   La. Civ. Code Art. 3544 (2) *(a)* provides that, "when both the injury and the conduct that caused it" occurred in the domicile of one party, the law of that state governs. For discussion, see Symeonides, "Louisiana's New Law of Choice of Law for Tort Conflicts: An Exegesis", 66 *Tul. L. Rev.* 677, 726-729 (1992). For an identical rule, see Article 47 of the Puerto Rico Draft Code.

118.   *Barkanic* v. *General Administration of Civil Aviation of the People's Republic of China*, 923 F. 2d. 957, 962 n. 5 (2d Cir. 1990).

119.   See La. Civ. Code Arts. 3547 ("exceptional cases"; *supra* footnote 54) and 3548 ("corporate tortfeasors"; *supra* footnotes 54, 80). Furthermore, the Louisiana rule is confined to disputes between the victim and the tortfeasor and does not encompass disputes between or among tortfeasors.

conduct and the injury must occur in the tortfeasor's home state for that state's law to govern.

Professor Cavers's Principle 2 would also reach the same results. It provides that

> "[w]here the liability laws of the state in which the defendant acted and caused an injury set a lower standard of ... financial protection than do the laws of the home state of the person suffering the injury, the laws of the state of conduct and injury should determine the standard of conduct or protection applicable to the case."[120]

As Cavers reasoned, "[i]nhabitants of [that state] should not be put in jeopardy of liabilities exceeding those [its] law creates simply because persons from states with higher standards of financial protection choose to visit there"[121]. As the preceding discussion illustrates, most courts have arrived at the same conclusion.

(b)   Pattern 4: Split-domicile cases in which the conduct, the injury, and the victim's domicile are in a state whose law favours the victim

(1)   The cases

142. Pattern 4 is the converse of Pattern 3, in that here the conduct and the injury are both in the *victim's* home state, which has a law that favours the victim, while the defendant's home state has a law that favours the defendant. One category of cases involving this pattern are cases in which a governmental entity that enjoys immunity from suit under the law of its home state engages in conduct in another state that does not accord such immunity, and causes injury there.

Nevada v. *Hall*[122] is the most well-known of these cases. In *Hall*, an employee of the University of Nevada, an entity that enjoyed sovereign immunity under Nevada law, drove to California on official university business and caused an accident there, injuring a California domiciliary. The California court refused to recognize Nevada's immunity, or Nevada's $25,000 limitation on damages. The court recognized Nevada's interest in protecting the financial well-being of Nevada entities, but found this interest to be much weaker than California's interest "in providing

---

120. D. Cavers, *The Choice-of-Law Process*, 146 (1965). The principle is accompanied by an exception for cases in which the parties had a pre-existing relationship. See *id.*

121. *Id.* at 148-149. Professor Posnak endorses a similar presumptive rule under interest analysis. He states that "if the parties are not from the same state but a significant portion of the probative facts took place in the home state of *only* one of the parties, its laws should presumptively apply to all the issues". B. Posnak, "The Restatement (Second): Some Not So Fine Tuning for a Restatement (Third): A Very Well-Curried Leflar over Reese with Korn on the Side (or Is It Cob?)", 75 *Ind. LJ* 561, 565 (2000). Professor Sedler believes that the rule emerging from the cases depends on where the action is filed. The courts apply the law of the defendant's home state when the action is filed there, but they are divided when the action is filed in the plaintiff's home state. See R. Sedler, "Choice of Law in Conflicts Torts Cases: A Third Restatement or Rules of Choice of Law?", 75 *Ind. LJ* 615, 623-625 (2000).

122. 44 US 410 (1979).

full protection to those who are injured on its highways through the negligence of both residents and non residents"[123]. The court contrasted this case with *Bernhard v. Harrah's Club*[124] and concluded that California had an even stronger interest in applying its law because, unlike *Bernhard* in which the defendant's conduct had occurred in Nevada, in *Hall* both "the State of Nevada's activities and the [victim's] injuries took place in California"[125]. The court continued: "By thus utilizing the public highways within our state to conduct its business, Nevada should fully expect to be held accountable under California laws."[126]

The United States Supreme Court upheld the constitutionality of the California court's decision after noting, *inter alia*, California's "substantial" interest in "providing full protection to those who are injured on its highways"[127]. Many years later, in *Franchise Tax Bd. of California v. Hyatt*,[128] the shoe was on the other foot. The Supreme Court affirmed the constitutionality of Nevada's refusal to accord sovereign immunity to a California tax assessing agency that was claimed to have caused injury to a Nevada domiciliary in Nevada through acts committed in both Nevada and California. In the intervening years between *Hall* and *Hyatt*, many state courts have also refused, as a choice-of-law matter, to recognize another state's immunity under similar circumstances[129].

---

123. *Hall* v. *Nevada*, 141 Cal. Rptr. 439 at 442 (Cal. App. 1977).

124. 546 P. 2d 719 (1976). *Bernhard* is discussed *supra* 67 and *infra* 179.

125. *Hall*, 141 Cal.Rptr. at 442.

126. *Id.* See also *id.* ("Given the fact that Nevada has chosen to engage in governmental and business activity in this state, the necessary acquisition of additional insurance coverage to protect itself during such an activity is an entirely foreseeable and reasonable expense").

127. *Hall*, 440 US at 423.

128. 538 US 488 (2003).

129. See, e.g., *Struebin* v. *Iowa*, 322 NW 2d 84 (Iowa 1982) (refusing to uphold Illinois' immunity and damages-limitation in a case arising from Iowa accident caused by Illinois' negligence in maintaining a bridge in Iowa. See *id.* at 87: "Iowa's interest in full compensation outweighs Illinois' interest in extending its statutory limitation to its Iowa torts"); *Laconis* v. *Burlington County Bridge*, 583 A. 2d 1218 (Pa. Super. 1990) (refusing to apply New Jersey immunity law to action filed against a New Jersey county by a Pennsylvania domiciliary who was injured on the Pennsylvania side of bridge connecting Pennsylvania to New Jersey and maintained by New Jersey county); *Church* v. *Massey*, 697 So. 2d 407 (Miss. 1997) (refusing to apply Alabama's immunity law to action of Mississippi domiciliary arising from Mississippi accident caused by an Alabama state employee); *Peterson* v. *Texas*, 635 P. 2d 241 (Colo. App. 1981) (Texas not immune from Colorado suit arising from Colorado tort injuring Colorado plaintiff); *Wendt* v. *County of Osceola*, 289 NW 2d 67 (Minn. 1979) (refusing to recognize Iowa's immunity in action arising from Minnesota injury); *Mianecki* v. *Second Judicial Dist. Court*, 658 P. 2d 422 (Nev. 1983) (refusing to recognize Wisconsin's immunity in action arising from Nevada injury).

. *Harris* v. *City of Memphis*, 119 F. Supp. 2d 893 (ED Ark. 2000), is one of the few cases that went the other way by applying the law of the defendant's home state, but it was based on comity, rather than on choice-of-law principles. *Harris* applied Ten-

143. One other sub-category of cases that also reached the same result involve police car chases that began in one state and ended in another, causing injury in the latter state. In one of those cases, *Biscoe* v. *Arlington County*[130], a policeman employed by the defendant, a Virginia county, began chasing a suspected bank robber in that county. The chase continued into the District of Columbia where it ended in an accident injuring plaintiff, an unsuspecting bystander[131]. Under the law of Virginia, but not D.C., the Virginia county would be immune from liability.

The court concluded that neither the Constitution's full faith and credit clause nor principles of comity required the District of Columbia to honour the immunity of the Virginia county. The court held that, under choice-of-law principles, D.C. law governed because "the District's policies would be substantially more seriously thwarted by nonapplication of its law ... than would those of Virginia"[132]. The court found that "Virginia's concern for the economic well-being of its counties ... [was] not an especially compelling one"[133]. In contrast, the District's "interests in deterrence of potential tortfeasors and compensation of injured parties"[134] were "strongly implicated"[135] because the District was "the site of the most relevant conduct and all the injury"[136], and the "defendants' acts created ... danger to District life and property"[137].

---

nessee immunity law to an Arkansas plaintiff's action against a Tennessee city for failure to maintain adequate lighting on the Arkansas side of a bridge connecting Arkansas with Tennessee, which the city had contractually agreed to maintain. *Hansen* v. *Scott*, 687 N.W.2d 247 (ND 2004), also invoked the principle of comity, but it is distinguishable on two additional grounds: (1) it arose out of conduct that occurred in the defendants' home state (Texas) rather than the plaintiff's (North Dakota) (the defendants were Texas parole officials and were charged with negligence in failing to properly supervise a Texas parolee, who then committed a murder in North Dakota); and (2) despite claims to the contrary, it did not *actually* defer to the immunity law of the defendant's home state. The court held the Texas defendants "immune from suit to the same extent the State of North Dakota would grant immunity to its employees under North Dakota law". *Id.* at 251.

130. 738 F. 2d 1352 (DC Cir. 1984).

131. The victim, though a Maryland domiciliary, was working in the District of Columbia and the court treated him as a DC domiciliary, because of the "special and largely unique interest of the District in protecting persons who live in the surrounding suburbs and work in the District". *Id.* at 1361.

132. *Id.* at 1362.

133. *Id.* at 1361.

134. *Id.*

135. *Id.*

136. *Id.*

137. *Id.*

Other cases involving this pattern and similar facts reached the same result as *Biscoe*[138]. The only case that reached the opposite result is *Lommen* v. *The City of East Grand Forks*[139]. In this case, a Minnesota police officer began chasing a stolen car in Minnesota and continued into North Dakota where he collided with another car injuring its passenger, a North Dakota domiciliary[140]. In a brazen display of parochialism, the Minnesota court applied Minnesota immunity law under Leflar's choice-influencing considerations. The court completely discounted the plaintiff's argument that, when a North Dakota domiciliary is injured in North Dakota she has a valid expectation that the consequences of her injury will be determined under that state's law. Instead, the court found that the officer and his employer "had a substantial expectation of on-the-job tort immunity"[141], which apparently they can carry with them on a high speed chase into other states. The court concluded that Minnesota law should govern because "Minnesota's ability to define the immunity of its officials should not vary according to the fortuitous facts of either the location of the accident or the citizenship of the injured party"[142].

Apparently, the court did not realize that this argument could easily be turned around – the rights of an innocent North Dakota citizen, who is maimed in North Dakota, "should not vary according to the fortuitous facts of either ... the citizenship of the [maimer or his employer]"[143]. Indeed, whether it is the result of naivety or blind provincialism, *Lommen* cannot withstand the scrutiny of logic. It is discussed here for purposes of illustration, not emulation.

---

138. See, e.g., *Skipper* v. *Prince George's County*, 637 F. Supp. 638 (DDC 1986) (police car chase from Maryland to District of Columbia, where the chased car injured DC resident – relying on *Biscoe* and applying DC law denying defendant the immunity Maryland law provided). For cases involving other issues, see *Pelican Point Operations* v. *Carroll Childers Co.*, 807 So. 2d 1171 (La. App. 2002) (applying Louisiana's pro-recovery law to a Louisiana plaintiff's action for injury caused to its Louisiana property by a Texas defendant who used self-help in repossessing property in violation of Louisiana law); *Mihalic* v. *K-Mart of Amsterdam, N.Y.*, 363 F.Supp.2d 394 (NDNY 2005) (applying New York law and allowing a New York third-party plaintiff to claim contribution from a Pennsylvania employer in a case arising from a New York work-site accident. Pennsylvania law did not allow contribution).

139. 522 NW 2d 148 (Minn. App. 1994).

140. The victim sued both the officer and his employer, a Minnesota municipality. Under Minnesota law, both the officer and his employer were immune from liability, unless the officer's actions were "willful or malicious". Under North Dakota law, the officer would not be immune if his acts were "grossly negligent", and, regardless of the officer's immunity, his employer was not immune. Thus, to the extent it pertained to the police officer, this case fell within Pattern 4, because the officer acted within North Dakota. To the extent it pertained to the Minnesota employer, this case fell within Pattern 7, *infra*, because the employer's acts or omissions occurred in Minnesota.

141. 522 NW 2d at 150.

142. *Id.* at 152.

143. See *supra* text at footnote 142.

144. Fortunately, no other cases can be found that emulate the *Lommen* analysis, or the result, in situations involving Pattern 4. To the contrary, even cross-border tort cases in which the tortfeasor's conduct occurred *outside* the victim's home state and injured the victim in the latter state applied the pro-plaintiff law of that state. These cases fall within Pattern 7, which is discussed later in this chapter for non-products cases[144], and in Chapter VIII for products liability cases[145]. These cases suggest that, *a fortiori*, the same result is appropriate in Pattern 4 cases in which the tortfeasor's conduct takes place *within* the victim's home state[146]. A person injured in her home state by conduct in that state should be able to rely on the protection of that state's law, regardless of whether the tortfeasor is from that state or from another state whose law protects the tortfeasor.

As Cavers explained, "the system of physical and financial protection [of the victim's domicile] would be impaired if a person who enters the territory of [that] state were not subject to its laws"[147]. That state's domiciliaries "should not be put in jeopardy in [that state] simply because [an out-of-stater] ... had come into [that state] from a state whose law provides a lower standard of financial protection"[148]. The out-of-state defendant who is held to the higher standard of the state of injury "is not an apt subject for judicial solicitude. He cannot fairly claim to enjoy whatever benefits a state may offer those who enter its bounds and at the same time claim exemption from the burdens"[149]. To quote *Bledsoe* again, "[t]he maxim 'When in Rome do as Romans do' bespeaks the common sense view that it is the traveler who must adjust"[150].

(2) Summary and rule

145. For the reader's convenience, the following table depicts the 14 Pattern 4 cases discussed above, and uses shading to denote the state whose law the court applied.

---

144. See *infra* 152-157.
145. See *infra* 213-214, 216, 226.
146. See *Nevada v. Hall*, at text accompanying footnote 125 *supra*.
147. D. Cavers, *The Choice-of-Law Process*, 140 (1965).
148. *Id.* at 142.
149. *Id.* at 141.
150. *Bledsoe* v. *Crowley*, 849 F. 2d 639, 647 (DC Cir. 1988) (Williams, J., concurring).

Table 10. Pattern 4 cases

#	Case name	Forum state	Contact states and their laws			
			P's Dom **Pro-P**	Injury **Pro-P**	Conduct **Pro-P**	D's Dom Pro-D
1	Hall	CA	CA	CA	CA	NV
2	Hyatt	NV	NV	NV	NV	CA
3	Biscoe	DC	DC	DC	DC	VA
4	Struebin	IA	IA	IA	IA	ILL
5	Laconis	PA	PA	PA	PA	NJ
6	Church	MS	MS	MS	MS	AL
7	Peterson	COL	COL	COL	COL	TX
8	Wendt	MN	MN	MN	MN	IA
9	Mianecki	NV	NV	NV	NV	WS
10	Skipper	DC	DC	DC	DC	MD
11	Pelican	LA	LA	LA	LA	TX
12	Mihalic	NY	NY	NY	NY	PA
13	Lommen	MN	ND	ND	ND	MN
14	Harris	ARK	ARK	ARK	ARK	TN

All 14 cases present the true conflict paradigm, in that they all involved situations in which the two states had conflicting laws that protected their respective domiciliaries. Thirteen of the 14 cases applied the law of the forum. However, only one of these cases, *Lommen*, exhibits a Currie-like forum favouritism, although the court did not admit any influence from Currie's theory. In the remaining 12 cases, the forum state had three additional contacts, which would justify the application of that state's law even if it were not the forum.

Twelve of the 14 cases applied the law of the victim's home state, which was also the place of conduct and injury[151]. If one were to restate the above results in the form of a rule, this rule would provide as follows:

RULE III. *When the conduct and injury occur in the victim's home state and that state's law favours the victim, that law applies* (even if the law of the tortfeasor's home state favours the tortfeasor).

---

151. The two exceptions are *Lommen* and *Harris*. Unlike *Lommen*, which is an example of forum favouritism, *Harris* was based on comity. The court decided to defer to the interest of the defendant's home state in immunizing the defendant (a public entity) from civil liability. See *supra* footnote 129.

Neumeier Rule 2b produces the same results as the above stated rule[152], as does the Louisiana codification[153] and Cavers's Principle 1[154].

2.   No-interest or unprovided-for cases

146. The converse of Patterns 3 and 4 cases are those cases in which the conduct, the injury, and one party's domicile are in a state whose law favours the *other* party. These "inverse" conflicts can be subdivided into two patterns:

(1)   *Pattern 5*: Cases like *Neumeier* v. *Kuhner*[155] and *Erwin* v. *Thomas*[156] in which the conduct and the injury occur in the victim's home state, which has a law that favours the tortfeasor who is domiciled in another state; and

(2)   *Pattern 6*: Cases like *Hurtado* v. *Superior Court*[157] in which the conduct and the injury occur in the tortfeasor's home state, which has a law that favours the victim who is domiciled in another state.

Under Currie's assumptions, especially his "personal-law" principle,[158] both patterns present the no-interest paradigm on the theory that neither state would have an interest in protecting the domiciliary of the other state. Currie argued that in these cases the court should apply the law of the forum *qua* forum.[159] Yet, as the following discussion illustrates, only one case, *Erwin* v. *Thomas*, followed Currie's prescription as such, although more cases applied the law of the forum on other grounds.

(a)   Pattern 5: The *Neumeier* pattern

147. *Erwin* was an action for loss of consortium filed by a Washington woman whose husband was injured in Washington by the conduct of an Oregon defendant. Oregon law favoured the Washington plaintiff by allowing such an action, whereas Washington law favoured the Oregon defendant by denying the action.

---

152.   Rule 2b provides that "when the guest was injured in the state of his own domicile and its law permits recovery, the driver who has come into that state should not – in the absence of special circumstances – be permitted to interpose the law of his state as a defense." See *supra* 93.

153.   See La. Civ. Code Art. 3544 (2) *(a)*, *supra* footnote 117.

154.   Principle 1 provides that, when the laws of the state of injury "set a higher standard of ... financial protection against injury than do the laws of the state where the person causing the injury ... had his home" then the laws of the former state should determine "the standard and the protection applicable to the case". D. Cavers, *The Choice-of-Law Process* 139 (1965). The principle is subject to an escape for cases in which the parties had a pre-existing relationship. See *id.* Professor Posnak endorses a similar presumptive rule under interest analysis. See *supra* footnote 121.

155.   286 NE 2d 454 (NY 1972), discussed *supra* 93.

156.   506 P. 2d 494 (Or. 1973), discussed *infra* 147.

157.   522 P. 2d 666 (Cal. 1974), discussed *infra* 149.

158.   See *supra* 18.

159.   See *supra* 22.

The court concluded that "neither state ha[d] a vital interest in the outcome of this litigation"[160]. Washington's defendant-favouring policy was not implicated because this case did not involve a Washington defendant, and Oregon's plaintiff-favouring policy also was not implicated because this case did not involve an Oregon plaintiff[161]. Thus, as Currie said, "neither state cares what happens"[162], and hence, said the court, "an Oregon court does what comes naturally and applies Oregon law"[163].

Labree v. *Major*[164], another old case involving the same pattern, also reached the same result, but under a different theory. *Labree* refused to apply the Massachusetts guest statute to an action arising from a Massachusetts accident involving a Massachusetts guest-passenger, the plaintiff, and a Rhode Island host-driver, the defendant. Instead the court applied Rhode-Island's pro-plaintiff law on the theory that, when the defendant driver is domiciled in a state whose law provides recovery, "the plaintiff should recover no matter what the law of his residence or the place of the accident"[165].

While this was a conclusion in search of a reason, at least it was not self-serving insofar as it benefited a foreign plaintiff at the expense of a forum defendant. In contrast, in cases like *Erny* v. *Estate of Merola*[166], which involved a forum plaintiff and foreign defendants, such a conclusion warrants more scrutiny. *Erny* involved the same pattern as *Erwin* and *Labree* in that the plaintiff was domiciled in the accident state (New Jersey) which had a pro-defendant statute, and the defendants were domiciled in another state (New York), which had a pro-plaintiff statute.[167] The only difference was that in *Erny* the accident state was also the

---

160. *Erwin* v. *Thomas*, 506 P. 2d 494, 496 (Or. 1973).

161. See *id.* ("[I]t is stretching the imagination more than a trifle to conceive that the Oregon Legislature was concerned about the rights of all the nonresident married women in the nation whose husbands would be injured outside of the state of Oregon.")

162. B. Currie, *Selected Essays*, 152.

163. *Erwin*, 506 P. 2d at 496-497. The court also noted that Washington would not object to the application of Oregon law. See *id.* at 496:

    "Washington has little concern whether other states require non-Washingtonians to respond to such claims. Washington policy cannot be offended if the court of another state affords rights to a Washington woman which Washington does not afford, so long as a Washington defendant is not required to respond."

164. 306 A. 2d 808 (RI 1973).

165. *Id.* at 818.

166. 792 A. 2d 1208 (NJ 2002).

167. The two defendants, both New Yorkers, were driving separate cars registered and insured in New York, when they collided with plaintiff's car in New Jersey. The defendants were found 60 and 40 percent at fault, respectively. Under New York's joint and several liability statute, the plaintiff could recover 100% of her damages from either joint tortfeasor, whereas under the New Jersey statute the plaintiff could recover only from the tortfeasor who was 60% at fault (but who was insolvent). In dollar terms, this meant that the New Jersey plaintiff would recover about $290,000 less under New Jersey law than under New York law.

forum statute. In a tortured analysis, the New Jersey court managed to classify this as a false conflict in which New Jersey was uninterested and New York was interested in applying its law.

The court found that the New Jersey statute was designed to protect certain defendants and to reduce the costs of car insurance and, since neither defendant was domiciled in New Jersey nor drove a car insured there, New Jersey did not have an interest in applying the statute.   In contrast, "New York placed more value in protecting the innocent victim ... than reducing the cost of automobile insurance"[168]. But, while New Jersey was interested only in its own defendants, New York was interested in plaintiffs anywhere and from everywhere as long as they sue New York defendants. As the court put it, New York's policy was "aimed at protecting innocent victims of New York vehicle registrants, whether injured or harmed in New York *or elsewhere*"[169], and regardless of whether they were *domiciled* in or *outside New York.*[170] In addition, said the court, the New York statute "encourages [New York] drivers to insure more adequately their vehicles and, inferentially, to drive with care"[171]. Thus, the New York statute "expresses a weightier interest in both compensation and deterrence than does the New Jersey statute"[172] and should be applied for this reason.[173]

In concluding that New York had an interest in protecting non-New York victims injured outside New York, the *Erny* court relied on a 1970 federal district court case[174] and conveniently overlooked New York's later authoritative decision in *Neumeier v. Kuhner*[175], which had held to the contrary in a similar case. And, as

---

168. *Erny*,792 A. 2d at 1218.
169. *Id.* at 1219 (emphasis added).
170. *Id.* at 1220 (emphasis added).
171. *Id.*
172. *Id.*
173. For similar cases decided the same way, see *Farrell v. Davis Enter., Inc.*, 1996 WL 21128 (Pa. Super. 1996) (applying Pennsylvania's pro-plaintiff joint and several liability law, rather than New Jersey's pro-defendant law described in *Erny*, to a New Jersey plaintiff's action against two Pennsylvania joint tortfeasors arising out of New Jersey accident. The court found that Pennsylvania law was in part designed to deter Pennsylvania tortfeasors); *Butkera v. Hudson River Sloop "Clearwater", Inc.*, 693 A. 2d 520 (NJ Super. 1997) (applying New York's non-immunity rule to the action of New Jersey plaintiffs injured in New Jersey by the acts of a New York charitable corporation that was immune under New Jersey law); *Stevens v. Shields*, 499 NYS 2d 351 (NY Sup. Ct. 1986) (following the *Neumeier* rule 3 escape and applying Florida's pro-plaintiff vicarious liability law to a New Yorker's action against a Florida defendant arising from a New York accident. The court found that Florida had a significant interest in applying its law to its domiciliaries, and that this would not impair New York's interest in protecting its residents from liability because a New York defendant was not involved in the case).
174. See *Erny*, 792 A. 2d at 1219 (relying on *Johnson v. Hertz Corp.*, 315 F. Supp. 302, 304 (SDNY 1970)).
175. 286 NE 2d 454 (NY 1973), discussed *supra* 93.

if to dispel any doubts, *Neumeier* also quoted with approval a statement that New York law was "[*not*] intended to be manna for the entire world"[176]. This message was well-received, or at least received, by the lower court in *Erny* when it rejected the premise "that New York would welcome another state's imposition of full responsibility on its resident solely because New York law would permit it"[177]. The court concluded that "[i]t would indeed be anomalous to apply foreign law solely to gain access to a deep pocket when local law denies that access"[178]

Indeed, at least in close cases, the argument that a state has an interest in deterring a particular class of defendants is less likely to be self-serving and thus more likely to be credible when it is made by courts in the defendants' home state than when (as in *Erny*) it is made by courts in the plaintiff's home state. *Kaiser-Georgetown Community Health Plan, Inc.* v. *Stutsman*[179] illustrates this proposition. *Kaiser* was a medical malpractice action filed by a Virginia plaintiff against a District of Columbia corporation arising from treatment in defendant's Virginia hospital. The District of Columbia court decided to apply D.C.'s unlimited-compensatory-damages rule, rather than Virginia's corresponding rule which limited the amount of damages, because D.C. had "a significant interest ... in holding [D.C.] corporations liable for the full extent of the negligence attributable to them"[180]. However, the court also based its decision on an additional ground – although domiciled in Virginia, the plaintiff was employed in D.C. and had chosen the defendant's hospital only because her employer's HMO would not allow other choices[181]. Under these facts, the court concluded that D.C. had an interest in "protecting a member of its work force who contracts for health services with a District of Columbia corporation within this forum and then is injured by the negligence of that corporation's agents"[182].

---

176. *Id.* at 458-59 (quoting Professor Willis Reese).

177. *Erny* v. *Russo*, 754 A. 2d 606, 615 (NJ Super. 2000).

178. *Id.* at 614.

179. 491 A.2d 502 (DC 1985).

180. *Id.* at 509.

181. For a similar case, see *Bucci* v. *Kaiser Permanente Fnd'n Health Plan*, 278 F.Supp.2d 34 (DDC 2003) (refusing to apply Virginia's limited-damages law in an action arising from a medical malpractice in Virginia because, although the plaintiff was a Virginia domiciliary, she was employed in D.C. and her choice of a medical care provider was controlled through a plan provided by her D.C. employer; holding that D.C.'s unlimited-damages law governed because of D.C.'s strong interest in "protecting its workforce and promoting corporate accountability"). *Id.* at 36.

182. *Id.* at 510.Three years later, when the plaintiff's husband sued the same defendants for loss of consortium resulting from his wife's death, the same court concluded, in *Stutsman* v. *Kaiser Found. Health Plan*, 546 A. 2d 367 (DC App. 1988), that Virginia was interested in applying its pro-defendant law, even though that law denied a Virginia plaintiff a remedy that DC law allowed. The court thought that Virginia's denial of loss of consortium actions was not intended to protect defendants or hospitals operating in that state, but was instead designed to "regulat[e] the legal rights of married

Thus, the fact that both the defendant and the plaintiff were affiliated with the forum jurisdiction made this case similar to the *Babcock* common-domicile pattern discussed earlier and allowed the court to ground the application of the law of the forum on *two affirmative* interests in (1) deterring forum defendants; and (2) protecting plaintiffs employed in the forum's territory. This distinguishes *Kaiser* from both *Erwin*, which applied forum law despite finding that the forum had no interest in applying its law, and *Erny*, which applied the law of the *other* state which favored the citizens of the form state.

148. In contrast to the above cases, other Pattern 5 cases have reached the opposite result by doing what *Neumeier* did, even without following its precise rationale. They applied the pro-defendant law of the state that, besides being the plaintiff's home state, was also the state in which both the conduct and the injury occurred. They did so on a variety of rationales, ranging from a territorial presumption, with or without reliance on the Restatement Second, to a different reading of the respective interests of the involved states.[183]

In one of these cases, *Miller* v. *Gay*[184], a guest-statute case that was the converse of *Cipolla*[185], the court concluded that neither state's relationship was more significant, and that reliance on state interests could not resolve the conflict. The court quoted *Cipolla's* statement that defendants acting in their home state "should not be put in jeopardy of liability exceeding that created by their state's laws just because a visitor from a state offering higher protection decides to visit there"[186]. The *Miller* court turned this statement around by concluding that "inhabitants of a state (here Delaware) should not be accorded rights not given by their home states, just because a visitor from a state offering higher protection decides to visit there"[187].

---

couples domiciled in Virginia ... by giving a married woman the exclusive right to sue for damages for her personal injuries". *Id.* at 374.

183. See, e.g., *Waddoups* v. *Amalgamated Sugar Co.*, 54 P.3d 1054 (Utah 2002) (applying Idaho's pro-defendant law, rather than Utah's pro-plaintiff law, to an action for wrongful termination and infliction of emotional distress filed against a Utah employer by Idaho domiciliaries who were hired in Idaho for work in defendant's Idaho plant and were also fired in Idaho); *Buglioli* v. *Enter. Rent-A-Car*, 811 F. Supp. 105 (EDNY 1993), aff'd without op., 999 F. 2d 536 (2d Cir. 1993) (following *Neumeier* Rule 3 and applying New Jersey pro-defendant common-law rule to New Jersey plaintiff's action against a New York car-rental company that rented the car to a New Jersey driver who caused the New Jersey accident; a New York statute imposed liability on the car-rental company).

184. 470 A. 2d 1353 (Pa. Super. 1984).

185. See *supra* 139. *Miller* arose out of a Delaware accident involving a Pennsylvania host-driver and a Delaware guest-passenger. Delaware, but not Pennsylvania, had a guest statute. The court applied the Delaware guest statute, barring the action.

186. See *supra* 139 at footnote 91.

187. *Miller*, 470 A. 2d at 1356.

Nodak Mutual Insurance Co. v. *American Family Mutual Insurance Co.*[188] illustrates that, even cases decided under Minnesota's choice-influencing considerations may end up applying the pro-defendant law of the accident state in Pattern 5 situations. *Nodak* was an insurance subrogation dispute arising from a North Dakota accident involving a North Dakota driver and a Minnesota driver[189]. North Dakota law favoured the Minnesota insurer, while Minnesota law favoured the North Dakota insurer. Predictably, each insurer invoked the law of the other state. The North Dakota insurer argued that Minnesota law should govern because Minnesota had a "strong interest in not allowing its insurers to recover no-fault benefits from out-of-state insurers"[190] when such benefits are not recoverable under Minnesota law so as to prevent those insurers from receiving "a windfall"[191].

The court appropriately turned the argument around by pointing out that, if Minnesota law were applied, then it would be the North Dakota insurer who would receive a windfall, because it would be able "to avoid paying ... money that it might otherwise have to pay"[192] under North Dakota law. In the end, the court applied the law of North Dakota, in part because, in the absence of special circumstances, "the state where the accident occurred has the strongest governmental interest"[193].

Finally, in *Boomsma* v. *Star Transport, Inc.*[194], the court reached a similar result by applying Wisconsin's pro-defendant law, rather than Illinois' pro-plaintiff law, to a wrongful death action arising from a Wisconsin accident involving Wisconsin victims and an Illinois driver. The court acknowledged that Wisconsin's cap on wrongful death damages was not intended to protect foreign defendants[195], but concluded that on balance Wisconsin law should govern because the plaintiffs failed to rebut the Second Restatement's *lex loci* presumption[196]. After noting that "plaintiffs had no 'justified expectation' that Illinois law would apply to their claims"[197], the court observed that application of Illinois law would endorse "a

---

188. 604 NW 2d 91 (Minn. 2000), discussed *supra* 78.
189. The North Dakota driver was insured by a North Dakota insurer through a policy delivered in North Dakota, and the Minnesota driver was insured by a Minnesota insurer through a policy delivered in Minnesota. After paying no-fault benefits to its Minnesota insured, the Minnesota insurer sought to recoup those benefits from the North Dakota insurer. North Dakota, but not Minnesota, provided for such recoupment.
190. 604 NW 2d at 95.
191. *Id.*
192. *Id.*
193. *Id.* at 96
194. 202 F. Supp. 2d 869 (ED Wis. 2002) (decided under Illinois conflicts law).
195. See *id.* at 878.
196. The court also noted that the presence of a Wisconsin third-party defendant also militated in favour of Wisconsin law. See *id.*
197. *Id.* at 879.

kind of lottery system"[198] for Wisconsin plaintiffs injured in Wisconsin in which "[t]he 'winners' ... would be those injured by states that do not cap wrongful death damages [and] [t]he 'losers' would be those injured by fellow Wisconsinites"[199].

(b)   Pattern 6: The *Hurtado* pattern

149. As said above, cases falling within Pattern 6 also qualify as no-interest cases, insofar as each state's law favours a litigant not domiciled in that state. However, this classification is more questionable here than in Pattern 5 because in Pattern 6 cases the law of the state of the conduct and injury *favours recovery*. If the court interprets that law as motivated by a policy of deterrence, then the pro-recovery state becomes interested in applying its law in order to deter that conduct. Thus, a potential no-interest case becomes a false conflict. Right or wrong[200], this was precisely the conclusion of the California court in *Hurtado* v. *Superior Court*[201].

Hurtado was a wrongful death action filed by the survivors of a Mexico domiciliary who was killed in a California accident caused by the negligence of a California driver. Mexico, but not California, limited the amount of wrongful-death damages. Under Currie's personal-law principle, this would have been a no-interest case. The court followed this principle when it concluded that Mexico did not have an interest in applying its defendant-protecting limited-damages rule to non-Mexican defendants at the expense of Mexican plaintiffs[202].

Based on the same principle, the court could have concluded that California also did not have an interest in applying its pro-plaintiff rule for the benefit of non-California plaintiffs at the expense of California defendants. However, the court found that the California rule was designed to deter negligent conduct in California. The court stated that California's "primary purpose" in creating a cause of action for wrongful death was not so much to compensate the victim as "to deter the kind of conduct within its borders which wrongfully takes life"[203], and that the unlimited-damages aspect of the rule simply "strengthen[ed] the deterrent aspect of the civil sanction"[204].

Thus, the court essentially reclassified the California rule as conduct-regulating. Once it did this, the court could not avoid the conclusion that California had an interest in applying the rule. As the court stated,

---

198. *Id.*

199. *Id.*

200. For a critique of *Hurtado* on this issue, see W. Reppy, "Eclecticism in Choice of Law: Hybrid Method or Mishmash?", 34 *Mercer L. Rev.* 645, 699 (1983).

201. 522 P. 2d 666 (Cal. 1974).

202. That law was designed to protect only Mexican defendants "from excessive financial burdens or exaggerated claims". 522 P. 2d at 670.

203. *Id.* at 671. This statement becomes semi-credible if one remembers that, historically, the common law did not recognize wrongful death actions until the nineteenth century, and that contemporary American law relies on civil rather than on criminal sanctions to a much greater extent than other legal systems.

204. *Id.*

"when the defendant is a resident of California and the tortious conduct ... occurs here, California's deterrent policy of full compensation is clearly advanced by application of its own law ... . California has a decided interest in applying its own law to California defendants who allegedly caused wrongful death within its borders."[205]

Thus, what might have been a no-interest case, became a false conflict[206].

The same was true in *Jett* v. *Coletta*[207], a medical malpractice action filed by an Idaho domiciliary and arising out of medical services rendered in a New Jersey hospital. The New Jersey court found that, although Idaho had no interest in applying its limited-damages rule which would benefit the New Jersey defendants[208], New Jersey had a "strong interest" in applying its unlimited-damages law so as to: (1) "deter[] negligent conduct in the medical profession"; (2) "promot[e] the competence of its medical practitioners"[209]; and (3) "ensur[e] that visitors to the state receive full compensation for their injuries"[210], particularly when the visitors' "presence is nonfortuitous."[211]

Finally, in *Arcila* v. *Christopher Trucking*[212], an action filed by New Jersey plaintiffs against Pennsylvania defendants arising out of a Pennsylvania accident, a Pennsylvania court applied Pennsylvania's pro-plaintiff compensatory damages law rather than New Jersey's pro-defendant law. The court reasoned that the application of New Jersey law would not promote New Jersey's interest in protecting defendants, but would "impair Pennsylvania's interest ... in deterring tortious conduct within its borders"[213]. The court also noted that, since the defendants were Pennsylvania domiciliaries and had acted in Pennsylvania, they were "on notice

---

205. *Id.* at 671-672.
206. For a similar conclusion in a case arising from the death of a Mexican domiciliary in an Arizona traffic accident, see *Villaman* v. *Schee*, 15 F. 3d 1095, 1994 WL 6661 (9th Cir. 1994). The court concluded that Mexico had no interest in applying its limited-damages law to benefit a foreign defendant acting outside Mexico. The court also concluded, however, that "Arizona tort law is designed in part to deter negligent conduct within its borders; thus Arizona has a strong interest in the application of its laws allowing for full compensatory and punitive damages". 1994 WL 6661 at *4.
207. 2003 WL 22171862 (DNJ 2003).
208. See *id.* at *4 (concluding that the Idaho rule was intended "to keep down insurance premiums in Idaho" rather than "[to] control[] liability insurance premiums in New Jersey for New Jersey defendants").
209. *Id.* at *3.
210. *Id.*
211. *Id.* The plaintiff, a 16-year old, was spending the summer in New Jersey with her grandmother when the plaintiff was treated in a New Jersey hospital. The court also found that New Jersey's contacts were "more substantial" than Idaho's, and thus New Jersey had a "much stronger relationship" and "a much greater incentive than Idaho to apply its law." Id. at 4.
212. 195 F. Supp. 2d 690 (ED Pa. 2002).
213. *Id.* at 694.

– at least constructively – of Pennsylvania's law governing remedies for injuries caused by negligent conduct"[214].

(c)   Summary and rule

150. Time now to summarize the discussion of cases falling within Patterns 5 and 6. For the reader's convenience, the following table depicts these cases and uses shading to denote the state whose law the court applied.

---

214. *Id.* at 695. See also *LaForge* v. *Normandin*, 551 NYS 2d 142 (App. Div. 1990) (New York traffic accident involving a Quebec plaintiff, two Quebec defendants, and four New York co-defendants. Under Quebec's no-fault law, the plaintiff could not recover damages from the Quebec defendants. The court held that, because of the presence of the New York co-defendants, *Neumeier* Rule 1 was inapplicable and Rule 3 applied. The court applied New York law even with regard to the Quebec defendants, reasoning that "New York's interest in protecting the contribution and apportionment rights of its domiciliaries is a significant interest". *Id.* at 143).

Table 11. Cases of Patterns 5 and 6

Pattern 5

#	Case name	Forum state	Contact states and their laws			
			P's Dom Pro-D	Injury Pro-D	Conduct Pro-D	D's Dom **Pro-P**
1	Neumeier	NY	On	On	On	NY
2	Stutsman	DC	VA	VA	VA	DC
3	Waddoups	UT	ID	ID	ID	UT
4	Miller	PA	DE	DE	DE	PA
5	Nodak	MN	ND	ND	ND	MN
6	Boomsma	WS	WS	WS	WS	ILL
7	Buglioli	NY	NJ	NJ	NJ	NY
8	Erwin	OR	WA	WA	WA	OR
9	Labree	RI	MA	MA	MA	RI
10	Kaiser	DC	VA/DC	VA	VA	DC
11	Bucci	DC	VA/DC	VA	VA	DC
12	Farrell	PA	NJ	NJ	NJ	PA
13	Erny	NJ	NJ	NJ	NJ	NY
14	Butkera	NJ	NJ	NJ	NJ	NY
15	Stevens	NY	NY	NY	NY	FL

Pattern 6

#	Case name	Forum state	Contact states and their laws			
			P's Dom Pro-D	Injury **Pro-P**	Conduct **Pro-P**	D's Dom **Pro-P**
16	Hurtado	CA	Mex	CA	CA	CA
17	Villaman	AZ	Mex	AZ	AZ	AZ
18	Jett	NJ	ID	NJ	NJ	NJ
19	Arcila	PA	NJ	PA	PA	PA

The above table and preceding discussion support the following observations.

1. All of the 19 cases discussed above would qualify as no-interest cases under Currie's classificatory scheme. However, only one case, *Erwin v. Thomas*, followed Currie's classification and rationale. *Erwin* concluded that both involved states were uninterested because their respective laws disfavoured their domiciliaries, and applied the law of the forum as the residual law. In all other cases, the court found that one of the involved states was interested, despite the fact that its law disfavoured its own domiciliary.

2. Of the 19 cases, ten cases applied the law of the forum, but except for *Erwin*, they based the application of forum law on the existence of affirmative forum interests or forum contacts, rather than on either the primacy or the residuality of the *lex fori*.

3. All four of the cases of Pattern 6 applied the law of the state that had three of the four pertinent contacts other than the forum, i.e., conduct, injury, and

defendant's domicile. Of the 15 cases of Pattern 5, seven cases applied the law of the state that had three of the contacts, i.e., conduct, injury and plaintiff's domicile, and eight cases applied the law of the state that had only one contact. However, for reasons discussed earlier, some of the latter cases, such as *Erny* and *Butkera* are poorly reasoned, while other cases, such as *Kaiser* and *Bucci*, are exceptional because of the plaintiff's affiliation with both states. Even without discounting these cases, a slight majority of the 19 cases applied the law of the state that had three of the four contacts, i.e., conduct, injury, and the domicile of either the plaintiff or the defendant.

If one were to restate the above results in the form of a rule, that rule would provide as follows:

RULE IV. *When both the conduct and the injury occur in the home state of one of the parties, that state's law applies* (even if it does not favour that party).

Neumeier Rule 3 as well as the Louisiana codification produce the same results as the above stated rule, while also providing the necessary flexibility for judicial deviation in appropriate cases. The *Neumeier* rule calls for the application of the *lex loci delicti*, unless the application of another law "will advance the relevant substantive law purposes without impairing the smooth working of the multistate system or producing great uncertainty for litigants"[215]. The Louisiana rule, which is phrased narrowly as to capture only cases in which both the conduct and the injury are in the home state of one of the parties[216], is also accompanied by flexible escapes[217] that are more likely to be utilized in Pattern 5 cases like *Kaiser* than in Pattern 6 cases[218].

---

215. *Neumeier* Rule 3, *supra* 93.
216. See La. Civ. Code Art. 3544 (2) (a), which provides that split-domicile cases in which both the conduct and the injury occur in the home state of one party are governed by the law of that state. See also Puerto Rico Draft Code, Art. 47 (b) (1). For discussion, see Symeonides, "Louisiana's New Law of Choice of Law for Tort Conflicts: An Exegesis", 66 *Tul. L. Rev.* 677, 726-729 (1992). Split-domicile *and* split-conduct-injury cases (other than those in which the injury occurred in the domicile of the victim whose law protects her, see *infra* 152-57) are not subjected to an a priori rule.
217. See La. Civ. Code. Art. 3547, which, in "exceptional cases", authorizes a judicial deviation from Article 3544 (and other articles), if such deviation is appropriate under the general principles of the Louisiana conflicts codification. La. Civ. Code Art. 3548 provides another escape with regard to corporate tortfeasors.
218. Yet, *Duhon* v. *Union Pacific Res. Co.*, 43 F. 3d 1011 (5th Cir. 1995), applied the escape in a Pattern 6 case. *Duhon* arose out of a Texas employment accident injuring a Louisiana worker who had been hired in Louisiana by a Texas subcontractor to work in Texas for a Texas general contractor. After receiving worker's compensation benefits through the subcontractor's carrier under Louisiana law, the worker sued the Texas general contractor in tort. Texas, but not Louisiana, allowed this action. Under La. Civ. Code art. 3544 (2) *(a)*, this case would be governed by Texas law because the

It should be noted that, although the escapes can and should be employed in a content-oriented fashion, the above rules are obviously jurisdiction-selecting – they call for the application of the law of the state with the three contacts regardless of whether that law favors the tortfeasor (Pattern 5) or the victim (Pattern 6). And that is precisely why these rules are bound to encounter criticism. While most of the critics do not object to the application of the pro-victim law in the cases of the *Hurtado* pattern (Pattern 6) cases, they object to the application of the pro-defendant law in the cases of the *Neumeier* pattern (Pattern 5).

For example, Professor Louise Weinberg believes that it is "unwise to protect the defendant if his own state would not"[219], as the proposed rule does in Pattern 5 cases. On the other hand it is not unwise to protect a plaintiff whose own state does not protect her because "the plaintiff-favoring law in an unprovided-for case is likely, at least, to reflect general policies both states share ... [such as] favoring compensation, deterrence, and risk-spreading"[220]. In contrast, pro-defendant laws often consist of "[d]efenses ... [that] embody special local concerns that may not reflect substantive policies that are as widely shared"[221]. If this is true, then, as Weinberg argues, the application of the pro-plaintiff law of the defendant's home state serves the above common policies whereas the application of the pro-defendant law of the plaintiff's home state defeats "for no reason" the plaintiff's "presumptively meritorious claim"[222] and is an obvious "denial of material justice"[223].

Professor Robert Sedler agrees that the case law supports a rule like the one proposed here for Pattern 6 cases, and he endorses such a rule[224]. For Pattern

---

conduct and the injury occurred in the defendant's home state. However, the court invoked the escape of Article 3547 and applied Louisiana's pro-defendant law after finding that Louisiana's policies would be more seriously impaired if its law were not applied to this issue. Although it confused contacts with interests, the court recognized the close interdependence between a rule that requires an employer to provide worker's compensation benefits and a rule that relieves that employer from tort liability. Because of this interdependence, allowing the worker to pick and choose would have resulted in an inappropriate *dépeçage*, which the court decided to avoid.

219. L. Weinberg, "Theory Wars in the Conflict of Laws", 103 *Mich. L. Rev.* 1631, 1651 (2005). Professor Weinberg does not discuss the proposed rule per se, but rather the cases from which the rule is derived. She finds those results "appalling" and "irrational" and expresses surprise that this author reports them "without dismay". *Id* at 1650.

220. *Id.*

221. *Id.*

222. *Id.*

223. *Id.* at 1650.

224. See R. Sedler, "Choice of Law in Conflicts Torts Cases: A Third Restatement or Rules of Choice of Law?", 75 *Ind. LJ* 615, 628 (2000) ("When a plaintiff from a non-recovery state is involved in an accident with a defendant from a recovery state, and the accident occurs in the defendant's home state, recovery is allowed."). For Professor Posnak's proposed presumptive rule, which is similar to the one stated in the text, see supra footnote 121.

5 cases, Sedler recognizes the split in authority[225] and proposes to resolve it by resorting to the "common policy" of both states. His solution is also grounded on the premise that pro-defendant laws are "exceptions" to a general policy of compensation that both involved states otherwise share. In Pattern 5 cases, Sedler argues, "the state whose law represents an exception to that common policy has no interest in having its law applied ... [and thus] the common policy should come to the fore, and the exception should not be recognized"[226]. Thus in a case like *Neumeier* v. *Kuehner*, the Ontario guest statute would be the exception to the general compensatory policy of both Ontario and New York. Since Ontario would have no interest in applying its guest statute to a case that does not involve an Ontario host-driver, "the common policy of both states in favor of recovery should prevail"[227].

These are creative, out-of the-box ideas. The problem is that not all pro-defendant laws can be characterized as "defenses" or "exceptions" to a compensatory policy; even when they are, they can nevertheless reflect affirmative, deliberate policy choices that cannot be construed away through creative accounting. For example, in *Erwin* v. *Thomas*, Washington's refusal to grant wives an action for loss of consortium was not a statutory exception to a common-law policy of compensation. Rather it was the result of the common-law's (as understood in Washington) stubborn refusal to recognize such an action: "the wife could not maintain such an action at common law, and no statute of this state gives her such a right"[228], said the Supreme Court of Washington in refusing to recognize the action. On the other hand, in *Stutsman*, Virginia had abolished by statute the husband's previously recognized common-law right to sue for his wife's loss of consortium[229]. Similarly, in *Buglioli*[230] and *Stevens* v. *Shields*[231], it was the pro-plaintiff rule that was the exception to the common policy. The common law of both states had adhered to a pro-defendant rule until the defendant's home state

---

225. See Sedler, *supra*, at *id*. ("When the accident occurs in the plaintiff's home state, recovery will usually be allowed, but sometimes the courts apply the law of the plaintiff's home state denying recovery".).

226. R. Sedler, "The Governmental Interest Analysis to Choice of Law: An Analysis and a Reformulation", 25 *UCLA L. Rev.* 181 (1977).

227. *Id*.

228. *Ash* v. *S.S. Mullen, Inc.*, 261 P.2d 118, 118 (Wash. 1953). *Ash* was the decision on which *Erwin* relied for the proposition that Washington did not allow loss-of-consortium actions. See *Erwin* v. *Thomas*, 506 P.2d 494, 495 (Or. 1973) ("Washington, by court decision, has followed the common law rule that no cause of action exists by a wife for loss of consortium. Ash v. S. S. Mullen, Inc., 43 Wash.2d 345, 261 P.2d 118 (1953)"). In Oregon, the right of married women to sue for loss of consortium was conferred by statute. See *Erwin*, *id*. at 495, (citing ORS 108.010).

229. See *Stutsman* v. *Kaiser Found. Health Plan of Mid-Atlantic*, 546 A.2d 367, 372 (D.C. 1988) (citing Va. Code Ann. § 55-36).

230. *Buglioli* v. *Enter. Rent-A-Car*, 811 F. Supp. 105 (EDNY 1993), aff'd without op., 999 F. 2d 536 (2d Cir. 1993) (described *supra* footnote 183).

231. 499 NYS 2d 351 (NY Sup. Ct. 1986) (described *supra* footnote 173).

introduced a pro-plaintiff rule through a statute imposing vicarious liability on the defendant.

This is one of those many areas in conflicts law in which there is plenty of room for disagreement, but it is difficult to accept that these, often coincidental, differences in the origin or wording of these pro-defendant or pro-plaintiff rules should determine the outcome of the conflicts between them. It is also difficult to accept that the outcome should depend on whether the pro-defendant rule is that of the forum or instead of the other involved state, as both of these scholars seem to suggest.

The truth is that, ironically, the no-interest cases are more problematic for interests analysts than are true conflicts. It is perfectly logical and consistent to resolve a true conflict by applying the law of the state that has the greatest or strongest interest, or whose interests would otherwise suffer the most serious impairment. But what is one to do in the no-interest cases? Try to find the most uninterested state? This is just another way of saying that interest analysis, being built around the notion of state interests, runs into an impasse when neither state has an interest. This means that, to resolve the conflict, one must look for options outside the framework of interest analysis rather than simply re-calibrate state interests and search for phantom common policies. In this sense, Currie's solution of applying the law of the forum as the residual law is a solution that lies *outside* the framework of interest analysis. The same is true with Professor Weinberg's suggestion of resorting to material justice and applying the law that favors the plaintiff. These solutions may be good or bad, but they are not consistent with interest analysis.

Once it is understood that the solution to the no-interest conundrum must be sought outside the framework of interest analysis, then other options become more palatable. One of them is to fall back on territorialism, which has been the established system before the advent of interest analysis. In like of this long tradition, it is not unreasonable to say that these particular no-interest cases should be governed by the law of the state in which both the conduct and the injury occurred and where one of the parties is domiciled. These are not "insignificant contacts"[232], and yes "they can serve as neutral tie-breakers"[233].

E.   Split-Domicile Cases – Cross-Border Torts

151. Split-domicile cases in which the conduct occurs in one state and the injury in another state present a variation of Patterns 3 through 6. Examples of such cross-border torts are products liability cases, which are discussed in Chapter VIII, as

---

232. L. Weinberg, "Theory Wars in the Conflict of Laws", 103 *Mich. L. Rev.* 1631, 1650 (2005) (stating that "an aggregation of contacts, albeit insignificant contacts, in Symeonides' view, is useful in otherwise unprovided-for cases. Even insignificant contacts can serve as neutral tie-breakers").

233. *Id.*

well as cases involving wrongful emissions, defamation, fraud, or other torts that may be committed from a distance.

The most likely scenarios involving two states are those in which the conduct occurs in the tortfeasor's home state and the injury in the victim's home state. Depending on the content of each state's law, these cases can be divided into two patterns, which are discussed below: *(1)* cases in which each state favours its own domiciliary (Pattern 7); and *(2)* cases in which each state favours the domiciliary of the other state (Pattern 8).

1.   Pattern 7: Cases in which the conduct and the tortfeasor's domicile are in a state whose law favours the tortfeasor, while the injury and the victim's domicile are in a state whose law favours the victim

(a)   The cases

152. Pattern 7 is similar to Patterns 3 and 4, inasmuch as in all three patterns each state has a law that favours its own domiciliary. This similarity explains why Pattern 7 poses at least as much of a true conflict as do Patterns 3 or 4. The difference is that in Patterns 3 and 4 both the conduct and the injury occur in one of the domiciliary states, whereas in Pattern 7 the conduct occurs in the tortfeasor's domicile and the injury occurs in the victim's domicile. In other words, both the personal contacts (domiciles) and the territorial contacts (conduct and injury) are now evenly split, with a concomitant bearing on both state policies and party expectations.

This difference makes Pattern 7 cases more difficult than those of Patterns 3 or 4. In Pattern 3, both the conduct and the injury occur in the tortfeasor's home state, and this explains why most courts apply the law of that state[234]. In Pattern 4, both the conduct and the injury occur in the victim's home state, and this explains why most courts apply the law of that state[235]. Pattern 7 is the exact middle point between Patterns 3 and 4, which suggests that Pattern 7 cases could go in either direction, i.e., apply the law of either the tortfeasor's home state and place of conduct or the victim's home state and place of injury.

Nevertheless, American courts have generally shown little hesitation in applying the law of the victim's home state, thus equating Pattern 7 cases with Pattern 4 cases. For reasons explained below, this resolution is appropriate, *provided* that the circumstances are such that the defendant should have foreseen the application of that law[236].

---

234. See Table 9, *supra* 141.
235. See Table 10, *supra* 145.
236. But see L. Weinberg, "Theory Wars in the Conflict of Laws", 103 *Mich. L. Rev.* 1631, 1654 (2005) (arguing that the foreseeability factor has been overstated: "Given the near universality of liability insurance among suable defendants, it is somewhat unreal to speak of 'unfair surprise' to tort defendants. They have insured against liability precisely because they anticipate it under some state's laws". See also *id.* ("[A] defendant's insurer is the paradigmatic actuarial expert, and has every opportunity

153. Many of the cases falling within Pattern 7 are products liability cases which are discussed separately in Chapter VIII, *infra*. Suffice it to say that the majority of those cases applied the pro-plaintiff law of the plaintiff's home state and place of injury, rather than the pro-defendant law of the defendant's home state and place of manufacture[237]. In all of these cases, the product had reached the plaintiff's home state through ordinary commercial channels and hence the defendant could not claim to be unfairly surprised by the application of that state's law.

---

to structure the insured's coverage accordingly. It has every opportunity to adjust the defendant's premiums to take into account this and other risks").

237. See *Eimers* v. *Honda Motor Co. Ltd*, 785 F. Supp. 1204 (W.D. Pa. 1992) (applying New York's pro-plaintiff law to an action by a New York plaintiff injured in New York by a motorcycle acquired in that state and manufactured by a Japanese defendant in Japan); *Savage Arms, Inc.* v. *Western Auto Supply Co.*, 18 P. 3d 49 (Alaska 2001) (successor-liability conflict applying the pro-plaintiff law of Alaska, which was the victim's home state and injury, and the place of the product's acquisition); *Tune* v. *Philip Morris, Inc.*, 766 So. 2d 350 (Fla. App. 2000) (applying Florida's pro-plaintiff law to an action filed against a tobacco manufacturer by a Florida domiciliary who was diagnosed with lung cancer in Florida after using tobacco products there and in New Jersey, his previous domicile); *R-Square Inv.* v. *Teledyne Indus., Inc.*, 1997 WL 436245 (ED La. 1997) (applying Louisiana's pro-plaintiff law to an action of a Louisiana plaintiff injured in Louisiana by a product acquired in Minnesota and manufactured in Alabama by an Alabama manufacturer); *Allstate Ins. Co.* v. *Wal-Mart*, 2000 WL 388844 (ED La. 2000) (applying Louisiana's pro-plaintiff law to an action of a Louisiana plaintiff injured in Louisiana by a product acquired in Oklahoma and manufactured in Minnesota by a Minnesota manufacturer); *In re Masonite Corp. Hardboard Siding Prod. Liab. Litig.*, 21 F. Supp. 2d 593 (ED La. 1998) (noting Florida's strong interest in applying its law to protect its citizens from building materials that were sold and used in that state and could not withstand that state's extreme weather conditions); *Hoover* v. *Recreation Equip. Corp.*, 792 F. Supp. 1484 (ND Ohio 1991) (applying Ohio's pro-plaintiff law to both products liability and successor liability claims by an Ohio resident injured in Ohio by a product manufactured in Indiana by an Indiana corporation which was acquired by another Indiana corporation). But see *Poust* v. *Huntleigh HealthCare*, 998 F. Supp. 478 (DNJ 1998) (applying New Jersey's pro-defendant compensatory damages law to products liability action filed against a New Jersey manufacturer by a Pennsylvania plaintiff who was injured by the product in Maryland).

Many other cases involving other cross-border torts[238], including professional malpractice[239], fraud and deceptive practices[240], or defamation,[241] as well as more complex disputes between joint tortfeasors[242], have also applied the pro-

---

238. See, e.g., *Monroe v. Numed, Inc.*, 680 NYS 2d 707 (NYApp.Div. 1998) (applying Florida's pro-plaintiff law to a loss-of-consortium action arising out of the death of a Florida child whose death during surgery in Florida was attributed to a defective medical device manufactured in New York by a New York defendant); *Caruolo v. A C & S, Inc.*, 1998 WL 730331 (SDNY 1998) (asbestosis case applying Rhode Island's pro-plaintiff law to a loss of consortium action by a Rhode Island plaintiff injured in Rhode Island); *Brown v. Harper*, 647 NYS 2d 245 (NYApp.Div.1996) (applying New York's pro-plaintiff law to impose liability on a Pennsylvania dealer who has sold car to uninsured driver who caused New York accident injuring New York domiciliary); *Drinkall v. Used Car Rentals, Inc.* 32 F. 3d 329 (8th Cir. 1994) (applying Iowa's pro-plaintiff law to impose liability on Nebraska car rental company that rented a car in Nebraska to an unlicensed driver that caused an accident in Iowa injuring an Iowa domiciliary).

239. See, e.g., *Bankers Trust Co. v. Lee Keeling & Assoc., Inc.*, 20 F. 3d 1092 (10th Cir. 1994) (discussed *supra* 99; applying New York law to a case arising out of injury in New York sustained by a New York plaintiff and caused by the conduct of an Oklahoma defendant in Oklahoma); *David B. Lilly Co., Inc. v. Fisher*, 18 F. 3d 1112 (3rd Cir. 1994) (applying Delaware law to Delaware plaintiff's action for legal malpractice committed outside Delaware by out of state attorneys).

240. See *Bombardier Capital, Inc. v. Richfield Housing Center, Inc.*, 1994 WL 118294 (NDNY 1994) (applying Vermont's pro-plaintiff law to an action brought by a Massachusetts/Vermont corporation against New York defendants for fraud in the inducement of a contract).

241. See, e.g., *Condit v. Dunne*, 317 F. Supp. 2d 344 (SDNY 2004) (applying California's pro-plaintiff law rather than New York's pro-defendant law to a California congressman's defamation action against a journalist for statements made in television and radio talk shows broadcast from New York to a national audience; the court found that, although New York had an interest in regulating the conduct of journalists in New York, California also had an interest in applying its law to protect its citizens from defamation and that was "the most significant interest". *Id.* at 355.

242. See, e.g., *Glunt v. ABC Paving Co., Inc*, 668 NYS 2d 846 (NYApp.Div. 1998) (reverse *Cooney*-type case arising out of a New York traffic accident involving an Ohio victim, his Ohio employer, and a New York defendant; following *Neumeier* Rule 2 and applying New York law allowing the New York defendant to obtain indemnification from the Ohio defendant who would be immune from indemnification under Ohio law); *Venturini v. Worldwide Marble & Granite Co.*, 1995 WL 606281 (SDNY 1995) (third-party actions for contribution and indemnification filed by New York company and Michigan company against a New Jersey company arising out of injury sustained in Michigan by a truck driver employed by the New Jersey company; applying Michigan law under "the second *and* third Neumeier rules", *id.* at *3 (emphasis added) and denying contribution, which would be available under New York law); *Mascarella v. Brown*, 813 F. Supp. 1015, (SDNY 1993) (third-party action by a New York defendant against a New Jersey corporation seeking contribution and indemnification for medical malpractice committed in New York by the New York defendant; applying New York law and allowing contribution, which was not available under New Jersey law); *Bader v. Purdom*, 841 F. 2d 38 (2d Cir. 1988) (action by a New York minor bitten by

plaintiff law of the plaintiff's home state and place of injury. Table 12 depicts these cases by using shading to denote the state whose law the court applied.

Table 12. Pattern 7 cases

#	Case name	Forum state	States' Contacts and Laws			
			P's Dom Pro-P	Injury Pro-P	Conduct Pro-D	D's Dom Pro-D
1	Kuehn	WS	WS	WS	CA	CA
2	Troxel	PA	PA	PA	DE	DE
3	Eimers	NY	NY	NY	Japan	Japan
4	Savage	AK	AK	AK	---	---
5	Hoover	OH	OH	OH	IN	IN
6	Tune	FL	FL	FL	---	---
7	Nelson	NJ IN	IN	IN	NJ	NJ
8	R-Square	LA	LA	LA	AL	AL
9	Allstate	LA	LA	LA	MN?	MN?
10	Monroe	NY	FL	FL	NY	NY
11	Brown	NY	NY	NY	PA	PA
12	Drinkall	IA	IA	IA	NE	NE
13	Bankers	NY OK	NY	NY	OK	OK
14	Lilly	DE	DE	DE	NY/MO	NY
15	Bombardier	NY	VT	VT	NY	NY
16	Condit	NY	CA	CA	NY	NY

One representative case from Pattern 7 is *Kuehn* v. *Children's Hospital, Los Angeles*[243], which was decided under Wisconsin's choice-influencing considerations. *Kuehn* was an action filed by the parents of a Wisconsin child who died in Wisconsin as a result of the negligence of a California hospital in improperly shipping to Wisconsin a package containing the child's bone marrow[244]. Under California

---

defendant's dog in Ontario. Defendants third-partied the minor's parents claiming contribution and indemnification for their negligent supervision of the child. Such claim was permitted by Ontario law, but not by New York law. Apparently thinking of the main action, rather than the third-party claim for contribution, the court concluded that this case fell within the scope of Rule 3 and applied Ontario law. A concurring judge pointed out that, more properly, the case fell within the scope of Rule 2b).

243. 119 F. 3d 1296 (7th Cir. 1997).

244. Pursuant to an agreement between the California hospital and a Wisconsin hospital, employees of the first hospital extracted bone marrow from the child and then shipped it to the Wisconsin hospital where it was to be reinserted into the child's bones. The marrow was improperly packaged and arrived in unusable condition. This necessitated a second procedure which did not succeed in saving the child's life. This action was only for the negligence in improperly shipping the marrow and involved only a claim for the child's pre-death pain and suffering.

law, the action did not survive the victim's death. Under Wisconsin law it did. In an opinion authored by Judge Posner, the court held that Wisconsin law governed based in part on Wisconsin's interest "in obtaining for its residents the measure of relief that the state believes appropriate in tort cases"[245].

However, the court also took care to explain why the California hospital should have foreseen the occurrence of the injury in Wisconsin, and thus the possibility of having to account under Wisconsin law – the hospital had shipped the package to Wisconsin based on a contractual arrangement with a Wisconsin hospital. Moreover, said the court, the only difference between California and Wisconsin law was "in the scope of liability for negligence, not in the standard of care. It [was] not as if California had required one method of packing and shipping bone marrow and Wisconsin another"[246].

154. In contrast, in *Troxel* v. *A.I. duPont Institute*[247], a medical malpractice case, the foreseeability element was somewhat tenuous, and this may have been part of the court's reason for reaching the opposite result. Another reason may have been that, unlike *Kuehn* which involved the negligent shipping of a package, *Troxel* arose out of actual in-patient treatment and thus was a true medical malpractice action. In *Troxel*, a Delaware hospital treated a Pennsylvania patient after referral from a Pennsylvania doctor. The patient returned to Pennsylvania and, unaware that she was suffering from a contagious disease, communicated that disease to her pregnant friend, the plaintiff, whose *in utero* child died as a result of the disease. The plaintiff sued the hospital for failure to inform its patient of the contagious nature of her disease and of the risk to pregnant women who might come into contact with her.

The Pennsylvania court recognized Pennsylvania's interest in protecting its citizens, but concluded that this interest was "superseded by Delaware's interest in regulating the delivery of health care services in Delaware"[248] and in protecting defendants who acted in that state[249]. The court said that "the qualitative contacts of Delaware were greater and more significant than those of Pennsylvania"[250], and that, when acting in Delaware, defendant was "entitled to rely on the duties and

---

245. *Kuehn*, 119 F. 3d at 1302.

246. *Id.* After examining the case under Leflar's five-choice influencing considerations followed in Wisconsin, the court concluded that "[s]o strongly do the other considerations besides predictability favor Wisconsin law in this case that the application of that law was predictable – thus completing the sweep". *Id.* at 1303.

247. 636 A. 2d 1179 (Pa. Super. 1994), appeal denied 647 A. 2d 903 (Pa. 1994).

248. 636 A. 2d at 1181.

249. See *id.*:

   "Insofar as the instant claim is focused upon [defendants] because of services rendered to a Pennsylvania resident in Delaware by a Delaware health care provider, the State of Delaware has the greater interest in the application of its law ... In treating [the patient] ... the hospital was required to follow and abide by the laws of Delaware. As such, [defendants] were entitled to rely on the duties and protections provided by Delaware law."

250. *Id.* at 1182.

protections provided by Delaware law"[251]. The court also stated that any rule that would allow patients to carry with them the protective law of their domicile when they travel to another state for medical care "would be wholly unreasonable, for it would require hospitals and physicians to be aware of and be bound by the laws of all states from which patients came to them for treatment"[252].

155. This discussion of state interests simply confirms that Pattern 7 cases are veritable true conflicts, which in turn means that the two states' interests are more or less equally strong and pertinent. One element that can tip the scales in one direction or the other is the actor's ability to reasonably foresee where the act will manifest its direct consequences. In *Kuehn*, it was beyond question that the California hospital should have foreseen that the consequences of its negligence in sending a package to Wisconsin would have been felt in Wisconsin.

Certainly, one could make the same argument in *Troxel* – the Delaware doctors should have foreseen that, when they send an uncured and uniformed contagious patient back to her home in Pennsylvania, the consequences of that negligence would have been felt in Pennsylvania. The fact that the *Troxel* court did not accept this argument suggests that the court believed strongly that, from a systemic perspective, medical malpractice conflicts should be resolved invariably under the law of the place where the medical services are rendered, regardless of any other factors. As seen earlier, cases like *Bledsoe* have adopted this very concept.

However, there is a difference between cases like *Bledsoe*, in which a patient chooses to go to an out-of-state hospital for treatment, and cases like *Troxel* in which the victim has no relation with the hospital. In the latter cases, the court should look at the case from the perspective of the victim, who has never left her home state and has been injured there, and ask whether she deserves to rely on the protective law of her own state. Stated another way, foreseeability has two sides – that of the tortfeasor, and that of the victim. When, as in *Bledsoe*, both sides can foresee the eventuality of the injury occurring in the victim's home state, the foreseeability criterion may be less critical in resolving the conflict. But when, as in *Troxel*, only the tortfeasor is in a position to foresee this eventuality and the victim cannot, the scale tips against the tortfeasor, not the victim[253].

(b) A rule

156. Subject to the above caveat regarding foreseeability, the results reached in the majority of Pattern 7 cases can be summarized as follows:

---

251. *Id.* at 1181.

252. *Id.* In a subsequent decision, the court allowed the plaintiff's action to proceed against the Pennsylvania referring doctor. See *Troxel v. A.I. duPont Institute*, 675 A. 2d 314 (Pa. Super. 1996), appeal denied 685 A. 2d 547 (Pa. 1996).

253. Cf. P. Nygh, "The Reasonable Expectations of the Parties as a Guide to the Choice of Law in Contract and Tort", 251 *Recueil des cours* 269, 296 (1995) ("The expectation of compensation is ... reasonable and fundamental, as is the converse expectation that the liability be foreseeable.").

RULE V. *When conduct originating in one state injures in another state a person domiciled in the latter state, the law of the latter state applies if it is more favourable to the injured person and if the occurrence of the injury in that state was objectively foreseeable.*

The Louisiana codification contains a rule to this effect, which expressly subjects the application of the pro-recovery law of the victim's domicile to an objective foreseeability proviso[254]. Professor Cavers, who also advocated the same result subject to the same proviso[255], offered the following rationale for it:

"Th[e] system of physical and financial protection [of the state of injury] would be impaired ... if actions outside the state but having foreseeable effects within it were not also subject to its law... . [T]he fact that [the defendant] would be held to a lower standard of ... damages back in the state where he had his home (or in the state where he acted) or, indeed, the fact that he enjoyed an immunity there, all would ordinarily seem matters of little consequence to the state of the injury ... . If he has not entered the state but has caused harm within it by his act outside it, then, save perhaps where the physical or legal consequences of his action were not foreseeable, it is equally fair to hold him to the standards of the state into which he sent whatever harmful agent, animal, object or message caused the injury."[256]

As explained earlier[257], the *Neumeier* rules were not designed for cross-border torts, but rather for guest-statute conflicts in which the conduct and the injury usually occur in the same state. The decision of the *Schultz* court to extend the scope of these rules to cross-border torts generates a potential conflict between *Neumeier* Rules 2a and 2b in the cross-border cases of Pattern 7. For example,

---

254. La. Civ. Code Art. 3544 (2) *(b)* provides that

"when the injury and the conduct that caused it occurred in different states, ... the law of the state in which the injury occurred [applies], provided that (i) the injured person was domiciled in that state, (ii) the person who caused the injury should have foreseen its occurrence in that state, and (iii) the law of that state provided for a higher standard of financial protection for the injured person than did the law of the state in which the injurious conduct occurred".

A similar defense is provided for products liability conflicts. See La. Civ. Code Art. 3545(2), which provides that Louisiana products liability law shall not apply "if neither the product that caused the injury nor any of the defendant's products of the same type were made available in this state through ordinary commercial channels".

255. Professor Sedler extracts a similar rule from the cases but phrases it in unilateral terms. His rule provides that,"[w]hen a forum resident suffers injury in the forum ... because of an act done elsewhere that creates a foreseeable risk of harm in the forum, the forum will apply its own law allowing recovery". R. Sedler, "Choice of Law in Conflicts Torts Cases: A Third Restatement or Rules of Choice of Law?", 75 *Ind. LJ* 615, 622 (2000).

256. D. Cavers, *The Choice-of-Law Process*, 140, 141 (1965).

257. See *supra* 95, 99.

when a defendant acts in his home state, whose law protects him, and causes injury to the victim in her home state, whose law protects her, Rule 2a calls for the application of the law of the former state, whereas Rule 2b calls for the application the law of the latter state[258].

As previously discussed, even after *Schultz*, New York courts have failed to differentiate between conduct and injury. They continue to speak of the "locus of the tort" and, uncritically relying on dicta contained in *Schultz*, place this "locus" in the state "where the last event necessary to make the actor liable occurred"[259] – at the state of the injury[260]. This means that, in Pattern 7 cases, the place of conduct becomes irrelevant. More importantly, it means that Rule 2b trumps Rule 2a, thus resulting in the application of the pro-recovery law of the victim's home state and place injury. For reasons explained above, this result is proper, except for the lack of a foreseeability proviso. Fortunately, Rule 2b contains an escape of sorts – "in the absence of special circumstances"[261] – which allows courts to consider the foreseeability factor.

157. Private international law codifications in the rest of the world have adopted rules that produce the same result as the one described above, even for cases in which the injured person is *not* domiciled in the state of injury. One example of these rules, which are usually presented and defended under the rubric of *favor laesi*[262], is Article 45(2) of the Portuguese Civil Code . It provides that, if the law of the state of injury holds the actor liable but the law of the state where he acts does not, the law of the injury state governs "provided the actor could foresee the occurrence of damage in that state as a consequence of his act or omission"[263].

---

258. See *id.* Similarly, if in the same case the injury occurs in a third state, a conflict arises between Rule 2a and Rule 3. Rule 2a calls for the application of the law of the state of conduct, whereas Rule 3 calls for the application of the law of the state "where the accident occurred" (meaning perhaps the place of injury) subject to the escape contained in that rule.

259. *Schultz*, 480 NE 2d at 683.

260. See *Bankers Trust Co.* v. *Lee Keeling & Assoc., Inc.*, 20 F. 3d 1092 (10th Cir. 1994), discussed *supra* 99; *Kramer* v. *Showa Denko K.K.*, 929 F. Supp. 733 (SDNY 1996). See also *Hamilton* v. *Accu-Tek*, 47 F. Supp. 2d 330, 337 (EDNY 1999): "In cases where the defendant's tortious conduct and the plaintiff's injury occur in different states 'the place of the wrong is considered to be the place where the last event necessary to make the actor liable occurred'", quoting *Schultz*, and citing *Pescatore* v. *Pan American World Airways, Inc.*, 97 F. 3d 1, 13 (2d Cir.1996), and *Kush* v. *Abbott Lab.*, 655 NYS 2d 520, 521 (NYApp.Div. 1996).

261. See *supra* 93.

262. See P. Nygh, "The Reasonable Expectations of the Parties as a Guide to the Choice of Law in Contract and Tort", 251 *Recueil des cours* 269, 292-293 (1995); F. Vischer, "General Course on Private International Law", 232 *Recueil des cours* 9, 119 (1992).

263. Portuguese Civ. Code Art. 45(2). An identical provision is contained in Art. 2097 of the Peruvian Civil Code. The Belgian PIL Code contains a similar provision for defamation cases. Art. 99(2)(1) allows the plaintiff to choose the most favorable law subject to a foreseeability exception in favor of the defendant.

Other codifications fail to include an express foreseeability proviso. For example, the Hungarian codification authorizes the application of the law of the state of injury "[i]f it is preferable to the injured party"[264] over the law of the conduct state, while the Italian and Venezuelan codifications do the reverse by applying the law of the injury state, unless the victim requests the application of the law of the state of conduct[265]. The German EGBGB has a similar provision (Art. 40.1) but also provides escapes (Art. 41) that would enable courts to avoid harsh results. Finally, less problematic are the provisions of the Swiss[266] and Quebec[267] codifications which include a foreseeability proviso, but do not condition the application of the law of the injury state on whether that law is favourable to the victim or the tortfeasor. Obviously, the foreseeability proviso is needed only when that law is unfavourable to the tortfeasor.

2.   Pattern 8: Cases in which the conduct and the tortfeasor's domicile are in a state whose law favours the victim, while the injury and the victim's domicile are in a state whose law favours the tortfeasor

158. Pattern 8 is similar to Patterns 5 and 6, inasmuch as in all three patterns the tortfeasor is domiciled in a state whose law favours the victim, while the victim is domiciled in a state whose law favours the tortfeasor. This explains why, under interest analysis, Pattern 8 presents the no-interest paradigm as do Patterns 5 and 6. However, in Patterns 5 and 6 both the conduct and the injury occur in the home state of one of the parties, whereas in Pattern 8 these two contacts are divided, with the conduct occurring at the tortfeasor's home state and the injury at the victim's home state. This division makes Pattern 8 cases more difficult than the cases of Pattern 5 or 6.

To be sure, as in the cases of Pattern 6 (the *Hurtado* pattern), a court may choose to characterize the pro-recovery law of the tortfeasor's home state and place of conduct as partly conduct-regulating. If so, the no-interest case becomes a "false" conflict. Several products liability cases discussed in Chapter VIII have done precisely that. They applied the pro-plaintiff law of the manufacturer's home state and place of manufacture, rather than the pro-defendant law of the plaintiff's home state and injury[268].

---

264. Hungarian PIL Act of 1979, Art. 32(2).

265. See Italian PIL Act of 1995, Art. 62; Venezuelan PIL Act of 1998, Art. 32 (2).

266. See Swiss PIL Act of 1987, Art. 133 (2). See also *id.* Arts. 136-139 regarding antitrust, emissions, and injuries to rights of personality.

267. Quebec Civ. Code, Art. 3126. But see *id.* Art. 3129, which requires the application of Quebec law for injuries caused outside Quebec as a result of exposure to raw materials originating in Quebec.

268. See, e.g., *Gantes v. Kason Corp.*, 679 A. 2d 106 (NJ 1996); *McLennan v. American Eurocopter Corp.*, Inc., 245 F. 3d 403 (5th Cir. 2001); *Mahne v. Ford Motor Co*, 900 F. 2d 83 (6th. Cir. 1990), cert. denied, 498 US 941 (1990); *Davis v. Shiley*, 75 Cal. Rptr. 2d 826 (Cal. App. 1998); *Marchesani v. Pellerin-Milnor Corp.*, 269 F. 3d 481 (5th Cir.

Similarly, as *Ardoyno* v. *Kyzar*[269] illustrates, a court may articulate a state's interests in a way that dissociates them from the parties' domiciles. *Ardoyno* was an action for interference with contract filed by a Louisiana plaintiff against a Mississippi defendant whose conduct in Mississippi caused injury to plaintiff in both states. Mississippi, but not Louisiana, allowed such an action. The court reasoned that the Louisiana rule which prohibited the action was geared not toward protecting defendants as such, but rather toward fostering competition with regard to employment contracts. Since the contract in question was entered into in Louisiana, the court concluded that Louisiana had an interest in applying this rule, even though a Louisiana plaintiff resisted, and a Mississippi defendant benefited from the rule's application.

However, in many Pattern 8 cases the above avenues may be unavailable. If so, these will remain "no-interest" cases which, by definition, cannot be resolved on the basis of state interests. One option is to fall back to territorial factors or to a presumptive *lex loci* rule (with its "last event" sub-rule) as other no-interest cases have done. The majority of product liability cases that fall within Pattern 8 applied the pro-defendant law of the plaintiff's domicile and place of injury under a variety of rationales[270]. However, in most of those cases, that state was also the state of the product's acquisition. For courts that tend to think in quantitative

---

2001); *Baxter* v. *Sturm, Ruger & Co., Inc.*, 644 A. 2d 1297 (Conn. 1994). These cases are discussed *infra* at 222-223. See also *Zenaida-Garcia* v. *Recovery Sys. Tech., Inc.*, 115 P. 3d 1017 (Wash. App. 2005); *Lewis-De Boer* v. *Mooney Aircraft Corp.*, 728 F. Supp. 642 (D. Colo. 1990); *Champlain Enter., Inc.* v. *United States*, 945 F. Supp. 468 (NDNY 1996); *Magnant* v. *Medtronic, Inc.*, 818 F. Supp. 204 (WD Mich. 1993). These cases are discussed *infra* 228. See also *Torrington Co.* v. *Stutzman*, 646 SW 3d 829 (Tex. 2000) (*infra* 239).

269. 426 F. Supp. 78 (ED La. 1976).

270. See, e.g., *Dorman* v. *Emerson Elec. Co.*, 23 F. 3d 1354 (8th Cir. 1994), cert. denied, 1994 US Lexis 7600 (1994); *Hall* v. *Gen. Motors Corp.*, 582 NW 2d 866 (Mich. App. 1998); *Farrell* v. *Ford Motor Co.*, 501 NW 2d 567 (Mich. App. 1993), app. denied, 519 NW 2d 158 (Mich. 1994); *Vestal* v. *Shiley Inc.*, 1997 WL 910373 (CD Cal. 1997); *Rice* v. *Dow Chem. Co.*, 875 P. 2d 1213 (Wash. 1994); *Walls* v. *Gen. Motors*, 906 F. 2d 143 (5th Cir. 1990); *Walters* v. *Warren Eng'g Corp.*, 617 NE 2d 170 (Ill. App. 1993); *In re Eli Lilly & Co. Prozac Products Liab. Litig.*, 789 F. Supp. 1448 (SD Ind. 1992); *Burleson* v. *Liggett Group Inc.*, 111 F. Supp. 2d 825 (ED Tex. 2000); *Hughes* v. *Wal-Mart Stores, Inc.*, 250 F. 3d 618 (8th Cir. 2001); *Nesladek* v. *Ford Motor Co.*, 46 F. 3d 734 (8th Cir. 1995), cert. denied, 516 US 814 (1995); *Clark* v. *Favalora*, 722 So. 2d 82 (La. App. 1998); *Orleans Parish Sch. Bd.* v. *United States Gypsum Co.*, 1993 WL 205091 (ED La. 1993); and *Jefferson Parish Hosp. Dist. # 2* v. *W.R. Grace*, 1992 WL 167263 (ED La. 1992); *K.E. Pittman* v. *Kaizer Aluminum & Chem. Corp.*, 559 So. 2d 879 (La. App. 1990); *Harlan Feeders* v. *Grand Labs., Inc.*, 881 F. Supp. 1400 (ND Iowa 1995). These and other similar cases are discussed *infra* at 217-221. See also *Denman* v. *Snapper Div.*, 131 F. 3d 546 (5th Cir. 1998), reh'g denied en banc, 137 F. 3d 1353 (5th Cir. 1998); *McKinnon* v. *F.H. Morgan & Co. Inc.*, 750 A. 2d 1026 (Vt. 2000); *Land* v. *Yamaha Motor Corp., USA.*, 272 F. 3d 514 (7th Cir. 2001); *Normann* v. *Johns-Manville Corp.*, 593 A. 2d 890 (Pa. Super. 1991), appeal denied, 607 A. 2d 255 (Pa. 1992). These cases are discussed *infra* at 227.

terms even when proclaiming otherwise, this additional contact tips the scale in the direction of the state with the most contacts.

Currie's solution to Pattern 8 cases was to apply the law of the forum *qua* forum. This is no doubt an efficient solution. It is also a solution that more often than not favours plaintiffs, because they can choose to sue in the defendant's home state whenever it has a pro-plaintiff law.

159. On balance, a better option is to concede that Pattern 8 cases are not susceptible to *a priori* solutions. A court that has the opportunity to consider the totality of the circumstances of the particular case, including factors such as the parties' relationship, if any, is likely to reach a better result than a result preformulated *ex ante*.

The Louisiana codification adopts this very position. Rather than imposing an *a priori* solution, the codification relegates these cases to the flexible approach of Article 3542[271], which contains a list of policies, factors, and contacts not unlike those of §6 of the Second Restatement.

Under the *Neumeier* Rules, Pattern 8 cases will fall within Rule 3, and thus will be presumptively governed by the law of the *lex loci* state which, under New York case law, is deemed to be the state of the "last event", i.e., the injury. To the rescue comes the Rule 3 escape, which can lead to the application of another state's law.

F.   Split-Domicile Conflicts Involving Three States

160. When the tortfeasor and the victim are domiciled in different states and the tort is committed in whole or in part in a third state, the resulting conflict can be quite complex. Depending on the content of the laws of the three states, these cases can present the false conflict, true conflict, or no-interest paradigms, but the involvement of the third state usually adds to the difficulty of resolving the conflict.

Budget Rent-A-Car System, Inc. v. *Chappell*[272] is a recent example of a tri-state conflict in which the laws of each state would produce a different outcome. Besides being a true conflict, this case had all the drama and some of the complexity of an exam question. Joseph, a domiciliary of Michigan rented in that state a car from the defendant company and, one day before Valentine's day, drove it to New York to deliver roses and a bracelet to Nicole, a New York domiciliary. He was driving back to Michigan through Pennsylvania with Nicole as his passenger when he fell asleep at the wheel. The resulting accident left Nicole a paraplegic. The rental-car company brought an action in Pennsylvania, seeking a declaratory judgment freeing it from vicarious liability arising from its ownership of the rented car. The company would be entitled to such a declaration under the law of Pennsylvania but not of Michigan or New York, both of which had statutes imposing on car owners civil liability for injuries caused by persons using the car

---

271. See *supra* 102.

272. 407 F 3d 166 (3rd Cir. 2005) (decided under Pennsylvania conflicts law).

with the owner's consent. However, unlike the New York statute, the Michigan statute limited the owner's liability to $ 20,000.

The court found that Pennsylvania had no interest in limiting the company's liability, while Michigan had some interest which, however, was "uncertain and tenuous"[273] under the circumstances of this case. In contrast, the court found that New York's interest was "clear, direct and compelling"[274], because all of the reasons for which New York enacted the pertinent statute were directly implicated in this case – New York had an interest in "(1) [Nicole's] full recovery from a financially responsible party, (2) the compensation of New York vendors who furnish medical and hospital care to [Nicole], and (3) recouping the State's welfare expenses"[275].

In characteristic simplicity, *Neumeier* Rule 3 submits *all* tri-state conflicts[276] to a presumptive *lex loci delicti* rule accompanied by an escape that authorizes displacement of the *lex loci*, if this would "advance the relevant substantive law purposes without impairing the smooth working of the multistate system or producing great uncertainty for litigants."[277] This escape came in handy in the part of *Schultz* v. *Boy Scouts of America*[278] that involved the second defendant, the Franciscan Brothers, that had their principal place of business in Ohio. Through this escape, the court managed to avoid the application of the pro-plaintiff law of the "locus of the tort" (New York) and thus to treat this defendant as favorably as the other defendant, Boy Scouts.

In *Gilbert* v. *Seton Hall University*[279], another tri-state conflict involving the same New Jersey charitable immunity rule and a New York injury, the court again avoided the *lex loci*, but through a different route. The defendant university was a non-profit New Jersey corporation protected by New Jersey's charitable immunity rule. The plaintiff was a Seton Hall student who was severely injured during

---

273. *Chappell* 407 F 3d at 178.

274. *Id.* at 177.

275. *Id.* *Knight* v. *Dawson*, 2004 WL 2334187 (NY Sup.Ct. 2d. 2004), involved the same New York statute, a New York rental-car and an accident in Ohio that resulted in the death of a New York passenger. After characterizing the New York statute as loss-allocating, the court invoked the escape of *Neumeier* Rule 3 and applied New York law. Noting that both the victim and the driver were New York domiciliaries and the car owner was a corporation authorized to do business in New York, the court concluded that "New York's interest in ensuring responsible ownership of vehicles subject to regulation in New York is served by the application of New York law ... and [since] the vehicle was only traveling through Ohio ... , the multi-state system will not be affected and litigants will not be subject to great uncertainty as a result of the departure from the general rule". *Id.* at *1.

276. For a table illustrating the many fact patterns that fall within the scope of Rule 3, see S. Symeonides, "Choice of Law in the American Courts in 1994: A View 'From the Trenches'", 43 *Am. J. Comp. L.* 1, 5 (1995).

277. *Neumeier* Rule 3, *supra* 93.

278. 480 NE 2d 679 (N.Y.1985), discussed *supra* 94-95.

279. 332 F.3d 105 (2d Cir. 2003) (decided under New York conflicts law).

a school rugby game held in New York. He was domiciled in Connecticut which, like New York, had abolished charitable immunity. The court noted that the case fell within the scope of *Neumeier* Rule 3, but, barely mentioning this rule again, proceeded to a full-fledged interest analysis that ended with the conclusion that New Jersey law should govern because New Jersey had a strong interest to apply it law, while New York did not. The court discounted the plaintiff's Connecticut domicile and treated his decision to attend a New Jersey school as equivalent to a choice of a domicile in New Jersey[280]. This made the case functionally analogous to a common-domicile case[281], which *Neumeier* Rule 1 subjects to the law of the common domicile[282].

The plaintiff invoked *Cook v. Goodhue*,[283] a lower-court case that held that the *lex loci* presumption of Rule 3 is rebutted by showing that the non-application of the *lex loci* would advance the policies of *all* other involved states—not just one. The *Gilbert* court rejected the argument, stating that "[n]othing in *Schultz* evi-

---

280. The court reasoned that the plaintiff "benefitted from the charitable immunity law of New Jersey by virtue of his voluntary decision to attend university in that state", *id.* at 110, and hence "New Jersey ha[d] a strong interest in having him bear a related burden." *Id.* Conversely, Connecticut's interest "in according [plaintiff] the benefits of its charitable [non-]immunity policy is reduced because ... he has avoided the policy's concomitant burden of paying the increased fees that a Connecticut institution, subject to negligence liability, must charge." *Id.*

281. In *Danan v. Sinai Special Needs Inst.*, 793 NYS 2d 419 (NYApp.Div.2005), which involved a New York plaintiff, the court distinguished *Gilbert* on this ground. The court held the New Jersey immunity rule inapplicable to this plaintiff's action against her New Jersey non-profit school for sexual abuse committed during a sleepover at a teacher's New York apartment.

282. In *O'Connor v. U.S. Fencing Ass'n*, 260 F.Supp.2d 545 (EDNY 2003), the home states of both parties (New York and California) allowed recovery, but the state of the accident did not. Thus, the analogy with the *Babcock* pattern was even clearer. Recognizing the analogy, the court held that allowing recovery would be consistent with the parties' expectations since both parties had "chosen to identify themselves in the most concrete form possible, domicile, with jurisdiction[s] that have weighed the [pertinent] interests ... and resolved the conflict in favor of recovery." *Id.* at 559 (quoting *Schultz*, 480 NE 2d at 686). For a similar case decided the same way, see *Diehl v. Ogorewac*, 836 F.Supp. 88 (EDNY 1993) (New Jersey defendant (driver), New York plaintiff (passenger), North Carolina traffic accident; North Carolina law favorable to defendant, New Jersey and New York law favorable to plaintiff; analogizing with common-domicile cases and, following escape from Rule 3, allowing recovery).

283. 842 F.Supp. 1509 (NDNY 1994). *Cook* arose out of a New York traffic accident involving a Texas plaintiff and an Ontario defendant. The Ontario defendant invoked Ontario's damages limitation and argued that since application of that limitation would promote Ontario's policy in protecting its domiciliaries, he met the requirements for the Rule 3 escape. "This is not so [said the court] ... . There is no 'either' in the rule ... . Defendant must show that the purposes of *all* relevant substantive laws will be advanced by application of [Ontario's] limit". *Id.* at 1511 (emphasis added).

dences so numerical an approach,"[284] and pointing out that *Schultz* applied New Jersey's charitable immunity rule even though both other involved states, New York and Ohio, had a non-immunity rule.

In *Bodea* v. *Trans Nat Express, Inc.*[285], New York was again the locus of the tort and its law favored the plaintiff more than *both* of the other involved states. The case arose out of a New York traffic accident involving an Ontario plaintiff and a Quebec defendant, driving in separate cars. The conflict involved the issue of damages for non-economic losses. Quebec did not allow such damages, Ontario allowed them but limited the amount, and New York allowed them without limits. The defendant invoked the Rule 3 escape and, apparently realizing that his chances of convincing the court to apply Quebec law were limited, made a more modest argument in favour of Ontario law. The court rejected the argument because it found "no reason why"[286] a Quebec resident "would expect that the laws of the Province of Ontario would apply to an accident that occurred in New York"[287]. The court noted that the analysis would differ if Ontario and Quebec had the same law but, since they did not, "the situs of the accident (New York) 'is appropriate as a 'tie breaker'"[288].

161. Should the *lex loci* be the tie breaker in these tri-state conflicts? This is a question on which reasonable minds can differ. For example, in drafting the Louisiana codification, this author concluded that: (1) the judicial experience accumulated at that time did not permit the articulation of even presumptive rules derived from that experience; and (2) rather than imposing such rules by legislative fiat, one should provide courts with the power and guidance to develop them. For this reason, the Louisiana codification relegates these cases, and other complex cases such as those involving joint tortfeasors, to the flexible approach of the residual article of the codification which lists the factors and policies the courts should consider in selecting the applicable law on a case-by case basis[289].

Two decades later, the author continues to subscribe to the same view. As the cases discussed in this section illustrate, one is hard pressed to identify clear patterns or solutions from which one can extract rules of any generality. This is the reason for which, unlike most of the preceding sections, this section does not conclude with a rule extracted from the case law.

The *Neumeier* court took a different route, which is both bolder and more conservative at the same time. It subjected these cases to a presumptive *lex loci*

---

284. *Gilbert*, 332 F.3d at 112.

285. 731 NYS 2d 113 (NYApp.Div. 2001).

286. *Id.* at 118.

287. *Id.*

288. *Id.* The court also noted that "both plaintiffs and defendants have purposefully associated themselves with the laws of New York", *id.*, and that their presence there was not fortuitous. The plaintiff traveled regularly through New York on his way to his apartment and job in Maryland, while the defendant, who was a truck-driver, drove frequently through New York.

289. See La. Civ. Code Art. 3542, discussed in Symeonides, *Exegesis*, 692-699.

rule qualified by an open-ended escape, the phrasing of which is deliberately vague. This is a sensible combination of certainty and flexibility. However, more than three decades after *Neumeier*, it is doubtful whether one can identify with any certainty the patterns that emerge in applying the Rule 3 escape. In *Gould Electronics Inc.* v. *United States*[290], a federal court attempted to summarize the circumstances under which New York courts displace the *lex loci* under *Neumeier* Rule 3. According to this summary, displacement is more likely when one or more of the following factors are present: (1) when the parties' contacts with the locus state are a matter of fortuity rather than voluntary action; (2) when the tort does not occur in the domicile of either party; (3) when displacement will not encourage forum shopping nor create the appearance of favouring local litigants; (4) when the parties are domiciled in states with similar laws; or (5) when the other state has a stronger interest than the locus state in applying its law[291].

This summary is eminently plausible. Whether it is also entirely accurate is another question. For example, one need not be facetious to suggest that, all other factors being equal, the *lex loci* is less likely to be displaced when it favours recovery than when it does not. Indeed, cases involving this tri-state pattern and decided by lower New York courts after *Schultz* suggest a certain pro-recovery bent. With the notable exception of *Gilbert*, and unlike the *Schultz* and *Neumeier* cases (both of which denied recovery in a *two*-state conflict of the no-interest paradigm), most of these lower-court cases have allowed recovery either by following the *lex loci* part of Rule 3[292], or by utilizing the escape contained in that

---

290. 220 F. 3d 169 (3d Cir. 2000) (decided under New York conflicts law).

291. *Id.* at 187.

292. For cases following the *lex loci* part of Rule 3 and allowing recovery, see, *Cook* v. *Goodhue*, 842 F. Supp. 1509 (NDNY 1994) (*supra* footnote 283); *McCann* v. *Somoza*, 933 F. Supp. 362 (SDNY 1996) (allowing recovery in a conflict among the no-fault statutes of Connecticut (the accident state), New Jersey (the plaintiff's state), and New York (the defendant's state). The first two states allowed recovery); *Simons* v. *Marriott Corp.*, 1993 WL 410457 (SDNY 1993) (personal injury action by a New York plaintiff against a Texas hotel owner, arising out of plaintiff's "slip and fall" in that hotel); *Weisberg* v. *Layne-New York Co.*, 517 NYS 2d 304 (Super. Ct. 1987) (damages for the wrongful death of a New York domiciliary resulting from a New Hampshire accident caused by a New Jersey defendant); *Gleason* v. *Holman Contract Warehouse, Inc.*, 681 NYS 2d 664 (NYApp.Div. 1998) (applying New Hampshire law and denying contribution between two foreign employers arising out of an injury in New Hampshire sustained by a New York employee); *Mihalic* v. *K-Mart of Amsterdam, N.Y.*, 363 F.Supp.2d 394 (NDNY 2005) (allowing contribution under New York law in third-party actions filed by non-New York subcontractors against Pennsylvania employer in case arising out of New York work-site accident. Pennsylvania law did not allow contribution). For a case refusing to apply the exception and denying recovery under the *lex loci*, see *Gopysingh* v. *Santiago*, 2002 WL 1586885 (SDNY 2002) (refusing to apply New York's car-owner statute to action of New York passenger injured in New Mexico while riding as passenger in a car rented in New Jersey).

rule[293]. It remains to be seen whether this trend will continue, and whether it will meet the approval of the New York Court of Appeals.

G.   Summary and Rules for Loss-Distribution Conflicts

162. This chapter has provided a fairly comprehensive[294] picture of the current state of American case law in loss-distribution conflicts. It covers cases decided by state and federal courts throughout the United States during the last three decades, under all modern choice-of-law methodologies. If one looks beyond the diversity of methodology and focuses on the actual results reached by the cases, one can discern a surprising degree of consistency if not uniformity – so much so that, for most patterns of cases, these results can be compressed into a few sentences of descriptive rules. This chapter has provided such rules for seven of the eight patterns discussed here.

If one were to assemble these rules and integrate them into a single rule, this rule would provide as follows[295]:

When, in a tort case that has pertinent contacts with more than one state, the loss-distribution laws of these states would produce a different outcome, the applicable law is determined as designated below, in the following order:

---

293. See, e.g., *Knight* v. *Dawson*, 2004 WL 2334187 (NY Sup.Ct. 2004) (*supra* footnote 275); *O'Connor* v. *U.S. Fencing Ass'n* , 260 F.Supp.2d 545 (EDNY 2003) (*supra* footnote 282); *Diehl* v. *Ogorewac*, 836 F. Supp. 88 (EDNY 1993) (*supra* footnote 282); *Murphy* v. *Acme Markets*, 650 F. Supp. 51 (EDNY 1986) (action by a New York plaintiff injured at a New Jersey job site owned by a Pennsylvania defendant, while working for a New York employer. New York's comparative negligence rule was more favourable to plaintiff than the New Jersey rule; applying New York law under the Rule 3 escape, because New York had an interest in protecting New Yorkers injured outside New York, while New Jersey had little interest in applying its loss-allocation rules when none of the parties were New Jersey domiciliaries); *Armstead* v. *Nat'l R.R. Passenger Corp.*, 954 F. Supp. 111 (SDNY 1997) (applying New York's pro-plaintiff comparative negligence law to action of New Yorker injured in Virginia on property belonging to a D.C. domiciliary, because of New York's "obvious interest in enforcing its determination that its own domiciliary whose own negligence is only partially responsible for her injuries should not go uncompensated". *Id.* at 112. Virginia had an all-or-nothing contributory negligence rule).

294. Although the review is comprehensive, it may not be 100% exhaustive. The author has made every effort to identify and discuss all major cases, but it is possible that some cases may have escaped his attention.

295. Any similarity between this rule and Article 3544 of the Louisiana Codification is purely coincidental.

(1) *(Common-Domicile Cases). If the injured party and the party whose conduct caused the injury (tortfeasor) are domiciled[296] in the same state[297], the law of that state governs* [whether it favours the victim (Pattern 1) or the tortfeasor (Pattern 2)];

(2) *(Split-Domicile Cases). If the injured party and the tortfeasor are domiciled in different states and both the tortfeasor's conduct and the victim's injury occurred in one of those states, the law of that state governs* [whether it favours the victim (Patterns 4 and 6) or the tortfeasor (Patterns 3 and 5)];

(3) *(Split-Domicile Cross-Border Cases). If conduct originating in one state has injured in another state a party domiciled in the other state, the law of the latter state governs if it is more favourable to the injured party and if the occurrence of the injury in that state was objectively foreseeable.* [(Pattern 7)].

163. As the bracketed phrases indicate, the above three rules cover seven of the eight typical patterns discussed in this chapter. In turn, these patterns represent the majority of loss-distribution conflicts. Each rule reflects the results reached by the majority of cases falling within the patterns covered by the rule. In some instances, this majority approaches unanimity (as in Pattern 1), in others it is overwhelming (as in Patterns 2, 3, 5 and 7), and in others it is simply a clear majority (as in Patterns 4 and 6). In this sense, all of the above rules are "restatements" of the case law.

Although these rules cover many cases, they do not cover all cases. They are deliberately elliptical. For example, the rules do not cover: (1) the cases falling within Pattern 8; (2) most cases involving three states; and (3) all disputes between joint tortfeasors in all patterns. Judicial experience thus far has not produced clear solutions for any of these categories. Although one can detect certain weak trends, it would be premature to give them the status of either a descriptive, or especially a prescriptive, rule.

The above rules are not phrased with the precision and the degree of detail that is necessary or customary for statutory rules. Furthermore, because they are descriptive rather than prescriptive, the above rules are not accompanied by any escape clause authorizing judicial deviations in exceptional cases. Such a clause would be necessary, however, if one were to put these rules in statutory language[298].

164. All three of the above rules are forum-neutral. Rules 1 and 2 are also content-neutral, namely, they are phrased in terms that, on their surface, do not

---

296. As used here, domicile is intended to cover other equivalent terms, such as habitual residence, "home-state", or principal place of business. See *supra* 125.

297. When the victim and the tortfeasor are domiciled in different states the laws of which produce the same result, the law of either state may be applied. See *supra* 135-136.

298. The similarly phrased rules of the Louisiana codification are accompanied by escapes. See *supra* footnotes 54, 80, 119, 217.

take account of the content of the involved states' laws. They provide for the application of the law of the designated state, regardless of whether that law favours the victim or the tortfeasor. In this sense, Rules 1 and 2 are "jurisdiction-selecting" rules. In contrast, Rule 3 is a content-dependent or content-oriented rule, because it provides for the application of the law of the designated state only if that law has a certain content, i.e., it favours the victim.

The reason for the difference is not an *a priori* preference, but rather the judicial experience accumulated during the revolution, and a careful study and analysis of that experience. For example, as the reader will recall, the above discussion divided the common-domicile cases covered by Rule 1 into two patterns (1 and 2), based precisely on the content of the involved states' laws. However, after collecting and analysing the cases of each pattern, the conclusion emerged that this content did not affect the outcome of the cases. Similarly, the cases covered by Rule 2 were divided into four patterns (3-6), again based on the content of the involved states' laws. Again, in the majority of cases that content proved to be immaterial in affecting the outcome.

In contrast, in the remaining two patterns (Patterns 7 and 8), the content of the involved states' laws did make a difference. The majority of cases applied the law of the victim's home state when that law favoured the victim (Pattern 7), but not when it favoured the tortfeasor (Pattern 8). For this reason, Rule 3 has been phrased narrowly so as to encompass Pattern 7, but not Pattern 8, cases.

165. Finally, as one author described them, the above rules are "derived" rather than "devised"[299]. They are descriptive of what the courts have been doing rather than prescriptive in the sense of seeking to re-orient the courts' path[300]. But this begs the question of whether they *should* be prescriptive. Should the rules reproduce the past, or should they improve on it[301]? After all, "'what the courts are really doing' might not always be an appropriate solution"[302]. Whether on not this is true in this case is a question that admits different answers because reasonable people may disagree on the merits of these rules.

---

299. L. Weinberg, "Theory Wars in the Conflict of Laws", 103 *Mich. L. Rev.* 1631, 1648 (2005) (concluding that this book's author "is not so much interested in inventing solutions and then proposing and advocating them ... as he is in changing our minds about the sources of rule-based solutions. He is not interested in devising rules. Rather, he wants to derive them …. His ambition is to put in rule form what courts actually do").

300. See *id.* (concluding that, rather than trying to "change what courts are doing", this book's author apparently believes that "whatever courts say they are doing – they will tend to gravitate toward established patterns of choice of law"). See also *id.* at 1650 ("[the author] is not in the business of criticizing these cases. To him, they speak volumes. These cases, just or unjust, rational or not, are authority".).

301. See *id.* (stating that this book's author "acts on the principle that what courts do, and their measure of agreement in what they do, are phenomena to be taken very seriously indeed ... [and] has the strong conviction that to glean truth from reality one has to handle a great deal of reality, and to do so with utmost care".).

302. E. Scoles, P. Hay, P. Borchers and S. Symeonides, *Conflict of Laws* 106 (4th ed. 2004).

For what it is worth, this author's opinion is that these rules are not only a good mirror of the past but also a good guide for the future. But while this opinion hardly matters, what is clear is that since they are derived from and reflect the results of the majority of cases, these rules are as good or bad as those results. The point is that, if these rules had been in place, the courts would have reached the same good or bad results, but in a less laborious, and much more direct, economical, and predictable way. In turn, this would have benefited the litigants (including those who lost) and the choice-of-law system at large. If this is true, it is worth asking whether one should seek to secure these benefits for future cases. We shall return to this question in Chapter X.

Chapter VII   Conduct-Regulation Tort Conflicts

A.   Introduction

166. This chapter discusses conflicts between conduct-regulating rules, namely rules that, in the words of the New York Court of Appeals, "have the prophylactic effect of governing conduct to prevent injuries from occurring"[1]. As explained in Chapter V, whether a particular rule falls within this category depends on the rule's *primary* purpose or function as determined by the court through the interpretative process. "Rules of the road" as well as those rules that prescribe the civil sanctions for violating rules of the road, and rules that prescribe safety standards for work sites, buildings, and other premises are examples of rules whose primary function is to regulate conduct, even if they ultimately also have a bearing on loss-distribution.

One peculiarly American example of conduct-regulating rules are rules that impose punitive or exemplary damages for egregious conduct. Punitive-damages rules go beyond the normative goal of deterrence that characterizes all conduct-regulating rules in that they seek to civilly punish the individual wrongdoer and set an example for others. In the words of one American court, these rules aim for "deterrence through public condemnation"[2]. Because of these special features, punitive-damages conflicts are reserved for separate discussion in part C of this chapter. Part B discusses cases involving other conduct-regulating rules or, in any event, rules that the courts classified as conduct-regulating rules.

B.   Generic Conduct-Regulation Conflicts

1.   The pertinent contacts and typical patterns

167. Unlike loss-distributing rules which focus both on people and on territory, conduct-regulating rules are primarily territorial. For example, a state has an interest in enforcing its traffic rules, without regard to who violates them and who suffers from the violation. A foreigner who enters the territory may not claim

---

1.   *Padula* v. *Lilarn Props. Corp.*, 644 NE 2d 1001, 1002 (NY 1994) (discussed *supra* 118).

2.   *Horowitz* v. *Schneider Nat'l Inc.*, 708 F. Supp. 1573, 1577 (D. Wyo. 1989).

exemption from these rules and, when injured by conduct that violates them, he may not be denied the benefit of their protection.

This suggests that, as a general proposition, the parties' domiciles are a far less significant factor in conduct-regulation conflicts than in loss-distribution conflicts. This is not to say that domicile is an irrelevant contact. For example, if the violator of a conduct-regulating rule is a domiciliary of the enacting state, this state has an additional reason to insist on the rule's application. Similarly, if the victim of the violation is a domiciliary of the enacting state, this state has an additional reason to insist on the rule's application. The point is, however, that a state has a general interest in enforcing its conduct-regulating rules even if neither the violator nor the victim resides in that state. For this reason, conduct-regulating conflicts should be analysed and resolved by focusing more on the spatial aspects of the conduct and the injury, and less on the parties' domiciles.

The reference to both the conduct and the injury underscores the possibility that these two events may occur in different states. Indeed, cross-border torts are more common today than ever before. In such torts, the old phrase "locus of the tort" becomes ambiguous. When conduct in one state produces injury in another, either state may qualify as the locus of the tort. Rather than retreating to outmoded and artificial "last-event" notions, one should be prepared to accept the premise that, when the conduct and the injury are not in the same state, both of these contacts deserve due consideration.

With this premise in mind, as well as the premise that the parties' domiciles are not a significant *a priori* factor in conduct-regulation conflicts, these conflicts can be classified into the following four patterns:

(1)   Cases in which the conduct and the injury occur in the same state *(Pattern 1)*;
(2)   Cases in which the conduct and the injury occur in different states, and in which:
    (a)   the two states prescribe the same standards of conduct *(Pattern 2)*; or
    (b)   the two states prescribe different standards (designated with the adjectives "high" and "low"), and in which the particular conduct:
        (i)   violates the ("higher") standards of the state of conduct, but not the ("lower") standards of the state of injury *(Pattern 3)*; or
        (ii) does not violate the ("lower") standards of the state of conduct, but does violate the ("higher") standards of the state of injury *(Pattern 4)*.

The table below depicts these patterns, with uppercase letters denoting a state with a high standard of conduct and lowercase letters denoting a state with a low standard of conduct.

Table 13. Patterns in conduct-regulation conflicts

Pattern	Conduct	Injury
1	A	A
2	A	B
3	A	b
4	a	B

2.   Pattern 1: Conduct and injury in same state

168. Ordinarily, the cases of Pattern 1 are so obviously false conflicts that they should not occupy us here. As long as the issue in question clearly qualifies as one of conduct-regulation, the state in which both the injurious conduct and the resulting injury occurred has the exclusive claim to apply its law. As the *Babcock* court stated, in these cases, "it would be almost unthinkable to seek the applicable rule in the law of some other place"[3]. Indeed, even the Restatement Second abandons its characteristic equivocalness and declares that, "[w]ith respect to issues relating to the standards of conduct, the local law of the state of conduct and injury has been *invariably* applied"[4].

Yet, perhaps because of the increased importance of the parties' domiciles in loss-distribution conflicts, it is easy to forget that the parties' domiciles are simply irrelevant in conduct-regulation conflicts. It therefore bears repeating that the principle that the state of conduct and injury has the "dominant interest" to apply it law holds true even when one *or both* of the parties are domiciled in such "other place".

---

3.   *Babcock* v. *Jackson*, 191 NE 2d at 280. See also *supra* 91, 108.

4.   Restatement Second, Conflict of Laws, § 146 cmt d., Reporters Note (emphasis added). See also *id.* § 145 cmt. d ("subject only to rare exceptions, the local law of the state where conduct and injury occurred will be applied to determine whether the actor satisfied minimum standards of acceptable conduct and whether the interest affected by the actor's conduct was entitled top legal protection").

Cases confirming this proposition are countless. They involve issues of not only traffic safety[5] and work site safety[6], but also premises liability[7], contributory

---

5.   See *Bertram* v. *Norden*, 823 NE 2d 478 (Ohio App. 2004) (discussed *infra* 169); *Bonelli* v. *Giguere*, 2004 WL 424089 (Conn. Super. Ct. 2004) (discussed *infra* 170); *Johnson* v. *Ford Motor Co., Inc.*, 2003 WL 22317425 (ND Ill.2003) (discussed *infra* 170); *Tkaczevski* v. *Ryder Truck Rental, Inc.*, 22 F. Supp. 2d 169 (SDNY 1998) (negligent parking of car that contributed to causing an accident); *Ellis* v. *Parto*, 918 P. 2d 540 (Wash. App. 1996), review den. 930 P. 2d 1229 (Wash. 1997) (traffic rules); *FCE Transp. Inc.* v. *Ajayem Lumber Midwest Corp.*, 1988 WL 48018 (Ohio App. 1988) (traffic rules); *Chang* v. *Chang*, 2004 WL 2095116 (Conn.Super. 2004) (statute imposing treble damages on drivers who knowingly operate car with defective mechanisms); *Hadley* v. *Bacchiocchi*, 18 Mass.L.Rptr. 282, 2004 WL 2341343 (Mass.Super.,2004) (car-lessor's liability statute); *Baca* v. *New Prime, Inc.*, 763 NE 2d 1014 (Ind. App. 2002) (applied Indiana's guest statute to an Indiana accident involving Missouri parties, in part because, in the court's opinion, that statute was conduct-regulating in that it "establish[ed] the standard of care owed by a driver to certain guests". *Id.* at 1019).

6.   See *Augello* v. *20166 Tenants Corp.*, 648 NYS 2d 101 (NYAD 1 Dept. 1996) (scaffolding law); *Thompson* v. *Int'l Bus. Mach.*, 862 F. Supp. 79 (SDNY 1994) (scaffolding law).

7.   See *Spinozzi* v. *ITT Sheraton Corp.*, 174 F. 3d 842 (7th Cir. 1999) (discussed *infra* 169); *Najarian* v. *Nat'l Amusements, Inc.*, 768 A. 2d 1253 (RI 2001); *Taylor* v. *Massachusetts Flora Realty, Inc.*, 840 A.2d 1126 (RI 2004); *Kirschbaum* v. *WRGSB Assoc.*, 243 F. 3d 145 (3rd Cir. 2001); *Olson* v. *Empire Dist. Elec. Co.*, 14 SW3d 218 (Mo. App. 2000); *Judge* v. *Pilot Oil Corp.*, 205 F. 3d 335 (7th Cir. 2000); *Wal-Mart Stores, Inc.* v. *Manning*, 788 So. 2d 116 (Ala. 2000); *Ramey* v. *Wal-Mart, Inc.* 967 F. Supp. 843 (ED Pa. 1997); *Schechter* v. *Tauck Tours, Inc.*, 17 F. Supp. 2d 255, (SDNY 1998); *Scheerer* v. *Hardee's Food Sys., Inc.* 92 F. 3d 702 (8th Cir. 1996); *Scott* v. *Pilot Corp.* 1996 WL 588038 (Wis. App. 1996); *Smith* v. *Florida Gulf Airlines, Inc.*, 1996 WL 156859 (ED La. 1996); *Leane* v. *Joseph Entm't Group, Inc.*, 642 NE 2d 852 (Ill. App. 1994); Johnson v. Travelers Ins. Co., 486 N.W.2d 37 (Wis. Ct. App. 1992); *Burns* v. *Geres*, 409 N.W.2d 428 (Wis. Ct. App. 1987); *Barrett* v. *Foster Grant Co, Inc.*, 450 F. 2d 1146 (1st Cir. 1971); *Murphy* v. *Thornton*, 746 So. 2d 575 (Fla. App. 1999). For cases involving hotels in particular, see *infra* footnotes 26-27.

negligence[8], interference with contract[9], misappropriation of trade secrets[10], and other issues[11]. In all of these cases, the courts applied the law of the state in which both the conduct and the injury occurred, without considering the parties' domiciles. Conversely, some cases have held that the forum's conduct-regulating rule

---

8.   See, e.g., *Dist. of Columbia v. Coleman*, 667 A. 2d 811 (DC 1995); *Matson by Kehoe v. Anctil*, 979 F. Supp. 1031 (D. Vt. 1997); *Moye v. Palma*, 622 A. 2d 935 (NJ Super.1993); *Gray v. Busch Entm't Corp.*, 886 F. 2d 14 (2nd Cir. 1989); *Kirby v. Lee*, 1999 WL 562750 (ED Pa. 1999); *Edwards v. McKee*, 76 P.3d 73 (Okla.Civ.App.2003); *Sabbatino v. Old Navy, Inc.*, 2003 WL 21448822 (N.Y.City Civ.Ct.2003) (finding that a New Jersey rule that barred recovery if the plaintiff was found at least 50% negligent was conduct-regulating because its intent was "to encourage people to act more carefully and to take responsibility for their own actions", *id.* at *5; applying the rule to the case of a New Yorker patron who was injured in a New Jersey shop – "it is not reasonable to conclude that ... by opening its doors to customers from New York [the New Jersey shop owner] was also inviting in New York's law". *Id.*).

9.   In *Abogados v. AT&T, Inc.*, 223 F. 3d 932 (9th Cir. 2000) (decided under California's comparative impairment), which involved an interference with a Mexican contract, the court found "nonsensical" the plaintiff's argument that "Mexico has no interest in regulating conduct that affects contracts made in Mexico". *Id.* at 935. The court concluded that Mexico had an interest in determining "the point at which it will attach tort liability to conduct occurring within its borders" and that such determination "is designed ... to protect potential defendants – including foreign defendants who might otherwise avoid doing business in Mexico – from liability for conduct that Mexico does not consider wrongful". *Id.* at 935-936. In *Bridas Corp. v. Unocal Corp.*, 16 SW 3d 893 (Tex. App. 2000) (decided under the Second Restatement), the interferences occurred in Turkmenistan and Afghanistan. The plaintiff argued that, because the defendant's acts were conceived in and directed from its Texas headquarters, Texas had an interest in applying its law to ensure compliance with its standards of conduct. The court, focusing more on contacts than on interests, rejected this argument after finding that "the parties and the subject matter of this litigation ha[d] a more significant relationship to the nations of Turkmenistan and Afghanistan than to Texas". *Id.* at 899. In *EA Oil Serv., Inc. v. Mobil Explor. & Prod. Turkmenistan, Inc.*, 2000 WL 552406 (Tex. App. 2000), which involved very similar facts and issues, the court reached the same result. The court noted Texas's interest in protecting the Texas plaintiff but also spoke of "Turkmenistan's interest in controlling its oil wealth", *id.* at *3, and concluded that, because the conduct and injury occurred in Turkmenistan, that country had the most significant relationship and its law should govern, thus barring plaintiff's action.

10.   See *BP Chem. Ltd. v. Formosa Chem. & Fibre Corp.*, 229 F. 3d 254 (3d Cir. 2000) (holding that Taiwanese law should govern misappropriation claim because Taiwan had the greatest interest in setting standards for determining whether trade information licensed in Taiwan and used there was protectable, and in determining whether the defendant acted tortiously in acquiring that information in Taiwan from another Taiwanese corporation).

11.   See, e.g., *Richardson v. Michelin N. Am., Inc.*, 1998 WL 135804 (WDNY 1998) (strict liability); *Troxel v. A.I. duPont Inst.*, 636 A. 2d 1179 (Pa. Super. 1994) (medical malpractice);.

was inapplicable to an out-of-state accident involving exclusively forum domiciliaries[12].

169. *Bertram v. Norden*[13] is a recent example of the controlling interest of the state of conduct and injury to apply its law, even when the tortfeasor and the victim have a joint domicile and a preexisting relationship in another state. *Bertram* arose from a snowmobiling collision in Michigan between two young Ohio domiciliaries who had traveled together to Michigan for a weekend of snowmobiling activities. A Michigan statute barred the plaintiff's action, providing that "[e]ach person who participates in the sport of snowmobiling accepts the risks associated with that sport insofar as the dangers are obvious and inherent"[14]. Ohio permitted the action. Following the Second Restatement and its presumption in favor of the law of the state of injury, the Ohio court applied the Michigan statute, holding for the defendant.

The court reasoned that the parties' common domicile and relationship in Ohio did not overcome the presumption in favor of Michigan law, because Michigan had a special interest in applying its snowmobiling statute to snowmobiling activity within its borders. Noting that Michigan is a well-known snowmobiling destination, the court found it "important that Michigan has created a law specifically regulating the operation of snowmobiles ... and ... recogniz[ing] a rider's own assumption of risk"[15]. The court concluded that Michigan law should govern "[b]ecause ... the place where the conduct causing ... injury occurred in Michigan

---

12. See *Padula v. Lilarn Prop. Corp.*, 644 NE 2d 1001 (NY 1994), discussed *supra* 118; *Huston v. Hayden Bldg. Maint. Corp.*, 617 NYS 2d 335 (NYAD 2 Dept. 1994); *Salsman v. Barden & Robeson Corp.*, 564 NYS 2d 546 (NYAD 3 Dept. 1990); *Zangiacomi v. Saunders*, 714 F. Supp. 658 (SDNY 1989); *Clarke v. Sound Advice Live, Inc.*, 633 NYS 2d 490 (NYAD 2 Dept. 1995); *Hardzynski v. ITT Hartford Ins. Co.*, 643 NYS 2d 122 (NYAD 2 Dept. 1996); *Florio v. Fisher Dev., Inc.*, 765 NYS 2d 879 (NYAD 2003). See also *Svege v. Mercedes Benz Credit Corp.*, 182 F. Supp. 2d 226 (D Conn. 2002) (holding that Connecticut's car owner's liability statute was conduct-regulating and thus did not apply to non-Connecticut owners and non-Connecticut accidents); *Cruz v. Teto*, 2003 WL 1963187 (Conn. Super. 2003) (similar case and analysis and same result); but see *Chang v. Chang*, 2004 WL 3105970 (Conn. Super. 2004) (holding the same Connecticut statute applicable to an accident in Florida involving a car rented there and a Connecticut driver and passenger); and *Chang v. Chang*. 2004 WL 2095116, 37 Conn. L. Rptr. 730 (Conn. Super. Ct. 2004) (holding inapplicable in the same case another Connecticut statute that imposed treble damages on persons driving a car with a defective mechanism).

13. 823 NE 2d 478 (Ohio App. 2004), appeal not allowed 824 NE 2d 541 (Ohio 2005).

14. Mich. Comp. Laws § 324.82126(6) (2004).

15. *Bertram*, 823 NE 2d at 484. See also *id.*: "Such a public policy creates a system that is certain, predictable and uniform in its result ... [and] allows for ease in the determination and application of the law as it applies to snowmobiling and snowmobiling related accidents, as well as protecting justified expectations".).

and Michigan has enacted specific legislation involving the risks of snowmobiling"[16].

Spinozzi v. *ITT Sheraton Corporation*[17], a case involving the issue of premises liability, is another good illustration of how irrelevant the parties' domicile is
in conduct-regulation conflicts. *Spinozzi* was an action by an Illinois domiciliary
who was injured in an American-owned hotel while on vacation in Mexico[18]. The
plaintiff, who was contributorily negligent, could recover under Illinois' comparative negligence rule, but not under Mexico's contributory negligence rule. The
plaintiff argued that, because defendant had solicited the plaintiff in Illinois, the
defendant should be deemed to have caused the injury in Illinois, and that this
"contact", together with the plaintiff's Illinois domicile, made Illinois the state with
the most significant relationship.

Writing for the court, Judge Posner thought that this argument was tantamount to saying that "each guest be permitted to carry with him the tort law of his
state or country, provided that he is staying in a hotel that had advertised there"[19].
The plaintiff could not have thought, said the judge, that he was

> "carrying his domiciliary law with him, like a turtle's house, to every foreign country
> he visited ... [nor could he, while] eating dinner with a Mexican in Acapulco, feel him-
> self cocooned in Illinois law, like citizens of imperial states in the era of colonialism
> who were granted extraterritorial privileges in weak or dependent states."[20]

Acceptance of the plaintiff's argument, said Posner, would subject a hotel operator like Sheraton "to a hundred different bodies of tort law"[21], each imposing potentially inconsistent duties of care. "A resort might have a system of firewalls that

---

16. *Id.* In *Schumacher* v. *Schumacher*, 676 NW 2d 685 (Minn. Ct. App. 2004), another
common-domicile case, the issue straddled the line between conduct-regulation and
loss-allocation, but again the court applied the law of the state of conduct and injury
(Iowa) rather than that of the parties' common domicile (Minnesota). The plaintiff
was injured in Iowa by one of his father's show horses. Iowa, but not Minnesota, immunized the owner of domesticated animals from liability for injury "resulting from
the inherent risks of a domesticated animal activity". While noting Minnesota's interest in compensating tort victims, the court found that Iowa also had a "substantial
governmental interest ... [in] encouraging participation in agricultural activities ...
such as horse shows, ... [which] bring[] people and money to the state", *id.* at 691, and
concluded that to apply Minnesota law "in the face of such an economic and public
policy would indicate disrespect for Iowa law". *Id.*
17. 174 F. 3d 842 (7th Cir. 1999) (decided under Illinois conflicts law).
18. The defendant ITT Sheraton was a Delaware corporation that had its principal place
of business in Massachusetts.
19. 174 F. 3d at 845.
20. *Id.* at 846. See *id.* ("Law is largely territorial, and people have at least a vague intuition
of this. They may feel safer in foreign hotels owned by American chains, but they do
not feel that they are on American soil and governed by American law").
21. *Id.* at 845.

under the law of some states or nations might be considered essential to safety and in others might be considered a safety hazard"[22]. These dangers are avoided, said Posner, by the application of the *lex loci delicti*, which is "the only choice of law that won't impose potentially debilitating legal uncertainties on businesses that cater to a multinational clientele while selecting the rule of decision most likely to optimize safety"[23]. For, in the absence of unusual circumstances, said Posner, the state where the tort occurred is the state that has "the greatest interest in striking a reasonable balance among safety, cost, and other factors pertinent to the design and administration of a system of tort law"[24]. As noted elsewhere[25], Posner's witty statements are correct, provided they are confined to issues of conduct regulation. For these issues, – and often for other issues as well – the cases have consistently, if not invariably[26], applied the law of the state in which the hotel or other building is situated, which is the state of both the conduct and the injury[27].

---

22.   *Id.* See also *id.* ("Illinois residents may want a higher standard of care than the average hotel guest in Mexico, but to supplant Mexican by Illinois tort law would disserve the general welfare because it would mean that Mexican safety standards (insofar as they are influenced by tort suits) were being set by people having little stake in those standards".)

23.   *Id.* at 846.

24.   *Id.* at 845.

25.   See S. Symeonides, "Choice of Law in the American Courts in 1999: One More Year", 48 *Am. J. Comp. L.* 143, 152 (2000).

26.   One of the very few cases to go the other way is *Brandt* v. *Starwood Hotels & Resorts Worldwide, Inc.*, 2004 WL 2958661 (ED Mich. 2004). In this case, a Michigan patron who was injured in a Florida hotel argued for the application of Florida's pro-plaintiff law, while the hotel owner argued for the application of Michigan's pro-defendant law. Following Michigan's *lex fori* approach, the court applied Michigan law because "Florida's interest in protecting a foreign tourist is no greater than Michigan's interest in applying its law to its own citizens ... especially ... when the business entity against which liability is sought operates a hostelry within this State". *Id.* at *4. This reasoning makes no sense except to the extent it confirms the absurdity of the *lex fori* approach.

27.   For example, in *Bauer* v. *Club Med Sales, Inc.*, 1996 WL 310076 (ND Cal. 1996), a similar case involving a California vacationer and another American-owned hotel in Mexico, the court applied Mexican law because, although California had a "cognizable interest in the application of its own stringent building and construction standards in order to protect its citizens traveling abroad", *id.* at *4, that interest should be subordinated to "Mexico's sovereignty interest in enforcing its own construction standards within its borders". *Id.* As noted *supra* at 135, Bauer involved an additional issue – the amount of damages for the victim's wrongful death. On this issue, the court took note of the parties' domicile, including defendant's status as an American corporation, and held that California's pro-recovery law should govern. For other cases applying the law of the place where the hotel is situated, see *Cummings* v. *Club Mediterranée, S.A.*, 2003 WL 22462625 (ND Ill.2003); *Guidi* v. *Inter-Continental Hotels Corp.*, 2003 WL 1907901 (SDNY 2003); *Beatty* v. *Isle of Capri Casino, Inc.*, 234 F.Supp.2d 651 (ED Tex. 2002); *Marzoni* v. *Hyatt Corp.*, 2002 WL 31001833 (ED La. 2002); *Garvin* v. *Hyatt*

170. Finally, like *Bertram* and *Spinozzi*, countless other cases involving issues of road safety ignore the parties' domiciles and focus instead on the state of
conduct and injury. As noted earlier, this category of issues is much broader than
commonly assumed. It includes not only traffic rules, but also the presumptions,
inferences, and other legal consequences and sanctions that states impose on violators of those rules[28]. For example, although all states of the United States require
car drivers and passengers to wear seat belts, many states differ on some of the
legal consequences of violating this requirement. Some states allow evidence of
failure to use a seatbelt to establish the parties' relative fault and mitigate civil
damages, while other states prohibit such evidence[29]. Depending on their specific
language and history, these seatbelt rules can be procedural or substantive[30], and,
if the latter, they can be either loss-distributing[31] or conduct-regulating. If they
fall into the latter category, then they apply to all persons driving or riding in the
enacting state, regardless of their domicile.

    Corp., 2000 WL 798640 (Mass. App. 2000); *McGovern v. Marriott Int'l, Inc.* 1996 WL
    470643 (ED La. 1996); *Greco v. Grand Casinos of Mississippi, Inc.* 1996 WL 617401 (ED
    La. 1996); *DeMyrick v. Guest Quarters Suite Hotels*, 944 F. Supp. 661 (ND Ill. 1996);
    Nagghiu v. Inter-Continental Hotels Group, Inc., 165 FRD 413 (D Del. 1996).

28.   See *supra* 120.

29.   "At present, 12 states provide that seatbelt evidence is not admissible. Only two states
    permit its introduction for purposes of determining the relative fault of the parties,
    and seven states, including the aforesaid two, permit its introduction for purposes
    of apportioning damages. In other states, the question at present is left largely unre-
    solved". R. Kohlman, "The Seatbelt Defense", 35 *Am. Juris. Trials* 349 § 29 (2005).

30.   In *Barron v. Ford Motor Co. of Canada Ltd.*, 965 F.2d 195 (7th Cir. 1992), cert. de-
    nied, 506 US 1001 (1992), the court stated that a North Carolina rule that prohibited
    evidence of a plaintiff's failure to wear a seat belt would be procedural if it was "mo-
    tivated by concern that jurors attach too much weight to a plaintiff's failure to wear
    his seatbelt" and substantive if it was "designed not to penalize persons who fail to
    fasten their seatbelts". *Id.* at 199. The court concluded that the rule was substantive
    because, according to North Carolina precedents, "it is founded on the desire of the
    North Carolina courts not to penalize the failure to fasten one's seatbelt, because
    nonuse is so rampant in the state that the average person could not be thought care-
    less for failing to fasten his seatbelt". *Id.* at 200. See also *Brown v. Ford Motor Co.*, 67
    F.Supp.2d 581 (ED Va. 1999) (characterizing a similar Virginia rule as substantive for
    some purposes and procedural for other purposes).

31.   See *Garcia v. Gen. Motors Corp.*, 990 P.2d 1069 (Ariz.App. 1999), review denied (1/04/
    2000) (applying Arizona rule allowing evidence of seatbelt nonuse rather than Idaho
    rule prohibiting such evidence in a case involving Arizona plaintiffs injured in Idaho,
    after finding that both rules were designed to affect the amount of plaintiffs' damages
    rather than the conduct of drivers or passengers); *Noble v. Moore*, 2002 WL 172665
    (Con. Super. 2002) (applying Connecticut rule prohibiting evidence of seatbelt non-
    use rather than New York rule allowing such evidence but only for mitigation of dam-
    ages (not for liability) in a case arising out of a New York accident involving only
    Connecticut parties, after finding that both rules were designed to affect the amount
    of damages available to plaintiffs rather than the conduct of drivers or passengers).

Johnson v. *Ford Motor Co., Inc.*[32], is a case on point. In this product-liability action arising out of a Kentucky accident, the court held that Illinois's pro-plaintiff law should govern most issues, except the issue of the seatbelt defense. Illinois prohibited the introduction of evidence of seatbelt non-use while Kentucky allowed such evidence to establish the plaintiff's contributory fault. "Kentucky has a strong interest in maintaining driver safety"[33], said the court, and "one way Kentucky chooses to enforce its seatbelt laws is by assessing comparative fault for a failure to wear a seatbelt"[34]. The court concluded that since "the Plaintiffs engaged in this actionable conduct in Kentucky where they were injured and acting contrary to Kentucky law ... Kentucky has a strong interest in enforcing its seatbelt laws"[35] and its law should govern this issue.

In *Bonelli* v. *Giguere*[36], the laws were reversed. The state of the accident, Connecticut, prohibited evidence of seatbelt non-use, while the plaintiff's home state, New York, allowed evidence of non-use for the purpose of mitigating damages. The court rejected the Canadian defendant's argument that the New York rule should apply. The court found that this rule was a "regulatory law specifically aimed at drivers traveling upon New York roadways"[37], and thus New York had "no interest" in applying it "beyond its borders ... on Connecticut roadways"[38]. Conversely, the court concluded, Connecticut had the exclusive interest in applying its own "regulatory laws regarding roadway travel"[39].

3.   Pattern 2: Conduct and injury in different states that prescribe the same standards of conduct

171. Cases in which the conduct and the injury occur in different states also present the false conflict paradigm if the two states prescribe the same standard of conduct. In policy terms, these cases are virtually indistinguishable from Pattern 1 cases. Whether the court applies the law of the one state or the other state, the outcome will be the same. Hence, applying the law of the conduct state is both sensible and non-controversial.

---

32.   2003 WL 22317425 (ND Ill. 2003).
33.   *Id.* at *4.
34.   *Id.*
35.   *Id.* See also *id.* at *5 ("The Plaintiffs cannot reasonably expect that a foreign state's law will govern the allocation of any possible damages award in a single-car incident merely because an accident fortuitously occurs outside of Illinois, but they know they are subject to the traffic laws of another state when driving in that state".).
36.   2004 WL 424089 (Conn. Super. Ct. 2004).
37.   *Id.* at *3. (Compare with *Noble* v. *Moore*, 2002 WL 172665 (Con.Super. 2002), *supra* footnote 31).
38.   *Id.*
39.   *Id.*

For example, in *Pardey* v. *Boulevard Billiard Club*[40], both the conduct state, Rhode Island, and the injury state, Massachusetts, had a dram shop act imposing civil liability on a tavern owner whose intoxicated patrons cause injury to another. A Massachusetts patron caused such injury in Massachusetts after becoming intoxicated in defendant's Rhode Island tavern. The court noted Rhode Island's "substantial governmental interest"[41] in applying the Rhode Island act to violations occurring in that state, even when the resulting injury occurs in another state. The court also noted that Massachusetts would not be "offended" by the application of the Rhode Island dram shop act because Massachusetts also had a dram shop act. Indeed, the court concluded, "[a]pplication of Rhode Island law therefore effectuates, rather than frustrates, the policies of *both* states".[42]

Other dram shop act cases have recognized this elementary principle and have reached the same result under similar circumstances[43].

172. Another group of Pattern 2 cases involves statutes that impose vicarious liability on car owners for injuries caused by a driver using the car with the owner's consent (hereafter referred to as "car-owner statutes"). Although some courts have characterized these statutes as loss-distributing[44], others have characterized them as conduct-regulating[45]. Accepting for now the latter characterization, Pattern 2 appears when both the state of the critical conduct, i.e., the state in which the owner consented to the use of the car by another, and the state in which the driver caused the injury have such statutes. In such a case, the court can apply the statute of either state without altering the outcome.

In *Elson* v. *Defren*[46], two of the involved states, Idaho and New York[47], had similar car-owner liability statutes. The only difference was that the text of the

---

40. 518 A. 2d 1349 (RI 1986).

41. *Id.* at 1352.

42. *Id.* (emphasis added).

43. See *Rutledge* v. *Rockwells of Bedford, Inc.*, 613 NYS 2d 179 (NYAD 1994) (applying New York's dram shop act to an action arising from a Connecticut accident caused by a driver who became intoxicated in defendant's New York tavern. Connecticut had a dram shop act similar to New York's); *Platano* v. *Norm's Castle, Inc.*, 830 F. Supp. 796 (SDNY 1993) (same pattern and same result on dram shop act liability, but awarding compensatory damages under Connecticut's more generous standards so as to better effectuate the deterrence policy embodied in New York's act); *Trapp* v. *4-10 Investment Corp.*, 424 F. 2d 1261 (8th Cir. 1970). For another case involving exposure to asbestos in one state and injury in another, see *Zimko* v. *American Cyanamid,* 905 So. 2d 465 (La.App. 2005) (finding a false conflict because both states had the same standards of liability).

44. See *infra* 175 footnote 64.

45. See, e.g., *Svege* v. *Mercedes Benz Credit Corp.*, 182 F. Supp. 2d 226 (D Conn. 2002), and other cases discussed *infra* 175, 179 at footnote 113.

46. 726 NYS 2d 407 (NYAD 2001).

47. This case also involved a third state, Washington, where a New York domiciliary rented the car. He then drove the car to Idaho with plaintiffs, also New York domiciliaries, riding as passengers. The court did not discuss Washington law, for two

New York statute limited its application to cars that had certain New York connections which were absent in this case. The court found that, because of this territorial limitation, the New York statute was inapplicable, but that the outcome remained the same because, "under the law of both Idaho and New York, when a vehicle is involved in an accident within their respective borders, the owner of the vehicle is vicariously liable"[48]. Accordingly, said the court, "without further inquiry, we apply Idaho law to effectuate the public policy reflected in the statutes of both jurisdictions"[49].

173. *Downing* v. *Abercrombie & Fitch*[50] illustrates the similarity between cases of Patterns 1, 2, and 3. In this case, the conduct in question, a misappropriation of a person's picture and name for commercial purposes, occurred in California, where the defendant published a commercial catalogue containing plaintiffs' picture. The injury occurred in California and in Hawaii, which was the plaintiffs' domicile. California, but not Hawaii, provided a statutory cause of action for this offence, but arguably the plaintiffs could recover under Hawaii's common law. Thus, to the extent that the injury occurred in California, this case fell within Pattern 1. To the extent that the injury occurred in Hawaii, this case fell within Pattern 2 (if Hawaii law provided a cause of action) or within Pattern 3 (if Hawaii did not provide such an action). Under any of these possibilities, the application of California law would be proper. The court applied California law after concluding that this was a false conflict because – unlike Hawaii, which was uninterested[51]

---

possible reasons: *(a)* the court treated the defendant (a rental company that had its principal place of business in New York) as a New York domiciliary and may have implicitly assumed that its conduct occurred in New York; and *(b)* the court treated the two statutes as loss-distributing and thus focused on the parties' domicile rather than the place of conduct.

48. 726 NYS 2d at 412.
49. *Id.* In a similar case, *Boatwright* v. *Budak*, 625 NW 2d 483 (Minn. App. 2001), both the parties' home state (Minnesota) and the accident state (Iowa) had such a statute. However, the Minnesota statute limited the owner's liability to $100,000, while the Iowa statute imposed no limit. The plaintiff argued that the Minnesota statute was inapplicable because its language confined it to accidents occurring within Minnesota and, consequently, the case should be decided under the Iowa statute, without any choice-of-law analysis. The court agreed that the Minnesota statute was inapplicable, but concluded that a choice-of-law analysis was necessary because, in its opinion, the inapplicability of the Minnesota statute meant that there would be no vicarious liability at all under Minnesota law and unlimited vicarious liability under Iowa law. Following a full-fledged choice-of-law analysis, the court held that the Iowa statute governed.
50. 265 F. 3d 994 (9th Cir. 2001).
51. See *id.* at 1007 ("Hawaii had no interest in limiting the extent of relief that its residents could obtain from a wrongful act against them in California ... . It is pure fancy to believe that Hawaii would wish to restrict its residents from recovery that others could obtain in California solely because it has not enacted a statute like California's to complement its common law action for the same offense").

– California had an interest in applying its law to deter this misconduct within it borders[52].

4. Pattern 3: Conduct in state with higher standard and injury in state with lower standard of conduct

174. The false conflict paradigm is also present in the cross-border torts falling within Pattern 3, *supra*, namely cases in which the tortfeasor's conduct violates the "higher" standard of the conduct-state but not the "lower" standard of the injury-state. *Schmidt* v. *Driscoll Hotel*[53], and *Rong Yao Zhou* v. *Jennifer Mall Restaurant, Inc.*[54], are two well-known dram shop act cases that exemplify this pattern. In both cases the tortious conduct, the serving of the liquor to an intoxicated patron, occurred in a state that had a dram shop act that imposed civil liability on tavern owners for this conduct, while the resulting injury occurred in a state that did not impose such liability. Both cases properly applied the dram shop act of the conduct-state, after concluding that only that state had an interest in deterring this conduct, while the injury state did not have a countervailing interest in protecting the conduct[55]. As the *Rong Yao Zhou* court stated, it, any interest the injury-state might have in protecting tavern owners from civil liability was "not implicated where the [tavern] is situated in [another state] and the unlawful conduct occurred therein"[56].

Indeed, the application of the dram shop act of the conduct-state promotes the policy of that state in policing conduct within its borders, without subordinating the policies of the law of the injury-state. The effectiveness of the conduct-regulating rule of the conduct-state would be seriously impaired if the rule exceptions were made for cross-border torts in which the injury occurs in another state. Such exceptions are not warranted by the fact that the injury-state adheres to a lower standard, because the lower standard is designed to protect conduct within, not outside, that state. Moreover, there is nothing unfair in subjecting a tortfeasor to the law of the state in which he acted. Having violated the standards

---

52. See *id.* at 1006.
53. 82 NW 2d 365 (Minn. 1957) (applying Minnesota's dram shop act to impose civil liability on a Minnesota tavern owner whose intoxicated customer caused an accident in Wisconsin injuring plaintiff, also a Minnesota resident. Wisconsin did not have a dram shop act).
54. 534 A. 2d 1268 (DC App. 1987) (applying the District of Columbia's dram shop act to impose civil liability on a DC tavern owner whose intoxicated customer caused an accident in Maryland. Maryland did not have a dram shop act).
55. In both cases, the victim was also a domiciliary of the conduct state. Thus the application of that state's law could have also been based on that state's compensatory interests. However, even in the absence of such interests, the application of the law of the conduct state would be justified for reasons stated in the text.
56. 534 A. 2d at 1271.

of that state, the tortfeasor should bear the consequences of such violation and should not be allowed to invoke the lower standards of another state[57].

In *Patton* v. *Carnrike*[58], the court again imposed liability under the higher standards of the state of conduct, New York, and refused to allow the New York defendant to avail himself of a defense under the law of the state of injury, Pennsylvania. Two 17-year-old Pennsylvanians had driven to New York and purchased beer from defendant's New York store in violation of the drinking-age provisions of the New York dram shop act. While drinking the beer on their return trip, the two youths were involved in a single-car accident in Pennsylvania that caused the death of one of them. When his parents sued the New York liquor vendor under the New York act, the vendor asserted the defense of improper parental supervision under Pennsylvania law. The court applied the New York act and refused to allow the Pennsylvania defense because this would undermine "the efficacy of [New York's] Dram Shop Act"[59]. The court reasoned that "New York ha[d] a compelling interest in maintaining the integrity of the Act's deterrent effect"[60] and that the "goal of deterring unlawful sales [was] well served by preserving the vendor's complete liability irrespective of where the injury occurred"[61] and irrespective of the "fortuity that the purchasers were residents of Pennsylvania"[62].

175. Many cases involving car-owner liability statutes have reached similar results by applying the statute of the state in which the owner consented to the use of the car, even though the accident occurred in a state that did not have such

---

57. See, e.g., Professors Cavers's third "principle of preference", which provides that
      "[w]here the state in which a defendant acted has established special controls, includ-
      ing the sanction of civil liability, over conduct of the kind in which the defendant was
      engaged when he caused a foreseeable injury to the plaintiff in another state, the plain-
      tiff ... should be accorded the benefit of the special standards of conduct and of finan-
      cial protection in the state of the defendant's conduct, even though the state of injury
      had imposed no such controls or sanctions". D. Cavers, *The Choice-of-Law Process* 159
      (1965).
      Cavers illustrates the application of this principle by discussing a dram shop act case
      similar to *Pardey* v. *Boulevard Billiard Club*, 518 A. 2d 1349 (RI 1986), *supra* 171, as
      well as a case in which the defendant engages in blasting operations in a state that
      imposes strict liability for such operations and causes injury in a state that follows
      a negligence rule. Cavers concludes that in both cases it is appropriate to apply the
      law of the place of conduct, so as to effectuate the deterrent and regulatory purposes
      of that law. When that law is violated by substandard conduct occurring within that
      state, such conduct "is just as bad when the victim is an outsider as an insider", Cav-
      ers, *supra* at 160, regardless of whether the injury materializes within or outside that
      state. See also *id.* at 160-66.
58. 510 F. Supp. 625 (NDNY 1981).
59. *Id.* at 629.
60. *Id.*
61. *Id.*
62. *Id.* at 630.

a statute. An old example is *Levy v. Daniels U-Drive Auto Renting Co.*[63], which was decided as a contract case through a manipulative characterization under the traditional theory. Recent cases, decided under a variety of modern approaches, have reached the same result directly[64].

For example, in *Veasley v. CRST International, Inc.*[65], the court applied Iowa's car-owner statute to a case arising from an accident in Arizona, which did not have such a statute. The plaintiff was an Iowa domiciliary who was injured in the accident while riding in a truck driven by his co-employee and owned by an Iowa company. The court found that one of the purposes of the Iowa statute was "to make vehicle owners responsible for the actions of others to whom they have entrusted their motor vehicle"[66], and that to not apply this statute because the accident occurred in another state "would undermine the effectiveness of th[is] important statute"[67]. Following the Second Restatement, the court held that the Iowa statute should govern because, "based on the deterrence policy underlying [the statute,] ... Iowa ha[d] a substantial connection regarding the responsibility of all persons or corporations with a local nexus that loan or lease motor vehicles to other entities"[68].

In *Burney v. PV Holding Corporation*[69], a Michigan court applied Michigan's car-owner statute to a case in which the driver rented the car in Michigan and caused an accident in Alabama, a state that did not have such a statute. The court found that Michigan had an interest in effectuating the purpose of its car-owner statute, which was "to place the risk of damage or injury on the person with ultimate control of the vehicle and thereby promote safety in transportation"[70]. The court noted that this purpose "cannot be fully effectuated unless the owner's liability statutes are given uniform application to residents of this state traveling

---

63. 143 A. 163 (Conn. 1928).
64. See, e.g., *Sexton v. Ryder Truck Rental, Inc.*, 320 NW 2d 843 (Mich. 1982); *Farber v. Smolack*, 229 NE 2d 36 (NY 1967); *McKinney v. S & S Trucking, Inc.* 885 F. Supp. 105 (DNJ 1995); *Haggerty v. Cedeno*, 653 A. 2d 1166 (NJ Super. Ct. App.Div. 1995); *Stathis v. Nat'l Car Rental Sys.*, 109 F. Supp. 2d 55 (D Mass2000); *Aponte v. Baez*, 2002 WL 241456 (Conn. Super. 2002). However, some New York cases characterized New York's car-owner liability statute as a loss-distributing rule. See, e.g., *Janssen v. Ryder Truck Rental, Inc.*, 667 NYS 2d 369 (NYAD 1998); *Tkaczevski v. Ryder Truck Rental, Inc.*, 22 F. Supp. 2d 169 (SDNY 1998); *Aboud v. Budget Rent A Car Corp.*, 29 F. Supp. 2d 178 (SDNY 1998); *Elson v. Defren*, 726 NYS 2d 407 (NYAD 2001); *Knight v. Dawson*, 2004 WL 2334187 (NY Sup. Ct. 2004). See also *Oliver v. Davis*, 679 So. 2d 462 (La. App. 1996), writ den. 682 So. 2d 773 (La. 1996). For a recent comprehensive discussion of why Connecticut's equivalent statute is conduct-regulating, see *Svege v. Mercedes Benz Credit Corp.*, 182 F. Supp. 2d 226 (D Conn. 2002).
65. 553 NW 2d 896 (Iowa 1996).
66. *Id.* at 899.
67. *Id.*
68. *Id.*
69. 553 NW 2d 657 (Mich. App. 1996), *appeal denied* 572 NW 2d 9 (Mich. 1997).
70. 553 NW 2d at 660.

outside of Michigan as well as persons within our state"[71], and that "[t]o enforce the[se] ... statutes on the basis of where the accident occurred would undermine the[ir] effectiveness"[72].

Gaither v. *Myers*[73] involved a different type of car-owner's liability statute. The place of conduct, the District of Columbia, imposed civil liability on owners who leave their cars unattended without locking them and removing the keys. The state of injury, Maryland, would not impose liability under the circumstances of this case. The plaintiff, a Maryland domiciliary, was injured in a Maryland accident caused by a car owned by the defendant, a DC resident. The defendant had left the ignition key in his car in DC, where it was presumably stolen and driven into Maryland.

The court concluded that this was a false conflict in which only DC was interested and its law should govern. The court reasoned that the main purpose of the DC rule was not to prevent theft for the sake of car owners, but rather "to promote the safety of the public in the streets ... [and] to make streets safer by discouraging the hazardous conduct [the rule] forbids"[74]. Thus, DC had a "significant"[75], indeed "powerful"[76], interest in applying the rule "to an actor who leaves his car keys to a thief in the District"[77], and sets in motion the chain of events that will likely lead to injury. The fact that this injury occurred in Maryland did not diminish DC's interests, nor did it generate a Maryland interest in applying its defendant-protecting rule. Whatever interest Maryland had in protecting car owners, "would not seem to extend to an owner like our defendant, who is not a citizen of Maryland ... especially ... where it is a Maryland citizen who is being compensated for his injuries"[78].

176. *Pittman* v. *Maldania, Inc.*[79] is illustrative of cases involving other conduct-regulation issues. In this case, the defendant operated a water-ski rental office on the Delaware side of the Delaware/Maryland border. The state line runs exactly in front of the office door, so that one must enter Delaware to rent the skis but would use them in Maryland. The laws of both states prohibited renting to persons under age 16, but (unlike Maryland) Delaware also required the showing of a valid driver's licence. After misrepresenting their ages, two Pennsylvania vacationers, ages 14 and 15, rented skis from defendant's Delaware office, and, while riding the skis in Maryland, collided with each other resulting in injury to the

---

71. *Id.*
72. *Id.*
73. 404 F.2d 216 (DC Cir.1968).
74. *Id.* at 222. The court also noted that the DC rule also had a compensatory purpose in that it protects victims by shifting the burden to the car owner. See *id.* at 223.
75. *Id.* at 223.
76. *Id.*
77. *Id.*
78. *Id.* at 224.
79. 2001 WL 1221704 (Del.Super. 2001).

14-year-old, the plaintiff. The plaintiff invoked Delaware law, while the defendant store-owner invoked Maryland law.

Following the Second Restatement, the Delaware court held that Delaware law should govern, despite the presumption of Restatement §146 in favour of the place of injury. The court found that: (1) this presumption was rebutted because the precise issue in this case was the defendant's conduct in renting the skis in Delaware to an underage person; (2) the Delaware statute reflected "a clear policy against renting jet skis to people who are unable to produce a valid driver's licence"[80]; (3) this policy was "part of a comprehensive statute on boating safety"[81]; and (4) a "statute regulating conduct should be enforced throughout the state"[82]. The court also found that: (1) "Maryland ha[d] no conflicting policy"[83]; (2) Delaware's law "[did] not interfere in any way with Maryland's regulation of water safety in its state"[84], and (3) the defendant, having acted in Delaware, could not complain about the application of Delaware law[85].

177. Finally, *D'Agostino* v. *Johnson & Johnson, Inc.*[86] is another illustration that a state's interest in deterring substandard conduct within its territory is not diminished by the fact that the conduct produces its effects in another state. In *D'Agostino*, the wrongful conduct occurred in New Jersey and had its impact in Switzerland. Executives of a New Jersey corporation allegedly "orchestrated" the retaliatory firing of an American citizen (who was employed by their wholly-owned Swiss subsidiary) for refusing to bribe Swiss officials in charge of regulating the licensing of pharmaceuticals in Switzerland. If proven, this conduct would violate the Federal Corrupt Practices Act, which New Jersey cases had incorporated into New Jersey law. Under Swiss law, the alleged bribes would be considered "consulting fees" and would be lawful, as would be the employee's firing.

In a unanimous opinion applying interest analysis, the New Jersey Supreme Court held that New Jersey's interests in deterring wrongful conduct in New Jersey "outweigh the Swiss interest in the at-will employment relationship that would not seek to deter such conduct through its civil law"[87]. The court emphasized that

---

80. *Id.* at *4

81. *Id.*

82. *Id.*

83. *Id.*

84. *Id.*

85. *Id.* The court also noted that this holding was confined to the narrow issue of renting the skis, and that if other issues were present in this case, a different conclusion might have followed.

86. 628 A. 2d 305 (NJ 1993).

87. *Id.* at 307. The court noted that, although the fired employee was at all times a resident of Switzerland, and had signed an at-will employment contract in that country containing a Swiss choice-of-law clause, and although Switzerland had an interest in regulating the employment relationship between a Swiss company and a Swiss resident, Switzerland did "not have an interest in condoning corporate bribery orchestrated beyond its boundaries". *Id.* at 316.

this case was "not about regulating just Swiss employment relationships ... [but rather] about regulating the conduct of parent companies in New Jersey that engage in corrupt practices through subsidiary employees"[88]. The court concluded that the strength of New Jersey's commitment to deterring commercial bribery, coupled with the "extensive New Jersey contacts"[89], suggested a "strong public interest" in applying New Jersey law and that "[a]ny opposing interest involving extraterritoriality"[90] did not outweigh New Jersey's "interests in preventing bribery, which could have a negative impact on public health and safety in New Jersey"[91].

5.   Pattern 4: Conduct in state with lower standard and injury in state with high standard

178. Pattern 4 involves the most difficult cross-border torts. In this pattern the conduct in question does not violate the "lower" standard of the state of conduct, but violates the "higher" standard of the state of injury. In interest analysis terminology, these cases usually present the true conflict paradigm because each state would have an interest in applying its own law. The first state has an interest in protecting conduct that is lawful there, while the second state has an interest in ensuring reparation for injuries occurring there and preventing future injuries.

As in all true conflicts, the choice of either law is bound to encounter disagreement. However, the argument for applying the higher standard of the state of injury is stronger in cases involving intentional torts than in negligence cases. Indeed, not many people would question the right of a state to punish conduct that is intended to produce, and does produce, detrimental effects within its territory, even when that conduct takes place outside the state. As Justice Holmes stated almost a century ago, "[a]cts done outside the jurisdiction, but intended to produce and producing detrimental effects within it, justify a state in punishing the cause of the harm"[92].

---

88. *Id.* at 311. This was "not exporting New Jersey employment law so much as applying New Jersey domestic policy ... to a domestic company". *Id.* at 318.

89. *Id.* at 316.

90. *Id.* at 315.

91. *Id.* at 315. In *Mehlman* v. *Mobil Oil Corp.*, 707 A. 2d 1000 (NJ 1998), the same court applied New Jersey's "Whistle-Blower Act" to an action by a New Jersey employee of Mobil Oil who was fired in New Jersey for publicly commenting in Japan that the gasoline sold by one of Mobil's Japanese subsidiaries contained excessive quantities of benzene. The percentage of benzene was significantly higher than that permitted for gasoline sold in the United States, but was not expressly prohibited by Japanese law. The court noted that the pertinent conduct was the New Jersey employer's retaliatory discharge, which occurred in New Jersey, that such conduct fell entirely within the intended scope of the Act, and that the Act's application to such conduct would not be extraterritorial. The Act protects employees from retaliatory discharge for refusing to violate applicable law.

92. *Strassheim* v. *Daily*, 221 US 280, 284 (1911).

To this end, federal courts have developed the so-called "effects doctrine", at least for acts committed abroad and producing intended injuries in the United States. For example, in *Hartford Fire Ins. Co.* v. *California*[93], the United States Supreme Court held that federal antitrust legislation, the "Sherman Act", applied to "foreign conduct that was meant to produce, and did in fact produce, some substantial effects in the United States"[94]. The Court applied the Act to British insurance underwriters who, while in London, engaged in conduct designed to affect the California insurance market.

Several lower-court cases have applied the Sherman Act in the same fashion[95], and one case, *United States* v. *Nippon Paper Industries*[96], went as far as to uphold under the Act a criminal prosecution of a Japanese defendant for conduct in Japan (price-fixing) that was intended to, and did, produce detrimental effects in the United States. The court rejected defendant's argument that the presumption against extraterritoriality operates with greater force in the criminal arena than in civil litigation, and appeared unconcerned by the lack of precedent for criminal prosecution for wholly extraterritorial conduct[97]. The court was equally unsympathetic to defendant's comity argument. According to *Hartford Fire*, said the court, comity concerns militate against the exercise of jurisdiction "only in those few cases in which the law of the foreign sovereign required a defendant to act in a manner incompatible with the Sherman Act or in which full compliance with both statutory schemes was impossible"[98]. Because in this case the defendant's conduct was illegal under both Japanese and American laws, there was "[no] concern about [defendant] being whipsawed between separate sovereigns"[99].

---

93. 509 US 764 (1993).

94. *Id.* at 795-796.

95. See *United States* v. *Aluminum Co. of Am.*, 148 F. 2d 416 (2d Cir. 1945); *Filetech S.A.* v. *France Telecom S.A.*, 157 F. 3d 922 (2d Cir. 1998); *Zenith Radio Corp.* v. *Matsushita Elec. Indus. Co., Ltd.*, 494 F.Supp. 1161 (DC Pa. 1980); *Mannington Mills, Inc.* v. *Congoleum Corp.*, 595 F.2d 1287 (3rd Cir. 1979). See also Restatement (Third) of Foreign Relations § 402.

96. 109 F. 3d 1 (1st Cir. 1997).

97. See *id.* at 6. The court also pointed out that there was sufficient precedent for applying a state's criminal statute to conduct occurring entirely outside the state's borders, as well as applying federal anti-drug statutes to wholly foreign conduct. See *id.*

98. *Id.* at 8.

99. *Id.* Pointing out the serious nature of the government charges according to which the defendant had orchestrated a conspiracy with the object of rigging prices in the United States, the court concluded that, if the charges were proven, then principles of comity should not prevent prosecution. Said the court: "We live in an age of international commerce, where decisions reached in one corner of the world can reverberate around the globe in less time than it takes to tell the tale. Thus, a ruling in [defendant's] favour would create perverse incentives for those who would use nefarious means to influence markets in the United States, rewarding them for erecting as many territorial firewalls as possible between cause and effect". *Id.*

A concurring judge examined whether the prosecution was reasonable under the standards prescribed by §§402 and 403 of the 1987 Restatement (Third) of the Foreign Relations Law of the United States and compatible with principles of international law. The judge reached an affirmative answer, but only after comparing the interests of the two countries. He found the Japan did not have an interest nor an incentive to apply its law because "Japanese consumers in this case ... were unaffected by the alleged conspiracy" which had targeted "only North American markets". In contrast the United States had "a strong interest in protecting United States consumers, who were affected by the increase in prices". Indeed, the court concluded that "only the United States ha[d] sufficient incentive to pursue the alleged wrongdoers, thereby providing the necessary deterrent to similar anticompetitive behavior"[100].

179. In cases involving negligent conduct, the argument for applying the higher standard of the state of injury may be less powerful psychologically, but it is still a fairly strong one, provided that the actor could have foreseen that his conduct in one state would produce injury in the other state. *Bernhard* v. *Harrah's Club*[101], which was discussed earlier, is a well-known example of such a case.

Bernhard applied California law and imposed civil liability on a Nevada tavern owner for conduct in Nevada that caused injury in California. Nevada law did not impose such liability. An important factor in justifying the application of California law was that the defendant should have foreseen that its conduct in Nevada would produce detrimental effects in California. The geographic proximity of the defendant's operation to the California-Nevada border, the defendant's active solicitation of California patrons, and the composition of defendant's clientele made it foreseeable that tavern patrons might drive into California and cause an accident there. It is this foreseeability factor that tips the scales and makes the application of the law of the injury-state an appropriate solution to these otherwise difficult true conflicts.

Similarly, in *Hoeller* v. *Riverside Resort Hotel*[102], which was decided under the Second Restatement, the court applied Arizona's common law which imposed civil liability on a Nevada casino owner under circumstances identical to those in *Bernhard*[103]. The court compared Nevada's interest in "free[ing] tavern owners, and other alcohol purveyors such as casinos, from the cost and inconvenience of incurring either civil or criminal liability in the operation of their businesses"[104] with Arizona's "strong interest in providing an opportunity for its residents to recover full compensation from persons and business that contribute to automobile accidents on Arizona highways ... [and] in holding tortfeasors responsible for

---

100. *Id.* at 12.
101. 546 P. 2d 719 (Cal. 1976), discussed *supra* 67.
102. 820 P. 2d 316 (Ariz. App. 1991).
103. An Arizona domiciliary became intoxicated in the Nevada casino and on his return to Arizona caused an accident injuring plaintiff, another Arizona domiciliary.
104. 820 P. 2d at 320.

their actions' foreseeable effects in Arizona"[105].The court also noted the casino's proximity to the Nevada/Arizona border and pointed out that the casino had gone to great lengths to attract Arizona clientele[106]. Under these circumstances, the court reasoned, the casino should have known that "many of the patrons it seeks, many of those who sit at its tables and drink its [free] liquor, have come to the casino from Arizona and will return to Arizona ... in an intoxicated condition and ... may cause accidents that injure third persons in Arizona"[107].

Other dram shop act cases have reached the same result under similar circumstances[108]. In one of them, *Young* v. *Players Lake Charles, L.L.C.*[109], the conduct-state, Louisiana, had enacted an "anti-dram shop act" that expressly insulated liquor servers from liability. A patron who became intoxicated in the defendant's river-boat casino, drove into Texas and caused injury there. The court noted that Louisiana's "appalling insulation of casino boats who use free or discounted liquor as the bait to entice gamblers, while ignoring the consequences when those predictably intoxicated gamblers hit the streets in lethal vehicles"[110], was within Louisiana's prerogatives, but only as long as the consequences of that decision were felt exclusively in Louisiana. However, the court concluded, this was not so

---

105. *Id.* The court also took note of the high number of accidents caused by drunk drivers (as well as the high number of drunk drivers arrested) in the particular Arizona county and surmised that many of these drivers "were given free alcohol at casinos in Nevada". *Id.* at 318 (quoting from the trial court opinion).

106. The casino maintained a parking lot on the Arizona side of the border (which consists of the Colorado River) and provided free ferry transportation to and from the lot to the casino. The casino may also have contributed to the cost of building a bridge across the river.

107. *Id.* at 321.

108. See *Zygmuntowicz* v. *Hospitality Inv., Inc.*, 828 F. Supp. 346 (ED Pa. 1993) (applying Pennsylvania's dram shop act against a New Jersey tavern owner for injury caused by one of his intoxicated patrons in Pennsylvania: "[T]he Defendant specifically targeted the Pennsylvania market and should, therefore, have expected and planned for possible suits under Pennsylvania law". *Id.* at 349); *Sommers* v. *13300 Brandon Corp.*, 712 F. Supp. 702 (ND Ill. 1989) (applying Indiana's dram shop act against an Illinois tavern owner for injury caused by one of his intoxicated patrons in Indiana); *Carver* v. *Schafer*, 647 SW 2d 570 (Mo. App. 1983) (allowing unlimited recovery under Missouri law to the survivors of a Missouri domiciliary who was killed in a Missouri accident caused by a Missouri domiciliary who became intoxicated in defendant's Illinois tavern. Illinois law also imposed liability but limited the amount); *City of Hastings* v. *River Falls Golf Club*, 1999 WL 535225 (8th Cir. 1999). But see *Estates of Braun* v. *Cactus Pete's, Inc.* 702 P. 2d 836 (Idaho 1985).

109. 47 F.Supp.2d 832 (SD Tex. 1999).

110. *Id.* at 834. See also *id.* at 837 (speaking of defendants's use of free alcohol for "the creation of a party atmosphere in which patrons are encouraged to freely spend their money gambling and then hit the road when they have exhausted their funds, regardless of their physical condition. Defendants are essentially giving alcohol away in express furtherance of that goal, arguably under the smug misconception that Louisiana law insulates them from the predictable and tragic consequences").

in this case in which Louisiana casino-owners "entice[d] residents of Texas and other states to flock in huge numbers to their casinos to drink too much and return home in a murderous condition"[111].

Blamey v. *Brown*[112], which was decided under Minnesota's better-law approach, was a closer case, if only because it was not an "enticement" case. The defendant, who operated a small tavern on the Wisconsin side of the Wisconsin/Minnesota border, did not advertise in Minnesota nor attempt to attract Minnesota customers. However, he occasionally sold liquor to Minnesota residents as in the present case in which he sold liquor to a Minnesota minor who drove back to Minnesota and caused an accident there injuring another Minnesota domiciliary. The court concluded that the bar's proximity to the border and the defendant's knowledge that some of his customers were Minnesotans allowed Minnesota courts to assume jurisdiction and to apply Minnesota's "better" law, which imposed liability on the bar owner.

Fu v. *Fu*[113], a case involving a car-owner's liability statute, was an even closer case. *Fu* arose out of a New York accident involving New Jersey domiciliaries who had rented a car in New Jersey from defendant, a rental company[114]. New York, but not New Jersey, had a car-owner liability statute. The New Jersey court characterized the New York statute as conduct regulating[115], because its main purpose was to "regulate the conduct of automobile owners by 'discourag[ing] owners from lending their vehicles to incompetent or irresponsible drivers'"[116]. The court held that the New York statute should govern because, "[w]hen the tort rule primarily serves a deterrent purpose, the state where the harmful conduct took place will likely have the dominant interest with respect to that rule"[117].

---

111. *Id.* at 837. Technically, this case applied federal maritime law because the casino boat was in navigable waters. However the language and tenor of the opinion leave no doubt that the court would have applied Texas state law which, like maritime law, imposed civil liability on tavern owners under these circumstances.

112. 270 NW 2d 884 (Minn. 1978), cert. denied, 444 US 1070 (1980).

113. 733 A. 2d 1133 (NJ 1999).

114. The defendant was a Delaware corporation that conducted business in New Jersey but had its principal place of business in Pennsylvania.

115. See 733 A. 2d at 1149:

 "Although vicarious liability rules, broadly defined, serve a loss-allocating function, there is no question that from its inception [the New York statute] also was intended to regulate irresponsible car lending practices, and it is that underlying governmental purpose that guides our inquiry. That the rule regulates highway safety indirectly, by providing an incentive for responsible business practices, rather than directly by stating a 'rule of the road' is irrelevant to the strength of New York's policy".

116. *Id.* at 1139.

117. *Id.* at 1141. The court also concluded that the New York statute should govern even if it was a loss-distributing rule, so as to ensure that local medical care providers will be compensated for their services and to avoid the possibility that indigent non-resident victims would become public wards. See *id.* at 1144-1145. The court failed to note that

Of course, the court's statement assumes that the pertinent conduct in this case was the conduct of the driver, which occurred in New York, rather than the conduct of the rental agency, which occurred in New Jersey[118]. It would be more accurate to concede that the pertinent conduct was the rental company's renting of the automobile and then to argue that, although that conduct occurred in New Jersey, it had a predictable effect in New York, if only because the company was expressly informed that the rented car was to be driven into New York. Under these circumstances, the application of New York law was foreseeable, and thus it was not unfair to the defendant. As the court noted, "[g]iven the not unlikely possibility that a car rented from a New Jersey agency for the purpose of traveling to New York might be involved in an accident there, New Jersey car rental agencies reasonably should anticipate potential exposure to liability under New York's motor vehicle laws"[119].

6.   *Summary and rule for conduct-regulation conflicts*

180. The following table summarizes and portrays the results that the courts reached in the principal cases discussed in the preceding text[120].

---

the New York Court of Appeals discounted this interest in *Schultz* v. *Boy Scouts of Am., Inc.*, 480 NE 2d 679, 685-86 (NY 1985).

118. Indeed, the court so concluded by stating that "[t]he event giving rise to vicarious liability was not the rental transaction, but the automobile accident, which occurred in New York", 733 A. 2d at 1145, and that "an accident in New York arising from negligent permissive use is the very underlying conduct [the New York statute] is designed to regulate". *Id.* Thus, the court concluded, "New York's governmental interests are compelling in this instance because both the conduct giving rise to liability and the injury occurred in that state". *Id.* at 1148.

119. *Id.* at 1148.

120. The table does not portray the cases discussed, summarized, or cited in the footnotes. Suffice it to say that, for each case discussed in the text, the footnotes document several more cases that reached the same result.

Table 14. Conduct-regulation conflicts

#	Case name	Forum state	States' contacts			
			P's Dom	Injury	Conduct	D's Dom

I. INTRASTATE TORTS
Pattern 1. Conduct and injury in same state

#	Case name	Forum state	P's Dom	Injury	Conduct	D's Dom
1	Padula	NY	NY	MA	MA	NY
2	Bertram	OH	OH	MI	MI	OH
3	Spinozzi	IL	IL	MEX	MEX	MA
4	Johnson	IL	IL	KY	KY	MI
5	Bonelli	CN	NY	CN	CN	CA

II. CROSS-BORDER TORTS
Pattern 2. Conduct and injury in different states that have same law

#	Case name	Forum state	P's Dom	Injury	Conduct	D's Dom
6	Pardey	RI	MA	MA	RI	MA
7	Elson	NY	NY	ID	NY	NY
8	Downing	CA	HI	HI CA	CA	OH

Pattern 3
Conduct in state with high standard, injury in state with lower standard

#	Case name	Forum state	P's Dom	Injury	Conduct	D's Dom
9	Schmidt	MN	MN	WIS	**MN**	MN
10	Rong	DC	DC	MD	**DC**	DC
11	Patton	NY	PA	PA	**NY**	NY
12	Veasley	IO	IO	AZ	**IO**	IO
13	Burney	MI	AL	AL	**MI**	MI
14	Gaither	DC	MD	MD	**DC**	DC
15	Pittman	DEL	PA	PA	**DEL**	DEL
16	D'Agostino	NJ	SWS	SWS	**NJ**	NJ

Pattern 4
Conduct in state with low standard, injury in state with higher standard

#	Case name	Forum state	P's Dom	Injury	Conduct	D's Dom
17	Hartford Fire	US	US	**US**	UK	UK
18	Nippon Paper	US	US	**US**	JPN	JPN
19	Bernhard	CA	CA	**CA**	NV	NV
20	Hoeller	AZ	AZ	**AZ**	NV	NV
21	Young	TX	TX	**TX**	LA	LA
22	Blamey	MN	MN	**MN**	WS	WS
23	Fu	NJ	NJ	**NY**	NJ	NJ

The shaded cells indicate the state whose law the court applied. In many of these cases, that state had more contacts than the one represented by the shaded cell. For example, in 17 of the 23 cases portrayed in the table, that state was also the forum. However, that factor should not and did not influence the court's choice-of-law decision, except of course subconsciously. Likewise, in eight of the 23 cases, that state was also the domicile of the plaintiff and in eight cases it was the domicile of the defendant. Again, however, these additional contacts did not play a decisive role in the court's choice.

In other words, the shaded cells represent the contacts that explain, in whole or in part, why the court chose to apply that state's law. In the cases of Patterns 1 and 2, that is the whole explanation, whereas in cases of patterns 3 and 4 it is a partial explanation that becomes complete only when one looks at the content of the law of the contact state.

In the cases of Pattern 1, the court applied the law of the state where both the conduct and the injury occurred, even when neither party was domiciled there and regardless of whether that state provided a higher or a lower standard than the parties' domicile or domiciles. In the cases of Pattern 2, the state of conduct and the state of injury had the same law, so it did not matter which of the two state's law the court applied. Finally, for reasons explained earlier, in the cases of Patterns 3 and 4, the courts applied the law of that state that established the *higher* standard of conduct (indicated by underlining).

One can compress the results of the above cases into the following one-sentence rule, as follows:

> *Conflicts between conduct-regulating rules are governed by the law of the state of conduct, except when the injury foreseeably occurs in another state that imposes a higher standard of conduct, in which case the law of the latter state governs.*

This rule is simple, predictable, and balanced. It resolves the false conflicts cases of Patterns 1-3 in the only logical – and thus non-controversial – way possible. The rule resolves the true conflicts of Pattern 4 in a way that favours plaintiffs and thus may appear to negate the claim that it is balanced. This claim is valid, however, considering the fact that the rule subjects the application of the plaintiff-protecting law of the state of injury to the foreseeability proviso[121]. Because of this proviso, one can defend the application of that state's law not so much on the basis of that state's interest or the *favor laesi* principle, but on basic principles of accountability. One who predictably causes harm in a state whose law considers that harm tortious should be held accountable under that law.

---

121. If the occurrence of the injury in that state could not have been foreseen, this rule is inapplicable and the case must be resolved under general principles.

In the United States, the Louisiana codification has adopted such a rule[122], and so has the Puerto Rico Draft Code[123]. As documented elsewhere[124], a rule essentially producing the same result also appears in most codifications enacted in the last decades of the twentieth century. For example, the Portuguese codification contains rules which are confined to conduct-regulation issues and which are virtually identical to the above rule[125]. Other codifications contain rules which, though not confined to conduct-regulation issues, resolve cross-border torts in the same way. The Dutch, Swiss, Quebec, and Russian codifications provide that, in cross-border cases, the law of the injury-state applies if its occurrence there was foreseeable, but they do not explicitly condition such application on whether that law provides for a higher or lower standard than the conduct-state[126]. The German, Hungarian, and Tunisian codifications and a Chinese Draft Law provide for the application of the law of the state of conduct, but allow the application of the law of the state of injury at the request of the victim, without conditioning such application on foreseeability[127]. Finally, the Italian and Venezuelan codifications and the proposed Rome II Regulation do the reverse. They provide for the application of the law of the state of injury, but also allow the application of the law of the state of conduct if the victim so requests[128].

---

122. Although phrased differently, the first two paragraphs of Article 3543 of the Louisiana codification contain the same rule as the one stated in the text. A third paragraph contains a unilateral exception in favour of forum law and litigants which Weintraub has justifiably criticized. See R. Weintraub, "The Contributions of Symeonides and Kozyris to Making Choice of Law Predictable and Just: An Appreciation and Critique", 38 *Am. J. Comp. L.* 511, 515-516 (1990). The reasons for this politically motivated exception are explained in S. Symeonides, "Louisiana's New Law of Choice of Law for Tort Conflicts: An Exegesis", 66 *Tul. L. Rev.* 677, 713-714. (1992).

123. See Puerto Rico Draft Code Art. 46. See also Professors Cavers's first "principle of preference", which provides in part that "[w]here the liability laws of the state of injury set a higher standard of conduct ... than do the laws of the state where the person who caused the injury has acted ... the laws of the place of injury shall determine the standard ... applicable to the case ...". D. Cavers, *The Choice-of-Law Process* 139 (1965).

124. See E. Scoles, P. Hay, P. Borchers and S. Symeonides, *Conflict of Laws* 850-852 (4th ed. 2004).

125. See Portuguese Civil Code, Art. 45 (1)-(3).

126. See Art. 3(2) of [Dutch] Act of 2001 Regarding Conflict of Laws on Torts; Arts. 133(2), 137, 135, 139, 142 (2) of Swiss Federal Law of PIL of 1987; Quebec Civil Code, Art. 3126 (1); Art. 1219(1) of Civil Code of the Russian Federation as enacted in 2001.

127. See EGBGB, Arts. 40(1), 44; Hungarian PIL Decree of 1979, §§32-33; Tunisian Code of PIL of 1998, Art. 70(2); Chinese Society of Private International Law, Model Law of Private International Law of the People's Republic of China (6th Draft, 2000), Art 112. The Belgian PIL Code (Art. 99(2)(1)) gives plaintiffs a similar choice in defamation cases, but also provides defendants with a foreseeability defense.

128. For Italy, see PIL Act of 1995, Art. 62.1. For Venezuela, PIL Act of 1998, Art. 32.The proposed Rome II Regulation gives this option only for environmental torts. See, Commission of the European Communities, Proposal for a Regulation of the Euro-

C.   Punitive-Damages Conflicts

1.   *Introduction*

181. Punitive or exemplary damages are money damages assessed against a defendant in a civil action for misconduct that the legal system regards as heinous or egregious[129]. They have been part of American law since at least the 19th century, when many states began introducing them for certain cases of aggravated or egregious misconduct. Today, all but one state allow punitive damages, at least in some cases[130].

The adjectives "punitive" and "exemplary" are often used interchangeably and express the two purposes of punitive damages: punishment and deterrence. Punishment or retribution is individual but backward looking, in that it focuses on the individual wrongdoer and his or her specific misconduct. The degree of punishment depends on both the egregiousness of the specific misconduct, and the wrongdoer's financial capacity to bear and internalize the punishment. Deterrence or prevention is more general and forward looking, in that it focuses not only on the individual wrongdoer, but on others who might consider engaging in similar misconduct in the future. Deterrence is achieved by attaching to certain conduct a price tag that is much higher than the gains one might expect from engaging in that conduct. Thus, punitive damages differ in important respects from compensatory damages, which are designed to compensate the victim, and hence are proportional to the victim's harm or loss[131].

---

pean Parliament and the Council on the Law Applicable to Non-Contractual Obligations, Art. 7, COM(2003) 427 final, 2003/0168(COD), Brussels, 22.7.203.

129.   For the standard treatises on punitive damages, see G. Boston, *Punitive Damages in Tort Law* (1993); J. Ghiardi & J. Kircher, *Punitive Damages Law and Practice* (1994); L. Schueter. & K. Redden, *Punitive Damages* (2d ed. 1989). For a state-by-state survey, see R. Blatt, R. Hammersfahr. & L. Nugent, *Punitive Damages: A State-by-State Guide to Law and Practice* (2002 ed.).

130.   See D. Owen, M. Madden & M. Davis, *Madden & Owen on Products Liability*, v. 2, § 18:1 n.41 (3d ed. 2002). Only one state, Nebraska, prohibits punitive damages in *all* cases. Even the mixed jurisdiction of Louisiana allows punitive damages for injury caused by drunk drivers, and for sexual abuse of minors. See La. Civ. Code arts. 2315.4 and 2315.7. Although most American states allow punitive damages in general, these states often disagree on the specific cases, causes of action, or other circumstances in which punitive damages are available. When such disagreements exist, the resulting conflicts are as intense as they come, if only because they involve large sums of money.

131.   See *State Farm Mut. Auto. Ins. Co.* v. *Campbell*, 538 U.S. 408, 123 S.Ct.1513, 1519 (2003) ("[I]n our judicial system compensatory and punitive damages, although usually awarded at the same time by the same decisionmaker, serve different purposes [..]. Compensatory damages are intended to redress the concrete loss that the plaintiff has suffered by reason of the defendant's wrongful conduct ... . By contrast, punitive damages serve a broader function; they are aimed at deterrence and retribution") (internal quotation marks omitted).

The very fact that compensatory damages should be proportional to the victim's loss explains why they often cannot effectively punish or deter economically powerful wrongdoers, especially corporate offenders who have the ability to pass this additional cost to the consumers. One might ask, why not employ the tools of criminal or administrative law enforcement? The American answer to this question is that these tools are largely inadequate and inefficient as a means of "control[ling] ... the villainous rich, though [they] may work to control the villainous poor"[132]. For example, corporate offenders, some of whom command more resources than the GNP of many nations and certainly more than those of the average prosecutor, often can either avoid conviction or reduce the severity of the penalty, especially in intricate, hard-to-prove cases[133]. In a system in which, by design or by default, government is "too small and too overstretched to regulate every area of life"[134], the pursuit of punitive damages by private plaintiffs can function as "a partial offset to weak administrative controls"[135], which are often "spottily enforced"[136]. Private plaintiffs and their enterprising attorneys fill the vacuum by acting as private attorneys-general or, one might say, bounty hunters[137]. The possibility of winning high awards gives them the financial incentive to invest and risk substantial resources in the investigation and prosecution of corporate wrongdoing that might otherwise remain undetected or unpunished. Thus, punitive damages can be a "means for social control and moral sanction of economically formidable wrongdoers"[138], and may serve a "vital function for which neither criminal punishment nor administrative controls can substitute[139].

182. The fact that punitive damages are awarded to a private plaintiff in a civil trial indicates their differences from criminal and civil fines, both of which inure to a public fund. Although a recent movement to direct a portion of punitive damages to a public fund tends to blur this distinction, that movement

---

132. M. Galanter & D. Luban, "Poetic Justice: Punitive Damages and Legal Pluralism", 42 Am. U. L. Rev. 1393, 1444 (1993). The authors also state that the poor tend to be prosecuted more frequently and convicted more easily. See id. at 1426 ("Criminal punishment is imposed mostly on the poor and marginal").

133. See M. Galanter & D. Luban, supra footnote 132, at 1443 (explaining the difficulties of prosecuting corporate white collar wrongdoers and why "corporate criminal offenders are not severely punished when they are convicted").

134. Id. at 1445.

135. Id. at 1426.

136. Id. at 1442.

137. See id. at 1441-42: "Contingency fee lawyers have an unsavory reputation, but that is not surprising: they are professional bounty hunters, and bounty hunters are not nice people [..]. But that is irrelevant. Society needs the bounty hunter because without inducing wealthy private parties such as lawyers and law firms to invest substantial resources in the investigation of wrongdoing, we would end up with something much worse [..] [namely] wrongdoing that goes merrily along on its illegal and devastating way because nobody is around to blow the whistle".

138. Id. at 1395.

139. Id. at 1426.

has had only limited success so far[140]. At the same time, the fact that, in a civil trial, the defendant does not enjoy certain procedural protections of the criminal law (such as proof beyond a reasonable doubt, the right against self-incrimination, and the protection from double jeopardy and excessive fines) is one of the reasons for which punitive damages are controversial. Yet, precisely because punitive damages are sought, and their prerequisites proven, by private plaintiffs rather than by the state, one could argue that the above procedural protections of the criminal law are largely unnecessary and perhaps inappropriate[141]; for private plaintiffs possess neither the coercive power of the state nor its superior investigatory resources. Moreover, while punitive damages can carry severe economic consequences, they do not endanger the defendant's life or liberty. In any event, many states have recently raised the burden of proof for punitive damages from "preponderance of the evidence" (which is the typical standard in civil cases) to "clear and convincing evidence"[142].

In any event, punitive damages have always been a subject on which opinions differ, and differ sharply. To some, punitive damages are "a responsible instrument of government [that] discourages private reprisals, restrains the strong, influential, and unscrupulous, vindicates the right of the weak, and encourages recourse to, and confidence in, the courts of law by those wronged or oppressed by acts or practices not cognizable in, or not sufficiently punished, by the criminal law"[143]. To others they are a "monstrous heresy ... an unsightly and unhealthy excrescence, deforming the symmetry of the body of law[144].

183. The latter view has many adherents even in the United States, but it has many more adherents in the rest of the world. For example, the vast majority of civil-law systems continue to reject punitive damages and to regard them as an aberration if not an abomination. Naturally, this is a judgment these systems are entitled to make for themselves. Indeed, the history, philosophy, and contemporary structure of most civil-law systems make their rejection of punitive damages for fully domestic cases entirely predictable and understandable. What is debatable, however, is whether this rejection should encompass all those multistate cases that, under the forum's choice-of-law rules, are governed by a foreign law that imposes punitive damages. Many civil-law systems have taken this very position. For example, some recent private international law codifications contain blanket prohibitions against awarding punitive damages under any circumstanc-

---

140. See S. Symeonides, "Resolving Punitive Damages Conflicts", 5 *Ybk of Priv. Int'l L.* 1, 2-3 (2003).

141. For an excellent exposition of this argument, see M. Galanter & D. Luban, *supra* footnote 132.

142. See S. Symeonides, *supra*, footnote 140. One state, Colorado, has further raised the standard to 'beyond reasonable doubt', which is the criminal law standard.

143. *Luther* v. *Shaw*, 147 NW 18, 20 (Wis. 1914).

144. *Fay* v. *Parker*, 53 NH 342, 382 (1872).

es[145]. The same hostility towards punitive damages surfaces in recent efforts to draft a new convention on judgment recognition under the auspices of the Hague Conference of PIL[146].

It seems that implicit in these prohibitions is an *a priori* legislative assumption that punitive damages are so fundamentally repugnant to the forum's sense of justice and fairness that a forum court should not be allowed to contaminate itself by even considering the possibility of permitting them in multistate cases. This assumption operates even if the forum country has no connections (besides the jurisdictional nexus) that would implicate its prohibition of punitive damages, such as an affiliation with the defendant or the occurrence of critical events within its territory. These prohibitions revoke in advance any and all discretion a court has in employing the traditional *ordre public* reservation, and effectively erase all the fine classical distinctions between *ordre public interne* and *ordre public international*. The fact that these systems have not taken such an *a priori* position against, for example, slavery, racism, or polygamy is indicative of the hostility that punitive damages encounter in some quarters.

One can question the wisdom, or even the morality, of a scheme in which such an important public-law function depends on the efforts of private enforcers. Nonetheless, for better or worse, this is the scheme that most states of the United States have chosen to adopt, after trial and error for more than two centuries. The scheme is subject to continuous scrutiny and correction, as it should be[147]. The function of private international law is not to gauge the wisdom of a state's substantive law, but rather to delineate the multistate cases to which this law should properly apply. As explained later, a blanket refusal to apply a law that imposes punitive damages solely because the forum state disapproves of them is

---

145. For example, Articles 135(2) and 137(2) of the Swiss PIL codification provide that, in products liability and obstruction to competition cases governed by foreign law, "no damages may be awarded in Switzerland other than those provided [..] under Swiss law". Similarly, Article 40(3) of the EGBGB (Rev. 1999) prohibits non-compensatory or "excessive" damages, while Article 34 of the Hungarian PIL Decree of 1979 provides somewhat more cryptically that Hungarian courts "shall not [..] impose legal consequences not known to Hungarian law".

146. See Art. 33 of the Hague Preliminary Draft Convention on Jurisdiction and Recognition of Foreign Judgments in Civil and Commercial Matters of 30 October 1999 (providing that a foreign judgment that awards exemplary damages shall be recognized, but only to the extent that similar or comparable damages could have been awarded in the recognizing state).

147. In a series of cases decided since the early 1990s, the United States Supreme Court enunciated standards for determining the constitutionality of punitive damages under the Due Process clause of the 14th Amendment of the US Constitution. See *Pacific Mut. Life Ins. Co.* v. *Haslip*, 499 US 1 (1991); *TXO Prod. Corp.* v. *Alliance Res. Corp.*, 509 US 443 (1993); *BMW of N. Am., Inc.* v. *Gore*, 517 US 559 (1996); *Cooper Indus., Inc.* v. *Leatherman Tool Group, Inc.*, 532 US 424 (2001); *State Farm Mut. Auto. Ins. Co.* v. *Campbell*, 538 US 408 (2003). These cases are discussed in S. Symeonides, *supra* footnote 140, 9-14.

not justified, unless the forum state has those connections with the case or the parties that would implicate its policy of prohibiting such damages.

2.   The pertinent contacts and typical patterns

184. As said at the beginning, rules imposing punitive damages are *par excellence* conduct-regulating rules. Thus, the place or places of the conduct and injury are contacts that are as pertinent in punitive-damages conflicts as in generic conduct-regulation conflicts. The state of the conduct has the right to regulate (police, punish, deter, or protect) conduct within its borders, and the state where this conduct produces its effects – the injury – has a right to determine what sanctions are appropriate for such conduct.

However, as the word "punitive" suggests, these rules have a greater sting than generic conduct-regulation rules, in that they seek to *punish* the individual tortfeasor, as well as to deter other potential tortfeasors. Thus, the tortfeasor's domicile is another pertinent contact in punitive-damages conflicts. When the law of the tortfeasor's home state imposes punitive damages, the application of that law serves its underlying purpose of punishing that tortfeasor and deterring him and other potential tortfeasors from engaging in similar conduct in the future. Similarly, when that law prohibits punitive damages, then its application would serve its underlying purpose of protecting that tortfeasor from excessive financial exposure.

This then leaves the domicile of the victim. If it is true that punitive damages are designed to punish and deter tortfeasors rather than to compensate victims (and their attorneys) who, *ex hypothesi*, are made whole through compensatory damages, then the victim's domicile should, in principle, be irrelevant in punitive-damages conflicts.

Thus, the contacts pertinent in identifying the concerned states in punitive damages conflicts are: *(a)* the place of conduct; *(b)* the place of injury; and *(c)* the tortfeasor's domicile or principal place of business.

Putting factual contacts and substantive laws[148] in the mix produces eight typical patterns of potential or actual punitive-damages conflicts. These patterns

---

148. The following discussion assumes that a state either imposes or does not impose punitive damages for the particular conduct. It is true that in some cases, states that impose punitive damages may differ on the available or permissible amounts. For example, one state may limit the amount, either through an absolute cap or in proportion to compensatory damages. These cases present a choice-of-law problem only if the claimant requests, and the court is prepared to grant, an amount exceeding this limit. Similarly, two states that allow punitive damages may differ on the applicable burden of proof. See, e.g., *Bank Saderat Iran* v. *Telegen Corp.*, 2002 WL 188935 (9th Cir. 2002) (conflict on burden of proof for imposing punitive damages resolved under standard of New York, which was state of defendant's domicile and place of conduct, rather than under California's higher standard ("clear and convincing evidence")). Even so, these cases are few and far between. For the sake of simplicity, this section does not discuss these issues.

are depicted in the following table. The last three columns represent the state or states that have the relevant contacts: the place of injury, the place of the tortfeasor's (hereafter "defendant") conduct, and the defendant's domicile or principal place of business. The previous two columns representing the forum state and the plaintiff's home state, respectively. These columns are left blank in order to underscore the point that the punitive-damages laws of these states are, or should be, irrelevant in resolving punitive-damages conflicts.

Table 15. Patterns in punitive damages conflicts

Pattern	Forum	Plaintiff	Injury	Conduct	Defendant
1	---	---	Pun.	Pun.	Pun.
2	---	---	No pun.	Pun.	Pun.
3	---	---	Pun.	Pun.	No pun.
4	---	---	Pun.	No pun.	Pun.
5	---	---	No pun.	No pun.	Pun.
6	---	---	No pun.	Pun.	No pun.
7	---	---	Pun.	No pun.	No pun.
8	---	---	No pun.	No pun.	No pun.

As discussed below, American courts have awarded punitive damages in cases falling within each one of the above eight Patterns. However, the majority of cases that awarded punitive damages fall within Patterns 1-4. The thesis of this section is that the award of punitive damages is:

(1)   entirely appropriate in cases falling within Patterns 1-4;
(2)   defensible in cases falling within Patterns 5-7; and
(3)   entirely inappropriate in cases falling within Pattern 8.

The balance of this essay examines the cases of each Pattern, in the above order.

3.   Three- or two-contact patterns

(a)   Pattern 1: All three contacts

185. In cases involving Pattern 1, a state that has all three pertinent contacts (or three states each of which have a pertinent contact) imposes punitive damages. For example, a defendant acts in his home state and causes injury in that state to a domiciliary of another state. If the law of the former state imposes punitive damages for that conduct, that state has every interest in applying its law to punish that defendant and to deter other defendants from engaging in similar conduct

in the future[149]. Even if the victim's home state prohibits punitive damages, such a prohibition need not be heeded, because it is designed to protect tortfeasors acting or domiciled in that state, rather than to prevent victims domiciled there from recovering punitive damages.

The same rationale should apply if the state that denies punitive damages is the forum state, whether or not it is also the victim's home state. In most cases, the forum's denial of punitive damages is designed to protect either forum defendants or forum conduct, or both, and in this case the forum has neither of these contacts. Thus, the award of punitive damages under the law of the other state in these cases does not undermine the forum's policies.

186. In the United States, this solution is widely accepted, even in states like Louisiana which prohibits punitive damages in the vast majority of cases[150]. As said earlier, most civil law systems take exactly the opposite position. One example is Switzerland. Article 135 of the Swiss codification, which provides that products liability claims are governed, at the choice of the injured party, by the law of the defendant's place of business or, subject to an escape, the law of the place where the product was acquired. However, the same article also provides that, when a products liability claim is governed by foreign law, "no damages may be awarded in Switzerland other than those provided for such damage under Swiss law"[151]. Because Swiss substantive law does not allow punitive damages, the quoted phrase effectively functions as a prohibition of punitive damages. This prohibition protects defendants – primarily Swiss defendants, because they are more likely to be sued in Switzerland[152] – but also restores a certain balance to an article that is unduly skewed in favor of plaintiffs. However, this prohibition also protects foreign defendants who have "a place of business" (but not their "principal" place of business) in Switzerland, as well as defendants who either acted in Switzerland or caused injury there. Moreover, the same prohibition also applies to cases in which the plaintiff does not have the option of choosing the products liability law that Article 135 provides.

---

149. For a recent case that fits this pattern, see *Cranfill* v. *Brew Bros., Inc.*, 2005 WL 1420876 (WD Tenn. 2005).

150. See La. Civ. Code art. 3546, which provides that punitive damages may be awarded if such damages are available under the law of a state or states that have any two or all of the following contacts: place of conduct, place of injury, or defendant's domicile. For discussion of the rationale of this article by its drafter, see S. Symeonides, "Louisiana's New Law of Choice of Law for Tort Conflicts: An Exegesis", 66 *Tul. L. Rev.* 677, 735-749 (1992).

151. Swiss PIL Act, Art. 135(2). For a similar provision, see Art. 137 of the same Act, which applies to claims for obstruction to competition governed by foreign law. Interestingly, the articles dealing with other tort conflicts do not contain a prohibition against punitive damages. See Arts. 133 (general), 134 (traffic accidents) 136 (unfair competition), 138 (emissions), and 139 (injury to rights of personality).

152. See *id.* Art. 129(1) (providing that Swiss courts have jurisdiction if the defendant has a domicile, habitual residence, or place of business in Switzerland).

Suppose for example that, while studying in Princeton, New Jersey, a Swiss student purchases a pharmaceutical manufactured and marketed in New Jersey by a New Jersey manufacturer. While back in Switzerland during the Christmas break, the student ingests the product which produces severe side effects. She sues the manufacturer in Switzerland. With regard to liability and other issues, the Swiss court will have to apply New Jersey law because the plaintiff's choices under Article 135 are confined to New Jersey law. With regard to punitive damages, however, the same article requires the court to apply Swiss law and deny punitive damages. The same requirement would apply if the plaintiff had used the product in New Jersey and had suffered the injury there[153]. In so doing, Article 135 protects a New Jersey manufacturer who had acted in New Jersey and caused injury there, even though New Jersey has a strong policy, demonstrated by New Jersey precedents[154], of punishing that manufacturer and deterring others from engaging in similar conduct in the future.

To be sure, one may counter that Switzerland's denial of punitive damages in such a case is not motivated by an affirmative policy of protecting defendants as such, but rather by a philosophical, if not moral, opposition to the very notion of punitive damages[155]. Ordinarily, such an opposition is relevant by mere virtue of the fact that a Swiss court is called upon to assess punitive damages. Even so, one should juxtapose this policy to the policy of New Jersey, which, rightly or wrongly, assumes that punitive damages are the only effective means of punishing the tortfeasor and deterring such conduct in the future. In such a conflict, if a conflict it is, one should give due regard to the fact that New Jersey has most, if not all, of the relevant contacts.

(b)   Pattern 2: State(s) of defendant's domicile and conduct impose(s) punitive damages

187. In Pattern 2, the tortfeasor is domiciled in a state that imposes punitive damages and, while in that state, engages in conduct that causes injury in another state

---

153.   In such a case, Swiss courts would have jurisdiction if the New Jersey defendant had a "place of business" though not the "principal" place of business in Switzerland. See Art. 129(1). Jurisdiction would also exist if the plaintiff sues the manufacturer's insurer in a direct action under article 131.

154.   See, e.g., *Gantes* v. *Kason Corp.*, 679 A.2d 106 (N.J. 1996) (discussed *infra* 222; applying New Jersey pro-plaintiff law to a wrongful death action filed on behalf of a Georgia woman killed in Georgia by a machine manufactured by a New Jersey defendant in New Jersey; stating that New Jersey had a "strong interest in encouraging the manufacture and distribution of safe products for the public and, conversely, in deterring the manufacture and distribution of unsafe products within the state". *Id.* at 111-12); *D'Agostino* v. *Johnson & Johnson, Inc.*, 628 A.2d 305 (1993) (discussed *supra* 177).

155.   One might also invoke the lack of a procedural mechanism and experience in assessing punitive damages in the context of a civil trial.

that does not impose punitive damages[156]. This case presents the false conflict paradigm. The first state has an interest in applying its punitive-damages law so as to punish the tortfeasor who engaged in egregious conduct in that state, and to deter similarly situated potential tortfeasors. As Judge Weinstein once said, that state has "an obvious and substantial ... interest in ensuring that it does not become either a base or a haven for law breakers to wreak injury [elsewhere]"[157]. In contrast, the state of injury does not have an interest in applying its non-punitive damages law, because that law is designed to protect tortfeasors who are either domiciled in, or act in that state, neither of which is the case here. Thus, the application of the law of the first state promotes the deterrence policies of that state without impairing the defendant-protecting policies of the state of injury.

188. Many cases involving this pattern have reached this precise result. One example is *In re Air Crash Disaster at Stapleton Int'l Airport, Denver*[158], a case arising from the crash of a passenger plane in Colorado. In this case, Texas was both the airline's principal place of business and the place of the conduct most likely responsible for the crash. Texas, but not Colorado, provided for punitive damages in wrongful death actions.

The court reiterated a principle articulated by the Seventh Circuit in *In re Air Crash Disaster Near Chicago, Illinois*[159] and since followed in most air disaster cases to the effect that, "[b]ecause the place of injury is much more fortuitous than the place of misconduct or the principal place of business, its interest in and ability to control behavior by deterrence or punishment, or to protect defendants from liability is lower than that of the place of misconduct or the principal place of business."[160]

The *Stapleton* court concluded that, because Texas was both the site of the critical conduct and the defendants' principal place of business, "its relationship to this litigation is most significant"[161]. The court acknowledged that Colorado might have an interest in regulating the conduct of corporations entering its territory to do business but concluded that this interest was "somewhat lessened when a foreign corporation attempts to shield itself from the more onerous laws of its home state by seeking refuge under Colorado law"[162]. Conversely, said the court, the knowledge that the law of a corporation's principal place of business will be

---

156. A functionally analogous variation of this pattern appears when the tortfeasor acts outside his home state, but in a state that also imposes punitive damage.

157. *In re Simon II Litig.*, 2002 WL 31323751 at *95 (EDNY 2002), vacated and remanded on grounds not relevant here, 407 F.3d 125 (2nd Cir. 2003)

158. 720 F. Supp. 1445 (D Colo. 1988).

159. 644 F. 2d 594 (7th Cir.) *cert. denied sub nom.* 454 US 878 (1981).

160. 720 F. Supp. at 1453.

161. *Id.*

162. *Id.*

applied in the event of litigation was "not likely to discourage corporations like [the defendant airline] from doing business in Colorado"[163].

Another example is *Jackson* v. *Travelers Ins. Co.*[164], a case involving an action for bad faith insurance practices. In this case, the court held that Iowa's punitive-damages law applied to the insurer's conduct in that state[165], even though the resulting injury to the Nebraska plaintiff had occurred in Nebraska, which did not allow such damages. The court found that "it [was] not in the interest of the Nebraska legislature to extend protection to all insurance companies nationwide regardless of whether they are Nebraska businesses"[166], and that Nebraska "ha[d]

---

163. *Id.* For similar cases, see, e.g., *Lewis-De Boer* v. *Mooney Aircraft Corp.*, 728 F. Supp. 642 (D Colo. 1990) (action by Colorado plaintiffs against the Texas manufacturer of a small airplane that crashed in Colorado, killing its Colorado passengers; Texas, but not Colorado, imposed punitive damages; after dismissing as fortuitous the occurrence of the injury in Colorado, the court concluded that Texas, as the place of the defendant's conduct and principal place of business, "ha[d] a greater policy interest in applying its laws and providing deterrence than Colorado ha[d] in preventing a windfall to its citizens". *Id.* at 645); *Offshore Logistics, Inc.* v. *Textron*, 1995 WL 555593 (ED La. 1995) (product liability case arising out of helicopter crash in Louisiana, which did not allow punitive damages; awarding punitive damages under the law of Texas, which was the place of the defendant's domicile and conduct).

Two product liability cases involving this pattern have applied the non-punitive damages law of the state of injury. In the first case, *Kemp* v. *Pfizer, Inc.*, 947 F. Supp. 1139 (ED Mich. 1996), the product, a heart valve, was manufactured in California by a California corporation and caused the death of a Michigan patient in Michigan. The court acknowledged California's interest in applying its punitive damages law to "punish its corporate defendants and deter future misconduct", *id.* at 1143. However, the court concluded that, because the defendant was also doing business in Michigan, Michigan had an interest in extending to defendant the benefit of its defendant-protecting law. The court resolved the dilemma under Michigan's *lex fori* approach and applied Michigan law. In the second case, *Rufer* v. *Abbott Lab.*, 2003 WL 22430193 (Wash. App.2003), affirmed in part, reversed in part, 2005 WL 1528792 (Wash. 2005), a medical malpractice and product liability action by a Washington domiciliary who was injured in Washington by a medical devise manufactured by an Illinois defendant in Illinois, the court upheld the lower court's refusal to impose punitive damages under Illinois law, which, unlike Washington law, permitted such damages. The court acknowledged that, since the manufacturer's misconduct occurred in Illinois, Illinois had an interest in deterring that misconduct. However, said the court, "this purpose is not one that is abjured by Washington but rather is shared; the two states simply differ in their policies as to how best to serve this purpose". 2003 WL 22430193 at *10. Without explaining this statement, the court concluded that "Washington law is more appropriate than that of Illinois", because "[t]he number of contacts in Washington is significant". *Id.*

164. 26 F. Supp. 2d 1153 (SD Iowa 1998).

165. The insured was a nationwide company that did business in Iowa, but all decisions in this case were made at the company's offices in Iowa.

166. 26 F. Supp. 2d at 1162.

no interest in preventing punitive damages awards from other states to Nebraska citizens"[167].

On the other hand, said the court, because Iowa "was the location of the *cause* of the injuries[,] ... Iowa ha[d] a significant interest in using punitive damages to punish bad faith conduct that occurs in Iowa"[168], and "failure to apply Iowa law ... would wholly frustrate Iowa's interest in deterring outrageous conduct"[169].

(c)   Pattern 3: State(s) of conduct and injury impose(s) punitive damages

189. In Pattern 3 cases, a tortfeasor domiciled in a state that does not impose punitive damages, engages in conduct in another state that imposes such damages, and causes injury in the latter state[170] This pattern presents a true conflict because both states have an interest in applying their laws. The first state has an interest in protecting its domiciliary tortfeasor from punitive damages, whereas the second state has a strong interest in deterring conduct in that state that causes injury there. On balance, the application of the law of the latter state is entirely justified. The fact that the defendant acted outside his home state weakens any argument that he relied on that state's law, and the fact that he acted in the other state destroys any argument of unfair surprise from the application of the latter state's law.

Cases involving this pattern have reached the result suggested above by applying the punitive-damages law of the state of conduct and injury. For example, in *Horowitz* v. *Schneider Nat'l Inc.*[171], the court applied Wyoming's punitive-damages law to an action arising from a Wyoming traffic accident, even though none of the parties were Wyoming domiciliaries. The court found that Wyoming had a "paramount interest 'in the manner in which its highways are used and the care

---

167.   *Id.* at 1165.

168.   *Id.* (emphasis added).

169.   *Id.* at 1164. For a similar case, see *Cunningham* v. *PFL Life Ins. Co.*, 42 F. Supp. 2d 872 (ND Iowa 1999) (holding that Iowa punitive-damages law applied to action against an Iowa defendant who engaged in bad faith insurance practices in Iowa, causing injury to insureds domiciled in several states). For a slander case, see *Ardoyno* v. *Kyzar*, 426 F. Supp. 78 (ED La. 1976) (applying Mississippi law and allowing punitive damages in a slander action filed by a Louisiana plaintiff against a Mississippi defendant who made defamatory statements about plaintiff in Mississippi).

For a case involving the same pattern as *Jackson* and reaching the opposite result, see *Northwestern Mut. Life Ins. Co.* v. *Wender*, 940 F. Supp. 62 (SDNY 1996). In this action for bad faith insurance practices filed by a New York insured against a Wisconsin insurer, the court applied New York law which did not allow punitive damages, because, although the defendant company acted from Wisconsin and had its principal place of business there, it also did business in New York, and New York had an interest in protecting it.

170.   A functionally analogous variation of this pattern is when the injury occurs in a third state that also imposes punitive damages.

171.   708 F. Supp. 1573 (D Wyo. 1989).

exercised by drivers'"[172]. The court reiterated that "[t]he policy behind ... punitive damages is not compensation of the victim ... [but rather] deterrence through public condemnation"[173].

Likewise, in *Isley* v. *Capuchin Province*[174], an action for sexual abuse arising out of events in Wisconsin and filed against an out-of-state religious order, a Michigan court applied Wisconsin law, which imposed punitive damages. The court concluded that "Wisconsin's interest outweigh[ed] Michigan's interest"[175], because Wisconsin had a "strong interest in protecting minors in Wisconsin from sexual abuse and in punishing those found guilty"[176].

Finally, in *Schoeberle* v. *United States*[177], the court held that the law of Iowa, which was the state of both the pertinent conduct and the injury, should govern the question of punitive damages, even though the plaintiffs and some of the defendants were domiciled in Wisconsin, which did not allow such damages for the conduct in question. The court concluded that Wisconsin's interest in protecting its resident corporate defendant from excessive liability was "outweighed by Iowa's interest in applying its punitive damages law to conduct within its borders"[178]. The court reasoned that, "[w]hen a balance between punishment and deterrence on the one hand and protection from excessive liability on the other must be

---

172. *Id.* at 1577 (quoting *Brown* v. *Riner*, 500 P. 2d 524, 526 (Wyo. 1972)).

173. *Id.* In *Villaman* v. *Schee*, 15 F. 3d 1095, 1994 WL 6661 (9th Cir. 1994), an Arizona court applied Arizona punitive-damages law to a wrongful death action filed by the estate of a Mexican domiciliary who was killed in an Arizona accident caused by a non-Arizona defendant. The court found that "Arizona tort law is designed in part to deter negligent conduct within its borders; thus Arizona has a strong interest in the application of its laws allowing ... punitive damages". 1994 WL 6661 at **4. Similarly, in *Wang* v. *Marziani*, 885 F. Supp. 74 (SDNY 1995), the court, after reiterating that "the imposition of punitive damages is a conduct-regulating rather than loss-allocating rule", *id.* at 77, held that Pennsylvania's punitive damages rule applied to a Pennsylvania traffic accident involving out-of-state parties, because Pennsylvania had an "overwhelming interest in regulating the conduct within its borders". *Id.* at 77-78. See also *Townes ex rel. Estate of Townes* v. *Cove Haven, Inc.*, 2004 WL 2403467 (SDNY 2004) (applying Pennsylvania punitive-damages law to an action filed by a New York guest against the Florida owner of a Pennsylvania resort for injury suffered at the premises: "the state in which the tort occurred has strong interests in deterring future tortious conduct within its jurisdiction and in protecting the reasonable expectations of the parties that their actions would be regulated by the state in which they were acting". *Id.* at *2).

174. 878 F. Supp. 1021 (ED Mich. 1995).

175. *Id.* at 1023.

176. *Id.* at 1024. See also *Rice* v. *Nova Biomedical Corp.*, 38 F. 3d 909 (7th Cir. 1994) (applying Illinois law to a defamation action filed against a Massachusetts defendant who defamed an Illinois plaintiff by statements made in Illinois; Illinois, but not Massachusetts, imposed punitive damages).

177. 2000 WL 1868130 (ND Ill. 2000).

178. *Id.* at *14.

struck, 'it is fitting that the state whose interests are more deeply affected should have its local law applied.'"[179]

That state was Iowa, said the court, because, as the place of both the conduct and the injury, Iowa had an "obvious interest ... in punish[ing] those responsible for [the] misconduct ... [and] in deterring such misconduct and occurrences in the future"[180].

In re Aircraft Accident at Little Rock, Arkansas[181] reached the same result in a more complicated case arising from the crash-landing of an American Airlines passenger plane in Little Rock, Arkansas, while en route from Texas to Arkansas. Arkansas imposed unlimited punitive damages on an employer for the acts of its employees while Texas capped the amount of punitive damages generally, and did not allow punitive damages against an employer who had not authorized or ratified the employee's wrongful act. The court found that the critical conduct that caused the crash was pilot error, which occurred in Arkansas airspace as the aircraft approached the Little Rock airport. The court held that Arkansas law should govern the availability of punitive damages. The court acknowledged that Texas had an interest in shielding the defendant airline from punitive damages. However, the court concluded that "Arkansas' interest in both punishing and deterring allegedly egregious conduct that occurs within its borders and which is harmful to its citizens is much stronger than Texas' interest in protecting its business from liability for acts committed outside Texas"[182].

(d) Pattern 4: State(s) of injury and defendant's domicile impose(s) punitive damages

190. In Pattern 4, a defendant domiciled in a state that imposes punitive damages engages in conduct in another state that does not impose punitive damages, and causes injury in the defendant's home state. This scenario is factually uncommon, but a variation of it is not as unlikely – when, in the same case, the defendant's conduct causes injury in a third state that also imposes punitive damages.

In re Air Crash Disaster at Washington D.C.[183] involved the latter pattern. The defendant, a Florida-based airline, engaged in conduct in Virginia that caused its airplane to crash a few hundred yards into the District of Columbia. Both Florida and D.C., but not Virginia, imposed punitive damages. The court correctly applied D.C. law, allowing punitive damages. It is true that, when the conduct occurs in a state that does not allow punitive damages, that state has a certain interest

179. *Id.* at *13 (quoting *In Re Air Crash Disaster Near Chicago*, 644 F. 2d 594, at 613 (7th Cir. 1981)).
180. *Id.*
181. 231 F.Supp.2d 852 (ED Ark. 2002), affirmed 351 F.3d 874 (8th Cir. 2003).
182. 231 F.Supp 875. The court also noted that the Arkansas legislature had rejected efforts to limit punitive damages, and concluded that Arkansas' punitive-damages rule was "better" than Texas's limited damages rule, because the latter deprived a jury of the ability to effectively deter a defendant as powerful as American Airlines.
183. 559 F. Supp. 333 (DDC 1983).

to apply its law so as to protect that conduct. However, the fact that the consequences of that conduct are felt in another state, and are caused by a tortfeasor
domiciled in a third state that also imposes punitive damages, suggests that, ultimately, the interests of the conduct state must give way to the interests of the
other two states.

4.   Single-contact patterns

191. Several cases have applied the punitive-damages law of a state that had only
one of the above three contacts, even though the other two contacts were in a
state or states that did not allow punitive damages. However, for every case that
did so, there is at least one other case that reached the opposite result. These cases
are discussed below.

(a)   Pattern 5: Defendant's home state

192. In Pattern 5, the defendant's home state imposes punitive damages and thus
has an interest in punishing the defendant and deterring others from engaging
in similar conduct in the future. However, both the defendant's conduct and the
resulting injury occur in another state (or states) that does not impose punitive
damages. In such a case, one could argue that the latter state has an interest in
protecting, if not the defendant as such, at least the defendant's activity within its
territory, which may be beneficial in other ways, such as by providing jobs for the
local population. The resulting conflict is not an easy one, and this is why courts
encountering such conflicts have reached different results. While most courts
deny punitive damages[184], a few courts have allowed them by applying the law of
the defendant's domicile.

Among the latter cases is *Fanselow* v. *Rice*[185], a traffic-accident case in which
the state of injury had only a fortuitous connection with the defendants. *Fanselow*

---

184. See, e.g., *In re Air Crash Disaster Near Chicago, infra* 193 at footnote 196 (with regard
to the plane's manufacturer); *In re Air Crash Disaster Near Monroe, Michigan on
January 9, 1997*, 20 F.Supp.2d 110 (ED Mich. 1998) (holding that actions arising out of
Michigan crash of airplane operated by an airline headquartered in Kentucky, which
allowed punitive damages, were governed by Michigan law, which did not allow such
damages); *In re San Juan Dupont Plaza Hotel Fire Litig.*, 745 F.Supp. 79 (DPR 1990)
(applying Puerto Rico law, which did not allow punitive damages, to actions arising
out of Puerto Rico hotel fire and filed against non-Puerto Rico defendants domiciled
in states that allowed punitive damages); *George Lombard & Lomar, Inc.* v. *Econ. Dev.
Admin. of Puerto Rico*, 1995 WL 447651, (SDNY 1995) (applying Puerto Rico law and
denying punitive damages for Puerto Rico conduct and injury).

185. 213 F.Supp.2d 1077 (D Neb. 2002). Another case that also applied the punitive damages law of the defendant's principal place of business is *Bryant* v. *Silverman*, 703 P.2d
1190 (Ariz. 1985), a case arising out of an airplane crash in Colorado, which prohibited
punitive damages. However, in this case the court was influenced by the fact that
the record did not reveal the place of the critical conduct (as between Arizona and
Colorado), and that the victim was also an Arizona domiciliary. The court concluded

arose out of a Nebraska two-car collision that injured two Colorado domiciliaries riding in one of the cars. The defendants were the driver of the other car, a Texas domiciliary who moved to Oregon after the accident, and his employer, a Minnesota-based corporation. Of the four involved states, only Nebraska disallowed punitive damages. The court did not discuss the place of conduct, but one can assume that although the driver's conduct occurred in Nebraska, his employer's conduct or omission occurred in Minnesota. Focusing only on the domicile of the defendants, the court held that Minnesota law governed the plaintiffs' punitive damages claims against the employer, and Oregon law governed their claims against the driver.

The court correctly noted that the purpose of a rule imposing punitive damages is to punish defendants and to deter them and others from future wrongdoing, while the purpose of a rule prohibiting punitive damages is to protect defendants from excessive financial liability and to encourage entrepreneurial activity through lowering the cost of doing business in the state. For this reason, the court reasoned that the plaintiffs' home state did not have an interest in imposing punitive damages subjecting the defendants to punitive damages as long as the plaintiffs were adequately compensated. Thus, the only states concerned with punitive damages are those states "with whom defendants have contacts significant for choice of law purposes"[186]. In *Fanselow*, those states were Nebraska, Minnesota, and Oregon. The court found that Nebraska's policy of protecting defendants from punitive damages was not implicated in this case because the defendants' only connection with that state was the occurrence of the accident there. In contrast, the court reasoned, the case implicated the policies of both Minnesota and Oregon in punishing and deterring defendants, because the defendants were domiciled in those two states[187].

(b) Pattern 6: State of conduct

193. In Pattern 6, the state of conduct imposes punitive damages (and thus has an interest in punishing and deterring the particular conduct), while the defendant's domicile and the place of injury are in a state, or states, that do not impose punitive damages (and thus have an interest in protecting the defendant). This results in a true conflict between the laws of the state of conduct and the state of the

---

that, "[s]ince this case involves an Arizona corporate defendant causing injury to an Arizona domiciliary, Arizona has the dominant interest in controlling [defendant's] conduct". *Id.* at 1196.

186. 213 F.Supp.2d at 1084. The court rejected the argument that those states are interested in imposing punitive damages only when their residents are injured, as well as the argument that, because Nebraska's prohibition of punitive damages was contained in its Constitution, Nebraska had a stronger interest in denying punitive damages than Minnesota or Oregon had in allowing them.

187. The court acknowledged that, insofar as the driver was not an Oregon domiciliary at the time of the accident, Oregon had less of an interest in punishing him. However, the court concluded that, because the driver was a *current* Oregon domiciliary, Oregon had an interest in deterring his future misconduct.

defendant's domicile, with the state of injury simply playing a secondary role. As the cases discussed below indicate, one can find cases applying the law of any one of these three states.

For example, in *Long v. Sears Roebuck & Co.*[188], a products liability case, the court applied the law of the place of wrongful conduct, which the court assumed to be the sale of a defective mower and a misrepresentation of its safety features. Both of these acts occurred in the District of Columbia[189]. The buyer, a Maryland domiciliary, was injured in Maryland while using the mower. The court applied D.C. law after concluding (a) that Maryland did not have an interest in applying its law, which disallowed punitive damages, because that law was not intended to protect foreign defendants; and (b) that the District of Columbia had an interest in deterring and punishing, through its punitive damages law, those defendants who engaged in reprehensible conduct in the District by selling unsafe products there and misrepresenting their safety features[190].

In contrast, in *Harlan Feeders v. Grand Laboratories, Inc.*[191], a product liability action for injury that occurred in Nebraska, the court applied Nebraska law, which prohibited punitive damages, rather than Iowa law, which allowed them. The product was manufactured in Iowa and was sold to the Nebraska plaintiff in Nebraska. Noting that "Nebraska has made a policy choice that punitive damages are inappropriate"[192], the court equated that choice to a state "interest" and concluded that that interest was not outweighed by Iowa's contrary interest in imposing punitive damages as a deterrent, "at least not ... where the plaintiff is a resident of Nebraska, not Iowa, where the alleged injury occurred in Nebraska, not Iowa, as a result of use of a product manufactured by a South Dakota, not an Iowa corporation, even when the corporation physically produced the product in Iowa"[193].

In *In re Air Crash Disaster at Sioux City, Iowa*[194], a multiparty case involving wrongful death and survival actions arising from the crash of a passenger plane in Iowa, the pertinent contacts were scattered in several states. Correctly discount-

---

188. 877 F. Supp. 8 (DDC 1995).

189. The mower had been manufactured in South Carolina, but neither party invoked that state's law.

190. In *Danziger v. Ford Motor Co.*, 2005 WL 1630082 (DDC 2005), the court also allowed punitive damages under the law of Maryland, the state in which the victims acquired the defective product (a car), on the theory that the sale of a defective product was the pertinent and critical conduct. The defendant, a company headquartered in Michigan, had designed the car in Michigan (which prohibited punitive damages) and manufactured it in Kentucky. The victims were Virginia and DC domiciliaries, and the accident occurred in Nebraska, which also prohibited punitive damages. After completion of the manuscript, the court reversed its decision and applied Michigan law, denying punitive damages. See 402 F.Supp.2d 236 (DDC 2005).

191. 881 F. Supp. 1400 (ND Iowa 1995).

192. *Id.* at 1410.

193. *Id.*

194. 734 F. Supp. 1425 (ND Ill. 1990).

ing the victims' domiciles, the court held that the liability of the manufacturers of the plane and engines for punitive damages should be governed by the law of the states of manufacture, rather than the defendants' principal places of business. The engine manufacturer had its principal place of business in New York, which allowed punitive damages, and had manufactured the engines in Ohio, which allowed such damages in survival actions, but not in wrongful death actions. The plane manufacturer had its principal place of business in Missouri, the law of which is not given by the court, and manufactured the plane in California, which allowed punitive damages in survival actions but not in wrongful death actions[195].

In re Air Crash Disaster Near Chicago[196], a similar case arising out of a passenger plane crash in Illinois, involved actions against both the plane's manufacturer and the airline company. The manufacturer's home state, Missouri, allowed punitive damages, but the state of manufacture, California, did not. The airline's home state, New York, did not allow punitive damages, but the state in which it maintained the aircraft, Oklahoma, allowed such damages. Examining each conflict separately for each defendant, the court found a true conflict between the states that allowed and those prohibited punitive damages. The court broke the tie by applying the law of a third state, Illinois, which was the place of injury and which did not allow punitive damages. The court further noted that Illinois had a "strong interest in having airlines fly in and out of the state, and ... in protecting [them] by disallowing punitive damages"[197].

(c) Pattern 7: State of injury

194. In Pattern 7, the state of the injury imposes punitive damages, but the state (or states) of the defendant's conduct and domicile prohibits such damages. Again, there is little doubt that this pattern presents the true conflict paradigm. The first state has an interest in punishing and deterring conduct and actors that cause injury within its territory, while the latter state has an interest in protecting its domiciliary actor from the heavy financial price of punitive damages.

On balance, the application of the law of the state of injury (and the award of punitive damages under that law) is a perfectly sensible resolution to these conflicts, *provided* it meets two conditions. The first is the general requirement of

---

195. With regard to the third defendant, the airline, the court held that Illinois law, which did not allow punitive damages, should govern. Illinois was the airline's principal place of business and the place where the corporate decisions regarding the maintenance of the aircraft and the training of its flight crew were made.

196. 644 F. 2d 594 (7th Cir. 1981), cert. denied 454 US 878 (1981).

197. 644 F. 2d at 615-616. Similarly, in *Freeman* v. *World Airways, Inc.*, 596 F. Supp. 841 (D Mass. 1984), a case arising out of an airplane crash in Massachusetts, the court found that Massachusetts, which did not allow punitive damages, "ha[d] a significant interest in regulating conduct (deterrence or encouragement) of planes arriving at [its airports] during the winter". *Id.* at 847. The negligent conduct that caused the crash arguably had occurred in other states that imposed punitive damages.

avoiding unfair surprise to the party who is adversely affected by the application of the law of the state of injury, here the defendant. Since here we are dealing with cross-border torts, the court should not apply the law of that state if the defendant demonstrates that one could not reasonably have foreseen the occurrence of the injury *in that state* (objective foreseeability). The second condition is more specific to punitive damages. It has been enunciated by the United States Supreme Court in *BMW of North America, Inc.* v. *Gore*[198]. *Gore* provides that, in assessing the amount of punitive damages, the court should consider only the conduct that caused detrimental effects *in the state of injury*, and not the conduct that caused such effects in other states.

Naturally, whether a particular case satisfies the foreseeability condition depends on the facts of that case but, for example, in the most common cross-border torts, products liability, this condition is satisfied unless the manufacturer demonstrates that its products were not available in the state of injury through ordinary commercial channels. Judging by how rarely manufacturers even choose to raise this argument[199], one can conclude that this condition is easy met. Indeed, in all the product liability cases that allowed punitive damages under the law of the state of injury, this condition has been met. This includes cases like *Kramer* v. *Showa Denko K.K.*[200], which involved a foreign manufacturer[201].

In *Kramer*, the court awarded punitive damages under the law of the state of injury, New York (which was also the victim's domicile) against a Japanese defendant who manufactured a car in Japan, a country that does not allow punitive damages. However, the car had reached the New York market through ordinary commercial channels, and the victim bought and used it in that state. Thus, the imposition of the financial burden of punitive damages under New York law was a foreseeable and insurable risk, which the manufacturer should expect to bear in exchange for deriving financial benefits from the New York market.

---

198. 517 US 559 (1996)(holding that, although in assessing the degree of reprehensibility of the defendant's conduct, Alabama may consider evidence of the defendant's non-Alabama conduct, nevertheless, in fixing the amount of punitive damages, Alabama may not punish the defendant for non-Alabama conduct that produced injuries outside of Alabama). For a discussion of this case and the test it articulated, see S. Symeonides, "Resolving Punitive Damages Conflicts", 5 *Ybk of Priv. Int'l L.* 1, 9-11 (2003).

199. See S. Symeonides, "Choice of Law for Products Liability: The 1990s and Beyond", 78 *Tul. L. Rev.* 1247, 1321 (2005) (showing that in none of the cases decided between 1989 and 2004 did the manufacturer invoke the defense of commercial unavailability).

200. 929 F.Supp. 733 (SDNY 1996).

201. For non-products cases awarding punitive damages under the law of the injury-state while also meeting the foreseeability requirement, see, e.g., *Cooper* v. *Am. Express Co.*, 593 F.2d 612 (5th Cir. 1979) (awarding punitive damages under the law of the state of injury and victim's domicile, even though the law of the defendant's domicile and place of conduct prohibited such damages); *Ashland Oil, Inc.* v. *Miller Oil Purchasing Co.*, 678 F.2d 1293 (5th Cir. 1982) (same)).

195. The same was true in *Apple* v. *Ford Motor Company*[202], which also awarded punitive damages under the law of the injury-state, Pennsylvania. The product in question was again a car, which was designed and manufactured in Michigan, a state that did not allow punitive damages, by defendant Ford, a company headquartered in Michigan. What was unusual was that, coincidentally, the victim was also a Michigan domiciliary who had driven the car to Pennsylvania for a short visit. The Pennsylvania court concluded that neither the victim's status as a non-resident nor the fact that he shared a Michigan affiliation with the defendant detracted from Pennsylvania's interest in applying its punitive-damages rule. The court reasoned that the purpose and policy of that rule was "to protect Pennsylvania residents and visitors to the state by deterring manufacturers from manufacturing products which may enter Pennsylvania that are defective and dangerous"[203] and that this policy was "equally furthered by awarding punitive damages to [a] plaintiff who is a Pennsylvania resident and to the plaintiff who is a resident of another state"[204].

A few years earlier, in *Kelly* v. *Ford Motor Co.*[205], a federal court in Pennsylvania reached the opposite result in a similar case. Actually, *Kelly* had better reasons to apply Pennsylvania law because the victim both lived in Pennsylvania and bought the car there. The court acknowledged Pennsylvania's interests "in punishing defendants who injure its residents and ... in deterring them and others from engaging in similar conduct which poses a risk to Pennsylvania's citizens"[206]. However, the court also found that Michigan had "a very strong interest"[207] in denying such damages, so as to ensure that "its domiciliary defendants are protected from excessive financial liability"[208]. By insulating companies such as Ford, who conduct extensive business within its borders, said the court, "Michigan hopes to promote corporate migration into its economy ... [which] will enhance the economic climate and well being of the state of Michigan by generating revenues"[209].

---

202. 2004 WL 3218425 (Pa. Commw. Ct. 2004).

203. *Id.* at *1.

204. *Id.*

205. 933 F.Supp. 465 (ED Pa. 1996).

206. *Id.* at 470.

207. *Id.*

208. *Id.*

209. *Id. Kelly* is discussed again *infra* at 201 and 215. For other cases applying the non-punitive damages law of the defendant's home state (rather than the punitive damages law of the state of injury), see *Selle* v. *Pierce*, 494 NW 2d 634 (SD 1993) (defamation action refusing to apply punitive damages law of place of injury and applying instead non-punitive damages law of state of conduct and defendant's domicile); *Beals* v. *Sipca Securink Corp.*, 1994 WL 236018 (DDC 1994) (product liability action applying Virginia law, which limited punitive damages (rather than District of Columbia law, which did not) in case arising from injury in D.C. caused by product manufactured by Virginia defendant in Virginia).

Without mentioning *Kelly*, the *Apple* court turned the migration argument around by saying that "Pennsylvania's public policy would be thwarted by applying the public policy of another state that seeks to encourage manufacturers to leave Pennsylvania"[210]. In *Danziger* v. *Ford Motor Company*[211], another court also addressed the migration argument by quoting with approval a comment from the Restatement Second to the effect that the place of conduct is less significant when "a potential defendant might *choose* to conduct his activities in a state whose tort rules are favorable to him"[212]. The court concluded by stating that "State sovereignty ... prevents Michigan from protecting its resident corporations from punishment"[213] in this way and that the interests of other states in protecting consumers who buy defective products sold in their territory "outweighs Michigan's interest in promoting its economy by shielding its corporate citizens from excess liability"[214].

196. *In re Air Crash Disaster at Washington D.C.*[215], was a more complex, multiparty case arising from the crash of an Air Florida plane in the District of Columbia. The case encompassed both product liability claims against Boeing, the company that manufactured the airplane in its home state of Washington, and other tort claims against Air Florida, the Florida-based company that owned and operated the airplane at the time of the crash. Boeing argued that Washington law, which prohibited punitive damages (rather than D.C. law which allowed them) should govern the claims against Boeing. The court rejected the argument by pointing out that, while Washington had chosen to protect manufacturers at the expense of victims, "the sovereignty of other states prevents [Washington] from placing on the scales the rights of those injured elsewhere"[216].

The court then focused on the actions against the airline, which was allegedly negligent in overseeing the de-icing of the plane before takeoff from the airport, which is located on the Virginia side of the Virginia-D.C. border. Virginia (unlike D.C.) prohibited punitive damages. The District of Columbia court found that, as between these two jurisdictions, D.C. had "the most significant relationship ... [because] the injurious effects of the [Virginia] conduct were predominantly felt in the District"[217].

---

210. *Apple*, 2004 WL 3218425 at *1.
211. 2005 WL 1630082 (DDC 2005).
212. Id. at *4 (quoting Restatement (Second) of Conflict of Laws § 145 cmt. e.) (emphasis added).
213. *Id.*
214. *Id.* After completion of the manuscript, the court reversed its decision and applied Michigan law, which did not allow punitive damages. See 402 F.Supp.2d 236 (DDC 2005).
215. 559 F.Supp. 333 (DDC 1983).
216. *Id.* at 359.
217. *Id.* at 356.

5.   Pattern 8: None of the above (victim's nationality or domicile)

197. Finally, in Pattern 8, the three pertinent contacts are in a state or states that do not impose punitive damages for the conduct in question. In such a case, there is little justification for awarding punitive damages, even if, for example, the victim's home state imposes such damages, and even if that state is also the forum state[218].

A case on point is *Phillips* v. *General Motors Corp.*[219], in which the Montana Supreme Court awarded punitive damages to a Montana plaintiff under Montana law, even though Montana did not have any other pertinent contacts and the other involved states did not allow or limited such damages. *Phillips* was a products liability action filed against a Michigan manufacturer for injuries caused by one of its trucks that was manufactured in Michigan. The court reasoned that, because "punitive damages serve to punish and deter conduct deemed wrongful – in this case, placing a defective product into the stream of commerce which subsequently injured a Montana resident"[220] – Montana had a strong interest in "deterring future sales of defective products in Montana and encouraging manufacturers to warn Montana residents about defects in their products as quickly and as thoroughly as possible"[221].

---

218. For cases following this line of reasoning, see *Gonzalez* v. *Univ. Sys. of New Hampshire*, 2005 WL 530806 (Conn.Super.2005) (holding that the action of a Connecticut student against her New Hampshire college for injuries sustained during cheerleading exercises at the defendant's campus was governed by New Hampshire law, which prohibited such damages, rather than Connecticut law which permitted them); *Guidi* v. *Inter-Continental Hotels Corp.*, 2003 WL 1907901 (SDNY 2003) (holding that Egyptian law, which did not allow punitive damages, governed in an action filed against an Egyptian hotel owner for injury to an American hotel guest);*Tubos de Acero de Mexico, S.A.* v. *Am. Int'l Inv. Corp., Inc.*, 292 F.3d 471 (5th Cir. 2002) (denying punitive damages because the defendant was a Mexican corporation and the pertinent conduct and injury had occurred either in Mexico or in Louisiana, and neither jurisdiction allowed punitive damages); *Gadzinski* v. *Chrysler Corp.*, 2001 WL 629336 (ND Ill. 2001) (applying Indiana law limiting punitive damages to the action of an Illinois plaintiff who was injured in Indiana by a car he bought there); *Calhoun* v. *Yamaha Motor Corp., U.S.A.*, 216 F.3d 338 (3rd Cir. 2000) (applying Puerto Rico law, which prohibited punitive damages, rather than Pennsylvania law which allowed them, in an action by Pennsylvania plaintiffs injured in Puerto Rico while using a rented Japanese-made watercraft); *Hernandez* v. *Aeronaves de Mexico, S.A.*, 583 F.Supp. 331 (ND Cal. 1984) (applying Mexican law and denying punitive damages in actions arising from the crash in Mexico of a Mexican airliner and resulting in death of California domiciliaries, but applying California's more generous compensatory damages law).

219. 995 P.2d 1002 (Mont. 2000).

220. *Id.* at 1012.

221. *Id.* For another case awarding punitive damages under the law of the plaintiff's domicile, see *Thiele* v. *Northwest Mut. Ins. Co.*, 36 F.Supp.2d 852 (ED Wis. 1999) (applying Wisconsin law as the better law in an action for bad faith insurance practices filed by

However, the sale of the product took place not in Montana, but rather in North Carolina, which did not impose punitive damages. The purchaser was a North Carolina domiciliary who sold the truck to another North Carolina domiciliary, the victim, who later moved his domicile to Montana. He was killed not in Montana, but in Kansas (which limited punitive damages), while driving the car from Montana to North Carolina. Montana's interests in protecting its domiciliaries from harm was fully satisfied by applying Montana's compensatory damages law, which the court applied. Under the facts of this case, any additional interest Montana might have had in deterring conduct that injured Montana domiciliaries is far weaker than the contrary interests of Michigan in shielding from punitive damages Michigan companies that manufacture products in Michigan.

198. Similar to *Phillips*, but more defensible, are certain cases decided under federal "antiterrorist" statutes, such as the Antiterrorist and Effective Death Penalty Act of 1996 (AEDPA)[222]. This Act imposes punitive damages for death or personal injury of United States citizens who are victims of attacks sponsored or aided by states designated as sponsors of terrorism. Thus, the Act authorizes the award of punitive damages under the law of the victim's nationality, even when the conduct, the injury, and the defendant's domicile are all in another state that does not allow such damages.

One such case is *Flatow* v. *Islamic Republic of Iran*[223], which arose out of the death of an American student killed in a suicide bomb attack in the Gaza Strip. The court held that the AEPDA applied extraterritorially because Congress enacted it with the express purpose of "affect[ing] the conduct of terrorist states outside the United States, in order to promote the safety of United States citizens traveling overseas"[224], and that this express purpose negated the usual presumption against extraterritoriality[225]. The court awarded $42 million in compensatory damages and $225 million in punitive damages.

Another similar case is *Wagner* v. *Islamic Republic of Iran*[226], which arose out of the death of a U.S. serviceman during the 1984 car-bombing of the U.S. Embassy in Beirut, Lebanon. The court applied federal substantive law and awarded $12 million in compensatory damages and $300 million in punitive damages. Taking note of the September 11 attacks, the court said that "now, more than ever, ... the

---

a Wisconsin insured against a Michigan insurer who insured plaintiff's barn house in Michigan. Michigan did not allow punitive damages).

222. 28 U.S.C. § 1605(a)(7). This Act lifts the sovereign immunity of foreign states designated by the U.S. State Department as sponsors of terrorism and provides a cause of action for U.S. citizens killed or injured by acts of terrorism sponsored or aided by these states.

223. 999 F.Supp 1 (DDC 1998).

224. *Id*. at 15 (citing legislative history).

225. *Id*. at 16. See also *id*. at 15 n. 7 (stating that such extraterritorial exception is consistent with international law, based on the principles of passive personality, protective, and universal).

226. 172 F.Supp.2d 128 (DDC. 2001).

acts of terrorists and their sponsors must be punished to the full extent to which civil damage awards might operate to suppress such activities in the future"[227].

The reason that cases like *Wagner* are more defensible than cases like *Phillips* is that, while the victim's Montana domicile in *Phillips* was no more than a coincidence, the victim's U.S. citizenship in *Wagner* was anything but a coincidence--the victim was a target of the attack *because* of his citizenship. Under these circumstances, the application of American punitive-damages law is defensible.

6.   *Summary and rule*

199. The preceding discussion provides a wide ranging sample of tort cases involving punitive damages conflicts. These cases have been decided under a variety of modern choice-of-law methodologies, such as the Restatement Second, interest analysis, and Leflar's choice-influencing considerations. However, as in many other tort conflicts, the use of one or another methodology does not appear to have had a perceptible bearing on the outcome of the cases. Consequently, it is unnecessary to dwell much on methodology and more fruitful to focus on the outcomes of cases.

As the above discussion indicates, American courts have awarded punitive damages in cases involving each of the eight patterns depicted in the above table. Following the same order as the table, these cases can be grouped into cases in which the court awarded punitive damages under the law of:
(1)   a state that had two or more pertinent contacts (Patterns 1-4);
(2)   a state that had one of the three pertinent contacts (Patterns 5-7); and
(3)   a state that did not have any of the three pertinent contacts, but had other contacts, such as the victim's domicile or nationality (Pattern 8).

If one were to compress these results into a *descriptive* choice-of-law rule, the rule would provide as follows:

> *Subject to some exceptions, American courts award punitive damages if such damages are imposed by one or more of the following states: (1) the state of*

---

227.   *Id.* at 138. For another AEDPA case, see *Surette v. The Islamic Republic of Iran*, 231 F.Supp.2d 260 (DDC 2002) (awarding compensatory and punitive damages against Iranian governmental agencies in action by the estate of an American hostage killed in Lebanon in 1985). See also *Doe v. Saravia*, 348 F.Supp.2d 1112 (ED Cal. 2004) (action filed under Torture Victim Protection Act (TVPA) awarding compensatory and punitive damages against former leader of Salvadoran paramilitary death squads for coordinating the 1980 assassination of Salvadoran Archbishop Oscar Romero in El Salvador); *Mehinovic v. Vuskovic*, 198 F.Supp.2d 1322 (ND Ga. 2002) (TVPA action against former Bosnian Serb police officer – finding defendant liable for war crimes and crimes against humanity, and awarding plaintiffs multimillion-dollar compensatory and punitive damages).

> *the defendant's domicile or principal place of business; (2) the state of the*
> *defendant's conduct; or (3) the state of the injury*[228].

This rule does not include cases falling within Pattern 8 (the domicile cases) because these cases are both uncommon and extreme, but it does include the cases falling within Patterns 5-7 (one contact), which are more common and more defensible.

However, while being "defensible" is an acceptable attribute of de facto practice, it is not a sufficient attribute of a *prescriptive* rule, namely a rule that seeks to guide future practices. One who attempts to draft a prescriptive rule should aspire to a higher standard – a rule that has a solid foundation in judicial practice *and* takes a more evenhanded position towards these sharp conflicts, keeping in mind the severity of punitive damages, when compared to other conduct-regulating rules. For this reason, a less liberal rule might be more appropriate for punitive damages than for other conduct-regulating issues. The view of this author is that such a rule must be grounded on the cases of Patterns 1-4, which are both more numerous and better-reasoned.

Such a rule can be modelled after the rule adopted by the Louisiana codification of 1991[229] and later by the ALI's Complex Litigation Project of 1994[230]. Although phrased differently, both of these rules are based upon the three contacts discussed above: the place of conduct, the place of the defendant's domicile, and the place of injury. These rules provide that:

---

228. If punitive damages are available only in the state of injury, the application of that state's punitive damages law is subject to the proviso that the occurrence of the injury in that state must have been objectively foreseeable. See *supra* 194.

229. See La. Civ. Code Art. 3546. For discussion of the rationale of this article by its drafter, see S. Symeonides, "Louisiana's New Law of Choice of Law for Tort Conflicts: An Exegesis", 66 *Tul. L. Rev.* 677, 735-749 (1992). Interestingly, the Puerto Rico Draft, although prepared by the same drafter as the Louisiana codification, does not contain a separate article for punitive damages. This means that punitive damages conflicts are governed by Article 46 of the Draft which applies to other conduct-regulating conflicts and which allows punitive damages more easily, i.e., whenever they are allowed under the law of either the state of conduct or the state of injury (in the latter case, subject to a foreseeability defense).

230. See American Law Institute, *Complex Litigation: Statutory Recommendations and Analysis* §6.06 (1994). For a discussion of this provision, see F. Juenger, "The Complex Litigation Project's Tort Choice-of-Law Rules", 54 *La. L. Rev.* 907 (1994); P. Kozyris, "The Conflicts Provisions of the ALI's Complex Litigation Project: A Glass Half Full?" 54 *La. L. Rev.* 953 (1994); J. Nafziger, "Choice of Law in Air Disaster Cases: Complex Litigation Rules and the Common Law", 54 *La. L. Rev.* 1001 (1994); R. Sedler, "The Complex Litigation Project's Proposal for Federally-Mandated Choice of Law in Mass Torts Cases: Another Assault on State Sovereignty", 54 *La. L. Rev.* 1085 (1994); S. Symeonides, "The ALI's Complex Litigation Project: Commencing the National Debate", 54 *La. L. Rev.* 843 (1994).

Punitive damages may be awarded if all three, or any two, of the above con-
tacts are located in a state or states that allow such damages.

Thus, these rules steer a middle course between outright hostility and undue lib-
erality toward punitive damages. For this reason, they can be challenged from
both the left and the right, i.e., to the effect that the two-contacts requirement is
either too restrictive or not restrictive enough.

200. The critics from the right tend to oppose punitive damages on substantive grounds and thus have great difficulty accepting the award of such damages
in any multistate cases, i.e. in all of the above patterns, except perhaps Pattern
1 in which *all* involved states would impose punitive damages. This viewpoint
has been sufficiently addressed earlier in this chapter[231], as well as elsewhere in
defending the similar rule of the Louisiana codification, which also employs the
two contact- approach[232].

The critics from the left would argue that punitive damages should be awarded in any case in which they are allowed by the law of any state that has even *one*
of the three contacts listed above, as in Patterns 5-7, above, (or perhaps other
contacts, such as the victim's domicile). Besides finding respectable support in
the case law, these critics can also support their position with reasonable policy
arguments. Indeed, in each of these patterns, there is a good reason to award
punitive damages:

(a)   in Pattern 5, the award of punitive damages would advance the policy of the
      tortfeasor's home state in punishing the tortfeasor and deterring other po-
      tential tortfeasors (even if neither the conduct nor the injury occurred within
      its territory);

(b)   in Pattern 6, the award of punitive damages would advance the policy of the
      state of conduct in punishing those engaging in substandard conduct within
      its territory (even if the injury occurs outside that territory) and deterring
      similar conduct in the future; and

(c)   in Pattern 7, the award of punitive damages would advance the policy of the
      state of injury in punishing defendants who cause injury within its territory
      (even if the conduct occurs elsewhere) and to deter similar conduct in the
      future.

201. A case involving the last pattern but refusing to follow this logic is *Kelly* v.
Ford Motor Co.[233], which was discussed earlier. *Kelly* applied Michigan law (which
denied punitive damages) rather than Pennsylvania law (which allowed them) in
a Pennsylvania products liability action arising from the death of a Pennsylvania
woman who was killed in Pennsylvania by a car manufactured by a Michigan defendant in Michigan. *Kelly* is an unsympathetic case that provides an easy target

---

231. See *supra* 181-183, 185-186.
232. See S. Symeonides, "Louisiana's New Law of Choice of Law for Tort Conflicts: An
      Exegesis", 66 *Tul. L. Rev.* 677, 742-749 (1992).
233. See *supra* 195 at footnote 205.

for commentators. One of them, Professor Phaedon Kozyris finds the *Kelly* result "plainly unacceptable under any reasonable approach"[234]. Another commentator, Professor Louise Weinberg, also finds *Kelly* nothing short of outrageous, and seems to criticize the undersigned author for not criticizing *Kelly*[235].

Weinberg correctly notes that Pennsylvania's interests were "at least as compelling as Michigan's"[236], which is why *Kelly* was a true conflict, and then provides her own good reasons for which the court should have applied Pennsylvania law. One of these reasons seems to be an appeal to material-justice: "Egregiously causing the death of a Pennsylvania woman on a Pennsylvania road is certainly conduct that cries out for punitive damages"[237]. By denying such damages, the *Kelly* court "failed to impress upon the defendant the gravity of conduct that caused a death far from the place of manufacture, failed to punish the defendant for it, failed to deter future such conduct, with foreseeable impact on road safety, and failed to pressure the defendant to pay the costs of maintaining better standards"[238]. All of this is true as is Weinberg's statement that Pennsylvania was "under *no obligation* to subordinate its own law and policies ... to another state's interests in protecting its local industry's egregious wrongdoing, and certainly not where the result is an unsafe condition on Pennsylvania's roads, and the death of a Pennsylvanian"[239].

---

234. P. Kozyris, "Conflicts Theory for Dummies: *Après le Deluge*, Where Are We on Producers Liability", 60 *La. L. Rev.* 1161, 1178 n. 39 (2000).

235. See L. Weinberg, "Theory Wars in the Conflict of Laws", 103 *Mich. L. Rev.* 1631, 1657 (2005) (stating that "Symeonides ... praises the *Kelly* court for resisting the 'all-too-common temptation' to apply forum law to favor the local bereaved".) Actually, this author simply found Kelly "*noteworthy* for resisting the all-too-common temptation ... ." See the first edition of this book in 298 *Recueil des Cours* 9, 309 (2003) (emphasis added).

236. Weinberg, *supra* footnote 235, at 1658.

237. *Id.*

238. *Id.* at 1659.

239. *Id.* at 1658-1659 (emphasis added). Professor Weinberg also believes that *Kelly*'s application of Michigan law "discriminat[ed] irrationally between two classes of Pennsylvania's decedents – those who could recover because the product that killed them at home in Pennsylvania was made in Pennsylvania, and those who could not because the product that killed them at home in Pennsylvania was sent into Pennsylvania". *Id.* at 1660. Weinberg does not argue that this discrimination is unconstitutional. She is also fully aware (see *id.* at 1653 n.55) that the alternative to this "intrastate" discrimination (i.e., applying Pennsylvania law) is "interstate" discrimination, which carries its own price tag. In cases like *Kelly* in which the application of either state's law is constitutional and thus neither discrimination is unconstitutional, the question becomes one of choice, i.e., which is the better choice. Applying forum law avoids the problem of intrastate discrimination, which concerns Weinberg, but it can lead to interstate discrimination, particularly under Weinberg's approach which does not allow tort defendants the defense of unfair surprise because "tort cases are actuarially predicted by the tortfeasor's insurer, an acknowledged expert with every opportunity to take into account the range of likely choices of law, and to set premiums accordingly". *Id.* at 1663.

Surely, Pennsylvania had no *constitutional* obligation to apply Michigan law. Conversely, had *Kelly* applied Pennsylvania law, the decision would not only be entirely constitutional but also entirely defensible from a choice-of-law perspective. In other words, we are in that middle area in which applying the law of either state is both constitutional and defensible from the choice-of-law perspective. On the other hand, if the question is which is the *better* choice-of-law decision in such a true conflict, then this is not only a question on which reasonable people can disagree, but also a question on which people can change their minds, as the undesigned author has.

In drafting the Louisiana codification, this author proposed a rule that, for reasons similar to those advanced by Professor Weinberg, would have allowed punitive damages in a case such as *Kelly*, that is, whenever such damages are imposed by the law of the state of injury and as long as the occurrence of the injury in that state was objectively foreseeable[240]. However, encouraged by a powerful industry lobby in a state that has always been hostile to punitive damages, the legislature of that state would not adopt such a "liberal" rule. Two years later, there emerged a compromise consisting of the two-contact rule described above. This may well be a case of the "Stockholm syndrome", but, fifteen years later, this author continues to believe that this rule was not simply the only possible exit from a political dead-end, but is also an objectively good formula for resolving these difficult conflicts, a formula that can survive the scrutiny of a rigorous non-political academic debate in which one does not have to make compromises.

---

240. The Reporter's original draft provided one rule for all conduct-regulating conflicts (including punitive damages), what later became La. Civ. Code Art. 3543, which is described *supra* at footnote 122 and is similar to the rule proposed earlier in this chapter for generic conduct-regulating conflicts other than punitive damages. See also the equivalent scheme of the Puerto Rico Draft Code, *supra* footnote 229. Article 4546 of the Louisiana Civil Code, which deals with punitive-damages conflicts, was added later. See S. Symeonides, "Louisiana's New Law of Choice of Law for Tort Conflicts: An Exegesis", 66 *Tul. L. Rev.* 677, 735 *et seq.* (1992).

Chapter VIII Products Liability

A. Introduction

1. Scope of the chapter

202. The law of products liability as a distinct body of law, at least partly independent from general tort and contract law from which it grew, is a relatively new phenomenon. Coincidentally, in the United States, its life parallels that of the American choice-of-law revolution – it was born in the 1960s, emancipated in the '70s, grew by leaps and bounds in the '80s when it also influenced the laws of other countries, and then began slowing down in the '90s[1]. This chapter discusses the experience of American courts in resolving product-liability conflicts since 1990.

Although this period coincides with a period of substantive and numerical retrenchment, it has nevertheless produced a number of product liability cases that is unrivaled in the rest of the world[2]. Indeed, it is no secret that, for a variety of reasons[3], "Americans use their product liability law a lot while victims and

---

1. For the substantive development and numerical growth of American products liability law, see J. Zekoll, "Liability for Defective Products and Services", in *American Law in a Time of Global Interdependence: U.S. National Reports to the XVIth International Congress of Comparative Law*, 121 (S. Symeonides & J. Reitz eds., 2002). The author reports that the number of personal-injury products liability filings in federal courts alone grew from 2,393 in 1975 to 32,856 in 1997 and then began to slow down to 26,886 in 1998, 18,781 in 1999, and 14,428 in 2000. See *id.* at 148-49. These numbers do not include filings in state courts where the numbers are lower. *Id.*

2. Professor Reimann reports that, on average, about 30,000 products liability actions (about one for every 90,000 inhabitants) are filed annually in the United States, whereas, for example, the European Commission reports "barely 100 court decisions ... in all the [EU] member states together", over a fifteen-year period". M. Reimann, "Liability for Defective Products and Services: Emergence of a Worldwide Standard?" *General Report to the XVIth Int'l Congress of Comp. L.* 57, 54 (Brisbane 2002).

3. For a discussion of the reasons, *see* the incisive analyses of M. Reimann, *supra* footnote 2, at 63-84; and J. Zekoll, *supra* footnote 1, at 143-59.

courts elsewhere don't"[4]. Naturally, the higher the number of product liability lawsuits, the higher the likelihood that many of them will have multistate elements, thus producing conflicts of laws. This is particularly true in the United States, which is essentially a single market, yet artificially segregated by state boundaries into multiple diverse products-liability regimes. Thus, for better or worse, American courts have had and continue to have the lion's share of product liability conflicts, and they have had to handle these conflicts with virtually no legislative guidance[5]. This Chapter examines the experience of American courts in handling these conflicts and attempts to identify the common patterns, trends, and lessons that emerge from this experience.

203. In order to keep the length of this Chapter within manageable limits, certain chronological and substantive limitations became necessary. Thus, this Chapter is confined to cases decided in the last fifteen years (1990 to 2005, inclusive) and, within that period, excludes: (1) class actions[6]; (2) cases decided as contract conflicts[7]; (3) cases in which both the plaintiff and the defendant were

---

4.   Reimann, *supra* footnote 2, at 53. See also *id.* at 57 ("products liability litigation in the United States is big business while it is of marginal importance in the rest of the world").

5.   The only exception are the cases decided under the 1991 Louisiana conflicts codification, specifically La. Civ. Code Art. 3545. For a discussion of this article by its drafter, see S. Symeonides, "Louisiana's New Law of Choice of Law for Tort Conflicts: An Exegesis", 66 *Tul. L. Rev.* 677, 749-759 (1992).

6.   Class actions are excluded because in most of them the choice-of-law discussion is limited to whether the application for class certification meets the commonality and predominance requirements, which depend in part on whether the same or similar laws would govern the claims of the members of the entire class or of manageable subclasses. See S. Symeonides, "Choice of Law in the American Courts in 2000: As the Century Turns, 49 *Am. J. Comp. L.* 1, 25-28 (2001); S. Symeonides, "Choice of Law in the American Courts in 2001: Fifteenth Annual Survey", 50 *Am. J. Comp. L.* 1, 83-88 (2002).

7.   Typically, these cases involve defective products that have not caused physical injury to a person or to property other than the product itself. See, e.g., *Rocky Mountain Helicopters, Inc.* v. *Bell Helicopter Textron, Inc.*, 24 F.3d 125 (10th Cir. 1994) (negligence and breach of warranty action for damage to a helicopter caused by its defective design; employing contract analysis and applying the law of Texas, which was the manufacturer's principal place of business and place of manufacture); *R-Square Inv., Inc.* v. *Teledyne Indus., Inc.*, 1997 WL 436245 (ED La. 1997) (case involving a defective airplane engine that caused damage to the plane; employing contract analysis to claim for damage to the engine, and tort analysis to claim for damage to the plane; applying Minnesota law to the former and Louisiana law to the latter claim); *Skansi Marine LLC* v. *Ameron Int'l Corp.*, 2003 WL 22852221 (ED La. 2003) (same analysis in case involving defective boats); *Thornton* v. *Cessna Aircraft Co.*, 886 F.2d 85 (4th Cir. 1989) (applying the law of the accident state to plaintiff's tort claims, and the law of the place of the product's acquisition, and also plaintiff's domicile, to his breach of warranty claims); *Boudreau* v. *Baughman*, 368 SE 2d 849 (1988) (breach of warranty case resolved under UCC § 1-105(1) and applying the law of the state of injury, which

affiliated with the same state or with states whose laws produced the same out-come[8]; and (4) cases in which the choice-of-law question remained undetected or uncontested or the court's discussion of it was cursory or inconsequential[9].

On the other hand, this Chapter includes lower court cases that either have not been appealed or have been affirmed by a higher court without opinion. For, even if lacking in precedential value, these cases represent the final resolution of the particular conflict, and thus help compose a more complete picture of the reality of American conflicts law.

The above limitations reduce the total number of cases to exactly 100[10], a manageable number that is also high enough to permit the drawing of some gen eral conclusions. This Chapter discusses all of these cases.

2.   The pertinent connecting factors

(a)   The list

204.The abandonment of the *lex loci delicti* rule has allowed courts to consider multiple factual contacts, or connecting factors, in the process of identifying the concerned jurisdictions. In product liability conflicts, these contacts are:
(1)   the domicile, habitual residence, or "home state" of the party injured by the product (hereafter interchangeably referred to as "plaintiff" or "victim");
(2)   the place where the injury occurred;

---

was also the place of the sale and use of the product); *Premix-Marbletite Mfg. Corp.* v. *SKW Chems., Inc.*, 2001 WL 673454 (SD Fla. 2001) (applying Florida law under UCC § 1.105(1) to an action by Florida buyer against Georgia seller of defective product purchased and used in Florida, because Florida had an appropriate relation to the transactions at issue, being the place of negotiation, purchase, and delivery of the product and the buyer's domicile and injury); *Robinson* v. *Am. Marine Holdings, Inc.*, 2002 WL 873185 (ED La. 2002) (breach of warranty and redhibition action).

8.   See, e.g., *Winsor* v. *Glassworks PHX, LLC*, 63 P.3d 1040 (Az. App. 2003) (applying Arizona law to a case in which the only non-Arizona contact was the incorporation of the defendant's successor).

9.   Also excluded are cases disposed on *forum non conveniens* grounds, and cases in which the choice-of-law discussion, though substantial, is not related to the manu-facturer's liability, e.g., whether the proceeds of a survival action belong to the estate or to the heirs or other beneficiaries.

10.   This number may be too round and convenient not be suspect, but no cases have been excluded or included in order to round up the number. Although the number of years the study encompasses was purposefully extended to 1990 (and stopped on July 31, 2005), no cases decided during this period and meeting the above parameters were excluded in order to reach this number. It is also worth noting that the findings and conclusions from the 100 cases discussed here do not differ, except in minor measure, from those drawn from the 70 cases discussed in the first edition of this book (written in 2002), or from the 80 cases discussed in S. Symeonides "Choice of Law for Products Liability: The 1990s and Beyond" 78 *Tul. L. Rev.* 1247 (2004) (writ-ten in 2003).

(3)   the place where the product was sold as such, either to the eventual victim (as in the case of most consumer products) or to a third party who owned the product at the time of the injury (as in the case of industrial machinery or public transportation means). This place is referred to hereafter as the "place of acquisition";

(4)   the place where the product was manufactured or designed (even though these two contacts do not always coincide in the same state); and

(5)   the principal place of business of the manufacturer (hereinafter referred to as "defendant")[11].

(b)   Qualifications

205. The above list calls for explanation and qualification. First, the list should not lead to the inference that *all* of these contacts arc taken into account in *all* cases. For example, cases decided under the *lex loci delicti* rule do not consider, and often do not mention, the other contacts.

Second, in some cases, one or more of these contacts may be located in more than one state. Thus, in the case of certain products used over long periods in several states, the injury may be peripatetic. Examples from recent experience include pharmaceuticals[12], breast implants, or tobacco products[13] that the victims

---

11.   In some cases, parties other than the manufacturer, such as a distributor or retailer, may be defendants. Nevertheless, all but six of the cases discussed in this Chapter involve lawsuits against manufacturers. The six cases in which the defendant was the retailer are *Hughes* v. *Wal-Mart Stores, Inc.*, 250 F.3d 618 (8th Cir. 2001); *Long* v. *Sears Roebuck & Co.*, 877 F.Supp. 8 (DDC 1995); *Danielson* v. *Nat'l Supply Co.*, 2003 WL 22332982 (Minn. App. 2003); *Gadzinski* v. *Chrysler Corp.*, 2001 WL 629336 (ND Ill. 2001); and *McKinnon* v. *F.H. Morgan & Co. Inc.*, 750 A.2d 1026 (Vt. 2000). In the last two cases, the retailer had also serviced the product.

12.   *Braune* v. *Abbott Labs.*, 895 F. Supp. 530 (EDNY 1995), is a typical example of peripatetic injury caused by a pharmaceutical product. In the 1950s, a drug known as DES and designed to prevent miscarriages was prescribed by doctors to pregnant women living in several states. The plaintiffs in *Braune* were among the daughters of those women, and had been exposed to DES during gestation in their mothers' wombs. As a result of that exposure, plaintiffs gradually developed various abnormalities in their reproductive organs, including infertility, miscarriages, and cervical cancer, which became evident when the plaintiffs reached child-bearing age. The plaintiffs, like their mothers, had lived in several states since the mothers had used the drug, thus raising difficult questions on when and where the injuries occurred. The court concluded that the injuries occurred in the states in which they were diagnosed. See also *Millar-Mintz* v. *Abbott Labs.*, 645 NE 2d 278 (Ill. App. 1994) (applying Illinois's pro-plaintiff law to an action filed by a plaintiff whose mother had used DES in the 1940's while domiciled in Illinois. The plaintiff had lived in New York, California, and then in Illinois, where she was first advised of her infertility and its causal relation to her mother's use of DES).

13.   See *Tune* v. *Philip Morris, Inc.*, 766 So.2d 350 (Fla. App. 2000) (action against tobacco manufacturer brought by a plaintiff who used tobacco products for many years while domiciled in two states and who was diagnosed with lung cancer while domiciled

used over long periods of time while residing in several states. Similarly, in many cases, the manufacturing process takes place in different phases in different states. The product is designed in one state, tested in another[14], approved in another, and manufactured and assembled in yet another state[15].

Third, each of the above contacts may be fortuitous in a given case, such as the place of injury in an airplane crash[16], or the place of acquisition in the case of a product purchased by a tourist in a distant state[17].

Fourth, the above contacts are not necessarily of equal weight or pertinence. For example, the place of the product's acquisition is generally less pertinent when a party other than the victim acquired the product, or when the victim was not the original acquirer. Likewise, in today's world of multistate corporate mobility, the manufacturer's principal place of business is justifiably given less weight[18], and in some cases – though not as many as one might expect – the defendant is not

---

in the second state); *Philip Morris, Inc.* v. *Angeletti*, 752 A.2d 200 (Md. 2000) (class action against tobacco manufacturers by former and current Maryland domiciliaries who were addicted to tobacco products – decertifying class because it was unlikely that the "deleterious" effect of nicotine had taken effect upon the bodies of all plaintiffs in the same state).

14. For the problem of testing products in a state "chosen because of its low liability laws", see J. Fawcett, "Products Liability in Private International Law: A European Perspective", 238 *Recueil des Cours* 9, 127 (1993).

15. See, e.g., *Dorman* v. *Emerson Elec. Co.*, 23 F.3d 1354 (8th Cir. 1994), cert. denied, 115 S. Ct. 428 (1994) (involving a miter saw manufactured in Taiwan by a Taiwanese corporation under license from a Missouri corporation that had designed and tested that line of products in Missouri); *Rutherford* v. *Goodyear Tire & Rubber Co.*, 943 F.Supp. 789 (WD Ky. 1996), aff'd, 142 F.3d 436, (6th Cir. 1998) (involving a car tire that was manufactured in Kansas by Goodyear, an Ohio corporation, purchased by Ford Motor Company, a Michigan corporation, and installed on a Ford car in Ford's Kentucky assembly plant); *Crouch* v. *Gen. Elec. Co.*, 699 F.Supp. 585 (SD Miss. 1988) (involving helicopter engine designed and manufactured in Massachusetts and installed in helicopter in Connecticut).

16. See, e.g., *In re Air Crash Disaster at Sioux City, Iowa*, 734 F.Supp. 1425 (ND Ill. 1990) (discounting as fortuitous the occurrence of the injury in Iowa in a case involving a flight from Denver to Chicago).

17. See, e.g., *Danielson* v. *Nat'l Supply Co.*, 2003 WL 22332982 (Minn. App. 2003) (involving a step-ladder that a Minnesota trailer-owner purchased while traveling through Texas).

18. See, e.g., *In re Air Crash Disaster at Sioux City, Iowa*, 734 F.Supp. 1425 (ND Ill. 1990) (noting that New York was General Electric's principal place of business only because the company's other holdings, unrelated to manufacture, were located in that state; discounting this contact for this reason); *Crouch* v. *Gen. Elec. Co.*, 699 F.Supp. 585 (SD Miss. 1988) (involving a defendant that had its principal place of business in New York, its headquarters in Connecticut, its engine manufacturing division's headquarters in Ohio, and its engine design and manufacturing division in Massachusetts).

the manufacturer but rather the seller of the product[19]. Finally, it has been argued that the place of manufacture should not be a pertinent contact[20].

A final qualification affecting the relative pertinence of some of the above contacts has to do with the inherent breadth of the very term "product" in encompassing things of widely diverse qualities and uses. For example, certain products, such as industrial or similar production-equipment, are intended for use in one state, while other products, such as airplanes or other means of public transportation, are intended for use in more than one state. In-between the two categories are consumer products, such as pharmaceuticals, appliances, foods, cosmetics, and personal vehicles that are used primarily, but not exclusively, in one state. While products of the last category are usually purchased directly by the user and eventual victim of the product, the products of the first two categories are purchased by someone other than the victim, and are usually not subject to the victim's control. The nature of the product often determines the relative pertinence of each of the above contacts. For example, the place of injury is given significant weight in cases of industrial machinery, especially one attached to a building, and much less weight in the case of an airplane crash. Similarly, as said above, the place of acquisition is given more weight when the acquirer is the victim than when it is not.

Despite these qualifications, the above list of contacts remains a useful vehicle through which to catalogue and analyze products liability conflicts. The analysis, or at least the description of it, can be further facilitated by grouping these contacts into plaintiff-affiliating and defendant-affiliating contacts. Thus, the plaintiff's domicile and the place of injury are plaintiff-affiliating contacts, while the defendant's principal place of business and the place of the manufacture are defendant-affiliating contacts. The remaining contact, the place of the product's acquisition, is where, figuratively speaking, the two sides meet each other. However, at least when the product is acquired by the victim rather than by a third party (as in the case of an airplane acquired by an airline company), this contact can be considered as a victim-affiliated contact and is treated as such in the discussion below.

---

19.   See *supra* footnote 11.

20.   See P. Kozyris, "Values and Methods in Choice of Law for Product Liability: A Comparative Comment on Statutory Solutions", 38 *Am. J. Comp. L.* 475, 500 (1990) ("[T]he mere making of a product, however defective, does not create the risk of causing harm ... . Production is only a preparatory act which does not rise to the level of the wrongful conduct. The tort does not commence until the product is placed in a position to cause harm, i.e., is distributed to a potential user"); *Rutherford* v. *Goodyear Tire & Rubber Co.*, 943 F. Supp. 789, 793 (WD Ky. 1996) ("Legal claims do not arise at the time or at the place of manufacture. They arise when an injury occurs. Thus, the place of injury, not the place of manufacture is the central focus of the cause of action"); *Maly* v. *Genmar Indus., Inc.*, 1996 WL 28473 (N D Ill. 1996) (the court does not even mention the place of manufacture, apparently because of the court's conclusion that the critical conduct was "the placement of a defective product in the stream of commerce". *id.* at *2).

Chart 11. The pertinent contacts in product-liability conflicts

(c) Dispersement of contacts

206. Although today's products travel great distances both before and after the time of purchase, it appears that most of the individual product-liability lawsuits involve cases that have contacts with only two or three states. For example, in 70 of the 100 cases, the five contacts listed above were grouped in either two or three states[21]. In 51 cases, three of the five contacts were in the same state. In 42 cases, both the acquisition of the product and the eventual injury occurred in the plaintiff's home state. As we shall see later, the vast majority of the latter cases applied the law of the latter state[22].

3. *The content of the contact states' laws*

207. One important lesson of the modern American conflicts experience is that one cannot resolve conflicts intelligently and rationally without considering the substantive content of the laws of each involved state, and without making that content an integral part of the whole choice-of-law process. This fundamental premise should be kept in mind, not only by the judge in resolving conflicts, but also by the commentator in discussing and analyzing them.

Product-liability laws may be categorized in many different ways, but at the most basic level these laws either favor the manufacturer or they favor the person injured by the product. This chapter refers to the former laws as pro-defendant laws and to the latter as pro-plaintiff laws.

The most common examples of pro-defendant laws are statutes of repose that bar lawsuits against manufacturers when filed after a specified number of years from the date the product entered the stream of commerce ("first use"), regardless of when the injury occurs. Other examples are rules that prohibit punitive damages, require the plaintiff to prove the manufacturer's negligence, or accord manufacturers special defenses such as "state of the art", or shield a manufacturer's successor from liability for the predecessor's products.

Conversely, among the clearest examples of pro-plaintiff laws are the absence of a statute of repose protecting manufacturers, and rules that impose strict liability, punitive damages, unlimited compensatory damages, or corporate successor liability on manufacturers.

---

21. The five contacts were grouped in two states in 36 cases, and in three states in 34 cases.

22. See *infra* 247.

4.   Typical patterns of product-liability conflicts

208. The combination of pertinent contacts and product-liability laws produces three typical patterns of product-liability conflicts (depicted below), depending on the laws of the involved states and on whether each state has contacts affiliating it only with the plaintiff, only with the defendant, or with both parties.

Table 16. The three major patterns of product-liability conflicts

Patterns	Plaintiff-Affiliating Contacts			Defendant-Affiliating Contacts	
	P's domicile	Injury	Acquisition	Manufacture	D's PPB
Direct conflicts	Pro-P	Pro-P	Pro-P	Pro-D	Pro-D
Inverse conflicts	Pro-D	Pro-D	Pro-D	Pro-P	Pro-P
Mixed conflicts	Pro-P	Pro-D	Pro-D	Pro-P	Pro-D
	or other combinations			other combinations	

The first pattern (hereafter called "*direct* conflicts") encompasses cases in which all three plaintiff-affiliating contacts are located in a state or states that have pro-plaintiff laws, while both defendant-affiliating contacts are located in a state or states that have pro-defendant laws.

The second pattern (hereafter called "*inverse* conflicts") encompasses cases in which all three plaintiff-affiliating contacts are located in a state or states that have pro-defendant laws, while both defendant-affiliating contacts are located in a state or states that have pro-plaintiff laws.

The third pattern is the residual pattern. It encompasses all the remaining combinations, such as situations in which the three plaintiff-affiliating contacts (domicile, injury, and product acquisition) are located in different states the laws of which favor a different party. Hereafter, these cases are called *mixed* conflicts.

209. In the prevailing conflicts jargon introduced by Brainerd Currie, direct conflicts would be called *true conflicts* and inverse conflicts would be called *no-interest* or *unprovided-for* cases. Even if one agrees with Currie's assumptions, his labels for these categories are problematic because they forejudge the answer to the basic question – whether in fact a state has an interest in applying its law to the particular case – a question that reasonable minds often answer differently. Indeed, as the discussion in this Chapter will show: most courts do not subscribe to Currie's assumptions; many courts do not employ his labels; and courts that employ these labels reach different conclusions regarding each state's interests than Currie would have reached. For example, in many inverse conflicts – which Currie would label as no-interest cases – the court concluded that one of the involved states did in fact have an interest[23], and this conclusion would move these cases

---

23.   See, e.g., *Gantes* v. *Kason Corp.*, 679 A.2d 106 (NJ 1996) (discussed *infra* 222; concluding that, although each party was affiliated with a state whose law favored the

from the no-interest category to the false conflict category. While it is true that many courts are likely to treat most direct conflicts as true conflicts and many inverse conflicts as no-interest cases, other courts may reach different conclusions.

For this reason, it is better to employ categorizations that are descriptive but non prescriptive. The terms "direct" and "inverse" conflicts meet this requirement. Rather than being dependent on largely subjective assumptions about each state's ostensible or real interests, these terms describe objectively the content of each state's substantive laws: *Direct* conflicts are those in which the application of each state's law would favor the party affiliated with that state ("each for its own"), while *inverse* conflicts are those in which the application of each state's law favors the party affiliated with the *other* state ("each for the other"). These terms are also non prescriptive, because they do not forejudge the court's own categorization of the conflict nor its ultimate outcome.

210. The only problem with these two terms is that, in product-liability conflicts, these terms can be under inclusive insofar as they only cover cases in which the contacts affiliated with one party are situated either in the same state or in states whose laws favor the *same* party. Because the number of relevant contacts in product-liability conflicts is as high as five, many cases do not fit the above specification. One example is cases in which the three plaintiff-affiliating contacts (domicile, injury, and place of acquisition) are located in two or three different states and one of those states has a law that favors the plaintiff while the other favors the defendant. Considering that the same possibility exists with regard to the two defendant-affiliating contacts, many more permutations are possible. Depending on the other factors, these permutations may present a direct conflict with regard to one pair of states and an inverse conflict with regard to another pair of states. For the purposes of this Chapter, all of these permutations are placed in one residual category which, for lack of a better term are called *mixed* conflicts.

5.   One hundred cases (1990-2005)

211. In order to facilitate the understanding of these complex cases, but also to enable the reader to verify the author's observations and conclusions, this Chapter frequently resorts to the use of tables. The next table depicts the100 cases decided during the survey period of 1990-2005[24]. The table lists the name of the case, the forum state, the states that had the five pertinent contacts, as well as an abbrevi-

---

other party, this was not a no-interest case but rather a false conflict because one of the two states had an interest in applying its law). See also cases ## 36-42, and 53-56 in Table 17, *infra*. See also *Jones* v. *SEPTA*, 1993 WL 141646 (ED Pa. 1993) (discussed *infra* at 239; concluding that, although each party was affiliated with a state whose law favored that party, this was not a true conflict but rather a false conflict because one state's interest was attenuated).

24.   The cases are numbered consecutively from 1 to 100, and this numbering is retained in subsequent tables and is used in the subsequent discussion.

ated description of their respective substantive laws[25]. The use of shading denotes the state whose law the court applied.

Table 17. Product-liability conflicts, 1990-2005

#	Case name	Forum state	Plaintiff-affiliating contacts			D-affiliating contacts	
			P's domicile	Injury	Acquisition	Manufacture	D's PPB
1. Cases in which the P's domicile, injury, and acquisition were in same state (42)							
A. Direct conflicts (each for its own) (9)							
a. Applying Pro-P law (8)							
1	Custom	KY Pro-D	CAN Pro-P	CAN Pro-P	CAN Pro-P	KY Pro-D	KY Pro-D
2	Kramer	NY Pro-P	NY Pro-P	NY Pro-P	NY Pro-P	Japan Pro-D	Japan Pro-D
3	Eimers	NY Pro-P	NY Pro-P	NY Pro-P	NY Pro-P	Japan Pro-D	Japan Pro-D
4	Savage	AK Pro-P	AK Pro-P	AK Pro-P	AK Pro-P	---	---
5	Hoover	OH Pro-P	OH Pro-P	OH Pro-P	OH Pro-P	IN ---	IN --
6	Tune	FL Pro-P	FL Pro-P	FL Pro-P	FL Pro-P / NY ---	---	--
7	Nelson	N.J. Pro-D / IN Pro-P	IN Pro-P	IN Pro-P	IN Pro-P	N.J. Pro-D	N.J. Pro-D
8	Kardas	NY Pro-D	VT Pro-P	VT Pro-P	VT Pro-P	---	NY Pro-D
b. Applying Pro-D law (1)							
9	Kelly	PA Pro-P	PA Pro-P	PA Pro-P	PA Pro-P	MI Pro-D	MI Pro-D
B. Inverse conflicts (each for the other) (33)							
a. Applying Pro-D law (25)							
10	Kemp	MI Pro-D	MI Pro-D	MI Pro-D	MI Pro-D	CA Pro-P	CA Pro-P
11	Burleson	TX Pro-D	TX Pro-D	TX Pro-D	TX Pro-D	Tobacco States ---	
12	Clark	LA Pro-D	LA Pro-D	LA Pro-D	LA Pro-D	CA Pro-P	CA Pro-P
13	Pittman	LA Pro-D	LA Pro-D	LA Pro-D	LA Pro-D	CA Pro-P	CA Pro-P
14	Jeff.Parish	LA Pro-D	LA Pro-D	LA Pro-D	LA Pro-D	--- Pro-P	--- Pro-P
15	Orl.Parish	LA Pro-D	LA Pro-D	LA Pro-D	LA Pro-D	--- Pro-P	--- Pro-P
16	Campofiore	CN Pro-D	CN Pro-D	CN Pro-D	CN Pro-D	NJ Pro-P	NJ Pro-P
17	Dorman	MO Pro-P	B.C. Pro-D	B.C. Pro-D	B.C. Pro-D	Taiwan ---	MO Pro-P
18	Walls	MS Pro-P	OR Pro-D	OR Pro-D	OR Pro-D	OH Pro-P	DEL Pro-P
19	Hughes	AR Pro-P	LA Pro-D	LA Pro-D	LA Pro-D	AR Pro-P	AR Pro-P
20	Hall	MI Pro-P	N.C. Pro-D	N.C. Pro-D	N.C. Pro-D	OH Pro-P	MI Pro-P
21	Farrell	MI Pro-P	N.C. Pro-D	N.C. Pro-D	N.C. Pro-D	MI Pro-P	MI Pro-P
22	Vestal	CA Pro-P	N.C. Pro-D	N.C. Pro-D	N.C. Pro-D	CA Pro-P	CA Pro-P
23	Nesladek	MN Pro-P	NEB Pro-D	NEB Pro-D	NEB Pro-D	MI ---	MI ---
24	Rice	WA Pro-P	WA Pro-P / OR Pro-D	OR Pro-D	OR Pro-D	---	---
25	Bain	TX Pro-P	B.C.? Pro-D	B.C. Pro-D	B.C.? Pro-D	---	TX Pro-P
26	Lilly	IN Pro-P	CA Pro-D	CA Pro-D	CA Pro-D	IN Pro-P	IN Pro-P
		KY	IN	IN	IN	KS / KY	MI

---

25.   Pro-plaintiff laws are abbreviated as "Pro-P" and pro-defendant laws as "Pro-D". The use of "---" means that the case contains no information on the particular state or its law.

#	Case name	Forum state	P-s domicile	Injury	Acquisition	Manufacture	D-s PPB
27	Rutherford	Pro-P	Pro-D	Pro-D	Pro-D	Pro-P	Pro-P
28	Harlan Feeders	IA Pro-P	NEB Pro-D	NEB Pro-D	NEB Pro-D	IA Pro-P	SD ---
29	Walters	IL Pro-P	KS Pro-D	KS Pro-D	KS Pro-D	TN/IL --/Pro-P	OH/IL --/Pro-P
30	Heindel	NJ Pro-P	PA Pro-D	PA Pro-D	PA Pro-D	NJ Pro-P	NJ Pro-P
31	White	OH Pro-P	GA Pro-D	GA Pro-D	GA Pro-D	OH Pro-P	OH Pro-P
32	Jones v. Cooper	PA Pro-P	VA Pro-D	VA Pro-D	VA Pro-D	OH Pro-P	OH Pro-P
33	Michaud	DEL Pro-P	QU Pro-D	QU Pro-D	QU Pro-D	--- ---	DEL Pro-P
34	Lupoli	MA Pro-P	NH Pro-D	NH Pro-D	NH Pro-D	MA Pro-P	MA Pro-P
	b. Applying Pro-P law (8)						
35	Gantes	N.J. Pro-P	GA Pro-D	GA Pro-D	GA Pro-D	N.J. Pro-P	N.J. Pro-P
36	McLennan	TX Pro-P	CAN Pro-D	CAN Pro-D	CAN Pro-D	TX Pro-P	TX Pro-P
37	Mahne	MI Pro-P	FL Pro-D	FL Pro-D	FL Pro-D	MI Pro-P	MI Pro-P
38	Davis	CA Pro-P	OR Pro-D	OR Pro-D	OR Pro-D	CA Pro-P	CA Pro-P
39	Marchesani	LA Pro-P	TN Pro-D	TN Pro-D	TN Pro-D	LA Pro-P	LA Pro-P
40	Baxter	CN Pro-P	OR Pro-D	OR Pro-D	OR Pro-D	CN Pro-P	CN Pro-P
41	Glover	MN Pro-P	IL Pro-D	IL Pro-D	IL Pro-D	NJ ---	NJ ---
42	Stupak	WS Pro-P	MI Pro-D	MI Pro-D	MI Pro-D	NJ ---	DEL ---

#	Case name	Forum state	Plaintiff-affiliating contacts			D-affiliating contacts	
			P-s domicile	Injury	Acquisition	Manufacture	D-s PPB
	2. Cases in which P-s domicile and injury were in same state (16)						
	A. Direct conflicts (each for its own) (5)						
	a. Applying Pro-P law (5)						
43	Smith	DEL Pro-P	DEL Pro-P	DEL Pro-P	MD Pro-D	MI? 	MD Pro-D
44	R-Square	LA Pro-P	LA Pro-P	LA Pro-P	MN Pro-D	AL ---	AL ---
45	Allstate	LA Pro-P	LA Pro-P	LA Pro-P	OK ---	MN? Pro-D	MN? Pro-D
46	Fisher	NEV Pro-P	NEV Pro-P	NEV Pro-P	UT Pro-D	ITA Pro-D	ITA Pro-D
47	Goede	MO Pro-P	MO Pro-P	MO Pro-P	CA? Pro-D	CA? Pro-D	CA Pro-D
	B. Inverse conflicts (each for the other) (11)						
	a. Applying Pro-D law (6)						
48	Egan	LA Pro-D	LA Pro-D	LA Pro-D	--- 	OH Pro-P	---
49	Land	IN Pro-D	IN Pro-D	IN Pro-D	KY Pro-P?	Japan Pro-D	Japan Pro-D
50	Denmann	MS Pro-P	N.C. Pro-D	N.C. Pro-D	MS Pro-P	GA ---	GA ---
51	McKinnon	VT Pro-P	Qu Pro-D	Qu Pro-D	VT Pro-P	VT Pro-P	VT Pro-P
52	Normann	PA Pro-P	PA / NY Pro-P / Pro-D	NY Pro-D	--- 	--- 	OH
	b. Applying Pro-P law (5)						
53	Zenaida-	WA	OR	OR	WA	WA	WA

	Case name	Forum state	P-s domicile	Injury	Acquisition	Manufacture	D-s PPB
		Pro-P	Pro-D	Pro-D	Pro-P	Pro-P	Pro-P
54	Magnant	MI / Pro-D	MI / Pro-D	MI / Pro-D	MN / Pro-P	MN / Pro-P	MN / Pro-P
55	Champlain	NY / Pro-D	NY / Pro-D	NY / Pro-D	KS / Pro-P	KS / Pro-P	KS / Pro-P
56	Lewis-DeBoer	CO / Pro-D	CO / Pro-D	CO / Pro-D	--- / ---	TX / Pro-P	TX / Pro-P
57	Sanchez	TX / Pro-P	MEX / Pro-D	MEX / Pro-D	TX / Pro-D	Japan / Pro-D	Japan / Pro-D
58	Long	D.C. / Pro-P	MD / Pro-D	MD / Pro-D	D.C. / Pro-P	S.C. / ---	DE / ---

3. Cases in which the P-s domicile and acquisition were in same state (14)

	Case name	Forum state	Plaintiff-affiliating contacts			D-affiliating contacts	
			P-s domicile	Injury	Acquisition	Manufacture	D-s PPB
59	Alexander	GA / Pro-P	GA / Pro-P	VA / Pro-D	GA / Pro-P	MI / ---	MI / ---
60	Etheredge	AL / Pro-P	AL / Pro-P	N.C. / Pro-D	AL / Pro-P	--- / ---	--- / ---
61	Kramer v Acton.	MA / Pro-P	MA / Pro-P	CN / Pro-D	MA / Pro-P	JAP / Pro-D	JAP / Pro-D
62	Mann	NY / Pro-P	NY / Pro-P	QU / Pro-D	NY / Pro-P	GA / ---	OH/TN / ---
63	Aguiniga	TX / Pro-P	TX (Pro-P) / MEX (Pro-D)	MEX / Pro-D	LA (---) / TX (Pro-P)	MI / ---	MI / ---
64	Thomson v Reinco	DEL / Pro-D	DEL / Pro-D	MD / Pro-P	DE (Pro-D) / PA (Pro-P)	NJ / ---	NJ / ---
65	Garcia	AZ / Pro-D	AZ / Pro-D	ID / Pro-P	AZ / Pro-D	MI / --	MI / --
66	Maly	IL / Pro-D	IL / Pro-D	WIS / Pro-P	IL / Pro-D	FL / ---	FL / ---
67	Thornton	AK (Pro-P) / IN (Pro-D)	IN / Pro-D	AK / Pro-P	IN / Pro-D	France / ---	CA / ---
68	Bonti	MS / Pro-P	N.C. / Pro-D	S.C. / Pro-D	N.C. / Pro-D	KY/MI / ---	MI / ---
69	Martin	WA / Pro-P	OR / Pro-D	WA / Pro-P	OR / Pro-D	OH / ---	OH / ---
70	Apple	PA / Pro-P	MI / Pro-D	PA / Pro-P	MI / Pro-D	MI / Pro-D	MI / Pro-D
71	Harsh	PA / Pro-P	VA / Pro-D	PA / Pro-P	VA / Pro-D	MI / ---	MI / ---
72	Fitts	AL / Pro-P	AL / Pro-P	FL / Pro-D	AL? / Pro-P	--- / ---	--- / ---

4. Cases in which the acquisition was in the state of Injury (16)

	Case name	Forum state	Plaintiff-affiliating contacts			D-affiliating contacts	
			P-s domicile	Injury	Acquisition	Manufacture	D-s PPB
73	Roll	NY (Pro-P) / NV (Pro-P)	NY / Pro-P	NV / Pro-P	NV / Pro-P	TX / Pro-D	TX / Pro-D
74	Johnson v. Ranch	IL / Pro-D	KS / ---	CO / Pro-P	CO / Pro-P	IL / Pro-D	IL / Pro-D
75	Gadzinski	IL / Pro-P	IL / Pro-P	IN / Pro-D	IN / Pro-D	---	IN / Pro-D
76	Romani	MA / Pro-P	MA / Pro-P	CN / Pro-D	CN / Pro-D	KS / ---	KS / ---
77	Tanges	NY / Pro-P	NY / Pro-P	CN / Pro-D	CN / Pro-D	--- / ---	--- / ---
78	LeJeune	PA / Pro-P	PA / Pro-P	DEL / Pro-D	DEL / Pro-D	--- / ---	--- / ---
79	Allison	MS	MS	TN	TN	PA	PA

		Pro-P	Pro-P	Pro-D	Pro-D	---	---
80	Schmidt	PA	PA	N.J.	N.J.	IL	IL
		Pro-P	Pro-P	Pro-D	Pro-D	---	---
81	Cianfrani	N.J.	PA	DEL	DEL	CA	CA
		Pro-P	Pro-P	Pro-D	Pro-D	---	---
82	Calhoun	PA	PA	P.R.	P.R.	Japan	Japan
		Pro-P	Pro-P	Pro-D	Pro-D	---	---
83	Beals	D.C.	VA	D.C.	D.C.	VA	VA
		Pro-P	Pro-P	Pro-P	Pro-P	Pro-D	Pro-D
84	Cosme	MA	MA	CN	CN	MA	MA
		Pro-P	Pro-P	Pro-D	Pro-D	Pro-P	Pro-P
85	Lou	MA	MA	CHI	CHI	CHI	MA
		Pro-P	Pro-P	Pro-D	Pro-D	Pro-D	Pro-P
86	Judge	FL	FL	MEX	MEX	MX | MI	MI
		Pro-P	Pro-P	Pro-D	Pro-D	Pro-D | Pro-P	Pro-P
87	Calhoun	PA	PA	P.R.	P.R.	Japan	Japan
		Pro-P	Pro-P	--	--	---	---
88	LaPlante	R.I.	R.I.	CO	CO	Japan	Japan
		Pro-P	Pro-P	Pro-D	Pro-D	Pro-D	Pro-D

			5. The Rest (12)				
			Plaintiff-affiliating contacts			D-affiliating contacts	
	Case name	Forum state	P-s domicile	Injury	Acquisition	Manufacture	D-s PPB
89	Torrington	TX	N.C.	MI/NE	TX	TX	TX
		Pro-P	---	Pro-D	Pro-P	Pro-P	Pro-P
90	Mitchell	TX	N.M./KY	N.C.	TX	TX	MD/CA
		Pro-P	---	Pro-D	Pro-P	Pro-P	---
91	Offshore	LA	---	LA	---	TX	TX
		Pro-D	---	Pro-D	---	Pro-P	Pro-P
92	Jones v. SEPTA	PA	IL	PA	---	NE	NE
		Pro-P	---	Pro-P	---	Pro-D	Pro-D
93	Mahoney	N.C.	AZ	N.C.	KY/AZ	N.C.	N.C.
		Pro-D	Pro-P	Pro-D	---	Pro-D	Pro-D
94	Huddy	TX	TX	GA	TN	PA	MI
		Pro-P	Pro-P	Pro-P	Pro-P	Pro-P	Pro-D
95	MacDonald	TN	N.D.	TN	KS	MI	MI
		---	Pro-P	---	Pro-D	---	---
96	Pollack	CN	CN	OH	KS	IL	OH
		Pro-P	Pro-P	Pro-D	--	--	Pro-D
97	Danielson	MN	MN	AZ	TX	--	CO
		Pro-P	Pro-P	Pro-D	Pro-D		--
98	Johnson v. Ford	IL	IL	KY	OK	KY	MI
		Pro-P	Pro-P	Pro-D	--	Pro-D	--
99	Phillips	MT	MT	KS	N.C.	MI	MI
		Pro-P	Pro-P	Pro-D	Pro-D	Pro-D	Pro-D
100	Danziger	DC	DC	NEB	MD	MI	MI
		Pro-P	Pro-P	Pro-D	Pro-P	Pro-D	Pro-D

B. Cases in Which the Three Plaintiff-Affiliating Contacts Were in the Same State

1. The cases

212. The discussion of cases begins with those that fit in the most frequent pattern: cases in which three of the five pertinent contacts – the ones affiliated with the plaintiff – were situated in the same state. As the above table indicates, the first 42 of the 100 cases fall within this category, that is, they involved situations in which the plaintiff's injury and the acquisition of the product were in the plain-

tiff's home state. In 14 of these cases, that state was also the forum state. In 33 or 79% of the 42 cases, the court applied the law of the state that had the three plaintiff-affiliating contacts. In 13 or 39% of the 33 cases, that state was also the forum state.

2.   Direct conflicts (each for its own)

213. The first nine of the 42 cases presented the direct or true conflict pattern, because the state with the three plaintiff-affiliating contacts had a pro-plaintiff law, while the state with the defendant-affiliating contacts had a pro-defendant law. Under the assumptions of interest analysis, the fact that each of the three plaintiff-affiliating contacts is in a state that has a pro-plaintiff law generates an interest on the part of that state to apply its law: the injured plaintiff's domicile in a state brings into play that state's interest in financially repairing the consequences of the injury for the victim and the victim's dependents; the occurrence of the injury within a state brings into play that state's interest in determining the legal consequences of the injury and minimizing similar injuries in the future; and the sale of the product in a state implicates that state's interest in ensuring that products marketed there conform with certain minimum standards of safety. By the same token, the fact that the state with the defendant-affiliating contacts has a pro-defendant law also generates an interest in applying its law to protect its manufacturers and through them its own economic welfare.

According to Currie's interest analysis, all of these true conflicts should be resolved by applying the law of the forum if the forum state is one of the interested states. Indeed, six of the eight cases in this category applied the law of the forum state[26], and this would seem to be a vindication of Currie's analysis. However,

---

26.   These cases are: *Kramer* v. *Showa Denko K.*, 929 F.Supp. 733 (SDNY 1996) (applying New York law and imposing punitive damages against a Japanese company that manufactured the product in Japan and sold it in New York where it injured plaintiff, a New York domiciliary; Japan did not allow punitive damages); *Eimers* v. *Honda Motor Co. Ltd*, 785 F.Supp. 1204 (WD Pa. 1992) (applying New York's pro-plaintiff law to an action by a New York plaintiff injured in New York by a motorcycle acquired in that state and manufactured by a Japanese defendant in Japan); *Savage Arms, Inc.* v. *Western Auto Supply Co.*, 18 P.3d 49 (Alaska 2001) (successor-liability conflict resolved under the Second Restatement and applying the pro-plaintiff law of Alaska, which was the victim's domicile, as well as the place of injury and the product's acquisition); *Hoover* v. *Recreation Equip. Corp.*, 792 F.Supp. 1484 (ND Ohio 1991) (following the Second Restatement and applying Ohio law to both products-liability and successor-liability claims of an Ohio resident injured in Ohio by a slide manufactured in Indiana by an Indiana corporation that was acquired by another Indiana corporation); *Tune* v. *Philip Morris, Inc.*, 766 So.2d 350 (Fla. App. 2000) (applying Florida's pro-plaintiff law to an action filed against a tobacco manufacturer by a Florida domiciliary who was diagnosed with lung cancer in Florida after using tobacco products in Florida and New Jersey, his previous domicile); and *Nelson* v. *Sandoz Pharm. Corp.*, 288 F.3d 954 (7th Cir. 2002). In *Nelson*, the action was filed in New Jersey, was transferred to Indiana, and was decided under New Jersey conflicts law under *van Dusen* v. *Barrack*,

the fact that in all six of those cases the forum state also had all three plaintiff-affiliating contacts may have been more determinative than the fact that it was the forum. Indeed, a perusal of the above table suggests that, whenever the three plaintiff-affiliated contacts are all in the same state, the law of that state will likely govern, regardless of whether that state is also the forum state or its law favors the plaintiff or the defendant, and regardless of the methodology the court follows.

214. *Custom Products, Inc.* v. *Fluor Daniel Canada, Inc.*[27], is one of three cases in this pattern that did *not* apply the law of the forum state[28]. This is noteworthy because: (a) the forum state officially follows a *lex fori* approach[29]; and (b) the application of forum law would have benefitted a forum defendant. The case also illustrates the strategy that many manufacturers now employ in hopes of taking advantage of choice-of-law approaches that favor the *lex fori*. Rather than waiting to be sued for injuries their products caused, manufacturers strike first by filing actions for declaratory judgments in a favorable forum. In *Custom Products*, this forum was Kentucky, which "no doubt ... prefers the application of its own laws over those of another forum"[30] and applies forum law whenever the forum has "significant contacts – not necessarily the most significant contacts"[31]. In this case, those contacts were the manufacture of the product and the manufacturer's principal place of business. The victim's domicile, place of injury, and the product's acquisition were all in Canada, the law of which favored the victim. Thus, under Currie's assumptions, this was a true conflict in that Kentucky would have an interest in applying its pro-manufacturer law to protect the Kentucky manufacturer, while Canada would have an interest in applying its pro-victim law to protect the Canadian victim injured in Canada. The court agreed that Canada had an "overwhelming interest"[32], but rejected the manufacturer's arguments

---

376 US 612 (1964). The court applied Indiana's pro-plaintiff discovery rule, rather than New Jersey's pro-defendant rule, to an Indiana plaintiff's action against a New Jersey manufacturer for injury caused in Indiana by a product sold there. It is unclear whether federal transfer cases like *Nelson* should be credited for or against the Currie column. Because Currie died before *van Dusen* articulated the obligation of the transferee court to act as surrogate for the transferor court, Currie did not have the opportunity to explain how his *lex-fori* preference would work in federal transfer cases. Under *van Dusen* the Indiana court is to act as a surrogate for the New Jersey federal court, which under *Klaxon* is to act as a surrogate for the New Jersey state court, which according to Currie should apply New Jersey law, whenever New Jersey has an interest. *Nelson* applied Indiana law.

27. 262 F.Supp.2d 767 (WD Ky.2003)
28. The other two cases are *Kelly*, which is discussed *infra* 215 and *Kardas* v. *Union Carbide Corp.* 784 NYS2d 921 (NY Supr. Ct. 2004) (applying Vermont's pro-plaintiff products liability law to action of a Vermont plaintiff who was exposed in that state to toxic substances manufactured and used by defendant).
29. For Kentucky's *lex fori* approach, see *supra* 68, 71.
30. *Rutherford* v. *Goodyear Tire & Rubber Co.*, 943 F.Supp. 789, 789 (WD Ky. 1996).
31. *Foster* v. *Leggett*, 484 SW 2d, 827, 829 (Ky. 1972).
32. *Custom Products*, 262 F.Supp.2d at 775.

that Kentucky had either "significant contacts" or significant interests. The court noted that the Kentucky manufacturer, albeit being the nominal plaintiff, was not the *"injured party"*[33] and was, "[f]or all practical purposes"[34], the defendant[35]. The court found "no evidence that Kentucky's law was intended to shield [such] a party when they ... cause injury in [another] jurisdiction, and then seek to avoid paying damages"[36], and concluded that "[t]he law of the forum cannot merely always follow the products of Kentucky corporations whenever they may cause injury in other jurisdictions"[37].

215. While *Custom Products* refused to extend the benefit of the forum's pro-manufacturer law to a forum-state manufacturer, *Kelly* v. *Ford Motor Co.*[38] refused to extend the benefit of the forum's pro-victim law to a victim domiciled and injured in the forum state. *Kelly* was a wrongful death action arising from the death of a Pennsylvania resident who was killed in Pennsylvania while driving a car he acquired in that state. Defendant Ford, a Michigan-based corporation, had designed, tested, and manufactured the car in Michigan. Pennsylvania, but not Michigan, imposed punitive damages on the manufacturer. The court acknowledged Pennsylvania's interests "in punishing defendants who injure its residents and ... in deterring them and others from engaging in similar conduct which poses a risk to Pennsylvania's citizens"[39]. However, the court also found that Michigan had "a very strong interest"[40] in denying such damages, so as to ensure that "its domiciliary defendants are protected from excessive financial liability"[41]. By insulating companies such as Ford, who conduct extensive business within its borders, said the court, "Michigan hopes to promote corporate migration into its economy ... [which] will enhance the economic climate and well being of the state of Michigan by generating revenues"[42]. On balance, the court concluded that, if faced with such a conflict, the Pennsylvania Supreme Court would "adopt a test that focuses on either the place of the defendant's conduct or the defendant's ...

---

33. *Id.* at 773.
34. *Id.* at 774.
35. For this reason, and to facilitate comparison with the other cases, Table 17, *supra*, places the contacts affiliated with the "plaintiff", i.e. the victim, in Canada, and the contacts affiliated with the "defendant", i.e., the manufacturer, in Kentucky.
36. *Custom Products*, 262 F.Supp.2d at 774. Noting that the Kentucky party "beat [the Canadian party] to the courthouse door", *id.*, the court found that Kentucky had a "greater interest ... in deterring the type of lawsuit which might seek a choice of law advantage". *Id.*
37. *Id.* at 775.
38. 933 F.Supp. 465 (ED Pa. 1996).
39. *Kelly*, 933 F.Supp. at 470.
40. *Id.*
41. *Id.*
42. *Id.*

principal place of business"[43], both of which were situated in Michigan, and would apply Michigan law.

The first edition of this book described *Kelly* as "noteworthy for resisting the all-too-common temptation of favoring the local victim who is favored by local law"[44]. While "noteworthy" is not the same as "praiseworthy", as some authors have assumed[45], it is necessary to explain that the reason *Kelly* is defensible rather than wrong is because it involved *only* the issue of punitive damages. Because the purpose of punitive damages is not to compensate victims, but rather to punish and deter tortfeasors, the victim's domicile is not a pertinent contact, but the places of injury, conduct, and tortfeasor's domicile are pertinent. For reasons discussed in Chapter VII[46], it is permissible and appropriate in cases of this pattern to apply the law of the state that has the latter two contacts, here, Michigan. On the other hand, for issues of loss-distribution, such as compensatory damages, in which the victim's domicile is again a pertinent contact and an important one, it would *not* be appropriate in such a case to apply the law of Michigan. For reasons explained in Chapter VI[47], the proper choice-of-law would be to apply the pro-plaintiff law of the victim's home state and place of injury, here, Pennsylvania, as long as the occurrence of the injury in that state was objectively foreseeable, which it was in this case[48]. For the record, the *Kelly* court indicated its readiness to apply Pennsylvania law to the loss-distribution aspects of the case[49].

216. Except for *Kelly*, all the other product-liability cases falling within this pattern involved issues other than punitive damages and, as the above table demonstrates, they all reached the opposite result – they applied the pro-plaintiff law of the plaintiff's home state, which was also the place of injury and the product's acquisition. This result is entirely appropriate, whether or not that state is also the forum, and regardless of whether one thinks in terms of state interests, party expectations, or factual contacts. As long as the product reached the particular state through ordinary commercial channels, then the application of that state's law is fair to the victim and not unfair to the defendant. A consumer who is injured in her home state by a product she has purchased there is entitled to the protection of that state's law, regardless of where the product was manufactured or by whom. Correspondingly, in a global market with free and predictable circulation

---

43.   *Id.* at 469.

44.   See 298 *Recueil des Cours*, 9, 309 (2003).

45.   See L. Weinberg, "Theory Wars in the Conflict of Laws", 103 *Mich. L. Rev.* 1631, 1657 (2005).

46.   See *supra* 194-196, 199-201.

47.   See *supra* 152-155.

48.   Professor Weinberg, supra footnote 45, at 1654, 1658-1660 , does not believe that it is necessary to accord product-liability defendants a foreseeabilty defense.

49.   Indeed, in a subsequent phase of the case, the same court dismissed the defendant's challenge against a Pennsylvania statute that provided that a driver's failure to wear his seatbelt should not be considered contributory negligence. See *Kelly* v. *Ford Motor Co.*, 1996 WL 639832 (ED Pa. 1996).

of goods, the manufacturer who chooses to market his products in the plaintiff's state may not reasonably expect to carry with him the protective laws of the state of manufacture. One of the tradeoffs in entering a particular market and benefit-ting from it is the foreseeable and insurable risk of being held accountable under the higher product liability standards of that market. As Peter Nygh put it, "[a] manufacturer should not be allowed to escape a higher risk by establishing itself in a low risk haven as a base for its activities"[50].

3.   *Inverse conflicts (each for the other)*

217. In 33 of the 100 cases, the state with the three plaintiff-affiliating contacts had a pro-defendant law, while the state with the defendant-affiliating contacts had a pro-plaintiff law[51]. Thus, these cases presented the inverse conflict pattern because each state's law favored the party affiliated with the other state. Accord-ing to Currie, these are the unprovided-for or no-interest cases in which neither state has an interest in applying its law because neither state wishes to protect non-domiciliaries at the expense of local domiciliaries. Thus, again according to Currie, all of these cases should be resolved by applying the law of the forum in its role as the residual law.

As Table 17 indicates, slightly more than half of the cases (18 of 33) did *not* apply forum law, including three cases decided in states that officially follow the *lex fori* approach[52]. The remaining 15 cases applied forum law[53], but, except for *Kemp* v. *Pfizer, Inc.*[54], none of them based that application on Currie's advocacy of the dominant role of the forum *qua* forum. Rather, they based that application on the forum state's contacts with the case and, in some instances, its *affirmative* interest – rather than its lack of interest – in applying its law[55]. Moreover, in all 15 cases, the application of the law of the forum benefitted a foreign litigant, and in 13 of those cases it worked to the detriment of a local litigant. In short, none of these cases bought Currie's "personal-law principle" that a state whose law favors the non-local litigant or disfavors the local litigant necessarily has no interest in applying it[56].

---

50.   P. Nygh, "The Reasonable Expectations of the Parties as a Guide to the Choice of Law in Contract and Tort", 251 *Recueil des Cours* 269, 369 (1995).

51.   See cases ## 10-42 in Table 17, *supra*.

52.   The cases that did not apply forum law are cases ## 17-34, in Table 17, *supra*. The three cases decided under the *lex-fori* approach are *Hall* (#20), *Farrell* (#21), and *Ruther-ford* (#26).

53.   See cases ## 10-16, 35-42 in Table 17, *supra*.

54.   *Kemp* is discussed *infra* 218 at text.

55.   One case (*Glover*, discussed *infra* at footnote 111) based the application of the forum's pro-plaintiff statute of limitation on the traditional procedural characterization of these statutes.

56.   However, once in a while, one finds statements suggesting partial adoption of this principle. For example, in *In re Eli Lilly & Co. Prozac Prod. Liab. Litig.*, 789 F.Supp.

(a)   Applying the pro-defendant law of a plaintiff-affiliated state

218. Three-fourths (or 25) of the 33 inverse conflicts applied the pro-defendant law of a state that had all three plaintiff-affiliating contacts[57]. For the reader's convenience, these cases are depicted in the following table, which is extracted from Table 17, above.

1448 (SD Ind. 1992), an action by California residents, injured in California by a drug acquired and used in California, against an Indiana defendant who manufactured the drug in Indiana, the court reasoned that "Indiana would have no interest in the application of [its] more pro-plaintiff rule to ... cases in which plaintiffs have no connection to Indiana and the Indiana connections all involve the business of the defendant". *Id.* at 1454. This reasoning made Indiana an uninterested state and, since California would also be uninterested in applying its pro-defendant law for the benefit of an Indiana defendant and at the expense of California plaintiffs, then, under Currie's prescriptions, one should apply Indiana law as the default law for no-interest cases. Instead, the *Lilly* court applied California law. For similar statements suggesting partial adoption of Currie's personal law principle, see, *Rutherford* v. *Goodyear Tire & Rubber* Co., 943 F.Supp. 789 (WD Ky. 1996) (discussed *infra* 221); *Mahne* v. *Ford Motor Co*, 900 F.2d 83 (6th. Cir. 1990) (discussed *infra* 223).

57.   See cases ## 10-34 in Table 17, *supra*.

Table 18. Cases applying the pro-defendant law of the victim's home state,
and place of acquisition and injury

#	Case name	Forum state	Plaintiff-affiliating contacts			D-affiliating contacts	
			P's domicile	Injury	Acquisition	Manufacture	D's PPB
10	Kemp	MI Pro-D	MI Pro-D	MI Pro-D	MI Pro-D	CA Pro-P	CA Pro-P
11	Burleson	TX Pro-D	TX Pro-D	TX Pro-D	TX Pro-D	Tobacco States ---	 ---
12	Clark	LA Pro-D	LA Pro-D	LA Pro-D	LA Pro-D	CA Pro-P	CA Pro-P
13	Pittman	LA Pro-D	LA Pro-D	LA Pro-D	LA Pro-D	CA Pro-P	CA Pro-P
14	Jeff.Parish	LA Pro-D	LA Pro-D	LA Pro-D	LA Pro-D	--- Pro-P	--- Pro-P
15	Orl.Parish	LA Pro-D	LA Pro-D	LA Pro-D	LA Pro-D	--- Prn-P	--- Pro-P
16	Campofiore	CN Pro-D	CN Pro-D	CN Pro-D	CN Pro-D	NJ Pro-P	NJ Pro-P
17	Dorman	MO Pro-P	B.C. Pro-D	B.C. Pro-D	B.C. Pro-D	Taiwan ---	MO Pro-P
18	Walls	MS Pro-P	OR Pro-D	OR Pro-D	OR Pro-D	OH Pro-P	DEL Pro-P
19	Hughes	AR Pro-P	LA Pro-D	LA Pro-D	LA Pro-D	AR Pro-P	AR Pro-P
20	Hall	MI Pro-P	N.C. Pro-D	N.C. Pro-D	N.C. Pro-D	OH Pro-P	MI Pro-P
21	Farrell	MI Pro-P	N.C. Pro-D	N.C. Pro-D	N.C. Pro-D	MI Pro-P	MI Pro-P
22	Vestal	CA Pro-P	N.C. Pro-D	N.C. Pro-D	N.C. Pro-D	CA Pro-P	CA Pro-P
23	Nesladek	MN Pro-P	NEB Pro-D	NEB Pro-D	NEB Pro-D	MI ---	MI ---
24	Rice	WA Pro-P	WA OR Pro-P Pro-D	OR Pro-D	OR Pro-D	--- ---	--- ---
25	Bain	TX Pro-P	B.C.? Pro-D	B.C. Pro-D	B.C.? Pro-D	--- ---	TX Pro-P
26	Lilly	IN Pro-P	CA Pro-D	CA Pro-D	CA Pro-D	IN Pro-P	IN Pro-P
27	Rutherford	KY Pro-P	IN Pro-D	IN Pro-D	IN Pro-D	KS/KY Pro-P	MI Pro-P
28	Harlan Feeders	IA Pro-P	NEB Pro-D	NEB Pro-D	NEB Pro-D	IA Pro-P	SD ---
29	Walters	IL Pro-P	KS Pro-D	KS Pro-D	KS Pro-D	TN/IL --/Pro-P	OH/IL --/Pro-P
30	Heindel	NJ Pro-P	PA Pro-D	PA Pro-D	PA Pro-D	NJ Pro-P	NJ Pro-P
31	White	OH Pro-P	GA Pro-D	GA Pro-D	GA Pro-D	OH Pro-P	OH Pro-P
32	Jones v. Cooper	PA Pro-P	VA Pro-D	VA Pro-D	VA Pro-D	OH Pro-P	OH Pro-P
33	Michaud	DEL Pro-P	QU Pro-D	QU Pro-D	QU Pro-D	--- ---	DEL Pro-P
34	Lupoli	MA Pro-P	NH Pro-D	NH Pro-D	NH Pro-D	MA Pro-P	MA Pro-P

In the first seven of those cases, that state was also the forum state[58]. *Kemp* v. *Pfizer, Inc.*[59], which was decided under Michigan's *lex fori* approach, is representative of these cases[60]. In *Kemp*, the plaintiff's decedent, a Michigan domiciliary, died in Michigan as result of a malfunction of a heart valve manufactured in California and implanted in him in a Michigan surgical procedure. California, but not Michigan, imposed punitive damages. The court found that, as the place of both the defendant's principal place of business and the product's manufacture, California had an interest in applying its punitive-damages law so as to "punish its corporate defendants and deter future misconduct"[61]. However, the court concluded that, because the defendant was also doing business in Michigan, Michigan had an interest in extending to the defendant the benefit of its defendant-protecting law. Thus, rather than viewing this as a no-interest case, the court characterized it as a true conflict in which both states had an interest. The court felt relieved from having to engage in the "admittedly abstruse exercise" of determining "which state's interest is greater" because, under Michigan's *lex fori* approach, "where Michigan has a strong interest in applying its laws ..., the Michigan courts would not displace its own laws in favor of the law of a foreign state"[62]. Thus, to the extent it relied on the *lex fori* presumption, *Kemp* is consistent with Currie's method. However, to the extent it extended the benefit of the forum's pro-defendant law to a foreign defendant and at the expense of a forum victim, *Kemp* rejected Currie's "personal law principle" which assumes that a state is never interested in protecting non-domiciliaries at the expense of local domiciliaries.

219. In the remaining 18 cases, the state with the three plaintiff-affiliating contacts (domicile, injury, and acquisition) had a pro-defendant law, but the fo-

---

58. See cases ## 10-16.

59. 947 F.Supp. 1139 (ED Mich. 1996).

60. Of the remaining six cases, two were decided under the Second Restatement and four under the Louisiana codification which requires the application of the law of the forum state if that state is also the victim's home state, place of injury, and place of acquisition. See *Clark* v. *Favalora*, 722 So.2d 82 (La. App. 1998); *Orleans Parish Sch. Bd.* v. *U.S. Gypsum Co.*, 1993 WL 205091 (ED La. 1993); *Jefferson Parish Hosp. Dist. # 2* v. *W.R. Grace*, 1992 WL 167263 (ED La. 1992); *K.E. Pittman* v. *Kaizer Aluminum & Chem. Corp.*, 559 So.2d 879 (La. App. 1990) (same result under pre-codification law).The two cases decided under the Second Restatement are *Burleson* v. *Liggett Group Inc.*, 111 F.Supp.2d 825 (ED Tex. 2000) (applying a Texas statute that barred suits against tobacco manufacturers on the ground that the statute was meant to protect foreign manufacturers, even vis a vis plaintiffs who were domiciled in Texas and were injured there); and *Campofiore* v. *Wyeth*, 2004 WL 3105962 (Conn. Super. 2004) (applying Connecticut's slightly pro-defendant law to the action of a Connecticut plaintiff who was injured in Connecticut by a drug manufactured by a New Jersey defendant in New Jersey).

61. *Kemp*, 947 F.Supp. at 1143.

62. *Id.*

rum state had a pro-plaintiff law[63]. All of these cases applied the law of the former state and none applied the law of the forum.

Three of these cases were transparent attempts at forum shopping, which, however, did not pay off. For example, in *Nesladek* v. *Ford Motor Co.*[64], the plaintiff candidly admitted that Minnesota's pro-plaintiff law was part of the reason for which she moved to Minnesota from Nebraska, after a Nebraska accident that resulted in her son's death. Her Minnesota lawsuit was barred by Nebraska's ten-year statute of repose but could have been maintained under Minnesota's "useful life" statute. The defendant Ford did business in Minnesota and a critical component of the car that caused the accident had been installed in the car in Ford's assembly plant in Minnesota. The court applied Nebraska's statute of repose and dismissed the action under it, partly "[b]ecause of the distinct presence of forum shopping"[65].

In *Jones* v. *Cooper Tire & Rubber Co.*[66], neither the plaintiffs nor the case had any connection with the forum state of Pennsylvania. The plaintiff was a Virginia domiciliary who was injured in Virginia by a motorcycle tire he purchased in that state. The tire was manufactured by an Ohio-based corporation, apparently in Ohio. After enumerating all the Virginia contacts and noting the lack of Pennsylvania contacts, the court wondered aloud why the plaintiffs chose a Pennsylvania forum and seemed to doubt the reason offered by plaintiffs – "because Plaintiffs 'have friends and family in the Philadelphia area, and visit here frequently'" [67]. The court applied Virginia law, which favored the defendant[68].

220. In all but one[69] of the remaining 15 cases, the defendant had significant contacts with the forum state, such as maintaining its principal place of business or manufacturing the product there, in whole or in part[70]. The existence of these contacts refutes any accusation that the plaintiffs engaged in forum shopping merely because they sued in a state that had a pro-plaintiff law. Even if this were forum shopping, however, it did not pay off because all of these cases applied the pro-defendant law of the non-forum state that had the plaintiff-affiliating contacts. In turn, the fact that that law favored a defendant who had contacts with

---

63.   See cases ## 17-34, in Table 17, *supra*.

64.   46 F.3d 734 (8th Cir. 1995), cert. denied, 516 US 814 (1995).

65.   46 F.3d at 740. A dissenting judge criticized the majority for "offer[ing] a sanction or punishment rather than an analysis as to choice of law". *Id.* at 741.

66.   2004 WL 503588 (ED Pa. 2004).

67.   *Id.* at #3 n.4.

68.   In *Walls* v. *Gen. Motors Corp.*, 906 F.2d 143 (5th Cir. 1990), an Oregon plaintiff, injured in Oregon by a car he purchased there, sued the defendant in Mississippi, hoping to take advantage of the latter state's longer statute of limitation. This strategy did not pay off since the court applied Oregon's statute of repose barring the action.

69.   This case is *Rice* v. *Dow Chem. Co.*, 875 P.2d 1213 (Wash. 1994), which is discussed *infra* at footnote 77.

70.   See cases ##1, 19-22, 25-31, 33-34.

the forum state might lead one to conclude that the choice of non-forum law was not altogether innocent.

In most of these cases, however, the court's choice was influenced heavily by the aggregation of three contacts in one state. Among these cases, *Dorman v. Emerson Electric Co.*[71] is representative of cases decided under the Second Restatement, particularly §146, which establishes a presumption in favor of the place of the injury[72]. The injury occurred in British Columbia, which was also the plaintiff's domicile and the place where he acquired the product. The product, a miter saw, was manufactured in Taiwan by a Taiwanese corporation under license from defendant, a Missouri corporation, that had designed and tested that line of products in Missouri[73]. Unlike Missouri, British Columbia did not impose strict li-

---

71.   23 F.3d 1354 (8th Cir. 1994) (decided under Missouri conflicts law), reh'g denied, 1994 U.S. App. Lexis 13588 (8th Cir. 1994), and cert. denied, 1994 U.S. Lexis 7600 (1994).

72.   For other cases decided under a similar presumption or a significant-contacts approach that lead to the same result, see *Bain* v. *Honeywell Int'l, Inc.*, 257 F.Supp.2d 872 (ED Tex. 2002) (applying British Columbia's pro-defendant law to the action of an Australian residing in British Columbia and arising from an injury there); *Michaud* v. *Fairchild Aircraft Inc.*, 2004 WL 1172897 (Del. Super. 2004) (applying Quebec's pro-defendant compensatory-damages law to wrongful death actions arising from the crash of a small airplane in Quebec that involved only Quebec flights and victims); *Walls* v. *Gen. Motors*, 906 F.2d 143 (5th Cir. 1990), described *supra* footnote 68; *Walters* v. *Warren Eng'g. Corp.*, 617 NE 2d 170 (Ill. App. 1993) (applying Kansas law to action of a Kansas plaintiff who was injured in Kansas by a machine partly manufactured in Illinois); *White* v. *Crown Equip. Corp.*, 827 NE 2d 859 (Ohio App. 2005) (applying Georgia's statute of repose baring an action against an Ohio defendant who manufactured in Ohio a lift truck that injured the Georgia plaintiff in Georgia); *Lupoli* v. *N. Util. Natural Gas, Inc.*, 2004 WL 1195308 (Mass. Super. 2004) (applying New Hampshire's pro-defendant parental consortium law to an action filed on behalf of a New Hampshire worker who was injured in that state by a gas burner manufactured in part by defendant in Massachusetts); *In re Eli Lilly & Co. Prozac Prod. Liab. Litig.*, 789 F.Supp. 1448 (SD Ind. 1992) (described *supra* footnote 56; decided under Indiana's significant-contacts approach).

For a case reaching the same result under Leflar's better-law approach, see *Hughes* v. *Wal-Mart Stores, Inc.*, 250 F.3d 618 (8th Cir. 2001). In *Hughes*, the defendant, an Arkansas retailer, sold a product in Louisiana to a Louisiana plaintiff whose child was injured in Louisiana while using the product. The plaintiff could recover under Arkansas law, but not under Louisiana law. The court held that Louisiana law governed because only one of the five Leflar factors was dispositive – "maintenance of interstate and international order" – and this factor pointed to Louisiana, because that state had nearly all the significant contacts. Arkansas had no interest in applying its pro-plaintiff law against an Arkansas defendant when the plaintiff was not a resident of Arkansas and the injury did not occur there. Neither was the "better-law" factor dispositive, because Louisiana law was not particularly "archaic and unfair" and thus, said the court, "our subjective view of which law represents the more reasoned approach would not persuade us that Arkansas law should apply". *Id.* at 622.

73.   The miter saw had been purchased by a Canadian corporation affiliated with defendant and sold to a Canadian retailer without ever having entered the United States.

ability on manufacturers. The plaintiff argued that, because the saw was designed in Missouri, that state had an interest in deterring substandard conduct within its territory. The court acknowledged the existence of this interest but found it insufficient to rebut the *lex loci* presumption. The court enumerated the contacts of British Columbia and, without articulating any corresponding interests, concluded that those contacts were "at least as substantial as Missouri's"[74].

Considering the starting point of the court's analysis, the application of British Columbia law is not surprising, not only because the court began with the *lex loci* presumption, but also because the court assumed that only state contacts, not state interests, may rebut the presumption. However, there is more room for disagreement when the court purports to base the application of the pro-manufacturer law of the victim's home state on the ostensible "interests" of that state.

221. One such case is *Hall v. General Motors Corp.*[75], in which a Michigan court held that North Carolina had an "obvious and substantial interest"[76] in applying its statute of repose to bar an action brought by a North Carolina domiciliary[77] against a Michigan-based manufacturer (GM)[78] who was *not* protected by Michigan law. This reading of North Carolina's interests, however, is doubly

---

74.   *Dorman*, 23 F.3d at 1361.

75.   582 NW 2d 866 (Mich. App. 1998).

76.   *Id.* at 869.

77.   The plaintiff was domiciled in North Carolina at the time of the injury, and in Michigan at the time he filed the action. While acknowledging that the record did not reveal the plaintiff's motives for changing his domicile, the court decided to discount the change of domicile because of the potential for encouraging forum shopping. See *id.* at 870.

   In *Rice v. Dow Chem. Co.*, 875 P.2d 1213 (Wash. 1994), the plaintiff was exposed to an herbicide while domiciled and working in Oregon, but moved his domicile to Washington before the injury manifested itself. His action was timely under Washington's twelve-year statute of repose, but was barred by Oregon's eight-year statute of repose. The court concluded that Oregon's statute applied because Oregon had a more significant relationship given that, except for the manifestation of the disease in Washington, all other contacts were with Oregon. After rejecting plaintiff's argument that the manifestation of the disease in Washington would make that state the place of the injury, the court examined the respective interests of the two states and concluded that "Oregon's interest ... in providing repose for manufacturers doing business in Oregon and whose products are used in Oregon", *id.* at 1219, was not extinguished by the plaintiff's subsequent move to Washington. Although Washington had an interest in protecting its residents, "[r]esidency in the forum state alone has not been considered a sufficient relationship to the action to warrant application of forum law". *Id.* The court reasoned that "[a]pplying Oregon law achieves a uniform result for injuries caused by products used in the state of Oregon and predictability for manufacturers whose products are used or consumed in Oregon". *Id.* Neither party offered evidence of the place of design, testing, or manufacture of the product, or of the defendant's principal place of business or state of incorporation. See *id.* at 1218.

78.   The product in question, a car, was designed in Michigan and manufactured in Ohio, but neither party urged the application of Ohio law.

suspect in that: (1) it emanates from a court that purports to adhere to a *lex fori* approach; and (2) it conveniently serves one of Michigan's three major automakers. With regard to (1), the court concluded that the strong presumption in favor of Michigan law was rebutted because "Michigan ha[d] only a minimal interest in the matter"[79]. With regard to (2), the court opined that: (a) North Carolina had an "obvious and substantial interest in shielding GM from 'open ended products liability claims'"[80], so as to "encourage GM to do business in its state'"[81]; and (b) Michigan had "no interest in affording greater rights of tort recovery to a North Carolina resident than those afforded by North Carolina [since] Michigan [was] merely the forum state and situs of defendant's headquarters"[82]. Needless to say, the statement regarding Michigan's lack of interest raises the corollary question of why North Carolina had any interest in affording a Michigan defendant greater protection than that afforded by Michigan[83].

Three other cases, decided in the manufacturer's home state under an interest analysis of sorts, also reached the same result[84]. In *Rutherford* v. *Goodyear Tire*

---

79.   *Hall*, 582 NW 2d at 868.

80.   *Id.* at 869.

81.   *Id.*

82.   *Id.* But see *id.* at 870 (Matuzak, J., concurring) ("GM's commercial relationship with [North Carolina] is insignificant when compared to its enormous economic presence in Michigan and consequential effect on this state ... . GM's headquarters and a significant part of its operations are located in Michigan".)

83.   Concurring Judge Matuzak saw "no good reason to extend the benefits of the North Carolina statute of repose to defendant", an out-of-state manufacturer, "for ... wrongs alleged to have been committed in Michigan or Ohio", *id.* at 870-871 (Matuzak, J., concurring), and pointed out that, because of defendant's enormous presence in Michigan, applying Michigan law "should not defeat defendant's expectations". *Id.* See also the court's analysis of Florida's statute of repose in a virtually identical case, *Mahne* v. *Ford Motor Co*, 900 F.2d 83 (6th. Cir. 1990), cert. denied, 498 US 941 (1990) (discussed *infra* 223).

In *Harlan Feeders* v. *Grand Labs., Inc.*, 881 F.Supp. 1400 (ND Iowa 1995), the court refused to apply Iowa law, which imposed punitive damages, and applied Nebraska law, which did not allow such damages. The product was manufactured in Iowa and was sold to a Nebraska plaintiff in Nebraska and caused injury there. Said the court: "Nebraska has made a policy choice that punitive damages are inappropriate, and that interest is not outweighed by Iowa's contrary interest in imposing punitive damages as a deterrent, at least not .. where the plaintiff is a resident of Nebraska, not Iowa, where the alleged injury occurred in Nebraska, not Iowa, as a result of use of a product manufactured by a South Dakota, not an Iowa corporation, even when the corporation physically produced the product in Iowa". *Id.* at 1410.

84.   One of these cases, *Farrell* v. *Ford Motor Co.*, 501 NW 2d 567 (Mich. App. 1993), app. denied, 519 NW 2d 158 (Mich. 1994), involved another one of Michigan's "big three" manufacturers. *Farrell* was a product liability action arising from a North Carolina accident in which a North Carolina domiciliary was killed while using a car manufactured in Michigan by Ford, a Michigan-based manufacturer. The action was timely in Michigan, but was barred by North Carolina's statute of repose. The court applied this

& Rubber Co.[85] which was decided under Kentucky's *lex fori* approach, the court applied the pro-defendant law of Indiana, which was the plaintiff's home state and place of injury and, indirectly, the place of the product's acquisition. The product, a car tire, had been manufactured in Kansas by Goodyear, an Ohio corporation, and was purchased by Ford, a Michigan corporation, and mounted on a car in Ford's assembly plant in Kentucky. The car was sold to an Indiana motorist who, while driving in Indiana, collided with a car driven by another Indiana motorist, the plaintiff. Indiana, but not Kentucky, had a statute of repose that barred the action. While acknowledging Kentucky's strong preference for the *lex fori*, the court concluded that in this case this preference was not warranted by the forum's

---

statute after concluding that North Carolina had "an obvious and substantial interest in shielding Ford from open-ended products liability claims ... and [in] encourag[ing] manufacturers, such as Ford, to do business in North Carolina". 501 NW 2d at 572. The court thought that this interest was "[no] less compelling solely by virtue of the fact that the defendant does not have a manufacturing plant [in] North Carolina". *Id.* On the other hand, the court concluded, Michigan was "merely the forum state and situs of defendant's headquarters" and "ha[d] little or no interest ... in affording greater rights of tort recovery to a North Carolina resident than his own state affords him". *Id.* at 572-73.

North Carolina's statute of repose was also applied in *Vestal* v. *Shiley, Inc.*, 1997 WL 910373 (CD Cal. 1997), to bar a product liability action by a North Carolina domiciliary against a California manufacturer of heart valves implanted in plaintiff during a North Carolina surgery. The court concluded that the application of California's statute of limitation, which allowed the action, "would impair North Carolina's effort to protect manufacturers who sell goods within its borders". *Id.* at *3. The court noted California's potential interest in deterring California manufacturers from manufacturing defective products within its borders, but concluded that this interest was adequately served by applying California law to the numerous actions filed by California plaintiffs. *Id.*

Heindel v. *Pfizer, Inc.*, 2004 WL 1398024 (DNJ 2004), was a consumer fraud action filed by Pennsylvania consumers who used in that state a drug that was manufactured in New Jersey by the defendants, New Jersey-based corporations. The court noted that, since the plaintiffs were not New Jersey domiciliaries, New Jersey did not have a "compelling reason", *id.* at *12, to extend to them the benefit of New Jersey's pro-plaintiff law, but New Jersey did have an interest "in governing the conduct of its corporate citizens and encouraging truthful marketing and advertising of products", *id.* at *11. However, the court thought that Pennsylvania had a "competing interest in ensuring that its own citizens are compensated for their injuries", *id.*, (even if its law would not compensate them), and in applying its rules regulating drug sales, doctors, and pharmacies within its borders. The court concluded that "'the deterrence interest of New Jersey as the domicile and locus of the defendant manufacturer must yield in this case to the compensation interest' of Pennsylvania'". *Id.* at *12 (internal quotations are from *Gantes* v. *Kason Corp.*, 679 A.2d 106, 115 (NJ 1996), which in fact reached the opposite result by applying New Jersey's pro-plaintiff law for the benefit of a foreign plaintiff and at the expense of a domestic defendant. *Gantes* is discussed *infra* 222).

85.   943 F.Supp. 789 (WD Ky. 1996).

contacts or interests and was outweighed by Indiana's "overwhelming interest"[86]. In contrast to the *Custom Products* court which concluded that Kentucky's pro-defendant law was not intended to shield Kentucky manufacturers who caused injury outside Kentucky[87], the *Rutherford* court reasoned that Kentucky's statute of limitation was "designed primarily to protect its own citizens or those injured within its boundaries ... [and not to] regulat[e] products assembled within its boundaries"[88]. The court opined that a certain "federalist concept", which the court did not define, "inherently limits the reach of any state's perceived interest to matters which occur within its boundaries or which impact its citizens"[89]. The court rejected the plaintiff's plea to choose the law of the place where the product was manufactured or assembled, because such a choice would create practical difficulties in cases in which the design, testing, manufacture, and assembly take place in different states, and because: "Legal claims do not arise at the time or at the place of manufacture. They arise when an injury occurs. Thus, the place of injury, not the place of manufacture is the central focus of the cause of action"[90].

(b) Applying the pro-plaintiff law of a defendant-affiliated state

222. One can usefully contrast cases like *Hall* and *Rutherford* with eight of the 33 inverse conflicts that reached the opposite result[91]. These cases, which are shown again in the Table below, applied the pro-plaintiff law of a state that was both the manufacturer's principal place of business and the place of manufacture. The fact that, in all six cases, that state was also the forum state means that these cases applied the forum's pro-plaintiff law for the benefit of a foreign plaintiff and at the expense of a forum defendant.

---

86.   *Id.* at 793.
87.   See *supra* 214 at footnotes 36-37.
88.   *Rutherford*, 943 F.Supp. at 792.
89.   *Id.*
90.   *Id.* at 793.
91.   See cases ## 35-42, in Table 17, *supra* and Table 19, *infra*.

Table 19. Cases applying the pro-plaintiff law of the plaintiff's home state,
and place of acquisition and injury

#	Case name	Forum state	Plaintiff-affiliating Contacts			D-affiliating contacts	
			P's domicile	Injury	Acquisition	Manufacture	D's PPB
35	Gantes	N.J. Pro-P	GA Pro-D	GA Pro-D	GA Pro-D	N.J. Pro-P	N.J. Pro-P
36	McLennan	TX Pro-P	CAN Pro-D	CAN Pro-D	CAN Pro-D	TX Pro-P	TX Pro-P
37	Mahne	MI Pro-P	FL Pro-D	FL Pro-D	FL Pro-D	MI Pro-P	MI Pro-P
38	Davis	CA Pro-P	OR Pro-D	OR Pro-D	OR Pro-D	CA Pro-P	CA Pro-P
39	Marchesani	LA Pro-P	TN Pro-D	TN Pro-D	TN Pro-D	LA Pro-P	LA Pro-P
40	Baxter	CN Pro-P	OR Pro-D	OR Pro-D	OR Pro-D	CN Pro-P	CN Pro-P
41	Glover	MN Pro-P	IL Pro-D	IL Pro-D	IL Pro-D	NJ ---	NJ ---
42	Stupak	WS Pro-P	MI Pro-D	MI Pro-D	MI Pro-D	NJ ---	DEL ---

Gantes v. *Kason Corp.*[92], is representative of these cases. *Gantes* was an action brought by the survivors of a Georgia woman who was killed in Georgia while working with a machine that was manufactured thirteen years earlier in New Jersey by a New Jersey-based corporation. Georgia's ten-year statute of repose barred the action, which was timely under New Jersey's two-year statute of limitations. Relying on a Georgia case, the New Jersey court noted that the Georgia statute was designed "'to address problems generated by the open-ended liability of manufacturers so as to ... stabilize products liability underwriting'"[93]. Assuming that the Georgia statute was "intended only to unburden Georgia courts and to shield Georgia manufacturers"[94], the court concluded that Georgia had no interest in applying that statute, because the defendant was not a Georgia manufacturer, and Georgia courts were not involved in this case. Plaintiffs' Georgia domicile brought into play Georgia's general policy "of fair compensation for injured domiciliaries"[95]. The Georgia statute subordinated that policy to the policy of protecting manufacturers, but only in those cases that involved Georgia manufacturers. Since the defendant in this case was not a Georgia manufacturer, Georgia had no real interest in applying its statute.

In contrast, said the court, New Jersey had a "cognizable and substantial interest in deterrence that would be furthered by the application of its statute of limitations"[96]. The court noted that the goal of tort law in general and products

---

92.   679 A.2d 106 (NJ 1996).

93.   *Id.* at 109 (quoting *Chrysler Corp.* v. *Batten*, 450 SE 2d 208, 212 (Ga. 1994)).

94.   *Id.* at 114-115.

95.   *Id.* at 115.

96.   *Id.* at 113. The court described the policies embodied in that statute which, as a result of a judicially-engrafted discovery rule, is permeated by "flexible, equitable consider-

liability law in particular is "to encourage reasonable conduct, and, conversely, to discourage conduct that creates an unreasonable risk of injury to others"[97]. The court concluded that, because the machine had been "manufactured in, and placed into the stream of commerce from, [New Jersey]"[98], New Jersey had a "strong interest in encouraging the manufacture and distribution of safe products for the public and, conversely, in deterring the manufacture and distribution of unsafe products within the state"[99]. The court rejected the lower court's conclusion that this interest in deterrence was outweighed by the possibility of unduly discouraging manufacturing in New Jersey[100]. Thus, by reading the forum's interests in a non-protectionist way, the court concluded that what might have been a no-interest case under Currie's analysis was in fact a false conflict in which only the forum state had an interest in applying its law.

223. Like the other cases in this group, *Gantes* applied a law that favored a foreign victim at the expense of a local manufacturer, but did so not so much for the sake of protecting the foreign victim, but rather in pursuance of the forum's own policy of deterring the manufacture of substandard products within its territory. While some commentators[101] and some courts[102] have questioned this policy, other courts have espoused it[103], including courts sitting in states with defendant-

---

ations based on notions of fairness to the parties and the justice in allowing claims to be resolved on their merits". *Id.* at 110.

97. *Id.* at 111.

98. *Id.*

99. *Id.* at 111-12.

100. The court also dismissed the forum-shopping argument because, as shown by the defendant's contacts with the forum state, the plaintiff had legitimate reasons to sue there.

101. *See, e.g.*, P. Kozyris, "Values and Methods in Choice of Law for Product Liability: A Comparative Comment on Statutory Solutions", 38 *Am. J. Comp. L.* 475, 501 (1990) (stating that: (1) "[the assumption] that imposing the stricter standards of the state of production to the-out-of-state distribution and harm may indirectly improve the in-state component as well ... is ... questionable in its logic of prohibiting what should be lawful to deter what is unlawful"; (2) that "[a] purported 'moral' concern of the state of production about local activities which endanger people worldwide ... is [also] not persuasive"; and (3) "Preferring the law of the state of production over those of distribution, harm and personal connections of the parties would be inconsistent with considerations both of allocating sovereign authority and of fairness to the parties".)

102. See, e.g., *Vestal* v. *Shiley Inc.*, 1997 WL 910373 (CD Cal. 1997), *supra* footnote 84; *Hall* v. *Gen. Motors Corp.*, 582 NW 2d 866 (Mich. App. 1998), discussed *supra* 221; *Farrell* v. *Ford Motor Co.*, 501 NW2d 567 (Mich. App., 1993), app. denied, 519 NW 2d 158 (Mich. 1994), *supra* footnote 84.

103. In addition to the cases discussed in the text, see, e.g., *Lewis-DeBoer* v. *Mooney Aircraft Corp.*, 728 F.Supp. 642 (D Colo. 1990), (discussed *infra* at footnote 134; concluding that Texas, as the place of the defendant's conduct and principal place of business, "ha[d] a greater policy interest in applying its laws and providing deterrence than Colorado ha[d] in preventing a windfall to its citizens". *Id.* at 645. Colorado was the victim's home state and place of injury.).

affiliating contacts. For example, in *Mitchell* v. *Lone Star Ammunition, Inc.*[104], the court concluded that Texas had a "substantial interest" in applying its pro-plaintiff law "as an incentive to encourage safer design and to induce corporations to control more carefully the manufacturing processes"[105]. In *McLennan* v. *American Eurocopter Corp., Inc.*[106], the court concluded that Texas had a strong interest in enforcing its strict product-liability law against manufacturers operating in that state, while noting that the application of that law did not impose an unexpected burden on a Texas-based manufacturer. In *DeGrasse* v. *Sensenich Corp.*[107] the court concluded that applying Pennsylvania law, which favored an Arkansas plaintiff at the expense of a Pennsylvania manufacturer, was in line with Pennsylvania's interests because "Pennsylvania's policy involves the attainment of broader objectives than simply ensuring full recovery for its domiciliary plaintiffs ... [such as] deterring the manufacture of defective products by, and assigning responsibility for such an activity to, Pennsylvania manufacturers"[108]. Finally, in *Lacey* v. *Cessna Aircraft Co.*[109], the court concluded that the application of Pennsylvania's strict liability law to a case involving a product that was manufactured in Pennsylvania and caused injury in British Columbia would "further Pennsylvania's interest in deterring the manufacture of defective products ... but would not impair British Columbia's interest in fostering industry within its borders"[110].

Even more numerous are the cases in which, without expressly articulating this policy, the courts allowed claims against a forum manufacturer that were barred by the statute of repose of the other, plaintiff-affiliated, state[111]. They did

---

104. 913 F.2d 242 (5th Cir. 1990) (applying Texas law and allowing action against a defendant who manufactured the product in Texas in an action brought by foreign plaintiffs and arising from injury that occurred in a state whose statute of repose would bar the action).

105. *Id.* at 250.

106. 245 F.3d 403 (5th Cir. 2001) (decided under Texas conflicts law and applying Texas pro-plaintiff law to an action of a Canadian domiciliary injured in Canada by a product manufactured by a Texas manufacturer in Texas).

107. 1989 WL 23775 (ED Pa. 1989).

108. *Id.* at *4. The plaintiff was injured in Alabama.

109. 932 F.2d 170 (3d Cir. 1991).

110. *Id.* at 188.

111. In two cases, the action was filed, not in the manufacturer's home state, but in a third state. One of these cases, *Glover* v. *Merck & Co., Inc.*, 345 F.Supp.2d 994 (D Minn. 2004), was a clear example of forum shopping. An Illinois consumer who was injured in Illinois by a drug she bought and used in that state, sued the New Jersey manufacturer in Minnesota. The action would be barred by the statute of limitation of Illinois, but not of Minnesota. Relying on old Minnesota precedents that characterized that state's limitation statute as procedural, the court applied that statute, thus allowing the action.

Despite contrary appearances, the second case, *Stupak* v. *Hoffman-La Roche, Inc.*,287 F.Supp.2d 968 (ED Wis. 2003), was not a forum-shopping case. The plaintiff's products-liability claim against a New Jersey drug manufacturer was intertwined with a

so either by characterizing the foreign statute as procedural[112], or by concluding, as *Gantes* did, that the foreign repose statute was not intended to protect forum manufacturers. Thus, in *Mahne* v. *Ford Motor Co.*[113], the court concluded that Florida's statute of repose was intended to protect Florida manufacturers, not Michigan manufacturers such as the ones involved in this case. The latter "cannot argue that applying Michigan law would defeat their expectations", said the court, and "[t]hus, there is simply no reason to extend the benefits of the Florida statute of repose to the Michigan defendants"[114].

---

medical malpractice claim against a Wisconsin doctor who prescribed the drug to the Michigan plaintiff's son. The plaintiff sued both the manufacturer and the doctor in Wisconsin, after her son committed suicide in Michigan, apparently because of the drug's side-effects. The parties limited their arguments to the laws of Michigan, which barred actions against manufacturers of FDA approved drugs, and Wisconsin, which allowed such actions. The court found that the product liability and medical malpractice claims were "inextricably intertwined", *id.* at 972, and, since the latter claims were clearly governed by Wisconsin law, the court reasoned that the former claims should also be governed by the same law because otherwise a Wisconsin doctor would have to shoulder "the entire burden of a loss for which ... [the manufacturer] bears substantial, if not primary, responsibility". *Id.* The court reasoned that Wisconsin's interest in fully and fairly adjudicating medical malpractice claims against Wisconsin doctors "outweighs the interest Michigan may have in having its prohibition on suits against FDA-approved drug manufacturers applied to New Jersey and Delaware corporate defendants whose drug was prescribed by a Wisconsin doctor who is now facing a malpractice action in Wisconsin". *Id.* at 973-974. Moreover, the application of Wisconsin law was not unfair to the defendant, because "as the manufacturer of a product placed in the stream of commerce, [the defendant] surely would have understood that it would be subject to suit in any state where its drug was available. It can come as no surprise that it would be required to defend itself in a forum in which resident physicians are prescribing its product". *Id.* at 973.

112. See *Baxter* v. *Sturm, Ruger & Co., Inc.*, 644 A.2d 1297 (Conn. 1994) (holding that, under Connecticut's characterization standards, Oregon's statute of repose was procedural and thus did not bar a Connecticut action that was timely under Connecticut's statute of limitation and was filed by an Oregon plaintiff against a Connecticut gun manufacturer for injury caused by the gun in Oregon).

113. 900 F.2d 83 (6th. Cir. 1990), reh'g den, en banc, *Mahne* v. *Ford Motor Co.*, 1990 US App. Lexis 10, 121 (6th Cir. 1990), and cert. denied, Ford Motor Co. v. Mahne, 498 US 941 (1990).

114. *Mahne*, 900 F.2d at 88-89. See also *Dabbs* v. *Silver Eagle Mfg. Co.*, 779 P.2d 1104 (Or. App. 1989) review denied, 784 P.2d 1101 (Or. 1989) (action of a Tennessee resident injured in Tennessee by a product acquired there and manufactured in Oregon by an Oregon-based defendant; concluding that Tennessee had no interest in applying its shorter statute of limitation barring the action, because no Tennessee defendant was involved in this case; applying Oregon's longer statute of limitation permitting the action); *Marchesani* v. *Pellerin-Milnor Corp.*, 269 F.3d 481 (5th cir. 2001) (applying Louisiana statute of limitations and allowing a products liability action that was barred by Tennessee's statute of repose – the action was brought against a Louisiana manufacturer by a Tennessee domiciliary who was injured in Tennessee by a product

C.   Cases in Which Two Plaintiff-Affiliating Contacts Were in the Same State

224. In the cases discussed in subdivision B, all three plaintiff-affiliating contacts were congregated in one state, while the two defendant-affiliating contacts were in one or two other states. Subdivision C discusses cases in which only two of the three plaintiff-affiliating contacts were in the same state, while the remaining three contacts were in one or more other states[115]. Under a quantitative significant-contacts or Second Restatement analysis, one can easily conclude that the state with the three plaintiff-affiliating contacts has a more significant relationship than the state or states with the two defendant-affiliating contacts. One would expect that such a conclusion would be more difficult in cases in which the first state has only two plaintiff-affiliating contacts. However, as the following discussion indicates, most courts confronted with such cases have not acknowledged this difficulty. Indeed, 30 of the 47 cases that belong to the latter group applied the law of the state that had the two plaintiff-affiliating contacts. Lest one mistakes this for a pro-plaintiff tilt, it should be noted that in more than half of the 30 cases (17), that state had a pro-defendant law.

1.   Plaintiff's domicile and injury

225. In the first 16 of these cases, the plaintiff's domicile and injury were in the same state, while the other three contacts were in another state or states[116]. The first 10 of those cases applied the law of the state with the two plaintiff-affiliating contacts[117] while the remaining six cases applied another state's law.

(a)   Direct conflicts

226. The first five of those cases presented the direct conflict pattern in that the state with the plaintiff-affiliating contacts had a pro-plaintiff law, while the state with the defendant-affiliating contacts had a pro-defendant law. The following table depicts those cases.

---

manufactured in Louisiana). In *Davis* v. *Shiley*, 75 Cal.Rptr.2d 826 (Cal.App. 1998), Oregon, the place of the victim's domicile and injury, had a statute of repose barring the action, whereas California, the state of manufacture and defendant's principal place of business, did not. The court allowed the action after finding the Oregon statute inapplicable because of Oregon's lack of interest in applying it to protect a foreign manufacturer at the expense of an Oregon domiciliary.

115.   See cases ## 43-88, in Table 17, *supra*.

116.   See cases ## 43-58.

117.   See cases ## 43-52.

Table 20. Direct conflicts applying the pro-plaintiff law of the plaintiff's home state and place of injury

#	Case name	Forum state		Plaintiff-affiliating contacts			D-affiliating contacts	
				P's domicile	Injury	Acquisition	Manufacture	D's PPB
43	Smith	DEL Pro-P		DEL Pro-P	DEL Pro-P	MD Pro-D	MI?	MD Pro-D
44	R-Square	LA Pro-P		LA Pro-P	LA Pro-P	MN Pro-D	AL ---	AL ---
45	Allstate	LA Pro-P		LA Pro-P	LA Pro-P	OK ---	MN? Pro-D	MN? Pro-D
46	Fisher	NEV Pro-P		NEV Pro-P	NEV Pro-P	UT Pro-D	ITA Pro-D	ITA Pro-D
47	Goede	MO Pro-P		MO Pro-P	MO Pro-P	CA? Pro-D	CA? Pro-D	CA Pro-D

All five cases applied the pro-plaintiff law of the former state. In four of those cases, the product was commercially available in that state, thus negating any argument of unfair surprise on defendant's part[118]. In one of those cases, the court noted that the Maryland defendant, who was located "a few miles from the Delaware line"[119], knowingly sold the product to a Delaware domiciliary and "[could] not reasonably expect to be subject only to the laws of Maryland"[120].

In the fifth case, *Goede* v. *Aerojet General Corp.*[121], it was unclear whether the defendant's products had ever entered the state of the victim's domicile and injury, Missouri. The victim moved to that state two years before she was diagnosed with mesothelioma, from which she died a year later, and which was claimed to have been caused by her father's exposure to asbestos dust during his employment by defendant in California thirty years earlier. The court affirmed the ap-

---

118. The four cases are: *Smith* v. *DaimlerChrysler Corp.*, 2002 WL 31814534 (Del. Super. 2002) (decided under the Second Restatement; applying Delaware's pro-plaintiff law to a Delaware plaintiff's action against a Maryland dealer and a Michigan manufacturer arising out of an accident in Delaware); *R-Square Inves.* v. *Teledyne Indus., Inc.*, 1997 WL 436245 (ED La. 1997) (applying Louisiana's pro-plaintiff law to an action of a Louisiana plaintiff injured in Louisiana by a product acquired in Minnesota and manufactured in Alabama by an Alabama manufacturer); *Allstate Ins. Co.* v. *Wal-Mart*, 2000 WL 388844 (ED La. 2000) (applying Louisiana's pro-plaintiff law to an action of a Louisiana plaintiff injured in Louisiana by a product acquired in Oklahoma and manufactured in Minnesota by a Minnesota manufacturer); *Fisher* v. *Prof'l Compounding Ctrs. of Am., Inc.*, 311 F. Supp. 2d 1008 (D Nev. 2004) (decided under Nevada's *lex-fori* approach; applying Nevada's pro-plaintiff law to the action of a Utah domiciliary who bought and used a diet drug in Utah and then moved to Nevada where she suffered the injury; the product was manufactured in Italy by an Italian defendant).

119. *Smith*, 2002 WL 31814534 at *1.

120. *Id.*

121. 143 SW 3d 14 (Mo. App. 2004), transfer denied (Sep 28, 2004).

plication of Missouri's pro-plaintiff compensatory damages law[122] because, with regard to the issue of damages, Missouri had the most significant relationship[123]. The court concluded that Missouri had an interest in compensating Missouri domiciliaries in accordance with its laws and that there was "no overwhelming interest in California having its laws regarding compensation applied to the claims of non-resident plaintiffs"[124].

(b) Inverse conflicts

227. The remaining 11 cases presented the inverse conflict pattern in that the state with the plaintiff-affiliating contacts had a pro-defendant law, while the state with the defendant-affiliating contacts had a pro-plaintiff law[125]. The following table depicts those cases.

Table 21. Inverse conflicts in which the plaintiff's home state was also the place of injury

#	Case name	Forum state	Plaintiff-affiliating contacts			D-affiliating contacts	
			P's domicile	Injury	Acquisition	Manufacture	D's PPB
a. Applying Pro-D law							
48	Egan	LA / Pro-D	LA / Pro-D	LA / Pro-D	--- / ---	OH / Pro-P	--- / ---
49	Land	IN / Pro-D	IN / Pro-D	IN / Pro-D	KY / Pro-P?	Japan / Pro-D	Japan / Pro-D
50	Denmann	MS / Pro-P	N.C. / Pro-D	N.C. / Pro-D	MS / Pro-P	GA / ---	GA / ---
51	McKinnon	VT / Pro-P	Qu / Pro-D	Qu / Pro-D	VT / Pro-P	VT / Pro-P	VT / Pro-P
52	Normann	PA / Pro-P	PA / Pro-P NY / Pro-D	N.Y. / Pro-D	--- / ---	--- / ---	OH / ---
b. Applying Pro-P law							
53	Zenaida-Garcia	WA / Pro-P	OR / Pro-D	OR / Pro-D	WA / Pro-P	WA / Pro-P	WA / Pro-P
54	Magnant	MI / Pro-D	MI / Pro-D	MI / Pro-D	MN / Pro-P	MN / Pro-P	MN / Pro-P
55	Champlain	N.Y. / Pro-D	N.Y. / Pro-D	N.Y. / Pro-D	KS / Pro-P	KS / Pro-P	KS / Pro-P
56	Lewis-DeBoer	CO / Pro-D	CO / Pro-D	CO / Pro-D	--- / ---	TX / Pro-P	TX / Pro-P
57	Sanchez	TX / Pro-P	MEX / Pro-D	MEX / Pro-D	TX / Pro-P	Japan / Pro-D	Japan / Pro-D
58	Long	D.C. / Pro-P	MD / Pro-D	MD / Pro-D	D.C. / Pro-P	S.C. / ---	DE / ---

---

122. The trial court had applied California law to liability and Missouri law to damages. The defendant appealed the application of Missouri law and argued for the application of California law, which disallowed pain and suffering damages in wrongful-death actions and held joint tortfeasors only severally liable for non-economic damages.

123. The court noted that the disease manifested itself after the victim had moved to Missouri, that the ultimate injury for which the pain and suffering was claimed (the victim's death) also occurred in Missouri, and that the surviving claimants were also domiciled in Missouri

124. 143 SW 3d at 27.

125. See cases ## 48-58 in Table 17, *supra.*

The first five of these cases applied the pro-defendant law of the plaintiff-affiliated state. These cases were decided under the Second Restatement[126], a significant-contacts approach[127], or other approaches that did not consider state interests[128]. One case, *Denman v. Snapper Div.*[129], was decided under a presumptive *lex loci* rule. In this case, a Mississippi domiciliary purchased in Mississippi a lawn mower that he later lent to his son, who used it in North Carolina and was injured there[130]. The plaintiff's action in Mississippi was timely under that state's statute of limitation, but was barred by North Carolina's statute of repose. The court noted that under Mississippi conflicts law, "the law of the place of injury is presumed to apply unless another state has a more significant relationship"[131]. The court concluded that the sale of the mower in Mississippi was "an insufficient basis for finding that Mississippi ha[d] a more significant relationship than North

---

126. See *McKinnon v. F.H. Morgan & Co. Inc.*, 750 A.2d 1026 (Vt. 2000). In this case, the plaintiff, a Quebec domiciliary, was injured in Quebec while riding a bicycle sold and serviced by the defendant in Vermont. The plaintiff invoked Vermont's pro-plaintiff law, but was apparently unprepared to rebut the presumption of Restatement (Second) §146 in favor the place of injury. The court applied the law of Quebec because, in addition to being the place of injury, Quebec was also the plaintiff's domicile and Vermont's contacts were not more significant.

127. See *Land v. Yamaha Motor Corp., U.S.A.*, 272 F.3d 514 (7th Cir. 2001) (decided under Indiana's significant-contacts approach). This case involved an action by an Indiana domiciliary injured in Indiana by a product manufactured in Japan by a Japanese manufacturer. The product was sold through a Kentucky dealer to an Indiana domiciliary who, many years later, sold it to another Indiana domiciliary. The court applied Indiana's statute of repose, barring the action, because Indiana's approach allows departure from the *lex loci delicti* only when the *locus delicti* has an "insignificant" relationship to the lawsuit. The court found that Indiana's relationship was not insignificant because Indiana was the place of the injury, the domicile of the victim as well as the product's owner, and the place where the product had been used for more than a decade.

128. See *Normann v. Johns-Manville Corp.*, 593 A.2d 890 (Pa. Super. 1991), review denied, 607 A.2d 255 (Pa. 1992) (action by a Pennsylvania resident who was exposed to defendant's asbestos products while employed and domiciled in New York; New York, but not Pennsylvania, allowed defendant to assert the "state of the art" defense (defendant was an Ohio corporation but Ohio law was not described in the opinion); noting that New York would have an interest in making this defense available to foreign corporations doing business in New York; applying New York law because New York had a closer relationship and "by far a greater interest", 593 A.2d at 894, than Pennsylvania); *Egan v. Kaizer Aluminum & Chem. Corp.*, 677 So. 2d 1027 (La. App. 1996), writ denied, 684 So. 2d 930 (La. 1996) (decided under pre-codification Louisiana conflicts law).

129. 131 F.3d 546 (5th Cir. 1998), reh'g denied en banc, 137 F.3d 1353 (5th Cir. 1998).

130. The defendant, a Georgia-based corporation, had manufactured the mower in Georgia, but neither party urged the application of Georgia law.

131. *Denman*, 131 F.3d at 550.

Carolina"[132] and that "the fact that the mower entered the stream of commerce in Mississippi [did] not tip the balance in favor of applying Mississippi law"[133].

228. Of the remaining six cases, four cases applied the pro-plaintiff law of the state with the defendant-affiliating contacts[134]. In only one of those cases, *Zenaida-Garcia v. Recovery Systems Technology, Inc.*[135], did that state have the additional contact of being the forum, but this was not the basis for the court's decision. Rather the court based its decision on that state's affirmative and "strong"[136] interest in "deterring the design, manufacture and sale of unsafe products within its borders"[137] and the lack of a countervailing interest on the part of the state of the victim's domicile and injury to "merely limit [the victim's] ability to recover"[138]. As another one of these cases noted, the state of manufacture had a greater interest in providing deterrence than the other state had "in preventing a windfall to its

---

132. *Id.*
133. *Id.* For cases reaching the opposite conclusion on this point, see *Sanchez* and *Long*, discussed *infra* at 228.
134. These cases are: *Magnant v. Medtronic, Inc.*, 818 F.Supp. 204 (WD Mich. 1993) (applying Minnesota's pro-plaintiff strict-liability law to an action of a Michigan plaintiff against a Minnesota manufacturer for injury sustained in Michigan and caused by a defect in one of defendant's heart pacemakers designed, manufactured, and implanted in plaintiff in Minnesota; The court noted that the defendant "cannot complain that application of Minnesota law is unfair or contrary to its expectations", *id.* at 206, and that Michigan, which did not impose strict liability, would have no objections either "because [plaintiff] would receive more rights under Minnesota law than under Michigan law". *Id.*); *Champlain Enter's, Inc. v. United States*, 945 F.Supp. 468 (NDNY 1996) (action for recovery of pure economic loss filed by a New York plaintiff whose plane crashed in New York, against a Kansas defendant who manufactured the plane in Kansas; applying Kansas's pro-plaintiff law, but holding for defendant on the merits; noting that in cases involving mobile products such as airplanes, the place of injury is fortuitous); *Lewis-DeBoer v. Mooney Aircraft Corp.*, 728 F.Supp. 642 (D Colo. 1990) (action by Colorado plaintiffs against the Texas manufacturer of a small airplane that crashed in Colorado, killing its Colorado passengers; aside from punitive damages, which were permitted in Texas but not in Colorado, Texas law was generally more generous to the plaintiff with regard to compensatory damages and the burden of proof; after dismissing as fortuitous the occurrence of the injury in Colorado, the court concluded that Texas, as the place of the defendant's conduct and principal place of business, "ha[d] a greater policy interest in applying its laws and providing deterrence than Colorado ha[d] in preventing a windfall to its citizens". *Id.* at 645); *Goede v. Aerojet Gen. Corp.*, (discussed *supra* at 226).
135. 115 P.3d 1017 (Wash. App. 2005).
136. *Id.* at 1022.
137. *Id* at 1023.
138. *Id.*

citizens"[139]. Moreover, as another case noted, the defendant could not complain against the application of the laws of its home state[140].

Finally, the last two cases – *Sanchez* v. *Brownsville Sports Ctr., Inc.*[141] and *Long* v. *Sears Roebuck & Co.*[142] – applied the pro-plaintiff law of the state in which the victim acquired the product, even though that state had no other contacts with the case. In *Sanchez*, the product in question, an all-terrain vehicle (ATV), was manufactured by a Japanese defendant in Japan and was sold through a Texas dealer, and then resold second-hand to plaintiff in Mexico, nine years later. The plaintiffs' child was killed while driving the vehicle in Mexico. The defendant argued for the application of Mexican law, which limited compensatory damages and favored the defendant in other respects, while the plaintiff invoked the law of Texas, which provided for strict liability and more generous compensatory damages.

Following §§ 145 and 6 of the Second Restatement, the court held that Texas law should govern. The court implicitly concluded that Mexico's interest in protecting defendants by limiting the amount of damages was attenuated in this case that involved non-Mexican defendants, at least when compared to Texas' countervailing interest resulting from the fact that Texas was the place where the particular product was first introduced into the stream of commerce. The court reasoned that, by adopting strict products liability laws, Texas had "expressed a clear interest in protecting its consumers and in regulating the quality of products in its stream of commerce"[143], and that, although the ATV eventually ended up in Mexico, "the key factor is that the ATV was originally placed in the stream of commerce in Texas"[144]. This gave Texas a "strong interest" to apply its law "as an incentive to encourage safer design and to induce corporations to control more carefully their manufacturing processes"[145].

Long involved the same pattern and reached the same result. However, the case also involved the issue of punitive damages, and to that extent the outcome is more difficult to defend. In *Long*, the plaintiff was injured in his home state of Maryland by a lawn mower he bought from the defendant in the District of Columbia. As in *Sanchez*, the defendant invoked the pro-defendant law of the state of injury, Maryland, but not the law of the state of manufacture, South Carolina. The court concluded that Maryland law, which limited non-economic damages and did not allow punitive damages, was not intended to protect foreign defendants who did not conduct business in Maryland nor engage in conduct there.

---

139. See *Lewis-DeBoer* v. *Mooney Aircraft Corp.*, 728 F.Supp. 642, 645 (D Colo. 1990) (discussed *supra* footnote 134).

140. See *Magnant* v. *Medtronic, Inc.*, 818 F.Supp. 204 (WD Mich. 1993) (discussed *supra* footnote 134).

141. 51 SW 3d 643 (Tex. App. 2001).

142. 877 F.Supp. 8 (DDC 1995).

143. *Sanchez*, 51 SW 3d at 669.

144. *Id.*

145. *Id.* at 670 (internal quotations omitted).

In contrast, said the court, the District of Columbia had an interest in deterring and punishing, through its unlimited compensatory and punitive damages, defendants who engage in reprehensible conduct in the District by selling unsafe products there and misrepresenting the product's safety features.

2.   Victim's domicile and product acquisition

229. In 14 of the 100 cases, the product was acquired in the victim's home state but the injury occurred in another state[146]. In these cases, the parties did not plead the law of the state with the defendant-affiliating contacts and thus the choice was confined to the laws of the victim's home state and place of acquisition on the one hand, and the state of injury on the other. Ten of the 14 cases applied the law of the former state[147], and four applied the law of the latter state[148]. The following table depicts these cases.

Table 22. Cases in which the plaintiff's home state was also the place of the product's acquisition

#	Case name	Forum state	Plaintiff-affiliating contacts			D-affiliating contacts	
			P's domicile	Injury	Acquisition	Manufacture	D's PPB
59	Alexander	GA / Pro-P	GA / Pro-P	VA / Pro-D	GA / Pro-P	MI / ---	MI / ---
60	Etheredge	AL / Pro-P	AL / Pro-P	N.C. / Pro-D	AL / Pro-P	---	---
61	Kramer v Acton.	MA / Pro-P	MA / Pro-P	CN / Pro-D	MA / Pro-P	JAP / Pro-D	JAP / Pro-D
62	Mann	NY / Pro-P	NY / Pro-P	QU / Pro-D	NY / Pro-P	GA / ---	OH/TN / ---
63	Aguiniga	TX / Pro-P	TX Pro-P / MEX Pro-D	MEX / Pro-D	LA --- / TX Pro-P	MI / ---	MI / ---
64	Thomson v Reinco	DEL / Pro-D	DEL / Pro-D	MD / Pro-P	DE Pro-D / PA Pro-P	NJ / ---	NJ / ---
65	Garcia	AZ / Pro-D	AZ / Pro-D	ID / Pro-P	AZ / Pro-D	MI / --	MI / --
66	Maly	IL / Pro-D	IL / Pro-D	WIS / Pro-P	IL / Pro-D	FL / ---	FL / ---
67	Thornton	AK Pro-P / IN Pro-D	IN / Pro-D	AK / Pro-P	IN / Pro-D	France / ---	CA / ---
68	Bonti	MS / Pro-P	N.C. / Pro-D	S.C. / Pro-D	N.C. / Pro-D	KY/MI / ---	MI / ---
69	Martin	WA / Pro-P	OR / Pro-D	WA / Pro-P	OR / Pro-D	OH / ---	OH / ---
70	Apple	PA / Pro-P	MI / Pro-D	PA / Pro-P	MI / Pro-D	MI / Pro-D	MI / Pro-D
71	Harsh	PA / Pro-P	VA / Pro-D	PA / Pro-P	VA / Pro-D	MI / ---	MI / ---
72	Fitts	AL / Pro-P	AL / Pro-P	FL / Pro-D	AL? / Pro-P	---	---

---

146. See cases ## 59-72, in Table 17, *supra*.

147. See cases ## 59-68, In Table 17, *supra*.

148. See cases ## 69-72.

(a) Applying the pro-plaintiff law of the victim's domicile and place of acquisition

230. In seven of the 14 cases, the state of the victim's domicile and acquisition was also the forum state and had a pro-plaintiff law, while the state of injury had a pro-defendant law[149]. Six of the seven cases applied the law of the former state.

The only case that did *not* do so, the Alabama case of *Fitts* v. *Minnesota Min. & Mfg. Co.*[150], was decided by a court that adhered to the *lex loci delicti* rule *and* was unwilling to escape from it. Three years later, in *Etheredge* v. *Genie Indus., Inc.*[151], the same court found a way to avoid the pro-defendant statute of repose of the *locus* state by characterizing it as procedural, thus freeing the court to apply the statute of limitation of the forum state[152].

In *Alexander* v. *General Motors Corp.*[153], a case decided under Georgia's *lex loci* regime, the court used the *ordre public* exception as the device for avoiding the pro-defendant negligence rule of the locus state of Virginia. This freed the court to apply the pro-plaintiff strict-liability rule of Georgia, which was also the plaintiff's domicile and the place where he bought the car involved in the Virginia accident[154]. In contrast, three virtually identical cases decided in states that have abandoned the *lex loci* rule have reached the same result more directly without resorting to intellectual gymnastics. In one of these cases, *Kramer* v. *Acton Toyota, Inc.*[155], the court found that the victim's home state and place of acquisition

---

149. See cases ## 59-64, 72, in Table 17, *supra*.

150. 581 So.2d 819 (Ala. 1991) (applying the pro-defendant law of Florida to a products liability action arising from the crash of a small airplane in Florida that caused the death of Alabama domiciliaries. The court did not mention the state of manufacture of the airplane or of a suspect instrument).

151. 632 So.2d 1324 (Ala. 1994).

152. In *Etheredge*, the plaintiff's domicile and place of acquisition were in Alabama, which had a statute of limitation favoring the plaintiff, while the place of injury was in North Carolina, which had a statute of repose favoring the defendant. The opinion does not disclose the place of manufacture and the defendant's principal place of business.

153. 478 SE2d 123 (Ga.1996).

154. A dissenting judge in the court of appeals offered affirmative and more realistic reasons for applying Georgia law. He reasoned that Georgia had an interest in protecting Georgia consumers who acquire in Georgia products marketed in that state. Since the defendant had made the car available for sale there, Georgia's "policy of placing the burden on the manufacturer who markets a new product to take responsibility for injury to members of the consuming public for whose use and/or consumption the product is made" was implicated in this case, even though the actual injury had fortuitously occurred in Virginia. *Alexander* v. *Gen. Motors Corp.*, 466 SE 2d 607, 613 (Ga. App.1995) (McMurray, J., dissenting).

155. 2004 WL 2697284 (Mass. Super. 2004). This case arose out of a Connecticut accident involving a Japanese-made car that the victim bought in his home state, Massachusetts. The dispute centered on the victim's contributory negligence, and the discussion was limited to the laws of Massachusetts (pro-victim) and Connecticut (pro-defendant). Following the forum's "functional approach", but also relying on the Second Restatement, the court applied Massachusetts law.

had "a strong interest in the manner in which its residents are compensated for injuries sustained as a result of allegedly faulty products sold within its borders, regardless of where those products ultimately failed"[156]. In contrast, the state of injury had "no significant interest in allocating responsibility for injuries, suffered by [non- residents] ... caused by a product ... purchased in [another state]"[157]. Since the defendant did not invoke the law of its own home state or the state of manufacture, the court could easily resolve the conflict in favor of the law of the victim's domicile and place of acquisition[158].

(b) Applying the pro-defendant law of the victim's domicile and place of acquisition

231. In the next eight cases, the law of the plaintiff's home state and place of acquisition favored the defendant, while the law of the state of injury favored the plaintiff[159]. Five of these cases applied the law of the former state[160], and three applied the law of the latter state[161].

It is noteworthy that in four of the five cases in the first group, the application of the forum's pro-defendant law favored a foreign defendant at the expense of a forum victim[162]. In one of those cases, *Maly* v. *Genmar Indus., Inc.*[163], an Illinois plaintiff was injured in Wisconsin by a product he purchased in Illinois.

---

156. *Id.* at *3 at *3.

157. *Id.*

158. The other two cases are *Ford Motor Co.* v. *Aguiniga*, 9 SW 3d 252 (Tex. App.1999) (applying Texas' unlimited compensatory-damages law to an action by Texas domiciliaries arising from a Mexico accident involving a car acquired by plaintiffs in Louisiana but inspected in Texas. The defendants invoked Mexico's ceiling on damages, but did not invoke the law of the state of manufacture, apparently because that law did not impose such a ceiling); and *Mann* v. *Cooper Tire Co.*, 761 NYS 2d 635 (NYAD 2003) (applying New York's pro-plaintiff law to a case arising from a Quebec traffic accident caused by a car tire manufactured in Georgia and installed on a car in New York).

159. See cases ## 64-71 in Table 17, *supra.*

160. See cases ## 64-68.

161. See cases ## 69-71.

162. In the fifth case, *Bonti* v. *Ford Motor Co.*, 898 F. Supp. 391 (SD Miss. 1995), aff'd without op., 85 F.3d 625 (5th Cir. 1996), none of the states affiliated with either the plaintiff or the defendant had a pro-plaintiff law. The forum state of Mississippi had a pro-plaintiff statute of limitation and this was the reason the plaintiff sued there, after a single-car accident in South Carolina that caused the death of her husband, a North Carolina domiciliary. The car was designed in Michigan, assembled in Kentucky, and sold to plaintiff in North Carolina. Five years after the accident and eight years after the purchase of the car, the plaintiff sued Ford in Mississippi, a state that had no contacts with the case other than that Ford was doing business there. North Carolina's statute of repose and South Carolina's three-year statute of limitation barred the action. Following the Second Restatement, the court concluded that North Carolina had the most significant relationship and its repose statute barred the action.

163. 1996 WL 28473 (N.D.Ill. 1996).

Unlike Wisconsin, the forum state of Illinois had a statute of repose barring the action. The manufacturer was a Florida corporation, but the court did not mention the place of manufacture, apparently because of the court's conclusion that the critical conduct was "the placement of a defective product in the stream of commerce"[164], which occurred in Illinois.

Confining its analysis to the policies of Illinois and Wisconsin, the court found them irreconcilable. Illinois' policy was "pro business: to reduce the cost to manufacturers and distributors of doing business in Illinois by cutting legal costs caused by old strict liability lawsuits which are particularly difficult to defend due to loss of witnesses, poor record keeping, and changes in legal and technical standards on products"[165]. Wisconsin's policy, on the other hand, "favors consumers over manufacturers, and apparently does not view proliferating products liability litigation a sufficient reason to deny consumers a cause of action in strict liability for injuries resulting from defective old products"[166]. After examining the contacts of the two states, the court concluded that Illinois had the most significant relationship, because "[t]he conduct complained of happened in Illinois to an Illinois resident and the relationship of the parties occurred in Illinois"[167]. Thus, the court concluded, "[t]here is no reason to rank Illinois' pro-business tort policy as less significant than Wisconsin's pro-consumer policy"[168].

In *Garcia* v. *General Motors Corp.*[169], the plaintiffs were Arizona domiciliaries who were injured in an Idaho accident while riding in a car they had rented in Arizona. The car was manufactured in Michigan by a Michigan defendant, but the parties did not plead Michigan law. Thus the conflict was between Idaho law, which did not allow evidence of the plaintiffs' failure to wear their seatbelts, and Arizona law, which permitted such evidence. The court held that Arizona had an interest "in encouraging its residents to wear seatbelts even outside its borders, as injuries resulting from not using seatbelts may well require medical care upon the residents' return to Arizona"[170]. The court also reasoned that it would be "incongruous to allow Idaho's desire to 'fully' compensate nonresident Arizona plaintiffs to control in an Arizona court, when Arizona courts would permit the jury to consider whether to reduce the recovery of Arizona plaintiffs who fail to wear seatbelts"[171].

---

164. *Id.* at *2.
165. *Id.*
166. *Id.*
167. *Id.*
168. *Id.*
169. 990 P.2d 1069 (Ariz. App. 1999).
170. *Garcia*, 990 P.2d at 1078.
171. *Id.* In *Thornton* v. *Sea Quest, Inc.*, 999 F.Supp. 1219 (ND Ind. 1998), the action was filed in Arkansas, transferred to Indiana, and decided under the conflicts law of both states. The victim, an Indiana domiciliary, bought scuba diving equipment that was manufactured in France and sold in Indiana by a California manufacturer and distributor. The victim died in Arkansas, while using the equipment. The issue was wrong-

(c)   Applying the pro-plaintiff law of the state of injury

232. Finally, three cases applied the pro-plaintiff law of the state of injury[172], which was also the forum state, rather than the pro-defendant law of the victim's home state and place of acquisition[173]. In all three cases, the application of that law benefitted a non-forum victim at the expense of a non-forum defendant.

In one of these cases[174], *Martin* v. *Goodyear Tire & Rubber Co.*[175], the fact that the product was acquired in the victim's home state was totally coincidental. The acquirer was a truck driver unrelated to the victim but domiciled in Oregon, the same state as the victim. The product was a wheel assembly that the truck driver installed on his truck in Oregon. While the truck was driven in the state of Washington, a metal ring separated from the assembly and struck and killed an Oregon domiciliary who was riding in another car. Oregon's, but not Washington's, statute of repose barred the plaintiff's action against the manufacturer of the assembly. Noting that the Oregon statute was intended to protect Oregon defendants, the court concluded that "Washington's interest in protecting persons from injuries from defective products within its borders outweighs Oregon's interest in protecting a [non-Oregon] manufacturer whose product arrives in Oregon through the stream of commerce and subsequently causes injury to a third party in another state"[176]. The court applied the Washington statute.

---

ful death recovery, and Arkansas law was more favorable to plaintiffs than Indiana law. Neither party pleaded French or California law. The court held that Indiana law should govern because Indiana had a more significant relationship than Arkansas, as well as "a strong interest in preventing the sale of supposedly defective products within its borders". *Id.* at 1224. In *Thompson* v. *Reinco, Inc.*, 2004 WL 1426971 (Del. Super. 2004), the court applied the law of the place of the product's delivery in a case in which the product was manufactured in New Jersey, sold in Pennsylvania, delivered in Delaware, and caused injury in Maryland. The court concluding that "it was the delivery of the product to a Delaware resident for use in Delaware that provides the pivotal moment which ultimately brought all the parties together. Having determined that the place of injury was fortuitous, the relationship between all the parties is predominantly centered on the delivery and intended use in Delaware". *Id.* at *2.

172.   For a case that applied the pro-defendant law of the state of injury in the converse scenario, see *Fitts* v. *Minnesota Min. & Mfg. Co.*, *supra* footnote 150.

173.   See cases ## 69-71, in Table 22, *supra*.

174.   The other two cases are *Apple* v. *Ford Motor Co.*, 2004 WL 3218425 (Pa. Commw. Ct. 2004) (discussed *supra* 195; awarding punitive damages in an action arising from a Pennsylvania accident involving a car manufactured by a Michigan defendant in Michigan, which was also the victim's domicile, and acquired by the victim in that state); and *Harsh* v. *Petroll*, 840 A 2d 404 (Pa. Cmmw.Ct 2003) (applying Pennsylvania's pro-plaintiff law to wrongful death actions filed on behalf of Virginia domiciliaries who were killed in Pennsylvania in a car purchased in Virginia and manufactured by a Michigan defendant in Michigan).

175.   61 P.3d 1196 (Wash. App .2003).

176.   *Id.* at 1201.

3. Injury and product acquisition

233. In 16 of the 100 cases, the injury occurred outside the plaintiff's home state but the product was acquired in the state of injury, either by the victim's employer or by the victim while temporarily in that state[177]. The following table depicts these cases.

Table 23. Cases in which the acquisition and the injury were in the same state

#	Case name	Forum state	Plaintiff-affiliating contacts			D-affiliating contacts	
			P's domicile	Injury	Acquisition	Manufacture	D's PPB
73	Roll	NY Pro-P / NV Pro-P	NY Pro-P	NV Pro-P	NV Pro-P	TX Pro-D	TX Pro-D
74	Johnson v. Ranch	IL Pro-D	KS ---	CO Pro-P	CO Pro-P	IL Pro-D	IL Pro-D
75	Gadzinski	IL Pro-P	IL Pro-P	IN Pro-D	IN Pro-D	---	IN Pro-D
76	Romani	MA Pro-P	MA Pro-P	CN Pro-D	CN Pro-D	KS ---	KS ---
77	Tanges	NY Pro-P	NY Pro-P	CN Pro-D	CN Pro-D	---	---
78	LeJeune	PA Pro-P	PA Pro-P	DEL Pro-D	DEL Pro-D	---	---
79	Allison	MS Pro-P	MS Pro-P	TN Pro-D	TN Pro-D	PA ---	PA ---
80	Schmidt	PA Pro-P	PA Pro-P	N.J. Pro-D	N.J. Pro-D	IL ---	IL ---
81	Cianfrani	N.J. Pro-P	PA Pro-P	DEL Pro-D	DEL Pro-D	CA ---	CA ---
82	Calhoun	PA Pro-P	PA Pro-P	P.R. Pro-D	P.R. Pro-D	Japan ---	Japan ---
83	Beals	D.C. Pro-P	VA Pro-D	D.C. Pro-P	D.C. Pro-P	VA Pro-D	VA Pro-D
84	Cosme	MA Pro-P	MA Pro-P	CN Pro-D	CN Pro-D	MA Pro-P	MA Pro-P
85	Lou	MA Pro-P	MA Pro-P	CHI Pro-D	CHI Pro-D	CHI Pro-D	MA Pro-P
86	Judge	FL Pro-P	FL Pro-P	MEX Pro-D	MEX Pro-D	MX Pro-D / MI Pro-P	MI Pro-P
87	Calhoun	PA Pro-P	PA Pro-P	P.R. --	P.R. --	Japan ---	Japan ---
88	LaPlante	R.I. Pro-P	R.I. Pro-P	CO Pro-D	CO Pro-D	Japan Pro-D	Japan Pro-D

In most of these cases, the parties did not plead the laws of the states of manufacture or the manufacturers' principal place of business. Thus, the courts' choice was confined to the laws of the victim's home state on the one hand, and the state of injury and the product's acquisition on the other.

The first ten of these cases applied the law of the latter state. That law favored the plaintiff in two cases[178] and the defendant in the remaining eight cases.

---

177. See cases ## 73-88 in Table 23, *supra*.

178. See *Roll* v. *Tracor, Inc.*, discussed *infra* at 134, and *Johnson* v. *Ranch Steamboat Condo. Ass'n*, 1999 WL 184068 (ND Ill. 1999). In *Johnson*, a Kansas domiciliary was injured in

234. In *Roll* v. *Tracor, Inc.*[179], the plaintiff, a New York serviceman, was injured at a military base in Nevada by flares acquired by the base authorities in Nevada and manufactured in Texas by a Texas manufacturer. The laws of these states differed on the issue of corporate successor liability, with Nevada and New York laws favoring the plaintiff and Texas law favoring the defendant. The court classified this as a true conflict between the law of Texas, on the one hand, and the laws of New York and Nevada, on the other[180]: (1) Texas had an interest in applying its rule of successor non-liability, because both the defendant and its predecessor corporation had their principal place of business in Texas; (2) New York had an interest in applying its successor-liability rule so as to provide a remedy to its injured domiciliary; and (3) Nevada had a parallel interest in applying its successor-liability rule so as to provide a remedy to a person injured within its borders.

The court concluded that the defendant did not rebut the presumption in favor of the law of the place of injury because the occurrence of the injury in Nevada was not fortuitous and the contacts with Nevada were not insignificant and the defendant could have foreseen the occurrence of the injury in that state [181]. Under these circumstances, the court reasoned, "[i]t would be unreasonable for [defendant] to expect that Texas law would automatically shield it from successor liability in every state of the Union. It would be unjust to allow a corporation to escape liability and leave potential plaintiffs without a remedy by simply giving itself a reorganizational facelift, and at the same time carry on the same business and manufacture the same product while using the same name, the same plant, and the same personnel"[182].

235. In the next eight cases, the state of injury and place of the product's acquisition had a pro-defendant law[183]. All eight cases applied that law[184], although

---

Colorado by a product acquired in Colorado and manufactured in Illinois. Colorado law favored the plaintiff, and Illinois law favored the defendant. Following the Second Restatement, the court acknowledged Illinois' interest in protecting Illinois corporations that manufacture products in that state, but concluded that Colorado's interest in protecting consumers injured in that state by products sold there was more compelling.

179. 140 F.Supp.2d 1073 (D Nev. 2001). This action, which was originally filed in New York and then transferred to Nevada, was decided under New York conflicts law.

180. The court also characterized the successor-liability issue as one of tort law and specifically as one pertaining to loss-allocation rather than conduct-regulation.

181. The plaintiff was stationed in Nevada for some time and the defendant's products were used in Nevada's multiple military bases for many years, thus making foreseeable the occurrence of the injury in that state and the application of that state's law.

182. *Roll*, 140 F.Supp.2d at 1083.

183. See cases ## 75-82, in Table 23, *supra*.

184. In addition to the cases discussed in the text, these cases are: *Allison* v. *ITE Imperial Corp.*, 928 F.2d 137 (5th Cir. 1991) (decided under Mississippi conflicts law; applying Tennessee's statute of repose, rather than Mississippi's statute of limitation, and barring the action of a Mississippi plaintiff for a Tennessee injury caused by a defective electrical circuit breaker sold and installed in Tennessee, but manufactured by a

in all but one of them[185] that law disfavored a forum victim and favored a non-forum defendant. In *Romani* v. *Cramer, Inc.*[186], the victim was domiciled in Massachusetts, but was employed in Connecticut and was injured there while using a chair supplied by his employer[187]. Unlike Massachusetts, Connecticut had a statute of repose barring the plaintiff's action. The court found that the victim's domicile in Massachusetts did not give that state a sufficient interest to override "Connecticut's superior interest on all other fronts"[188]. Connecticut's interest was superior because "Connecticut enacted its statute [of repose] to protect manufacturers from liability for products whose useful lives have expired ... [and to] encourage[] manufacturers to freely sell products within its borders"[189]. The court also noted that, as the place of the injury, Connecticut was the state whose law presumptively applied under § 146 of the Second Restatement, unless another state had a more significant relationship. The court found that Massachusetts did not have such a relationship.

In *LeJeune* v. *Bliss-Salem, Inc.*[190], a Pennsylvania court refused to apply the strict-liability law of the victim's home state of Pennsylvania, and applied instead the negligence law of Delaware, which was the place of the accident and the place of the product's acquisition. The court compared Pennsylvania's interest in "protect[ing] its citizens from defective products"[191], with Delaware's interest in "encouraging economic activity in the state ... and lowering costs to consum-

---

Pennsylvania-based defendant in Pennsylvania; the court did not describe Pennsylvania law); *Tanges* v. *Heidelberg N. Am., Inc.*, 687 NYS 2d 604 (NY 1999) (applying Connecticut's statute of repose barring an action brought by a New York domiciliary injured by a printing press while working for his employer in Connecticut); *Gadzinski* v. *Chrysler Corp.*, 2001 WL 629336 (ND Ill. 2001) (applying Indiana's pro-defendant law to an action by an Illinois plaintiff who was injured in Indiana by a product he purchased from an Indiana dealer); *Schmidt* v. *Duo-Fast, Inc.*, 1995 WL 422681 (ED Pa. 1995) (applying New Jersey pro-defendant law to the claim of a Pennsylvania worker injured in a New Jersey construction accident caused by a tool purchased from Pennsylvania but shipped directly to New Jersey: "[T]he accident happened in New Jersey and 'departures from the territorial view of torts ought not to be lightly undertaken.'" *Id.* at *1); *Calhoun* v. *Yamaha Motor Corp., U.S.A.*, 216 F.3d 338 (3rd Cir. 2000) (action by Pennsylvania plaintiffs for injury they sustained in Puerto Rico while using a rented Japanese-made watercraft; holding that plaintiffs' claims for punitive damages were governed by Puerto Rico law (which does not allow such damages) because "Puerto Rico's interest in regulating the activity that occurs in its territorial waters ... is more dominant". *Id.* at 348).

185. In one case, *Cianfrani* v. *Kalmar-Ac Handling Sys., Inc.*,1995 WL 563289 (DNJ 1995), the applicable law favored a foreign defendant at the expense of a foreign plaintiff.
186. 992 F.Supp. 74 (D Mass. 1998).
187. The chair had been manufactured by a Kansas corporation, apparently in Kansas, but neither party urged the application of Kansas law.
188. *Id.* at 79.
189. *Id.* at 78.
190. 85 F.3d 1069 (3d Cir. 1996).
191. *Id.* at 1071.

ers"[192]. The court concluded that, because most of the conduct had occurred in Delaware, and the occurrence of the injury in that state was not fortuitous, Delaware's contacts were "qualitatively" more important and thus "Delaware ha[d] the greater interest in having its law applied"[193].

Similarly, in *Cianfrani* v. *Kalmar-Ac Handling Systems, Inc.*[194], a New Jersey court refused to apply the strict-liability law of Pennsylvania, the plaintiff's home state, and instead applied Delaware's negligence law to an action arising from an accident in plaintiffs' Delaware employment site. The accident was caused by a defective forklift leased by plaintiff's employer in Delaware. Although recognizing Pennsylvania's interest in protecting its domiciliary plaintiff, the court held that, because this case involved a question of liability rather than damages, Delaware had a greater interest "in defining the circumstances under which people who do business in or ship goods to Delaware will be exposed to liability"[195].

236. Finally, the remaining six cases went the other way by applying the law of the victim's home state rather that of the state of injury and acquisition[196]. In four of those cases, the defendant had its principal place of business in, or had a similar affiliation with the victim's home state that made these cases analogous to common-domicile cases[197].

For example, in *Cosme* v. *Whitin Mach. Works, Inc.*[198], the plaintiff, a Massachusetts domiciliary, was injured in Connecticut while using machinery that defendant, a Massachusetts corporation, had manufactured in Massachusetts and had delivered to plaintiff's employer in Connecticut. Connecticut's statute of repose barred the action, which was timely under Massachusetts' statute of limitation. The court allowed the action after finding that Massachusetts had a more significant relationship and a greater interest in applying its law than did Connecticut.

In *Lou ex rel. Chen* v. *Otis Elevator Co.*[199], the product was an escalator manufactured and installed in a building in China, but the court again applied Massachusetts' pro-victim law because the victim was a Massachusetts domiciliary and the defendant was an American corporation with significant connections with Massachusetts. The court found that China had no interest in the parties, partly because, under Chinese conflicts law, a Chinese court would have applied the

---

192. *Id.* at 1072.
193. *Id.*
194. 1995 WL 563289 (DNJ 1995).
195. *Id.* at *6.
196. See cases ## 83-88, in Table 17, *supra*.
197. In three of those cases, discussed in the text *infra*, that state had a pro-plaintiff law. In the fourth case, *Beals* v. *Sipca Securink Corp.*, 1994 WL 236018 (DDC 1994), that state had a pro-defendant law. *Beals* applied Virginia's pro-defendant law to an action by Virginia plaintiffs against a Virginia manufacturer of ink that was manufactured in Virginia and caused injury in the District of Columbia.
198. 632 NE 2d 832 (Mass. 1994).
199. 2004 WL 504697 (Mass. Super., 2004).

law of the parties' common domicile, and thus the defendant "cannot say it has a settled expectation that Chinese law would apply"[200]. After noting the practical difficulties of applying Chinese law, the court concluded that Massachusetts had a "stronger public policy interest than China ... both in the compensation of a Massachusetts citizen ... and in holding accountable a United States company doing business in Massachusetts"[201].

In *Judge* v. *American Motors Corp.*[202], the parties were domiciled in different states (Florida for the plaintiff and Michigan for the defendants) which, however, had the same law on one important issue – the availability of a wrongful death action and the amount of compensatory damages[203]. All the other contacts were in Mexico, the law of which did not allow an action for wrongful death. The plaintiff's decedents were killed in Mexico while using a car manufactured there but designed by defendants in Michigan. The court characterized this as an essentially intra-U.S. case in which "a United States plaintiff sues three United States defendants in a United States court for tortious acts committed by the United States defendants"[204]. The court concluded that, although Mexico might have a slight interest in applying its pro-defendant law to shield defendants doing business in Mexico, that interest was "slight"[205], while the interests of Florida and Michigan were more significant. The court remanded the case to the trial court for determining which of those states had a more significant relationship[206].

237. The remaining two cases applied the pro-plaintiff law of the plaintiff's home state despite that state's lack of any other contacts[207]. One of them, *LaPlante* v. *Am. Honda Motor Co., Inc.*[208], which was decided under Rhode Island's better-law approach[209], is particularly indefensible[210]. In this case, a Rhode Island domiciliary who was stationed in Colorado was injured in Colorado by a Honda all-ter-

---

200. *Id.* at *4.

201. *Id.*

202. 908 F.2d 1565 (11th Cir. 1990).

203. These two states differed on the availability of punitive damages (allowed in Florida, but not in Michigan), but the court did not decide this issue.

204. *Judge*, 908 F.2d at 1573.

205. *Id.* at 1572.

206. Apparently the case was settled because there is no reported subsequent decision of the district court.

207. See cases ## 87-88 in Table 17, *supra*.

208. 27 F.3d 731 (1st Cir. 1994) (decided under Rhode Island conflicts law).

209. While stating that the better-law criterion did "not weigh heavily in either state's direction", *id.* at 743, the court opined that the Rhode Island Supreme Court would "undoubtedly favor a compensatory damage standard without limits". *Id.*

210. The second case, *Calhoun* v. *Yamaha Motor Corp., U.S.A.*, 216 F.3d 338 (3rd Cir. 2000), applied Pennsylvania's pro-plaintiff comparative negligence law to an action against a Japanese manufacturer arising from an accident in Puerto Rico that resulted in the death of a Pennsylvania child. This holding is more balanced than it appears considering that, in another holding in the same case, the court applied Puerto Rico's pro-defendant law denying punitive damages. See *supra* footnote 184.

rain vehicle he acquired in that state[211]. Colorado, but not Rhode Island, limited compensatory damages to $250,000. The court assumed that the purpose of this limit was "to increase the affordability and availability of insurance by making the risk of insured entities more predictable ... [and] improve the predictability of risks faced by insurance companies"[212]. However, said the court, "[t]he concern of an insurance company is the risk associated with insuring each individual insured, not with denying an injured person damages that may be paid by another insurance company or person"[213]. Hence, there was "no reason why the Colorado legislature would be concerned with the affordability of insurance to a multinational Japanese corporation"[214]. After noting that the defendant sold its products in all fifty states, the court observed that "Colorado's damages law plays, at best, an insignificant role in setting [defendant's] insurance rates"[215] and that defendant had not "ceased doing business in any state because of a failure by that state to limit the amount of damages a plaintiff may recover"[216]. The court applied Rhode Island law.

D.   The Rest of the Cases

238. Of the remaining 12 cases[217], no two cases are alike. Most of these cases present the mixed conflict pattern in that the plaintiff-affiliating contacts were located in different states, some of which had a pro-plaintiff law while others had a pro-defendant law. The following table depicts these cases.

---

211. The vehicle had been designed and manufactured in Japan by a Japanese corporation. The defendant did not plead the law of Japan, but did plead the law of Colorado.
212. *LaPlante*, 27 F.3d at 743.
213. *Id.*
214. *Id.*
215. *Id.*
216. *Id.*
217. See cases ## 89-100 in Table 17, *supra* and Table 24, *infra*.

Table 24. The remaining cases

#	Case name	Forum state	Plaintiff-affiliating contacts			D-affiliating contacts	
			P's domicile	Injury	Acquisition	Manufacture	D's PPB
89	Torrington	TX Pro-P	N.C. ---	MI/NE Pro-D	TX Pro-P	TX Pro-P	TX Pro-P
90	Mitchell	TX Pro-P	N.M./KY ---	N.C. Pro-D	TX Pro-P	TX Pro-P	MD/CA ---
91	Offshore	LA Pro-D	--- ---	LA Pro-D	--- ---	TX Pro-P	TX Pro-P
92	Jones v. SEPTA	PA Pro-P	IL ---	PA Pro-P	--- ---	NE Pro-D	NE Pro-D
93	Mahoney	N.C. Pro-D	AZ Pro-P	N.C. Pro-D	KY/AZ	N.C. Pro-D	N.C. Pro-D
94	Huddy	TX Pro-P	TX Pro-P	GA Pro-P	TN Pro-P	PA Pro-P	MI Pro-D
95	MacDonald	TN ---	N.D. Pro-P	TN ---	KS Pro-D	MI ---	MI ---
96	Pollack	CN Pro-P	CN Pro-P	OH Pro-D	KS --	IL --	OH Pro-D
97	Danielson	MN Pro-P	MN Pro-P	AZ Pro-D	TX Pro-D		CO --
98	Johnson v. Ford	IL Pro-P	IL Pro-P	KY Pro-D	OK --	KY Pro-D	MI --
99	Phillips	MT Pro-P	MT Pro-P	KS Pro-D	N.C. Pro-D	MI Pro-D	MI Pro-D
100	Danziger	DC Pro-P	DC Pro-P	NEB Pro-D	MD Pro-P	MI Pro-D	MI Pro-D

239. In the first four cases, the parties did not plead the laws of the plaintiffs' domiciles and confined their arguments to the laws of the state of injury on the one hand and the defendant-affiliated states on the other[218]. In *Torrington Co.* v. *Stutzman*[219] and *Mitchell* v. *Lone Star Ammunition, Inc.*[220], the products were acquired in the state of manufacture and both cases applied the pro-plaintiff law of that state. In *Mitchell*, the product was manufactured and sold in Texas by defendants who had their principal places of business in Maryland and California, respectively. The plaintiffs were the survivors of Kentucky and New Mexico servicemen who were killed in North Carolina by defendants' defective munitions. North Carolina, but not Texas, had a statute of repose barring the plaintiffs' actions.

---

218. In the fifth case, *Mahoney* v. *Ronnie's Road Serv.*, 468 SE 2d 279 (NC App. 1996), review denied 476 SE 2d 118 (NC 1996), the plaintiff did plead the law of his home state, Arizona, but three of the other contacts were located in the same other state, North Carolina – the plaintiff was injured in North Carolina by a product manufactured in that state by a North Carolina defendant. The court concluded that North Carolina had a more significant relationship and applied its statute of repose to bar an action that was timely under Arizona law.

219. 46 SW 3d 829 (Tex. 2000) (applying Texas pro-plaintiff compensatory damages law to an action filed against a Texas-based corporation that manufactured a helicopter in Texas; the place of injury and the victims' domiciles were in three different states).

220. 913 F.2d 242 (5th Cir. 1990).

The court concluded that North Carolina did not have an interest in applying its statute to protect foreign manufacturers and to deprive persons injured in that state of remedy. In contrast, the court concluded that Texas had a substantial interest in encouraging the manufacture of safe products and that this interest was "particularly strong" in this case because "the defective product in question was manufactured and placed in the stream of commerce in the state of Texas"[221].

In *Offshore Logistics, Inc.* v. *Bell Helicopter Textron*[222] and *Jones* v. *SEPTA*[223], the place of the product's acquisition was not mentioned and the choice was confined to the laws of the state of manufacture and the state of injury. Both cases applied the law of the former state, which was also the manufacturer's principal place of business. Unlike *Offshore*, which was a very cursory opinion, *Jones* provided reasons for this choice. In *Jones*, the defendant-affiliating contacts (defendant's domicile and place of manufacture) were situated in Nebraska, the law of which favored the defendant, while the victim-affiliating contacts were split between Illinois (victim's domicile) and Pennsylvania (place of injury). The plaintiff invoked Pennsylvania's successor-liability law, which was favorable to him, but not Illinois law, which apparently was not favorable. The court found that Pennsylvania's interest in ensuring adequate compensation for persons injured within its borders was "less pronounced" because the plaintiff was not a Pennsylvania domiciliary. The court recognized Pennsylvania's interest in "seeing that corporations whose products ... cause injury in the state not escape the liability that the state imposes on successor corporations"[224] but concluded that, in the absence of other contacts, this interest was "more remote than Nebraska's interest in determining the tort liability of its successor corporations"[225], and that Nebraska had "a more significant relationship ... and a greater interest"[226] in applying its law[227].

240. The next six cases applied the pro-plaintiff law of the plaintiff's home state, even though that state did not have any other contacts with the case[228]. However, in all but one of these cases, the five pertinent contacts were dispersed

---

221. *Id.* at 250. See also *id.* (concluding that Texas had a "substantial interest" in applying it pro-plaintiff law "as an incentive to encourage safer design and to induce corporations to control more carefully the manufacturing processes").

222. 1995 WL 555593 (ED La. 1995) (applying Texas pro-plaintiff law to an action arising out of a Louisiana crash of a helicopter manufactured in Texas by a Texas defendant).

223. 1993 WL 141646 (ED Pa. 1993).

224. *Jones*, 1993 WL 141646 at *23.

225. *Id.*

226. *Id.* at *25.

227. The court noted that, since both corporations were from Nebraska and the succession agreement had been made in that state, the successor corporation "may have a justified expectation that Nebraska law of successor non-liability ... will apply to it even when an injury for which its predecessor ... may have been liable occurred in another state". *Id.* at *21.

228. See cases ## 94-99, in Table 24, *supra*.

in four or five different states[229]. In one case, *Huddy* v. *Fruehauf Corp.*[230], except for the defendant's principal place of business, all other involved states had a pro-plaintiff law[231].

In three cases – *Pollack* v. *Bridgestone/Firestone, Inc.*[232], *MacDonald* v. *General Motors Corp.*[233], and *Danielson* v. *National Supply Co.*[234], – the defendants

---

229. The only exception is *Johnson* v. *Ford Motor Co.,* 2003 WL 22317425 (ND Ill. 2003). In this case, the defendant pleaded the law of the state of manufacture, Kentucky, which by coincidence was also the state of injury. The plaintiffs were injured in Kentucky while returning from Florida to Illinois on a car they rented in Illinois. The court reasoned that, because of the fortuity of the accident's locale, the fact that Kentucky had two contacts with the case did not give it any greater interest in applying its law to issues of compensatory damages than the plaintiff's home state, which would bear the social consequences of non-recovery. "It cannot be reasonably inferred", said the court, "that Ford chose to manufacture in Kentucky to obtain the benefits of Kentucky tort laws". *Id.* at *3. The court held, however, that Kentucky law should govern issues of conduct regulation – specifically whether plaintiffs' failure to wear seatbelts would reduce their recovery.

230. 953 F.2d 955 (5th Cir. 1992).

231. The plaintiff was a former Texas domiciliary who was injured in Georgia while driving a car his employer purchased in Tennessee. The defendant invoked the pro-defendant negligence law of its principal place of business, Michigan, but the product in question had been manufactured in Pennsylvania, the law of which favored the plaintiff, as did the law of all the other involved states. The court concluded that this was an insufficient reason to apply Michigan law and applied Texas' pro-plaintiff strict-liability law.

232. 939 F.Supp.151 (D Conn. 1996) (applying Connecticut's pro-plaintiff liability law to an injury suffered by a Connecticut domiciliary in an Ohio accident caused by a tire manufactured in Illinois by an Ohio corporation).

233. 110 F.3d 337 (6th Cir. 1997) (decided under Tennessee's conflicts law). *MacDonald* was a wrongful death action arising from a Tennessee traffic accident caused by a brake defect in a van manufactured by GM in Michigan and sold in Kansas to the University of Kansas. The victim was a student from North Dakota who was a passenger in the van. Kansas, but not North Dakota, limited wrongful-death damages. Neither party argued for the application of Tennessee or Michigan law and the court found the contacts of those states to be inconsequential. The court concluded that, as the domicile of the decedent and the plaintiffs, "North Dakota has the most significant relationship to the measure of damages", *id.* at 344, that its pro-plaintiff law reflected "a strong interest in assuring that next of kin are fully compensated for the tortious death of its domiciliaries", *id.* at 345, and that "applying the Kansas statute would frustrate North Dakota's policy of fully compensating its domiciliaries for their injuries". *Id.* The court acknowledged that Kansas' ceiling on damages reflected an interest in protecting defendants from excessive jury verdicts, but concluded that this interest was not sufficiently compelling.

234. 2003 WL 22332982 (Min. App. 2003). In *Danielson*, the laws of both the state of injury (Arizona) and the state of acquisition (Texas) favored the defendant retailer, but their connections with the case were rather transient. The plaintiff, a Minnesota domiciliary, was injured during his Arizona vacation while using a step ladder that he bought

pleaded only the laws of states with plaintiff-affiliating contacts. Thus, the courts' choices were confined between the laws of the victim's home state and the state of injury, as in *Pollack*, or between the victim's home state and the state of the product's acquisition, as in *MacDonald*.

241. All of the above cases are easier to defend than *Phillips* v. *General Motors Corp.*[235]. *Phillips* was an action by the survivors of a Montana family who perished in an accident in Kansas while on a trip from Montana to North Carolina, when their car exploded upon colliding with another car. The defendant, General Motors, a Michigan-based corporation, manufactured the car in Michigan and sold it in North Carolina where one of the victims purchased it while domiciled there. The defendant invoked the law of Kansas, which had a statute of repose that barred the action, allowed certain defenses not available to manufacturers elsewhere, and limited the amount of compensatory and punitive damages[236]. The plaintiffs invoked the law of Montana, which had no statute of repose, disallowed the manufacturer's defenses, and imposed no limits on compensatory or punitive damages.

The court held that Montana had a more significant relationship and that its law should govern all issues of liability and damages. The court found that the purpose of Kansas' products liability law was "to regulate the sale of products in that state and to prevent injuries incurred by that state's residents due to defective products"[237], and that this purpose "could not be implicated by the facts of this case as it involves neither a sale in Kansas nor an injury to a Kansas resident"[238].

---

for his motor home while driving through Texas. The retailer who sold him the ladder had a similar store in Minnesota and the plaintiff claimed that this was the reason for which he visited the particular store in Texas. At issue was the timeliness of the plaintiff's action, which was barred by the statutes of limitation of Texas and Arizona but allowed by Minnesota's statute. The court held that the Minnesota statute should govern, either because it was procedural, or because Minnesota had a greater interest in providing a forum to its injured domiciliary than the other two states had in avoiding litigation of stale claims.

235. 995 P.2d 1002 (Mont. 2000). Also difficult to defend is the very last of the 100 cases – *Danziger* v. *Ford Motor Co.*, 2005 WL 1630082 (DDC 2005), another case involving a car designed by the same defendant, a Michigan-based company, in Michigan and manufactured in Kentucky. The victims bought the car in Maryland while domiciled in the District of Columbia and were injured in an accident in Nebraska. Nebraska prohibited punitive damages, but the parties confined their arguments to the laws of Michigan, which also prohibited punitive damages, and Maryland, which allowed them. The court allowed punitive damages under the law of the Maryland, reasoning that the sale of a defective product was the most pertinent and critical conduct. After completion of the manuscript the court reversed its decision and applied Michigan law. See 402 F.Supp.2d 236 (DDC 2005).

236. The defendant also invoked the laws of North Carolina and Michigan, but did not adequately brief the court on the content of those laws.

237. *Phillips*, 995 P.2d at 1009.

238. *Id.*

Curiously, the court followed the same rationale even with regard to those rules of Kansas products liability law that protected the manufacturer, such as its statute of repose or the state-of-the art defense. The court concluded that these rules "were not enacted in order to grant a defense to a manufacturer when a non-Kansas resident is injured by a product not purchased in Kansas"[239].

Regarding compensatory damages, the court concluded that Kansas' limitations on the amount of wrongful-death damages were intended "to alleviate a perceived crisis in the availability and affordability of liability insurance"[240] and that, because no Kansas residents were involved in this case, Kansas had no interest in insisting on those limitations.

242. Finally, regarding punitive damages, the court focused more on the fact that Kansas law allowed such damages, rather than on the fact that it limited their amount to $5 million. Noting that the purpose of punitive damages is "to punish or deter conduct deemed wrongful when ... compensatory damages are considered an insufficient punishment or deterrence"[241], the court concluded that Kansas was uninterested because the manufacturer's conduct did not occur in Kansas.

As to where the manufacturer's conduct occurred, the defendant pointed to two states with pro-defendant laws, Michigan, where the car had been manufactured, and North Carolina, where the car had been introduced into the market and then resold to the victim. Using a *renvoi*-type syllogism, the court concluded both of those states would be uninterested. North Carolina would not be interested, the court reasoned, in applying its law because, under the *lex loci delicti* rule followed in that state, a North Carolina court would have applied Kansas law. Thus, said the court, "any expectation General Motors had that the law of North Carolina would govern ... would not be justified"[242]. The court also invoked a similar Michigan case that found that Michigan had "little interest in applying its law when its only contact with the dispute is the location of the manufacturer"[243].

---

239. *Id.* at 1009-1010. The court disposed in a similar manner defendant's argument regarding plaintiff's contributory negligence, which would have reduced plaintiff's recovery under Kansas law. While noting that the record contained no evidence of plaintiff's contributory negligence or where such negligence occurred, the court concluded that Kansas's comparative negligence rule was loss-allocating rather than conduct-regulating and that Kansas had "no interest in allocating responsibility for the injuries suffered by Montana residents and caused by a product purchased in North Carolina". *Id.* at 1010.

240. *Id.*

241. *Id.*

242. *Phillips*, 995 P.2d at 1013.

243. *Id.* at 1011, citing *Farrell v. Ford Motor Co.* 501 NW 2d 567 (Mich. App. 1993), appeal denied, 519 NW 2d 158 (Mich. 1994). *Farrell* is discussed *supra* footnote 84. While it is true that some Michigan cases have reached this result, (see, e.g., *Hall v. Gen. Motors Corp.*, 582 NW 2d 866 (Mich.App. 1998) (discussed *supra* 221), other cases reached the opposite result (see, e.g., *Mahne v. Ford Motor Co*, 900 F.2d 83 (6th. Cir. 1990), cert. denied, 498 US 941 (1990), discussed *supra* 223). Moreover, in the Michigan

Even if Michigan had such an interest, the court reasoned, Michigan law should not be applied because its application "would tend to leave victims under compensated as states wishing to attract and hold manufacturing companies would raise the threshold of liability and reduce compensation"[244]. This would be "inherently unfair"[245], said the court, because it would allow a state with a high concentration of industry to "capture all of the benefits of a high threshold of liability and a low level of compensation ... by attract[ing] and retain[ing] manufacturing firms ... within its borders while placing the costs of its legislative decision, in the form of less tort compensation, on the shoulders of nonresidents injured by its manufacturers' products"[246].

Thus, after discounting the interests of the states of injury, conduct, and the defendant's domicile, the court considered the interests of the victims' home state, Montana, the law of which favored the victims on liability, as well as compensatory and punitive damages. The court found that Montana's interests predominated in all respects. After noting that Montana's strict liability standard was intended to "afford 'maximum protection for consumers ... [regardless of] the manufacturer's conduct or knowledge'"[247], the court stated that "the focus of Montana law is not only on the regulation of products sold in Montana, but also on providing the maximum protection and compensation to Montana residents"[248]. The court reasoned that, because the victims in this case were Montana residents, the application of Montana's law of strict liability and full compensation "would further the purposes of Montana law by insuring that the costs to Montana residents ... are fully borne by the responsible parties"[249] and would have "the salutary effect of deterring future sales of defective products in Montana and encouraging manufacturers to warn Montana residents about defects in their products as quickly and as thoroughly as possible"[250]. The court reasoned that the application of Montana's punitive-damages law would serve the same policy of deterrence because "punitive damages serve to punish and deter conduct deemed wrongful – in this case, placing a defective product into the stream of commerce which subsequently injured a Montana resident"[251]. Thus, the court concluded, Montana had a more significant relationship than Kansas and this displaced the *lex loci* presumption.

---

cases that did not apply Michigan law, Michigan law favored a foreign victim at the expense of a Michigan manufacturer. Thus, those cases did not present the converse and more difficult true-conflict between the pro-plaintiff law of the plaintiff's home state and the pro-manufacturer law of the state of manufacture.

244. *Phillips*, 995 P.2d at 1011-1012.
245. *Id.* at 1012.
246. *Id.*
247. *Id.* at 1012 (quoting *Sternhagen v. Dow Co.*, 935 P.2d 1139, 1144 (Mont. 1997)).
248. *Id.*
249. *Id.*
250. *Id.*
251. *Id.*

243. It is worth noting that, even under the most pro-plaintiff choice-of-law rules in the world, those of the Swiss, Italian, and Quebec codifications, *Phillips* would have been decided in favor of the defendant[252]. With regard to liability and compensatory damages, one can appreciate the *Phillips* result: besides the equities of the case (a whole family perishing with only one minor child surviving), the five contacts were spread in four states, the occurrence of the injury in Kansas was fortuitous, and the product, though purchased in North Carolina, was commercially available throughout the United States, including in Montana. On the other hand, one cannot defend *Phillips* to the extent it imposed punitive damages, at least beyond the limits imposed by Kansas law.

E.   General Observations

244. The cases discussed in this chapter are sufficiently numerous, methodologically and substantively diverse, and geographically dispersed to permit one to draw some general conclusions. This part of the chapter attempts to do so, beginning with a brief discussion of the role that state policies and factual contacts played in the courts' choice-of-law decisions.

1.   The role of state policies and interests

245. The 100 cases discussed here have been decided under a variety of choice-of-law methodologies, including primarily the Second Restatement, the significant-contacts approach, interest analysis, Leflar's better-law approach, as well as the traditional method. With the exception of cases decided under the traditional method, the majority of the other cases subscribe, explicitly or implicitly, to two basic premises: (1) that states do have an interest in the outcome of multistate product-liability disputes between private parties; and (2) to properly resolve these disputes, one should take account of these interests, albeit not to the exclusion of other factors, such as factual contacts and party expectations. Because of this, a casual observer might conclude that Brainerd Currie's interest analysis is still alive and well among the courts. However, such a conclusion would be inaccurate because the courts do not seem to subscribe to two essential ingredients of Currie's analysis: (a) his "personal-law" principle; and (b) the primacy of the *lex fori*.

As noted earlier, the personal-law principle describes Currie's assertion that a state always has an interest in protecting its own domiciliaries but is never interested in protecting similarly situated out-of-staters. As the preceding discussion in this chapter documents, very few cases subscribe to this self-centered proposition. For example, several cases (1) applied the forum's pro-plaintiff law even though that law favored a plaintiff who was not a forum domiciliary and

---

252. These codifications are discussed *infra* at 272.

disfavored a defendant affiliated with the forum state[253]; or (2) applied the forum's pro-defendant law for the benefit of a non-forum defendant and at the expense of a forum plaintiff[254].

Currie's approach assigned a primary role to the *lex fori*, because he argued that the law of the forum should govern, *inter alia*, in *all* true conflicts before an interested forum, and in all no-interest cases. As will be explained later[255], the vast majority of the 100 cases fall into one or the other of these two categories (called direct and inverse conflicts, respectively), yet only a slight majority of them (56%) applied the law of the forum.

For this reason, it is safe to conclude that, although many cases speak the language of interest analysis – or more accurately policy analysis – most cases do not subscribe to the most controversial specifics of the particular approach that Currie advocated. If anything, most courts seem to be more impressed with the number of factual contacts a state has with the case than with an advocate's sophisticated analysis of state interests. The discussion now turns to an inevitably tedious, yet necessary, "contacts analysis" of all the cases.

2.   A contacts analysis

246. This section looks at the cases from two slightly different perspectives: Subsection (a) looks at how the pertinent contacts were congregated or dispersed among the involved states, and with what frequency; Subsection (b) focuses on the contacts of the state whose law the court applied.

(a)   Aggregation of contacts and law applied

247. The reader who has the patience to count the cases depicted in Table 17, *supra*, will notice the high number of cases in which all three plaintiff-affiliating contacts were situated in one state – the product was sold in the plaintiff's home state and caused the injury in that state. More than a third of the cases (42 out of 100) fall in this category[256], and more than two thirds of them (33 out of 42 or 79%) applied the law of that state. That state was also the forum in 13 of those cases and had a pro-defendant law in 25 or 76% of the 33 cases. Chart 12, and Table 25, *infra*, depict these results.

---

253. See, e.g., cases ## 35-40, 53, 89-90, in Table 17, *supra*. See also case # 1, which applied non-forum law which favored a non-forum plaintiff and disfavored a forum defendant, and case # 9, which applied non-forum law which favored a non-forum defendant and disfavored a forum plaintiff.

254. See , e.g., cases ## 10-16, 48-49, 64-67, in Table 17, *supra*.

255. *See infra* 266-267.

256. See cases ## 1-42 in Table 17, *supra*. Nine of the 42 cases presented the direct conflict pattern because that state had a pro-plaintiff law, while the remaining 33 cases presented the inverse conflict pattern because that state had a pro-defendant law.

Chart 12. Cases in which the victim's home state was also the place of injury
and product acquisition

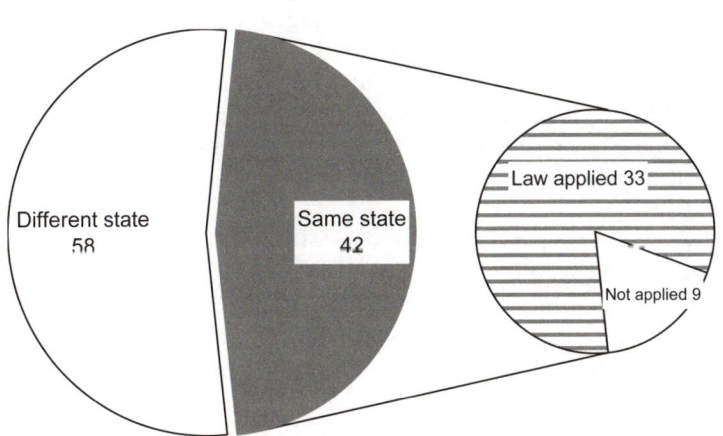

In 16 of the 100 cases, the injury occurred in the plaintiff's home state, but the product was acquired outside that state[257]. That state had a pro-plaintiff law in five cases, and the court applied it in all five cases. The same state had a pro-defendant law in 11 cases, and the court applied that law in five of those cases. Altogether, 10 of the 16 cases applied the law of the state of the victim's domicile and place of injury[258].

Table 25. Aggregation of contacts and law applied

Contacts	Cases and Law		Applied	Forum
Domicile Injury and Acquisition	All cases	42	33	13
	Pro-P	9	8	
	Pro-D	33	25	
Domicile and Injury	All cases	16	10	7
	Pro-P	5	5	
	Pro-D	11	5	
Domicile and Acquisition	All cases	14	10	8
	Pro-P	6	5	
	Pro-D	8	5	
Injury and Acquisition	All cases	16	10	1
	Pro-P	3	2	
	Pro-D	13	8	
The rest		12		
Totals		100		

---

257. See cases ## 43-58 in Tables 17, 20-21, *supra*.
258. See Table 25, *infra*.

In 14 of the 100 cases, the product was acquired in the plaintiff's home state, but the injury occurred elsewhere[259]. That state had a pro-plaintiff law in 6 cases and a pro-defendant law in 8 cases. Ten of the 14 cases applied that state's law.

In 16 of the 100 cases, the injury and the place of the product's acquisition were in the same state, but not the plaintiff's home state[260]. The former state had a pro-plaintiff law in three cases and a pro-defendant law in 13 cases. Ten of the 16 cases applied the law of that state, while the remaining six cases applied the law of the plaintiff's home state, which, in four of these cases, also had contacts with the defendant.

In the remaining 12 cases, the three plaintiff-affiliating contacts were located in three different states, although in 5 of those cases the defendant-affiliating contacts were located in the same state[261]. The five cases applied the law of the state with the defendant-affiliating contacts, while the remaining six cases applied the law of the plaintiff's home state, which did not have any other contact.

(b)   The contacts of the state whose law the court applied

248. The following table focuses on the state whose law the court applied. The first column shows the number of cases in which a patten occurred, and then the shaded cells show the number of cases in which the courts applied the laws of the states corresponding to those cells. The last four columns show the number of cases in which the law applied was that of the forum state, and whether it favored the plaintiff or the defendant.

---

259. See cases ## 59-72 in Tables 17, 22, *supra*.
260. See cases ## 73-88 in Tables 17, 23 *supra*.
261. See cases ## 89-100 in Tables 17, 24 *supra*.

Table 26. The contacts of the state whose law applied

Occurrences	P's Dom	Injury	Acqu.	Mnfg.	D's PPB	Forum	Non-Forum	Pro-P	Pro-D
Three contacts (41 cases)									
42		33				13	20	8	25
5			4			2	2	4	0
2	2			2		1	1	1	1
1		1		1		1	0	0	1
1			1		1	0	1	0	1
Two contacts only (42 cases)									
16	10					7	3	5	5
14	10		10			8	2	5	5
16		9				1	8	2	7
1				1		1	0	1	0
65				10		6	4	8	2
3	2				2	2	0	2	0
One contact only (15 cases)									
--	8					7	1	8	0
--			3			2	1	3	0
--		4				3	1	3	1
No contact (2 cases)									
2						2	0	2	0
Cases	65	58	61	18	20	56	44	52	48

249. *Three Contacts.* As the above table indicates, 41 of the 100 cases applied the law of a state that had three of the five contacts identified as pertinent in this Article. (See the shaded cells).

In 33 of those cases, the three contacts were the plaintiff's domicile, the place of injury, and the place of the product's acquisition[262]. In 13 of those cases, that state was also the forum state. It had a pro-plaintiff law in 8 cases and a pro-defendant law in 25 cases.

In 4 of the 41 cases, the three contacts were the place of the product's acquisition, the place of manufacture, and the defendant's principal place of business[263]. In all four cases, that state had a pro-plaintiff law, and in two of them it was also the forum state.

In the remaining 4 cases, the three contacts were congregated as shown in Table 17, *supra*[264].

---

262. See cases ## 1-8, 9-34, in Tables 17, 18, *supra*.
263. See cases ## 53-55, 89, in Tables 17, 21, 24, *supra*.
264. See cases ## 75, 83-84, 93 in Tables 17, 23, 24, *supra*.

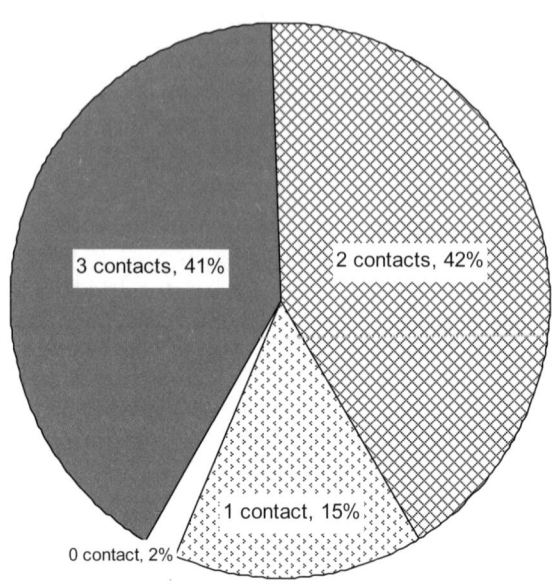

Chart 13. Number of contacts of state whose law applied

250. *Two contacts.* In 42 of the 100 cases, the court applied the law of a state that had two contacts, as follows: (a) the plaintiff's domicile and the place of injury in 10 cases[265]; (b) the plaintiff's domicile and the place of the product's acquisition in 10 cases[266]; (c) the place of injury and the product's acquisition in 9 cases[267]; (d) the defendant's principal place of business and the place of manufacture in 10 cases[268]; (e) the plaintiff's and the defendant's domiciles in two cases[269]; and (e) the places of manufacture and acquisition in one case[270].

251. *One contact.* Fifteen of the 100 cases applied the law of a state that had only one contact[271]. In all but one of those cases, that state had a pro-plaintiff law.

265. See cases ## 43-52 in Table 17, 20, 21, *supra*. In 7 of these cases, that state was also the forum; in 5 cases it had a pro-plaintiff law; and in 5 cases it had a pro-defendant law.

266. See cases ## 59-68, in Table 17, 22, *supra*. In 8 of those cases, that state was also the forum; it had a pro-plaintiff law in 5 cases and a pro-defendant law in 5 cases.

267. See cases ## 73-74, 76-82 in Tables 17, 23, *supra*. In 7 of those cases, that state had a pro-defendant law.

268. See cases ## 9, 35-40, 56 and 91-92 in Table 17, *supra*. In 6 of those cases, that state was also the forum, and in 8 cases it had a pro-plaintiff law.

269. See cases # 85 and 86, in Tables 17, 23, *supra*. In the latter case, the parties' domiciles were in different states but the two states had the same law, which was equally different from the law of the state of injury.

270. See case # 90, in Table 17, *supra*. That state was also the forum and had a pro-plaintiff law.

271. See cases ## 57-58, 69-72, 87-88, and 94-100, in Table 17, *supra*.

In 8 of those cases, the five pertinent contacts were dispersed in four or five states. In 8 of the cases, that state was the plaintiff's home state and had a pro-plaintiff law and in 7 cases it was also the forum state[272].

In 77 of the 100 cases, the court applied the law of a state that had only plaintiff-affiliating contacts, but in 43 or 56% of those cases that state had a pro-defendant law[273]. In 10 of the 100 cases, the court applied the law of a state that had only defendant-affiliating contacts, but in 8 of those cases that state had a pro-plaintiff law. In 11 of the 100 cases, the court applied the law of a state that had both plaintiff- and defendant-affiliating contacts, and in 9 of those cases that state had a pro- plaintiff law[274].

(1)   Plaintiff-affiliating contacts and laws

252. *Plaintiff's domicile.* In 65 of the 100 cases, the court applied the law of a state in which the plaintiff was domiciled[275]. However, in all but 8 of those cases, that state had one or two additional contacts[276]. This is not a tilt towards the plaintiff because, in more than half of those cases (36 cases out of 65 or 55%), that state had a pro-defendant law. In any event, the plaintiff's domicile, especially when coupled with another contact, appears to be an important contact in product liability conflicts.

---

272. In two cases, that state was the place of the product's acquisition and also the forum and had a pro-plaintiff law. In four cases, that state was the place of the injury and it had a pro-plaintiff law in three of the cases. Finally, two cases applied the law of a state that had none of the pertinent contacts besides being the forum. One of these cases, *Glover* (case #41), did so on the ground that the issue at stake (statute of limitations) was a procedural one, and the second case, *Stupak* v. *Hoffman-La Roche, Inc.* (case # 42), applied forum law because the products liability claim was closely interconnected with a medical malpractice claim that was governed by forum law.
273. In 33 of the 100 cases, the court applied the law of a state that had all three plaintiff-affiliating contacts, but in 25 or 76% of those cases that state had a pro-defendant law. In 29 cases, the court applied the law of a state that had two plaintiff-affiliating contacts, but in 17 or 59% of those cases that state had a pro-defendant law. Fifteen cases applied the law of a state that had only one plaintiff-affiliating contact, and in 14 of those cases that state had a pro-plaintiff law. Eight of the 15 cases applied the pro-plaintiff law of the plaintiff's home state, which in 7 of those cases was also the forum state. Two cases applied the pro-plaintiff law of the state of the product's acquisition, one case applied the pro-plaintiff law of the state of injury and another state applied the pro-defendant law of the state of injury.
274. In the remaining two cases (cases ## 41-42), the court applied the law of the forum state which had none of the contacts considered pertinent in this chapter, although it did have the contacts necessary for the court's jurisdiction.
275. See chart 14, *infra*.
276. It had two additional contacts in 35 cases, and one additional contact in 22 cases. See Chart 14, *infra*.

Chart 14. Cases applying the law of the state with the listed contacts

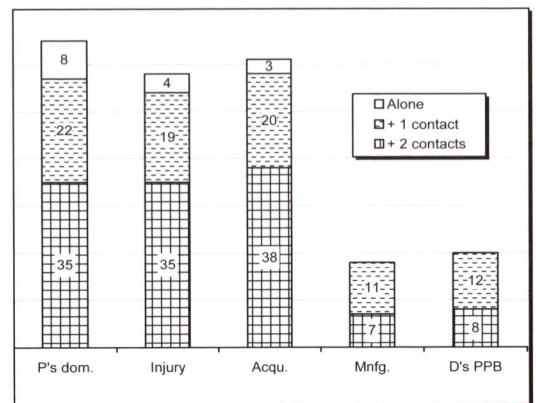

253. *Place of injury.* In 58 of the 100 cases, the court applied the law of the state in which the injury occurred[277]. This does not entail a return to the *lex loci* rule. Although it suggests that the place of the injury remains an important contact, this is true only when the state of the injury has at least one additional contact. Indeed, in all but four of the 58 cases, the state of injury had one or two additional contacts[278]. In any event, the application of the law of the state of injury favored defendants by a wide margin (40 of the 58 cases or 69%).

254. *Place of the product's acquisition.* In 61 of the 100 cases, the court applied the law of a state that was the place of the product's acquisition, but in all but three of those cases that state had one or two additional contacts[279]. Again, this is not a tilt toward the plaintiff because, in 38 or 62% of the 61 cases, that state's law favored the defendant. In any event, the place of acquisition has gradually gained in significance, although this significance varies considerably from case to case. As suggested at the beginning of the chapter, this contact is more important in cases involving consumer goods and other similar products acquired by the victim. It is less important in cases involving other products, such as transportation means or machinery acquired by a third party.

(2) Defendant-affiliating contacts and laws

255. In 65 of the 100 cases, the two defendant-affiliating contacts – the place of manufacture and the defendant's principal place of business – were in the same state. Yet, only 10 or of those cases applied the law of a state that had *only* those

---

277. See chart 14, *supra.*
278. The state of injury had two additional contacts in 35 cases, and one additional contact in 19 cases.
279. The state of acquisition had two additional contacts in 38 cases, and one additional contact in 20 cases. See chart 14, *supra.*

contacts and no others[280]. One reason for this low number is the fact that in most cases the defendants did not plead the law of that state (apparently because it was unfavorable) and instead relied on the more favorable law of a state with a plaintiff-affiliating contact. In many cases, it was the plaintiffs who invoked the law of the defendants' state and in some cases the plaintiffs prevailed – in 8 of the 10 cases, that state had a pro-plaintiff law. The second reason for the low numbers is the relative insignificance of one of these two contacts, i.e., the defendant's principal place of business, at least when compared to the other four contacts. This issue is discussed later.

State of manufacture. Only 18 of the 100 cases applied the law of the state of manufacture, but in all of them that state had either two additional contacts (7 cases) or one additional contact (11 cases). In 14 of the 18 cases, that state had a pro-plaintiff law.

Defendant's principal place of business. Only 20 of the 100 cases applied the law of the state of the defendant's principal place of business, but in all of them that state had either two additional contacts[281] or one additional contact[282]. Stated another way, no case applied the law of the manufacturer's principal place of business *as such.* Of the five pertinent contacts, this one appears to be the least significant, and appropriately so. In any event, in 15 of the 20 cases, the state of the defendant's principal place of business had a pro-plaintiff law.

3.   Forum shopping is neither common nor rewarding

256. The 100 cases of the survey period do not confirm the widespread impression that product-liability plaintiffs engage in rampant forum shopping. Obviously, the validity of this observation depends on one's definition of forum shopping[283], as well as the size and nature of the sample examined[284]. If one defines forum shopping as to include all cases in which the plaintiff sues in a state that has a favorable substantive law, then one could conclude that plaintiffs do engage in forum

---

280. Ten additional cases applied the law of a state that had one or both of those contacts *and* a plaintiff-affiliating contact.

281. This was so in 8 cases. The two additional contacts were the places of manufacture and acquisition (4 cases), the place of manufacture and the plaintiff's domicile (two cases), the places of manufacture and injury (one case), and the places of injury and acquisition (one case).

282. This was so in 12 cases. In 10 of those cases, the additional contact was the place of manufacture.

283. "Forum shopping is not a term of art". J. Fawcett, "Products Liability in Private International Law: A European Perspective", 238 *Recueil des Cours* 9, 96 (1993).

284. This Chapter is confined to cases that resulted in a choice-of-law decision that is either published or reported in Westlaw. One could argue that, insofar as courts dispose of many forum-shopping suits without issuing such a decision, this Chapter's sample is not representative enough with regard to this specific issue.

shopping inasmuch as in 79 of the 100 cases the forum state had a pro-plaintiff substantive law[285].

However, a more precise definition of forum shopping should encompass only those cases in which a plaintiff unfairly exploits the jurisdictional rules to sue in a state that does not have relevant contacts other than the jurisdictional nexus with the defendant (e.g., "doing business" and nothing else)[286]. Under this definition, *only five of the 100 cases involved forum shopping*. Two of these cases were filed in Mississippi in order to take advantage of that state's long statute of limitations[287], two cases were filed in Minnesota to take advantage of that state's better-law approach[288], and one case was filed in Pennsylvania to take advantage of that state's substantive law[289]. Two additional cases might qualify as "borderline" forum-shopping cases in that the forum's contacts were somewhat tenuous[290]. Even if one adds these cases, the percentage of forum-shopping cases rises to only 7%[291]. In any event, in 6 of the 7 cases, the plaintiff's forum shopping attempt did *not* succeed because the courts applied the pro-defendant law of a state other than the forum. It succeeded in the eighth case[292], but only because the federal court felt bound by state precedent that characterized the particular issue (statute of limitations) as procedural and thus as automatically governed by forum law.

257. On the other hand, when a plaintiff sues a defendant in a state with defendant-affiliating contacts (e.g., a state that is the manufacturer's principal place of business or the place of manufacture), the plaintiff does not unfairly exploit

---

285. This includes two federal transfer cases (*Roll* and *Thornton*) in which the original forum (transferor) had a pro-plaintiff law.

286. See Fawcett, *supra* footnote 283 at 97 ("[T]he defendant may be greatly inconvenienced in having to defend in a forum with which the parties and the dispute have little or no connection").

287. See *Bonti* v. *Ford Motor Co.*, 898 F. Supp. 391 (SD Miss. 1995), aff'd without op., 85 F.3d 625 (5th Cir. 1996) (discussed *supra* footnote 162), and *Walls* v. *Gen. Motors*, 906 F.2d 143 (5th Cir.1990) (discussed *supra* footnote 68).

288. See *Nesladek* v. *Ford Motor Co.*, 46 F.3d 734 (8th Cir. 1995), cert. denied, 516 U.S. 814 (1995) (discussed *supra* 219); *Glover* v. *Merck & Co., Inc.*, 345 F.Supp.2d 994 (D Minn. 2004) (discussed *supra* footnote 111).

289. See *Jones* v. *Cooper Tire & Rubber Co.*, 2004 WL 503588 (ED Pa. 2004) (discussed *supra* 219).

290. These contacts were, respectively, the place of the product's assembly (see *Rutherford*, case #27), and the principal place of business of a defendant who owned the defective equipment (see *Cianfrani*, case #81).

291. See Chart 15, *infra*. The chart indicates that in a total of 8 (rather than 7) out of the 100 cases the forum had none of the contacts considered pertinent here. However, in one of those cases, *Stupak* v. *Hoffman-La Roche, Inc.* (case #42), the forum had other contacts that negated the forum-shopping accusation. As discussed at footnote 111, *supra*, the product-liability claim in *Stupak* was closely interwoven with a medical malpractice claim that had all the pertinent contacts with the forum state

292. See *Glover* v. *Merck & Co., Inc.*, 345 F.Supp.2d 994 (D Minn. 2004) (discussed *supra* footnote 111).

the jurisdictional rules since the defendant can hardly complain for being forced to litigate at home[293]. More than a fourth of the cases (29 out of 100) were filed in states with defendant-affiliating contacts. Although in 23 of the 29 cases the forum had a pro-plaintiff law, the court applied that law in only 11 cases[294].

258. Conversely, when the plaintiff sues in a state with plaintiff-affiliating contacts (i.e., places of domicile, injury, or acquisition), the defendant may be subject to a certain degree of inconvenience depending on remoteness and other factors. However, this inconvenience is a fair price to pay in exchange for selling products in the forum's market[295]. When a consumer injured by one of these products exercises her right to sue in that state, the consumer is not necessarily engaging in inappropriate forum shopping, especially if that state has more than one of the above five contacts. In this context, one should note that, except for the eight aforementioned cases of actual or suspected forum shopping[296], in all the other cases in which the forum had a pro-plaintiff law, that state had at least one additional contact – three such contacts in 12 cases, two contacts in 29 cases, and one contact in 29 cases.

---

293. See, e.g., *Gantes* v. *Kason Corp.*, 679 A.2d 106 (N J1996) (discussed *supra* 222; rejecting the lower court's conclusion that a Georgia plaintiff who sued a New Jersey manufacturer for a Georgia injury caused by a product manufactured in New Jersey was engaging in forum shopping: "In essence, the policy against forum shopping is intended to ensure that New Jersey courts are not burdened with cases that have only 'slender ties' to New Jersey... . In this case, plaintiff does not seek to use New Jersey's court system to litigate a dispute that has only a slight link to New Jersey and where the only plausible reason to select this State is because it is a hospitable forum. This action is materially connected to New Jersey by the fact that the allegedly defective product was manufactured in and then shipped from this State by the defendant-manufacturer". *Id.* at 113).

294. See Chart 16, *infra*.

295. Cf. J. Fawcett, "Products Liability in Private International Law: A European Perspective", 238 *Recueil des Cours* 9, 97 (1993) ("The defendant has no ... cause to complain if the forum is one which has a strong connection with the parties and the dispute".).

296. As noted *supra* footnote 291, in one of those cases (*Stupak*) the forum did not have the pertinent contacts, but nevertheless this was not a forum-shopping case.

Chart 15. Forum's contacts and forum shopping

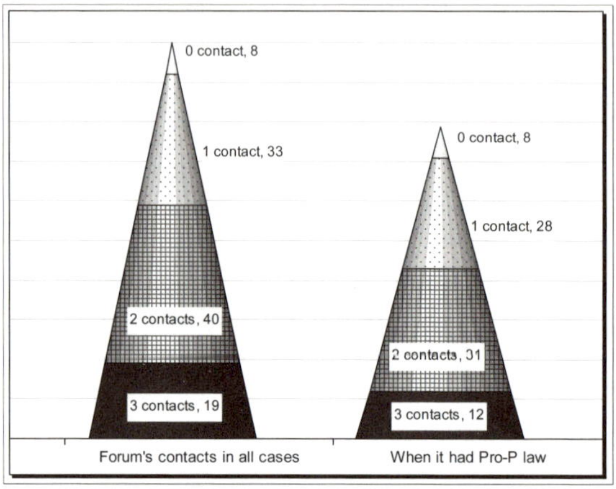

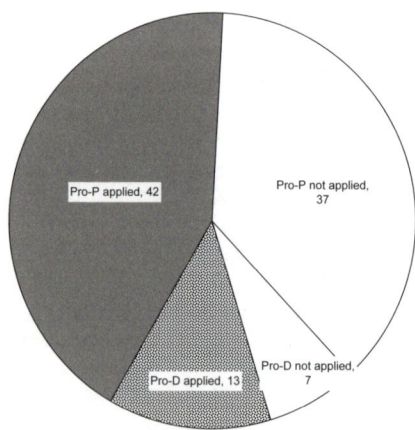

0 contact, 8

1 contact, 33

0 contact, 8

1 contact, 28

2 contacts, 40

2 contacts, 31

3 contacts, 19

3 contacts, 12

Forum's contacts in all cases   When it had Pro-P law

260. More importantly, even if one adopts the broadest definition of forum shopping to include all cases in which plaintiffs sue in states that have pro-plaintiff laws, this strategy does not succeed as frequently as one might think. Of the 79 cases in which the forum had a pro-plaintiff law, the court applied that law in only 42 cases or 53%[297] In contrast, of the 20 cases in which the forum had a pro-defendant law, the court applied that law in 13 cases or 65%. Thus, defendants have had a better chance in persuading a court to apply its pro-defendant law than plaintiffs had in persuading the court to apply its pro-plaintiff law[298].

Chart 16. Forum's law and law applied

Pro-P applied, 42

Pro-P not applied, 37

Pro-D applied, 13

Pro-D not applied, 7

---

297. In addition, one of the federal transfer cases, *Roll*, applied the law of the transferee state, which was identical to the law of the transferor state.

298. See Chart 16, *infra*

4.   Plaintiffs tend to sue at or close to home

261. The assumption that American courts are a magnet for foreign products-liability plaintiffs is both widespread and plausible. Nevertheless, of the 100 cases of this period, only 7 cases were filed by foreign plaintiffs and in all 7 cases the plaintiffs were domiciliaries of neighboring countries – Mexico or Canada. On the whole, the 100 cases suggest that most product-liability plaintiffs tend to sue close to home. Only 29 of the 100 cases were filed in defendant-affiliated states[299]. This may be because of distance and inconvenience (more likely the attorney's) since the manufacturer-affiliated states do not seem to have pro-defendant laws. In fact, in 63% of the cases that reveal the law of the state of manufacture (37 out of 59 cases), that state had a pro-plaintiff law.

Chart 17. Forum's contacts

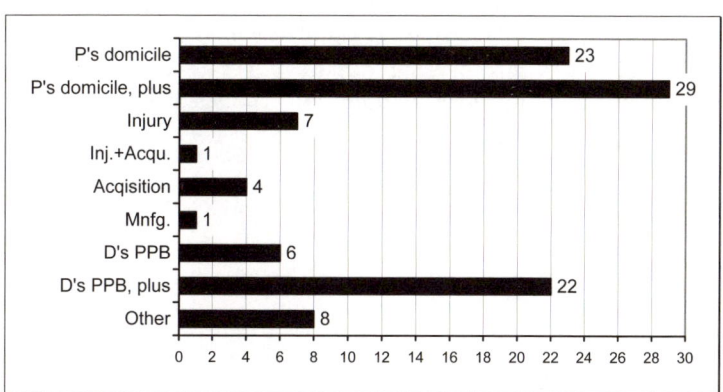

In 53 of the 100 cases, the plaintiffs sued in their home states. In more than half of those cases (29 out of 53) that state had either one additional contact (16 cases) or two additional contacts (13 cases).

In 38 or 72% of the 53 cases in which the plaintiffs sued in their home state, that state had a pro-plaintiff law. The court applied that law in 26 or 68% of the 38 cases. Perhaps more noteworthy are the remaining 15 of the 53 cases in which the plaintiffs sued in their home states even though their laws favored the defendants. Not surprisingly, 12 of those cases applied that state's law.

---

299. See Chart 17, *infra*. As this chart indicates, in 22 cases, the forum state was both the defendant's principal place of business and the place of manufacture. In 6 cases, the forum was the defendant's principal place of business, and in one case the place of manufacture. In all but 5 of the 29 cases, the forum state had a pro-plaintiff law, which the court applied in 11 cases.

In 12 of the 100 cases, the action was filed in states with other plaintiff-affiliating contacts, such as the place of injury[300]. The remaining 7 cases are the forum-shopping cases described earlier, which were filed in states that did not have any of the five contacts identified as pertinent in this chapter.

5.   No pro-plaintiff bias

262. The cases of this period do *not* support the widely-held assumption that, in their choice-of-law decisions, courts favor plaintiffs as a class. Plaintiffs continue to fare better in state courts[301], while defendants fare slightly better in federal courts[302], but on the whole the number of cases that applied a pro-plaintiff law (52 cases) barely exceeded the number of cases that applied a pro-defendant law (48 cases)[303]. Whether this is the outgrowth of the "tort reform" movement of the 1980s, or a series of conservative appointments to the federal bench during the same period, or a combination of these and other factors is unclear. What seems clear is that, at the beginning of the 21st century, products liability plaintiffs encounter more difficulties in recovering from manufacturers than in previous decades. This is as true in multistate as in domestic products liability litigation[304].

---

300. Seven cases were filed in the state of injury and three of them applied the law of that state. Four cases were filed in the state of the product's acquisition. In all four cases, that state had a pro-plaintiff law, which the court applied in three cases. One case (*Beals*) was filed in a state that was both the place of injury and the product's acquisition.

301. Of the 100 cases of this period, 43 cases were decided by state courts. They applied a pro-plaintiff law in 25 cases or 58%.

302. Of the 100 cases of this period, 57 cases were decided by federal courts. They applied a pro-defendant law in 29 cases or 51%.

303. See Chart 18, *infra*.

304. According to Reimann, "American products liability law has become distinctly more cautious in the 1980s and 1990s... . [C]ourts have become significantly more conservative in practice. After favoring plaintiffs and pushing the boundaries of liability for decades, as of the 1980s, they began to protect defendants, refused to expand liability further, and in fact often retreated to earlier positions". M. Reimann, "Liability for Defective Products and Services: Emergence of a Worldwide Standard?" *General Report to the XVIth Int'l Congress of Comp. L.*, 52 (Brisbane 2002).

Chart 18. Do courts favor plaintiffs?

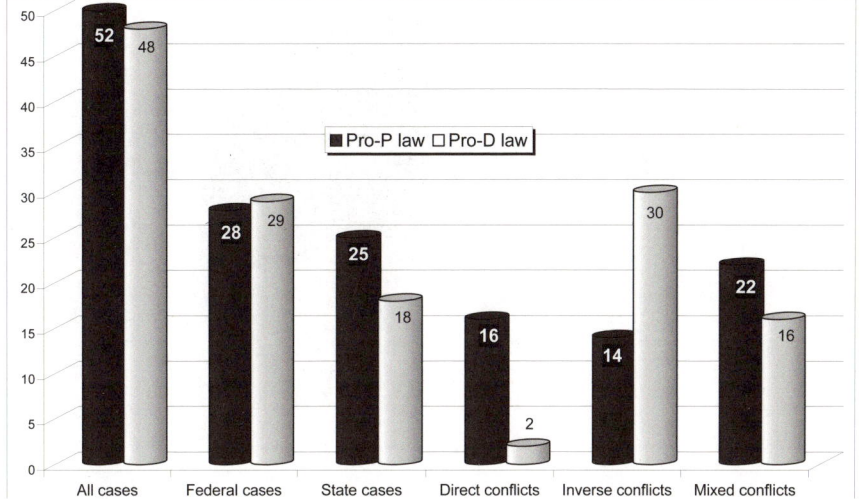

263. Plaintiffs do enjoy a significant advantage in direct or true conflicts. Of the 18 conflicts that fall within this category, 16 applied a pro-plaintiff law[305]. However, the inverse conflicts, which are more numerous, close the gap. Of the 44 cases that fall in this category, 30 cases applied a pro-defendant law[306].

Even if one focuses only on the cases in which the forum had a pro-plaintiff law (78 out of 100 cases), the plaintiff's success was short of spectacular. Only 42 of the 78 cases, i.e., 54%, applied that law. The remaining 46% applied the law of another state that favored the defendant.

264. Thus, it is more accurate to say that most courts apply the law of a state or states that have plaintiff-affiliating contacts (domicile, injury, and acquisition), *whether or not* that law favors the plaintiff. Indeed, as noted earlier, 77 of the 100 cases applied the law of a state with the plaintiff-affiliating contacts, but in 43 or 56% of those cases that state had a pro-defendant law.

6. No favoritism towards forum domiciliaries

265. Another surprising finding is the apparent lack of favoritism towards the local litigant (plaintiff or defendant). As the following chart illustrates, only 41 of the 100 cases applied a law that favored the local litigant. Of these cases, 28 favored a local plaintiff and 13 favored a local defendant.

---

305. Plaintiffs also enjoyed an advantage in mixed conflicts. Of the 38 cases that fall in this category, 22 cases applied a pro-plaintiff law and 16 applied a pro-defendant law.

306. For example, in 21 or 64% of the 33 inverse conflicts in which the forum had a pro-plaintiff law, the court applied the law of another state that favored the defendant.

Chart 19. Do courts favor local litigants?

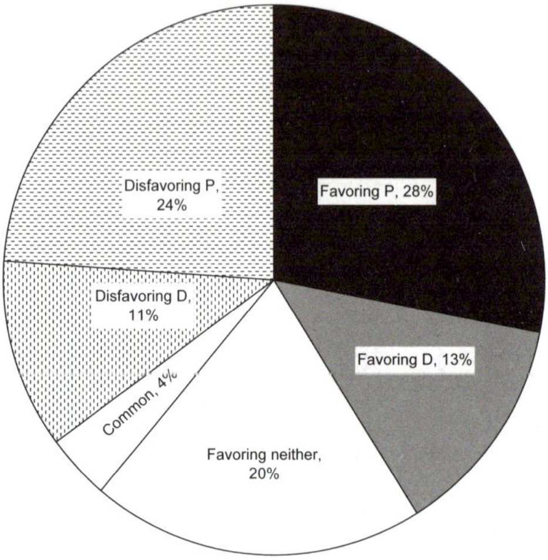

Even more surprising, a comparable number of cases, 35 out of 100, applied a law that *disfavored* the local litigant. Of these cases, 24 cases applied a law that disfavored a local plaintiff, and 11 cases applied a law that disfavored a local defendant[307] .

7. No pro-forum law bias

266. Another widely held assumption is that "courts employing the new [choice-of-law] theories have a very strong preference for forum law that frequently causes them to manipulate the theories so that they end up applying forum law"[308].

The 100 cases of this period do not support this assumption. Although the cases that applied forum law outnumber the cases that applied foreign law, the margin is too narrow to justify the above assumption. Of the 100 cases of this period, 56 applied forum law, and 44 applied foreign law[309]. The margin is even narrower if one excludes the three federal-transfer cases that applied the law of the transferee forum[310]. Moreover, in most of these cases, the forum state had significant aggregations of contacts that could justify the application of its law,

---

307. Of the remaining 24 cases, 20 cases applied a law that neither favored nor disfavored a local litigant and 4 cases applied a law that was common to both litigants.

308. *Sutherland* v. *Kennington Truck Serv., Ltd.*, 562 NW2d 466, 469-70 (Mich. 1997).

309. Federal courts applied forum law less frequently (49%) than state courts (67%). Of the 57 cases decided by federal courts, 28 cases applied forum law. Of the 43 cases decided by state courts, 29 cases applied forum law. See chart 21, *infra.*

310. The three cases are *Nelson* (#7), *Thornton* (#67), and *Roll* (#73). As noted earlier, see *supra* footnote 26, it is unclear whether these cases should be counted in or outside of the Currie column.

even if it was not the forum, and regardless of the choice-of-law theory the court followed. The forum state had three additional contacts in 17 cases, two additional contacts in 22 cases, and one additional contact in 15 cases[311].

Chart 20. Law applied and forum's contacts when applying its law

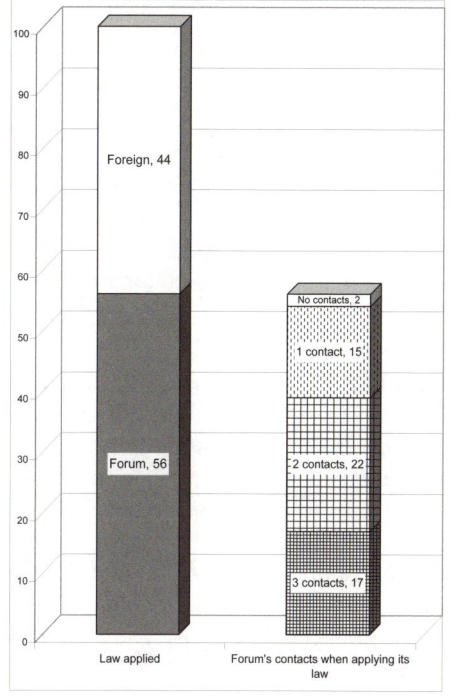

267. These numbers also exhibit lack of judicial support for Brainerd Currie's strong advocacy of the law of the forum. As noted earlier, Currie argued that the law of the forum should govern in all true conflicts in which the forum was one of the interested states and in all no-interest cases. According to Currie's assumptions about state interests, 62 of the 100 cases fall within one or the other of these categories and thus *all* 62 cases should be governed by the law of the forum. Instead only slightly half of those cases (32 out of 62 or 52%) applied forum law. Table 27 and Chart 21, *infra*, show the specifics.

---

311. See Chart 20, *infra*. In the remaining two cases, the forum did not have any one of the four pertinent contacts.

Table 27. Conflicts patterns and law applied

Pattern		Law applied	
Direct conflicts (True conflicts)	18	Forum	12 (67%)
		Non-forum	6 (33%)
Inverse conflicts (No-interest cases)	44	Forum	20 (45%)
		Non-forum	24 (54%)
Mixed conflicts	38	Forum	24 (63%)
		Non-forum	14 (37%)
Totals	100	Forum law	56 (56%)
		Non-forum law	44 (44%)

Direct or true conflicts. In 18 cases, the state with the plaintiff-affiliating contacts had a pro-plaintiff law and the state with the defendant-affiliating contacts had a pro-defendant law[312]. Under Currie's assumptions, these cases would qualify as true conflicts and all of them should be governed by the law of the forum. Indeed, 12 of those cases applied the law of the forum, but 6 cases did not.

Inverse conflicts or no-interest cases. In 44 cases, the state with the plaintiff-affiliating contacts had a pro-defendant law and the state with the defendant-affiliating contacts had a pro-plaintiff law[313]. Under Currie's assumptions, these cases would fall into the no-interest category, and *all* of them should be governed by the law of the forum. In fact, less than half of these cases (20 out of 44, or 45%) applied the law of the forum.

---

312. See cases ## 1-9, 43-47, 73-74, 92 and 94 in Table 17, *supra.*
313. See cases ## 10-42 and 48-58 in Table 17, *supra.*

Chart 21. Cases applying forum and foreign law

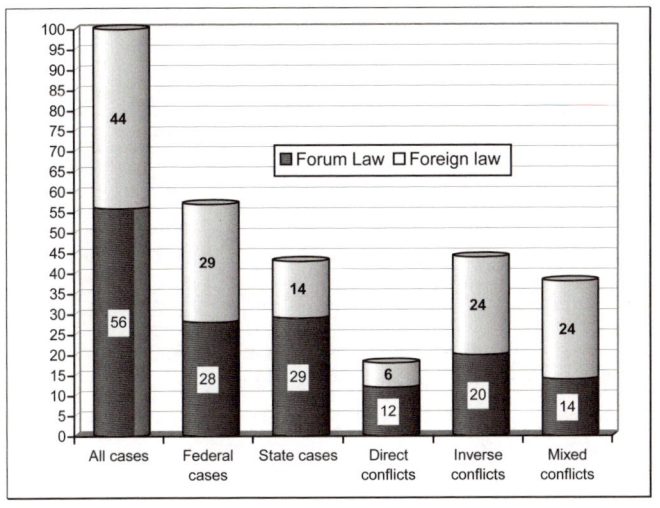

Mixed conflicts. The remaining 38 cases fell within the mixed conflict pattern because at least one of the plaintiff-affiliating contacts was located in a state that had a pro-plaintiff law and at least one such contact was located in a state with a pro-defendant law[314]. Under Currie's scheme all these cases would fall in either the true conflict category or the no-interest category and thus all of them should be governed by the law of the forum. In fact only 24 of the 38 cases applied forum law.

Thus, the cases as a whole do not support the impressionistic assertion that courts manipulate all modern choice-of-law approaches looking for excuses to apply the law of the forum.

8.   *No surprise to manufacturers*

268. As said above, several cases applied the pro-plaintiff law of a state with plaintiff-affiliating contacts, and in a few of those cases that state had only one such contact (e.g., the plaintiff's domicile). Yet in none of these cases, including the nine cases involving non-U.S. manufacturers[315], nor in any of the other cases, did the defendants assert that the product was unavailable in that state through ordinary commercial channels.

---

314. *See* cases ## 59-72, 75-91, 93, and 95-100 in Table 17, *supra*.
315. See cases ## 2-3, 17, 49, 57, 61, 82, 87-88 in Table 17, *supra*.

9.   The cases, on the whole

269. On the whole, the results of the cases appear pleasingly but suspiciously symmetrical: the cases that applied a pro-plaintiff law barely outnumber the cases that applied a pro-defendant law (52:48); the cases that applied the law of the forum outnumber by only a slim margin the cases that applied foreign law (56:44); and the number of cases that applied a law favoring a local litigant was not much higher than the number of cases that applied a law disfavoring a local litigant (41:35).

Does the symmetry of these numbers mean that the results are objectively good? Not necessarily. Suppose for example that (a) several cases that, by some objective standard, should have applied a pro-plaintiff law applied instead a pro-defendant law: and (b) that an equal number of cases that should have applied a pro-defendant law applied instead a pro-plaintiff law. In such a scenario, the fact that the "wrong" cases in the one group would cancel the "wrong" cases in the second group does not mean that the aggregate result is objectively good, especially from the perspective of the losing litigant in the "wrong" cases. For this reason, this chapter does not contend that each and every one of the 100 cases has been "correctly" decided, nor that all cases together have been correctly decided. The sole contention of this chapter is that, on the whole, the cases do not support certain widely held assumptions about the current state of American conflicts law, at least in product-liability conflicts. Despite impressions to the contrary, *courts do not favor plaintiffs as a class; courts do not favor local over non-local litigants; and courts do not unduly favor the law of the forum.*

The next question, and arguably the more pertinent one, is whether these results – whether they are good or bad – could have been reached more quickly and efficiently. The balance of the chapter addresses this question by examining first the extent to which any of the existing or proposed choice-of-law rules for product-liability conflicts would have produced the same results. The chapter concludes by proposing a new rule that seems to hold that promise.

F.   Comparison with Rules

270. Most of the above cases have been decided without the aid or the restraints of choice-of-law rules[316]. It might be helpful to inquire as to how these cases would have been decided if American courts were bound by rules, such as those in force elsewhere in the world. This section undertakes a brief inquiry to this end, beginning with the 1973 Hague Convention on the Law Applicable to Products Liability, and including some recent civilian codifications.

---

316. Only the Louisiana cases were decided under a statutory choice-of-law rule, La.Civ. Code Art. 3545.

1. The Hague Convention

271. The Hague Convention[317] provides that the law of the state of the victim's habitual residence governs, if that state is also: (a) the defendant's principal place of business; or (b) the place where the victim acquired the product[318]. If these conditions are not met, then the law of the state of injury governs, if that state is also: (a) the victim's habitual residence; or (b) the defendant's principal place of business; or (c) the place where the victim acquired the product[319]. When none of the above conditions are met, the victim may choose between the law of the state of injury and the law of the defendant's principal place of business[320].

If the Hague Convention had been adopted in the United States, it would have produced the same results as the American courts reached in 70 of the 100 cases [321]. This may come as a surprise to many, considering the fact that the Convention is based on a straight forward quantitative approach that eschews policy analysis and all the complications that go with it. Whether or not one likes the Convention *or* the results reached by the courts, one cannot ignore the fact that the Convention would have produced the same results, good or bad, in 70% of the cases, but with much less expenditure of judicial resources than in the actual cases. One might even predict that, had the Convention or a similar rule-system been in force in the United States, many of these cases would have been settled without litigation, thus conserving even more judicial resources.

However, before passing judgment on the Conventions, one should inquire as to how the Convention would have resolved *the remaining* 30 cases. It turns out that, in 25 of those cases, the Convention would have changed the result from pro-plaintiff to pro-defendant, and in two cases it would have changed the result in the opposite direction[322]. Because of these changes, the Convention would have produced a pro-defendant result in 73 cases and a pro-plaintiff result in 24 cases[323]. Thus the defendants would fare much better under the Convention than they did in the actual cases (73% vs 48%). This is one reason the Convention will never enjoy the support, or even the neutrality, of American trial lawyers.

---

317. The Convention is in force in ten European countries (Croatia, Finland, FYROM, France, Luxembourg, Netherlands, Norway, Slovenia, Spain, and Yugoslavia). See Conférence de La Haye de droit international privé, *Recueil des conventions* (1951-96).

318. *See* Convention Art. 5.

319. *Id.* Art. 4.

320. *Id.* Art. 6. The defendant may prevent the application of the law of the place of injury or of the victim's habitual residence by proving that he could not reasonably have foreseen that the product that caused the injury or his products of the same type would be made available in those states through commercial channels. *Id.* Art. 7.

321. See chart 22, *infra*.

322. In three cases, the change cannot be determined because the cases do not provide sufficient information.

323. See Chart 23, *infra*.

2.   Civilian codifications

272. Among recent private international law codifications, the Swiss and Italian codifications give the victim a choice between the laws of: (a) the state of the defendant's place of business or, in the absence thereof, his habitual residence; or (b) the state in which the product was acquired, "unless the defendant proves that the product has been marketed in that state without his consent"[324]. The Quebec codification gives the victim the same choices, but without the above quoted proviso[325].

Of the 100 cases discussed in this chapter, 32 cases do not provide sufficient information from which to determine how the victims would have exercised their choice. The application of the above codifications in the remaining 68 cases would have produced the same result in 35 cases, and a different result in 33 cases[326]. Because of the differences in the latter cases, these codifications would produce a pro-plaintiff result in 61 or 90% of 68 cases that provide sufficient information, and a pro-defendant result in only seven of those cases[327]. Even if one adds all of the 32 undeterminable cases to the pro-defendant column, the ratio would still be 61 to 39 in favor of plaintiffs.

3.   Professor Cavers's rule

273. Among academic commentators, the first to propose a choice-of-law rule for products liability was Professor David Cavers[328]. His rule would allow the plaintiff to choose from among the laws of: (a) the place of the product's production or ap-

---

324. *See* Swiss PIL Act of 1987, Art. 135; Italian PIL Act of 1995, Art. 63.

325. *See* Quebec Civ. Code, Art. 3128.The Russian codification adds a third choice – the victim's habitual residence or principal place of activity (subject to the same proviso). See Civil Code of the Russian Federation, Art. 1221 (federal law n. 146 of 26 November 2001, Rossyiskaya Gazeta, n. 49 item 4553, 28/11/2001). The Tunisian codification adds a fourth choice – the place of injury (without the proviso). See Code of Private International Law (Law N. 98-97 of 27 November 1998), Art. 72, Official Journal of the Republic of Tunisia, 1 December p. 2332.

326. See Chart 22, *infra*.

327. See Chart 23, *infra*.

328. For rules proposed by other authors, see F. Juenger, *Choice of Law and Multistate Justice* 197 (1993); R. Weintraub, *Commentary on the Conflict of Laws* 424-25 (4th ed. 2001); P. Kozyris, "Values and Methods in Choice of Law for Products Liability: A Comparative Comment on Statutory Solutions", 38 *Am. J. Comp. L.* 475, 492-93 (1990); P. Kozyris, "Conflicts Theory for Dummies: *Après le Deluge*, Where Are We on Producers Liability?" 60 *La. L. Rev.* 1161, 1173-83 (2000); M. McConnell, "A Choice-of-Law Approach to Products-Liability Reform", in *New Directions In Liability Law* (W. Olson ed. 1988); P. Nygh, "The Reasonable Expectations of the Parties as a Guide to the Choice of Law in Contract and Tort", 251 *Recueil des Cours* 269, 374-75 (1995). S. Symeonides, "The Need for a Third Conflicts Restatement (And a Proposal for Tort Conflicts)", 75 *Ind. LJ* 437, 450-51 (2000). For a comparison and analysis of these rules,

proval; or (b) the place of the plaintiff's habitual residence, if that place coincides with either the place of injury or the place where the plaintiff had acquired the product; or (c) the place of acquisition if that place is also the place of injury[329].

Of the 100 cases discussed in this chapter, 32 cases do not provide sufficient information from which to determine how the plaintiffs would have exercised their choice. The application of Cavers's rule to the remaining 68 cases would produce the same result as the courts in 36 cases and a different result in 32 cases[330]. Because of the differences in the latter cases, Cavers's rule would produce a pro-plaintiff result in 60 or 88% of the 68 cases, and a pro-defendant result in 8 cases[331]. Even if one adds all 32 undeterminable cases to the pro-defendant column, the balance would still be tilted in favor of plaintiffs in a 60 to 40 ratio.

4.   Lex Loci, lex fori, lex domicilii

274. The above inquiry may increase one's curiosity on whether simpler, mono-dimensional rules, such as the *lex loci delicti* or the *lex fori*, would have come closer to approximating the results in the 100 cases. This question is addressed below and the answers are depicted in Chart 22 (below).

If all 100 cases had been decided under the *lex loci delicti* rule (and assuming the *locus delicti* was deemed to be in the state of the injury), the result would have been the same in 58 of the cases[332]. However, because most of the remaining 42 cases would have been decided in favor of the defendant[333], the *lex loci* rule would have raised the overall pro-defendant number to 73 cases and would have lowered the pro-plaintiff number to 25% of the cases[334].

If all 100 cases had been decided under the *lex fori*, the result would have been the same in 56 cases[335]. However, because in most of the remaining 44 cases the forum had a pro-plaintiff law, the *lex fori* rule would have raised the overall

---

see E. Scoles, P. Hay, P. Borchers & S. Symeonides, *Conflict of Laws* 937-941 (4th ed. 2004).

329. See, D. Cavers, "The Proper Law of Producer's Liability", 26 *Int'l & Comp. L. Q.* 703, 728 (1977). However, the defendant may prevent the application of the laws of the states specified in (b) and (c) by showing that "he could not reasonably have foreseen the presence in th[ose] State[s] of his product which caused harm to the claimant or his property". *Id.*

330. See Chart 22, *infra.*

331. See Chart 23, *infra.*

332. See Chart 22, *infra.*

333. The *lex loci* rule would change the result from pro-plaintiff to pro-defendant in 33 cases, and from pro-defendant to pro-plaintiff in 7 cases. In two cases, the result would remain the same, although the law of a different state would govern. Two cases do not disclose the law of the state of injury, so it is unknown whether the result would change.

334. See Chart 23, *infra.* Two cases that applied a pro-plaintiff law do not disclose the content of the *lex loci.*

335. See Chart 22, *infra.*

pro-plaintiff number to 78 cases and would have lowered the pro-defendant number to 21 cases[336].

If all the 100 cases had been decided under the law of the plaintiff's home state (*lex domicilii*), the result would have been the same in 66 cases[337]. Because of the differences in the remaining 34 cases, this rule would lower the overall pro-plaintiff number to 42 cases and would raise the pro-defendant number to 53 cases[338].

Finally, if the 100 cases had been decided under the law of the state of the product's acquisition, the result would have been the same in 61 cases. As a result of the differences in the remaining 39 cases, this rule would have raised the pro-defendant number to 59 cases and would have lowered the overall pro-plaintiff number to 30 cases[339].

5.   *Comparing the comparisons*

275. The following charts depict the results that the rules discussed in the preceding paragraphs would produce in the 100 cases.

Chart 22 shows the number of cases in which these rules would lead to the application of the law of the same state as the actual cases, a different state, or an unknown state. As the chart indicates, the Hague Convention comes closer to approximating the results of the actual cases, insofar as it would lead to the application of the law of the same state in 70 of the 100 cases.

---

336. See Chart 23, *infra*. One case *(MacDonald, # 95)* does not disclose the law of the forum.
337. See Chart 22, *infra*.
338. See Chart 23, *infra*. The remaining five cases do not disclose the law of the plaintiff's home state. Thus it is unknown whether the result would be different.
339. See Chart 23, *infra*. Eleven cases do not disclose the law of the state of acquisition.

Chart 22. Comparing with rules: (same choice of law)

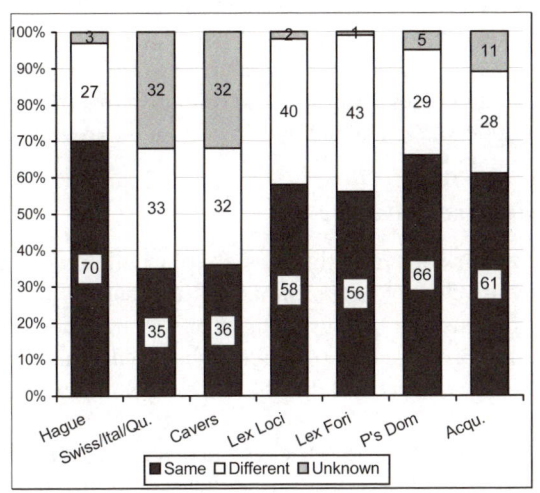

Chart 23 (below) compares the results in terms of which rules would apply a law that favors the plaintiffs or the defendants.

Chart 23. Comparing with rules: (Pro-P and Pro-D result)

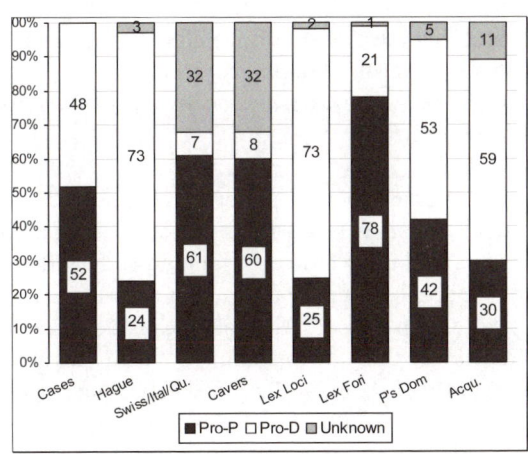

As the chart indicates, none of these rules comes close to approximating the results reached in the actual cases[340]. Three of those rules, including the *lex loci delicti* rule and the Hague Convention, would favor defendants much more than

---

340. The *lex domicilii* rule comes closer with a ratio of 42 pro-plaintiff results to 53 pro-defendant results, compared to a 52 to 48 ratio in the actual cases.

the actual cases, while three rules would favor plaintiffs much more than the actual cases. Predictably, the most pro-plaintiff rule is the *lex fori* rule because plaintiffs' lawyers tend to choose fora that have favorable substantive laws. The civilian codifications and Professor Cavers's rule would also be much more pro-plaintiff than the actual cases because these rules give plaintiffs an important role in choosing the applicable law, albeit within certain parameters.

6.   Articulating a descriptive rule

276. The above comparisons raise the question of whether a different, more complex rule would come closer to approximating the results of the actual cases. The short answer to this question is "yes, but not by much". Indeed, unlike other tort conflicts, the results produced by products liability cases cannot be easily compressed into a rule that can accurately reflect these results and still be functionally defensible.

If one were to accept as proper the results reached by the 100 cases and then articulate a contacts-based descriptive rule that would produce the same results in the majority of those cases, that rule might resemble the following:

1. *Apply the law of a state that has any three of the following contacts: (a) place of injury; (b) domicile of the injured party; (c) place of the product's acquisition; (d) place of manufacture; or (e) defendant's principal place of business.*
2. If two states have two of the above contacts each, apply the law of the state with the plaintiff-affiliating contacts.
3. *If no state has three contacts, and only one state has two contacts, apply the law of that state.*

The first paragraph of the rule covers a pattern that appeared in 56 of the 100 cases and would produce the same result in 42 cases[341]. The second paragraph covers a pattern that appeared in 27 cases and would produce the same result in 20 cases[342]. The third paragraph covers a pattern that appeared in 15 cases and would produce the same result in 9 cases[343]. All in all, the above rule covers 98 of the 100 cases[344] and would produce the same result in 71 of the cases and a different result in 27 cases. Because of these changes, the rule will produce pro-defendant results in 72 cases and pro-plaintiff results in 28 cases. Although these rates are slightly better than those of the Hague Convention, and although in many instances the results are more defensible than those in the actual cases, the improvement is only slight.

---

341. This rule would change the result from pro-plaintiff to pro-defendant in 12 cases, and from pro-defendant to pro-plaintiff in 2 cases.
342. This rule would change the result from pro-plaintiff to pro-defendant in 8 cases.
343. This rule would change the result from pro-plaintiff to pro-defendant in 5 cases.
344. The two cases not covered are *Fitts* and *Huddy.*

277. Frustrations like these often generate a nostalgia for the old *lex loci* rule. At least one court concluded that, because of its neutrality towards parties and substantive laws, the *lex loci* rule is the best alternative. In *Ness v. Ford Motor Co.*[345], the court, after considering other options, concluded that "[s]ometimes an apparently arbitrary choice – like *lex loci delicti* – is a reasonable way of dealing with the problem of conflict of interest between states"[346]. The court recognized that the plaintiff's home state had an interest in "seeing its citizens adequately compensated for their injuries"[347], but also noted that the state of manufacture had an interest in "seeing that product-liability plaintiffs are not overcompensated, resulting in higher insurance premiums for [its] manufacturers, higher costs, and lost jobs"[348]. A rule calling for the application of the law of the state of manufacture, said the court, "would tend to leave victims uncompensated as states wishing to attract and hold manufacturing companies would raise the threshold of liability and reduce compensation"[349]. Likewise, a rule applying the law of the victim's domicile "would permit a state with little manufacturing to endow its citizens with generous protection wherever they choose to travel without picking up any of the cost"[350]. After also rejecting the notion of applying the law of the place of the product's acquisition (because products may be resold in other states, and because product liability does not require privity), the court concluded that "[t]he traditional rule of *lex loci delicti* appears less objectionable once it is understood that there is no alternative that will yield a rational and fair result in all cases"[351].

Indeed, is there no other alternative? Was the conflicts revolution just a circuitous march that was bound to end with a return to the *lex loci* rule? No, we have come too far to return to a simplistic, mechanical rule that is oblivious to the hard-earned lessons of the American experience. As for the alternative, the alternative is to stop groping for mono-dimensional, all-or-nothing rules based on single connecting factors like the ones the *Ness* court considered, and to start thinking about more comprehensive and flexible formulae for these inherently complex conflicts.

Attaining a consensus on the precise ingredients of these formulae will not be easy, but the debate should begin sooner rather than later. While nobody has a monopoly on good ideas, academic authors can do their part by putting forward

---

345. 1993 WL 996164 (ND Ill.1993) (unpublished).

346. *Id.* at *2.

347. *Id.* The plaintiff was an Illinois resident who was injured in a single-car accident in Iowa, when the car in which he was a passenger rolled over. The car was manufactured by defendant Ford in Michigan, and was registered and garaged in Illinois. At the time of the accident, it was driven by another Illinois resident in a trip that began and was to end in Illinois.

348. *Id.*

349. *Id.*

350. *Id.*

351. *Id.* at *3.

their proposals on how these rules or formulae *should* look. The proposal described in the next section is this author's modest contribution to this end.

G.   A Proposed Rule

1.   *Proposing a forward-looking rule*

278. Product-liability conflicts are inherently difficult and, thus far, nobody has put forward the perfect formula for resolving them. This includes the undersigned author who, in the course of the last fifteen years, has drafted two statutory rules for such conflicts[352] and has proposed two *other* rules for the same purpose[353]. The fact that each of those rules differs from the others serves as this author's own admission that none of them are perfect. But the search for the better, if not the perfect, must continue. The rule proposed below is another attempt for the better.

I.   *LIABILITY.*
(1)   *Liability for injury caused by a product is determined, at the choice of the injured party, by the law of a state that has any two of the following contacts:*
   (a)   *the place of injury;*
   (b)   *the domicile or habitual residence of the injured party;*
   (c)   *the place in which the product was made; or*
   (d)   *the place in which the product was delivered to the first acquirer and final user.*
   The injured party's choice shall be disregarded upon proof that neither the product that caused the injury nor the defendant's products of the same type were available in the chosen state through ordinary commercial channels.
(2)   *If the injured party fails to make a choice under I(1), the defendant may choose the law of a state that has any three of the contacts listed in I(1).*
(3)   *Cases not disposed of under I(1) or I(2) are governed by the law chosen by the court under … [the general rules or approach for tort conflicts].*

II.   *DAMAGES.*
   If the defendant is liable under I, the injured party's right to compensatory or punitive damages and the amount of such damages shall be determined by the court under the law chosen under the general rules or approach for tort conflicts.

---

352.   See La. Civ. Code Art. 3545, discussed in Symeonides, *Exegesis*, 749-59; Puerto Rico Draft Code, Art. 48.

353.   See S. Symeonides, "The Need for a Third Conflicts Restatement (And a Proposal for Tort Conflicts)", 75 *Ind. L J* 437, 450-51, 472-74 (2000) and the first editions of this book in 298 *Recueil des Cours* 352-53 (2003).

2.   *General Features*

279. The main features of the proposed rule are that: (1) it differentiates between liability and damages; (2) it allows first the plaintiff and then the defendant to choose the state whose law will govern; and (3) it is built on four factual contacts and requires that the chosen state have *more than one* of these. These features are discussed below.

(a)   Defending party choice

280. From the perspective of American law, the idea of allowing *one* party to choose the applicable law, especially *after* the dispute arises, sounds novel and unilaterally suspicious[354]. Thus, the defense of this rule must begin with explaining and defending this notion.

Since the beginning of the history of conflicts law, the choice of the law governing multistate cases has been made by the lawgiver in advance through pre-formulated choice-of-law rules or by the judge in deciding the particular case, or through a combination of the two methods. In all cases, it was meant to be an unbiased choice by impartial public actors.

The will of private parties entered the picture relatively recently. In the last two centuries, most legal systems began resurrecting and gradually employing the ancient principle of party autonomy, namely the notion that parties to a multistate dispute can have a say in the choice of the law that would govern the dispute. By now, this principle is "perhaps the most widely accepted private international rule of our time"[355].

However, until recently, this notion has been limited to the law of contracts and contemplated a *pre-dispute* choice agreed to by *both* parties. If the parties to a contract agreed in advance on the law that would govern their future *contractual*[356] dispute, then a court would honor the agreement if it was otherwise valid and did not exceed certain public-policy limits. In recent years, many systems extended this principle to certain status-like contracts, such as those regulating the property relations of spouses (matrimonial regimes), and lately to the law of

---

354. Obviously, allowing both parties to agree on the applicable law after the dispute arises is far less problematic. For example, in the United States, when neither party argues for the application of non-forum law, most courts will decide the case under forum law, even if the forum's choice-of-law rules would normally point to non-forum law. See S. Symeonides, W. Perdue & A. von Mehren, *Conflict of Laws: American, Comparative, International* 107-111 (2nd ed. 2003).

355. R. Weintraub, "Functional Developments in Choice of Law for Contracts", 187 *Recueil des Cours* 239, 271 (1984). For a discussion of party autonomy and its limitations in contracts and torts, see E. Scoles, P. Hay, P. Borchers, & S. Symeonides, *Conflict of Laws* 947-987 (4th ed. 2004).

356. For a discussion of the ability of contracting parties to choose the law that will govern future non-contractual disputes arising from a contract, see Scoles, Hay, Borchers, & Symeonides, *supra*, 809-812; Symeonides, Perdue & von Mehren, *supra*, 358-59.

testate successions where the testator is now allowed within certain limits to des-ignate the law that will govern his or her succession[357].

In the latter case, the choice of law is made by a *single* party – the testator – who, however, besides being in an entirely different position than a litigant in adversary litigation, makes the choice *before* the dispute arises. In contrast, the proposed rule gives a *post-dispute* choice to *one* party who is already an actual or potential litigant. For this reason, one would be justified in assuming that such a rule is too generous to that party and thus unfair to the other party. However, closer examination reveals a more complex picture.

281. To begin with, the notion of a post-dispute choice by one party may be novel, but it is not unprecedented. In recent years, many legal systems have ad-opted it, even without the safeguards that the rule proposed here provides. For example, as noted earlier, certain recent PIL codifications give to the victim an almost unrestricted right to choose the law of a state that has only *one* contact[358]. Moreover, none of these codifications give a choice to defendants[359]. Similarly, in the last two decades, many codifications have extended the notion of post-dispute choice of law by the plaintiff to cross-border torts other than those arising from products liability. As noted earlier, these codifications provide that, when the in-jurious conduct and the resulting injury occur in different states, the injured party has the unqualified right to choose the law of either one of those states[360]. Finally, during the same period, many systems have extended the notion of favoring the presumptively weak party to areas other than torts. They adopted choice-of-law rules that expressly favor one party, such as children and maintenance obligees, by requiring courts to choose from among several laws the one most favorable to the obligee[361].

---

357. See S. Symeonides, *Private International Law at the End of the 20th Century: Progress or Regress?* 38-40, 56-57 (1999).

358. See *supra* 157, 180, 272.

359. These codifications provide defendants with the commercial unavailability defense. However, if the American cases are any indication, this defense will rarely be avail-able. As seen earlier (see *supra* 268) in none of the 100 cases discussed in this chap-ter, not even those involving non-U.S. manufacturers, did the manufacturer invoke a similar defense.

360. See *supra* 157, 180. Most of these codifications do not provide defendants with any defenses, such as a foreseeability proviso, for those cases in which the injured party chooses the law of the place of injury. Following the same principle of *favor laesi*, other codifications, such as those of Hungary and Portugal, produce the same result by requiring the court to choose between the above laws the one that is most favor-able to the injured party.

361. For example, subject to certain qualifications, article 18 of the German EGBGB pro-vides for the application of the law most favorable to the maintenance obligee from among the laws of the obligee's habitual residence, the common nationality of the obligor and the obligee, and the law of the forum. Similar rules are found in arts 1-3 of the 1956 Hague Convention on the Law Applicable to Maintenance Obligations Towards Children (choice between the *lex fori* and the law of the child's habitual

All of these rules serve as a reminder that conflicts law – like substantive law – often adopts rules designed to directly reach a specific substantive result, such as protecting a party whom the legal system considers to be in need of protection. Indeed, result-oriented choice-of-law rules, at least of the type that give the choice to the court, are by no means a recent phenomenon – they have been around for at least a century.

282. Thus, one could defend the rule proposed here as simply one additional result-oriented rule of the kind that so many systems have seen fit to adopt unapologetically[362]. However, such a defense would be selling the rule short. To begin with, to the extend it favors plaintiffs, the proposed rule does so to a much lesser degree than any of the other rules described above, in that: (1) it gives plaintiffs the right to choose a law only for the question of liability, not damages; and (2) it limits the plaintiffs' choices to states that have *two* pertinent contacts[363]. In many cases, the latter limitation will negate the plaintiff's choice and will shift the choice to the defendant. Secondly, the proposed rule provides not only plaintiffs but also defendants with a similar, albeit secondary, right to choose the applicable law[364].

---

residence); arts 4-6 of the 1973 Hague Convention on the Law Applicable to Maintenance Obligations, (choice between the *lex fori* and the law of the obligee's habitual residence, or the common national law of the obligor and the obligee); and several national or sub-national codifications. See, e.g., arts. 311-318 of the French *Code civil* (giving the choice to the child); Quebec Civ. Code, art. 3094 (choice between the law of the domicile of the obligee or the obligor); Hungarian codification, art. 46 (Hungarian law governs status, family relationships, and maintenance rights of children living in Hungary if it is more favorable than the otherwise applicable law).

362. For an equally unapologetic and eloquent defense of a pro-plaintiff choice-of-law regime, see L. Weinberg, "Theory Wars in the Conflict of Laws", 103 *Mich. L. Rev.* 1631, 1654 (2005):

> "Systematic choices of plaintiff-favoring law are better public policy than systematic choices of defendant-favoring law. When defendants engage in risky activities in reliance upon lax standards in their home states, shared public policies (favoring safety and fair dealing) would seem better served not by indulging such defendants in their race to the regulatory bottom, but rather by permitting plaintiffs injured by those activities to seek enforcement of higher legal standards. It is also sound public policy, universally recognized in American tort law, that innocent plaintiffs not bear the risk of their own injuries."

363. The rule also provides the defendant with the commercial unavailability defense stated in the second paragraph of I(1), which is a standard feature in all similar rules. The availability of this defense is a necessary safeguard, even though, in today's world, this defense will operate rather rarely. *See supra* 268.

364. To this author's knowledge, Professor Weintraub was the first to propose giving defendants a choice. See Weintraub, "Methods for Resolving Conflict-of-Laws Problems in Mass Tort Litigation", 1989 *U. Ill. L. Rev.* 129, 148 (1989). See also Symeonides, "The Need for a Third Conflicts Restatement (And a Proposal for Tort Conflicts)", 75 *Ind. LJ* 437, 450-51 (2000).

Admittedly, the two parties' choices may appear asymmetrical, not only because the plaintiff has the first choice, but also because the state the plaintiff chooses need only have two contacts, whereas the state the defendant chooses must have at least thee contacts. However, even with this asymmetry, the proposed rule is more balanced than the rules discussed above. Moreover, as explained later, this apparent asymmetry will probably not increase the rate of pro-plaintiff results that American courts have reached in the last decade. Even if it does, however, the result can be defended on the ground that an asymmetrical right to choose that favors plaintiffs can help equalize their position with that of manufacturers. To that extent, a tilt towards plaintiffs is not only permissible; it is also appropriate.

283. The remaining question is why give the choice to the parties rather than to the court. As the above description of choice-of-law rules demonstrates, some systems choose the one option, while other systems choose the other. And that is precisely the point: the two options are interchangeable. From a fairness perspective, it makes little difference whether a rule gives the choice of law directly to a party or instead to the court to be exercised for a party's benefit. If nothing else, giving the choice directly to a party obviates the need for a judicial answer to the question of whether a given law indeed favors a particular party. This is particularly helpful not only in cases in which that answer is unclear, but also in cases in which one state's law favors one party on some issues of liability and the other party on other issues. In these situations, the parties will have to carefully weigh all the pros and cons of exercising or not exercising their right to choose and, in either case, they would neither occupy the court's time nor be able to blame anybody else. In conclusion, therefore, one can say that the notion of giving the choice to a party is a smart cost-saving tool that would help conserve judicial resources.

(b) Differentiating between liability and damages

284. Unlike the rules discussed earlier, the rule proposed here imposes an important limitation on the parties' choice by confining it to the question of liability and excluding questions of damages. This limitation is designed to prevent either party from choosing a law that is favorable on both liability and damages. Moreover, as noted earlier, the choice must be for the *entire* question of liability, not some issues or aspects of it. In other words, neither party should be allowed to pick and choose.

These features protect both the defendant – when the plaintiff exercises the choice – and the plaintiff, when the defendant does likewise. By reserving the court's power to select the law governing damages, especially punitive damages, the proposed rule enables the court to guard against excesses and to re-equalize the position of the parties as explained later. For example, if Part I of the rule turns out to favor plaintiffs too much on liability, the court can use its power under Part II of the rule to reduce the impact on the defendant with regard to damages.

(c)   Redefining the pertinent contacts

285. Finally another important limitation to the parties' choice is the requirement that the chosen state must have more than one of the contacts considered pertinent in product liability conflicts – at least two of those contacts in the case of the plaintiff, and at least three contacts in the case of the defendant. Based on the study of decided cases, the proposed rule employs the following four factual contacts the pertinence of which is explained below: (1) the place of injury; (2) the domicile or habitual residence of the injured party; (3) the place in which the product was made; and (4) the place in which the product was delivered to the first acquirer and final user.

The place of injury. Obviously, the place of injury remains a relevant contact, if only because the injury is the very event that causes the dispute. The fact that this was the only contact that counted under the traditional *lex loci delicti* regime does not mean that this contact should be discounted now. No further explanation is needed on the pertinence of this contact.

The victim's domicile. The domicile or habitual residence, or "home state", of the injured party is a contact that has gained growing significance in recent years. It is obviously relevant here because the victim's home state experiences the social and economic impact of recovery or, especially, non-recovery. Readers familiar with modern private international law need no further explanation on this point.

286. *The making of the product.* Despite arguments to the contrary[365], the place of manufacture is relevant because – if the product is in fact defective – that is the place where the defect should have been detected. It is, in other words, the place of the critical act or omission that set in motion the chain of events that caused the injury. When the state in which the product was made has a law that favors the manufacturer, that state has an interest in applying that law to protect the manufacturer, an interest that must be juxtaposed to the interests of other states in protecting the persons injured by the product. When that state has a law that disfavors the manufacturer, that state may have an interest in deterring the manufacture of substandard products.

Admittedly, as noted earlier[366], the manufacture of a product often consists of several phases (design, testing, approval, assembly) which may occur in different states. By using the term "making" rather than "manufacture", the proposed Rule seeks to address some of these problems, but a more carefully drafted technical definition would be preferable.

287. *The product's acquisition.* The fourth contact, the place of the product's acquisition, requires some discussion. Although there is little doubt that this contact is pertinent, there are several questions about its precise meaning. For example, should one differentiate among situations in which the acquirer was the victim, another party on the victim's behalf, or a third party unrelated to the victim? Should one distinguish between consumer goods that are usually acquired by the victim in her home state, and goods like airplanes or other means of public trans-

---

365. *See supra* 205 footnote 20.
366. *See supra* 205 footnote 15.

portation that are often acquired in a state other than the victim's home state? These distinctions would be important if the place of acquisition *alone* would determine the applicable law. However, this is not the case under the rule proposed above. Under this rule, this contact becomes important only if the acquisition takes place in a state that has at least one other pertinent contact (in the case of a choice by the victim) or two pertinent contacts (in the case of a choice by the defendant). As long as this requirement is met, the above distinctions become less important.

Another question involves sales across state lines, which now are becoming even more common with the advent of the internet. By using the term "delivery to the ... acquirer", the proposed rule seeks to reduce the artificiality of this contact or its manipulation by one party. Similarly, by using the rather inelegant phrase "first acquirer *and* final user", the proposed rule seeks to exclude sales to intermediaries, as well as second-hand sales. To the extent that intermediaries, such as distributors or retailers, actually acquire a product (rather than holding it in consignment), they do so not for the purpose of using it as such, but rather for the purpose of selling it further. Consequently, for the purposes of this rule, which deals with tort liability, the place of acquisition by such intermediaries is irrelevant. The critical acquisition is the one by the acquirer *and* user. Similarly, since the rule deals with the liability of the producer rather than the liability of a non-professional seller, the critical acquisition is the one by the *first* acquirer and user, not the one to whom that party resells the product in used condition (second-hand sale).

288. *The defendant's principal place of business.* Finally, an explanation is due on why the proposed rule does *not* include the defendant's principal place of business among the pertinent contacts. The reason is simply because, as the cases discussed in this chapter demonstrate, this is the least relevant contact – no case has applied the law of the defendant's principal place of business *as such*[367].

This is hardly surprising. Most product producers are corporate entities with a multistate composition and multistate presence, but often without a real "home state" anywhere. Many of them engage in activities other than manufacturing and choose their principal place of business for reasons unrelated to this activity. For example, in one case involving the engines of a commercial airliner that crashed in Iowa, the court found that New York was the manufacturer's principal place of business only because the company's other holdings, unrelated to manufacture, were located in that state. The court disregarded this contact for that reason[368]. In another case involving a helicopter engine manufactured by the same company, the company's principal place of business was still in New York, but its headquarters were in Connecticut, its engine manufacturing division's headquarters were in Ohio, and its engine design and manufacturing division was in Massa-

367. See *supra* 255. Although 20 of the 100 cases have applied the law of a state that was the defendant's principal place of business, in all of these cases, that state had either one or two additional contacts.
368. *In re Air Crash Disaster at Sioux City, Iowa,* 734 F.Supp. 1425 (ND Ill. 1990).

chusetts[369]. Thus, to the extent that the principal place of business can serve as a proxy for the place of corporate decision-making, the relevant decision-making is often made elsewhere.

To be sure, one could analogize with natural persons and argue that, like a person's home state, the state of a corporation's principal place of business will feel the financial impact of a court decision imposing or not imposing liability, or assessing large amounts of damages, especially punitive damages. However, the analogy can only go so far. While in some cases that state may feel the impact in terms of jobs or tax revenue losses, the fact remains that the major losers are the corporation's shareholders most of whom could well have their domiciles elsewhere.

For these reasons, the proposed rule does not include the defendant's principal place of business in its part that gives the parties a choice for determining liability. However, this contact remains available for consideration by the court in choosing the law governing liability in those cases that are not disposed of through a party choice under Part I of the rule, or the law governing damages in all cases under Part II.

(d)   The content of the conflicting laws

289. Finally, as the discussion throughout this book illustrates, one of the major lessons of the American choice-of-law revolution is the notion that conflicts of laws can be resolved more intelligently by considering the content of these laws and making that content a criterion in the final choice of the governing law. Content-oriented law selection, as opposed to content-blind jurisdiction-selection, has justifiably become a major article of faith and an integral part of all modern American choice-of-law approaches.

However, a content-oriented choice need not be relegated to the judge in all cases. As some of the rules proposed earlier in this book illustrate, in some cases, this choice can be made in advance by the rule-drafter, after considering all possible permutations. The rule proposed here illustrates another possibility: content-oriented law-selection through the vehicle of party choice. After all, the reason a party will choose the law of a state that has the required contacts is not because of any particular affection for that state nor because of its contacts. Rather it is because the content of that law is such as to be favorable to that party's case. Whether that choice is also a good choice from a systemic perspective is a separate question, but if it is, then the device of having a party rather than the court choose the law accomplishes the objective of a content-oriented law selection while relieving the court from the burdens of an otherwise laborious choice-of-law analysis.

---

369. *Crouch v. Gen. Elec. Co.*, 699 F.Supp. 585 (SD Miss. 1988).

3.   The Rule's operation

290. This section illustrates the operation of the proposed rule, first with regard to liability and then with regard to damages, by first cataloguing the various combinations of contacts and laws that will allow each party to exercise its choice with regard to liability.

(a)   Liability

291. Part I of the rule (hereafter "Rule I") gives, first to the plaintiff and then to the defendant, the right to choose the state whose law will govern, provided that that state has the requisite factual contacts. Because each party will exercise this choice only if that state has a favorable law, it would be helpful to catalogue all the possible combinations of contacts and laws that would lead to a choice by the plaintiff or the defendant.

The table reproduced below depicts all possible combinations or patterns, a total of 14. The first ten patterns represent all the possible combinations that would favor the plaintiff (see gray cells). The last four patterns represent all the possible combinations that would favor the defendant (see white cells)[370].

---

370. It should be noted that, for either party to be eligible to choose, the requisite contacts must be in the *same state*. It does not suffice if they are in different states that have the same law. For example, if in a given case the four contacts are located in four different states, the first three of which have a pro-plaintiff law, the case would appear analogous to case # 1 in Table 28, and thus, one could argue, the plaintiff should have the same choice of a pro-plaintiff law as in case #1. However, the decisive counter-argument is that, even if the two cases are analogous in terms of state policies, they are not analogous in terms of the reliance and expectations of the parties. In case # 1, a person is injured in her home state by a product she acquired in that state. In arguing on the victim's behalf, one would be justified in saying that she is entitled to rely on the protection of that state's law. In contrast, in the hypothetical case described here, the victim acquires the product outside his home state and is injured in a third state. For this reason, a reliance argument is much weaker in such a case.

Table 28. The Parties' choices

#	Plaintiff's domicile	Injury	Delivery	Making	Occurrences
The Plaintiff's Choices					
1	Pro-P	Pro-P	Pro-P	Pro-D	9
2	Pro-D	Pro-P	Pro-P	Pro-P	0
3	Pro-P	Pro-D	Pro-P	Pro-P	0
4	Pro-P	Pro-P	Pro-D	Pro-P	0
5	Pro-P	Pro-P	Pro-D	Pro-D	5
6	Pro-D	Pro-P	Pro-P	Pro-D	4
7	Pro-D	Pro-D	Pro-P	Pro-P	6
8	Pro-P	Pro-D	Pro-P	Pro-D	7
9	Pro-P	Pro-D	Pro-D	Pro-P	1
10	Pro-D	Pro-P	Pro-D	Pro-P	0
The Defendant's Choices					
11	Pro-D	Pro-D	Pro-D	Pro-P	33
12	Pro-P	Pro-D	Pro-D	Pro-D	2
13	Pro-D	Pro-P	Pro-D	Pro-D	1
14	Pro-D	Pro-D	Pro-P	Pro-D	0
Total Actual Choices"					
Plaintiff: 32; Defendant: 36					

The fact that the plaintiff has ten possible choices, while the defendant only has four, suggests that the proposed rule is skewed towards the plaintiff. This is a distinct possibility, which, as noted earlier, one can defend on the merits as an attempt to bring some equilibrium to the otherwise unequal positions of manufacturers and consumers.

292. Such a defense may not be necessary, however. The fact that theoretically plaintiffs have a higher chance for a favorable combination of contacts and laws does not necessarily mean that plaintiffs have the same advantage in actuality. This would be true only if in real life each of the 14 patterns occurred with the same frequency. At least the 100 cases discussed in this chapter suggest otherwise. Specifically:

(1) of the ten combinations theoretically available to plaintiffs, only six combinations actually occurred, for a combined total of 32 occurrences; and

(2) of the four combinations theoretically available to defendants, only three combinations actually occurred, for a combined total of 36 occurrences.

The last column in Table 28, *supra*, indicates these occurrences.

Surprisingly, therefore, in these particular 100 cases, the proposed rule would give *defendants* a few more *actual* favorable choices than it would give plaintiffs. To be sure, this is not necessarily a virtue, but it does demonstrate that the rule is not as tilted in favor of plaintiffs as its language suggests. Whether it is also a good rule will depend on the actual results the rules will produce, as discussed below.

If the plaintiff does not choose a state under Rule I(1), for example because the case does not present any of the ten favorable combinations of contacts and laws[371], then Rule I(2) would give the defendant the right to choose a state that has any *three* of the pertinent contacts. Again, the defendant will likely exercise this choice if the case presents any one of the last four combinations depicted through the white cells of Table 28, *supra*.

If the case is not resolved through either Rule I(1) or Rule I(2), it will likely be because the case did not present the right combinations of contacts and laws to make it attractive for either party to choose the applicable law. As explained below, this occurred in 34 of the 100 cases. Under Rule I(3), these 34 cases would be resolved by the court under the general rule or approach the court follows in other tort conflicts.

(b) Damages

293. If the defendant is not liable under the law chosen through Rule I, the case will end there. If the defendant is found liable, then, under Rule II, the court will address the question of compensatory and punitive damages, if any, under the general choice-of-law rules or approach the court follows for tort conflicts.

Depending on the circumstances of the particular case, the court may choose the same law as the one that governs liability under Rule I, or the court may choose a different law. In choosing the former, the court should guard against giving one side too much through the same law. In choosing the latter, the court should guard against the possibility of giving one side the best of both worlds through an inappropriate *dépeçage*. Maintaining a balance between these two conflicting goals will be a delicate task, and this is precisely why the proposed rule assigns it to the court rather than to self-interested parties.

(c) Applying the rule to actual cases

294. If the 100 cases discussed in this chapter were to be decided under the proposed Rule[372], the part of the Rule that allows party choice would quickly produce the same result in 52 cases. Table 29, below, shows these cases[373]. The combination of contacts and laws is such that, in 27 of those cases, the plaintiffs will be able to choose the same pro-plaintiff law as the courts chose in the actual cases and the defendants will be able to do likewise in 25 cases.

---

371. Another possibility is that the defendant successfully invokes the commercial unavailability defense of the second paragraph of Rule I(1).

372. This exercise is subject to a caveat stemming from the fact that the proposed Rule distinguishes between liability and damages and gives parties a choice only with regard to liability. The 100 cases, at least as represented in Table 17, *supra*, do not always make this distinction. Some of the cases involved disputes on both liability and damages, while other cases involved a dispute only about damages because liability had been established or conceded. However, for the purposes of this exercise, it is assumed that in each of the 100 cases the involved states had the laws depicted in Table 17 on the issue of liability.

373. Table 28 is extracted from Table 17, *supra* at 211. Table 28 retains the same numbering of the cases as Table 17, so that the reader can track the cases.

Table 29. Cases in which the proposed rule will produce the same result through party choice (52 out of 100 cases)

Case name	Forum state	Plaintiff-affiliating contacts			D-affiliating contacts	
		P's domicile	Injury	Acquisition	Manufacture	D's PPB
A. Applying Pro-Plaintiff law (27 cases)						
1 Custom	KY Pro-D	CAN Pro-P	CAN Pro-P	CAN Pro-P	KY Pro-D	KY Pro-D
2 Kramer	NY. Pro-P	NY Pro-P	NY Pro-P	NY Pro-P	Japan Pro-D	Japan Pro-D
3 Eimers	NY Pro-P	NY Pro-P	NY Pro-P	NY Pro-P	Japan Pro-D	Japan Pro-D
4 Savage	AK Pro-P	AK Pro-P	AK Pro-P	AK Pro-P	--- 	---
5 Hoover	OH Pro-P	OH Pro-P	OH Pro-P	OH Pro-P	IN ---	IN --
6 Tune	FL Pro-P	FL Pro-P	FL Pro-P	FL NY Pro-P ---	--- ---	--- --
7 Nelson	N.J. IN Pro-D | Pro-P	IN Pro-P	IN Pro-P	IN Pro-P	N.J. Pro-D	N.J. Pro-D
8 Kardas	NY Pro-D	VT Pro-P	VT Pro-P	VT Pro-P	--- 	--
43 Smith	DEL Pro-P	DEL Pro-P	DEL Pro-P	MD Pro-D	MI? 	MD Pro-D
44 R-Square	LA Pro-P	LA Pro-P	LA Pro-P	MN Pro-D	AL ---	AL ---
45 Allstate	LA Pro-P	LA Pro-P	LA Pro-P	OK ---	MN? Pro-D	MN? Pro-D
46 Fisher	NEV Pro-P	NEV Pro-P	NEV Pro-P	UT Pro-D	ITA Pro-D	ITA Pro-D
47 Goede	MO Pro-P	MO Pro-P	MO Pro-P	CA? Pro-D	CA? Pro-D	CA? Pro-D
53 Zenaida-Garcia	WA Pro-P	OR Pro-D	OR Pro-D	WA Pro-P	WA Pro-P	WA Pro-P
54 Magnant	MI Pro-D	MI Pro-D	MI Pro-D	MN Pro-P	MN Pro-P	MN Pro-P
55 Champlain	NY Pro-D	NY Pro-D	NY Pro-D	KS Pro-P	KS Pro-P	KS Pro-P
59 Alexander	GA Pro-P	GA Pro-P	VA Pro-D	GA Pro-P	MI ---	MI ---
60 Etheredge	AL Pro-P	AL Pro-P	N.C. Pro-D	AL Pro-P	--- ---	--- ---
61 Kramer v Acton.	MA Pro-P	MA Pro-P	CN Pro-D	MA Pro-P	JAP Pro-D	JAP Pro-D
62 Mann	NY Pro-P	NY Pro-P	QU Pro-D	NY Pro-P	GA ---	OH/TN ---
63 Aguiniga	TX Pro-P	TX MEX Pro-P | Pro-D	MEX Pro-D	LA TX --- | Pro-P	MI ---	MI ---
73 Roll	NY NV Pro-P | Pro-P	NY Pro-P	NV Pro-P	NV Pro-P	TX Pro-D	TX Pro-D
74 Johnson v. Ranch	IL Pro-D	KS ---	COL Pro-P	COL Pro-P	IL Pro-D	IL Pro-D
75 Gadzinski	IL Pro-P	IL Pro-P	IN Pro-D	IN Pro-D	--- 	IN Pro-D
84 Cosme	MA Pro-P	MA Pro-P	CN Pro-D	CN Pro-D	MA Pro-P	MA Pro-P
89 Torrington	TX Pro-P	N.C. ---	MI/NEB Pro-D	TX Pro-P	TX Pro-P	TX Pro-P
90 Mitchell	TX Pro-P	N.M./KY ---	N.C. Pro-D	TX Pro-P	TX Pro-P	MD/CA ---
B. Applying Pro-D law (25 cases)						
9 Kemp	MI Pro-D	MI Pro-D	MI Pro-D	MI Pro-D	CA Pro-P	CA Pro-P
11 Burleson	TX	TX	TX	TX	Tobacco States	

	Pro-D	Pro-D	Pro-D	---	---
12 Clark	LA / Pro-D	LA / Pro-D	LA / Pro-D	LA / Pro-D	CA / Pro-P	CA / Pro-P
13 Pittman	LA / Pro-D	LA / Pro-D	LA / Pro-D	LA / Pro-D	CA / Pro-P	CA / Pro-P
14 Jeff.Parish	LA / Pro-D	LA / Pro-D	LA / Pro-D	LA / Pro-D	--- / Pro-P	--- / Pro-P
15 Orl.Parish	LA / Pro-D	LA / Pro-D	LA / Pro-D	LA / Pro-D	--- / Pro-P	--- / Pro-P
16 Campofiore	CN / Pro-D	CN / Pro-D	CN / Pro-D	CN / Pro-D	NJ / Pro-P	NJ / Pro-P
17 Dorman	MO / Pro-P	B.C. / Pro-D	B.C. / Pro-D	B.C. / Pro-D	Taiwan / ---	MO / Pro-P
18 Walls	MS / Pro-P	OR / Pro-D	OR / Pro-D	OR / Pro-D	OH / Pro-P	DEL / Pro-P
19 Hughes	AR / Pro-P	LA / Pro-D	LA / Pro-D	LA / Pro-D	AR / Pro-P	AR / Pro-P
20 Hall	MI / Pro-P	N.C. / Pro-D	N.C. / Pro-D	N.C. / Pro-D	OH / Pro-P	MI / Pro-P
21 Farrell	MI / Pro-P	N.C. / Pro-D	N.C. / Pro-D	N.C. / Pro-D	MI / Pro-P	MI / Pro-P
22 Vestal	CA / Pro-P	N.C. / Pro-D	N.C. / Pro-D	N.C. / Pro-D	CA / Pro-P	CA / Pro-P
23 Nesladek	MN / Pro-P	NEB / Pro-D	NEB / Pro-D	NEB / Pro-D	MI / ---	MI / ---
24 Rice	WA / Pro-P	WA / Pro-P OR / Pro-D	OR / Pro-D	OR / Pro-D	---	---
25 Bain	TX / Pro-P	B.C.? / Pro-D	B.C. / Pro-D	B.C.? / Pr-D	---	TX / Pro-P
26 Lilly	IN / Pro-P	CA / Pro-D	CA / Pro-D	CA / Pro-D	IN / Pro-P	IN / Pro-P
27 Rutherford	KY / Pro-P	IN / Pro-D	IN / Pro-D	IN / Pro-D	KS / Pro-P	MI / Pro-P
28 Harlan Feeders	IA / Pro-P	NEB / Pro-D	NEB / Pro-D	NEB / Pro-D	IA / Pro-P	SD / ---
29 Walters	IL / Pro-P	KS / Pro-D	KS / Pro-D	KS / Pro-D	TN/IL / --/Pro-P	OH/IL / --/Pro-P
30 Heindel	NJ / Pro-P	PA / Pro-D	PA / Pro-D	PA / Pro-D	NJ / Pro-P	NJ / Por-P
31 White	OH / Pro-P	GA / Pro-D	GA / Pro-D	GA / Pro-D	OH / Pro-P	OH / Pro-P
32 Jones v. Cooper	PA / Pro-P	VA / Pro-D	VA / Pro-D	VA / Pro-D	OH / Pro-P	OH / Pro-P
33 Michaud	DEL / Pro-P	QU / Pro-D	QU / Pro-D	QU / Pro-D	---	DEL / Pro-P
34 Lupoli	MA / Pro-P	NH / Pro-D	NH / Pro-D	NH / Pro-D	MA / Pro-P	MA / Pro-P

Rules I(1) and I(2) will change the result in 14 cases. In 4 cases, the change will be from a pro-defendant to a pro-plaintiff law, and in 10 cases the change will be from a pro-plaintiff to a pro-defendant law. Table 29, below, depicts these cases. The shaded cells show the state whose law the court applied in the actual cases. The use of underlining and bold-face type indicates the law that would be chosen under proposed Rules I(1) or I(2). Each of these changes can be defended as a change for the better, although space limitations do not allow for this discussion here.

Table 30. Cases in which the proposed rule will change the result (14 cases)

Case name	Forum state	Plaintiff-affiliating contacts			D-affiliating contacts	
		P's domicile	Injury	Acquisition	Manufacture	D's PPB
A. From Pro-D to Pro-P Law (4)						
9 Kelly	**PA** / **Pro-P**	**PA** / **Pro-P**	**PA** / **Pro-P**	**PA** / **Pro-P**	MI / Pro-D	MI / Pro-D
51 McKinnon	**VT** / **Pro-P**	Qu / Pro-D	Qu / Pro-D	**VT** / **Pro-P**	**VT** / **Pro-P**	VT / Pro-P
72 Fitts	**AL** / **Pro-P**	**AL** / **Pro-P**	FL / Pro-D	**AL?** / **Pro-P**	--- / ---	--- / ---
83 Beals	**D.C.** / **Pro-P**	VA / Pro-D	**D.C.** / **Pro-P**	**D.C.** / **Pro-P**	VA / Pro-D	VA / Pro-D
B. From Pro-P to Pro-D Law (10)						
35 Gantes	N.J. / Pro-P	**GA** / **Pro-D**	**GA** / **Pro-D**	**GA** / **Pro-D**	N.J. / Pro-P	N.J. / Pro-P
36 McLennan	TX / Pro-P	**CAN** / **Pro-D**	**CAN** / **Pro-D**	**CAN** / **Pro-D**	TX / Pro-P	TX / Pro-P
37 Mahne	MI / Pro-P	**FL** / **Pro-D**	**FL** / **Pro-D**	**FL** / **Pro-D**	MI / Pro-P	MI / Pro-P
38 Davis	CA / Pro-P	**OR** / **Pro-D**	**OR** / **Pro-D**	**OR** / **Pro-D**	CA / Pro-P	CA / Pro-P
39 Marchesani	LA / Pro-P	**TN** / **Pro-D**	**TN** / **Pro-D**	**TN** / **Pro-D**	LA / Pro-P	LA / Pro-P
40 Baxter	CN / Pro-P	**OR** / **Pro-D**	**OR** / **Pro-D**	**OR** / **Pro-D**	CN / Pro-P	CN / Pro-P
41 Glover	MN / Pro-P	**IL** / **Pro-D**	**IL** / **Pro-D**	**IL** / **Pro-D**	NJ / ---	NJ / ---
42 Stupak	WS / Pro-P	**MI** / **Pro-D**	**MI** / **Pro-D**	**MI** / **Pro-D**	NJ / ---	DEL / ---
70 Apple	PA / Pro-P	**MI** / **Pro-D**	PA / Pro-P	**MI** / **Pro-D**	**MI** / **Pro-D**	**MI** / **Pro-D**
85 Lou	MA / Pro-P	MA / Pro-P	**CHI** / **Pro-D**	**CHI** / **Pro-D**	**CHI** / **Pro-D**	MA / Pro-P

295. By adding up the cases in Tables 29 and 30, one can see that, through the medium of party choice, Rules I(1) and I(2) will quickly resolve 56 of the 100 cases. Rule I(1) will produce a pro-plaintiff result in 31 of those cases (compared to 33 in the actual cases). Rule I(2) will produce a pro-defendant result in 35 cases (compared to 29 in the actual cases).

Thus, despite their pro-plaintiff appearance, Rules I(1) and I(2) will actually produce results that favor defendants more than plaintiffs and more than in the actual cases. As shown above, in the actual cases, the ratio was 52% to 48% in favor of plaintiffs. Under Rules I(1) and I(2), the ratio will be 47% to 53% in favor of *defendants*. The following chart depicts these percentages.

Chart 24. Effect of party choice under proposed rule

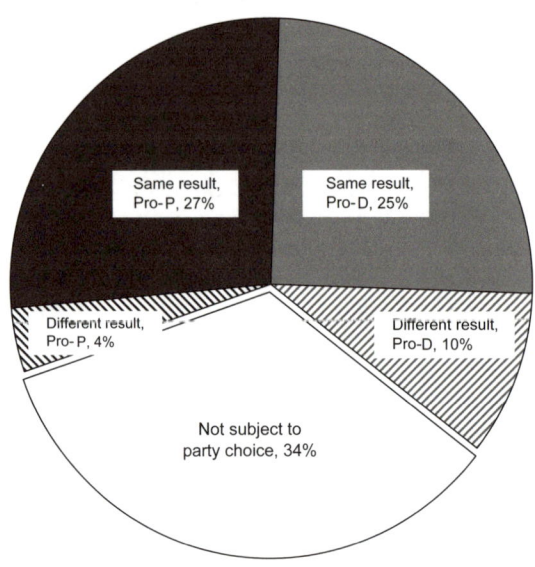

296. The remaining 34 of the 100 cases would not have been resolved through the medium of party choice, because they did not present the right combinations of contacts and laws to make it attractive for either party to exercise the choices Rules I(1) and I(2) provide. Under Rule I(3), these cases would have to be resolved by the courts under the general choice-of-law approach the courts would normally follow for such cases. If these courts were to follow the same approaches as in the actual cases (and there is little reason to assume otherwise), then the courts would reach the same results as in the actual cases. If this is true, then Rule I:

(1)   would have produced the same result in 86 of the 100 cases[374].
(2)   would change the result from pro-defendant to pro-plaintiff in 4 cases and from pro-plaintiff to pro-defendant in 10 cases[375]; and
(3)   all together, the proposed rule would have lead to the application of a pro-plaintiff law in 47 of the 100 cases (compared to 52 in the actual cases), and a pro-defendant law in 53 cases (compared to 48 in the actual cases). The following chart depicts these results.

---

374. See Chart 24, *supra*.
375. See Chart 24, *supra*.

Chart 25. Comparing the results: The 100 cases under the proposed rule

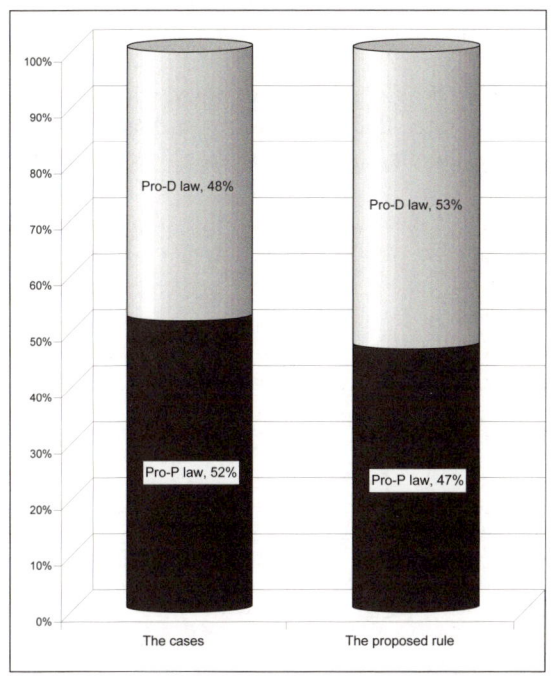

Thus, the proposed rule comes much closer than any of the existing or proposed rules in reproducing the results reached by the courts in the United States in the period 1990-2005.

297. To be sure, one could argue that the results of the cases are themselves bad and, to the extent the proposed rule reproduces the same results, the rule simply replicates a bad system. Even if this were true, however (and there is no reason to assume that it is), there is still much to be said about the benefits of having a rule that makes these results predictable, reduces litigation expenses, and lightens the courts' choice-of-law burdens. Indeed, one could argue that, if a rule like Rule I were in effect, it would have facilitated early settlements in most of these cases without resort to litigation, thus conserving precious judicial resources. Knowing beforehand what the applicable liability law would be is an added incentive to avoid litigation. Even if litigation is not avoided, Rule I will reduce the court's choice-of-law burden, while Rule II will allow the court to remain in control on the question of damages.

H.   Conclusions

298. This chapter provides a comprehensive review of American product-liability conflicts cases decided during the period of 1990 to 2005. Although this was not its goal, the review produced some surprising findings that dispute certain widely

held assumptions about the current state of American conflicts law, especially in the area of tort conflicts. Among these findings are the following:

(1) Although today's products travel great distances, most multistate product-liability cases (88%) involve only two or three states. In a clear plurality of cases (42%), the victim's domicile and injury, and the product's acquisition were in the same state. The vast majority of those cases (79%) applied that state's law, and in the majority of those cases (76%) that law favored the defendant;

(2) Forum-shopping is neither as common nor as rewarding as critics assume. Of the 100 cases, only 5 cases involved actual forum shopping, and 2 cases involved borderline forum shopping. Only one of these cases applied the pro-plaintiff law of the forum;

(3) Most product-liability plaintiffs tend to sue in their home state. They did so in 52 of the 100 multistate cases discussed in this chapter;

(4) Most cases (77 out of 100) applied the law of a state that had only plaintiff-affiliating contacts, but in most of those cases (43 or 56%) that state had a pro-defendant law;

(5) In their choice-of-law decisions, courts do not unduly favor plaintiffs as a class. The number of cases that applied a pro-plaintiff law (52) barely exceeded the number of cases that applied a pro-defendant law (48);

(6) Courts do not unduly favor the domiciliaries of the forum state (plaintiffs or defendants). In fact, more than half of the cases applied a law that did *not* favor the local litigant;

(7) Courts do not unduly favor the law of the forum. The percentage of cases that applied forum law was only 10% higher than the cases that applied foreign law, and the cases that exhibited undue forum-law favoritism are no more than a handful.

299. All in all, a review of all the cases reveals that the record of American courts in handling these most difficult of conflicts is much better than one might assume from a selective reading of a few cases. Indeed, this is one of those situations in which the whole is better than any of its parts separately considered.

Nevertheless, this record comes at a high cost in litigation expenses for the parties and a heavy utilization of judicial resources that are needed elsewhere. Long delays in resolving a conflict and high uncertainties regarding the final outcome commensurably reduce the value of even a good outcome. Predictability of outcomes is as important in this area of the law as it is elsewhere.

In an effort to reduce this uncertainty, this Chapter has proposed a choice-of-law rule that would produce nearly the same results as the actual cases, but much more quickly and at a much lower cost. In about two thirds of the cases, the proposed rule will enable the parties to know in advance which law will determine liability. This knowledge will increase the incentive for early negotiations on the question of damages and would increase the chances of early settlements without resort to litigation. In turn, this would benefit both parties and the system at large.

300. While the proposed rule will clearly be more efficient than the present regime of non-rules, one should not be content with efficiency but should also strive for fairness. In the field of conflict of laws, fairness is a particularly elusive concept, if only because the very name of the subject implies the existence of conflicting notions of fairness. This author claims no particular insight in defining fairness. However, one of the most astute students of product liability conflicts, Professor Phaedon Kozyris has put forward five general propositions for testing the fairness and overall soundness of choice-of-law rules on this subject. The balance of this section discusses whether the rule proposed in this Chapter conforms to these propositions.

Proposition # 1 is that "it is unfair for a person to be subjected to the burdens of the law of a state with which he has no deliberate and meaningful 'affiliating circumstances'"[376]. Since this is primarily a defendant-protecting proposition, it should be tested against the part of the proposed rule that allows the plaintiff to choose the applicable law, namely Rule I(1)[377]. This rule complies with Proposition #1 because the rule requires that the state the plaintiff chooses must have at least two of the listed contacts and only one of those contacts (the plaintiff's domicile) is presumptively unaffiliated with the defendant. For example, when the plaintiff chooses the pro-plaintiff law of his home state, that state must have the defendant-affiliating contacts of the occurrence of the injury[378], or place of delivery, or the making of the product. Even if the rule did not require these additional contacts, the commercial availability defense of the second paragraph of Rule I would suffice to ensure compliance with Kozyris' first proposition.

Proposition # 2 is that "it is not just for a person to receive the benefits of the law of a state with which he also has no [deliberate and meaningful 'affiliating circumstances']"[379]. The reference to "receiv[ing] benefits" leads to the inference that this proposition is concerned primarily with compensatory laws which confer benefits to plaintiffs. If this is true, it leaves out conduct-regulating rules which are designed to deter particular conduct for the benefit of society at large rather than of particular plaintiffs as such. In any event, regardless of the correctness of this inference or the soundness of Proposition #2, the proposed rule complies with it because the rule: (a) requires the concurrence of at least two of the listed contacts in the state chosen by either the plaintiff or the defendant; and (b) two of the four contacts (delivery and injury) are affiliated with both parties while each of the other two is affiliated with one party only. For example, when the plaintiff chooses the pro-plaintiff law of the place of manufacture, that state must have

---

376. P. Kozyris, "Conflicts Theory for Dummies: *Après le Deluge*, Where Are We on Producers Liability?" 60 *La. L. Rev.* 1161,1175 (2000).

377. Even if this were viewed as a plaintiff-protecting proposition, it will always be satisfied by the requirement of Rule I(2) that the state chosen by the defendant must have at least three contacts of which at least one will always be plaintiff-affiliating.

378. The fact that the the injury was caused by one of the defendant's products should be considered a defendant-affiliating circumstance under Kozyris' propositions.

379. Kozyris, *supra* footnote 376, at *id.*

one of the other contacts, all of which are plaintiff-affiliating contacts, namely the plaintiff's domicile, or injury, or the place of the product's delivery.

Proposition # 3 is that "there should be no substantive bias in favor of recovery, except in the most residual no-other-choice sense"[380]. As the preceding discussion documents, the proposed rule satisfies this proposition insofar as the rule would produce fewer pro-plaintiff results than the actual cases (47 vs. 52) and would keep those results below the fifty-percent line. In any event, this rule is much less pro-plaintiff than many of the enacted or proposed rules, such as those of the civilian codifications discussed earlier.

If anything, the proposed rule raises the opposite question of whether it unduly favors defendants insofar as it produces more pro-defendant than pro-plaintiff results. The answer should be negative. It seems that the reason the rule produces more pro-defendant results is simply because, since the early 1990s, more states have pro-defendant substantive laws than pro-plaintiff substantive laws. If this is true, then a choice-of-law rule, even one that gives plaintiffs more choices, can only go so far in compensating for this imbalance.

Proposition # 4 is that "an effort should be made to apply the chosen law as a whole, avoiding *dépeçage*"[381]. The proposed rule entails the possibility of *dépeçage* to the extent it differentiates between liability and damages. However, this does not mean that *dépeçage* will be inevitable or even frequent, or that it will be inappropriate when it occurs. As explained earlier, in choosing the law governing damages under Rule II, the court should guard against an inappropriate *dépeçage* by making sure it does not give one party the best of both worlds. Thus, the proposed rule complies with the desideratum of avoiding excessive or inappropriate *dépeçage*.

Finally, the proposed rule conforms with *Proposition # 5*, which provides that "the territorial connections should predominate over the personal"[382]. Here they do because three of the four listed contacts are territorial and only one (the plaintiff's domicile) is arguably non-territorial.

In summary, the rule proposed here seems to satisfy all five general propositions that Professor Kozyris articulated for guiding the search for proper resolutions to product-liability conflicts. While this fact alone does not promise perfection, it may suggest that the quest for the optimum is headed in the right direction.

---

380. *Id.*
381. *Id.*
382. *Id.*

Chapter IX   The American Choice-of-law Revolution: A Macro View

A.   Introduction

301. The sheer number of cases that a book of this type encompasses poses the risk that either the author or the reader can be lost in a sea of casuistry. To minimize this risk, one should, after having studied and described each tree, pause to survey the entire forest.

Each of the previous three chapters has attempted a similar undertaking by seeking to extract from case holdings the trends and principles that can be recast in the form of rules. This chapter undertakes a broader and more ambitious task. It surveys the philosophical infrastructure of the American choice-of-law revolution – scholastic and judicial – and then explores the all-important question of "what next"?

To this end, this chapter returns to the basic philosophical and methodological dilemmas of the choice-of-law process. Naturally, reasonable people may disagree in choosing and defining these dilemmas. With due respect to other view points, this chapter explores the following six, partly-overlapping, basic dilemmas: (1) unilateralism versus bilateralism; (2) territoriality versus non-territoriality; (3) interstate or international uniformity versus ethnocentricism or forum-favouritism; (5) "jurisdiction-selection" versus "content-oriented" law-selection; (5) "conflicts justice" versus "material justice"; and (6) legal certainty versus flexibility.

B.   Unilateralism versus Multilateralism

1.   The two misnamed branches of selectivism

302. If one accepts the assumption that most multistate conflicts should be resolved by choosing the law of one of the involved states[1], then one must identify

---

1.   This assumption is not inevitable. For example, the "substantivist" method of the Roman *praetor peregrinus* and its subsequent versions, proceeded on the premise that multistate conflicts should be resolved by constructing a new substantive rule of decision derived from the domestic laws of the involved states. For a discussion of this method in American and comparative private international law, see S. Symeonides, "American Choice of Law at the Dawn of the 21st Century", 37 *Willamette L. Rev.* 1,

the criteria that will guide the choice. One of the sub-questions in this process is whether the choice of law should be based: (a) on the respective "claims" of each involved state to apply its law; or (b) on predefined neutral criteria that are indifferent to these claims. The first option is the basis of unilateralism, whereas the second is the basis of multilateralism.

The term unilateralism sounds inherently chauvinistic and arbitrary, while its historical antipode, multilateralism, sounds conciliatory and cooperative. For example, in international relations, unilateralism is defined as "[t]he doctrine that nations should conduct their foreign affairs individualistically without the advice or involvement of other nations"[2], while multilateralism is defined as "the principle or belief that several nations should be cooperatively involved in the process of achieving something"[3]. The unqualified transplantation of these two terms in the field of private international law may lead the uninitiated to conclude that:

(1)   Unilateralism is the approach in which the forum state chooses the governing law based exclusively on the forum's own notions and preferences and in complete disregard of those of the other state or states involved in the conflict; and

(2)   Multilateralism is the approach in which the choice of law is made in a cooperative fashion after consulting with, or at least inquiring into, the wishes of the other involved state or states.

Although these conclusions are intuitive and etymologically justified, they are largely incorrect; so much so that reversing them would bring each one closer to the truth. Indeed, both of the above labels are misplaced. This is hardly surprising since the label "unilateralism" was chosen not by those who first proposed that approach, i.e., the Italian statutists of the 12th century, but rather by their 19th century critics who self-righteously called themselves "multilateralists". Besides creating unnecessary confusion[4], this mislabeling has severely handicapped the choice-of-law approach caricatured as unilateralism.

4, 11-16 (2000); S. Symeonides, *Private International Law at the End of the 20th Century: Progress or Regress?* 9-12, 18-21 (2000). In contrast to this method, the "conflictual" or "selectivist" methods that dominate contemporary private international law proceed on the premise that the way to resolve multistate problems is by selecting and applying the domestic law of one or another of the involved states.

2.   *Webster's Online Dictionary: The Rosetta Edition* (2005) See also, *The American Heritage Dictionary of the English Language* (4th ed. 2000) ("A tendency of nations to conduct their foreign affairs individualistically, characterized by minimal consultation and involvement with other nations, even their allies."); *The New Dictionary of Cultural Literacy* (3rd ed. 2002) ("Action initiated or taken by a single nation rather than by two nations (see bilateralism) or several (see multilateralism).").

3.   *Encarta World English Dictionary* (North American Ed. 2005).

4.   According to one observer, part of the confusion is caused by "a failure to distinguish between judicial unilateralism and political unilateralism: between unilateralism as a strategy for the nation's political branches and unilateralism as an approach that courts might take in the conflict of laws". W. Dodge, "Extraterritoriality and Con-

This section attempts to facilitate a better understanding of this misnamed approach by looking behind the misplaced labels. It concludes by suggesting that, properly understood, unilateralism can appropriately complement multilateralism and can make valuable contributions to a rational resolution of choice-of-law problems.

2.   *The original unilateral method*

303. Historically, unilateralism preceded multilateralism. The Italian statutists developed the original unilateral method in the 12th century, and their French and Dutch successors improved upon it[5]. This method is based on two premises:
(1)   that conflicts of laws should be resolved on the basis of the involved states' respective claims to apply their law; and
(2)   that one can ascertain those claims by examining each involved state's relevant substantive statutes (*statuta*) and determining whether they were intended to reach the case at hand.

These premises are plausible even by today's standards, although they do not, for example, address the problems created by the inevitable statutory overlaps or gaps[6]. The problems lie in the implementation. The statutists, who were more grammarians than lawyers, assumed that they could delineate and catalogue in advance the intended reach of *all* statutes, and that the reach of a statute depended on its wording – worse yet, its first words. Proceeding on these simplistic assumptions, the early statutists classified all statutes into real (i.e., territorial) or personal (i.e., non-territorial), before adding a third category predictably called "mixed".

Later statutists attempted to cure the deficiencies of the original method by replacing grammar with teleology and suggesting that the classification of statutes should depend on the presumed and apparent *purpose* of those who enacted them[7]. With this improvement, the statutist method survived well into the nineteenth century when it was demolished by the writings of Friedrich Carl von Savigny[8], whose persuasive critique relegated unilateralism to the periphery of PIL history, at least for another century.

---

flict-of-Laws Theory: An Argument for Judicial Unilateralism", 39 *Harv. Int'l LJ* 101, 109 (1998).
5.   See E. Scoles, P. Hay, P. Borchers and S. Symeonides, *Conflict of Laws* 10-15 (4th ed. 2004); S. Symeonides, W. Perdue and A. von Mehren, *Conflict of Laws: American, Comparative, International*, 7-11 (2nd ed 2003).
6.   In the contemporary American conflicts lexicon, statutory overlaps generate "true" conflicts while statutory gaps generate "no-interest" cases.
7.   See S. Symeonides, W. Perdue & A. von Mehren, *supra* footnote 5, at 9.
8.   See F. C. von Savigny, *System des heutigen Römischen Rechts*, Vol. 8 (1849).

3.   The original multilateral method

304. Unlike previous critics of unilateralism, Savigny took the next step of articulating an alternative method of resolving conflicts of laws. This method, henceforth known as the multilateral method, began from the opposite end from that of the statutists. Rather than focusing on the conflicting laws and trying to ascertain their intended spatial reach, Savigny focused on categories of disputes or "legal relationships", and then sought to identify the state in which each relationship had its "seat", or in whose legislative jurisdiction it "belonged". Rather than classifying statutes, Savigny classified relationships. He then "localized" each relationship by assigning decisive importance to the geographical location of certain elements ("connecting factors") of each relationship in one state or another.

Savigny's classificatory scheme eschewed any pre-choice examination of the content of the conflicting laws, or of a state's "wishes" to apply them. In this scheme, the choice of the applicable law was to be made through a network of preformulated, multilateral choice-of-law rules that defined the reach of both forum and foreign law and placed both of them on equal footing. These rules were to be neutral and even-handed and should be suitable for adoption by all nations, without significant modifications. Savigny's dream was that all nations would adopt and uniformly apply these rules so that all nations would decide the same multistate dispute in the same way, thus producing an international uniformity of result *(internationaler Entscheidungseinklang)*.

By the beginning of the twentieth century, Savigny's multilateral method had almost completely displaced the unilateral method and dominated the international conflicts scene. In the meantime, the new movement had also reached the United States where, after an early attempt to import the statutist method failed[9], the multilateral approach found an articulate proponent in the seminal work of Joseph Story[10].

305. Despite the international dominance of multilateralism, Savigny's dream of international uniformity remains as far from reality today as it was during his time[11]. This is hardly surprising. For, even if Savigny's assumptions about seats and seat locations had the qualities of apocalyptic truth, nobody could guarantee their universal unqualified acceptance. In the absence of a supranational order empowered to impose international uniformity, each country claimed for itself the task of pursuing it.

As a result, and despite contrary rhetoric and perhaps intentions, multilateralism has become more unilateral than unilateralism ever has been. Multilateralism is supposed to be a forum-neutral system, but – as its hostility to *renvoi*

---

9.   See S. Symeonides, W. Perdue & A. von Mehren, *supra* footnote 5, at 12-13 (describing Samuel Livermore's efforts in the 1820s to introduce the statutist method to the United States); De Nova, "The First American Book on Conflict of Laws, 8 *Am. J. Legal Hist.*136 (1964).

10.   See J. Story, *Commentaries on the Conflict of Laws* (1834).

11.   See *infra* 332-335.

exemplifies – it is more of a forum-knows-best system. For example, when the forum adopts a bilateral choice-of-law rule such as the *lex loci contractus* rule, the forum assumes that the law of the country in which the contract was made is the most appropriate law to govern all disputes arising from that contract, even if the latter country holds the view that its law is the *least* appropriate one. Indeed, except for the limited circumstances in which it allows *renvoi*, multilateralism is totally indifferent to the views of countries other than the forum. Moreover, as will be explained later[12], in some cases, the seemingly neutral bilateral rules of which multilateralism prides itself may conceal deliberate policy choices designed to promote the forum's national interest.

306. In sum, even if all countries had the most altruistic of intentions – an assumption belied by experience – multilateralism could not produce international harmony. Instead, an international polyphony, if not cacophony, characterizes private international law a century-and-a-half since Savigny. In light of this less than ideal state of affairs, an approach to private international law that honestly acknowledges the reality of conflicting national interests may be more promising that an approach that naively assumes an angelic state of affairs.

This is where unilateralism can help; not Currie's imperialistic unilateralism, but rather a cooperative, *accommodative* unilateralism – an unilateralism that acknowledges that states do have interests in the outcome of multistate private-law disputes and attempts to accommodate these interests to the extent humanly possible. The following section sketches the parameters of this approach.

4.   *The resurgence of the unilateralism method*

(a)   Currie's unilateralism

307. During the twentieth century, the unilateral approach experienced a remarkable renaissance, especially in the United States[13]. It has appeared not only in academic doctrine, as one would expect, or in judicial opinions, but also in a series of little-known, yet important, state statutes which are discussed later[14].

In the academic world, the most outspoken proponent of unilateralism was Brainerd Currie[15]. Although Currie was probably unaware of other versions of uni-

---

12.   See *infra* 333.

13.   For the resurgence of unilateralism in other countries, see S. Symeonides, *Private International Law at the End of the 20th Century: Progress or Regress?* 15-18 (2000); Gothot, "Le renouveau de la tendance unilatérale en droit international privé", 60 *Rev. critique* 1, 209, 415 (1971).

14.   See *infra* 311-312.

15.   See *supra* 14-24. See also J. Dolinger, "Evolution of Principles for Resolving Conflicts in the Field of Contracts and Torts", 283 *Recueil des cours* 189, 306 (2000) (referring to Currie's approach as "the ultimate materialization of the unilateralist approach"). Another unilateralist, albeit one with less influence than Currie, was Professor Albert Ehrenzweig. For his voluminous work, see, *inter alia*, A. Ehrenzweig, *A Treatise on the Conflict of Laws* (1962); A. Ehrenzweig, *Private International Law*, Vol. I (1967); A. Ehrenzweig, "Specific Principles of Private Transnational Law", 125 *Recueil des*

lateralism[16], his theory of conflicts resolution was, in many of its central premises, remarkably similar to the statutist method. Currie postulated that, to properly resolve a conflict of laws, one should first ascertain whether each of the involved states would wish to apply their respective laws. To do so, one should examine the content of the conflicting laws, and seek to determine whether their underlying purposes or policies would be best effectuated by their application to the particular case – determine, in other words, through the interpretative process, whether the involved states have an interest in applying their law.

As noted earlier, only three American jurisdictions continue to follow Currie's approach, and even they have rejected some significant features of that approach, such as Currie's intense *lex-fori* favouritism and his proscription of interest weighing[17]. Similarly, Currie's direct influence on other academic approaches now seems to be at its lowest point ever. Nevertheless, as explained below, most other modern American choice-of-law approaches have adopted two Currie-like premises, and to this extent they have incorporated unilateralist elements. The two premises are: (1) that states have an "interest" in the outcome of multistate private-law disputes, and (2) that these "interests" must be taken into account, albeit together with other factors, in resolving these conflicts.

(b) The concept of state interests

308. This is not to say that the above premises have been accepted without opposition. In fact the premise that states have an interest in the outcome of multistate private-law disputes continues to encounter serious criticism. Among the many critics who rejected the notion of state interests[18], Professor Friedrich K. Juenger was the most categorical. He argued that the very notion of a state interest in this context is "a highly implausible construct"[19]. He rejected Currie's hypothesis that states have such an interest, or, as Juenger put it, that states have "a deep-seated concern in the implementation of their legal rules"[20], and criticized Currie and his followers for "[not] adducing empirical evidence for this hypothesis."[21] Echoing Juenger's critique, another scholar asked rhetorically: "Can anyone cite a case in which a state appeared as amicus curiae arguing the importance that its own

---

cours 170 (1969); A. Ehrenzweig, "A Proper Law in a Proper Forum: A 'Restatement' of the 'Lex Fori Approach'", 18 *Okla. L. Rev.* 340 (1965).

16. See S. Symeonides, *An Outsider's View of the American Approach to Choice of Law: Comparative Observations on Current American and Continental Conflicts Doctrine* 16-38 (1980).

17. See *supra* 20-23, 65-66.

18. Among the early critics, see A. Ehrenzweig, *Private International Law* 63 (v. I, 1967); P. Graulich, *Principes de droit international privé* 14 (1961); Kegel, "The Crisis of Conflict of Laws", 112 *Recueil des Cours* 91, 180-82 (1964); Rheinstein, "How to Review a Festschrift", 11 *Am. J. Comp. L.* 632, 664 (1962).

19. F. Juenger, *Choice of Law and Multistate Justice* 135 (1993).

20. *Id.*

21. *Id.*

law be applied?"[22] If it is true that "States often appear as amicus curiae asserting interests they do hold dear"[23], then – the argument goes – states would submit amicus curiae briefs urging a court to apply their respective laws. Do they?

Indeed they do; not in every case, but in more cases than one would think. For example, as documented elsewhere[24], in practically every major international maritime conflicts case that has reached the United States Supreme Court, at least one foreign government, and occasionally the United States government, has filed amicus curiae briefs bringing to the Court's attention their interests in the outcome of litigation between shipowners and seamen. This phenomenon is not confined to maritime conflicts. For example, in *Hartford Fire Insurance Co. v. California*[25], the British Government submitted an amicus brief urging the application of British law in a dispute involving British reinsurers.

Nor is this phenomenon confined to international conflicts. In *Clay* v. *Sun Insurance Office, Ltd.*[26], an interstate conflict involving an insurance dispute between private parties, the Florida Attorney General appeared before the US Supreme Court to defend Florida's interests in applying its law[27]. In *Bernhard* v. *Harrah's Club*[28], in which a California court applied California law imposing civil liability on a Nevada casino, the State of Nevada filed an amicus brief supporting the casino's petition for a writ of certiorari to the United States Supreme Court. Finally, such briefs are not uncommon in lower federal courts or in state courts. For example, in *Modern Computer Systems* v. *Modern Banking Systems*[29], the Minnesota Attorney General appeared as *amicus curiae* in a federal district court in Nebraska and argued for the application of Minnesota law to a franchise contract dispute between a Minnesota franchisee and a Nebraska franchisor[30].

---

22. M. Gottesman, "Adrift in the Sea of Indeterminacy", 75 *Ind. LJ* 527, 531 (2000).

23. *Id.*

24. See the authorities cited in S. Symeonides, "Maritime Conflicts of Law from the Perspective of Modern Choice of Law Methodology", 7 *Maritime Lawyer*, 223, 224-225, 228, 247 (1982).

25. 509 US 764 (1993).

26. 363 US 207 (1960).

27. *Clay* involved the question of whether Florida could constitutionally apply a statute that prohibited the contractual shortening of the limitation period for suing an insurer on a policy issued in Illinois to an insured who later moved to Florida and sustained the loss there. The US Supreme Court held that Florida could do so, in part because of its interests in protecting insureds who sustain losses in that state. The Court noted that: "Florida's particular interest in this very statute is shown by the fact that the Attorney General of the State filed briefs and participated in oral arguments to support the ... [statute's] constitutionality[.]" 363 US at 216.

28. 546 P. 2d 719 (Cal. 1976), cert. denied, 429 US 859 (1977). *Bernhard* is discussed *supra* at 67, 179.

29. 858 F. 2d 1339 (8th Cir. 1988) (decided under Nebraska conflicts law), reversed by *Modern Computer Sys.* v. *Modern Banking Sys.*, 871 F. 2d 734 (8th Cir. 1989).

30. For numerous additional examples of state attorneys general appearing on the side of a private litigant and advocating for their respective states' interests, see S. Syme-

To be sure, amicus briefs are not the only evidence of a state's interest in the application of its law. Even in the absence of such briefs, it is not difficult to see that the tax base of a state like Nevada, which depends heavily on the casino industry, is adversely affected when that industry is subjected to civil liability under the law of another state[31]; or that a state like Michigan, the home of the three large US auto makers, is adversely affected when they are subjected to punitive damages under the law of another state[32]; or that a country that depends heavily on its shipping industry is adversely affected if that industry is subjected to American operating and compensation standards[33]. It is *this adverse impact* that is the essence of the term state "interest".

309. Unfortunately, in articulating this valid concept, Currie used terms that implied an *active desire* on the part of a "government" to apply its law and, worse, a proclivity to assert that desire in an aggressive, imperialistic, "beggar thy neighbor" fashion[34].

Currie either erred or exaggerated. States do not have active desires regarding the outcome of private disputes. However, the policies, purposes, and values embodied in a state's law *can* be adversely affected when that law is *not* applied to a case the law was intended to reach. In this sense, speaking of a state's "interest" in applying its law is simply a shorthand way of describing this *adverse consequence*[35]. Whether one calls this an "interest" or a "concern" – or whether one opts

---

onides. "American Choice of Law at the Dawn of the Twenty-first Century", 37 *Willamette L. Rev.* 1, 23-24 (2000).

31.   Even the California court acknowledged this interest in *Bernhard*. See *supra* 67.

32.   See, e.g., *Kelly* v. *Ford Motor Co.*, 933 F. Supp. 465, 470 (ED Pa. 1996), discussed *supra* at 195, 201, 215 (stating that Michigan had "a very strong interest" in applying its law denying punitive damages so as to ensure that "its domiciliary defendants are protected from excessive financial liability", and that by protecting from punitive damages companies such as Ford, "Michigan hopes to promote corporate migration into its economy ... [which] will enhance the economic climate and well being of the state ... by generating revenues"); *Ness* v. *Ford Motor Co.*, 1993 US Dist. Lexis 9938 at *5 (ND Ill. 1993) ("Michigan has an interest in seeing that product-liability plaintiffs are not overcompensated, resulting in higher insurance premiums for Michigan manufacturers, higher costs, and lost jobs"); *In re Air Crash Disaster Near Chicago*, 644 F. 2d 594 (7th Cir. 1981), cert. denied 454 US 878 (1981) (emphasizing California's "substantial interest in the economic health of corporations ... which do business within its borders" and the ability of such corporations to "enhance[] the economic well-being of the state". 644 F. 2d at 614). For Michigan's protectionism of the three major automakers, see S. Symeonides, "Choice of Law in the American Courts in 1998: Twelfth Annual Survey", 47 *Am. J. Comp. L.* 327, 375-376 (1998), and authorities cited therein.

33.   See S. Symeonides, "Maritime Conflicts of Law from the Perspective of Modern Choice of Law Methodology", 7 *Maritime Lawyer* 223, 224-225, 228, 247 (1982).

34.   See S. Symeonides, "Revolution and Counter-Revolution in American Conflicts Law: Is There a Middle Ground?", 46 *Ohio St. LJ* 549, 558-563 (1985).

35.   At least two modern American approaches make this notion explicit – Weintraub's approach (see *supra* 31), and the approach of the Louisiana codification (see *supra* 102).

for a term such as "the most significant relationship", which the uninitiated may mistake for a mere geographical test – is really a secondary matter. The bottom line is that states are *not* indifferent to the resolution of conflicts between their respective laws. Consequently, a choice-of-law analysis that fails to take this factor into account is presumptively deficient.

This conclusion does not carry with it a wholesale, or even a partial, subscription to Currie's particular value-system, especially the narrow selfish perspective that Currie ascribed to the forum state, and his assumption that states are only interested in protecting their own citizens (the "personal law" principle)[36]. It is not that these tenets are unconstitutional, as some critics have charged[37]. Rather, they are antithetical to the goals of private interstate and international law[38]. To paraphrase John Donne, *no state is an island*, even if geographically it is. The selfish pursuit of the forum's interests is inimical to individual justice and state coexistence, as well as detrimental to the forum's own interests in the long run.

(c)   Unilateralism in other scholastic and judicial approaches

310. With the above clarifications or modifications, one can say that, despite differences in nomenclature, the majority of modern American academic and judicial approaches recognize the concept of state interests as an important choice-of-law factor. To this extent, most of these approaches are at least partially unilateral[39]. For some authors, this proves that Currie has "won the war"[40] even if he "may have

---

36.   See *supra* 18.

37.   See *id.*

38.   See, e.g., D. Cavers, *The Choice of Law Process* 151 n. 29 (1965) (charging that some of Currie's prescriptions are "more appropriate to a tribal system of law than to that prevailing in the American Union"). Currie explained that his analysis did "not imply the ruthless pursuit of self-interest by the states", and did not preclude what he called "rational altruism". B. Currie, *Selected Essays* 185, 186. See also *id.* at 549: ("In a federal union such as ours there is no room for the cycle of discrimination, retaliation, and reciprocity. Each state may and should extend the benefits of its laws to foreigners, not merely with the hope but with the assurance that all other states will reciprocate as a matter of course".) However, Currie never retracted his personal-law principle according to which a state's interest is confined to protecting only its own citizens. In short, he first elevated a faulty assumption into a choice-of-law principle, and then relied on "rational altruism" and self-restraint to resolve the resulting problems and curtail the inevitable excesses.

39.   As Professor von Mehren concedes, while "[m]any jurists who accept a functional and teleological approach to choice of law criticize the extreme unilateral-parochial form advocated by Currie ... [f]ew would deny ... the existence of a strong unilateral tendency in the contemporary theory and practice of choice of law in the United States". A. von Mehren, "American Conflicts Law at the Dawn of the Century, 37 *Willamette L. Rev.* 133, 139 (2000).

40.   H. Kay, "Currie's Interest Analysis in the Twenty First Century: Losing the Battle but Winning the War", 37 *Willamette L. Rev.* 123, 126 (2000). Kay's comment addresses Currie's war against the jurisdiction-selecting aspect of the traditional American approach (an issue on which Kay is right, even though Cavers had started that war long

lost the battle"[41]. Whether or not this is true, important elements of unilateralism are prominently present in virtually all contemporary choice-of-law approaches.

This is particularly true with the most widely followed of these approaches, the Second Restatement. The Restatement has all the appearances of a multilateral approach, including a Savignian-sounding exhortation to apply the law of the state of the "most significant relationship". However, an essential tool in the process of identifying that state is an unilateralist tool – the court must consider "the relevant policies of the forum ... [and] of other interested states ... in the determination of the particular issue"[42].

The same combination of multilateral and unilateral elements appears in other modern policy-oriented approaches. For example – even before Currie – Cook and Cavers argued that the choice-of-law process should consider the socioeconomic purposes underlying the competing substantive laws[43]. Weintraub, and von Mehren and Trautman, also regard state interests as relevant to the choice-of-law process, although – unlike Currie – they advocate weighing those interests[44]. Even Leflar's better-law approach contains an unilateralist element insofar as one of its "choice-influencing considerations" is the "[a]dvancement of the forum's governmental interests"[45]. Finally, "evaluating the strength and pertinence of the relevant policies of all involved states" and applying the law of "the state whose policies would be most seriously impaired if its law were not applied"[46] is the operating principle of the Louisiana codification.

Thus, as a knowledgeable observer recently concluded, "[t]he prevailing methodology in the United States, emerging from the conflicts revolution ... is a curious amalgam of the unilateral and multilateral methods"[47].

(d) Unilateralism in American statutes

311. The same amalgam can be seen in the real world of statutes, a world that academic writers often neglect. This neglect is puzzling if one recalls that a good part of the academic debate on interest analysis has focused on whether states have interests in multistate disputes, and whether legislatures have an intent regarding the spatial reach of the laws they enact. "[L]egislatures *have* no actual intent on

---

before Currie), but the comment can also apply to Currie's undeclared war against multilateralism.

41. *Id.*

42. Restatement Second § 6(2) *(b)* and *(c)*.

43. See *supra* 12-13.

44. See *supra* 30-31. Likewise, Baxter's comparative impairment advocates weighing of the impairments of state interests. See *supra* 25-26.

45. See *supra* 27.

46. See La. Civ. Code Arts. 3515, 3519, 3537, 3542. See *supra* 102.

47. C. Peterson, "American Private International Law at the End of the 20th Century: Progress or Regress?", in S. Symeonides, *Private International Law at the End of the 20th Century: Progress or Regress?* 430 (1999).

territorial reach"[48], says one commentator. Statutes "do not come equipped with labels proclaiming their spatial dimension"[49], says another. And a third asks rhetorically: "Has any state legislature declared it important that its substantive law be chosen in some defined category of cases having multistate contacts?"[50]

The answer is an emphatic "yes". A quick perusal of state statutes reveals the existence of several provisions that contain precisely such declarations. They proclaim that the law of the enacting state shall apply to transactions or events that have certain enumerated connections with the enacting state. Some of these statutes even expressly prohibit the contractual choice of another state's law. The following are simply some examples.

—   A Nevada statute provides that it applies to "1. *All* insurers authorized to transact insurance in this state; 2. *All* insurers having policyholders resident in this state; [and] 3. *All* insurers against whom a claim under an insurance contract may arise in this state."[51] Many other states have similar statutes[52] and many of them expressly prohibit the contractual choice of another state's law[53].

---

48.   L. Brilmayer, "Interest Analysis and the Myth of Legislative Intent", 78 *Mich. L. Rev.* 392, 393 (1980).

49.   F. Juenger, "Conflict of Laws: A Critique of Interest Analysis", 32 *Am. J. Comp. L.* 1, 35 (1984).

50.   M. Gottesman, "Adrift in the Sea of Indeterminacy", 75 *Ind. LJ* 527, 531 (2000).

51.   Nev. Rev. Stat. §696B.020 (1998) (emphasis added).

52.   For example, a Texas statute provides that

> "Any contract of insurance payable to any citizen or inhabitant of this State by any insurance company ... doing business within this State shall be ... governed by [the laws of this State] notwithstanding such ... contract ... may provide that the contract was executed and the premiums ... should be payable without this State." Tex. Ins. Code Ann. §21.42 (West 1999).

A North Carolina Statute provides that

> "[a]ll contracts of insurance on property, lives, or interests in this State shall be deemed to be made therein, and all contracts of insurance the applications for which are taken within the State shall be deemed to be made within this State and are subject to the laws thereof". N.C. Gen. Stat. §58-3-1 (1999).

A Wisconsin statute provides that "[e]very insurance against loss or destruction of or damage to property in this state or in the use of or income from property in this state is governed by the law of this state". Wis. Stat. §632.09 (1997).

For other similar statutes, see Minn. Stat. §60A.08(4) (2000) ("All contracts of insurance on property, lives, or interests in this state, shall be deemed to be made in this state"); Colo. Rev. Stat. §10-4-711 (1999); Fla. Stat. ch. 627.727 (1994); Okla. Stat. tit. 36 §3636 (1997); La. Rev. Stat. Ann. §§22:611, 22:655, 22:1406(D) (West 2000).

53.   For example, an Oregon statute provides that, for an insurance policy "delivered or issued for delivery in" Oregon, any "condition, stipulation or agreement requiring such policy to be construed according to the laws of any other state or country ... shall be invalid". Or. Rev. Stat. §§742.001 and 742.018. For similar statutes, see, e.g. La. Rev. Stat. Ann. 22:629 (West 2002); Tex. Ins. Code Ann. §21.42 (West 1999).

–   An Oregon statute provides that, in cases of insurance for environmental contamination, "Oregon law shall be applied in all cases where the contaminated property to which the action relates is located within the State of Oregon"[54]. Statutes in other states also require the application of forum law to cases arising from trans-boundary pollution[55].

–   An Iowa statute mandates the application of forum law to franchises operated in that state[56], prohibits a contractual choice of another state's law[57], and provides that a contractual choice of Iowa law does not alone render that statute applicable[58]. Other states have enacted similar statutes[59].

–   An Indiana statute requires the application of forum law to consumer credit transactions that have certain connections to that state and prohibits a contractual choice of another state's law[60]. Similar statutes are found in many other states[61].

–   A Louisiana statute requires the application of forum law to construction contracts to be performed in that state and prohibits the contractual choice of another state's law[62].

–   Finally, virtually every state's workers' compensation statutes contain provisions authorizing their extraterritorial application to injuries sustained outside the forum state, if the employee or the employment relationship have certain connections with the forum state[63].

312. The above statutes do not use phrases such as "conflict of laws" or "choice of law", and this is why they can easily elude an electronic word-search. But these

---

54.   Or. Rev. Stat. §465.480(2)(a). The statute continues as follows: "Nothing in this section shall be interpreted to modify common law rules governing choice of law determinations for sites located outside the State of Oregon." *Id.*

55.   See, e.g., Mich. Comp. Laws §324.1804 (1994) ("The law to be applied in an action or other proceeding brought pursuant to this part, including what constitutes 'pollution' is the law of this state, excluding choice of law rules."). For identical provisions, see Colo. Rev. Stat. §§13-1.5-104, 51-351b (1996); NJ Stat. Ann. §2A:58A-5 (1991); Wis. Stat. §299.33(4) (1997).

56.   See Iowa Code §523H.2 (1998).

57.   See *id.* §523H.14.

58.   See *id.* §523H.2.

59.   See, e.g., Minn. Stat. §80C.21 (2000) (franchises); *id.* §325.064 (farm equipment dealerships); § 325.064 (heavy equipment dealerships).

60.   See Ind. Code § 24-4.5-1-201 (1996).

61.   See, e.g., La. Rev. Stat. Ann. §§ 9:3511, 9:3563, 51:1418 (2000).

62.   See, e.g., *id.* § 9:2779. See also *id.* §§9:2778, 38:2196 (same with regard to contracts involving the state and its agencies or subdivisions).

63.   See, e.g., Ala. Code §25-5-35 (1996); Ariz. Rev. Stat. §23-904 (1995); Cal. Lab. Code §3600.5 (1991); Ind. Code §22-3-2-20 (1998); Ga. Code Ann. §34-9-242 (1998); Ky. Rev. Stat. Ann. §342.670 (1997); La. Rev. Stat. Ann. §23:1035.1 (West 2000); Md. Code. Ann. Lab. & Empl. §9-203 (1996); Okla. Stat. tit. 85 §4 (1997); Tenn. Code Ann. §50-6-115 (1999); Tex. Code Ann. §406.071 (West 1992).

statutes do provide conspicuous "labels proclaiming their spatial dimension"[64]. Thus, rather than speaking of a "myth of legislative intent"[65], perhaps we should be speaking of a "myth" of legislative inaction in the choice-of-law field[66]. In the awkward anthropomorphic terminology of interest analysis, these statutes proclaim the enacting state's "interest" (or *volonté d'application*) in regulating the enumerated multistate transactions. In the terminology of classic PIL, these statutes are veritable choice-of-law rules of the unilateral, inward-looking type.

The fact that academic writers often overlook these statutes does not render them unimportant. One indication of their practical importance is that they affect the lives of thousands of people and expeditiously dispose of hundreds of cases without the need for a laborious judicial choice-of-law analysis. But they are also important from a methodological perspective. They illustrate unilateralism's intuitive appeal to legislators. One reason for this appeal is that unilateral rules delineate the minimum spatial reach of the statute that contains them, but *without* prejudging the more difficult question of defining its *maximum* reach[67]. Thus, by employing unilateral rules, legislatures can protect the interests of the forum state without having to enter the "dismal swamp"[68] of conflicts law.

5.   *Understanding modern unilateralism*

313. As noted earlier, the word unilateralism has had an intrinsically negative connotation, even before its current use in the foreign policy context. Thus, it is not surprising that many commentators view the resurgence of the unilateral approach in conflicts law as a negative development.

This view is often based on any or all of the following assumptions: (1) that the unilateral method is a mechanical method; (2) that unilateralism is tantamount to parochialism; and (3) that unilateralism cannot coexist with multilateralism, and thus a system must choose one or the other, without the possibility of combining them.

---

64. F. Juenger, *supra* footnote 49.

65. L. Brilmayer, "Interest Analysis and the Myth of Legislative Intent", 78 *Mich. L. Rev.* 392, 430-431 (1980).

66. In fairness, Brilmayer's and Juenger's statements about lack of legislative intent regarding the spatial reach of statutes refer to substantive statutes, such as guest statutes, that are silent on this question. However, the statutes described in the text illustrate that legislatures often expressly declare their intent on the territorial reach of many statutes. The fact that legislatures often fail to do so in other statutes does not imply a "lack of intent" with regard to the latter statutes.

67. See, e.g., Or. Rev. Stat. §465.480(2)(a) (1999) (quoted *supra* footnote 54; relegating to the "common law rules governing choice of law", i.e., the judicial choice-of-law process, the question of what law governs insurance coverage with regard to contaminated sites located outside Oregon).

68. See M. Gottesman, "Draining the Dismal Swamp: The Case for Federal Choice of Law Statutes", 80 *Geo. LJ* 1 (1991); S. Symeonides, "Exploring the 'Dismal Swamp': Revising Louisiana's Conflicts Law on Successions", 47 *La. L. Rev.* 1029 (1987).

Although history partially justifies some of these assumptions, contemporary reality tends to negate them.

314. The first assumption derives from the fact that the original unilateral method of the Italian statutists was based on a mechanical classification of statutes into real and personal. However, this was a deficiency in interpretative technique, which was partially cured even before the advent of the multilateral approach. In any event, this deficiency is not characteristic of modern unilateralism. A good example is Currie's approach. His critics notwithstanding, Currie's approach was far from mechanical. Rather, it was based on a sophisticated, albeit biased, teleological method of statutory interpretation.

315. The parochial bias of the approaches of Currie and Ehrenzweig[69] gives credence to the second assumption that unilateralism and parochialism travel together. In truth, however, they can travel separately just as well. Parochialism is neither inseparable from unilateralism nor antithetical to multilateralism.

For example, Leflar's better-law approach is multilateral in appearance but can be parochial in its operation, if in applying that approach judges routinely conclude that forum law is better. Conversely, although a strong partiality towards the forum's interests was central in Currie's own thinking, that partiality is severable from the remainder of his basic analysis. Cases like *People* v. *One 1953 Ford Victoria*[70], *Bernkrant* v. *Fowler*[71], and more recent cases employing interest analysis[72] demonstrate that, when used by enlightened judges such as Justice Traynor, even Currie's approach can shed its pro-forum bias.

Other approaches such as those of von Mehren and Trautman, and to a lesser extent comparative impairment, illustrate that one can adopt some of unilateralism's basic postulates (such as inquiring into state interests, "concerns", or "impairments" before choosing the applicable law) without falling into the pit of parochialism. In fact, one can argue that, by inquiring into the interest of both the forum and the foreign state before choosing the applicable law, unilateralism has the *potential* of being more solicitous of foreign interests than a multilateral system that chooses that law *a priori*, before the questions are even known. Although Currie's unilateral method scorned this potential, other unilateral methods, both before and after Currie's, have not done so.

---

69. For Currie's forum-bias, see *supra* 23, and S. Symeonides, "Revolution and Counter-Revolution in American Conflicts Law: Is There a Middle Ground?", 46 *Ohio St. LJ* 549, 566-567 (1985). For Ehrenzweig's forum bias, see E. Scoles, P. Hay, P. Borchers & S. Symeonides, *Conflict of Laws* 38-43 (4th ed. 2004).

70. 311 P. 2d 480 (Cal. 1957) (California court applying Texas law, which favoured a Texas mortgagee at the expense of a California state entity).

71. 360 P. 2d 906 (Cal. 1961) (California court applying Nevada law, which favoured a Nevada claimant at the expense of a California estate).

72. See, e.g., *Eger* v. *Du Pont DeNemours Co.*, 539 A. 2d 1213 (NJ 1988) (discussed *supra* 66; applying South Carolina law, which favoured a foreign defendant at the expense of a forum plaintiff); *Kaiser-Georgetown Comm. Health Plan, Inc.* v. *Stutsman*, 491 A. 2d 502 (DC 1985) (discussed *supra* 66; applying forum law, which favoured a foreign plaintiff at the expense of local defendants).

316. Indeed, both the original unilateral method of the Italian statutists and certain contemporary codified systems that employ unilateral rules offer convincing evidence that parochialism is not an inherent characteristic of all versions of unilateralism. For example, the statutists did not oppose the application *in foro* of a foreign personal statute. Likewise, as documented elsewhere[73], countries that have sanctioned the concept of *règles d'application immédiate* have also demonstrated a willingness to yield to foreign mandatory rules in appropriate circumstances. Some countries have enacted outward-looking unilateral rules, and many of the countries that have enacted inward-looking unilateral rules have paired them with corresponding outward-looking unilateral rules.

A recent example of the latter phenomenon is the Louisiana codification, which contains several such pairings[74]. One of these pairings is seen in Articles 3533 and 3534, which provide for succession to immovables situated within and outside the forum state, respectively. The first article is an inward-looking unilateral rule that calls for the application of the law of the forum situs, while the second article is an outward-looking unilateral rule that calls for the application of the law of the foreign situs. Thus, the two articles together amount to a bilateral rule calling for the application of the law of the situs. The reason this idea was expressed through two unilateral rules rather than one bilateral rule is because, besides the issue of *renvoi*[75], the application of the situs law is subject to different exceptions against or in favour of the forum's forced heirship law in the two situations[76]. This and other examples[77] illustrate that unilateral rules need not be

---

73. See S. Symeonides, *Private International Law at the End of the 20th Century: Progress or Regress?* 15-18 (1999).

74. For detailed discussion of this issue, see S. Symeonides, "Les grands problèmes de droit international privé et la nouvelle codification de Louisiane", 81 *Rev. critique* 223, 260-263 (1992).

75. When the situs is in the forum state, the applicable law is the substantive law of that state, but when the situs is a foreign state the applicable law is the "whole law" of the latter state, including its conflicts law.

76. With regard to forum immovables, the forced heirship law of the forum state does *not* apply if neither the decedent nor the heirs were domiciled in that state at the time of death. See La. Civ. Code Art. 3533(2). With regard to foreign immovables, the forced heirship law of the forum state *does* apply if the decedent and the heirs were domiciled in the forum state at the time of death. See La. Civ. Code Art. 3544(2). The reasons for this differentiation are explained in S. Symeonides, "Exploring the 'Dismal Swamp': Revising Louisiana's Conflicts Law on Successions", 47 *La. L. Rev.* 1029, 1092-1097 (1987).

77. For another example, see Swiss PIL Act, Arts. 90 and 91. The first paragraph of Article 90 provides that Swiss law governs the succession of Swiss domiciliaries, while the second paragraph allows foreigners domiciled in Switzerland to elect their national law, within certain limits. Article 91 provides that the succession of foreign domiciliaries is governed by the whole law of their domicile, subject to certain restrictions. This is a carefully crafted, sophisticated scheme that could not have been constructed through bilateral rules.

parochial, and that the unilateral technique is a high precision tool that allows the drafting of more focused and nuanced rules than the bilateral technique.

Second, one should keep in mind that an inward-looking unilateral rule, even when not paired with a corresponding outward-looking unilateral rule, does not operate in isolation, especially when it is surrounded by multilateral rules. Another example from the Louisiana codification illustrates this point. Article 3545 contains an inward-looking unilateral rule in its first paragraph that calls for the application of forum law to product liability cases that have certain connections to the forum state (subject to a foreseeability exception provided in the second paragraph). The third paragraph provides that "[a]ll cases not disposed of by the preceding paragraphs are governed by the other Articles of the [torts] Title"[78]. The latter articles consist of bilateral rules, most of which provide the court with ample, but guided discretion in choosing the applicable law[79]. Here again, the use of the unilateral technique allows the drafter to delineate with precision the reach of the forum law without prejudging the reach of foreign law, and to do so in a non-parochial fashion.

Third, even when an inward-looking unilateral rule is not paired with a corresponding outward-looking rule nor complemented by a bilateral rule, the result is not necessarily parochialism. For example, a rule that, like Article 3 of the French *Code civil*, provides that forum law governs torts committed in the forum's territory does not foreclose – and indeed it suggests – the possibility of applying foreign law to torts committed outside the forum. Rather, the rule relegates the latter torts to the judicial case-by-case revolution, which may or may not be parochial, and which can lead to a judicial "bilateralization" of the rule, as it has in France[80].

Another example is the previously quoted Oregon statute that mandates the application of Oregon law to insurance conflicts arising from contaminated sites located in Oregon[81]. That statute does not address the question of which law applies with regard to non-Oregon sites. Instead it states that "[n]othing in this section shall be interpreted to modify common law rules governing choice of law determinations for sites located outside the State of Oregon"[82]. Thus, the statute wisely preserves the use of the ordinary choice-of-law process for non-forum sites and, with it, the courts' freedom to apply either forum law or foreign law, depending on all of the choice-of-law factors that are pertinent in the particular case.

---

78. La. Civ. Code Art. 3545 (3).
79. One of these articles, Article 3547, contains an escape that can displace even the unilateral rule of the first paragraph of Article 3545. For a detailed discussion of this scheme and its rationale, see S. Symeonides, "Problems and Dilemmas in Codifying Choice of Law for Torts: The Louisiana Experience in a Comparative Perspective", 38 *Am. J. Comp. L.* 431, 464-469 (1990); S. Symeonides, "Louisiana's New Law of Choice of Law for Tort Conflicts: An Exegesis", 66 *Tul. L. Rev.* 677, 749-757 (1992).
80. See B. Audit, *Droit international privé* 95, 160 (2nd ed., 1997).
81. See *supra* footnotes 54, , 67.
82. Or. Rev. Stat. §465.480(2)(a) (1999).

6. The present and future symbiosis of the multilateral and unilateral methods

317. The third misconception about unilateralism is the assumption is it cannot coexist with multilateralism because the two are antithetical[83]. This assumption finds some justification in the previous history of antagonism and successive displacement between these two methods.

However, as the preceding discussion illustrates, the twentieth century provides ample evidence of *de facto* coexistence and amalgamation. This is true in codified conflicts systems where unilateral rules are surrounded by multilateral rules. It is also true in the United States, where multilateralism and unilateralism cohabit within the confines of each of several modern choice-of-law approaches, and where unilateral state statutes are becoming common place.

The Second Restatement provides a most conspicuous example of such cohabitation. Its all-important §6 employs the basic tools of unilateralism insofar as it directs the court to consider the interests of the forum and non-forum states. At the same time, §6 directs the court to be mindful of values and factors with a peculiarly cosmopolitan and thus multilateral bent, such as "*(a)* the needs of the interstate and international systems, ... *(d)* the protection of justified expectations, ... [and] *(f)* uniformity of result"[84]. Whether this blend of unilateralism and multilateralism is a successful blend is a matter of opinion, but the success or failure of the Restatement did not depend on the fact that it drew from both of these schools of thought. Rather it depended on the merits of the particular choices the drafters made in formulating the Restatement's specific sections.

Similarly, over the last 50 years, state legislatures have propagated another blend of unilateralism and multilateralism. As illustrated above[85], there are literally hundreds of state statutes that contain unilateral conflicts rules interspersed with substantive rules. The blend results from the fact that these statutes presuppose the continuing use of the multilateral choice-of-law process as employed by the courts. Although academic authors tend to ignore these statutes, this reality will not disappear. If anything, the use of unilateral rules in substantive statutes is likely to increase in the future. Whether this will result from increasing protectionism or economic competition among states, a higher sophistication among lobbyists, or other causes, is immaterial. The fact remains that state legislatures prefer to specify whether a statute they are about to enact should apply to cases with enumerated connections with their state than to enter the "dismal swamp" of drafting full-fledged, comprehensive, multilateral choice-of-law rules.

318. These examples of unilateralism's resilience suggest that unilateralism will continue to be with us for the foreseeable future. Rather than ignoring this reality, academic writers can help shape it by using their persuasive powers to steer

---

83. See, e.g., F. Juenger, "A Third Conflicts Restatement?", 75 *Ind. LJ* 403, 410 (2000) ("[U]nilateralism and multilateralism are antithetical."

84. Restatement (Second) §6 (2).

85. See *supra* 311.

legislatures and courts towards the non-parochial use of unilateralism. A preliminary step in that direction would be to begin seeing this symbiosis of the multilateral and unilateral methods not as a symptom of decline, but rather as another healthy example of a *"pluralisme des méthodes"*[86] that can only enrich contemporary private international law. The fact is that virtually no contemporary conflicts system can claim methodological purity; and it is doubtful that any system yearns for it, or that it should. Perhaps the modern legal mind has come to realize that no single method is perfect, that no single method can solve all conflicts problems, and that, if properly coordinated with each other, the two methods *together* can produce a much better system than either method alone.

After more than a century of domination in the United States, Story's multilateral method ran into an impasse[87], particularly in the hands of one of his successors, Joseph Beale. Currie proposed his unilateral method as a complete substitute, but it too ran into its own impasse, especially in confronting the true-conflict and unprovided-for paradigms. What emerged from the clash of these two methods was a mutual accommodation that may prove more workable than either multilateralism or unilateralism alone.

7.   *Accommodative unilateralism*

319. In this new symbiosis, multilateralism will continue to provide the basic and outer framework of any approach to conflicts resolution. However, this approach can benefit from the essential core of unilateralism, namely the notion that, in selecting the applicable law, one should consider the purposes, policies, or interests underlying the laws from which the selection is to be made. This is a useful notion, if only because it helps identify and rationally resolve false conflicts. This is by no means a small accomplishment. In the centuries-old history of private international law, progress has come in slow, tiny steps. In this sense, empowering the decision-maker to separate false conflicts from other conflicts and to resolve the former by applying the law of the only interested state is one of few breakthroughs in the recent history of private international law. This is true even after conceding, as one should, that reasonable minds can differ on whether a particular case is in fact a false conflict or instead a true conflict or a no-interest case.

With good will and some effort, one can also resolve many true conflicts within the confines of unilateralism by resorting to principles of comparative im-

---

86.   H. Batiffol, "Le pluralisme des méthodes en droit international privé", 139 *Recueil des cours* 75, 106 (1973); B. Audit, "Le droit international privé français vers la fin du vingtième siècle: Progrès ou recul?", in S. Symeonides, *Private International Law*, 191 at 210 ("[L]e pluralisme des méthodes constitue une tendance dominante de l'évolution du droit international privé français au cours du XXe siècle").

87.   See A. von Mehren, "American Conflicts Law at the Dawn of the 21st Century", 37 *Willamette L. Rev.* 133, 137 (2000) (concluding that the bilateralism road "may be impassable").

pairment or "consequentialism"[88], namely by applying the law of the state whose interests would suffer the most serious adverse consequences if its law were not applied. The Louisiana codification[89] and the courts of California[90], New Jersey[91], and the District of Columbia[92] provide numerous examples of how this can be accomplished.

320. The common denominator between resolving false conflicts by applying the law of the only interested state and resolving true conflicts by applying the law of the state of the most impairment is the basic principle of *accommodation* of state interests. Rather than thinking in terms of *advancing* the interests of one state at the expense of those of another state, the decision-maker aspires to avoid frustrating the interest of the state that has the most to lose by an adverse choice of law. In false conflicts, that state is the only interested state. In true conflicts, it is the state with the strongest interest. This principle of accommodation is a unilateralist principle in that, rather than denying the existence of state interests, it openly acknowledges them. The fact that it then attempts to accommodate these interests makes it a benevolent or accommodative unilateralism as opposed to Currie's aggressive, imperialistic version.

Admittedly, even this accommodative unilateralism cannot resolve the remaining third category of conflicts cases, namely those in which none of the involved states has an interest in applying its law, i.e., the no-interest cases. Examples of such cases are tort cases in which the parties are domiciled in different states and in which both the conduct and the injury occurred (a) in the tortfeasor's home state whose law protects the victim; or (b) in the victim's home state whose law protects the tortfeasor[93]. To properly resolve these cases, one must look outside the confines unilateralism and employ other criteria of conflict resolution, such as the parties' justified expectations or reliance, and principles of territorial-

---

88. This term originated in theology to describe a doctrine according to which the morality of an act is to be judged solely by its consequences. In choice-of-law, consequentialism stands for the proposition that the quality of a choice-of-law decision is to be judged by the consequences it produces on the interests and values reflected in the conflicting laws. For contemporary iterations of this notion in the Louisiana codification and Professor Weintraub's approach, see *supra* 102 and 31, respectively.

89. *See* Book IV of the Louisiana Civil Code (Arts. 3515-49), enacted in 1991. For discussion, see Symeonides, "Louisiana's New Law of Choice of Law for Tort Conflicts: An Exegesis", 66 *Tul. L. Rev.* 677 (1992). For a specific example of such a resolution of true conflicts, see Articles 3543 and 3544 which provide that, subject to some qualifications, cases in which the tortfeasor's conduct occurred in one state and the victim's injury occurred in another state that had a higher standard of conduct or financial protection for the victim, are governed by the law of the latter state if the tortfeasor should have foreseen that the injury would occur in that state.

90. See, e.g., *Offshore Rental Co.* v. *Continental Oil Co.*, 583 P.2d 721 (Cal. 1978) (discussed *supra* at 67.

91. See the cases discussed *supra* at 66.

92. *See id.*

93. These cases are discussed *supra* at 146-150.

ism, which is to say multilateralism. Applying the law of the state in which both the conduct and the injury occurred, as Chapter VI suggested[94], is one example of how this can be done.

321. To summarize, the notion of accommodative unilateralism begins with the intuitive but important notion that, to intelligently resolve a conflict, any conflict, one must first ascertain the claims of each claimant. The fact that our topic deals with conflicts of *laws* and choice of law means that these claims cannot be ascertained, much less evaluated, without (a) examining the laws from which the choice is to be made, and (b) inquiring into their purposes or policies, or the interests underlying them.

This, however, is only the starting premise, not a complete formula. The complete formula consists of a conscious combination of accommodative unilateralism and multilateralism in which the choice-of-law inquiry begins with the first and ends with the second. The inquiry would proceed as follows:

(1)   If the examination of the laws of the involved states, in light of their contacts with the parties and the case, leads to the conclusion that only one state has an interest in applying its law, then that law should govern;

(2)   If more than one state has an interest, then the resulting conflict should be resolved by weighing the adverse consequences of the choice-of-law decision on the interests of each involved state and by choosing the law of the state that would suffer the most by an adverse choice; and

(3)   If the conflict cannot be resolved in this step of the process, or if the initial inquiry leads to the conclusion that none of the involved states has an interest in applying its law, then the governing law should be chosen by resorting to multilateral criteria such as the ones described above.

C.   Territoriality versus Non-Territoriality

1.   The question

322. The second major dilemma of private international law revolves around our understanding of how laws operate in terms of space. The question can be stated in different ways: (1) do laws attach to a territory as such or to the citizens or domiciliaries of that territory (territoriality versus personality)?; (2) does a law operate only within the enacting state's territory or also beyond that territory (territoriality versus extraterritoriality)?; or (3) does the application of a state's law within its territory necessarily exclude the application of the laws of other states?

Despite differences on the margins, the above formulations ask essentially the same core question. What all of them lack, however, is a cognizance that this is not an all-or-nothing proposition. For this reason, it is preferable to frame the question in terms of territoriality versus *non-territoriality*: when is the application of a state's law grounded on territorial factors, and when is it grounded on other, including personal, factors?

---

94.   See *supra* 150.

2.   Its past

323. The above core question has been answered differently in different periods of history, with the pendulum swinging from territoriality to personality and vice versa, but without one principle completely dislodging the other. For example, during the days of the Roman empire, the principle of personality was the dominant, but not exclusive, principle. In the days of the Italian statutists, the two principles coexisted, with personality embodied in "personal" statutes and territoriality embodied in "real" statutes[95].

With the emergence of modern nation states and Jean Bodin's sixteenth-century seminal works on territorial sovereignty[96], territoriality began gaining more ground, which Ulricus Huber expressed in two of his three famous axioms in the seventeenth century. According to these axioms: (1) the laws of each state have force within its territory but not beyond; and (2) these laws bind all persons found within the territory, whether permanently or temporarily[97]. Following Huber, Joseph Story gave his own ringing endorsement to territoriality in the nineteenth century[98], and Joseph Beale elevated it to a commanding position in the twentieth century. Beale believed that, "by its very nature[,] law must apply to everything and must exclusively apply to everything within the boundary of its jurisdiction"[99]. Thus, a state's law should govern all torts occurring, contracts made, and property located within its territory.

Even in Beale's doctrine, however, territoriality was not the exclusive principle, inasmuch as it was subject to exceptions, many of which were derived from the vested rights theory. In Beale's words, "[t]he law of a state prevails throughout its boundaries and, *generally speaking*, not outside them"[100]. The question was

---

95.   See *supra* 303.

96.   See J. Bodin, *Six livres de la république* (1576).

97.   U. Huber, *De conflictu legum diversarum in diversis imperiis*, in *Praelectiones Juris Romani et hodierni* (1689). Huber's third axiom (using the word "comity" by which his doctrine is known) was that, out of comity, foreign laws may be applied so that rights acquired under them can retain their force, provided that they do not prejudice the state's powers or rights.

98.   See J. Story, *Commentaries on the Conflict of Laws* 19, 21 (1834) ("[E]very nation possesses an exclusive sovereignty and jurisdiction within its territory ... [and its laws] affect, and bind directly all property, whether real or personal, within its territory and all persons, who are residents within it, ... and also all contracts made, and acts done within it ... . [N]o state or nation can, by its laws, directly affect, or bind property out of its own territory, or bind persons not resident therein ...").

99.   J. Beale, *Conflict of Laws* 46 (Vol. 1, 1935). See also *id.* at 45 ("Law operates by extending its power over acts done throughout the territory within its jurisdiction and creating out of those acts new rights and obligations ... . It follows also that not only must the law extend over the whole territory subject to it and apply to every act done there, but only one law can so apply.").

100.   *Id.* at 308 (emphasis added).

which cases qualified for such exceptions, and for Beale and his Restatement[101] the answer was "not many".

Indeed Beale's system allowed for much fewer "personal" or other exceptions than, say, most continental countries, which adopted the personality principle for most matters of capacity, personal status, and succession at death. Even in the 1930s, this was odd for a country like the United States which purported to be "one nation, indivisible", notwithstanding the state boundaries. With the advent of new transportation and communication means and the increased mobility of people, state boundaries became even less important[102], and Beale's insistence on territoriality as the dominant principle made even less sense than before. This is why, by the end of the twentieth century, the exceptions to territoriality have grown exponentially.

3.   Its present

324. First, in terms of general methodology, territoriality lost its dominant position the moment modern methodologies rejected the first Restatement's method of basing the choice of law on a single connecting factor, and instead relied on multiple factors. Most of the new factors, such as the parties' domicile and their pre-existing relationship, were non-territorial. This is true not only of the center-of-gravity approach and its contemporary equivalent, the significant-contacts approach, but also of the Second Restatement, interest analysis, the better law, and other contemporary approaches.

Secondly, in terms of specific solutions to conflicts problems, American courts have introduced major exceptions to territoriality in all areas of conflicts law, not only in torts, but also in contracts and even in property. For example, in contracts, territoriality lost its dominant position when courts abandoned the *lex loci contractus* rule and began choosing the applicable law on the basis of multiple factors, many of which are non-territorial. Territoriality's biggest loss came with the wider recognition and expansive utilization of the principle of party autonomy. This principle is non-territorial in a dual sense: (a) it focuses on the individual parties and makes their volition the supreme principle; and (b) it allows the parties to choose the governing law – including an a-national, non-territorial law – independently from territorial connections.

The extension of party autonomy to areas beyond contracts, such as successions and matrimonial property[103], is also another dramatic example of the retreat of territoriality. A less dramatic example is the gradual reduction of the scope of

---

101. See *Restatement of the Law, Conflict of Laws*, §1 ("No state can make a law which by its own force is operative in another state; the only law in force in the sovereign state is its own law, but by the law of each state rights or other interests in that state may, in certain cases, depend upon the law in force in some other state or states.").
102. See *supra* 7.
103. See S. Symeonides, *Private International Law at the End of the 20th Century: Progress or Regress?* 38-40, 48, 56-60 (1999).

the situs rule for immovables[104]. This reduction is so gradual that it is hardly noticeable, but it has occurred, and it is likely to continue.

In sum, in areas other than torts, American conflicts law is going through a correction period – correcting Beale's excessive reliance on territoriality as the grand guiding principle on how laws operate in terms of space. With some simplification, one can say that, with this correction, American conflicts law will arrive where European conflicts law has always been.

325. Ironically, however, in the area of tort conflicts, the retreat of territoriality has not been as major as it might appear on first sight. This should not be surprising because, as the *Babcock* court signaled[105], the revolution's goal was not to banish the *lex loci* rule from being used in tort conflicts, but rather to define the circumstances under which one should continue to employ that rule. Four decades after *Babcock*, 41 other jurisdictions have followed New York's lead and have abandoned the *lex loci* rule as the rule by which to resolve all tort conflicts[106]. In fact, one might argue that in most of these jurisdictions the rule *as such* has ceased to exist, in that the courts now rely on multiple contacts, factors, and policies which are antithetical to the single-mindedness of the *lex loci* rule.

Nevertheless, when one looks at the *results* that these multifaceted flexible approaches have produced since the *Babcock* days, one realizes that, in many categories and patterns of tort conflicts, these approaches have produced the same results that the *lex loci* rule would have produced: they applied the law of a state of injury, even if that state had additional contacts and even if the rationale for applying that law was partly based on those additional contacts or other factors.

In some other categories of cases, the courts applied the law of the place of conduct (rather than the place of injury) and thus produced a different result than the American version of the *lex loci* rule would produce. However, because the place of conduct is a territorial rather than a personal conduct, these cases remain in the territorialist column.

This means that, in terms of the results of actual cases (rather than in terms of underlying rationale or methodology), territoriality has lost relatively little ground as a result of the American choice-of-law revolution. The figure below attempts to depict the ground that territoriality continues to occupy and the ground it has lost to the principle of personality (see the shaded cells).

---

104. See S. Symeonides, "Exploring the 'Dismal Swamp': The Revision of Louisiana's Conflicts Law on Successions", 47 *La. L. Rev.* 1029, 1043, 1052-1054, 1075-1076, 1090-1092 (1987).

105. See *supra* 89 footnote 189 (*Babcock* court posing question of whether the *lex loci delicti* should "*invariably*" govern all tort conflicts and all their aspects).

106. See *supra* 128-133.

Issues	Conduct-Regulation		Loss Distribution		
Parties' domiciles	Irrelevant		Split-Domicile		Common domicile
Conduct & injury	Same state	Cross-Border	Cross-Border	Same state	Irrelevant
Principle	Territoriality		The remaining battle ground		Personality

4.   Conclusions

326. The study of the decisions of courts that have abandoned the *lex loci delicti* rule supports the following conclusions:

(1)   Territoriality continues to reign supreme in conflicts between conduct-regulating rules. In these conflicts, the courts disregard the parties' domiciles and focus on the two territorial contacts, i.e., the place of conduct and the place of injury. When both of these contacts are in the same state, the courts invariably apply the law of that state[107]. When these contacts are in different states, the courts choose one of those states, as explained above[108]. When they choose the law of the place of conduct, the result deviates from the *lex loci* rule as applied in the United States, but it is still a territorial result.

(2)   Territoriality has lost significant ground to personality in conflicts between loss-distribution rules. However, the ground lost is confined to one category of cases, namely, cases in which both the tortfeasor and the victim are domiciled or have significant affiliations with the same state and are involved in a tort that occurred in another state or states. In these "common-domicile cases", the courts have almost unanimously applied the law of the parties' common domicile[109]. Thus, one can say that the principle of personality reigns supreme in loss-distribution conflicts of the common-domicile pattern[110].

(3)   This leaves the middle ground of loss-distribution conflicts of the split-domicile pattern. This is the arena in which territoriality and personality continue to challenge each other. Although the courts that have abandoned the *lex loci* rule consider both the personal and the territorial contacts, the majority of courts end up applying the law of the state that has the territorial contacts (even if that state also has a personal contact) rather than the state that has

---

107. See *supra* 168-170.

108. See *supra* 171-180.

109. See *supra* 128-133.

110. The few products liability cases that applied the law of the plaintiff's home state when it did not have any other contacts are additional, if extreme, examples of exceptions to territoriality that are not even limited to loss-distribution issues. See *supra* 240-243. The same is true of the federal anti-terrorism statutes which, based on the passive personality principle, apply American law extraterritorially to cases in which the only connection to the United States is the victim's citizenship. See *supra* 197-198.

only a personal contact.[111] In that sense, one can say that, at least for now, territoriality continues to carry the day in these middle conflicts.

327. If one assumes that the goal of the American choice-of-law revolution was to banish territoriality from tort conflicts, one would have to conclude that the revolution has scored only a partial victory. However, as noted earlier, such an assumption would be incorrect. The revolution's goals were neither as deliberate nor as narrow. The chief goal was to free American choice-of-law from the shackles of a mechanical rule that inexorably required the application of the law of a state that had a single contact – which happened to be territorial – regardless of any other contacts or factors, and regardless of the issue involved in the conflict or the content of the conflicting laws. Judged in this light, the revolution has succeeded in demolishing not only this particular rule, but also the system that gave birth to it. Along the way, the revolution has brought about a new accommodation or equilibrium between territoriality and personality.

This equilibrium can form the basis for the next step in the evolution of American conflicts law, which, as explained later[112], should lead to the formulation of new, issue-directed, content-sensitive, flexible, and evolutionary choice-of-law rules based on the accumulated experience of American courts.

D.   Interstate versus Intrastate Uniformity

328. The third basic dilemma of private international law juxtaposes a lofty ideal to a down-to-earth materiality: Should the choice-of-law process aspire to ensure the same result regardless of where the case is litigated (interstate or international uniformity), or should the process cater to the interests of the involved states, and especially the forum state (ethnocentricism or forum-favouritism)?[113]

This dilemma parallels in part the dilemma between multilateralism and unilateralism[114]. Generally, multilateral methods are more concerned with interstate uniformity, whereas unilateral methods tend to be more forum-oriented and to favour intrastate over interstate uniformity. However, as previously explained, these are not inherent characteristics of these methods. For example, a method that, like Leflar's, instructs the judge to choose the "better law" is a multilateral

---

111. See *supra* 137-161.

112. See *infra* 370 *et seq*.

113. Cf. J. Dolinger, "Evolution of Principles for Resolving Conflicts in the Field of Contracts and Torts", 283 *Recueil des cours* 189, 240 (2000) (speaking of "a permanent struggle between ... rules that are universalistically minded ... and ... principles that tame the enthusiasm for international legal tolerance").

114. See A. von Mehren, "American Conflicts Law at the Dawn of the 21st Century", 37 *Willamette L. Rev.* 133, 137-138 (2000) (contrasting "parochial-unilateralism" with "cosmopolitan-bilateralism" and concluding that the bilateralism road "may be impassable", while the unilateralism road "could lead to increasingly unattractive forms of parochialism").

method in that it theoretically places forum law and foreign law on the same footing. However, in its actual operation, such a method can become quite parochial
if the judge routinely concludes that the forum's law is better. Likewise, although
Currie's unilateral approach was heavily biased in favour of the *lex fori*, this is
not necessarily true of all unilateral methods, including the archetypal unilateral
method of the Italian statutists. Nevertheless, historically, more unilateralists have
espoused ethnocentric or forum-centred ideologies, whereas more multilateralists (especially the founders of multilateralism, Savigny and Story) have professed
an internationalist ideology. This section discusses the two opposing ideologies
independently of unilateralism or multilateralism.

329. A less provocative, and perhaps fairer, way of framing the above dilemma is to think in terms of interstate versus intrastate uniformity: when a court
encounters a dispute with foreign elements, should the court try to resolve it: (1)
in the same way as would foreign courts; or (2) in the same way the court would
resolve similar intrastate disputes?[115]

Thus posed, the question is a much closer one than when phrased as a choice
between cosmopolitanism and parochialism[116]. At least since the days of Savigny,
conflicts specialists have assumed that interstate uniformity trumps intrastate
uniformity, an assumption that, at least for the uninitiated, does not appear self-
evident. As one author noted,

> "most conflicts specialists are anxious not to give the impression, right or wrong, that
> they support the primacy of forum law. With a few exceptions, they like to be seen as
> believers in the one true faith, that is: adherence to the equivalence of legal systems
> as the foundation of choice of law."[117]

---

115. Cf. J. Dolinger, "Evolution of Principles for Resolving Conflicts in the Field of Contracts and Torts", 283 *Recueil des cours* 189, 365 (2000) ("Conflicts law contains a peculiar conflict of principles ...: the conflict between securing a minimum of conflicting decisions on the same question in the forum country and in foreign States, on the
one side, and the principle of securing consistency of decisions in the forum country
itself, on the other side.")

116. See T. de Boer, "Facultative Choice of Law: The Procedural Status of Choice-of-Law
Rules and Foreign Law", 257 *Recueil des cours* 223, 419 (1996) (speaking of "the impossible combination of uniform results and substantive justice" and the impermissible
"compromise between domestic morality and unbiased internationalism"); A. von
Mehren, "Choice of Law and the Problem of Justice", 41 *Law & Contemp. Prob.* 27
(1977); A. von Mehren, "American Conflicts Law at the Dawn of the 21st Century", 37
Willamette L. Rev. 133, 137 (2000).

117. T. de Boer, *supra* footnote 116 at 256. See also *id.* ("One seldom reads a dissertation whose author professes an unadulterated forum bias."). See also L. Weinberg,
"Theory Wars in the Conflict of Laws", 103 *Mich. L. Rev.* 1631, 1645 (2005) ("Choices that yield forum law are considered parochial .... Choices that extend comity to
the (usually) defendant-favoring law of a sister state are considered illiberal, unjust,
and defense-oriented .... [T]he forum preference characteristic of interest analysis
is thought unacceptably indulgent to the plaintiff and the parochial, selfish state".).

1.   The classical view: Interstate (or international) uniformity

330. The prophet of the "true faith" was none other that Savigny[118] who in many respects is the intellectual father of modern European private international law. Savigny advanced the laudable idea that the choice-of-law process should seek to ensure international or interstate uniformity of decisions (*internationaler Entscheidungseinklang*), regardless of where the case is litigated. This meant that the process should not favour forum interests or litigants and, to the extent it relied on choice-of-law rules, it should employ rules that are neutral and evenhanded towards foreign law and litigants.

This became the classic view of private international law and, despite disagreements on the margins, it was firmly entrenched in most countries by the dawn of the twentieth century.

2.   The heretical view: Intrastate uniformity or ethnocentricism

331. Since then, however, many theorists have argued that, although uniformity is a laudable goal, it is largely unattainable, and thus the theory and practice of conflicts law should recognize and support other goals. Among the new goals put forward, the one most directly antithetical to international uniformity was the need or the desire to protect state or national interests, especially those of the forum state.

In the United States, the most outspoken proponent of this view was Brainerd Currie, who specifically dismissed the view that the "needs of the interstate and international system"[119] should guide a state's choice-of-law decisions. In his view conflicts law and the judges who apply it were instruments of state policy who, unless constitutionally prohibited, should apply forum law whenever such application would advance the forum's interest[120]. Thus, Currie's approach was ethnocentric both in conception and in result, insofar as it discarded international uniformity as a goal of the choice-of-law process and explicitly favored the application of the *lex fori* in the great majority of cases.

Even so, as Professor Weinberg's own publications illustrate, in the United States, the pro-forum viewpoint is hardly in isolation. See L. Weinberg, "On Departing from Forum Law", 35 *Mercer L. Rev.* 595 (1984); L. Weinberg, "Against Comity", 80 *Geo. LJ* 53 (1991).

118.   See *supra* 304-306.

119.   B. Currie, *Selected Essays* 614; H. Kay, "Currie's Interest Analysis in the Twenty First Century: Losing the Battle but Winning the War", 37 *Willamette L. Rev.* 123, at 128 (2000) ("[Currie] refused to permit forum court judges to sacrifice their state's interest in the hope of achieving a goal of uniformity that was not readily attainable in any event").

120.   See *supra* 21, 23.

3.   *The loss of innocence*

332. By the end of the twentieth century, Currie's *lex fori* favouritism and his per-sonal-law principle had been largely rejected as *de jure* propositions, both by the courts that otherwise follow interest analysis and by many otherwise sympathetic commentators[121]. However, according to many observers, a *de facto* forum favorit-ism, which predates Currie[122], continues to exist in many courts, and not just those that follow the *lex fori* approach[123]. If this is true, Currie may have given voice and rationalization to pre-existing homeward trends that the first Restatement tried unsuccessfully to suppress.

Moreover, as noted earlier, although Currie's particular methodology was eventually rejected, two of its basic premises have survived its rejection: (1) the notion that states do have an interest in applying their law to multistate cases, and (2) the notion that the choice-of-law process ought to take these interests into ac-count in resolving conflicts of laws.

Indeed, these two premises enjoy much wider judicial and academic support than Currie's particular methodology, even among those who vehemently dis-agree with Currie, or who do not attribute to him the paternity of these premises. To a lesser or greater extent, these two notions have made their way into most other contemporary choice-of-law approaches, including the widely followed Second Restatement. Although differing on the specifics, such as how to identify state interests, what weight to assign to those interests relative to other factors, and how to resolve the resulting conflicts, these approaches accept the premise that state interests must be included in the complex calculus of factors on which the final choice is to be based[124]. These approaches differ from Currie's in that they do not officially or openly favour the forum as Currie did. This, however, is simply a difference in intentions, which may or may not produce a difference in result. One could argue that, by freeing judges from the constraints of choice-of-law rules, and by requiring a policy analysis and evaluation, these other approaches unintentionally provide cover to the same homeward trends that Currie unabash-edly embraced and attempted to legitimize.

---

121.   See *supra* 65-66, 23-24, 310.

122.   See, e.g., the writings of Walter W. Cook, discussed *supra* 10.

123.   See P. Borchers, "The Choice-of-Law Revolution: An Empirical Study", 49 *Wash. & Lee L. Rev.* 354 (1992) (reporting the same frequency of pro-forum bias in cases de-cided under any one of the modern choice-of-law methodologies); M. Solimine, "An Economic and Empirical Analysis of Choice of Law", 24 *Ga. L. Rev.* 49 (1989) (same conclusions). But see *supra* 266-267 (finding no similar bias in products conflicts).

124.   See C. Peterson, "American Private International Law at the End of the 20th Century: Progress or Regress?", in S. Symeonides, *Private International Law* 418-423. See also *id.* at 432 ("Not only governmental interest analysis but most of the other theories which have emerged from the revolution are now policy-based, and there can be little doubt that this is now the prevailing view in the United States").

333. Yet, one should not assume that ethnocentricism or forum-favouritism is a peculiarly American phenomenon. As documented elsewhere[125], an increasing number of PIL systems that officially use the international-uniformity rhetoric have adopted rules and mechanisms designed to protect the forum's interests in derogation of the desideratum of international uniformity. Among these mechanisms are (1) the preference given to the forum's *lois d'application immédiate*[126], which one French author characterized as "imperialistic"[127] and an Australian author called "unilateralism triumphant"[128]; (2) the enactment of certain inward-looking unilateral rules specifically designed to protect forum interests[129]; and (3) certain *multilateral* rules that, although facially neutral, are carefully crafted to accomplish the same end[130]. Although these mechanisms are generally more subtle and/or exceptional[131] than Currie's unabashedly parochial approach, they signify that foreign legislatures, no less than American scholars or judges, are cognizant of national interests when entering the supposedly cosmopolitan field of private international law.

334. This is why the second half of the twentieth century can be described as the time in which conflicts law "lost its innocence"[132]. Although international

---

125. See S. Symeonides, *Private International Law* 64-74.

126. See *id.* at 69-70; P. Francescakis, "Lois d'application immédiate et règles de conflits", 3 *Riv. dir. int'le priv. proces.* 699 (1966).

127. Y. Loussouarn, "Cours général de droit international privé", 139 *Recueil des cours* 275, 333 (1973) ("Cet impérialisme de la loi de police").

128. P. Nygh, "The Reasonable Expectations of the Parties as a Guide to the Choice of Law in Contract and Tort", 251 *Recueil des cours* 269, 378 (1995).

129. See, e.g., Swiss PIL Act, Arts. 135 (2) and 137 (2) (requiring the application of Swiss damages law to product-liability and obstruction-to-competition cases that are otherwise governed by foreign law); Hungarian PIL Act, Art. 34 (providing that, regardless of the applicable law, a Hungarian court "shall not impose liability for ... conduct that is not unlawful under Hungarian law ... [nor] impose legal consequences not known to Hungarian law"). For a discussion of these and other similar European rules and an explanation of why these seemingly neutral rules are designed to protect the forum's interests, see S. Symeonides, *Private International Law*, 67-71.

130. Among the oldest examples are multilateral rules that designate the law applicable to matters of personal status. In countries with emigrating populations, that law is the law of the person's nationality, whereas in countries with immigrating populations that law is the law of the person's domicile. See S. Symeonides, *Private International Law*, 66-67.

131. Some commentators reject any similarity between Currie's approach and the concept of *lois d'application immédiate* on the ground that the latter are exceptional, whereas Currie's approach was an all-embracing theory. See, e.g., J. Dolinger, "Evolution of Principles for Resolving Conflicts in the Field of Contracts and Torts", 283 *Recueil des cours* 189, 309 (2000). While this is generally true, the similarity between the two notions is undeniable insofar as they both give precedence to the forum's interests.

132. "Le droit international privé a perdu son innocence." S. Vrellis, "Le droit international privé grec vers la fin du vingtième siècle: progrès ou recul?", in S. Symeonides, *Private International Law* 243 at 247.

uniformity has not been dethroned as the *official desideratum* of the choice-of-law process, it is now mostly a matter of symbolism and rhetoric[133], and even the rhetoric is tapering off[134]. As a notable Dutch author has acknowledged, "we preach the equivalence of all legal systems of the world, [while] at the same time applying our own law as often as we can"[135].

In any event, partly because of the realization that uniformity is elusive, but also because of the economic warfare that outlasted the Cold War, the theory and practice of private international law have come to recognize other goals that should be pursued, either in parallel to uniformity or in derogation therefrom.

In the United States, this rearrangement of goals has been openly and honestly debated, and would have been even more radical had Currie's ideology won the day. He would have placed the pursuit of state interests at the top, and uniformity in the basement, of the conflicts pyramid. In the end, he scored a partial victory by making the pursuit of state interests a legitimate goal of the choice-of-law process, side-by-side with the loftier goal of interstate uniformity.

In other countries, a similar rearrangement has occurred, although it may not be transparent. Many codified PIL systems have gradually come to the conclusion that consideration and, if possible, accommodation of national interests is a legitimate goal of the choice-of-law process, which belongs somewhere in the pyramid of goals. The difference then may be only a difference in degree. In these systems, consideration of national interests is, or is supposed to be, the exception rather than the rule[136] and is disguised rather than openly undertaken and explained.

335. While the "loss of innocence" is regrettable, it would be even more regrettable if we pretended that it has not occurred. A good understanding of reality is the first precondition of success in addressing the problem at hand. As we proceed down the path of the twenty-first century, we can expect that states will, even more boldly, assert their interest in multistate private-law disputes. Our discipline can serve the interstate and international legal order by recognizing the existence of state interests, recognizing when they truly conflict, and articulating principles and mechanisms that can provide a reasonable accommodation between these interests.

E. "Jurisdiction-Selection" versus "Law-Selection"

336. The fourth basic dilemma of private international law has received much more attention in the United States than elsewhere. It is described by the following question: Should the choice-of-law process seek to select a *state* (as the source

---

133. See T. de Boer, "Facultative Choice of Law: The Procedural Status of Choice-of-Law Rules and Foreign Law", 257 *Recueil des cours* 223, 285 (1996).

134. Cf. T. de Boer, *id.* ("If Savigny's theory was meant to bring about uniformity of result, or decisional harmony, it has failed miserably.")

135. T. De Boer, *id.* at 419.

136. See *supra* footnote 131.

of the applicable law) because of that state's factual connections to the case and without regard to the content of its law (the *"jurisdiction-selecting"*[137] method), or should the process seek to select a state's *law* because of its content and underlying policy (*"content-oriented"* law selection)?

This dilemma partly overlaps with the dilemma between multilateralism and unilateralism in that, historically, multilateral methods engaged in jurisdiction-selection, whereas unilateral methods aimed at a content-oriented law-selection. Again, however, these are not inherent characteristics of these methods. For example, the Second Restatement, which is largely a multilateral system[138], calls for a content-oriented law-selection in the great majority of cases. Conversely, Article 3 of the French *Code civil*, which is a classic unilateral rule, is also a classic jurisdiction-selecting rule[139].

1. *The difference*

337. The choice-of-law rules of the first Restatement, and of many other traditional systems, required the judge to select the state of the governing law without regard to that law's substantive content. Obviously, that content became relevant in cases that fell within the *ordre public* exception and some other exceptions, such as the penal or tax exceptions. In all other cases, however, the content (and much less the purpose and policy) of the potentially conflicting laws was not an *official* factor in the court's choice of the governing law. It was as if the choice was between states or "jurisdictions", rather than between their substantive laws. This is why some critics of traditional choice-of-law rules, like Professor Cavers, called them "jurisdiction-selecting" rules, a term that has come to be viewed as more or less synonymous with mechanistic, even arbitrary, rules.

These characterizations, though accurate with regard to most of the first Restatement's rules, should not be applied indiscriminately to all jurisdiction-selecting rules. Jurisdiction-selection was a well-intended, though not inevitable, by-product of the combination of multilateralism and internationalism. Multilateralism's insistence on focusing on legal relationships rather than on the conflicting laws, coupled with internationalism's yearning for evenhanded treatment of forum and foreign law and for international uniformity, led to a system of selection that relied heavily on territorial contacts and deliberately ignored the content of the conflicting laws.

---

137. The term jurisdiction-selection has been coined by Professor Cavers. See *supra* 13. In this context, Cavers uses the term "jurisdiction" not in its usual meaning of either adjudicatory or prescriptive jurisdiction, but rather in the sense of a territorially organized legal order or legal system.

138. This statement is true, except to the extent that the Restatement incorporated unilateralist elements as explained *supra* at 310.

139. Article 3 provides that the "[French] [l]aws of police and public safety obligate all those inhabiting the [French] territory".

It is unfortunate, though not surprising, that a well-intended effort to produce a neutral and evenhanded system produced instead a system of random and blind selection. As Cavers argued, one cannot make an intelligent choice of law without examining the content of the potentially conflicting laws and determining how their application would serve their underlying purposes and affect the outcome of the case[140]. Cavers advocated a transformation of the choice-of-law process from one of choosing between states without regard to the content of their laws, to one of choosing among the conflicting rules of law because of their content[141] and the result their application would yield in the particular case.

338. Currie essentially adopted Cavers's main thesis when he argued that courts should employ the "domestic method" of ordinary construction and interpretation for resolving conflicts of laws[142]. Yet, perhaps because Currie's style was more provocative than Cavers's, this thesis encountered more criticism in Currie's hands.

The critics charged: (1) that Currie's reliance on the "domestic method" of statutory construction and interpretation was misguided, if not suspect, because this method failed to recognize the differences between domestic and conflicts cases[143]; (2) that this method is incapable of pinpointing the policies underlying the conflicting rules of law[144] and (3) that, even if such policies can be ascertained, they cannot help delineate a law's intended territorial reach[145].

---

140. After all, Cavers asked rhetorically, "[t]he court is not idly choosing a law; it is deciding a controversy. How can it choose wisely without considering how that choice will affect that controversy?" D. Cavers, "A Critique of the Choice-of-Law Problem", 47 *Harv. L. Rev.* 173, 189 (1933).

141. This element of Cavers's approach is a unilateralist element. However, his approach as a whole, especially as eventually articulated in his "principles of preference", is a multilateral approach.

142. See *supra* 16.

143. See, e.g., L. Brilmayer, "Interest Analysis and the Myth of Legislative Intent", 78 *Mich. L. Rev.* 392, 417 (1980) ("[D]omestic interpretation and conflicts interpretation are different enterprises altogether"); R. Leflar, "Choice-of-law Statutes", 44 *Tenn. L. Rev.* 951, 954 (1977) ("The term 'statutory construction' is no more than a pretentious disguise for application of the court's conflicts law"); M. Rosenberg, "The Comeback of Choice of Law Rules", 81 *Colum. L. Rev.* 946, 947 (1981) (arguing that, by resorting to the domestic method, Currie "inescapably" implies that "the 'foreign elements' in a case do not call for a distinctive mode of refereeing").

144. See, *inter alia*, E. Bodenheimer, "The Need for a Reorientation in American Conflicts Law", 19 *Hastings LJ* 731, 737 (1978); L. Brilmayer, *supra* footnote 143, at 399, 417, 424; P. Hay, "Reflections on Conflict-of-Laws Methodology: A Dialogue", 32 *Hastings LJ* 1644, 1661 (1981); F. Juenger, "Conflict of Laws: A Critique of Interest Analysis", 32 *Am. J. Comp. L.* 1, 33-35 (1984); W. Reese, "Chief Judge Fuld and Choice of Law", 71 *Colum. L. Rev.* 548, 559-560 (1971); M. Rosenberg, "Two views on *Kell v. Henderson*: An Opinion for the New York Court of Appeals", 67 *Colum. L. Rev.* 459, 463-464 (1967).

145. See L. Brilmayer, *supra* footnote 143, at 393 ("legislatures *have* no actual intent on territorial reach"); F. Juenger, "Conflict of Laws: A Critique of Interest Analysis", 32 *Am. J. Comp. L.* 1, 35 (1984) ("policies do not come equipped with labels proclaiming

These criticisms would have been less surprising had they emanated from the traditionalist conflicts camp. Instead they have been advanced by scholars who have even more contempt for the conceptual systematics of the first Restatement. To the extent they are directed against Currie's forum favouritism[146], these criticisms are justified, although forum-favoritism is not a necessary attribute of the use of the "domestic method" in resolving conflicts cases.

To the extent they are directed at the domestic method's ability to ascertain state policies, these criticisms are less justified, at least to the extent they refer to forum policies. Indeed, "[t]he most important lesson taught in the first year of law school is that an intelligent decision to apply or not to apply a legal rule depends upon knowing the reasons for the rule"[147]. In this sense, Currie's domestic method is just another name for the teleological method[148], which ought to be beyond reproach, at least among the revolutionary ranks. Ascertaining the *telos* or purpose of a law is more difficult in conflicts cases than in ordinary domestic cases, but it is both a surmountable and a worthy task[149].

339. Equally unjustified is the criticism regarding the ability of the teleological method to help delineate the intended spatial reach of the interpreted laws.

---

their spatial dimension"). For counter arguments, see H. Kay, "A Defense of Currie's Governmental Interest Analysis", 215 *Recueil des cours* 9, 117-129 (1989); R. Sedler, "Interest Analysis and Forum Preference in the Conflict of Laws: A Response to the 'New Crits'", 34 *Mercer L. Rev.* 593, 606-620 (1983); R. Sedler, "Reflections on Conflict-of-Laws Methodology", 32 *Hastings LJ* 1628, 1632-1635 (1981); R. Weintraub, "Interest Analysis in the Conflict of Laws as an Application of Sound Legal Reasoning", 35 *Mercer L. Rev.* 629, 630-634 (1984).

146. See *supra* 23.

147. R. Weintraub, "Interest Analysis in the Conflict of Laws as an Application of Sound Legal Reasoning", 35 *Mercer L. Rev.* 629 at 631 (1984).

148. See H. Baade, "Counter-Revolution or Alliance for Progress? Reflections on Reading Cavers, *The Choice-of-Law Process*", 46 *Tex. L. Rev.* 141 at 149 (1967) ("governmental interest analysis is merely one of the many applications of teleological interpretation. It seeks to determine the pertinence of rules of law to multiple-contact cases through an analysis of the purposes behind these rules").

149. "In broad outline, the laws of the several states are remarkably similar, and the policies behind those laws are largely shared and thus presumptively familiar to the examining court. This familiarity enables the court, on comparing the points at which significant variations do occur, to identify the purpose or policy which objectively seems to be served by the variation and to assess the strength of that policy. This is not a search in legislative history but an observation based on common background. For the most part, the court is merely asked to think about why a rule exists and to consider whether that purpose should, or even can be given effect in this case." E. Scoles, P. Hay, P. Borchers and S. Symeonides, *Conflict of Laws* 47 (4th ed., 2000). On the other hand, *teleology* has its limits when the rule under interpretation is that of a foreign country with a legal tradition, language, and terminology different from our own. "Intra-mural speculation on the policies of other states has obvious limitations because of restricted information and wisdom." *Tooker* v. *Lopez*, 249 NE 2d 394, 411 (NY 1969) (Breitel, J., dissenting).

The vitality of this method has never depended on proof of *actual* legislative intent, as the critics have assumed. Without agreeing with Currie's method or with his particular inferences about the spatial reach of laws, one can still accept the notion that the spatial reach of laws is best determined by looking to their purpose and function, as long as it is understood that such determination is only half of the process of actually resolving a conflicts problem. The second half of the process, in which Currie's insights were much less inspiring, is to actually and rationally accommodate laws with overlapping spatial reach.

In sum, having gone down the road of completely rejecting the established choice-of-law system, Currie had the sense of turning to something equally established but more flexible and more resourceful – the domestic common-law method. This opened the way for introducing functionalism into choice-of-law thinking, allowing a more individualized approach to cases, and tempering the conflictual method by injecting into it considerations of substantive justice. Of all the elements of Currie's theory, this was the least problematic.

2.   *The gains of content-oriented law-selection in the United States*

340. Despite minor differences on the logistics, Cavers's basic notion that the choice-of-law process should consider the content of the competing substantive rules before choosing between them became "a major article of faith"[150] of all branches of the American conflicts revolution. In fact, it was one of the reasons *for* the revolution. It offered judges a more direct and honest route to resolving the impasses of the first Restatement, a route that rendered obsolete the manipulative escape devices judges employed before the revolution[151]. By freeing judges from the constraints of blindfold choice-of-law rules, this notion also placed on judges the responsibility of explaining the real reasons for their choices.

However, the radical transformation of the choice-of-law process that Cavers advocated[152] has not been completed, and may never be. Nevertheless, the all-important notion of a content-oriented law selection, as opposed to content-blind jurisdiction-selection, has become an integral part of all modern American choice-of-law approaches. These include Currie's interest analysis; the Second Restatement when properly applied; Leflar's better-law approach and other result-oriented approaches; von Mehren's and Trautman's functional analysis; and Weintraub's new consequences-based approach. Last but not least, this notion has been implemented in the Louisiana conflicts codification which consists primarily of content-oriented rules[153]. As Weintraub characterized it, "[a]n approach

150. H. Korn, "The Choice-of-Law Revolution: A Critique", 83 *Colum. L. Rev.* 772, 810 (1983).

151. See S. Symeonides, W. Perdue and A. von Mehren, *Conflict of Laws* 42-103 (2nd ed. 2003); E. Scoles, P. Hay, P. Borchers and S. Symeonides, *Conflict of Laws* 122-145, 722-726 (4th ed. 2004).

152. See *supra* 13, 337.

153. See *infra* 345.

to choice of law that focuses on consequences is consistent with the positions of almost all major American conflict-of-laws scholars"[154].

3. The next step in the United States: Consolidation

341. As documented elsewhere[155], the notion that conflicts of laws can be resolved more intelligently by considering the content of these laws has also gained considerable ground in codified conflicts systems outside the United States. This is so despite the fact that these systems are supposed to be negatively disposed toward this notion, as well as the fact that this notion appears not to be well-suited for statutory choice-of-law rules. Recent evidence disproves both assumptions. Indeed, recent experience illustrates that it is possible to construct a new breed of content-oriented choice-of-law rules that make the choice dependent in whole or in part on the content of the conflicting laws[156]. Content-oriented rules have proliferated in recent years, although they continue to be vastly outnumbered by jurisdiction-selecting rules. Considering that, even when applying jurisdiction-selecting rules, judges covertly consider the content of the conflicting laws in pondering whether to invoke any of the available escapes, one can conclude that the jurisdiction-selecting method has lost much more ground than is commonly believed.

342. One question worth considering is whether such content-oriented rules are feasible and desirable in the United States. For, although content-oriented law selection was a tremendous step forward, it has also brought with it a much more laborious, exacting, and sophisticated choice-of-law analysis, with all concomitant consequences on judicial resources.

The general need for rules that enable courts to rationally and expeditiously resolve conflicts without having to reinvent the wheel in each case is explored in detail later[157]. For now the question is a narrower one: Is it possible to craft content-oriented rules of a shape and content that are faithful to the lessons of the American conflicts experience? In this author's view, the answer is clearly affirmative and evidence supporting it comes from all directions – academic, judicial, and legislative.

343. In the academic world, the first to attempt to construct content-oriented rules was Cavers himself, and appropriately so. In his seminal 1965 book *The Choice of Law Process*[158], Cavers proposed five "principles of preference" for tort

---

154. R. Weintraub, *Commentary of the Conflict of Laws* 347 (4th ed. 2001). According to Weintraub, these scholars "differ primarily on whether or not it is feasible to attempt forum-neutral solutions when there is a true clash of state policies, and, if so, what form forum-neutral solutions will take". *Id.*

155. See S. Symeonides, *Private International Law at the End of the 20th Century: Progress or Regress?* 37-42 (1999).

156. See *id.*

157. See *infra* 371-389.

158. D. Cavers, *The Choice of Law Process* 139 et seq. (1965).

conflicts and two for contract conflicts. His first principle for torts covered situations in which the injury is in one state and either the conduct or the tortfeasor's domicile are in another state. The principle calls for the application of the law of the state of injury, but only if that law "set[s] a *higher standard* of conduct or of financial protection against injury *than* do the laws of the [other] state"[159]. His second principle covered situations in which the conduct and the injury are in one state and the victim's domicile is in another state. The principle called for the application of the law of the former state, if that law provides for "*a lower standard* of conduct or of financial protection *than* the victim's domicile"[160].

The italicized words signify the content-oriented element of these principles and are the basis of their rationale according to Cavers. His choice of law was not based on a state's physical contacts alone, but rather on the presence of the "right" *combination* of contacts *and* laws. For example when a state's law prescribes a high standard of conduct, but the state's only contact is the victim's domicile, this is not the right combination for applying that law. On the other hand, if that state's contact is that it is the place of the tortfeasor's conduct, then this is the right combination for applying that state's conduct-regulating rule, even in the absence of other contacts.

Among other scholars who followed Cavers's lead are Professor Weintraub, who proposed a plaintiff-favouring rule for tort conflicts[161] and a validation-favouring rule for contract conflicts[162], and the undersigned author who suggested a series of content-oriented rules for a proposed Third Conflicts Restatement[163].

344. In the judicial front, New York's *Neumeier* Rules 2a and 2b[164] are examples of content-oriented rules. Rule 2a covers situations in which the tortfeasor's conduct and domicile are in one state and the victim's domicile is in another. The rule calls for the application of the law of the former state *if that law favors the tortfeasor*. Rule 2b deals with the converse situation in which the tortfeasor's domicile is in one state and the injury and victim's domicile are in another. The rule calls for the application of the law of the latter state *if that law protects the victim*. Again, the italicized words signify the content-orientation of these rules.

---

159. *Id.* at 139 (emphasis added).
160. *Id.* at 146 (emphasis added).
161. See *supra* 31. For another content-and result-oriented rule proposed by Weintraub for product liability conflicts, see R. Weintraub, *Commentary on the Conflict of Laws* 424-425 (4th ed. 2001).
162. See *id.* at 480-481 (proposing a rule that favours the application of a law that validates the contract. The rule authorizes the application of the validating law of any state having a contact with the parties or with the transaction sufficient to make that state's validating policies relevant, "unless some other state would advance its own policies by invalidating the contract" and some other specified conditions are met.)
163. See S. Symeonides, "The Need for a Third Conflicts Restatement (and a Proposal for Tort Conflicts)", 75 *Ind. LJ* 437, 450-451 (2000).
164. See *supra* 93.

In other states, courts have not been as bold as the New York Court of Appeals in enunciating content-oriented (or, for that matter, any) choice-of-law rules in a quasi-legislative fashion. Nevertheless, these courts routinely take account of the content of conflicting laws in resolving conflicts cases. One who systematically studies these cases can easily recast their results into content-oriented rules. Examples of such rules are those proffered for conduct-regulation conflicts in Chapter VII[165], and one of the three rules proffered for certain split-domicile and cross-border loss-distribution conflicts in Chapter VI[166].

345. On the legislative front, the Louisiana codification illustrates that the notion of content-oriented law-selection is entirely compatible with statutory rules. Indeed, as noted earlier, the codification's content-oriented rules outnumber jurisdiction-selecting rules by a ratio of more than 3:1[167]. The same is true of the Puerto Rico Draft Code[168] and, to a lesser extent, the American Law Institute's proposed statute on Complex Litigation[169].

---

165. See *supra* 180. See also E. Scoles, P. Hay, P. Borchers and S. Symeonides, *Conflict of Laws* 850 (4th ed. 2004).

166. See *supra* 162. See also E. Scoles, P. Hay, P. Borchers and S. Symeonides, 842. For a similar effort to extract content-oriented rules of choice of law, see R. Sedler, "Choice of Law in Conflicts Torts Cases: A Third Restatement or Rules of Choice of Law", 75 *Ind. LJ* 615 (2000).

167. Twenty-seven out of the 35 articles of the Louisiana codification are content-oriented. See S. Symeonides, "Les grands problèmes de droit international privé et la nouvelle codification de Louisiane", 81 *Rev. critique* 223, 251-253 (1992). Examples of such content-oriented rules for tort cases are La. Civ. Code Arts. 3543 and 3544. The first article provides in part that issues pertaining to standards of conduct and safety are governed by the law of the state in which the injurious conduct occurred, if the injury occurred in that state "or in another state whose law did not provide for a *higher* standard of conduct". If the injury-state has such a higher standard, then its law applies "provided that the person whose conduct caused the injury should have foreseen its occurrence in that state". Article 3544 provides in part that in split-domicile cross-border torts the law of the injury-state applies (subject to the foreseeability proviso) if that state is also the victim's domicile and its law "provide[s] for a *higher* standard of financial protection for the injured person than did the law of the state in which the injurious conduct occurred". For a discussion of these rules by their drafter, see S. Symeonides, "Louisiana's New Law of Choice of Law for Tort Conflicts: An Exegesis", 66 *Tul. L. Rev.* 677, 705-735 (1992).

168. See Academia Puertorriqueña de Jurisprudencia y Legislacion, *Proyecto para la Codificación del Derecho internacional privado de Puerto Rico*, S. Symeonides & A. von Mehren, *Rapporteurs* (1991). For discussion, see S. Symeonides, "Revising Puerto Rico's Conflicts Law: A Preview", 28 *Colum. J. Transn'l L.* 413 (1990); S. Symeonides, "Codifying Puerto Rico's Choice-of-Law for Contracts", in *Law and Justice in a Multistate World: Essays in Honor of Arthur T. von Mehren*, 419-437 ((J. Nafziger and S. Symeonides, eds., 2002).

169. See American Law Institute, *Complex Litigation: Statutory Recommendations and Analysis* (1994). For a discussion of this Project, see a Symposium published in 54 *La. L. Rev.* 833 (1994) (containing articles by von Mehren, Trautman, Symeonides,

The above developments illustrate that content-oriented rules are feasible[170]. Demonstrating that they are also desirable is a more difficult undertaking, especially because of the traditional American hostility towards choice-of-law rules of *any* kind. This issue is revisited later[171].

4.   The limits of content-oriented law selection and its symbiosis with jurisdiction-selection

346. Despite its inherent merits and its significant gains during the twentieth century, content-oriented law-selection will never completely displace the jurisdiction-selection method; nor should it. This is particularly true in codified systems. The differences among state and national substantive laws are too many to be susceptible to being accurately catalogued and compressed into a few meaningful categories around which to build *all-encompassing* content-oriented rules. Thus, in codified systems, content-oriented rules are bound to remain the exception. As said elsewhere, the realistic challenge for the contemporary conflicts codifier is "not how to eliminate jurisdiction-selecting rules, but rather how to combine them with content-oriented rules in such a way that both sets of rules together may produce a rational system"[172]. In other words, a principled eclecticism is once again the name of the game. While each system may opt for a different mix between these two types of rules, most systems nowadays recognize the need to combine them as well as the feasibility of so doing. This was hardly true one generation ago.

347. Content-oriented selection should have an easier time in uncodified systems like the United States, but, even there, it will not displace jurisdiction-selection. First, despite its multiple advantages, content-oriented selection is a laborious process that imposes a considerable burden on judges. Some judges are unwilling or unable to bear this burden and prefer to engage in simply counting contacts. Contact-counting is the modern version of jurisdiction-selection, with the only difference being that the choice of law is based on more than one contact. Some courts engage in contact-counting even when applying the Second Restatement, which contemplates a content-oriented selection[173]. Thus, jurisdic-

---

Cooper, Juenger, Kalis, Kozyris, Mullenix, Nafziger, Sedler, Seidelson, Shreve and Wilkins).

170. See also A. von Mehren, "Recent Trends in Choice-of-Law Methodology", 60 *Cornell L. Rev.* 927, 966 (1975) ("[T]he results reached through policy-based analysis should be susceptible of generalization in a dispositive manner, that is to say, of statement as rules.").

171. See *infra* 371-389.

172. S. Symeonides, Les grands problèmes de droit international privé, *supra* footnote 167, at 250.

173. See S. Symeonides, "The Judicial Acceptance of the Second Conflicts Restatement: A Mixed Blessing", 56 *Md. L. Rev.* 1248, 1262-1263, 1272-1273 (1998).

tion-selecting tendencies will continue to reside within a segment of the judiciary for many years to come.

Secondly, even those who, like this author, strongly believe in the advantages of a content-oriented law selection should recognize that in some cases the content of the conflicting laws should *not* affect the final choice. Perhaps the best example emerges from the experience of American courts in dealing with loss-distribution conflicts involving the common-domicile pattern. As documented in Chapter VI[174], virtually all state supreme court cases involving conflicts between the loss-distribution rules of the accident state and the parties' common domicile applied the law of the common domicile, *both* when that law favoured recovery *and* when it did not. From this experience, one could justifiably conclude that the law of the common domicile governs *de facto*, whether it favours or disfavours recovery, i.e., *regardless of its content*. The New York Court of Appeals has adopted precisely such a rule (*Neumeier* Rule 1) as have the Louisiana codification and recent European codifications in the rest of the world[175].

Now, reasonable people may disagree on whether this rule should be content-neutral. For example, while virtually no one questions the wisdom of applying the common-domicile law in cases of the *Babcock* pattern (i.e., when that law favours the plaintiff), some commentators disagree with the automatic application of that law to cases of the converse pattern (i.e., when that law favours the defendant). These commentators would prefer a content-oriented rule that applies common-domicile law when it helps, but not when it hurts, the plaintiff. This view is more plausible than it appears at first sight. On the other hand, those who do not subscribe to this differentiation prefer a content-neutral common-domicile rule. They do so, not necessarily because they subscribe to jurisdiction-selection but rather because, after examining the consequences of the rule in each pattern, they find it equally appropriate to both. The point is that a choice-of-law rule need not wear content-orientation on its sleeve and that a rule that does not *explicitly* refer to the content of the conflicting laws can embody all the lessons of a modern functional choice-of-law thinking.

348. Another example is a rule like the one proposed in Chapter VII, which provides that conduct-regulation conflicts should be resolved by applying the law of the state in which both the conduct and the injury occurred[176]. This sounds like the old *lex loci delicti*, and it is – except that (1) it is limited to conduct-regulation issues for which the *locus delicti* is uniquely if not exclusively concerned; and (2) it applies only if both the conduct and the injury occurred in the same state. Again,

---

174. See *supra* 133, 164.

175. See *supra* 134.

176. See *supra* 180. A rule to this effect is contained in the Louisiana codification. See La. Civ. Code Art. 3543, discussed in S. Symeonides, "Louisiana's New Law of Choice of Law for Tort Conflicts: An Exegesis", 66 *Tul. L. Rev.* 677, 705-708 (1992). A similar rule is proposed in E. Scoles, P. Hay, P. Borchers and S. Symeonides, 850, and S. Symeonides, "The Need for a Third Conflicts Restatement (and a Proposal for Tort Conflicts)", 75 *Ind. LJ* 437, 450, 454-457 (2000).

while some people might argue that the application of the *lex loci* should depend on whether it provides for a lower or a higher standard of conduct than, say, the law of the parties' common domicile, the better view is that the content of the *lex loci* should make no difference. These are the cases for which the *Babcock* court said that "it would be almost unthinkable to seek the applicable rule in the law of some other place"[177]. If any confirmation of this elementary proposition is needed, the case law is replete with examples of cases holding to that effect[178]. Thus again, a rule stated in jurisdiction-selecting terms can embody the most modern content-oriented considerations.

In the final analysis, therefore, the challenge of conflicts scholars is to draw from the case law and to formulate more such rules, in which the sophisticated content-oriented analysis is done by the formulator, and which judges can apply without having to reinvent the wheel.

F. "Conflicts Justice" versus "Material Justice"

349. In contrast to the previous dilemmas, the dilemma between "conflicts justice" and "material justice" is more philosophical and less methodological. It is posed by the following question: should the choice-of-law process aim for: (1) the proper *law*, i.e., the law that has the most pertinent connections to the case without regard to the quality of the result it produces; or (2) the proper *result*, i.e., a result that produces the same quality of justice in the individual case as is expected in fully domestic, non-conflicts cases?

This dilemma partly overlaps with the dilemma between jurisdiction-selection and content-oriented law-selection, in the sense that jurisdiction-selecting methods are more likely to aim at conflicts justice, whereas content-oriented methods are more likely to aim at material justice. However, some jurisdiction-selecting rules are also result-oriented, such as those that instruct the judge to select the law of the state that produces a pre-selected substantive result, e.g., upholding the validity of a juridical act[179]. Conversely, while many content-oriented rules are motivated by considerations of material justice, this is not true of all such rules. For example, rules honouring a choice of law by both parties are motivated primarily by considerations of conflicts justice[180]. Put another way, while all result-oriented rules are content-oriented, the converse is not true. Moreover, many content-oriented approaches aim at conflicts justice rather than material justice. This is clearly true of Currie's approach[181] and even Cavers's ultimate method, his

---

177. *Babcock, supra* 108 footnote 13.

178. See *supra* 168-170.

179. See *infra* 353.

180. See S. Symeonides, *Private International Law at the End of the 20th Century: Progress or Regress?* 38-40 (1999).

181. See H. Kay, "Currie's Interest Analysis in the Twenty First Century: Losing the Battle but Winning the War", 37 *Willamette L. Rev.* 123, 123 (2000) (predicting that Currie "would respectfully decline the invitation to confront once again ... 'the dilemma be-

"principles of preference", which are among the best examples of a content-oriented method. Although Cavers was one of the harshest critics of the jurisdiction-selecting method and one of the first advocates of the pursuit of "justice in the individual case", he eventually opted for conflicts justice in formulating his "principles".

1.   The classical view: "Conflicts justice"

350. The classical, traditional view of private international law, going as far back as Savigny, is grounded on the basic premise that the function of conflicts law is to ensure that each multistate legal dispute is resolved according to the law of the state that has the "most appropriate" relationship with that dispute. Opinions on defining and especially assessing the "propriety" of such a relationship have differed over the years from one legal system to another and from one subject to the next. Despite such differences, however, all the versions of the classical school have remained preoccupied with choosing the proper *state* to supply the applicable law, rather than directly searching for the proper *law* or, much less, for the proper *result*.

Indeed, the implicit if not explicit assumption of the classical school is that, in the great majority of cases, the law of the proper state *is* the proper law. But in this context "propriety" is defined not in terms of the content of that law, or the quality of the solution it produces, but rather in geographical or spatial terms[182]. If the contacts between the state from which that law emanates and the multistate dispute at hand are such as to meet certain pre-defined choice-of-law criteria, then the application of that law is considered proper regardless of the qualities of the solution it produces. Whether the solution is "good" or "bad" depends on the inherent goodness or badness of the applicable law, and this is something beyond the domain of conflicts law. After all, conflicts exist because different societies have laws reflecting different value judgments on how to resolve legal disputes[183].

---

tween 'conflicts justice' and 'material justice', since he early on resolved that dilemma in favour of the judicial vindication of the policy of the forum state when its interests are at stake").

182. See G. Kegel, "The Crisis of Conflict of Laws", 112 *Recueil des cours* 91, 184-185 (1964) ("[W]hat is considered the best law according to its content, that is, *substantively*, might be far from the best spatially").

183. 1499. See A. von Mehren, "American Conflicts Law at the Dawn of the 21st Century", 37 *Willamette L. Rev.* 133, 134 (2000):

"[T]he difficulties posed for instrumental or teleological analysis are far greater when the controversies to be resolved are not localized in a single legal order that holds shared values and policies and has a unified administration of justice that can authoritatively weigh competing values and decide which shall prevails when conflicts arise."

See also *id.* at 137: "[T]he same degree of justice usually cannot be given in matters that concern more than one society as is provided in matters that concern only one society and its legal order"; A. von Mehren, "Choice of Law and the Problem of Justice", 41 *Law & Contemp. Prob.* 27, 42 (1977)

As long as multistate disputes are resolved by choosing the law of one state over the other, such a choice is bound to satisfy one society and one party and aggrieve another. This being so, the choice of the applicable law cannot afford to be motivated by whether it produces a "good" or "just" resolution of the actual dispute. Hence, while conflicts law should strive to ensure the application of the law of the proper state (conflicts justice), it cannot expect to ensure the same type and quality of justice as is pursued in fully domestic situations (material justice). In Gerhard Kegel's words, conflicts law "aims at the *spatially* best solution ... [while] substantive law aims at the *materially* best solution"[184].

2.   The second view: "Material justice"

351. A second view begins with the premise that multistate cases are not qualitatively different from domestic cases and thus judges should not abdicate their responsibility to resolve disputes *justly and fairly* when they discover that the case contains foreign elements. Resolving such disputes in a manner that is substantively fair and equitable to the litigants should be an objective of conflicts law as much as it is of internal law. Justice should not be dispensed in gradations, and conflicts law should not accept a lesser quality of justice. Thus, this view rejects the classical presumption that the law of the proper state is necessarily the proper law and instead directly scrutinizes the applicable law to determine whether it actually produces the proper *result*. Again, opinions differ on defining the "propriety" of the result, but all the various versions of this view agree that the propriety should be determined in material rather than in spatial terms.

This view is much older than is generally believed. Historical precedents include the Byzantine commentators' preference for the *philanthropoteron* result[185], the Italian statutists' preference for the forum's *statuta favorabilia* over foreign *statuta odiosa*[186], and Magister Aldricus' call for the application of the *potior et utilior* law[187]. However, for at least seven centuries, this view has remained in the periphery of choice-of-law thinking until the twentieth century, when it found a more hospitable climate.

3.   Inroads by material justice into conflicts justice

352. During the second half of the twentieth century, the material-justice view has gained significant ground at the expense of the classical view. This is particularly

---

184. G. Kegel, "Paternal Home and Dream Home: Traditional Conflict of Laws and the American Reformers", 27 *Am. J. Comp. L.* 615, 616-617 (1979).

185. See M. Maridakis, "L'inaplicabilité du droit étranger à Byzance", 2 *Mélanges Fredericq* 79 (1965). The Greek word *philanthropoteron* is the comparative form of the word *philanthropos* (which is the root of the English word philanthropic). It would loosely translate as the more philanthropic, humane, benevolent, or merciful result.

186. See 1 Lainé, *Introduction au droit international privé*, 146, 264 (1888).

187. See Code cisianus E.VIII. 218 §46.

true in the United States[188], where this view found enthusiastic support in the writings of Professors Leflar, Juenger, and McDougal[189], and a more qualified and targeted support in the early writings of Professors Cavers[190] and Weintraub[191].

353. However, closer examination reveals that in recent years the material justice view has made significant inroads even in codified private international systems[192], which usually are viewed as the bastions of the classical view. Recent codifications are replete with result-oriented choice-of-law rules *(règles de conflit à coloration matérielle)* which, in one form or another, aim to accomplish a certain substantive result that the drafters considered *a priori* as desirable. More often than not, this result is one favoured by the domestic law of not only the forum state, but also of most states that partake in the same legal tradition. This result may be one of the following: (1) favouring the formal or substantive validity of a juridical act, such as a testament, a marriage, or an ordinary contract; (2) favouring a certain status, such as the status of legitimacy or filiation, the status of a spouse, or even the dissolution of a status (divorce); or (3) favouring a particular party, such as a tort victim, a consumer, an employee, a maintenance obligee, or any other party whom the legal order considers weak or whose interests are considered worthy of protection[193].

The first two objectives (favouring the validity of a juridical act or favouring a certain status) are accomplished by choice-of-law rules that contain a list of alternative references to the laws of several states *(alternative-reference rules)* and allow the court to select a law that validates the juridical act or confers the preferred status[194]. The third objective (protecting a particular party) is accomplished through choice-of-law rules that: *(a)* provide alternative choices to the court as

---

188. For similar views in Europe, see T. de Boer, "Facultative Choice of Law: The Procedural Status of Choice-of-Law Rules and Foreign Law", 257 *Recueil des cours* 223, 293-297 (1996); K. Zweigert, "Zur Armut des internationalen Privatrechts an sozialen Werten", 37 *RabelsZ* 435 (1973). See also C. Joerges, *Zum Functionswandel des Kollisionsrecht, Die "Governmental Interest Analysis" und die "Krise des Internationalen Privatrechts"* (1971); J. González Campos, "Diversification, spécialisation et matérialisation des règles de droit international privé", 287 *Recueil des cours* 9 (2000); P. Gutzwiller, "Von Ziel und Methode des 'IPR'", *Ann. Suisse droit int'l* 161 (1968).

189. See *supra* 27.

190. See *supra* 14.

191. See *supra* 31. From the next generation, see J. Singer, "Pay No Attention to That Man Behind the Curtain: The Place of Better Law in a Third Conflicts Restatement", 75 *Ind. LJ* 659 (2000); L. Weinberg, "Theory Wars in the Conflict of Laws", 103 *Mich. L. Rev.* 1631, 1666-1669 (2005).

192. See S. Symeonides, *Private International Law at the End of the 20th Century: Progress or Regress?* 46-60 (1999).

193. See E. Jayme, "Internationales Familienrecht heute", in *Festschrift Müller-Freienfels* 341, 349-350 (1986); F. Pocar, "La protection de la partie faible en droit international privé", 188 *Recueil des cours* 340 (1984).

194. For discussion and documentation regarding these rules, see S. Symeonides, *Private International Law* 49-56.

above; *(b)* allow the protected party, either before or after the events that give rise to the dispute, to choose the applicable law from among the laws of more than one state[195]; or *(c)* protect that party from the adverse consequences of a potentially coerced or uninformed choice-of-law[196].

354. Of these rules, the ones that grant to one party the unilateral right to select the applicable law are among the most conspicuously result-oriented rules, since that party is likely to choose the law that he or she considers best. This is particularly true when the choice is exercised after the dispute, as in the case of certain tort disputes and child and spousal support disputes[197], but also when the choice is made in advance, as in the case of testate succession[198]. Indeed in some countries, the tort victim (or the court on the victim's behalf) may choose between the law of the place of the injurious conduct and the place of the resulting injury. This solution has been developed judicially in some countries[199], and has been sanctioned by statute in other countries, either for all torts[200] or for some torts[201]. In products liability conflicts, the Swiss, Italian, and Quebec codifications

---

195. See *id.* at 56-59.

196. See, e.g., Rome Convention, Arts. 5-6; German EGBGB, Arts. 29-30; Swiss, PIL Act, Art. 120 (2); Austrian PIL Act, §§ 41, 44 (3); Quebec C.C. arts. 3117-3118. For discussion, see S. Symeonides, *Private International Law* 56-60.

197. See, e.g., EGBGB, Art. 18, which, subject to certain qualifications, allows a choice of the law most favourable to the maintenance obligee from among the laws of the obligee's habitual residence, the common nationality of the obligor and the obligee, and the law of the forum. For similar rules, see French Code civil, Arts. 311-318; Hungarian PIL Act, Art. 46; Quebec Civ. Code, Art. 3094; Hague Convention on the Law Applicable to Maintenance Obligations Towards Children of 1956, Arts. 1-3; Hague Convention on the Law Applicable to Maintenance Obligations of 1973, Arts. 4-6; Inter-American Convention on Support Obligations of 1989, Art. 6.

198. Rules that allow a testator to select, within certain geographical and substantive limits, the law that will govern his or her succession can be found, *inter alia*, in Swiss PIL Act, Arts. 90.2, 91.2, 87.2, and 95.2.3; Quebec Civ. Code, Arts. 3098-3099; Italian PIL Act, Art. 46 (successions) and Art. 56 (donations); Article 5 of the 1989 Hague Convention on the Law Applicable to Estates, and the American Uniform Probate Code §2-602.

199. See S. Symeonides, *Private International Law* 58-59.

200. See EGBGB, Art. 40 (1); Italian PIL Act, Art. 62; Hungarian PIL Act, Art. 32(2); Quebec C.C., Art. 3126; Venezuelan PIL Act, Art. 32; Tunisian PIL Code, Art. 70(2); Yugoslav PIL Act, Art. 28. See also Chinese Society of Private International Law, Model Law of Private International Law of the People's Republic of China (6th Draft, 2000), Art 112.

201. See Swiss PIL Act, Art. 138 (applicable to injury resulting from emissions). See also *id.*, Art. 139, which, for injuries to rights of personality, allows a choice from among the laws of the tortfeasor's habitual residence or place of business, and – subject to a foreseeability defence – the victim's habitual residence or the place of the injury; Hungarian PIL Act, Art. 32 (4) (choice between the law of the place of injury and the tortfeasor's personal law for issues of culpability); Art. 10.2 (choice between the *lex loci* and the *lex fori* for damages in cases of violation of personal rights); EGBGB, Art.

allow the plaintiff to choose from among the laws of: *(a)* the tortfeasor's place of business or habitual residence, or *(b)* subject to a proviso, the place of the product's acquisition[202]. The Hague Convention on the Law Applicable to Products Liability also allows the plaintiff to choose between the laws of the tortfeasor's principal place of business or the law of the place of injury, if certain contingencies are met[203]. Similar rules have been proposed in the United States[204], although they have not as of yet received judicial or legislative sanction.

355. These developments may suggest that many of the differences between the American and the continental European approaches have more to do with the differences in the relative role of legislators and judges in their respective legal systems than with a genuine disagreement in fundamental policy. Indeed, it may not be too much of an oversimplification to say that much of what American approaches endeavour to do judicially, European systems endeavour to do legislatively. However, the very use of different implements tends to magnify the real and apparent differences in implementation. American solutions appear more *ad hoc*, more subjective, and more extreme. European solutions appear more objective, consistent, and moderate. Yet the real differences are often differences in degree rather than in substance[205].

4.   *Conflicts justice tempered by material justice*

356. Be that as it may, the fact that so many codified conflicts law systems, typically perceived as the bastions of conflicts justice, saw fit to enact so many choice-

---

44 (choice between the places of conduct and injury in cases involving emissions); Belgian PIL Code Art. 99(2)(1) (choice between the places of conduct and injury in defamation cases).

202. See *supra* 272.

203. See *supra* 271.

204. See the rule proposed by Professor Cavers, *supra* 273 (letting the plaintiff choose from among the laws of: *(a)* the place of manufacture; *(b)* the place of the plaintiff's habitual residence if that place coincides with either the place of injury or the place of the product's acquisition; or *(c)* the place of acquisition, if that place is also the place of injury); R. Weintraub, "Methods for Resolving Conflict-of-Laws Problems in Mass Tort Litigation", 1989 *U. Ill. L. Rev.* 129, 148 (1989) (giving both the victim and the tortfeasor a choice under certain circumstances); S. Symeonides, "The Need for a Third Conflicts Restatement (and a Proposal for Tort Conflicts)", 75 *Ind. LJ* 437, 450-451, 472-474 (2000) (same notion but different choices). Professor Juenger's proposed rule instructs the court to choose "the rule of decision that most closely accords with modern products liability standards." F. Juenger, *Choice of Law and Multistate Justice*, 197 (1993).

205. Indeed, many of the ideas that have been advocated in the United States during this second half of the twentieth century have also surfaced in Europe, usually in a more moderate form. This is not to say that the former have caused the latter. After all, capable independent minds confronted with similar problems are likely to come up with similar solutions, even if they function in isolation. See also *infra* 361-362.

of-law rules specifically designed to accomplish a particular substantive result suggests that either this perception is wrong, or the material-justice view has gained significant ground over the classical view. Indeed, during the course of the twentieth century, we have moved from an era in which material justice was officially unmentionable to an era in which it has become an important, and in some instances almost co-equal, goal with conflicts justice. At the dawn of the twenty-first century, the dilemma is no longer (and perhaps it never should have been) an "either or" choice between conflicts justice and material justice[206]. Rather, it is a question of *when*, *how*, and *how much* considerations of material justice should temper the search for conflicts justice.

357. Professor Juenger, one of the most articulate proponents of the material-justice view, concluded that the existence of so many result-oriented rules: (a) "contradicts the proposition that our discipline is value-free"[207]; *(b)* demonstrates that "teleology can be reduced to statutory form"[208]; and *(c)* strengthens his argument that "teleology" or result-orientation should be elevated into a controlling choice-of-law criterion, at least in uncodified conflicts law systems like the American system[209]. The first two propositions are not disputed here. Our discipline is not value-free; it is not and should not be indifferent to material-justice considerations; and contemporary legislatures are perfectly capable of taking cognizance of these considerations.

Juenger's third proposition, however, is far more debatable. The existence of the result-oriented rules described above neither signifies, nor militates for, a *wholesale* reorientation of conflict law towards material justice[210]. As important as they may be, these rules remain the exception. They cover a relatively small range of conflicts problems and, more importantly, they are designed to produce results that the *collective* will considers desirable and non-controversial. The existence of these rules demonstrates that even codified conflicts law systems are capable of making targeted adjustments where needed. In turn, this militates in favour of preservation and against condemnation and demolition of the system. Such adjustments are structurally and philosophically easier in uncodified systems, and the real value of the result-oriented rules described above is that they pinpoint the areas in which uncodified systems can make similar adjustments in favour of material justice.

But it is one thing to speak of selective pre-authorized adjustments in favour of material justice and quite another to advocate an *ad hoc* judicial method

---

206. Cf., e.g., B. Audit, "Le droit international privé français vers la fin du vingtième siècle: Progrès ou recul?", in Symeonides, *Private International Law* 191, 194: "La simple justice des conflits est susceptible de degrés". *Id.* at 195: "Il y a donc une 'justice de répartition'".
207. F. Juenger, *Choice of Law and Multistate Justice* 185 (1993).
208. *Id.* See also *id.* at 179 ("In legislation, as in adjudication, teleology can take various shapes.").
209. See *id.* at 179, 192-995, *et passim*.
210. See *id.* at 191ff.

in which material justice completely displaces conflicts justice. The fact that re-sult-orientation is often a realistic explanation of the outcome of most American conflicts cases does not militate in favour of ratifying this *de facto* state of affairs and elevating it to a *de jure* method of conflict resolution[211]. There is an important qualitative difference between result-selection in legislation and result-selection in adjudication. In the former, the desirable result is identified in advance and *in abstracto* through the consensus mechanisms of the democratic legislative pro-cesses. In the latter, the result is chosen *ex post facto* and *in concreto* and often by a single individual who, with the best of intentions, cannot easily avoid the dangers of subjectivity[212].

In summary, unguided, freewheeling result-selectivism in choice-of-law ad-judication is dangerous and objectionable. On the other hand, the selective, tar-geted use of result-oriented rules in choice-of-law legislation offers the best hope for an appropriate equilibrium between the established view of conflicts-justice and the re-emerging view of material justice.

G.   Legal Certainty versus Flexibility

358. Finally, the sixth basic dilemma of private international law, and of law in general, is the one between certainty and flexibility. Three decades ago, Willis Reese posed the same dilemma for American conflicts law[213]: whether the choice of law should be made through predefined, fixed rules designed to produce legal certainty and predictability, or rather through mere checklists of factors or guide-lines ("approaches") which provide flexibility at the expense of certainty.

1.   *The perennial tension*

359. The tension between the need for legal certainty, predictability, and uniform-ity on the one hand, and the desire for flexible, equitable, individualized solutions on the other, is as old as law itself. Aristotle described it more than twenty-three

---

211. "However much ... in practice the judge's choice of law may be influenced by his pref-erence for the content of one law or another, it is inadvisable to elevate a fact of human weakness to a principle of legislative policy." O. Kahn-Freund, "General Prob-lems of Private International Law", 143 *Recueil des cours* 139, at 466 (1974).

212. As Nygh pointed out, "one court's better law may be another's worse. It is only by ref-erence to an ideology that a court can in some cases make a choice as to which is the better law; there needs to be a commitment in some cases to allowing the 'collective good' to prevail". P. E. Nygh, *Conflict of Laws in Australia* 29 (6th ed., 1995).

213. See W. Reese, "Choice of Law: Rules or Approach", 57 *Cornell L. Rev.* 315, 315 (1972) ("The principal question in choice of law today is whether we should have rules or an approach.").

centuries ago when he spoke of the role of equity as a corrective of the written law[214]. As René David put it,

> "[t]here is and will always be in all countries, a contradiction between two requirements of justice: the law must be certain and predictable on one hand, it must be flexible and adaptable to circumstances on the other."[215]

The law of conflict of laws is not immune from this contradiction, and perhaps it is particularly susceptible to it.

Every legal system has wrestled with this contradiction and has striven to attain an appropriate equilibrium between these two competing, yet necessary, goals. Naturally, the equilibrium differs not only from system to system, but also from subject to subject and from time to time.

At the beginning of the twentieth century, most conflicts systems, especially those that relied on statutory rules, placed a higher premium on legal certainty than on flexibility. By the beginning of the twenty-first century, virtually all systems, and the American system more than any other, have moved in varying degrees toward flexibility[216].

2.   The American conflicts "revolution": Bad rules versus no rules

360. In the United States, the movement of conflicts law from certainty to flexibility has been impulsive, rash, and wholesale. Its banner became Brainerd Currie's revolutionary aphorism that "[w]e would be better off without choice-of-law rules"[217]. That this was an oversimplification has since been recognized by reputable scholars, some of whom subscribe to similar choice-of-law philosophies as Currie[218]. Nevertheless, this aphorism epitomizes the strong anti-rule sentiment

---

214. See Aristotle, *The Nicomachean Ethics*, V. x 4-7:
> "[T]he law always speaks in general terms, yet in many cases it is impossible to speak in terms that are both general and correct at the same time ... . [W]hen the law enunciates a general rule and thereafter a case arises that is not covered by the general rule, then it is proper, where the law-maker's pronouncement is defective because of its over-simplicity, to rectify the defect by deciding in the same way as the lawmaker would have decided ... had he been cognizant of the case ... . This is in essence the nature of equity *(epieikia)*: a corrective of the law when law is defective due to its generality." (Author's translation.)

215. R. David, *English Law and French Law* 24 (1980).

216. For a detailed discussion of this movement in American conflicts law, see S. Symeonides, "Exception Clauses in American Conflicts Law", in *Les Clauses d'Exception en matière de Conflits de Lois et de Conflits de Juridictions – ou le principe de proximité* (D. Kokkini-Iatridou, ed.) 77 (1994). For a comparative discussion, see S. Symeonides, *Private International Law*, 21-35.

217. B. Currie, *Selected Essays*, 183. See *supra* 15.

218. See, e.g., D. Cavers, *The Choice-of-Law Process*, 108-113, 121-123 (1965); R. Traynor, "War and Peace in the Conflict of Laws", 25 *Int'l & Comp. LQ* 121, 127 (1976). See also P.

that characterized American conflicts thinking during and shortly after the revolution. One after the other, American courts abandoned the first Restatement's rules for torts and contracts and replaced them with so-called "approaches" – formulae that do not prescribe solutions in advance, but simply enumerate the factors that one should take into account in the judicial fashioning of an *ad hoc* solution. Although these factors differ from one approach to the next, all such approaches are open-ended and call for an individualized, *ad hoc* handling of each case.

For some time, these approaches were looked upon as panacea. They were perceived as capable of resolving all problems without the aid of rules, not even those produced by the normal workings of precedent. At some point, American conflicts law began looking like "a tale of a thousand-and-one-cases"[219] in which "each case [was] decided as if it were unique and of first impression"[220]. We shall return to this point later, after a brief overview of European developments during the same period.

3.   *A quiet evolution: The European experience*

361. While American conflicts law was marching, or stumbling, through a loud revolution, private international law in the rest of the world and especially in Europe was going through a quiet evolution. The old choice-of-law rules were gradually repaired rather than abandoned. Of course, most of those rules were statutory, and virtually none of them were as bad as those of the first Restatement. Still, the first reaction against bad rules in the rest of the world was not to legislatively replace them or to judicially ignore them. Legislative interventions were few and exhaustively debated. Judicial corrections were careful, reserved, and respectful of the rule[221].

Hay, "Reflections on Conflict-of-Laws Methodology", 32 *Hastings LJ* 1644, 1672 (1981); P. Kozyris, "Interest Analysis Facing its Critics", 46 *Ohio St. LJ* 569, 577-580 (1985); W. Reese, "Choice of Law: Rules or Approach", 57 *Cornell L. Rev.* 315, 319 (1972); M. Rosenberg, "The Comeback of Choice-of-Law Rules", 81 *Colum. L. Rev.* 946 (1981).

219. P. Kozyris, "Interest Analysis Facing its Critics", 46 *Ohio St. LJ* 569, 578 (1985).

220. *Id.* at 580.

221. For the influence of the American conflicts revolution in Europe, but also for the reasons for which European PIL systems did not follow in the revolution's path, either in direction or in degree, see, e.g., B. Audit, "A Continental Lawyer Looks at Contemporary American Choice-of-Law Principles", 27 *Am. J. Comp. L.* 589 (1979); J. Dolinger, "Evolution of Principles for Resolving Conflicts in the Field of Contracts and Torts", 283 *Recueil des cours* 189, 381-386, 468-482 (2000); G. Kegel, "Paternal Home and Dream Home: Traditional Conflict of Laws and the American Reformers", 27 *Am. J. Comp. L.* 615 (1979); E. Jayme, "The American Conflicts Revolution and Its Impact on European Private International Law", in *Forty Years On: The Evolution of Postwar Private International Law in Europe*, 15 (1992); K. Siehr, "Ehrenzweigs lex-fori-Theorie und ihre Bedeutung für das amerikanische und deutsche Kollisionsrecht", 34 *RabelsZ* 583 (1970); F. Vischer, "New Tendencies in European Conflict of Laws and the Influ-

As one European commentator suggested, perhaps "European judges took advantage of the fact that they were to decide later than their American colleagues"[222], and thus they could selectively draw from the American experience without repeating its excesses. Moreover, by virtue of both training and temperament, European judges – and, on this subject, legislatures – tend to think in terms of repairing the existing rules, often by creating exceptions, rather than in terms of abandoning the rules. For example, when the German Federal Court confronted a case of the *Babcock* common-domicile pattern, the Court applied the law of the parties' common domicile[223], but also made it crystal clear that this was meant to be a mere exception from the *lex loci delicti* rule, which was to remain as the basic rule for tort conflicts. Eventually, the 1999 German codification preserved this very scheme, with the *lex loci* as the rule[224], and the *lex domicilii communis* as the exception[225], along with other exceptions, including that of the "substantially closer connection"[226].

362. A similarly smooth evolution occurred in England, which, until recently, had few statutory choice-of-law rules. As Professor Fentiman has stated,

> "unlike their counterparts in the United States, English lawyers have never – or have never entirely – lost faith in the effectiveness and validity of traditional conceptions of legal reasoning. Certainly, English law never experienced the challenge (and response) to formalism represented by the American realist movement ... . [I]f the American conflicts revolution is a realist revolution, it is striking how little English conflicts scholarship owes to both."[227]

The House of Lords faced its own *Babcock* scenario in *Boys* v. *Chaplin*[228] and reached the same result, which eventually found its way in the 1995 codification as a flexible exception from the *lex loci* rule[229].

---

ence of the US-Doctrine – A Short Survey", in *Law and Justice in a Multistate World: Essays in Honor of Arthur T. von Mehren*, 459 (J. Nafziger and S. Symeonides, eds., 2002); E. Vitta, "The Impact in Europe of the American 'Conflicts Revolution', 30 *Am. J. Comp. L.* 1 (1982). See also S. Symeonides, *An Outsider's View of the American Approach to Choice of Law: Comparative Observations on Current American and Continental Conflicts Doctrine* 159-374 (1980).

222. Jayme, *supra* footnote 221, at 22.

223. See BGH, 8.1.1985, *JZ* 144 (1985), note Werner Lorenz.

224. See EGBGB, Art. 40 (1).

225. See EGBGB, Art. 40 (2).

226. See EGBGB, Art. 41, which authorizes displacement of the law designated by Articles 38-40, "[i]f there is a substantially closer connection to the law of [another] state".

227. R. Fentiman, "English Private International Law at the End of the 20th Century: Progress or Regress?", in S. Symeonides, *Private International Law* 165, 169. See also *id.* at 173-174.

228. [1969] 3 WLR 322 (HL).

229. See Private International Law (Miscellaneous Provisions) Act of 8 November 1995 (c. 42) § 12. This section provides in part that the law applicable to a tort under the

In short, although in terms of specific substantive solutions, "American thinking has pervaded [European conflicts law] by osmosis"[230], European conflicts systems have not been tempted to abandon rules in favour of "approaches" in the American sense. Indeed, the prevailing, though not necessarily correct view, is that such approaches are incompatible with the very notion of codification[231]. Thus, for codified systems, the dilemma between "rules" or "approaches" that Willis Reese[232] posed for American law received an easy answer that overwhelmingly favoured rules[233].

363. However, as centuries of codification experience demonstrate, the decision to adopt statutory rules need not outlaw judicial discretion[234]. Many of the new conflicts codifications are replete with examples of express legislative grants

---

general rule of section 11 will be displaced,

> "[i]f it appears, in all the circumstances, from a comparison of *(a)* the significance of the factors which connect a tort or delict with the country whose law would be the applicable law under the general rule; and *(b)* the significance of any factors connecting the tort or delict with another country, that it is substantially more appropriate for the applicable law for determining the issues arising in the case, or any of those issues, to be the law of the other country".

230. Jayme, *supra* footnote 221, at 24. Although Jayme's statement refers only to the German codification, the statement can also be made about European conflicts law in general.

231. The only conflicts codification to defy this wisdom is one drafted on American soil – the Louisiana codification. See S. Symeonides, "Les grands problèmes de droit international privé et la nouvelle codification de Louisiane", 81 *Rev. critique* 223, 242 (1992) ("[C]ontrary to conventional wisdom, an 'approach' can play an extremely useful role in a PIL codification, at least as a gap-filler. Thus, Louisiana's answer to the dilemma 'rules vs. approach' is 'rules *and* an approach'. Through a combination of narrow rules and a flexible approach, the Louisiana codification attempts to strike an appropriate balance between specificity and generality and between certainty and flexibility."). Ten years later, a similar combination of rules and approach has been implemented in Oregon. See *supra* at 104.

232. See *supra* footnote 213.

233. See J. Kropholler and J. von Hein, "From Approach to Rule-Orientation in American Tort Conflicts", in *Law and Justice in a Multistate World: Essays in Honor of Arthur T. von Mehren*, 317, 331-339 (J. Nafziger and S. Symeonides, eds. 2002).

234. As early as 1804, the redactors of the Code Napoléon recognized the simple truth that had escaped the drafters of the Prussian Code of 1794: that for the *legislateur* "to anticipate everything is a goal impossible of attainment". Portalis, Tronchet, Bigot-Préameneu & Maleville, "Texte du discours préliminaire", in J. Locré, *La legislation civile, commerciale et criminelle de la France*, 251, 255 (Vol. 1, 1827). Consequently, the legislator's role is "to set, by taking a broad approach, the general propositions of the law, [and] to establish principles which will be fertile in application … . It is for the judge and the jurist, imbued with the general spirit of the laws to direct their application." *Id.*

of judicial discretion[235]. As demonstrated elsewhere[236], the "flexibility scale" has many steps or gradations, only one of which is the use of *ad hoc*, American-style approaches. The other gradations or techniques are: (1) rules employing alternative connecting factors; (2) rules relying on flexible or "soft" connecting factors; and (3) rules armoured with escape clauses.

Chart 26. The flexibility ladder

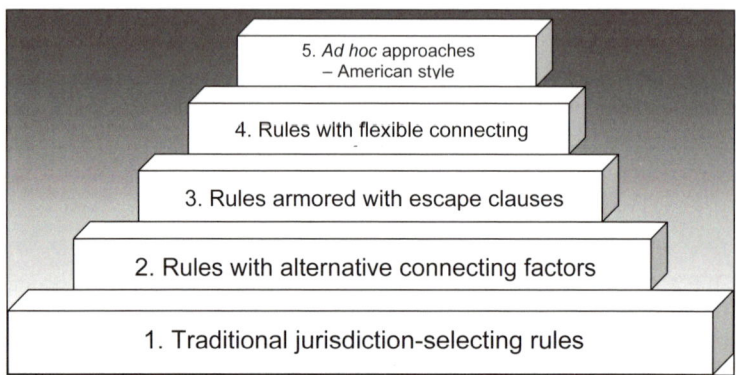

The most common technique, used by both recent and older codifications, is the use of the alternative-reference rules discussed earlier, which employ alternative connecting factors[237]. Another relatively recent but common technique is the replacement of pre-fixed, mono-directional, and rigid connecting factors (such as the *loci contractus* or the *loci delicti*) with open-ended, multi-directional and softer connecting factors, such as the "closest connection". Unlike the old rules, which almost inexorably pre-determined the applicable law, the new rules allow the judge considerable discretion in identifying the state whose "connection", "relationship", "link", or "tie" with the case is the "closest", the "strongest", the "most direct", or the "most appropriate"[238].

Finally, the most dramatic concession to flexibility, yet falling short of adopting an American-style approach, is the use of pre-authorized escapes from the

---

235. See S. Symeonides, *Private International Law Private International Law at the End of the 20th Century: Progress or Regress?* 26-30 (1999).

236. See *id.* at 28.

237. See *supra* 353. For detailed discussion, see Symeonides, *Private International Law* 28-29, 49-60. From the judge's perspective, these rules appear inimical to judicial discretion and thus to flexibility insofar as they deny the judge the freedom of choosing a law other than the one that produces the preselected *result*, e.g., upholding the contract. Nevertheless, from a systemic perspective, these rules provide flexibility in that – although they tie the system to a particular result – they do not tie the system to the law of a particular state.

238. Rules employing such factors are discussed in detail in S. Symeonides, *Private International Law* 29-31; S. Symeonides, "Exception Clauses in American Conflicts Law", 42 *Am. J. Comp. L.* 813 (1994).

results dictated by the forum's statutory choice-of-law rules. With some notable exceptions, most modern legislatures seem to have become aware of the inherent limitations in their ability to anticipate everything[239], and have learned to entrust judges with greater discretion than in the past. There seems to be an increasing realization that any pre-formulated rule, no matter how carefully or wisely drafted, may, "because of its generality"[240], or because of its specificity, produce results that are contrary to the purpose for which the rule was designed. In the words of Peter Hay, this "is a natural consequence of the difference between *law making* and *law application*"[241]. Contemporary rule-makers attempt to avert such undesirable results by expressly granting judges the authority to adjust or avoid altogether the application of the rule when the peculiarities of the individual case so dictate. This grant of authority takes the form of escape clauses attached to the rules[242].

One example of such a clause is Article 15 of the Swiss PIL Act, which authorizes the court to not apply the law specified in the Act's other choice-of-law rules "if, from the totality of the circumstances, it is manifest that the particular case has only a very slight connection to that law and has a much closer relationship to another law". Similar clauses are found in the codifications of Austria[243],

---

239. See Portalis, *et al.*, *supra* footnote 234.

240. Aristotle, *Nicomachean Ethics*, *supra* footnote 214.

241. P. Hay, "Flexibility versus Predictability and Uniformity in Choice of Law", 226 *Recueil des cours* 281, 291 (1991).

242. From the rich literature on the subject, see C. Dubler, *Les clauses d'exception en droit international privé* (1983); D. Kokkini-Iatridou, *Les clauses d'exception en matière de conflits de lois et de conflits de juridiction – ou le principe de proximité* (1994); S. Symeonides, *Private International Law* 31-34; J. González Campos, "Diversification, spécialisation et matérialisation des règles de droit international privé", 287 *Recueil des cours* 9, 214-308 (2000); P. Hay and R. Ellis, "Bridging the Gap between Rules and Approaches in Tort Choice of Law in the United States: A Survey of Current Case Law", 27 *Int'l Lawyer* 369 (1993); F. Mosconi, "Exceptions to the Operation of Choice of Law Rules", 217 *Recueil des cours*, 9, 189-195 (1989); K. Nadelmann, "Choice of Law Resolved by Rules or Presumptions with an Escape Clause", 33 *Am. J. Comp. L.* 297 (1985); A. von Overbeck, "Les questions générales du droit international privé à la lumière des codifications et projets récents", 176 *Recueil des cours* 9, 186-207 (1982); S. Symeonides, "Exception Clauses in American Conflicts Law", 42 *Am. J. Comp. L.* 813 (1994).

243. See Article 1 of the Austrian PIL Act, which provides that all the choice-of-law rules contained in the Act "shall be considered as expressions of th[e] principle" of the "strongest connection", thus obliquely authorizing the court to deviate from these rules if it concludes that they lead to a result that is inconsistent with the general principle of the strongest connection.

Belgium[244] Germany[245], England[246], Quebec[247], Louisiana[248], and Puerto Rico[249], as well as several international conventions[250]. Although these clauses differ in the specifics, all of them share one common denominator: they are pre-authorized legislative licences for displacing or adjusting statutory rules in appropriate circumstances. In this sense, these clauses provide safety valves that play a critical role in maintaining an appropriate equilibrium between legal certainty and flexibility, an equilibrium that legislators alone cannot hope to maintain.

4.   Comparison

364. The diverse experiences of European and American conflicts systems offer two different examples of the perennial and often cyclical struggle to attain an

---

244. See Belgian PIL Code Art. 19, which provides that the law of the state designated by the other articles of the Code does not apply if from the totality of the circumstances it is manifestly apparent that that the situation has a very slight connection with that state and a very closer connection with another state.

245. See EGBGB, Art. 41, *supra* footnote 226.

246. See English PIL Act of 1995 §12, *supra* footnote 229.

247. See Quebec C.C., Art. 3082, which provides the law designated by the codification's choice of law rules "is not applicable if, in the light of all attendant circumstances, it is clear that the situation is only remotely connected with that law and is much more closely connected with the law of another country".

248. See La. Civ. Code, Art. 3547, which provides that the law applicable under the other tort articles of the codification shall not apply if, "from the totality of the circumstances of an exceptional case, it is clearly evident under the principles of Article 3542 (the general article for tort conflicts), that the policies of another state would be more seriously impaired if its law were not applied to the particular issue". In such a case, the law of the latter state applies. For the history and meaning of this article, see Symeonides, "Louisiana's New Law of Choice of Law for Tort Conflicts: An Exegesis", 66 *Tul. L. Rev.* 677, 763-766 (1992).

249. See Article 45 of the Puerto Rico Draft Code of 1991, which enunciates the general approach for tort conflicts and then provides that when, in a particular case, the specific rules of the codification "would produce a result that is clearly contrary to the objectives of this Article, the applicable law is selected in accordance with this Article".

250. See, e.g., paragraph 5 of Article 4 of the Rome Convention, which provides that the presumptive rules or paragraphs 2-4 "shall be disregarded if it appears from the circumstances as a whole that the contract is more closely connected with another country"; Art. 6.2 *(b)* of the same Convention regarding employment contracts; Art. 8.3 of the Hague Convention for the Law Applicable to the International Sales of Goods (1985), which provides that "where, in the light of the circumstances as a whole ..., the contract is manifestly more closely connected with a law which is not the law which would otherwise be applicable to the contract ..., the contract is governed by that other law"; Article 3 of the 1989 Hague Convention on the Law Applicable to the Estates of Deceased Persons, which provides that "in exceptional circumstances" the principle of the closest connection may lead to the application of a law other than the one designated by the Convention.

optimum equilibrium between certainty and flexibility[251]. During the twentieth century, these systems have found themselves in different points of this cyclical movement. The European systems have moved slowly but steadily in one direction – from certainty to flexibility. They experienced no revolutions, they did not embark on drastic changes, and they did not abandon rules in favour of *ad hoc* "approaches." Instead, these systems injected small, controlled doses of flexibility through some new and some old and tested devices. The result is a new equilibrium between certainty and flexibility, with more of the former than of the latter.

During the same period, American conflicts law has careened from the one extreme of the rigidity of the 1930s to the other extreme of the total flexibility or anarchy of the conflicts revolution, when rules were denounced and legal certainty was demoted to a low-rank goal. Did the American movement toward flexibility go too far? If the answer is yes, the next question is whether a correction is desirable and feasible. The next chapter explores these questions.

H.   Up to the Present

365. In looking back at the state of American conflicts law before the revolution, one sees a system of rigid, territorially based, multilateral, jurisdiction-selecting, choice-of-law rules intended to provide legal certainty, attain conflicts justice, and promote interstate uniformity of result regardless of forum.

Four decades later, the landscape has changed considerably. Although this change cannot be easily quantified, much less pinpointed on a road map, the following chart attempts to do precisely that. At the risk of oversimplifying, the chart portrays the position of American conflicts law before and after the revolution on the six major dilemmas discussed above, with the opposing key terms of each dilemma occupying the opposite sides of the chart.

---

251.   Ironically, the much maligned Professor Joseph Beale understood well, and described insightfully, this cyclical movement, although he did not do much to contribute to an equilibrium during his time. See J. Beale, *A Treatise on the Conflict of Laws*, 50 (Vol. I, 1935); S. Symeonides, "Exception Clauses in American Conflicts Law", 42 *Am. J. Comp. L.* 813, 864-865 (1994).

Chart 27. The grand dilemmas of American Conflicts Law

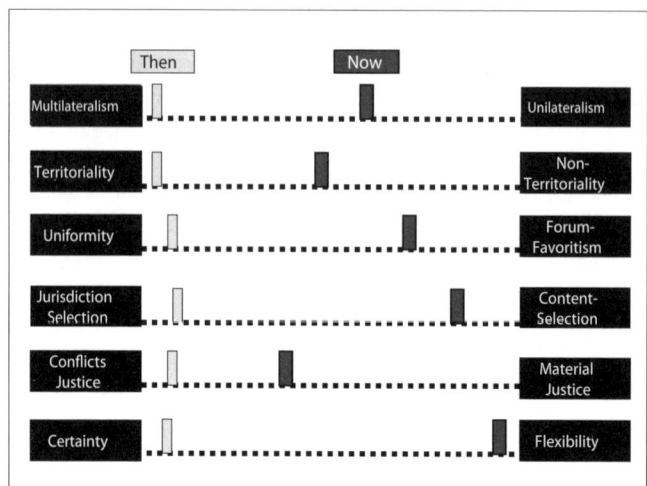

Before the revolution, American conflicts law was firmly entrenched at the far left side of the spectrum. It had adopted a method consisting of multilateral, mostly territorial, fixed, jurisdiction-selecting rules, designed to provide legal certainty, to attain conflicts justice, and to promote interstate and international uniformity.

366. With the revolution, American conflicts law moved toward the right end of the spectrum. The singled-minded, territorial, rigid, but also idealistic system has been replaced with a multitude of flexible, eclectic, and to some extent pragmatic approaches which, despite individual differences, tend to share the characteristics described below:

(1) Most of these approaches have moved from multilateralism towards unilateralism and, knowingly or not, have combined elements from both of these seemingly antithetical methods[252].

(2) All of these approaches have moved away from territoriality by choosing the applicable law on the basis of multiple factors, many of which are not grounded on territoriality.

(3) To a lesser or greater degree, most of these approaches subscribe to the view that, while interstate uniformity remains a desideratum of the choice-of-law process, the process should also take account of other factors, such as state interests, especially those of the forum state.

(4) All of these approaches have moved away from jurisdiction-selection and have embraced the notion of a content-oriented law selection. However, ju-

---

252. In addition, state legislatures have been routinely enacting unilateral rules interspersed in substantive statutes. See *supra* 311.

risdiction-selection remains the norm in those areas of conflicts law, such as property, that the revolution did not affect.

(5)   Most of these approaches continue to aspire to conflicts justice, but are becoming increasingly sensitive to material-justice considerations, with some of these approaches overtly advocating the direct pursuit of material justice in the choice-of-law process.

(6)   Finally, all of these approaches have moved away from fixed rules and seem to value flexibility much more than the need for certainty. However, as discussed in the next chapter, the pendulum may be about to begin its gradual swing back.

367. Predictably, opinions differ on which of these changes have been beneficial and which have been detrimental. This author's opinion is that some of these changes, such as the move away from territoriality and jurisdiction-selection, have been both beneficial and long overdue. Regarding the other changes, the more apt question is whether they were inevitable. Again, this author's view is that the concessions to unilateralism and conflicts justice were inevitable and that, if used with caution, they can be beneficial. The same is true of the notion that consideration of state policies and, yes, *interests*, is an appropriate criterion for resolving many conflicts of laws.

In sum, the only change that has been neither beneficial nor inevitable, is the complete denouncement of *all* rules in favour of *ad hoc* approaches. Even if this denouncement was understandable at the beginning of the revolution, it should be looked upon with much closer scrutiny four decades later. This is not a defense of the first Restatement's rules. However, it is one thing to denounce those particular rules and another thing altogether to denounce *all* rules. To do so would be to assume that the only rules possible are those drafted by Professor Beale. American conflicts law can do much better. The next chapter addresses this issue.

Chapter X   The Next Phase in Choice of Law

A.   The Revolution's Victory

368. Looking at sheer numbers, there is no doubt that the American conflicts revolution has *prevailed* over the traditional system[1]. However, to prevail is one thing and to *succeed* is another. Success should not be judged by numbers alone. Instead, one should ask whether the revolution has produced a new *system* to replace the old one, and how well the new system attends to the basic needs and aspirations of the choice-of-law process, such as the predictability, rationality, and uniformity of decisions. Although the revolution has changed American conflicts law in the beneficial ways noted in the previous chapter, the revolution has not succeeded in producing a new system, perhaps because it did not aspire to create one.

Rather than offering a unified vision for the future, the revolution offered conflicting theories, which the courts have merged together, often adding their own variations[2]. Thus, the academic polyphony that characterized the scholastic revolution produced an even more dissonant judicial polyphony. Moreover, in its zeal to cleanse the system from all the vestiges of the first Restatement, the revolution went too far in denouncing all choice-of-law rules.

369. One of the consequences of these developments was an unprecedented degree of judicial flexibility in choice-of-law decisions. To be sure, flexibility is preferable to uncritical rigidity, but too much flexibility can be as bad as no flexibility at all. Even Leflar, one of the revolution's protagonists, admitted that "flexibility is not a virtue for every type of conflicts case"[3]. *A fortiori*, it is not a virtue for *all* cases. When each case is decided *ad hoc* as if it were a case of first

---

1.   See *supra* 41-44 (listing the states that have abandoned the traditional system in tort and contract conflicts).

2.   Cf. F. Juenger, "A Third Conflicts Restatement?", 75 *Ind. LJ* 403, 403 (2000) ("[O]ne finds authors who are at doctrinal loggerheads peacefully united in a single footnote; one encounters prose so turgid and stilted that one suspects that the judge (more likely the law clerk who actually drafted the opinion) never really grasped the idea behind the particular conflicts approach the court purports to follow".).

3.   R. Leflar, "Choice-of-Law Statutes", 44 *Tenn. L. Rev.* 951, 952 (1977).

impression[4], multiple problems arise[5], including increased litigation costs[6], waste of judicial resources[7], and an increased danger of judicial subjectivism[8], which has been aptly described as "judicial particularistic intuitionism"[9] or "*impressionnisme juridique*"[10]. In turn, judicial subjectivism leads to dissimilar handling of similar cases[11], which in turn tests the citizens' faith in the legal system and tends to undermine its very legitimacy[12].

---

4.   See P. J. Kozyris, "Interest Analysis Facing Its Critics", 46 *Ohio St. LJ* 569, 580 (1985) ("any system calling for open-ended and endless soul-searching on a case-by-case basis carries a high burden of persuasion").

5.   See M. Rosenberg, "Comments on *Reich* v. *Purcell*", 15 *UCLA L. Rev.* 641, 644 (1968) ("The idea that judges can be turned loose in the three-dimensional chess games we have made of [conflicts] cases, and can be told to do hand-tailored justice, case by case, free from the constraints or guidelines of rules, is a vain and dangerous illusion.").

6.   See P. Borchers, "Empiricism and Theory in Conflicts Law", 75 *Ind. LJ* 509 (2000) ("[T]he extreme flexibility of the modern approaches probably brings increased litigation costs, in particular through the need to prosecute appeals. Because cases settle (at least for economically rational litigants) when the parties' assessments of the value of the case converge to within the expected cost of pursuing the case to judgment, the ever-present wild card of choice of law may discourage settlement.").

7.   See P. J. Kozyris, "The Conflicts Provisions of the ALI's Complex Litigation Project: A Glass Half Full?", 54 *La. L. Rev.* 953, 956 (1994) ("Conflicts theorists ... have been notoriously indifferent to the issue of efficiency, treating every case as a unique specimen calling for custom-made handling on the tacit assumption that litigation resources are infinite"); E. Scoles, P. Hay, P. Borchers and S. Symeonides, *Conflict of Laws* 107-108, 789-790 (4th ed. 2004); P. Borchers, "Back to the Past: Anti-Pragmatism in American Conflicts Law", 48 *Mercer L. Rev.* 721, 724 (1997); E. O'Hara and L. Ribstein, "From Politics to Efficiency in Choice of Law", 67 *U. Chi. L. Rev.* 1151 (2000); S. Wiegand, "Fifty Conflict of Laws 'Restatements': Merging Judicial Discretion and Legislative Endorsement", 65 *La. L. Rev.* 1 (2004). See also *Kaczmarek* v. *Allied Chem. Corp.*, 836 F. 2d 1055, 1057 (7th Cir. 1987) (Posner, J.).

8.   See E. Scoles, P. Hay, P. Borchers and S. Symeonides, *Conflict of Laws* 107 (4th ed. 2004) ("Contradictory results in the case law, confusion, and also the 'homeward trend' have been the resulting consequences.").

9.   P. J. Kozyris, "Interest Analysis Facing Its Critics", 46 *Ohio St. LJ* 569, 580 (1985).

10.   Y. Loussouarn and P. Bourel, *Droit international privé* 142-153 (7th ed. 2001).

11.   In this sense, the revolution may have forsaken not only interstate but also *intrastate* uniformity of result.

12.   See P. J. Kozyris, "Conflicts Theory for Dummies: Après le Deluge, Where Are We on Producers Liability?", 60 *La. L. Rev.* 1161, 1162 (2000) ("[T]elling the courts in each conflicts case to make a choice and fashion the applicable law 'ad hoc' and 'anew' (i.e., without legislative or precedential direction) on the basis of what is right (just, proper, good, suitable, interested, etc.), as is often done under the prevailing conflicts theories, appears to me to be not only inconsistent with the basic principles of separation of powers, not only burdensome and potentially arbitrary beyond reason, not only disorienting to the transacting person, but also essentially empty of meaning ... . [U]npredictable law is not law to begin with.").

While conflicts law is in some respects a field apart, it is not so different as to risk ignoring these fundamental values for long.

B.   From Victory to Success

370. Indeed, while polyphony and flexibility are both necessary and enriching in periods of transition and experimentation, they should not be the ultimate destination goals. Put another way, transitions and experimentations should not last forever[13].

A knowledgeable European observer has suggested that "the American conflicts revolution has remained perhaps no more than a 'protest song'"[14], and then spoke matter-of-factly of "the sunset of the American conflicts movement"[15]. The latter characterization may be premature, but it will become a reality if the revolution drags on much longer.

Indeed, four decades after the revolution began, it is high time to see how it should end. It is time to develop an exit strategy that consolidates and preserves the gains of the revolution and turns its victory into success.

It is also time to recognize that the revolution has gone too far in embracing flexibility to the exclusion of all certainty, just as the traditional system had gone too far toward certainty to the exclusion of all flexibility.

A correction is needed, and a new equilibrium should be sought between these two perpetually competing needs.

The view of this author is that it is now *necessary and possible* to articulate a new breed of smart, evolutionary choice-of-law rules that will accomplish both objectives: (1) restore a proper equilibrium between certainty and flexibility; and (2) preserve the substantive and methodological accomplishments of the revolution.

---

13.   In anthropomorphic terms, "[t]he conflicts revolution has been pregnant for too long. The conflicts misery index, which is the ratio of problems to solutions, or of verbiage to result, is now higher than ever". P. J. Kozyris, "Foreword and Symposium on Interest Analysis in Conflict of Laws: An Inquiry into Fundamentals with a Side Glance at Products Liability", 46 *Ohio St. LJ* 457, 458 (1985).

14.   E. Jayme, "The American Conflicts Revolution and Its Impact on European Private International Law", in *Forty Years On: The Evolution of Postwar Private International Law in Europe*, 15, 18 (1992).

15.   *Id.*

C.   The Need for New Rules

1.   Anti-rulism

371. Unlike other countries, any mention of rules encounters serious opposition in the United States[16]. This opposition comes in different gradations and intensities, some of which are grounded in the common law tradition in general, and some in the conflicts experience in particular. At one end of the spectrum stands Currie's categorical indictment of all choice-of-law rules as not only unhelpful but also as harmful[17]. Given Currie's penchant for hyperbole as well as the timing of the indictment, a time dominated by Beale's "unreasonable rules"[18], one can only hope that such an all-encompassing indictment would find little support today. The problem today is "to escape both horns of the dilemma by avoiding both unreasonable rules and an unruly reasonableness that is destructive of many of the values of law"[19].

Currie simply did not think that such an escape was possible in his time. Today it is. Thanks in part to his attacks, the unreasonable rules are dead. What has replaced them is clearly an unruly situation, which may or may not be reasonable, but which can be replaced by a principled and orderly reasonableness.

372. Today, much of the opposition to rules is less categorical than Currie's. Most rule opponents do not openly deny the general value of rules; rather they argue that it is premature to attempt to develop new rules at this time. Writing in 1977, Professor Leflar admonished that any attempt to formulate rules should wait "until the bench and the bar have achieved a much better understanding of conflicts theory and the conflicts law itself has come to be more completely stabilized in keeping with the socioeconomic and legal functions that it should serve."[20]

---

16.   The view that conflicts law is somehow inappropriate for, or insusceptible to, legislation is neither new, nor uniquely American. For awhile, this view was espoused even in that stronghold of codification, the European continent. See O. Kahn-Freund, *General Problems of Private International Law* 80-84 (1976); T. DeMaekelt, "General Rules of Private International Law in the Americas: New Approach", 177 *Recueil des cours* 193 (1982); Schwind, "Problems of Codification of Private International Law", 17 *Int'l & Comp. LQ* 428, 431 (1968); F. Rigaux, "Codification of Private International Law: Pros and Cons", 60 *La. L. Rev.* 1321 (2000). Nevertheless, this view has receded in the face of intense legislative activity that has produced more than twenty codifications in Europe and elsewhere, including England, the metropolis of the common law. See E. Scoles, P. Hay, P. Borchers and S. Symeonides, *Conflict of Law* 110-118 (4th ed. 2004). For England, see P. North, "Problems of Codification in a Common Law System", 46 *RabelsZ* 490 (1982) ("Codes are not monsters ... [and] [e]ven if they are, they can be trained.").

17.   See *supra* 15.

18.   M. Rosenberg, "Two Views on *Kell* v. *Henderson*: An Opinion for the New York Court of Appeals", 67 *Colum. L. Rev.* 459, 464 (1967).

19.   *Id.*

20.   R. Leflar, "Choice-of-Law Statutes", 44 *Tenn. L. Rev.* 951, 971 (1977).

This admonition was both well-intended and prudent, although one could argue that the need for rules is greater when the understanding of the bench and bar is lacking than when it is not. Be that as it may, more than a quarter of a century later, the bar's understanding of conflicts law has not improved, perhaps because the subject has been dropped from the bar examinations[21], and, according to some observers, the bench is not doing much better[22]. For example, one commentator concluded that American choice-of-law decisions are characterized by "confused and misguided thinking"[23], and their analysis "tends to be unsophisticated, unthoughtful, and often unreasoned"[24]. This is a harsh assessment, but if it is even half-accurate one should ask who is to blame. Should we blame judges, many of whom encounter conflicts cases only infrequently and thus do not have the opportunity or the incentive to develop the expertise[25]? Or should we blame the experts who have not communicated their expertise in language that judges can understand and follow?[26] As one treatise noted, "[c]ourts need and are entitled to more guidance than the iconoclastic literature has provided"[27].

Fortunately, and importantly, despite the lack of such guidance and the supposed lack of sophistication, judicial decisions have produced much more consistent *results* than the critics assume. In this sense, one of Leflar's preconditions for the development of rules has been satisfied in that conflicts law "has come to

---

21.   See R. Weintraub, "The Restatement Third of Conflict of Laws: An Idea Whose Time Has Not Come", 75 *Ind. LJ* 679, 679 (2000); F. Juenger, "What Now?", 46 *Ohio St. LJ* 509, 515 (1985).

22.   See F. Juenger, "A Third Conflicts Restatement?", 75 *Ind. LJ* 403, 403, 411 (2000); R. Weintraub, *supra* footnote 21, at 679-682.

23.   L. Kramer, "On the Need for a Uniform Choice of Law Code", 89 *Mich. L. Rev.* 2134, 2149 (1991).

24.   L. Kramer, "Choice of Law in the American Courts in 1990: Trends and Developments", 39 *Am. J. Comp. L.* 465, 466 (1991).

25.   See R. Weintraub, "Courts Flailing in the Waters of the Louisiana Conflicts Code: Not Waving but Drowning", 60 *La. L. Rev.* 1365, 1366 (2000) ("Judges are not stupid, just busy"); R. Weintraub, "The Restatement Third of Conflict of Laws: An Idea Whose Time Has Not Come", 75 Ind. LJ 679, 680 (2000) ("[A]ll courts, but especially state courts, encounter choice-of-law problems haphazardly at infrequent intervals. Changes in court personnel can cause a new court to reinvent the wheel that was invented at least a decade earlier, but this time not get it quite right"); A. von Mehren, "Recent Trend in Choice-of-Law Methodology", 60 *Cornell L. Rev.* 927, 966 (1975) ("Judicial experience with any given choice-of-law problem is usually more episodic than with analogous domestic-law problems.").

26.   See G. Shreve, "Conflicts Altruism", in *Law and Justice in a Multistate World: Essays in Honor of Arthur T. von Mehren* 383, 390 (J. Nafziger and S. Symeonides, eds. 2002) ("[T]he conflicts academy has not demonstrated ... more curiosity and concern about how lawyers and judges are faring as they grapple with the subject ... . Many appear indifferent to the workaday problems that lawyers and judges have with conflicts law.").

27.   E. Scoles, P. Hay, P. Borchers and S. Symeonides, *Conflict of Law* 108 (4th ed. 2004).

be more completely stabilized"[28]. After four decades of post-*lex loci* case law, and
"[w]ith centuries of experience and doctrinal elaboration behind us, we hardly
need more lab testing and narrow findings. Rather, we need to make up our minds
and make some sense out of the chaos"[29].

373. Another anti-rule objection that is sometimes phrased in terms of timing, and sometimes more generally, is that the formulation of rules will retard the
development of the law, or worse petrify it or freeze it in time[30]. This objection is
valid when directed against all-encompassing inflexible rules, such as those of the
first Restatement.

However, no one is advocating such rules today. Indeed, thanks to the first
Restatement, we now know what to avoid: broad, all-embracing, inflexible, mono-
lithic rules, based on a single connecting factor chosen on metaphysical grounds.
Thanks also to the choice-of-law revolution, we also know what to aim for: narrow, flexible, content-and issue-oriented rules, based on experience, with occasional built-in escape clauses that would allow these rules to grow and to adjust to
changing needs and values[31].

As said earlier, to assume that the only rules possible are those drafted seven
decades ago by Mr. Beale is to both ignore the rich rule-making experience gained
in the interim and to severely underestimate the capacity of American conflicts
law to renew itself. In the twenty-first century, the choice is not between excessive
rigidity and excessive flexibility, or between prefabricated mechanical prescriptions and *ad hoc* individualized dispensations[32]. As Cavers noted, "[t]he pursuit

---

28. R. Leflar, *supra* at footnote 20.

29. P. J. Kozyris, "Interest Analysis Facing Its Critics", 46 *Ohio St. LJ* 569, 578 (1985). See
    also W. Richman & W. Reynolds, "Prologomenon to an Empirical Restatement of
    Conflicts", 75 *Ind. LJ* 417, 426-27. (2000) ("[T]he theoretical debates are reaching the
    point of diminishing returns .... The theoretical scholarship, while adequate to dem-
    onstrate the faults of the First Restatement, does not seem to be able to produce
    consensus on the proper modern approach").

30. See, e.g., B. Currie, "Comments on *Babcock* v. *Jackson*", 63 *Colum. L. Rev.* 1233, 1241
    (1963) ("[N]ew efforts to find short cuts and syntheses should be sternly discouraged.
    We are beginning to recover from a long siege of intoxication resulting from overin-
    dulgence in generalities; for a while, at least, total abstinence should be enforced.").

31. Cf. R. Leflar, "Choice-of-Law Statutes", 44 *Tenn. L. Rev.* 951, 952 (1977) (recognizing
    that "flexibility can be built into a statute ... just as it can be and is more often pre-
    scribed in the common law"). See P. J. Kozyris, "Interest Analysis Facing Its Critics",
    46 *Ohio St. LJ* 569, 580 (1985) ("[F]ixed but revisable rules which lead to good results
    in the overwhelming majority of the cases, and which are supplemented by some
    general corrective principles to mitigate injustice in the remaining cases, are superior
    to, and incredibly more efficient than, a system in which each case is decided as if it
    were unique and of first impression.").

32. See P. Borchers, "Louisiana's Conflicts Codification: Some Empirical Observations
    Regarding Decisional Predictability", 60 *La. L. Rev.* 1061 (2000) (concluding that "the
    Louisiana codification ... is a hopeful indication that statutory solutions can allow for
    the reconciliation of predictability and other values in multistate cases").

of justice in the individual case does not require the abandonment of rules but rather the formulation of rules with their just operation in particular situations in view"[33].

The question then becomes one of degree, namely finding the optimum equilibrium between these two goals[34]. While reasonable people will disagree on the exact dosages that can produce this equilibrium, it is far more constructive to devote our energies to this task than to assume in advance that it is unattainable.

2.   *Overcoming the anti-rule syndrome*

374. In short, four decades after the revolution, it is time to rid ourselves of the strong anti-rule syndrome that the revolution propagated. Fortunately, even some of the revolution's protagonists have spoken in favour of rules, even while the revolution was at its peak[35]. For example, as early as 1965, Cavers became disillusioned with the uncertainty unleashed by the revolution and recognized the need to "provide rules ... under which the same cases will be decided the same way no matter where the suit is brought"[36]. He also showed the way by proposing his own "principles of preference" for tort and contract conflicts[37]. Professor Willis Reese, the chief drafter of the Second Restatement, also proclaimed that "the formulation of rules should be as much an objective in choice of law as it is in other ar-

---

33.   D. Cavers, "Legislative Choice of Law: Some European Examples", 44 *S. Cal. L. Rev.* 340, 360 n. 177 (1971).

34.   Cf. E. Bodenheimer, "The Need for a Reorientation in American Conflicts Law", 29 *Hastings LJ* 731, 745 (1978) ("Is it possible to find a solution to the problem which proceeds from the basic assumption that certainty and elasticity in legal methodology are not polar opposites, between which a clearcut choice must be made but complementary values, which in some fashion must be meshed together?").

35.   See C. Peterson, "New Openness to Statutory Choice of Law Solutions", 38 *Am. J. Comp. L.* 423, 442 (1990) ("Many observers and participants in the conflicts revolution have expressed the hope that a system of principled rules will emerge from the collective experience of the courts in attempting to grapple with this dynamic subject.").

36.   D. Cavers, *The Choice of Law Process* 22 (1965) ("We will not ... fulfill the objectives of the conflict of laws unless we can provide rules ... under which the same cases will be decided the same way no matter where the suit is brought.").

37.   See *id.* at 139-203; *supra* 13, 124, 135, 141, 144-145, 156, 174, 273.

eas of law"[38]. Other scholars have also advocated the development of rules[39], and some have proposed rules of their own[40].

In 1999, American conflicts professors devoted their annual meeting to discussing the need for a Third Conflicts Restatement[41], thus beginning a debate that continues today[42]. Although both the specific debate for a new Restatement and the more general debate about the need for rules are inconclusive, it seems that, even among academics, Currie's aphorism that "we are better off without choice

---

38. See W. Reese, "General Course on Private International Law", 150 *Recueil des cours*, 1, 61 *et passim* (1976). As early as 1976, Reese argued that the conflicts experience since the revolution had "reached the stage where most areas of choice of law can be covered by general principles subject to imprecise exceptions. We should press on, however, beyond these principles to the development, as soon as our knowledge permits, of precise rules." *Id.* at 62.

39. See, e.g., E. Scoles, P. Hay, P. Borchers and S. Symeonides, *Conflict of Laws* 105-110 (4th ed. 2004); R. Weintraub, *Commentary on Conflict of Laws* 355-357 (4th ed. 2001); M. Gottesman, "Draining the Dismal Swamp: The Case for Federal Choice of Law Statutes", 80 *Geo. LJ* 1 (1991); M. Gottesman, "Adrift in the Sea of Indeterminacy", 75 *Ind. LJ* 527 (2000); A. Hill, "For a Third Conflicts Restatement – But Stop Trying to Reinvent the Wheel", 75 *Ind. LJ* 535 (2000); L. Kramer, "On the Need for a Uniform Choice of Law Code", 89 *Mich. L. Rev.* 2134 (1991); M. Rosenberg, "Two Views on *Kell* v. *Henderson*: An Opinion for the New York Court of Appeals", 67 *Colum. L. Rev.* 459 (1967); R. Whitten, "Curing the Deficiencies of the Conflicts Revolution: A Proposal for National Legislation on Choice of Law, Jurisdiction, and Judgments", 37 *Willamette L. Rev.* 259 (2000); S. Wiegand, "Fifty Conflict of Laws 'Restatements': Merging Judicial Discretion and Legislative Endorsement", 65 *La. L. Rev.* 1 (2004).

40. See, e.g., the rules for product-liability conflicts proposed by Cavers, Weintraub, Juenger, Kozyris, and McConnell, supra 273. See also Sedler *supra* 134 footnote 60; Posnak, *id.*; Wiegand, *supra* footnote 39.

41. See "Symposium: Preparing for the Next Century – A New Restatement of Conflicts", 75 *Ind. LJ* 399 (2000) (containing an introduction by Shreve, articles by Juenger, Richman and Reynolds, Symeonides, and Weinberg, and commentaries by Borchers, Dane, Gottesman, Hill, Maier, Peterson, Posnak, Reimann, Reppy, Sedler, Silberman and Lowenfeld, Simson, Singer, Twerski, and Weintraub). This debate was initiated by this author in the previous annual meeting, which celebrated the silver anniversary of the Second Restatement. See S. Symeonides, "The Judicial Acceptance of the Second Conflicts Restatement: A Mixed Blessing", 56 *Md. L. Rev.* 1246 (1997).

42. See "Symposium: American Conflicts Law at the Dawn of the 21st Century", 37 *Willamette L. Rev.* 1 (2000) (containing articles by Symeonides, Juenger, Kay, von Mehren, Weinstein, Weintraub and commentaries by Cox, Nafziger, Sedler, Shreve, and Whitten). See also J. Kropholler and J. von Hein, "From Approach to Rule-Orientation in American Tort Conflicts", in *Law and Justice in a Multistate World: Essays in Honor of Arthur T. von Mehren* 317 (J. Nafziger and S. Symeonides, eds. 2002); S. Wiegand, *supra* footnote 39.

of law rules"[43] is no longer taken at face value[44]. The pendulum has begun swinging back.

375. Judges, especially federal judges who often adjudicate complex multidistrict cases, have also routinely advocated the enactment of federal choice-of-law legislation for such cases[45]. At least one judge has described modern American conflicts law as "a veritable jungle, [in] which, if the law can be found out, leads not to a 'rule of action' but a reign of chaos dominated in each case by the judge's 'informed guess'"[46].

At the state level, one of the most influential courts in the country, the New York Court of Appeals, has confronted this "chaos" by enunciating, in a quasi-legislative fashion, a set of rules (the *Neumeier* rules) for resolving certain tort conflicts[47]. Although much of the academic community remains skeptical if not outright hostile[48], the *Neumeier* rules have survived the demise of guest statutes for which the rules were originally devised and now apply to a wide range of loss-distribution issues.

376. At the legislative level, one state, Louisiana, attempted the unthinkable – it enacted a comprehensive conflicts codification in 1991. One decade later, Dean Borchers, after painstakingly comparing the affirmance rate in cases decided before and after the codification, concluded that the codification "has improved the affirmance rate, and by implication the predictability of decisions in conflicts cases"[49]. Borchers also concluded that these results are "hopeful and suggestive

---

43. B. Currie, *supra* 15.

44. See C. Peterson, "New Openness to Statutory Choice of Law Solutions", 38 *Am. J. Comp. L.* 423, 423 (1990) ("We may be seeing a sea change in the attitudes of American conflicts scholars with respect to the use of statutes in solving conflicts problems").

45. See, e.g., *In re Air Crash Disaster at Stapleton Int'l Airport, Denver*, 720 F. Supp. 1445, 1454-1455 (D. Colo. 1988) ("The choice of law problems inherent in air crash and mass disaster litigation cry out for federal statutory resolution ... . Uncertainty on the choice of law question requires a considerable expenditure of time, money and other resources ... by litigants and counsel. Federal law would eliminate costly uncertainty and create uniformity. This approach would lead to a quick and efficient resolution of mass disaster cases"); J. Weinstein, "Mass Tort Jurisdiction and Choice of Law In a Multinational World Communicating by Extraterrestrial Satellites", 37 *Willamette L. Rev.* 145, 153 (2000) ("A federal statute would help. An international treaty would be even better.").

46. *In Re Paris Air Crash of March 3, 1974*, 399 F. Supp. 732, 739 (CD Cal. 1975).

47. See *supra* 93.

48. See, e.g., R. Weintraub, *Commentary on the Conflict of Laws* 400-403 (4th ed. 2001); G. Simson, "The *Neumeier-Schultz* Rules: How Logical a 'Next Stage in the Evolution of the Law' after *Babcock*?", 56 *Alb. L. Rev.* 913 (1993).

49. P. Borchers, "Louisiana's Conflicts Codification: Some Empirical Observations Regarding Decisional Predictability", 60 *La. L. Rev.* 1061, 1068 (2000). See also *id.* (reporting that "the pre-codification ... affirmance rate was 52.9%" and that "for post-codification decisions ... the affirmance rate improved to 76.2%").

that comprehensive conflicts codifications can produce significant benefits"[50]. In the meantime, two other jurisdictions, Puerto Rico and Oregon, have embarked on similar codification efforts[51], while the American Law Institute has proposed a comprehensive set of choice-of-law rules for mass torts and mass contracts cases for enactment by the United States Congress[52].

Even more common are the various state statutes on specific narrow areas of conflicts law. As illustrated earlier, during the last 50 years, state legislatures have routinely been enacting unilateral choice-of-law rules interspersed with substantive rules in areas such as insurance contracts, franchises, dealerships, consumer protection, construction contracts, workers' compensation, public contracts, and other densely regulated areas[53]. Moreover, choice-of-law legislation is not confined to such areas, nor to unilateral rules. For example, in addition to the choice-of-law provisions in the Uniform Commercial Code (which is in force in all 50 states), several states have enacted bilateral choice-of-law rules on matters such as contractual choice of law and forum, statutes of limitation, interstate arbitration, decedents' estates, marital property, premarital agreements, partnerships, wrongful death, notice and proof of sister-state and foreign law, child and spousal support, proof of paternity, child custody, and even on the discipline of members of the bar[54].

377. Thus, choice-of-law statutes are not uncommon; they are piecemeal rather than comprehensive, and they tend to avoid tort conflicts, which are the focus of most academic commentaries. In any event, the existence of so many statutes contradicts the long-entrenched view among academics, which regards legislation and choice of law in antithetical terms[55]. We are told that "legislative direction is inherently incapable of capturing the nuance and sophistication necessary for just and satisfactory choice-of-law solutions"[56], and that "[n]o legislature, no matter how wise it may be, could envisage all of the almost endless possibilities"[57]. Whether they underestimate the ability of legislatures or overestimate the complexity of the subject matter, these assessments are unduly pessimistic.

---

50. *Id.* at 1062.

51. See *supra* 103-104. Professor Wiegand argues that other state should follow with their own choice-of-law codes. See S. Wiegand, "Fifty Conflict of Laws 'Restatements': Merging Judicial Discretion and Legislative Endorsement", 65 *La. L. Rev.* 1 (2004).

52. See *supra* 345.

53. See *supra* 311.

54. For documentation for all of these statutes, see S. Symeonides, "American Choice of Law at the Dawn of the 21st Century", 37 *Willamette L. Rev.* 1, 80-81 (2000).

55. See, e.g., B. Currie, "Comments on *Babcock* v. *Jackson*", 63 *Colum. L. Rev.* 1233, 1241 (1963); R. Leflar, "Choice-of-Law Statutes", 44 *Tenn. L. Rev.* 951 (1977); R. Sedler, "Reflections on Conflict-of-Laws Methodology", 32 *Hastings LJ* 1628, 1636 (1981).

56. D. Trautman, "Reflections on Conflict-of-Laws Methodology", 32 *Hastings LJ* 1612, 1621 (1981).

57. W. Reese, "Statutes in Choice of Law", 35 *Am. J. Comp. L.* 395, 396 (1987).

The difficulties one encounters in drafting, and especially passing, conflicts legislation are formidable[58]. Nevertheless, these difficulties are surmountable, provided there exist both the political will and the mental fortitude to undertake the task. As is often the case, the perfect is the enemy of the good, but as Willis Reese reminded us, "[t]he risk of failure should not deter an attempt at rule making in choice of law ... whenever there is good basis for the belief that a proposed rule would lead to good results under most circumstances ... . Perfection is not for this world"[59].

In any event, even if it is true that the task of drafting choice-of-law rules is too risky, this has not prevented legislatures from haphazardly inserting such rules in various substantive statutes. Academics may continue to lament this fact or ignore these statutes altogether, as many of them do[60], or they could use their formidable talents to assist legislatures in drafting better statutes in the future.

3. Three options for rules

378. Be that as it may, this is not the best place to argue for choice-of-law *legislation*, especially in light of the attendant political difficulties and cultural scepticism at the state level, and the constitutional complexities at the federal level[61]. The contentions of this chapter are modest, respectful of the revolution, and deferential to the judicial choice-of-law process, to wit: (1) American conflicts law has reached a point at which it needs, is ripe for, and is capable of producing, new choice-of-law rules; and (2) these rules can and should preserve the best gains of the revolution. The question of whether these rules should be enacted by statute

---

58. See F. Vischer, "Drafting National Legislation on Conflict of Laws: The Swiss Experience", 41 *Law & Contemp. Prob.* 131 (1977) ("[S]ince undertaking this task [of drafting the Swiss conflicts codification] ... I became aware how much more difficult the task of the legislator is in comparison with that of the scholar reviewing the work afterwards"); S. Symeonides, "Louisiana's New Law of Choice of Law for Tort Conflicts: An Exegesis", 66 *Tul. L. Rev.* 677, 742-748 (1992) (describing the political opposition to the enactment of a Louisiana conflicts rule on punitive damages).

59. W. Reese, "Choice of Law: Rules or Approach?", 57 *Cornell L. Rev.* 315, 322 (1972).

60. "American conflicts scholars must exhibit far more humility, cooperation, and real-world-curiosity than they have so far." G. Shreve, "Conflicts Altruism", in *Law and Justice in a Multistate World: Essays in Honor of Arthur T. von Mehren* 383, 388 (J. Nafziger and S. Symeonides, eds. 2002).

61. For arguments in favour of federal legislation, see M. Gottesman, "Draining the Dismal Swamp: The Case for Federal Choice of Law Statutes", 80 *Geo. LJ* 1 (1991); L. Kramer, "On the Need for a Uniform Choice of Law Code", 89 *Mich. L. Rev.* 2134 (1991). See also S. Symeonides, "The ALI's Complex Litigation Project: Commencing the National Debate", 54 *La. L. Rev.* 843, 852-854 (1994) (discussing the source of federal power to legislate on choice-of-law matters).

or embodied in a new Restatement, as this author has argued elsewhere[62], can remain open.

A third option is to do what some commentators[63], including this one in the previous three chapters, have attempted – to "privately" extract such rules from a study and comparison of decided cases and restate them in treatises or other academic publications[64].

379. Each of these options has advantages and drawbacks[65]. One drawback of the third option is that – unlike, for example, England – the United States tradition does not favour such privately articulated rules, unless they carry the imprimatur of a collective body like the American Law Institute. Secondly, even if painstakingly constructed, such rules have the inherent problem of reinforcing and reproducing the shortcomings of the status quo. For example, as Professor Juenger suggested, if the gist of judicial practice in tort conflicts can be stated in a single sentence "thou shalt not apply foreign law"[66], it would be undesirable to elevate this sentence to the status of a rule. Judicial practice is not as parochial as critics often assume, but Juenger was correct in implying that rule-makers should have higher aspirations than merely collecting and restating what courts have decided.

At the same time, the thankless job of collecting, sorting out, synthesizing, and recasting in systematic descriptive statements what the courts have done is helpful in at least two independent ways: (1) it helps sharpen academic theory and ground it on reality rather than intuition. Indeed, it is one thing to propagate a theory and then look for cases to support it, and another thing to read all the cases and then to formulate a theory; and (2) it is a necessary prerequisite to the

---

62. See S. Symeonides, "The Need for a Third Conflicts Restatement (and a Proposal for Tort Conflicts)", 75 *Ind. LJ* 437 (2000).

63. See, e.g., E. Scoles, P. Hay, P. Borchers and S. Symeonides, *Conflict of Laws* 841-842, 850 (4th ed. 2004); R. Sedler, "Rules of Choice of Law Versus Choice-of-Law Rules: Judicial Method in Conflicts Torts Cases", 44 *Tenn. L. Rev.* 975, 1033-1041 (1977); R. Sedler, "Choice of Law in Conflicts Torts Cases: A Third Restatement or Rules of Choice of Law?", 75 *Ind. LJ* 615 (2000); S. Symeonides, "Choice of Law in the American Courts in 1999: One More Year" 48 *Am. J. Comp. L.*, 143, 147-150, 155-516 (2000); S. Wiegand, "Fifty Conflict of Laws 'Restatements': Merging Judicial Discretion and Legislative Endorsement", 65 *La. L. Rev.* 1 (2004).

64. See R. Weintraub, *Commentary on the Conflict of Laws* 355 (4th ed. 2001) ("After a series of decisions dealing with similar conflicts issues, courts and commentators can summarize the results as a rule".). See also P. Hay and R. Ellis, "Bridging the Gap between Rules and Approaches in Tort Choice of Law in the United States: A Survey of Current Case Law", 27 *Int'l Law* 369 (1993).

65. For example, legislation is the most authoritative and can bring uniformity much more quickly, but it is politically difficult. A new Restatement *should* not be politically difficult, but it is non-binding, although in time it can gain in persuasive authority what it lacks in formal status. Privately extracted rules are even less authoritative, but they are also harmless.

66. F. Juenger, "A Third Conflicts Restatement?", 75 *Ind. LJ* 403, 411 (2000).

next step – articulating normative rules that can correct in the future what has been wrongly decided in the past. Thus, descriptive rules are a necessary foundation for prescriptive or normative rules, if one considers the latter desirable.

This author contends that this book has demonstrated that, at this stage in the development of American conflicts law, both descriptive and normative rules are feasible. Whether normative rules are also desirable is something that may or may not be demonstrable, if only because it largely depends on one's beliefs on whether it is generally preferable to resolve problems *ex post* rather than *ex ante*. Be that as it may, this author, having been involved in all three types of rule-articulation, has a preference for either of the first two options, and a strong aversion to doing nothing.

D.   The Shape of the New Rules

380. If the option of doing nothing is rejected, the next hurdle is to reach a consensus regarding the shape and content of the new rules. This hurdle is formidable, but it cannot be surmounted unless conflicts scholars begin a constructive debate putting forward their views[67]. The following suggestions are this author's initial contribution to this debate.

It is submitted that the new choice-of-law rules should possess the following characteristics:

(a) They should be narrow and issue-specific, sometimes regulating only a single issue, e.g., amount of damages, (rather than broad legal categories such as torts or contracts) so as to preserve the issue-by-issue analysis which is one of the revolution's main accomplishments[68].

(b) They should not attempt to regulate the entire field of conflicts law, but only those enclaves that have been sufficiently explored, and preferably settled, by precedent. The unexplored areas should be left to some general open-ended

---

67.   Fortunately, the debate has already begun in the context of discussing the desirability of a Third Conflicts Restatement. In addition to the excellent contributions contained in the *Indiana Law Journal* Symposium, see *supra* footnote 41, see S. Cox, "Substantive Multilateral, and Unilateral Choice of Law Approaches", 37 *Willamette L. Rev.* 171 (2000); J. Nafziger, "Making Choices of Law Together", 37 *Willamette L. Rev.* 209 (2000); R. Sedler, "Interest Analysis, 'Multistate Policies', and Considerations of Fairness in Conflicts Tort Cases", 37 *Willamette L. Rev.* 231 (2000); G. Shreve, "Conflicts Empiricism", 37 *Willamette L. Rev.* 247 (2000); L. Weinberg, "Theory Wars in the Conflict of Laws", 103 *Mich. L. Rev.* 1631 (2005); R. Whitten, "Curing the Deficiencies of the Conflicts Revolution: A Proposal for National Legislation on Choice of Law, Jurisdiction, and Judgments", 37 *Willamette L. Rev.* 259 (2000); S. Wiegand, "Fifty Conflict of Laws 'Restatements': Merging Judicial Discretion and Legislative Endorsement", 65 *La. L. Rev.* 1 (2004)

68.   See *supra* 90.

principles or approaches, which in due time will produce new rules through judicial application and the doctrine of *stare decisis*[69].

(c)   Some of the rules should be subject to escape clauses that would authorize the court to deviate from the predesignated result in appropriate cases[70].

(d)   While most of the rules should be phrased in multilateral terms delineating the reach of both forum and foreign law, the use of unilateral rules delineating the reach of forum law should not be ruled out. When surrounded by multilateral rules, unilateral rules can serve judicial economy without fostering unchecked parochialism. They help quickly dispose of some cases without a judicial choice-of-law analysis, but also without precluding such analysis for other cases. Furthermore, the careful and selective use of unilateral rules has the advantage of collectively delineating the precise circumstances under which the forum's policies should prevail over the policies of other states, rather than leaving that determination to an ad hoc judicial decision[71].

(e)   The new rules should aspire for interstate uniformity *whenever possible*. The italicized words signify the difference between the old and the new rules. The American experience demonstrates that uniformity is not readily attainable, and that states do take an interest in the outcome of multistate disputes between private parties[72]. Contemporary political and economic realities being what they are (and as long as choice of law remains a matter of state or national law, rather than federal or international law), one cannot expect states to abdicate their responsibility to protect important state interests. The same is equally true in the international arena. The key challenge is to carefully and moderately identify those cases in which these interests are in fact real and important. Once this is done, then the protection of these interests can be ensured by a combination of inward-and outward-looking unilateral rules, or by multilateral rules that take account of these interests.

(f)   The new rules should be based on the premise that the task of conflicts law is to choose between state *laws* rather than between *states* as such. Consequently, the new rules should be designed to achieve a content-oriented law-selection rather than jurisdiction-selection. However, this law-selection need not be relegated to the judge in all cases. In some cases it can and should be made in advance by the rule-drafter after considering all possible permutations. When this is done – and it can be done – the resulting rules

---

69.   Examples of cases that are not ripe for rules are certain loss-distribution conflicts involving the split-domicile cross-border pattern (see *supra* 158-159) and conflicts involving three states (see *supra* 160-161). Even the seemingly well-traversed area of common-domicile cases is not ripe for rules with regard to issues other than the rights of the victim and the tortfeasor vis a vis each other (e.g., vis a vis third parties or joint tortfeasors).

70.   See *supra* 363.

71.   See *supra* 316-321.

72.   See *supra* 308-309.

will have the appearance of jurisdiction-selecting rules, but they will be free of the defects of the old rules[73].

(g) Finally, the new rules should aspire for conflicts justice, but without being oblivious to the need for material justice. Again the key question is when to do what. One answer suggested above[74] is provided by comparative experience: the circumstances under which the pursuit of conflicts justice should be subordinated to the need for material justice should be defined in advance by the collective democratic process of rule-making rather than be left to an *ad hoc* judicial determination. Obviously, one cannot expect judges to completely repress their natural instinct to do justice in the individual case. Neither should they. However, the pursuit of justice-in-the-individual-case must take into account the *multistate* nature of that case.

381. The above are simply *general* guidelines; and they are eclectic, which in some circles is considered a mortal sin. Indeed, these guidelines do not subscribe to a single methodology, theory, or ideology. Eclecticism can be a serious flaw, if it is the result of uncritical or unprincipled choices. However, in a period of transition, eclecticism is inevitable, and, upon arrival to the destination, eclecticism can be a sign of maturity, if it is the result of considered and principled choices. Methodological or philosophical purity should not be an end in itself when dealing with complex multistate problems that by definition implicate conflicting national and societal values.

As is often the case, the devil will be in the details, but the difficulties should not be overestimated. For example, *all* of the above guidelines have been followed in drafting the Louisiana and Puerto Rico codifications, as well as in formulating the rules contained in the previous three chapters. That some, or many, academic commentators may find these guidelines faulty or these rules deficient, is both natural and healthy. A constructive debate on how to avoid these defects is much more preferable than interminable academic colloquia, or worse yet monologues, on guest-statute conflicts, or the transcendental nature of comity. The twenty-first century expects more from us.

---

73. See *supra* 346-348.
74. See *supra* 357.

Table of Cases

(All references are to paragraphs, not pages)

C

N

Bibliography

Allen, W., and E. O'Hara, "Second Generation Law and Economics of Conflict of Laws: Baxter's Comparative Impairment and Beyond", 51 *Stan. L. Rev.* 1011 (1999).

Audit, B., *Droit international privé*, 3rd ed., Paris, 2000.

___, "Le droit international privé en quête d'universalité", 305 *Recueil des cours* 9 (2004)

___, "Le droit international privé français à la fin du vingtième siècle: Progrès ou recul?", in S. Symeonides, *Private International Law at the End of the 20th Century: Progress or Regress?*, 191, The Hague, 2000.

___, "Le caractère fonctionnel de la règle de conflit", 186 *Recueil des cours* 219 (1985).

___, "A Continental Lawyer Looks at Contemporary American Choice-of-Law Principles", 27 *Am. J. Comp. L.* 589 (1979).

Baade, H., "The Operation of Foreign Public Law", 30 *Tex. Int'l LJ* 429 (1995).

___, "Counter-Revolution or Alliance for Progress? Reflections on Reading Cavers, *The Choice-of-Law Process*", 46 *Tex. L. Rev.* 141 (1967).

Baker, J., "Respecting a State's Tort Law, while Continuing its Reach to that State", 31 *Seton Hall L. Rev.* 698 (2001).

Ballarino, T., *Diritto internazionale Privato*, Padua, 1996.

___, "Questions de droit international privé et dommages catastrophiques", 220 *Recueil des cours* 289 (1990).

Basedow, J., "International Antitrust: From Extraterritorial Application to Harmonization", 60 *La. L. Rev.* 1037 (2000).

Batiffol, H., "Le pluralisme des méthodes en droit international privé", 139 *Recueil des cours* 75 (1973).

___, "La loi applicable à la responsabilité du fait des produits", 62 *Rev. critique* 252 (1973).

Batiffol, H., and P. Lagarde, *Droit international privé*, 8th ed., Paris 1983.

Baxter, W., "Choice of Law and the Federal System", 16 *Stan. L. Rev.* 1 (1963).

Beale, J., *A Treatise on the Conflict of Laws*, Vols. 1-3, New York, 1935.

Beitzke, G., "Les obligations délictuelles en droit international privé", 115 *Recueil des cours*, 67 (1965).

Bermann, G., *Transnational Litigation*, St. Paul (2003).

Berman, P., "Towards a Cosmopolitan Vision of Conflict of Laws: Redefining Governmental Interests in a Global Era", 153 *U. Pa. L. Rev.* 1819 (2005).

Bernasconi, C., "Civil Liability Resulting from Transfrontier Environmental Damage: a Case for the Hague Conference? 12 *Hague Ybk. Int'l L.* 35 (2000).

Blaikie, J., "Foreign Torts and Choice of Law Flexibility", 1995 *SLT* 23.

Bliesener, D., "Fairness and Choice of Law: A Critique of the Political Rights-Based Approach to the Conflict of Laws", 42 *Am. J. Comp. L.* 687 (1994).

Bodenheimer, E., "The Need for a Reorientation in American Conflicts Law", 19 *Hastings LJ* 731 (1978).

Boele-Woelki, K., "The Communitarization of Private International Law " 4 *Ybk. Priv. Int'l L.*1 (2002)

___, "Unification and Harmonization of Private International Law in Europe", in *Private Law in the International Arena – Liber Amicorum Kurt Siehr* 61 (J. Basedow, *et al.*, eds., 2000).

Boele-Woelki, K., C. Joustra, and G. Steenhoff, "Dutch Private International Law at the End of the 20th Century: Progress or Regress?", in S. Symeonides, *Private International Law at the End of the 20th Century: Progress or Regress?*, 295, The Hague, 2000.

Bogdan, M., "Aircraft Accidents in the Conflict of Laws" 208 *Recueil des cours* 9 (1988)

Boggiano, A., "The Law of the Relations Between Legal Systems: a Methodological Analysis" in *Private Law in the International Arena: Liber Amicorum Kurt Siehr* 79, The Hague, 2000.

Bolard, "Universalisme ou nationalisme: l'hésitation française", *Ann. Suiss. dip.* 83 (1977).

Bonomi, A., "The Italian Statute on Private International Law" 27 *Int'l J. Leg. Inf.* 247 (1999).

Borchers, P., "Louisiana's Conflicts Codification: Some Empirical Observations Regarding Decisional Predictability", 60 *La. L. Rev.* 1061 (2000).

___, "Empiricism and Theory in Conflicts Law", 75 *Ind. LJ* 509 (2000).

___, "Back to the Past: Anti-Pragmatism in American Conflicts Law", 48 *Mercer L. Rev.* 721 (1997).

___, "Choice of Law in the American Courts in 1992: Observations and Reflections", 42 *Am. J. Comp. L.* 125 (1994).

___, "Conflicts Pragmatism", 56 *Alb. L. Rev.* 883 (1993).

Borchers, P., and Zekoll, J. (eds.), *International Conflict of Laws for the Third Millennium: Essays in Honor of Friedrich K. Juenger*, Ardsley, NY 2000.

Bourel, P., "Du rattachement de quelques délits spéciaux en droit international privé" 214 *Recueil des cours* 251(1990).

Briggs, A., "Choice of Law in Tort and Delict", 1995 *LMCLQ* 519.

Brilmayer, L., "The Role of Substantive and Choice of Law Policies in the Formation and Application of Choice of Law Rules", 252 *Recueil des cours* 9 (1995).

___, "The Other State's Interests", 24 *Cornell Int'l LJ* 233 (1991).

___, "Rights, Fairness, and Choice of Law", 98 *Yale LJ* 127 (1989).

___, "Shaping and Sharing in Democratic Theory: Towards a Political Philo-sophy of Interstate Equality", 15 *Fla. St. L. Rev.* 389 (1987).

___, "Methods and Objectives in the Conflict of Laws: A Challenge", 35 *Mercer L. Rev.* 556 (1984).

___, "Interest Analysis and the Myth of Legislative Intent", 78 *Mich. L. Rev.* 392 (1980).

Bucher, A., "L'ordre public et le but social des lois en droit international privé", 239 *Recueil des cours* 9 (1993).

___, "Sur les règles de rattachement à caractère substantiel", *Liber Amicorum Adolf Schnitzer*, 37, Geneva, 1979.

Bucher A. and Bonomi, A., *Droit international privé*, Helbing & Lichtenhahn, Bâle, Genève, Munich, 2nd 2004.

Burián, L., "Hungarian Private International Law at the End of the 20th Century: Progress or Regress?", in S. Symeonides, *Private International Law at the End of the 20th Century: Progress or Regress?*, 263 (2000).

Buxbaum, H., "Conflict of Economic Laws: From Sovereignty to Substance", 42 *Va. J. Int'l L.* 931 (2002).

Camara, K., "Costs of Sovereignty", 107 *W. Va. L. Rev.* 385 (2005).

Carrillo Salcedo, A., "Le renouveau du particularisme en droit international privé", 160 *Recueil des cours* 181 (1978).

Carter, P., "Choice of Law in Tort: The Role of the Lex Fori", 54 *Cambridge LJ* 38 (1995).

Castel, J., *Canadian Conflict of Laws*, 4th ed., Toronto, 1997.

___, "Back to the Future! Is the 'New' Rigid Choice of Law Rule for Interpro-vincial Torts Constitutionally Mandated?", 33 *Osgoode Hall LJ* 35 (1995).

Cavers, D., *The Choice-of-Law Process*, Ann Arbor, U. of Michigan P., 1965.

___, "A Correspondence with Brainerd Currie, 1957-1958", 34 *Mercer L. Rev.* 471 (1983).

___, "The Proper Law of Producer's Liability", 26 *Int'l and Comp. LQ* 703 (1977).

___, "The Value of Principled Preferences", 49 *Tex. L. Rev.* 211 (1971).

___, "Cipolla and Conflicts Justice", 9 *Duq. L. Rev.* 360 (1971).

___, "Legislative Choice of Law: Some European Examples", 44 *S. Cal. L. Rev.* 340 (1971).

___, "Contemporary Conflicts Law in American Perspective", 131 *Recueil des cours* 75 (1970).

___, "Comments on *Reich* v. *Purcell*", 15 *UCLA L. Rev.* 467 (1968).

___, "Some of Ehrenzweig's Choice-of-Law Generalizations", 18 *Okla. L. Rev.* 357 (1965).

___, "Comments on *Babcock* v. *Jackson*", 63 *Colum L. Rev.* 1219 (1963).

___, "A Critique of the Choice-of-Law Problem", 47 *Harv. L. Rev.* 173 (1933).

Cheatham, E., "Conflict of Laws: Some Developments and Some Questions", 25 *Ark. L. Rev.* 9 (1971).

Cheatham, E., and H. Maier, "Private International Law and Its Sources", 22 *Vand. L. Rev.* (1968).

Cheatham, E., and W. Reese, "Choice of the Applicable Law", 52 *Colum. L. Rev.* 959 (1952).

Chen, J., "Australian Private International Law at the End of the 20th Century: Progress or Regress?", in S. Symeonides, *Private International Law at the End of the 20th Century: Progress or Regress?*, 83, The Hague, 2000.

Collins, L., *Dicey and Morris on the Conflict of Laws*, 13th ed., London 2000.

Cook, W., *The Logical and Legal Bases of the Conflict of Laws*, Cambridge, Mass., 1942.

___, "An Unpublished Chapter of the Logical and Legal Bases of the Conflict of Laws", 37 *U. Ill. L. Rev.* 418 (1943).

Cordero Moss, G., *International Commercial Arbitration*, Oslo 1999.

Corr, J. "The Frailty of Interest Analysis", 11 *Geo. Mason L. Rev.* 299 (2002).

Couch, H., "Is Significant Contacts a Choice-of-law Methodology?", 56 *Ark. L. Rev.* 745 (2004).

Cross, J., "The Conduct-Regulating Exception in Modern United States Choice-of-Law", 36 *Creighton L. Rev.* 425 (2003).

Cox, S., "Substantive Multilateral, and Unilateral Choice of Law Approaches", 37 *Willamette L. Rev.* 171 (2000).

Currie, B., *Selected Essays on the Conflict of Laws*, Durham, NC, Duke UP, 1963.

___, "The Disinterested Third State", 28 *Law & Contemp. Probs.* 754 (1963).

___, "Notes on Methods and Objectives in the Conflict of Laws", 1959 *Duke LJ* 171 (1959).

Currie, B., and H. Schreter, "Unconstitutional Discrimination in the Conflict of Laws: Privileges and Immunities", 69 *Yale LJ* 1323 (1960).

___, "Unconstitutional Discrimination in the Conflict of Laws: Equal Protection", 28 *U. Chi. L. Rev.* 1 (1960).

Dane, P., "Whereof One Cannot Speak: Legal Diversity and the Limits of a Restatement of Conflict of Laws", 75 *Ind. LJ* 511 (2000).

___, "Vested Rights, 'Vestedness', and Choice of Law", 96 *Yale LJ* 1191 (1987).

Davis, G., "Choice of Law in Tort at the Dawning of the 21st Century", 24 *Melb. UL Rev.* 982 (2000).

Deby-Gérard, F., *Le rôle de la règle de conflict dans le règlement des rapports internationaux*, Paris 1973.

de Boer, T., *Beyond Lex Loci Delicti: Conflicts Methodology and Multistate Torts in American Case Law*, Deventer, 1987.

___, "Facultative Choice of Law: The Procedural Status of Choice-of-Law Rules and Foreign Law", 257 *Recueil des cours* 223 (1996).

___, "Prospects for European Conflicts Law in the Twenty-First Century", in *International Conflict of Laws for the Third Millennium: Essays in Honor of Friedrich K. Juenger* 193 (P. Borchers and J. Zekoll, eds. 2000).

De Maekelt, T., "Venezuelan Private International Law at the End of the 20th Century: Progress or Regress?", in S. Symeonides, *Private International Law at the End of the 20th Century: Progress or Regress?*, 445 (2000).

de Nova, R., "Glancing at the Content of Substantive Rules under the Jurisdiction-Selecting Approach", 41 *Law & Contemp. Prob.* 1 (1977).

___, "Historical and Comparative Introduction to Conflict of Laws", 118 *Recueil des cours* 441 (1966).

___, "The First American Book on Conflict of Laws", 8 *Am. J. Leg. Hist.* 136 (1964).

Dolinger, J., "Evolution of Principles for Resolving Conflicts in the Field of Contracts and Torts", 283 *Recueil des cours* 189 (2000).

Droz, G., "Regards sur le droit international privé comparé", 229 *Recueil des cours* 9 (1991).

Dubler, C., *Les clauses d'exception en droit international privé*, Geneva, 1983.

Dutoit, B., *Droit international privé suisse: Commentaire de la loi fédérale du 18 décembre 1987*, 2nd ed., Bâle et Francfort-sur-le-Main, 1997.

Dutson, S., "Product Liability and Private International Law: Choice of Law in Tort in England", 47 *Am. J. Comp. L.* 129 (1999).

___, "Choice of Law in Tort in Domestic and International Litigation", 26 *Austl. Bus. L. Rev.* 238 (1998).

Eades, R., "Attempts to Federalize and Codify Tort Law", 36 *Tort & Ins. LJ* 1 (2000).

Ehrenzweig, A., *Private International Law*, Vol. 1, 1967.

___, *A Treatise on the Conflict of Laws*, St. Paul, 1962.

___, "Choice of Law in California – A 'Prestatement'", 21 *UCLA L. Rev.* 781 (1974).

___, "Conflict, Crisis and Confusion in Pennsylvania", 9 *Duq. L. Rev.* 459 (1971).

___, "The Value of Principled Preferences", 49 *Tex. L. Rev.* 236 (1971).

___, "Specific Principles of Private Transnational Law", 124 *Recueil des cours* 167 (1968).

___, "A Counter-Revolution in Conflicts Law? From Beale to Cavers", 80 *Harv. L. Rev.* 377 (1966).

___, "A Proper Law in a Proper Forum: A 'Restatement' of the 'Lex Fori Approach'", 18 *Okla. L. Rev.* 340 (1965).

___, "The Second Conflicts Restatement: A Last Appeal for Its Withdrawal", 113 *U. Pa. L. Rev.* 1230 (1965).

___, "Choice of Law: Current Doctrine and 'True Rules'", 49 *Calif. L. Rev.* 240 (1961).

___, "The Lex Fori-Basic Rule in the Conflict of Laws", 58 *Mich. L. Rev.* 637 (1960).

Einhorn, T., and Siehr, K. (eds), *Intercontinental Cooperation Through Private International Law: Essays in Memory of Peter Nygh*, The Hague 2004.

Ely, J., "Choice of Law and the State's Interest in Protecting its Own", 23 *Wm. and Mary L. Rev.* 173 (1981).

Evrigenis, D., *Idiotikon Diethnes Dikaion*, Thessaloniki, 1968.

___, "Tendances doctrinales actuelles en droit international privé", 118 *Recueil des cours* 313 (1966).

Fach Gómez, K., *La contaminacion transfrontieriza en Derecho Internacional Privado: Estudio de derecho applicable*, Barcelona 2002.

___, "The Law Applicable to Cross-Border Environmental Damage: From the European National Systems to Rome II", 6 *Ybk Priv. Int'l L.* 291 (2004).

Fallon, M., "Les règles d'applicabilité en droit international privé", *Mélanges Van der Elst* 285, Brussels,1986.

Fallon, M., and J. Meeusen, "Belgian Private International Law at the End of the 20th Century: Progress or Regress?", in S. Symeonides, *Private International Law at the End of the 20th Century: Progress or Regress?*, 109 (2000).

Fauvarque-Cosson, B., *Libre disponibilité des droits et conflits de lois*, Paris, 1996.

___, "Comparative Law and Conflict of Laws: Allies or Enemies? New Perspectives on an Old Couple", 49 *Am. J. Comp. L.* 407 (2001).

Fawcett, J., "Cross-Fertilization in Private International Law", 53 *Current Leg. Prob.* 303 (2000).

___, "Products Liability in Private International Law: A European Perspective", 238 *Recueil des cours* 9 (1993).

___, "Is American Governmental Interest Analysis the Solution to English Tort Choice of Law Problems?", 31 *Int'l & Comp. LQ* 31 (1982).

Felix, R., "Leflar in the Courts: Judicial Adoptions of Choice-Influencing Considerations", 52 *Ark. L. Rev.* 35 (1999).

Fentiman, R., "Foreign Law and *Forum Conveniens*", in *Law and Justice in a Multistate World: Essays in Honor of Arthur T. von Mehren*, 275 (J. Nafziger and S. Symeonides, eds., 2002).

___, "English Private International Law at the End of the 20th Century: Progress or Regress?", in S. Symeonides, *Private International Law at the End of the 20th Century: Progress or Regress?*, 165 (2000).

Fernández Arroyo, D., *La codificación del derecho internacional privado en América Latina*, Madrid, 1994.

Ferrer-Correia, A., "Les problèmes de codification en droit international privé", 145 *Recueil des cours* (1975).

Firorini, A., "The Codification of Private International Law: The Belgian Experience", 54 *ICLQ* 499 (2005).

Flessner, A., *Interessenjurisprudenz im internationnalen Privatrecht*, Tübingen, 1990.

Forget, L., *Les conflits de lois en matière d'accidents de la circulation routière*, 1973.

Francescakis, P., *La pensée des autres en droit international privé*, Thessaloniki, 1985.

___, *La théorie du renvoi et les conflits des systèmes en droit international privé*, Paris, 1958.

___, "'Lois d'application immédiate' et règles de conflits", 3 *Riv. dir. int. priv. proces.* 699 (1966).

___, "Quelques précisions sue les 'lois d'application immédiate' et leurs rapports avec les règles de conflit de lois", 55 *Rev. critique* 1 (1955).

Fuchs, A., H. Muir Watt and E. Pautaut (eds.), *Les conflits de lois et le système juridique communautaire*, Paris 2004.

Gannagé, P., "L'égalité de traitement entre la loi du for et la loi étrangère dans les codifications nationales de droit international privé" 63 *Ann. Inst. Dr. Int'l.* 293 (1990).

Glenn, H. P., "Codification of Private International Law in Quebec", 60 *RabelsZ* 231 (1996).

González Campos, J., "Diversification, spécialisation et matérialisation des règles de droit international privé", 287 *Recueil des cours* 9 (2000).

Gothot, P., "Phocion Francescakis et 'La pensée des autres'", Rev. Critique 711 (1987).

___, "Le renouveau de la tendance unilatérale en droit international privé", 60 *Rev. critique* 1, 209, 415 (1971).

Gottesman, M., "Adrift in the Sea of Indeterminacy", 75 *Ind. LJ* 527 (2000).

___, "Draining the Dismal Swamp: The Case for Federal Choice of Law Statutes", 80 *Geo. LJ* 1 (1991).

Grammatikaki-Alexiou, A., *Delictual Obligations in Private International Law* (in Greek), Thessaloniki, 1987.

___, "Substantive Conflicts Rules and Connecting Factors of a Substantive Character: Two Versions of Methodological Pluralism" (in Greek), *Rev. hellenique droit europ.* 299 (1986).

Grammatikaki-Alexiou, A., Z. Papassiopi-Passia, and E. Vassilakakis, *Idiotikon Diethnes Dikaion*, Thessaloniki, 1997.

Gray, A., "Flexibility in Conflict of Laws Multistate Tort Cases: The Way Forward in Australia", 23 *U. Queensl. L.J.* 435 (2004).

Greene, J., "Choice of Law in Tort – The Song that Never Ends", 26 *Fed. L. Rev.* 349 (1998).

Guedj, T.G., "The Theory of the lois de police, a Functional Trend in Continental Private International Law: A Comparative Analysis with Modern American Theories", 39 *Am. J, Comp. L.* 661(1991).

Guojian, X., "Torts in Chinese Private International Law: A Case Note", 40 *ICLQ* 684 (1991).

Gutzwiller, P., "Von Ziel und Methode des IPR", *Ann. suisse droit int.* 161 (1968).

Guzman, A., "Choice of Law: New Foundations", 90 *Geo. LJ* 883 (2002).

Hamza, G., "Some Reflections on the History of Private International Law" 34 *Act. Jur. Acad. Sci. Hung.* 195 (1992).

Hanotiau, B., *Le droit international privé américain*, Paris-Brussels, 1979.

Harris, J., "Choice of Law in Tort – Blending in with the Landscape of the Conflict of Laws?", 61 *Mod. L. Rev.* 33 (1998).

Hay, P., *Internationales Privatrecht*, 2nd ed. Munich 2002.

___, "From Rule-Orientation to 'Approach' in German Conflicts Law: The Effect of the 1986 and 1999 Codifications", 47 *Am. J. Comp. L.* 633 (1999).

___, "Flexibility versus Predictability and Uniformity in Choice of Law: Reflections on Current European and United States Conflicts Law", 226 *Recueil des cours* 281 (1991).

___, "Full Faith and Credit and Federalism in Choice of Law", 34 *Mercer L. Rev.* 709 (1983).

___, "Reflections on Conflict-of-laws Methodology: A Dialogue", 32 *Hastings LJ* 1644 (1981).

Hay, P., and R. Ellis, "Bridging the Gap between Rules and Approaches in Tort Choice of Law in the United States: A Survey of Current Case Law", 27 *Int'l Law.* 369 (1993).

Herzog, P., "The 'Conflict of Laws Revolution' in New York, and Where Did It Leave Us", 50 *Syr. L. Rev.* 1279 (2000).

___, "Constitutional Limits on Choice of Law", 234 *Recueil des cours* 239 (1992)

Hill, A., "For a Third Conflicts Restatement – But Stop Trying to Reinvent the Wheel", 75 *Ind. LJ* 535 (2000).

___, "After the Big Bang: Professor Sedler's Remaining Dilemma", 38 *Wayne L. Rev.* 1471 (1992).

___, "Governmental Interest and the Conflict of Laws – A Reply to Professor Currie", 27 *U. Chi. L. Rev.* 463 (1960).

Hiller, L., "The 'Most Significant Relationship' Test of the Second Restatement of Conflicts and Its Effect Outside the United States in the Area of Torts", 12 *NY Int'l L. Rev.* 55 (1999).

Horowitz, H., "The Law of Choice of Law in California – A Restatement", 21 *UCLA L. Rev.* 719 (1974).

___, "Toward a Federal Common Law of Choice of Law", 14 *UCLA L. Rev.* 1191 (1967).

Jaffey, A., *Topics in Choice of Law*, Norwich, 1996.

Jayme, E., *Ein Internationales Privatrecht für Europa*, Heidelberg, 1991.___, *Methoden der Konkretisierung des ordre public im Internationalen Privatrecht*, Heidelberg, 1989.

___, "Le droit international privé du nouveau millénaire: La protection de la personne humaine face à la globalisation", 282 *Recueil des cours* 9 (2000).

___, "Identité culturelle et intégration: Le droit international privé postmoderne", 251 *Recueil des cours* 9 (1995).

___, "The American Conflicts Revolution and Its Impact on European Private International Law", in *Forty Years On: The Evolution of Postwar Private International Law in Europe*, Centrum voor Buitenlands Recht en Internationaal Privaatrecht Universiteit van Amsterdam, 15 (1992).

___, "Considérations historiques et actuelles sur la codification du droit international privé", 177 *Recueil des cours* 9 (1982).

___, "Neue Kodifikation des Internationalen Privatrechts in Louisiana", *IPRax.* 1993, 80.

Joerges, C., *Zum Functionswandel des Kollisionsrecht, Die 'Governmental Interest Analysis' und die 'Krise des Internationalen Privatrechts'"*, Berlin, 1971.

Juenger, F., *Selected Essays on the Conflict of Laws*, Ardsley, NY, 2001.

___, *Choice of Law and Multistate Justice*, Dordrecht, Boston, 1993.

___, "How Do you Rate a Century?", 37 *Willamette L. Rev.* 89 (2000).

___, "A Third Conflicts Restatement?", 75 *Ind. LJ* 403 (2000).

___, "Choice of Law: How It Ought Not to Be", 48 *Mercer L. Rev.* 757 (1997).

___, "Contract Choice of Law in the Americas", 45 *Am. J. Comp. L.* 195 (1997).

___, "The Complex Litigation Project's Tort Choice-of-Law Rules", 54 *La. L. Rev.* 907 (1994).

___, "What's Wrong with Forum Shopping?", 16 *Sydney L. Rev.* 5 (1994).

___, "Forum Shopping: A Rejoinder", 16 *Sydney L. Rev.* 28 (1994).

___, "*Babcock* v. *Jackson* Revisited: Judge Fuld's Contribution to American Conflicts Law", 56 *Alb. L. Rev.* 727 (1993).

___, "Governmental Interests and Multistate Justice: A Reply to Professor Sedler", 24 *UC Davis L. Rev.* 227 (1990).

___, "Mass Disasters and the Conflict of Laws", 1989 *U. Ill. L. Rev.* 105 (1989).

___, "Conflict of Laws: A Critique of Interest Analysis", 32 *Am. J. Comp. L.* 1 (1984).

___, "Robert A. Leflar's Contribution to American Conflicts Law", 31 *SC L. Rev.* 413 (1980).

___, "Trends in European Conflicts Law", 60 *Cornell L. Rev.* 969 (1975).

___, "Choice of Law in Interstate Torts", 118 *U. Pa. L. Rev.* 202 (1969).

Josephs, H., "Book Review – Conflict of Laws: American, Comparative, International: Cases and Materials", 60 *La. L. Rev.* 1123 (2000).

Kahn-Freund, O., *General Problems of Private International Law*, Leyden, 1976.

___, "Delictual Liability and the Conflict of Laws", 124 *Recueil des cours* 1 (1968).

Kassir, W., *Réflexions sur le renvoi en droit international privé comparé*, Bruylant 2002.

Kay, H., "Currie's Interest Analysis in the 21st Century: Losing the Battle, But Winning the War", 37 *Willamette L. Rev.* 123 (2001).

___, "A Defense of Currie's Governmental Interest Analysis", 215 *Recueil des cours* 9 (1989).

___, "Chief Justice Traynor and Choice of Law Theory", 35 *Hastings LJ* 747 (1984).

___, "Theory into Practice: Choice of Law in the Courts", 34 *Mercer L. Rev.* 521 (1983).

Kaye, P. *Private International Law of Tort and Product Liability*, Aldershot, 1991.

Kegel, G., "Paternal Home and Dream Home: Traditional Conflict of Laws and the American Reformers", 27 *Am. J. Comp. L.* 615 (1979).

___, "The Crisis of Conflict of Laws", 112 *Recueil des cours* 91 (1964).

Kegel, G. and Schurig, K., *Internationales Privatrecht*, 9th ed., Munich 2003.

Kerameus, K., "Enforcement in the International Context", 264 *Recueil des cours* 179 (1997).

Kessedjian, C., "Codification du droit commercial international en droit international privé", 300 *Recueil des cours* 79 (2004).

___, "Le passé et l'avenir du droit international privé européen dans le cadre de l'intégration de l'Union européene, 4 *Rev. des affaires européennes* 411 (2001-02).

Kokkini-Iatridou, D., *Les clauses d'exception en matière de conflits de lois et de conflits de juridictions – ou le principe de proximité*, Dortrecht, Boston, London, 1994.

Korn, H., "Big Cases and Little Cases: *Babcock* in Perspective", 56 *Alb. L. Rev* 933 (1993).

___, "The Choice-of-Law Revolution: A Critique", 83 *Colum. L. Rev.* 772 (1983).

Kozyris, P., "Conflicts Theory for Dummies: Après le Deluge, Where Are We on Producers Liability?", 60 *La. L. Rev.* 1161 (2000).

___, "The Conflicts Provisions of the ALI's Complex Litigation Project: A Glass Half Full?", 54 *La. L. Rev. 953* (1994).

___, "Values and Methods in Choice of Law for Products Liability: A Comparative Comment on Statutory Solutions", 38 *Am. J. Comp. L.* 475 (1990).

___, "Interest Analysis Facing Its Critics", 46 *Ohio St. LJ* 569 (1985).

Kozyris, P., and S. Symeonides, "Choice of Law in the American Courts in 1989: An Overview", 38 *Am. J. Comp. L.* 601 (1990).

Kramer, L., "Choice of Law in Complex Litigation", 71 *NYU L. Rev.* 547 (1996).

___, "On the Need for a Uniform Choice of Law Code", 89 *Mich. L. Rev.* 2134 (1991).

___, "More Notes on Methods and Objectives in the Conflict of Laws", 24 *Cornell Int'l LJ* 245 (1991).

___, "Return of the Renvoi", 66 *NYU L. Rev.* 979 (1991).

___, "Rethinking Choice of Law", 90 *Colum. L. Rev.* 277 (1990).

___, "The Myth of the 'Unprovided For' Case", 75 *Va. L. Rev.* 1045 (1989).

___, "Interest Analysis and the Presumption of Forum Law", 56 *U. Chi. L. Rev.* 1301 (1989).

Kraus, M., "Product Liability and Game Theory: One More Trip to the Choice-of-Law Well", 2002 *B.Y.U. L.* Rev. 759 (2002).

Kropholler, J., *Internationales Privatrecht*, 5th ed., Tübingen, 2004.

___, *Europäisches Zivilprozessrecht*, Heidelberg 2002

Kropholler, J., and J. von Hein, "From Approach to Rule-Orientation in American Tort Conflicts", in *Law and Justice in a Multistate World: Essays in Honor of Arthur T. von Mehren*, 317 (J. Nafziger and S. Symeonides, eds., 2002).

Lalive, P., "Tendances et méthodes en droit international privé", 155 *Recueil des cours* 1 (1977).

Lagarde, P., "Le principe de proximité dans le droit international privé", 196 *Recueil des cours* 9 (1986).

Laycock, D., "Equal Citizens of Equal and Territorial States: The Constitutional Foundations of Choice of Law", 92 *Colum. L. Rev.* 249 (1992).

Lebedev, S., "New Russian Regulation on Private International Law", 4 *Ybk. Priv. Int'l L.* 117 (2002).

Leflar, R., "The Nature of Conflicts Law", 81 *Colum. L. Rev.* 1080 (1981).

___, "Choice of Law: A Well-Watered Plateau", 41 *Law and Contemp. Prob.* 10 (1977).

___, "Choice-of-Law Statutes", 44 *Tenn. L. Rev.* 951 (1977).

___, "The 'New' Choice of Law", 21 *Am. UL Rev.* 457 (1972).

___, "Choice-Influencing Considerations in Conflicts Law", 41 *NYU L. Rev.* 367 (1966).

___, "Conflicts of Law: More on Choice Influencing Considerations", 54 *Calif. L. Rev.* 1584 (1966).

Leflar, R., L. McDougal, and R. Felix, *American Conflicts Law*, 4th ed., Charlottesville, Va., 1986.

Little, L., "Hairsplitting and Complexity in Conflict of Laws: The Paradox of Formalism" 54 *Def. L.J.* 377 (2005).

Lookofsky, J., "Danish Private International Law at the End of the 20th Century: Progress or Regress?", in S. Symeonides, *Private International Law at the End of the 20th Century: Progress or Regress*, 147, Kluwer, 2000.

Lookofsky, J., and Hertz, K., *Transnational Litigation and Commercial Arbitration*, 2nd ed., Copenhagen 2004.

Lorenzen, E., "Territoriality, Public Policy, and the Conflict of Laws", 43 *Yale LJ* 736 (1924).

Loussouarn, Y., "Les vicissitudes de la codification du droit international privé français", in *E pluribus unum: Liber amicorum Georges A. L. Droz*, 191, The Hague, 1996.

Loussouarn, Y., and P. Bourel, *Droit international privé*, 7th ed., Dalloz, 2001.

Lowenfeld, A., "International Litigation and the Quest for Reasonableness: General Course of Private International Law" 245 *Recueil des cours* (1995).

Maier, H., "Finding the Trees in Spite of the Metaphorist: The Problem of State Interests in Choice of Law", 56 *Alb. L. Rev.* 753 (1993).

___, "The Utilitarian Role of a Restatement of Conflicts in a Common Law System: How Much Judicial Deference is Due to the Restaters or 'Who Are These Guys, Anyway?'", 75 *Ind. LJ* 541 (2000).

Mayer, P., "L'État et le droit international privé", 16 *Droits: Rev. Française de Théorie Juridique* 33 (1992)

___, Mayer, P., "Le rôle du droit public en droit international privé", *Rev. int'le droit comp.* 467 (1986).

Mayer, P. and Heuzé, V., *Droit international privé*, 7th ed., Paris, 2001.

McClean, D., "Perspectives on Private International Law at the Turn of the Century", 282 *Recueil des cours* 41 (2000).

McDougal, L., "Leflar's Choice-Influencing Considerations: Revisited, Refined and Reaffirmed", 52 *Ark. L. Rev.* 105 (1999).

___, "Toward the Increased Use of Interstate and International Policies in Choice-of-Law Analysis in Tort Cases under the Second Restatement and Leflar's Choice-Influencing Considerations", 70 *Tul L. Rev.* 2465 (1996).

___, "The Real Legacy of *Babcock* v. *Jackson*: Lex Fori Instead of Lex Loci Delicti and Now it's Time for a Real Choice-of-Law Revolution", 56 *Alb. L. Rev.* 795 (1993).

___, "Private International Law: Jus Gentium Versus Choice of Law Rules or Approaches", 38 *Am. J. Comp. L.* 521 (1990).

___, "Toward Application of the Best Rule of Law in Choice of Law Cases", 35 *Mercer L. Rev.* 483 (1984).

___, "Comprehensive Interest Analysis versus Reformulated Governmental Interest Analysis: An Appraisal in the Context of Choice-of-Law Problems concerning Contributory and Comparative Negligence", 26 *UCLA L. Rev.* 439 (1979).

___, "New Frontier in Choice of Law-Trans-state Laws: The Need Demonstrated in Theory and in the Context of Motor Vehicle Guest-Host Controversies", 53 *Tul. L. Rev.* 731 (1979).

___, "Choice of Law – Prologue to a Viable Interest-Analysis Theory", 51 *Tul. L. Rev.* 207 (1977).

McDougal, L., Felix, R. and Whitten, R., American Conflicts Law, 5th ed., Ardsley, NY 2001.

Meeusen, J., Pertegás, M., and Straetmans, G. (eds), *Enforcement of International Contracts in the European Union*, Antwerp 2004.

Morse, C.G.J. *Torts in Private International Law*, North-Holland, 1978.

___, "Torts in Private International Law: A New Statutory Framework", 45 *Int'l and Comp. L. Q.* 888 (1996).

___, "Choice of Law in Tort: a Comparative Survey", 32 Am. J. Comp. L. 51 (1984).

Mosconi, F., "A Few Questions on the Matter of International Uniformity of Solutions and Nationality as a Connecting Factor", in *Private Law in the International Arena: Liber Amicorum Kurt Siehr* 465, The Hague, 2000.

___, "Exceptions to the Operation of Choice of Law Rules", 217 *Recueil des cours* 9 (1989).

Moura Ramos, R., *Das relaçoes privadas internacionais*, Coimbra, 1995.

___, "Le droit international privé portugais à la fin du vingtième siècle: Progrès ou recul?", in S. Symeonides, *Private International Law at the End of the 20th Century: Progress or Regress?*, 349, The Hague, 2000.

Moustaira, A., *The Evolution of Private International Law in the United States: Tradition, Revolution, Counter-Revolution* (in Greek), Athens, 1996.

Muir Watt, H., "Aspect économiques du droit international privé" 3007 *Recueil des cours* 25 (2005).

___, "Globalisation des marchés et économie politique du droit international privé", 47 *Arch. phil. dr.* 243 (2003).

___, "Choice of Law in Integrated and Interconnected Markets", 9 *Colum. J. Eur. L.* 383 (2003).

___, "Law and Economics: Quelle contribution pour le droit international privé?" *Melanges J. Gestin* 685 (2000).

___, "La codification en droit international privé", 27 *Droits: Rev. Franç. théor. jurid.* 149 (1998)

___, "Les principes généraux en droit international privé français", 124 *J. dr. int'l* 403 (1997).

___, "Quelques remarques sur la théorie anglo-américaine des droits acquis", 75 *Rev. critique* 425 (1986).

Mullenix, L., "Mass Tort Litigation and the Dilemma of Federalization", 44 *De Paul L. Rev.* 755 (1995).

___, "Federalizing Choice of Law for Mass-Tort Litigation", 70 *Tex. L. Rev.* 1623 (1992).

Nadelmann, K., "Wächter's Essay on the Collision of Private Laws of Different States", 13 *Am. J. Comp. L.* 414 (1963).

Nafziger, J., "Oregon's Conflicts Law Applicable to Contracts", 38 *Willamette L. Rev.* 397 (2002).

___, "Avoiding Courtroom 'Conflicts' Whenever Possible", in *Law and Justice in a Multistate World: Essays in Honor of Arthur T. von Mehren*, 341 (J. Nafziger and S. Symeonides, eds., 2002).

___, "Making Choices of Law Together", 37 *Willamette L. Rev.* 209 (2000).

___, "Oregon's Project to Codify Choice-of-Law Rules", 60 *La. L. Rev.* 1189 (2000).

___, "Choice of Law in Air Disaster Cases: Complex Litigation Rules and the Common Law", 54 *La. L. Rev.* 1001 (1994).

Nafziger, J., and S. Symeonides, *Law and Justice in a Multistate World: Essays in Honor of Arthur T. von Mehren,*, New York, 2002.

Nagan, W.P., "Theory and Method in Private International Law: A Policy-Oriented, Internationalist Perspective", in *Liber Memorialis François Laurent* 907 (J. Erauw et al., eds.) Brussels, 1989.

North, P., *Essays in Private International Law*, Oxford, 1993.

___, "Private International Law: Change or Decay?", 50 *Int'l & Comp. LQ* 477 (2001).

North, P.M., "Reform, but not Revolution: General Course on Private International Law" 220 *Recueil des cours* 9 (1990).

North, P. and Fawcett, J., *Cheshire and North's Private International Law*, 13th ed., London 1999.

Nygh, P., *Conflict of Laws in Australia*, 6th ed., Sydney, Butterworths, 1995.

___, "The Reasonable Expectations of the Parties as a Guide to the Choice of Law in Contract and Tort", 251 *Recueil des cours* 269 (1995).

O'Hara, E., "Economics, Public Choice, and the Perennial Conflict of Laws", 90 *Geo. LJ* 941 (2002).

___, "Opting out of Regulation: A Public Choice Analysis of Contractual Choice of Law", 53 *Vand. L .Rev.* 1551 (2000).

O'Hara E., and L. Ribstein, "From Politics to Efficiency in Choice of Law", 67 *U. Chi. L. Rev.* 1151 (2000).

Opeskin, B., "The Price of Forum Shopping: A Reply", 16 *Sydney L. Rev.* 14 (1994).

Oppetit, B., "Les principes généraux en droit international privé", *Arch. Philos. Dr.* 179 (1987).

Pajor, T., "Polish Private International Law at the End of the 20th Century: Progress or Regress?", in S. Symeonides, *Private International Law at the End of the 20th Century: Progress or Regress?*, 329 (2000).

Pamboukis C., "Les clauses d'exception en matière de conflits de lois et de conflits de juridictions – Grèce", in *Les clauses d'exception en matière de conflits de lois et de conflits de juridictions – ou le principe de proximité* (D. Kokkini-Iatridou, ed.), Dortrecht, Boston, London, 1994.

___, "L'acte quasi public en droit international privé", 82 *Rev. critique* 565 (1993).

Papadopoulou, T., *The Role of the Judge in Private International Law* (in Greek) Athens, 2000.

Papassiopi-Passia, Z., *Rules of Immediate Application and Substantive Choice of Law Rules* (in Greek), Thessaloniki, 1989.

___, *New Trends in the Private International Law of Conventional Obligations* (in Greek), Thessaloniki, Athens, 1985.

Parra-Aranguren, G., *Codificacion del derecho internacional privado en America*, Vol. 2, Caracas, 1998.

___, *Monografias selectas de derecho internacional privado*, Caracas, 1984.

___, "General Course on Private International Law: Selected Problems", 210 *Recueil des cours* 9 (1988).

Patocchi, P., *Règles de rattachement localisatrices et règles de rattachement à caractère substantiel: De quelques aspects récents de la diversification de la méthode conflictuelle en Europe*, Geneva, 1985.

Perdue, W., "A Reexamination of the Distinction between 'Loss-Allocating' and 'Conduct-Regulating Rules'", 60 *La. L. Rev.* 1251 (2000).

Peterson, C., "Restating Conflicts Again: A Cure for Schizophrenia?", 75 *Ind. LJ* 549 (2000).

___, "American Private International Law at the End of the 20th Century: Progress or Regress?", in S. Symeonides, *Private International Law at the End of the 20th Century: Progress or Regress?*, 430, Kluwer, 2000.

___, "New Openness to Statutory Choice of Law Solutions", 38 *Am. J. Comp. L.* 423 (1990).

___, "Federalism and the Elusive Goal of Uniformity in American Conflicts Law, in *Liber Memorialis François Laurent* 943 (J. Erauw et al., eds.) Brussels, 1989.

___, "Particularism in the Conflict of Laws", 10 *Hofstra L. Rev.* 973 (1982).

Picone, P., *Diritto internazionale privato e diritto communtario*, Cedam 2004.

___, *La riforma italiana del diritto internazionale privato*, Padua, 1998.

___, "Les méthodes de coordination entre ordres juridiques en droit international privé", 276 *Recueil des cours* 9 (1999).

___, "Caratteri ed evoluzione del metodo tradizionale dei conflitti di leggi", *Riv. dir, int.* 5 (1990).

Pielemeier, J., "Choice of Law for Multistate Defamation - The State of Affairs as Internet Defamation Beckons", 35 *Ariz. St. L.J.* 55 (2003).

Posch, W., "The 'Draft Regulation Rome II' in 2004: Its Past and Future Perspectives", 6 *Ybk. Priv. Int'l L.* 129 (2004).

Pocar, F., *Il nuovo diritto internazionale privato italiano*, 2nd ed Milan 2002.

___, "La protection de la partie faible en droit international privé", 188 *Recueil des cours* 340 (1984).

Pocar, F., and C. Honorati, "Italian Private International Law at the End of the 20th Century: Progress or Regress?", in S. Symeonides, *Private International Law at the End of the 20th Century: Progress or Regress?*, 279 (2000).

Posnak, B., "The Restatement (Second): Some Not So Fine Tuning for a Restatement (Third): A Very Well-Curried Leflar over Reese with Korn on the Side (or Is It Cob?)", 75 *Ind. LJ* 561 (2000).

___, "Choice of Law – Interest Analysis: They Still Don't Get It", 40 *Wayne L. Rev.* 1121 (1994).

___, "Choice of Law: Interest Analysis and Its 'New Crits'", 36 *Am. J. Comp. L.* 681 (1988).

___, "Choice of Law: A Very Well-Curried Leflar Approach", 34 *Mercer L. Rev.* 731 (1983).

Princi, J., "Private International Law in Pursuit of Justice for Tort Choice of Law", 2002 *Australian Int'l L.J.* 237 (2002).

Prujiner, A., "Canadian Private International Law at the End of the 20th Century: Progress or Regress?", in S. Symeonides, *Private International Law at the End of the 20th Century: Progress or Regress?*, 127 (2000).

Pryles, M.C., "Tort and Related Obligations in Private International Law", 227 *Recueil des cours* 9 (1992).

Reed, A, "The Anglo-American Revolution in Tort Choice of Law Principles: Paradigm Shift or Pandora's Box?" 18 *Ariz. J. Int'l & Comp. L.* 867 (2001).

___, "The Private International Law (Miscellaneous Provisions) Act 1995 and the Need for Escape Devices", 15 *Civ. Just. Q.* 305 (1996).

Reese, W. "Statutes in Choice of Law", 35 *Am. J. Comp. L.* 395 (1987).

___, "The Second Restatement of Conflict of Laws Revisited", 34 *Mercer L. Rev.* 501 (1983).

___, "American Choice of Law", 30 *Am. J. Comp. L.* 135 (1982).

___, "American Trends in Private International Law: Academic and Judicial Manipulation of Choice of Law Rules in Tort Cases", 33 *Vand. L. Rev.* 717 (1980).

___, "Choice of Law in Torts and Contracts and Directions for the Future", 16 *Colum. J. Trans'l L.* 1 (1977).

___, "General Course on Private International Law", 150 *Recueil des cours* 1 (1976).

___, "Dépeçage: A Common Phenomenon in Choice of Law", 73 *Colum. L. Rev.* 58 (1973).

___, "Choice of Law: Rules or Approach", 57 *Cornell LQ* 315 (1972).

___, "Choice of Law", 71 *Colum. L. Rev.* 548 (1971).

___, "Chief Judge Fuld and Choice of Law", 71 *Colum. L. Rev.* 548 (1971).

Reimann, M., "Liability for Defective Products and Services: Emergence of a Worldwide Standard?", *General Report to the XVIth International Congress of Comparative Law*, Brisbane, 2002.

___, "Parochialism in American Conflict Law", 49 *Am. J. Comp. L.*, 369 (2001).

___, "Codifying Torts Conflicts: The 1999 German Legislation in Comparative Perspective", 60 *La. L. Rev.* 1297 (2000).

___, "A New Restatement-for the International Age", 75 *Ind. LJ* 575 (2000).

Reppy, W., "Codifying Interest Analysis in the Torts Chapter of a New Conflicts Restatement", 75 *Ind. LJ* 591 (2000).

___, "Eclecticism in Choice of Law: Hybrid Method or Mishmash?", 34 *Mercer L. Rev.* 645 (1983).

Reynolds, L., "Legal Process and Choice of Law", 56 *Md. L. Rev.* 1371 (1997).

Reynolds, W., "Robert Leflar, Judicial Process and Choice of Law", 52 *Ark. L. Rev.* 123 (1999).

Rheinstein, M., "How to Review a Festschrift", 11 *Am. J. Comp. L.* 632 (1962).

Ribstein, L., "From Efficiency to Politics in Contractual Choice of Law", 37 *Ga. L. Rev.* 363 (2003).

Richman, W., and W. Reynolds, *Understanding Conflict of Laws*, 2nd ed., 1992.

___, "Prologomenon to an Empirical Restatement of Conflicts", 75 *Ind. LJ* 417 (2000).

Richman, W., and D. Riley, "The First Restatement of Conflict of Laws on the Twenty-Fifth Anniversary of Its Successor: Contemporary Practice in Traditional Courts", 56 *Md. L. Rev.* 1196 (1997).

Rigaux, F., "Codification of Private International Law: Pros and Cons", 60 *La. L. Rev.* 1321 (2000).

___, "Droit privé matériel et règles de conflit de lois", *Rev. belge dr. int.* 385 (1991).

___, "Les situations juridiques individuelles dans un système de relativité' générale: Cours général de droit international privé", 213 *Recueil des cours* 9 (1989).

___, "Droit économique et conflits de souverainetés", 52 *RabelsZ* 104 (1988).

Rogerson, P. "Choice of Law in Tort: A Missed Opportunity?", 44 *Int'l Comp. LQ* 650 (1995).

Rosenberg, M., "The Comeback of Choice-of-Law Rules", 81 *Colum. L. Rev.* 946 (1981).

___, "Comments on *Reich* v. *Purcell*", 15 *UCLA L. Rev.* 641 (1968).

___, "Two views on *Kell* v. *Henderson*: An Opinion for the New York Court of Appeals", 67 *Colum. L. Rev.* 459 (1967).

Roosevelt, K., "Guantanamo and the Conflict of Laws: *Rasul* and Beyond", 153 *U. Pa. L. Rev.* 2017 (2005).

___, "The Myth of Choice of Law: Rethinking Conflicts", 97 *Mich. L. Rev.* 2448 (1999).

Schurig, K., "Interessenjurisprudenz contra Interessenjurisprudenz im IPR: Anmerkungen zu Flessners Thesen", 59 *RabelsZ* 229 (1995).

Scoles, E., P. Hay, P. Borchers, and S. Symeonides, *Conflict of Laws*, 4th ed., St. Paul, Minn., 2004.

Sedler, R., "American Federalism, State Sovereignty, and the Interest Analysis Approach to Choice of Law", in *Law and Justice in a Multistate World: Essays in Honor of Arthur T. von Mehren,* 369 (J. Nafziger and S. Symeonides, eds., 2002).

___, "The Louisiana Codification and Tort Rules of Choice of Law", 60 *La. L. Rev.* 1331 (2000).

___, "Choice of Law in Conflicts Torts Cases: A Third Restatement or Rules of Choice of Law?", 75 *Ind. LJ* 615 (2000).

___, "A Real World Perspective on Choice of Law", 48 *Mercer L. Rev.* 781 (1997).

___, "The Complex Litigation Project's Proposal for Federally-Mandated Choice of Law in Mass Torts Cases: Another Assault on State Sovereignty", 54 *La. L. Rev.* 1085 (1994).

___, "Interest Analysis, Party Expectations and Judicial Method in Conflicts Torts Cases: Reflections on *Cooney* v. *Osgood Machinery, Inc.*", 59 *Brook. L. Rev.* 1323 (1994).

___, "Interest Analysis, State Sovereignty, and Federally-Mandated Choice of Law in 'Mass Tort' Cases", 56 *Alb. L. Rev.* 855 (1993).

___, "Continuity, Precedent, and Choice of Law: A Reflective Response to Professor Hill", 38 *Wayne L. Rev.* 1419 (1992).

___, "Professor Juenger's Challenge to the Interest Analysis Approach to Choice-of-Law: An Appreciation and a Response", 23 *UC Davis L. Rev.* 865 (1990).

___, "Interest Analysis as the Preferred Approach to Choice of Law: A Response to Professor Brilmayer's 'Foundational Attack'", 46 *Ohio St. LJ* 483 (1985).

___, "Interest Analysis and Forum Preference in the Conflict of Laws: A Response to the 'New Crits'", 34 *Mercer L. Rev.* 593 (1983).

___, "Reflections on Conflict-of-Laws Methodology", 32 *Hastings LJ* 1628 (1981).

___, "Rules of Choice of Law versus Choice-of-Law Rules: Judicial Method in Conflicts Torts Cases", 44 *Tenn. L. Rev.* 975 (1977).

___, "The Governmental Interest Analysis to Choice of Law: An Analysis and a Reformulation", 25 *UCLA L. Rev.* 181 (1977).

___, "On Choice of Law and the Great Quest: A Critique of Special Multistate Solutions to Choice-of-Law Problems", 7 *Hofstra L. Rev.* 807 (1979).

___, "Interstate Accidents and the Unprovided-for Case: Reflections on *Neumeier* v. *Kuehner*", 1 *Hofstra L. Rev.* 125 (1973).

___, "The Truly Disinterested Forum in the Conflict of Laws", 25 *SC L. Rev.* 185 (1973).

Seidelson, D., "Resolving Choice-of-Law Problems through Interest Analysis in Personal Injury Actions: A Suggested Order of Priority among Competing State Interests and among Available Techniques for Weighing Those Interests", 30 *Duq. L. Rev.* 869 (1992).

___, "Section 6.01 of the ALI's Complex Litigation Project: Function Follows Form", 54 *La. L. Rev.* 1111 (1994).

___, "Interest Analysis: The Quest for Perfection and the Frailties of Man", 19 *Duq. L. Rev.* 207 (1981).

Shapira, A., *The Interest Approach to Choice of Law,* The Hague, Martinus Nijhoff, 1970.

___, "Territorialism, National Parochialism, Universalism and Party Autonomy: How does One Square the Choice of Law Circle?", 26 *Brooklyn J. Int'l L.* 199 (2000).

___, "Torts Choice of Law in Israel: Putting Order in a Methodological Chaos", in *Private Law in the International Arena – Liber Amicorum Kurt Siehr* 685 (J. Basedow, *et al..*, eds., 2000).

Sharkey, C., "Punitive Damages as Societal Damages", 113 *Yale LJ* 347 (2003)

Shreve, G., *A Conflict-of-Laws Anthology,* Anderson Publ., 1997.

___, "Conflicts Altruism", in *Law and Justice in a Multistate World: Essays in Honor of Arthur T. von Mehren,* 383 (J. Nafziger and S. Symeonides, eds., 2002).

___, "Every Conflicts Decision is a Promise Broken", 60 *La. L. Rev.* 1345 (2000).

___, "Notes from the Eye of the Storm", 48 *Mercer L. Rev.* 823 (1997).

___, "Choice of Law and the Forgiving Constitution", 71 *Ind. LJ* 271 (1996).

___, "Conflicts Law – State or Federal?", 68 *Ind. LJ* 907 (1993).

Siegel, D., "A Retrospective on *Babcock* v. *Jackson*: A Personal View", 56 *Alb. L. Rev.* 693 (1993).

Siehr, K., *Internationales Privatrecht*, Heidelberg, 2001.

___, *Das Internationale Privatrecht der Schweiz*, Zurich 2002.

___, "Revolution and Evolution in Conflicts Law", 60 *La. L. Rev.* 1353 (2000).

___, "Swiss Private International Law at the End of the 20th Century: Progress or Regress?", in S. Symeonides, *Private International Law at the End of the 20th Century: Progress or Regress?*, 389 (2000).

___, "Ehrenzweigs lex-fori-Theorie und ihre Bedeutung für das amerikanische und deutsche Kollisionsrecht", 34 *RabelsZ* 583 (1970).

Simon-Depitre, "Les règles matérielles dans le conflit de lois", 63 *Rev. critique* 591 (1974).

Simson, G., "The Choice-of-Law Revolution in the United States: Notes on Rereading von Mehren", 36 *Cornell Int'l L.J.* 125 (2003).

___, "State Interests, State Autonomy, and the Quest for Uniformity in Choice of Law", in *Law and Justice in a Multistate World: Essays in Honor of Arthur T. von Mehren*, 391 (J. Nafziger and S. Symeonides, eds., 2002).

___, "Leave Bad Enough Alone", 75 *Ind. LJ* 649 (2000).

___, "Resisting the Allure of Better Rule of Law", 52 *Ark. L. Rev.* 141 (1999).

___, "The *Neumeier-Schultz* Rules: How Logical a 'Next State in the Evolution of the Law' after *Babcock*?", 56 *Alb. L. Rev.* 913 (1993).

___, "Plotting the Next 'Revolution' in Choice of Law: A Proposed Approach", 24 *Cornell Int'l LJ* 279 (1991).

Singer, J., "Pay No Attention to that Man behind the Curtain: The Place of Better Law in a Third Restatement of Conflicts", 75 *Ind. LJ* 659 (2000).

___, "Justice and the Conflict of Laws", 48 *Mercer L. Rev.* 831 (1997).

___, "A Pragmatic Guide to Conflicts", 70 *BU L. Rev.* 731 (1990).

___, "Facing Real Conflicts", 24 *Cornell Int'l LJ* 197 (1991).

Solimine, M., "The Impact of *Babcock* v. *Jackson*: An Empirical Note", 56 *Alb. L. Rev.* 773 (1993).

___, "Choice of Law in the American Courts in 1991", 40 *Am. J. Comp. L.* 951 (1992).

___, "An Economic and Empirical Analysis of Choice of Law", 24 *Georgia L. Rev.* 49 (1989).

Sonnenberger, H., "Le droit international privé allemand à la fin du vingtième siècle: Progrès ou recul?", in S. Symeonides, *Private International Law at the End of the 20th Century: Progress or Regress?*, 221, The Hague, 2000.

Southerland, H., "Sovereignty, Value Judgments, and Choice of Law", 38 *Brandeis LJ* 451 (2000).

Stanivuković, M., "Yugoslavian Private International Law at the End of the 20th Century: Progress or Regress?", in S. Symeonides, *Private International Law at the End of the 20th Century: Progress or Regress?*, 461 (2000).

Starace, V., "Le champ de la juridiction selon la loi de réforme du système italien de droit international privé" 85 *Rev. critique* 67 (1996).

Stephan, P., "The Political Economics of Choice of Law", 90 *Geo. LJ* 957 (2002).

Sterk, S., "The New York Court of Appeals: 150 Years of Leading Decisions", 48 *Syracuse L. Rev.* 1391 (1998).

___, "The Marginal Relevance of Choice of Law Theory", 142 *U. Pa. L. Rev.* 949 (1994).

Story, J., *Commentaries on the Conflict of Laws*, Boston, 1834.

Strikwerda, L., "Interest Analysis: No More than a 'Protest Song'?", in *Law and Reality: Essays in Honour of Cornelius Carel Albert Voskuil* 301, Dordrecht, 1992.

Sucharitkul, S., "Unification of Private Law and Codification of International Law", *Rev. droit unif.* 693 (1998).

Symeonides, S., "The American Choice-of-Law Revolution in the Courts: Today and Tomorrow", 298 *Recueil des Cours* 1 (2003).

___, *Private International Law at the End of the 20th Century: Progress or Regress?*, The Hague, 2000.

___, *An Outsider's View of the American Approach to Choice of Law: Comparative Observations on Current American and Continental Conflicts Doctrine*, Cambridge, Mass. 1980.

___, "Accommodative Unilateralism as a Starting Premise in Choice of Law", in *Balancing of Interests –Liber Amicorum Peter Hay* 417-434, Verlag Recht und Wirtschaft GmbH, 2005.

___, "The Quest for the Optimum in Resolving Product-Liability Conflicts", in *Essays in Honor of P. John Kozyris* (2005).

___, "A Choice-of-Law Rule for Conflicts Involving Stolen Cultural Property", 38 *Vanderbilt J Transnat'l L.* 1177-98 (2005).

___, "Of Teleology, State Interests and Pluralism in Choice of Law: In Loving Memory of Friedrich K. Juenger", in Friedrich K. Juenger, *Choice of Law and Multistate Justice* xxxiii (spec. ed. 2005).

___, "Choice of Law in the American Courts in 2003: Eighteenth Annual Survey", 53 *Am. J. Comp. L* 919-994 (2005).

___, "Choice of Law for Products Liability: The 1990s and Beyond", 78 *Tul. L. Rev.* 1247 (2004).

___, "Tort Conflicts and Rome II: A View from Across", in *Festschrift für Erik Jayme* 935 (2004).

___, "Choice of Law in the American Courts in 2003: Seventeenth Annual Survey", 52 *American Journal of Comparative Law* 1-76 (2004)

___, "Territoriality and Personality in Tort Conflicts", in *Intercontinental Cooperation Through Private International Law: Essays in Memory of Peter Nygh*, (T. Einhorn & K. Siehr, eds) 401 (2004)

___, "Resolving Punitive-Damages Conflicts", 5 *Ybk. Priv. Int'l L.* 1 (2003)

___, "Codifying Choice of Law for Contracts: The Oregon Experience", 67 *RabelsZ* 726 (2003).

___, "Choice of Law in the American Courts in 2002: Sixteenth Annual Survey", 51 *Am. J. Comp. L.* (2003).

___, "Codifying Puerto Rico's Choice-of-Law for Contracts", in *Law and Justice in a Multistate World: Essays in Honor of Arthur T. von Mehren*, 419 (J. Nafziger and S. Symeonides, eds., 2002).

___, "Choice of Law in the American Courts in 2001: Fifteenth Annual Survey", 50 *Am. J. Comp. L.* 1 (2002).

___, "Choice of Law in the American Courts in 2000: As the Century Turns", 49 *Am. J. Comp. L.* 1 (2001).

___, "American Choice of Law at the Dawn of the 20th Century", 37 *Willamette L. Rev.* 1 (2000).

___, "Material Justice and Conflicts Justice in Choice of Law", in *International Conflict of Laws for the Third Millennium: Essays in Honor of Friedrich K. Juenger*, 125 (P. Borchers and J. Zekoll, eds., 2000).

___, "On the Side of the Angels: Choice of Law and Stolen Cultural Property", in *Private Law in the International Arena – Liber Amicorum Kurt Siehr* 649 (J. Basedow, *et al.*, eds. 2000).

___, "The Need for a Third Conflicts Restatement (and a Proposal for Tort Conflicts)", 75 *Ind. LJ* 437-474 (2000).

___, "Choice of Law in the American Courts in 1999: One More Year", 48 *Am. J. Comp. L.* 143 (2000).

___, "Covenant Marriage and the Conflict of Laws" (with K. Spaht), 32 *Creighton L. Rev.* 1085 (1999).

___, "Choice of Law in the American Courts in 1998: Twelfth Annual Survey", 47 *Am. J. Comp. L.* 327 (1999).

___, "Choice of Law in the American Courts in 1997", 46 *Am. J. Comp. L.* 233 (1998).

___, "The Judicial Acceptance of the Second Conflicts Restatement: A Mixed Blessing", 56 *Md. L. Rev.* 1246 (1997).

___, "Resolving Six Celebrated Conflicts Cases through Statutory Choice-of-Law Rules", 47 *Mercer L. Rev.* 837 (1997).

___, "Choice of Law in the American Courts in 1996: Tenth Annual Survey", 45 *Am. J. Comp. L.* 447 (1997).

___, "Choice of Law in the American Courts in 1995: A Year in Review", 44 *Am. J. Comp. L.* 181 (1996).

___, "Choice of Law in the American Courts in 1994: A View 'From the Trenches'", 43 *Am. J. Comp. L.* 1 (1995).

___, "Choice of Law in the American Courts in 1993 (and in the Six Previous Years)", 42 *Am. J. Comp. L.* 599 (1994).

___, "Louisiana Conflicts Law: Two 'Surprises'", 54 *La. L. Rev.* 497 (1994).

___, "The ALI's Complex Litigation Project: Commencing the National Debate", 54 *La. L. Rev.* 843 (1994).

___, "Exception Clauses in American Conflicts Law", 42 *Am. J. Comp. L.* 813 (1994).

___, "Private International Law Codification in a Mixed Jurisdiction: The Louisiana Experience", 57 *RabelsZ* 460 (1993).

___, "Louisiana's New Law of Choice of Law for Tort Conflicts: An Exegesis", 66 *Tul. L. Rev.* 677 (1992).

___, "Revising Puerto Rico's Conflicts Law: A Preview", 28 *Colum. J. Transn'l L.* 413 (1990).

___, "Choice of Law in the American Courts in 1988", 37 *Am. J. Comp. L.* 457 (1989).

___, "Exploring the 'Dismal Swamp': Revising Louisiana's Conflicts Law on Successions", 47 *La. L. Rev.* 1029 (1987).

___, "In Search of New Choice-of-Law Solutions to Some Marital Property Problems of Migrant Spouses: A Response to the Critics", 13 *Com. Prop. J.* 11 (1986).

___, "Revolution and Counter-Revolution in American Conflicts Law: Is there a Middle Ground?" 46 *Ohio St. LJ* 549 (1985).

___, "Maritime Conflicts Law from the Perspective of Modern Choice of Law Methodology", 7 *Mar. Law.* 223 (1982).

Symeonides, S., Perdue, W. and von Mehren, A., *Conflict of Laws: American Comparative International*, 2nd ed. St. Paul, Minn., Thomson-West 2003.

Swire, P., "Elephants and Mice Revisited: Law and Choice of Law on the Internet", 153 *U. Pa. L. Rev.* 1975 (2005).

Tetley, W., *International Conflict of Laws: Common. Civil and Maritime*, Montreal 1994.

___, "A Canadian Looks at American Conflict of Law Theory and Practice, Especially in Light of the American Legal and Social Systems (Corrective vs. Distributive Justice)", 38 *Colum. J. Transn'l L.* 299 (1999).

Thue, H., "Norwegian Private International Law at the End of the 20th Century: Progress or Regress?", in S. Symeonides, *Private International Law at the End of the 20th Century: Progress or Regress?*, 319 (2000).

Todd, J., "A Judge's View", 31 *SC L. Rev.* 435 (1980).

Trautman, D., "Toward Federalizing Choice of Law", 70 *Tex. L. Rev.* 1715 (1992).

___, "A Comment on Twerski and Mayer: A Pragmatic Step Towards Consensus as a Basis for Choice-of-Law Solutions", 7 *Hofstra L. Rev.* 833 (1979).

___, "The Relation between American Choice of Law and Federal Common Law", 41 *Law and Contemp. Prob.* 105 (1977).

___, "Two Views on *Kell* v. *Henderson*: A Comment", 67 *Colum. L. Rev.* 465 (1967).

Traynor, M., "Conflict of Laws, Comparative Law, and the American Law Institute", 49 *Am. J. Comp. L.* 391 (2001).

Traynor, R., "Is this Conflict Really Necessary?", 37 *Tex. L. Rev.* 658, 670 (1959).

Trooboff, P.D., "The Growing Interaction Between Private and Public International Law" 6 *Hague Ybk. Int'l L.* 107 (1994).

Twerski, A., "One Size Does Not Fit All: The Third Multi-Track Restatement of Conflict of Laws", 75 *Ind. LJ* 667 (2000).

___, "A Sheep in Wolf's Clothing: Territorialism in the Guise of Interest Analysis in *Cooney* v. *Osgood Machinery, Inc.*", 59 *Brook. L. Rev.* 1351 (1994).

___, "With Liberty and Justice for All: An Essay on Agent Orange and Choice of Law", 52 *Brook. L. Rev.* 341 (1986).

___, "*Neumeier* v. *Kuhner*: Where Are the Emperor's Clothes?", 1 *Hofstra L. Rev.* 93 (1973).

___, "Enlightened Territorialism and Prof. Cavers – The Pennsylvania Method", 9 *Duq. L. Rev.* 373 (1971).

Twerski, A., and R. Mayer, "Toward a Pragmatic Solution of Choice-of-Law Problems – At the Interface of Substance and Procedure", 74 *Nw. UL Rev.* 781 (1979).

Vallindas, P., "La structure de la règle de conflit", 101 *Recueil des cours* 327 (1960).

Vassilakakis, E., *Orientations méthologiques dans les codifications récentes du droit international privé en Europe*, Paris, 1987.

Verhoeven, J., "Droit international privé et droit international public: où est la différence", *Arch. Philos. Dr.* 23 (1987).

Vischer, F., "New Tendencies in European Conflict of Laws and the Influence of the US-Doctrine – a Short Survey", in *Law and Justice in a Multistate World: Essays in Honor of Arthur T. von Mehren*, 459 (J. Nafziger and S. Symeonides, eds., 2002).

___, "General Course on Private International Law", 232 *Recueil des cours* 9 (1992).

___, "Drafting National Legislation on Conflict of Laws: The Swiss Experience", 41 *Law & Contemp. Prob.* 131 (1977).

Vitta, E., "The Impact in Europe of the American 'Conflicts Revolution'", 30 *Am. J. Comp. L.* 1 (1982).

___, "Cours général de droit international privé", 162 *Recueil des cours* 9 (1979).

Volken, P., "Wenn Wächter mit Story", in *Private Law in the International Arena – Liber Amicorum Kurt Siehr* 815 (J. Basedow, *et al.*, eds., 2000).

von Bar, C., Environmental Damage in Private International Law", 268 *Recueil des cours* 291 (1997).

von Mehren, A., "American Conflicts Law at the Dawn of the 21st Century", 37 *Willamette L. Rev.* 133 (2000).

___, "Choice of Law and the Problem of Justice", 41 *Law & Contemp. Prob.* 27 (1977).

___, "Recent Trends in Choice-of-Law Methodology", 60 *Cornell L. Rev.* 927 (1975).

___, "Special Substantive Rules for Multistate Problems: Their Role and Significance in Contemporary Choice of Law Methodology", 88 *Harv. L. Rev.* 298 (1974).

___, "Conflict of Laws in a Federal System: Some Perspectives", 18 *Int. and Comp. LQ* 681 (1969).

___, "Book Review", 17 *J. Legal Ed.* 91 (1964) (reviewing B. Currie, *Selected Essays on the Conflict of Laws*, 1963).

___, "The Renvoi and its Relation to Various Approaches to the Choice-of-Law Problem", *XXth Century Comparative and Conflicts Law* 380 (1961).

von Mehren, A., and D. Trautman, *The Law of Multistate Problems* (1965).

von Overbeck, A., "De quelques règles générales de conflit de lois dans les codifications récentes", in *Private Law in the International Arena – Liber Amicorum Kurt Siehr* 545 (J. Basedow, *et al.*, eds., 2000).

___, "The Fate of Two Remarkable Provisions of the Swiss Statute on Private International Law", 1 *Ybk. of Priv. Int'l L.* 119 (1999).

___, "Les questions générales du droit international privé à la lumière des codifications et projets récents", 176 *Recueil des cours* 9 (1982).

von Savigny, F., *System des heutigen römischen Rechts*, Vol. 8, Berlin, 1849.

Voulgaris, I., "Réflexions sur l'approche comparative de la qualification en droit international privé" in *Mélanges en l'honneur de Denis Tallon*, 193, Paris, 1999.

Vrellis, S., "Le droit international privé grec vers la fin du vingtième siècle: progrès ou recul?", in S. Symeonides, *Private International Law at the End of the 20th Century: Progress or Regress?*, 243 (2000).

___, "La justice 'matérielle' dans une codification du droit international privé", in *E Pluribus Unum, Liber Amicorum Georges Droz*, 541, The Hague, 1996.

___, "Methodologikoi provlematismoi gia ten periptose metaboles tou ellenikou idiotikou diethnous dikaiou", 37 *Nomiko Vema* 33 (1989).

Wagner, G., "Ehrenschutz und Pressefreiheit im europäischen Zivilverfahrens- und Internationalen Privatrecht" 62 *RabelsZ* 243 (1998).

Walker, J., "'Are We There Yet?': Towards a New Rule for Choice of Law in Tort", 38 *Osgoode Hall LJ* 331 (2000).

___, "Choice of Law in Tort: the Supreme Court of Canada Enters the Fray", 111 *Law Q. Rev.* 397 (1995).

Weinberg, L., "Theory Wars in the Conflict of Laws", 103 *Mich. L. Rev.* 1631 (2005).

___, "Of Theory and Theodicy: The Problem of Immoral Law", in *Law and Justice in a Multistate World: Essays in Honor of Arthur T. von Mehren*, 473 (J. Nafziger and S. Symeonides, eds. 2002).

___, "A Structural Revision of the Conflicts Restatement", 75 *Ind. LJ* 475 (2000).

___, "Choosing Law and Giving Justice", 60 *La. L. Rev.* 1361 (2000).

___, "Mass Torts at the Neutral Forum: A Critical Analysis of the ALI's Proposed Choice Rule", 56 *Alb. L. Rev.* 807 (1993).

___, "Choosing Law: The Limitations Debate", 1991 *U. Ill. L. Rev.* 683 (1991).

___, "The Place of Trial and the Law Applied: Overhauling Constitutional Theory", 59 *U. Colo. L. Rev.* 67 (1988).

___, "On Departing from Forum Law", 35 *Mercer L. Rev.* 595 (1984).

___, "Choice of Law and Minimal Scrutiny", 49 *U. Chi. L. Rev.* 440 (1982).

___, "Conflicts Cases and the Problem of Relevant Time: A Response to the Hague Symposium", 10 *Hofstra L. Rev.* 1023 (1981).

Weinstein, J., "Mass Tort Jurisdiction and Choice of Law in a Multinational World Communicating by Extra-Terrestrial Satellites", 37 *Willamette L. Rev.* 145 (2000).

___, "Ethical Dilemmas in Mass Tort Litigation", 88 *Nw. UL Rev.* 469 (1994).

Weintraub, R., *Commentary on the Conflict of Laws*, 4th ed., New York, 2001.

___, "Getting the Conflict of Laws Y2K Ready", 37 *Willamette L. Rev.* 157 (2000).

___, "The Restatement Third of Conflict of Laws: An Idea Whose Time Has Not Come", 75 *Ind. LJ* 679 (2000).

___, "Flailing in the Waters of the Louisiana Conflicts Code: Not Waving but Drowning", 60 *La. L. Rev.* 1365 (2000).

___, "Choice of Law for Products Liability: Demagnetizing the United States Forum", 52 *Ark. L. Rev.* 157 (1999).

___, "'At Least to Do No Harm': Does the Second Restatement of Conflicts Meet the Hippocratic Standard?", 56 *Md. L. Rev.* 1284 (1997).

___, "An Approach to Choice of Law That Focuses on Consequences", 56 *Alb. L. Rev.* 701 (1993).

___, "The Contributions of Symeonides and Kozyris to Making Choice of Law Predictable and Just: An Appreciation and Critique", 38 *Am. J. Comp. L.* 511 (1990).

___, "A Proposed Choice-of Law Standard for International Products Liability Disputes", 16 *Brook. J. Int'l L.* 225 (1990).

___, "Methods for Resolving Conflict-of-Laws Problems in Mass Tort Litigation", *U. Ill. L. Rev.* 129 (1989).

___, "Interest Analysis in the Conflict of Laws as an Application of Sound Legal Reasoning", 35 *Mercer L. Rev.* 629 (1984).

___, "Functional Developments in Choice of Law for Contracts", 187 *Recueil des cours* 239 (1984).

Whincop, M., "The Market Tort in Private International Law", 19 *NW. J. Int'l L. & Bus.* 215 (1999).

Whitten, R., "Curing the Deficiencies of the Conflicts Revolution: A Proposal for National Legislation on Choice of Law, Jurisdiction, and Judgments", 37 *Willamette L. Rev.* 259 (2000).

___, "Improving the Better Law System: Some Impudent Suggestions for Reordering and Reformulating Leflar's Choice-influencing Considerations", 52 *Ark. L. Rev.* 177 (1999).

Wiegand, S., "Fifty Conflict of Laws 'Restatements': Merging Judicial Discretion and Legislative Endorsement", 65 *La. L. Rev.*1 (2004)

Wilde, C., "Dépeçage in the Choice of Tort Law", 41 *S. Cal. L. Rev.* 329 (1968).

Williams, F., "The Complex Litigation Project's Choice of Law Rules for Mass Torts and How to Escape Them", 1995 *BYU L. Rev.* 1081.

Yntema, H., "The Hornbook Method and the Conflict of Laws", 37 *Yale LJ* 468 (1928).

Zekoll, J., "Liability for Defective Products and Services", in S. C. Symeonides, and J. Reitz, *American Law in a Time of Global Interdependence: U.S. National Reports to the XVIth International Congress of Comparative Law*, 121 (2002).

Zweigert, K., "Zur Armut des internationalen Privatrechts an socialen Werten", 37 *RabelsZ* 435 (1973).

___, "Some Reflections on the Sociological Dimensions of Private International Law or: What Is Justice in the Conflict of Laws?", 44 *U. Colo. L. Rev.* 283 (1973).

Index

(All references are to paragraph numbers, not pages)

THE HAGUE ACADEMY OF INTERNATIONAL LAW MONOGRAPHS

1.   Ian Brownlie, *The Rule of Law in International Affairs: International Law at the Fiftieth Anniversary of the United Nations*, 1998   ISBN   90 411 1068 2

2.   Shabtai Rosenne, *The Perplexities of Modern International Law*, 2004
                                                          ISBN   90 04 13692 4

3.   Theodor Meron, *The Humanization of International Law*, 2006
                                                          ISBN   90 04 15060 9

4.   Symeon C. Symeonides, *The American Choice-of-Law Revolution: Past, Present and Future*, 2006   ISBN   90 04 15219 9